COUNSELING EMERGING COMPANIES
IN
GOING INTERNATIONAL

Alan S. Gutterman

Editor

Section of International Law and Practice
American Bar Association

Published under the direction of the Publications Committee of the Section of International Law and Practice.

Publications Committee Chair: John E. Noyes

Publications Director: Susan Frensilli Williams

COUNSELING EMERGING COMPANIES IN GOING INTERNATIONAL

TABLE OF CONTENTS

Part Four
Multilateral Initiatives and Government Programs Affecting International Business Activities

Part Five
Practical Considerations in Counseling Clients on International Business Activities

Part Six
Going International: Area Specific Summaries

FOREWORD

International business transactions designed to allow domestic firms to gain access to the customers and resources in new foreign markets have served as the basis for one of the most consistent and growing areas of modern legal practice. In spite of the number and popularity of these transactions, relatively few books exist which provide counsel and their clients with a clear and concise overview of all of the key legal and business considerations which should be taken into account in counseling companies in their efforts to "go international." This book provides a summary of some of the basic strategies for operating in international markets, the important domestic laws and regulations which impact international business activities, foreign laws and regulations which may confront the firm in a new foreign market, government programs which exist as a means for assisting domestic firms in international trade, some of the practical aspects of international business and a variety of country-specific studies written by practitioners chosen for their substantial experience in those areas. This book is by no means comprehensive. For example, the impact of the United States antitrust laws on international activities has not been covered, nor have foreign acquisition transactions. Moreover, readers with an interest in international joint ventures would benefit from a survey of the large amount of materials which have been written on that subject. Nonetheless, the book provides a starting point for the long adventure across many borders.

ALAN S. GUTTERMAN
July 1994

ACKNOWLEDGEMENTS

Publication of this book comes almost five years after the idea of conducting a National Institute program on the general topic of Counseling Emerging Companies on Going International was first conceived. My thanks go to all of the persons within the Sections of International Law and Practice and Business Law, as well as the National Institute staff, who helped make those programs a success. I am particularly grateful to Bob Rendell and Jim Silkenat for their trust in allowing me to organize the program, Bob Shanks for his able assistance as co-chair, and Ernestine Murphy for her support and know-how. I also want to thank all of the contributors for their work and patience in putting the materials together. Within the Section of International Law and Practice, I especially want to recognize Fred Brown, the immediate past chair of the Publications Committee, for his ongoing support and interest in the project, and Susan Frensilli Williams for her invaluable support in working with the contributors and shepherding the book through to publication.

ALAN S. GUTTERMAN
July 1994

OVERVIEW

Alan S. Gutterman

I. INTRODUCTION

ONE OF the definitions of "emerging" which seems to be relevant to the subject matter of this book is "arising as a natural or logical consequence." In the business arena, the decision to commence activities in a foreign jurisdiction has become a natural milestone for almost all growing businesses in the United States, regardless of their size in terms of employees, products, customers or revenues. Moreover, the issues relating to "going international" are raised anew whenever a business decides to enter a different country, since the variety of laws and customs around the world often makes it difficult to generalize regarding the appropriate legal and business strategy which should be taken in each country.

This book has been organized into six different parts. The organization was intended to focus the reader on most of the key legal considerations which must be taken into account when engaging in any particular international business transaction. The first five parts provide an overview of a variety of issues, while the last part includes materials on a number of different countries and regions. Obviously, the information included herein is not meant to be a complete substitute for advice from local experts. However, it is hoped that this book will serve as a good basic resource that will be consulted whenever an international issues comes into focus.

II. BASIC STRATEGIES FOR OPERATING IN INTERNATIONAL MARKETS

Introduction

While laws and regulations certainly have an impact on the structure of an international business transaction, in most cases the "going international" analysis begins with a decision about the basic strategy which the domestic firm wishes to follow as a means for becoming active in a given foreign market area. There are a number of basic strategies which might be considered, including a basic technology licensing arrangement designated to facilitate the transfer of the legal right to use intellectual property from one party to another, research and development arrangements, product purchase and manufacturing relationships, sales and distribution arrangements, joint ventures, outright acquisitions of one or more foreign entities and, finally, the formation of a new subsidiary in the foreign market to conduct business in a manner similar to any other local entity.

Licensing Arrangements

One of the most basic forms of international business agreement is a licensing agreement, which may cover patents, trade secrets, copyrights and trademarks. A license conveys to the licensee the right to use the licensed intellectual property right for the specific purposes described in the agreement without fear of being sued for infringement or misappropriation by the owner of the right. In effect, a license is a contractual exception to the otherwise exclusive rights of the owner. In some cases, the license will extend to subsequent improvements or enhancements to the original licensed subject matter.

While a license is appropriate when the licensee simply wishes to exploit its own technology without being "blocked" by the rights of the licensor, it is quite common to see a license used as a fundamental tool in one of the other forms of international business transactions. For example, in order for a party to manufacture and distribute the products developed by another party, it must generally be granted a license to make and sell the products. In such cases, the arrangement between the parties includes the basic technology license and an agreement covering the terms and conditions upon which the products will ultimately be sold to consumers.

Research and Development Arrangements

Research and development arrangements contemplate a coordinated effort by the parties to make fundamental changes in, or improvements to, specified core technologies. The research may be conducted under an agreement which provides for one party to fund the research work of another party in return for the rights to use the resultant technology in various applications. If the parties have complementary technical skills and assets, the development program may include cross-licensing agreements and sharing of scientific and engineering personnel. In recent years, many domestic firms have turned to foreign firms as new strategic partners in the conducting of basic research and development work on promising technologies. A research and development agreement is often the first step toward a broader arrangement covering the sale and distribution of products arising from the research work.

Purchasing and Manufacturing Arrangements

Another common and important type of technology transaction involves the purchase and manufacture of technology-based goods. For example, a firm may be able to realize greater efficiency in production by utilizing low-cost manufacturers overseas to make their products. The firm may achieve these cost savings by granting a license to the manufacturer to make the products and agreeing to repurchase the products at a fixed price, perhaps at some multiple of the manufacturer's actual cost. The license must include some agreement as to technical assistance, since the manufacturer must be trained in a manner which guarantees that its products are similar in quality to those that would otherwise be produced by the licensor.

Sales and Distribution Arrangements

Foreign markets are an important source of new potential revenues for domestic firms and the emerging companies may well seek out partners in foreign countries to assist them in the sale and distribution of their products. One basic form of distribution relationship would involve a sale of goods by the manufacturing entity to the distributing entity for resale by the distributor, combined with a license covering all the patents, trade secrets and trademarks required in order for the distributor to market and service the products. This type of arrangement will allow the manufacture to take advantage of the sales network of the distributor. In turn, the distributor gains access to new products without incurring the costs of internal development.

Joint Venture Arrangements

Rather than relying upon one or more of the contractual arrangements referred to above, the parties may choose to create a formal, commonly-owned joint venture company to conduct some or all of the activities relating to the technology. For example, a joint venture may be formed to conduct additional research and development projects, as well as to manufacture and distribute the various derivative products. A joint venture arrangement serves a number of purposes and, obviously, tends to bring the interests of the parties into much closer alignment than would be the case if the technology transfer simply consisted of a license agreement between two essentially unrelated parties.

The parties to a joint venture must resolve most of the issues that would otherwise arise in any of the basic contractual relationships. For example, if one party is performing research and development work for the joint venture, a research agreement will probably be used which sets out the objectives of the work and the compensation which the researching party will receive for the performance of the work. In addition, the parties must agree on a number of other issues which are particular to the use of the joint venture form, such as the control mechanisms for the joint venture, the form of contribution which each party must make in the form of patent licenses, technical information, technical and management assistance, training, cash, capital, labor and other similar items, and the procedures for terminating the venture.

Foreign Investments and Acquisitions

A domestic firm may sometimes decide to enter a new foreign market by purchasing a significant equity interest in an existing foreign entity or by purchasing the entity outright. Obviously, this type of strategy can involve a significant amount of cash and other resources and the success thereof may ultimately depend on the domestic firm's ability to retain key local employees and to continue to capitalize on the reputation and local contacts which the local firm has developed prior to the acquisition. A domestic firm may seek an investment or acquisition transaction after it has been involved with the target firm in one of the other business relationships referred to above, such as a distribution agreement.

Formation of a New Foreign Entity

In situations where there are no viable strategic partners in the specified market, the domestic firm may decide to actually go into the market by forming a new entity and attempting to establish an entirely new business. This strategy can be extremely risky unless the firm has substantial familiarity with the market and is able to recruit qualified local personnel to assist in the venture.

III. LEGAL AND REGULATORY CONSIDERATIONS

International business relationships can involve a number of disparate areas of law and regulation, both domestic and foreign. While the book has been organized in a manner which separates the domestic and foreign laws and regulations that effect international business transactions, the following list is informative:

- *Antitrust and Unfair Competition.* Entry into a new foreign market through one of the international business relationships can certainly have an impact upon the competitive conditions in the marketplace. Both domestic and foreign laws and regulations relating to antitrust and unfair competition call for scrutinizing each of the specified arrangements, including the formation of joint ventures, stock and asset acquisitions, patent and trade secret licenses and distribution agreements.
- *Export Controls.* The United States and many other developed countries have adopted export control laws which regulate the types of technology that can be exported to certain foreign countries.
- *Foreign Technology Transfer Laws.* Many developing countries have attempted to regulate the content of "inbound" technology transfer agreements, such as a license or technical assistance agreement between a large foreign enterprise as licensor and a local firm as the licensee. Common areas of concern include the amount of compensation to be paid for the license and the type of restrictions which can be imposed upon the licensee's use of the transferred technology.
- *Inbound Investment Laws.* Many countries in both the developed and developing worlds have laws and regulations dealing with inbound investment by foreign parties. For example, formation of an international joint venture or the acquisition of an ownership interest in a local firm may be subject to review by governmental authorities and approval may be subject to agreement to conditions on such things as personnel practices, local content and the repatriation of earnings in hard currency.
- *Foreign Agency and Distribution Laws.* Agreements with foreign sales agents

and distributors with respect to the sale and marketing of products in the local market may be subject to review and regulation under various agency and distribution laws. In many cases, the effect of these laws is to make it more difficult for the local agent or distributor to be terminated without the right to receive some additional compensation from the principal.

- *Tax and Accounting Considerations*. Any transfer of technology rights, whether it takes the form of a license under which royalties are to be paid or an outright sale of the intellectual property assets, may have significant tax and accounting consequences for both parties.

In addition, various types of transactions will raise issues relating to securities laws, such as when an investment is to be made or a firm is to be acquired in its entirety; corporation and partnership law, particularly when the parties are forming a joint venture; products liability law, in those cases where the agreement contemplates the manufacture and/or sale of products to consumers; and bankruptcy laws, especially if there is some concern regarding the financial stability of one or both of the parties.

IV. MULTILATERAL INITIATIVES AND GOVERNMENT PROGRAMS

The growing network of international business relationships has led to the promulgation of various laws and regulations which are designed to facilitate international trade between countries with varied legal and business customs. For example, the law of sales has been the subject of intense study, eventually leading to the promulgation of a model code which can be used to govern an international sales contract. In addition, growing recognition of the importance of international trade has led to the development of federal, state and local programs designed to assist domestic firms in marketing their goods overseas.

V. PRACTICAL CONSIDERATIONS AND COUNTRY-SPECIFIC MATTERS

In addition to the laws, regulations and basic business strategies involved in "going international," it is important to be cognizant of a number of practical matters, as well as the laws and customs which dictate the conduct of business activities in each of those countries in which the firm is active. In this book, we have included general discussions on evaluating business and market opportunities in foreign markets, selecting and using counsel in foreign jurisdictions, insuring against the risks associated with foreign market activities and international arbitration. Also, a variety of country-specific chapters have been included on areas from around the world, including the European Community, Latin America, the Pacific Rim, the Middle East, and Africa. As always, local assistance should be secured whenever difficult issues arise in any "going international" transaction.

PART ONE

BASIC STRATEGIES FOR OPERATING IN INTERNATIONAL MARKETS

INTERNATIONAL TECHNOLOGY LICENSE AGREEMENTS

Michael R. Oestreicher
Thomas F. Zych
Howard B. Gee

I. INTRODUCTION

TECHNOLOGY LICENSING often proves to be a popular and cost-effective approach for a company to expand internationally. It is perceived to be a vehicle by which a company can enter and penetrate foreign markets and achieve local production in such markets, without establishing its own operation or manufacturing facilities. Technology licensing also oftentimes is used by companies as a means of acquiring technology, whether by way of inbound licensing only or through cross-licensing/technology sharing arrangements.

All too often, however, pursuing an international licensing strategy underestimates the level of commitment required of a company if it hopes to transfer successfully, and then exploit profitably on an ongoing basis, its technology.

This chapter will explore the subject of technology licensing generally; and through its coverage of the various considerations involved in technology licensing, hopefully will demonstrate the level of commitment required of a successful licensor or licensee.

A technology license is a grant of the subsidiary right to use all or part of an intellectual property right. Stated otherwise, inasmuch as an intellectual property right carries with it the legal power to prohibit another from practicing the technology or expression embodied in the right, a license is a formal expression by the owner of the right permitting the use of the right by another notwithstanding the owner's legal right to prohibit such use. Therefore, the principal provision of a license agreement is the grant of the right to use the technology; the remaining terms regulate the consideration to be given to the grantor in exchange for its permission, the means, methods and procedures for the grantee's use of the technology, and compliance with applicable laws.

The term "technology transfer" connotes a related transaction, one in which a party with knowledge of a technology imparts that knowledge to another, usually for consideration. Because virtually all negotiated technology transfers occur with regard to technology that is the subject of a recognized property right, this chapter will discuss the general topic of technology licensing, recognizing that such transactions by necessity consist of or contain the transfer of a given technology from the grantor to the grantee.

3

The chapter will first discuss general considerations critical to the preparation of a valid and useful technology license agreement and specific provisions that should be considered in preparing the agreement. The chapter also will discuss the effects of various types of national and community laws that regulate or have an impact upon technology licensing agreements. For ease of reference, these laws will be discussed within the context of specific contractual provisions.

The chapter will not address in detail the important issues of tax, antitrust and competition, dispute resolution or capital repatriation issues (because they are treated in other chapters in this compilation). As to national and community laws, no attempt is made to differentiate in each instance between results required by established normative laws and rules derived largely from the practices of national governmental bodies whose approval or acquiescence is required. Indeed, the practices of governmental bodies frequently have the effect of nullifying recorded laws. In each instance, the reader is urged to consult the latest available research materials (especially in light of rapidly changing laws and practices driven by international trade developments) and consult with local counsel familiar with the nation's licensing laws and practices.

II. GENERAL CONSIDERATIONS

When to License

A license transaction is appropriate where the owner of protectable technology desires that the technology be exploited in whole or in part by another while retaining title to the technology. Where the owner has no interest in retaining title to the technology, an assignment of its interest is more appropriate.

In addition, a license is appropriate any time during the term of the legal protection afforded to the technology. For example, a patent license is appropriate during the statutory term of the patent, but after the expiration of the patent a license is unnecessary from the point of view of the transferee, at least as to the art covered by the patent disclosures. On the other hand, certain rights, such as trade secrets, have no fixed life span. So long as the technology is protectable as a trade secret, a license of the secret is appropriate.

What to License

The most basic term of a license is an accurate statement of what rights the licensee is granted. This requires, in turn, a firm understanding on the part of all contracting parties as to what rights exist in the technology. A given industrial process may embody a patented process or product, a trademark under which the end product is marketed, proprietary know-how not covered by the patent disclosures, and copyrighted works necessary to the practice of the technology such as blueprints, shop drawings and software. The parties must understand what rights exist to the technology and agree as to which of the rights will be the subject of the license.

Once an accurate inventory of existing rights is compiled, the next decision is whether the rights will be granted in their respective entirety or whether the licensee will be permitted to practice only a portion of the granted rights. For example, the licensee may be restricted to practicing the granted right only in a specified territory or within a limited field of use. Similarly, the licensee may be promised exclusivity or, on the other hand, may be required to compete with the proprietor or other licensees in exploiting the technology. The grant may be for a term shorter than the term of legal protection for the right, or may be coextensive with the right's life. Before a decision is made to license less than all of the rights subsisting in a particular article of intellectual property, however, care should be taken to consult applicable national and community laws that may prohibit or limit the division of rights in a license.

Consideration

The quid pro quo for the license is the consideration paid to the licensor. It is in this term that the parties may have the greatest latitude in fashioning the transaction, subject to applicable laws. Where permitted by law, the payment may be entirely in cash, paid either at the time of the grant, or over time or in a combination of the two approaches. The payment may be in a lump sum, based on a royalty computed by manufacture, use or sale, or a combination of the two. The consideration may be in kind, (in whole or in part) in the form of a cross-license of other technology, the supply of finished or processed goods, or in some other non-cash form. The principal limitations are applicable national and community laws and the economic desires of the parties as to cash-flow, tax and planning economics.

Applicable Laws

It is unusual for an international license agreement to be consummated without somehow being impacted by the applicable laws of the countries of domicile of the grantor and grantee. At a minimum, to the extent that the protection of the property right depends in the first instance upon governmental sanction, as with patents, the law of the country under which the patent is issued must be considered as should the patent laws of the grantee's country. In addition, the laws of the grantor's domicile must be considered as to whether the technology may be exported, and on what terms. Similarly the laws of the grantee's domicile must be considered in light of what technology may be imported and what protection can be assumed for that technology in the grantee's nation. It does little good to license technology into a nation whose laws frustrate the commercial designs of the parties or endanger the integrity of the technology itself.

III. KEY CONTRACTUAL PROVISIONS

No single form of license agreement will be adequate for every commercial setting. There are, however, critical transactional considerations that are best dealt with through carefully crafted contractual provisions rather than after-the-fact negotiations aimed at resolving disputes.

The Granting Clause

The clause granting the licensee the right to exploit the technology is the single most important term of the license. In most instances, practicing the technology of another without that party's permission is unlawful. The clause therefore should enumerate in detail the precise rights that are to be licensed. As noted above, the parties should have a firm understanding of all of the rights that exist in the technology before the drafting begins. With this understanding, the parties are in a good position to determine which rights will be transferred.

For example, if the technology is covered by an existing patent (or patent application) the parties should decide whether the licensee will be permitted to use all of the art disclosed in the patent or whether only a portion of it will be transferred. Similarly, where the technology is embodied in a copyrighted work, such as a computer program, the parties should decide whether all of the Section 106 rights (i.e., the exclusive rights granted to the owner of a copyright by 17 U.S.C. §106) are to be licensed, or whether the licensee is to be given only some of those rights (e.g., the reproduction, distribution or derivative works rights). From the licensor's point of view, the divisibility of intellectual property rights permits a careful decision as to whether the licensee is to be given access to the entire right, or whether, in the case of a patent or trademark license, the licensee is to be limited to a subsidiary role in the marketing of the fruits of the technology. For example, the licensee may have the right to manufacture the goods in question but not to sell or otherwise distribute them. Crafting the granting clause appropriately is an extremely important tool for maintaining control over the licensee's activities.

Conversely, the licensee needs to ensure that enough of the rights are transferred to permit the bargained-for commercial exploitation of the technology. A patent license may not be of much use, at least in the short term, where the patent does not disclose sufficient data to permit the economical manufacture of the patented article. A concomitant know-how license, included in the granting clause, will effectuate the transfer of the unpatented technology so as to permit the efficient use of the patented article.

Of necessity, an international license carries with it the need to transfer international rights. It is assumed for purposes of this discussion that the licensor has taken sufficient steps to protect its rights in the country into which the technology will be licensed. For example, it is assumed that the owner has secured patent rights in the target nation prior to, or as part of, the licensing of the patent rights into that nation. The granting clause should grant a license under the patent issued by the licensor's home nation and under the patent secured in the licensee's home nation so as to ensure the legal right to exploit fully the licensor's technology.

In most nations, a single agreement with a single granting clause is both sufficient and advisable. However, the laws of certain countries have required the execution (and governmental approval) of separate contracts for the license of patents, trademarks and "industrial technology" (i.e., know-how), each containing its own granting clause for the pertinent right.

Grant-Back Clauses

It is typical for the licensor to seek in the license agreement a promise from the licensee that any technology derived from the licensee's exploitation of the transferred technology be given to the licensor. For example, where a patent licensee develops improvements to the patented article or process, it is a natural desire for the grantor to seek either an assignment or license-back of the improvements. Such "grant-backs" may take several forms. The agreement may require that the licensee assign to the licensor all of the licensee's right, title and interest in the improvements (either during the life of the agreement or upon its termination) with or without an accompanying license of the improved technology to the licensee; it may require that the licensee grant back an exclusive license to the improvement to the licensor; or it may require that the improvement simply be made available to the licensor by a nonexclusive license-back or otherwise. In any event, the licensor's justification for such a provision is that the licensee could not have discovered or developed the improvement without access to the licensed technology, and the improvement often becomes an integral part of the current and commercially-expected version of the technology.

Many national and community laws, however, severely restrict the use of grant-back clauses. The rationale for such laws are that they can be used to entrench the dominant market position of the licensor and can extend the economic power of the licensor by limiting of access to technology that was not the subject of the original rights owned by the licensor. Mandatory grant-back clauses requiring an assignment of the improvement have been expressly prohibited either by law or governmental practice in numerous countries. Grant-backs have been permitted if effected by mutual license, for example under the EEC block exemptions for patent and know-how license agreements, and under various national laws. Grant-backs by license generally have been permitted in numerous other countries, and also have been allowed in others subject to regulations with regard to agreements affecting trade among member states of various trade blocks. The extreme case was Brazil which prohibited grant-back clauses on the one hand while requiring the licensor to grant to the licensee a royalty-free license as to improvements developed by the licensor on the other.

Warranties

The licensee typically will require warranties of title, validity and non-infringement, and warranties concerning the products' performance, together with corresponding indemnification provisions.

Warranty of Title

The licensee should request that the licensor warrant that it holds title to the transferred rights free and clear of conflicting claims of ownership. While this is no substitute for an effective title search (where possible), the warranty provides a vehicle for imposing liability on the licensor in the event it later discovers or determines that the licensor did not hold good title to the rights at the time of contracting, particularly in connection with unpatented know-how.

Warranty of Validity

Similarly, the licensee should request a warranty that the right is valid; i.e., that the exclusive intellectual property right under which the license is granted in fact exists. For example, a trade secret licensee should request a warranty that the information disclosed is, indeed, proprietary and confidential to the licensor, is not generally available to the industry and has not been disclosed in circumstances destroying the trade secrecy of the information. The breach of such a warranty leads to the unacceptable conclusion that the licensee has paid for a right that it could have exercised without the license.

Warranty of Non-Infringement

In order to avoid paying twice for the same right, the licensee also should request a warranty that the practice of the licensed technology will not infringe the rights of any third party.

Other Warranties

It is common for licensees to request specific performance-oriented or product capability warranties as well as Uniform Commercial Code-type warranties that the goods produced under the license will be merchantable and fit for their intended purpose, particularly where the goods are to be produced to the licensor's specifications.

The licensor is not required, however, to give any such warranties. It is entirely appropriate for the parties to leave the risks outlined above to be faced by the licensee. These risks should, however, be treated expressly in the license agreement and the various warranties either given or disclaimed in clear and enforceable terms.

Some warranties may be implied as a matter of law. For example, English law has been held to imply a warranty of quiet enjoyment in license agreements that is breached in the event a claim is made by a third party that the licensee's practice of the technology infringes the third party's rights. Governmental authorities of other countries have required the insertion of a clause providing for the indemnification by the licensor in the event that there is a failure in the efficacy of the technology.

Consideration

Most license agreements call for payment to the licensor in return for the grant of rights. As noted above, there is almost no limit to the conceptual range of payment mechanisms available to the parties, other than those imposed by applicable law. Once the parties have determined their respective financial and accounting goals with regard to the contractual payments (such as cash flow management, tax minimization and accounting and reporting obligations), there is virtually no limit to the form in which the consideration can be structured. As with the granting clause which should be carefully tailored to meet the needs of the parties with regard to the transferred technology, the consideration provisions should be tailored to the precise transaction at issue.

Most commonly, payment is made in cash. However, the laws of certain countries have required the payment of royalties in kind. Where currency is the medium of payment, the payments may be in one or more of the following forms: a single payment made at or near the time of execution (a "paid-up" license) payments of fixed periodic amounts with or without inflators (or deflators) or payments calculated with reference to a specified unit of manufacture, sale, or revenue. Commonly, the payment may be made in a combination of some or all of these forms, as in a license calling for a lump sum payment "up front" with a specified minimum annual royalty payment and a percentage revenue calculated on sales or revenues.

Where payment is to be made in cash, the currency of payment should be spelled out in the contract. In addition, the agreement should provide for exchange rate fluctuations, by indexing the royalty payments to recognized exchange rate fluctuations or otherwise. Where the payments are made upon activities in a nation with readily convertible currency with little or no legal restriction on currency export, the choice is dictated largely by the parties' preference, established banking relationships and the relative predictability in the value over time of the currencies under consideration. Where this is not the case, the choice may be dictated in whole or in part for the parties.

Minimum royalties not tied to actual commercial exploitation of the technology generally have been prohibited in numerous countries. In addition, some nations in the past have regulated royalty levels by declaring specific royalties "excessive" or "unfair," largely on a case-by-case basis. Historically, the Brazilian government further has prohibited the remittance of royalties by a Brazilian subsidiary to its foreign parent except in bona fide technical assistance agreements not involving the license of patents, trademarks, or know-how and has prohibited the payment of royalties on technology subject to a patent application until the patent is issued.

Where a royalty is calculated with reference to some unit of economic activity, such as sales or revenues, care must be taken in defining the elements of the equation. Terms that the parties may believe have general commercial definitions often are unsuitable and the sure subject of later dispute. Terms such as "net" "gross" and "profit" should not be used in the absence of clear definition. For example, "net" should not be used unless the agreement defines what items are excluded from the computational base used to derive the "net" figure. "Profit" has numerous meanings even within this country, and national norms and accounting standards vary from nation to nation (either formally or by convention) so as to make the term virtually meaningless unless a formula for calculating "profit" is spelled out in the contract. The better approach is to choose a purely objective variable, such as revenues, define what may be deducted from the pure gross (e.g. returns, allowances or warranty payments) and apply a percentage to the resulting figure.

The period during which royalty obligations may be imposed varies with the type of intellectual property licensed. The law in this country specifies that royalty obligations may not be imposed upon the use of a patented technology following the expiration of the patent, and a contractual provision imposing such an obligation constitutes patent misuse that may give rise to antitrust liability. In certain countries, for example, royalty payments with regard to patent licenses generally are limited to the first five years following issuance of a patent.

The United States Court of Appeals for the Fourth Circuit recently recognized the affirmative defense of copyright misuse in copyright infringement actions. This will functionally prohibit the imposition of royalty obligations as to an expired copyright. *Lasercomb America, Inc. v. Reynolds,* 1990-2 Trade Cas. ¶69,145 (4th Cir. 1990).

As with contractual payment obligations in general, it is advisable to incorporate some monitoring mechanisms to ensure the licensee's compliance. Most commonly, the licensor insists upon the right, either upon request or at specified intervals, to inspect the pertinent records relating to any activity that affects the royalty obligation. A concomitant obligation would require the licensee to maintain sufficient, detailed records (preferably in conformance with generally acceptable accounting standards and in a language readily understandable by the licensor) to make such auditing meaningful. The parties may allocate the responsibility for paying for the audit among themselves. A common compromise requires the licensor to pay for the audit unless a discrepancy of greater than a specified amount or percentage is found, in which case both the discrepancy and the cost of the audit are to be paid by the licensee.

It is conceivable that the consideration may be paid in kind. For example, a manufacturer may wish to move manufacturing operations off-shore, but without the heavy up-front capital investment required by such a move. An option is to grant a manufacturing license with restricted sales rights to a foreign licensee in return for the obligation to manufacture and deliver to the licensor a specified volume (or portion of the licensor's requirements) of manufactured goods at cost. One benefit to the licensor of such an arrangement is the savings of capital and costs. Similar economic considerations may justify other forms of in-kind royalties.

Sub-License

In the absence of a provision dealing with the right of the licensee to grant sub-licenses, it is generally understood that the licensee does not have the right to sublicense the rights conveyed in the license documents. Nevertheless, even if the parties implicitly understand that sub-licensing is not to be permitted, it is better practice to cover the issue explicitly in the license agreement. If the parties are in agreement that sub-licenses are to be prohibited, a single sentence so providing will suffice.

If, on the other hand, the parties agree to permit sub-licenses, then the terms and circumstances for such sub-licensing should be articulated. Common limitations (where permitted by law) provide for the requirement of approval both of the fact of the sub-license and of the particular sub-licensee. It is conceivable to spell out the criteria for the granting or withholding of approval, with a view to forestalling later disputes. A middle ground would provide that the approval should not unreasonably be withheld, but this invites disputes over what may be considered unreasonable.

The licensor should clarify the terms and conditions upon which the sub-license may be made, if possible in the form of an agreed-upon sub-license agreement (attached as an exhibit to the license agreement) which sets out the principal acceptable terms of the sub-license and prohibits the licensee from entering into sub-licenses that materially differ from those specified in the form agreement without the licensor's approval. In effect, such a clause ensures the licensor's participation in the negotiations of the sub-license. In addition, it may be appropriate to include a contractual provision requiring the licensee to disclose the identity of all persons and entities that solicit a sub-license. This may raise concerns on the part of the licensee with respect to the disclosure of confidential business relationships, causing resistence to a disclosure requirement. In addition, the licensor should anticipate some enforcement difficulties.

The licensee's sub-license revenues should be either explicitly included or excluded from the royalty formula, if there is one, rather than leaving the matter unclear.

More complicated questions arise where the licensed technology is likely to be subject to modification and improvement during the term of the license, whether by the licensor or the licensee. The sub-licensing clause should clarify whether the licensee has the right to sub-license all generations of the licensed technology or only some smaller subset of that technology. Where the license validly requires the grant-back of new versions of the technology, the sub-license provision should not create inconsistencies with the licensee's rights to the technology under the grant-back clause. Permitting the sub-licensing of technology otherwise covered by an exclusive grant-back clause, for example, creates a contractual ambiguity that is easily prevented.

Confidentiality

It is highly improbable that a technology license will be effective in the absence of the disclosure of technical, financial and other information that at least one of the parties wishes be kept in confidence. Because license relationships are not inherently confidential, the license agreement should specify both the type of information that should be kept in confidence (often an essential element in assuring the legal protection for the information), and the manner in which the information should be treated.

Generally, trade secrets consist of all proprietary commercial information that is not generally known in the relevant trade or industry and that provides its owner with a competitive advantage over those who do not know or use it. *Kewanee Oil Co. v. Bicron Corp.*, 416 U.S. 470, 474-75 (1974) (quoting Restatement of Torts § 757, comment b [1939]). In addition, the law permits contacting parties to designate as confidential data that otherwise that does not fit the legal definition of trade secrets and thereby extend the functional equivalent of trade secrecy to such information. The scope of that which is considered to be a trade secret normally will exclude (1) information that becomes generally known in the industry without the fault of the party to whom the initial disclosure is made; (2) information that is disclosed to that party by a person under no obligations of secrecy with regard to the information; and (3) information that is already known by the party to whom disclosure is made at the time of the disclosure.

The disclosing party should insist on tight and specific limitations on the use of the disclosed information. For example, not all of the licensee's employees need access to the disclosed technology; therefore, the license agreement should describe the classes of persons who may have access. Moreover, depending on the country involved, the agreement should contain provisions assuring the obligations of those employees who are granted access to such information to maintain the requisite confidentiality either as a matter of law or by separate agreement. Disclosure to affiliates of the licensee should be prohibited unless such affiliates are clearly bound to the same or greater obligations of confidentiality as is the licensee.

The licensor should consider national disclosure, or registration requirements with regard to the licensed technology, and assess the likelihood of the confidentiality provisions being negated by governmental disclosures. For example, Brazil has required not only the registration and approval of license agreements, but also the filing of periodic reports with details as to the progress of the exploitation of the technology. At a minimum, the licensor should require that the licensee notify the licensor in advance of any required disclosures to be made to a governmental body. Of course, such a provision should not be used to facilitate evasion of such requirements, but will allow the licensor to consider terminating the relationship (if contractually and economically feasible) rather than risking the possible loss of confidentiality.

Restrictions on Operations

Normally the licensor has taken great pains in designing its manufacturing, distribution and sales strategy in its own country. The licensor naturally will desire that the operations of foreign licensees at least not be in conflict with those strategies and, preferably, be complimentary to the overall approach to the exploitation of the technology chosen by the licensor. Accordingly, the licensor will seek to impose restrictions on the licensee's exploitation of the licensed technology. This is often the subject of the most intense negotiations and is the area in which compliance with national and community laws is both difficult and crucial.

Most foreign licensing is conceived of territorially. That is, the licensor is seeking to move its technology into new geographic markets. It is thus natural that the licensor views the licensee as exploiting the technology within a specific geographic market. The licensee, on the other hand, views the newly-licensed technology as an extension of its manufacturing or sales capacity, and if the licensee is engaged in or contemplates international business it does not share the licensor's geographically-restricted view of the licensing relationship.

It is thus extremely important for the licensing parties to spell out the territoriality of the license. First, the license should define the territory within which the licensee may use the technology. The most commonly used reference points are national, community or continental boundaries.

Next, the agreement should specify whether the fruits of the licensed activities may be exported out of the territory. It does not follow automatically that the prohibition on a licensee's ability to manufacture a patented or trademarked article outside of a specified territory carries with it an implicit prohibition on sales of that article outside of the territory. Any such provision should be explicit, if desired and lawful. EEC law of course prohibits export restrictions with regard to trade between Member States and the Treaty of Rome has been construed to prohibit restrictions on parallel imports within the Community, except in narrow circumstances where there is an appreciable difference in quality which justifies territorial restrictions so as to prevent consumer confusion as to the source and quality of the goods. On the other hand, the European Commission recently invalidated German beer purity laws to the extent they were used to prohibit imports of beer not meeting German beer purity laws.

Numerous countries traditionally have prohibited export restrictions. In others, export restrictions have been permitted where limited to areas in which the licensor has granted prior exclusive licenses or where the licensor is already working the technology itself.

Where territorial or export restrictions are either legally unavailable or not feasible, it may be possible to include a term limiting the quantity of goods or services that the licensee may manufacture or provide through use of the licensed technology. Such limitations may focus the licensee's exploitation on its local markets, since sales outside of that territory normally would carry greater cost burdens than within the territory and local profits could not be used to subsidize more costly distant sales without a one-for-one reduction in the more profitable local sales. However, volume limits will take a license agreement outside of the EEC's block exemptions for patent and know-how licenses, and volume limits have been prohibited under numerous national laws.

The agreement also should state whether the agreement is exclusive and, if so, as to which parties. The parties may either permit or prohibit the granting of similar licenses to others within the territory (licensee exclusivity) and may either permit or prohibit the licensee from entering into licenses with other parties with regard to similar technology (licensor exclusivity). Again, national and community laws frequently limit the parties' discretion in imposing exclusivity obligations. The EEC block exemptions for patent and know-how licenses permit exclusive licenses, but, as noted above, such a term cannot be used as a basis for prohibiting parallel imports. Certain national laws have prohibited exclusive licenses altogether.

A third type of exclusivity prohibits the licensee from dealing in technology of the type covered by the license through internal development. In effect, such a provision ensures that the licensor will be the sole source of the licensed technology, preempts the "make or buy" decision on the licensee's part, and ensures maximum royalties. More importantly, an internal exclusivity provision protects against the use of the license as a tool for reverse engineering where the licensee has the contractual right to terminate the agreement before substantial royalty revenues can be gained by the licensor.

Naturally, the licensor can expect that the licensee will be less than enthusiastic over contractually limiting its research and development activities. In addition numerous countries have prohibited the use of such controls over the licensee's internal research and development efforts, and such terms likely will be the subject of close scrutiny and possible objection where a governmental body is a party to the negotiations. The decision in *Lasercomb America, Inc. v. Reynolds*, discussed above, expressly disapproved a provision in a software copyright license agreement prohibiting the licensee from developing similar software programs itself.

The licensor also may request non-competition provisions in the license agreement.

Most commonly, the licensor will seek to prohibit the licensee from engaging in the trade of goods or services competitive with the business contemplated by the license agreement. The obvious purpose of a non-competition clause is to maximize the revenues generated from the licensing activities. Also, non-competition provisions prevent against the use of the licensed technology to assist in the manufacture, distribution and sale of competing goods and services, since it is very unlikely that the licensee's operations are so compartmentalized that the licensed and non-licensed portions of its business will not be served by the same pool of technological and personnel support. If possible, the licensee should be prohibited from avoiding the non-competition requirements by lodging the competing operations with an affiliate, such as a subsidiary or sister corporation. The agreement should define the period of time during which competitive activities are prohibited and whether the prohibition will survive the termination or expiration of the agreement and, if so, for how long. Various countries have prohibited restrictions on the licensee's use of the licensed technology after termination of the agreement, while others permit such restrictions except where the technology has entered the public domain. Of course, because a license is the grant of a right subsidiary to that of the licensor's, where the statutory right (such as a patent) continues in force after termination or expiration of the license, the right to preclude use by the licensee by law normally remains with the licensor.

Where articles produced through use of the licensed technology should bear a notice of the licensor's claim of right, such as a patent, trademark or copyright notice, the contract should require the licensee to apply the appropriate marking to any goods manufactured or sold by the licensee. Even where the technology consists solely of unpatented know-how, the licensor often will want to require that an appropriate indication of the licensing relationship appear on the products and in any accompanying literature.

The licensor also may require the right to supervise the activities of the licensee with regard to the licensed technology. With regard to trademark licenses, this is virtually mandatory, as the failure to supervise a trademark licensee's production or provision of the covered goods and services may be deemed to be an abandonment of the trademark. *E.g.*, *Kentucky Fried Chicken v. Diversified Packaging Corp.*, 549 F.2d 368 (5th Cir. 1977). Generally speaking, the supervision right is meant to ensure that goods or services manufactured or provided under the license are of acceptable quality and reliability so as to maintain the goodwill associated with the licensed technology. Accordingly, the supervision right should be tailored to meet this need rather than to extend general control over the licensee's business. Several nations have prohibited the use of such a clause to unduly control the licensee's operations, and some do not permit the imposition of quality requirements except to the extent necessary to the effective use of the licensed technology.

With regard to patent and know-how licenses, the agreement may restrict the field of uses to which the licensed technology may be put. Often a given technology may have several applications and one licensor may not be an appropriate vehicle for all of them. The licensor may desire to reserve one or more fields of use for itself or for other licensees. Field of use restrictions permit great latitude in managing internationally-useful technology over time. The European Commission has permitted field of use restrictions both in individual and block exemptions, and such provisions have been permitted under the laws of numerous countries.

An area of uncertainty with regard to such restrictions is the fact that various national authorities have invoked general prohibitions on undue restriction of the licensee's business to invalidate or prohibit restrictions as to which there is no general normative or written prohibition.

Technical Assistance

It is rare that licensed technology can be used off the shelf. Even though a patent, for example, must disclose the best method of use, few patents disclose all of the ins and outs of their exploitation. Accordingly, the licensee should insist on a term requiring the licensor to provide sufficient technical assistance to its personnel both in the form of start-up training and continuing consultation. Ideally, the contract will require on-site training and consultation, although the licensor fairly may insist on reimbursement for the expense of remote technical assistance. In any event, it is in both parties' interest that the licensee understand how to use the licensed technology.

However, even where the contract contains well-drafted confidentiality provisions, the licensor may not wish to disclose to the licensees, nor be obligated to provide technical assistance with regard to, particularly sensitive areas of technology but rather may wish to "black box" such sensitive components of the technology. In this event, the assistance clause should explicitly except such components from its obligations.

Certain laws prohibit any requirement that the licensee avail itself (at its own cost) of technology that is deemed unnecessary by the government.

Infringement

The licensed technology and its practice may either be subject to challenge or provide the basis for challenging activities of third parties. Because technology is so frequently the subject of litigation, the license agreement should spell out the parties' respective rights and obligations in the event of infringement of or by the transferred rights. At a minimum, the contract should require prompt disclosure of information that another is unlawfully practicing the licensed technology or has raised a claim of infringement of its rights. The obligation is two-way: the licensor desires to learn of claims or infringing activity affecting its rights and the licensee desires to know of challenges to the validity of the rights it has been granted.

Infringement of the Granted Rights

The agreement should specify which party bears the financial and logistical burden of prosecuting infringing activities occurring within the licensee's territory and which party has the right to supervise the response, including the right to institute and control infringement litigation. Normally, the party that pays is the party in control. Regardless of which party controls the handling of infringement claims against third parties, the other should be required to cooperate in the prosecution of the complaint and the agreement should spell out who pays for the cost of such cooperation. In addition, the license agreement should state which party is entitled to receive and retain any monetary relief obtained in infringement litigation. Conceptually, the relief should go to the licensor since it is the party whose rights were unlawfully used and who is damaged by the infringement most directly. However, a case may be made that some portion of the award should go to the licensee where the activities of the infringer occurred in a territory in which the licensee has exclusivity as the lost sales (if any) come out of the licensee's pocket. The remedial laws of the various nations as to the proper parties to and those entitled to relief in infringement actions differ to an extent beyond the scope of this paper, but the parties nevertheless should address the matter in the license wherever possible.

Improvement of Third-Party Rights

Where the practice of the licensed technology violates superior rights of a third party, liability under a warranty of non-infringement will be triggered if such a warranty is given by the licensor. In addition, the agreement should specify which party has the obligation to control the defense of the infringement claim and, again, the cooperation of each party in the defense should be explicitly required.

Remedies and Dispute Resolution

While the laws protecting the licensed technology in the first instance provide for substantial remedies for their misuse, it is advisable for the licensor to provide in the agreement for specific remedies, clearly deemed to be non-exhaustive, for the breach of particularly important obligations. The breach of non-competition, confidentiality or grant-back clauses and the breach of sub-license prohibitions or restrictions should be deemed to be remediable by immediate injunctive relief, as money damages obtained in the remote future are rarely a sufficient remedy for such a breach. Where allowed liquidated damages reduce the uncertainty in remedial laws, although they may be deemed to be an election of remedies and thereby unduly restrict available remedies. In any event, the specified remedies should be clearly stated to be in addition to, and not in lieu of, other available remedies.

Volumes have been written about the advisability of arbitrating international commercial disputes. Mechanisms and recognized tribunals exist in most parts of the world to arbitrate licensing disputes. Suffice it to say that there is no general agreement as to whether to include arbitration clauses in international technology licenses. If one is included, however, care must be taken to preserve other forms of judicial relief that are beyond the power of tribunals, such as injunctive and other coercive remedies backed up by the law enforcement powers ancillary to judicial bodies.

Some nations have prohibited the use of arbitration clauses requiring arbitration proceedings outside of that nation. Historically, for example, Brazilian authorities have gone so far as to require the removal of arbitration clauses entirely.

The parties may wish to choose a specific venue for actions arising out of or relating to the license agreement if resort to judicial relief is contemplated or allowed by the agreement. Where the licensee is permitted to trade in more than one country, this is particularly appropriate from the licensor's point of view so as to prevent forum shopping by the licensee, and provides both parties with some degree of legal predictability. Various countries prohibit the choice of a forum outside of that country.

Similarly, the parties may specify the law to govern the interpretation and performance of the agreement, understanding that it is not possible (and in some cases illegal) to contractually override entirely the laws of nations in which the licensed activities will occur. English and American laws generally recognize and enforce contractual choices of applicable law except where the law chosen is that of a nation without a substantial relation to the execution or performance of the contract. It should be noted that even where permitted a contractual choice of law will not carry with it an implied choice of forum, as most courts consider themselves competent to discern and apply the laws of another nation.

Term and Termination

The preferences of the parties with regard to the term and termination of the license presents one of the more contested provisions of license agreements. In the usual situation, the licensor desires to maintain as much flexibility in managing the long-term exploitation of its technology and may view the license arrangement as a temporary measure to generate revenues until it is in a position itself to exploit the technology. On the other hand, the licensee desires a term as long as possible to enable it to recoup its start-up capital and personnel investments and to permit long-term planning. The term provision represents (or should represent) a compromise between these positions. A fixed term is the first choice, and is a function of the considerations discussed immediately above. The agreement may then provide for renewal options or for automatic renewal barring notice of non-renewal, with or without specified criteria for non-renewal.

As with other provisions, national laws have substantial impact on the parties' choice of an agreed term. Several legal approaches are imposed. For example several nations require a minimum initial term long enough to permit the licensee to become familiar with and obtain financial benefits from the technology. On the other hand, some national laws have prescribed an outside limit for the term of the license. Others, for example, have deemed a patent license to be coextensive in term with the life of the licensed patent unless otherwise provided in the agreement.

Where the license is of technology covered by rights having several fixed dates of expiration, the agreement is of little use to the licensee after the last-tour expiration inasmuch as it has the legal right to practice the technology without a license after that time. The expiration date in this circumstance defines the outside limit of the term, particularly with regard to royalty obligations. Where mixed rights are granted, some of which have no fixed date of expiration (such as trade secret rights) the parties should consider the effect of the expiration of certain rights upon the viability of the license as a whole. In the absence of applicable contractual prohibitions, the licensee may be able to practice the technology solely by reference to the technology now in the public domain and its own know-how, and will want the license (with its payment obligations) to terminate upon the entry of the necessary technology into the public domain.

This raises the larger question of the parties' respective rights upon termination or non-renewal of the license. From the licensor's point of view, it wants all licensed rights to revert to it upon termination together with all physical embodiments (such as drawings, records, prints, formula cards and the like) constituting or revealing the technology. The licensee desires to relinquish only so much of the rights as is legally required, that is, to continue possession and use of everything that is not covered by the parameters of the previously licensed rights. As note above, many nations do not permit the licensor to restrict the post-termination activities of the licensee except as is implicit in statutory rights. The inclusion of post-termination confidentiality, non-use and non-competition covenants, together with explicit destruction or return obligations, is advisable where permitted as these subjects are not likely to be fruitful topics for negotiation after termination or expiration of the license arrangement.

The grounds for termination, or the right to terminate without any ground or cause, should be spelled out in detail. Commonly, the cessation of the licensee's business, the licensee's insolvency or bankruptcy, breaches of material terms of the agreement (such as confidentiality or royalty obligations) or other breaches of faith are deemed to be grounds for immediate termination of the agreement. Other breaches may be grounds for termination if not cured within a reasonable time after notice. From the licensee's point of view, the insolvency or cessation of the licensor's business may be deemed grounds for immediate termination, although the licensee must understand that the termination of the license may greatly impair its ability to continue operations requiring use of the licensed technology. In the absence of a notice provision, English law permits the termination of a license on reasonable notice.

Finally, the effect of termination or non-renewal should be deemed not to affect obligations (e.g., royalty payments) accrued at the time of the termination.

Miscellaneous Provisions

The license agreement should specify whether and by which party the agreement may be assigned. From the licensor's standpoint, the agreement is personal in that the identity of the licensee is very critical to the licensing decision. From the licensee's standpoint, the agreement is a vehicle for obtaining technology, and the licensor's identity is less important. Accordingly, it is entirely appropriate for the license to be assignable by the licensor but not by the licensee. National laws will have an impact in this area as well: in some countries a license is normally assignable unless otherwise provided; under others' laws, however, the licensee must have the licensor's permission to assign the license.

The agreement should specify the "official" language of the agreement as well as the language in which contractually-required notices and communications should be made. This is a term as to which the licensor's preference usually prevails. However, some countries require the use of their national language; others require that a local language version of the contract be given "equal authenticity" with the foreign translation. The use of translations should he undertaken with great care. For example, in

English and American practice the words "contract" and "agreement" are used almost interchangeably. In China, however, the word "hetong," which translates as "contract," refers to a binding legal obligation, while the word for "agreement" is "xieyi" which refers to a non-binding statement of intent.

The agreement may contain a "most-favored licensee" clause providing that the licensee will obtain at least as much of and as recent technology as do other licensees. This is most important to the licensee where the license is non-exclusive on the licensee's side. Similarly, the licensee may wish to include a most favored nation clause with regard to royalties, again particularly where the licensee will face competition from other licensees.

The licensee should be given the obligation to comply with all applicable local and national laws (including taxes, employment, duties and import and export requirements) as it is in the better positive to comply with such laws. The United States licensor should be aware that it has the burden of complying with United States export control requirements and in some cases imposing some restrictions on the licensee's use of the technology in light of existing or new trade restrictions.

Where the license calls for the manufacture or sale of goods made to specifications outside of the licensee's control, the licensee should request product liability indemnification from the licensor. This is accomplished through a legally implied warranty under English law.

Other boilerplate terms (e.g., integration clauses, method of notice clauses) are equally important in license agreements.

INTERNATIONAL SALES AGENCY AND DISTRIBUTION ARRANGEMENTS

Kathy Woeber Gardner[1]

I. INTRODUCTION

SELLING ABROAD via agents or distributors is one of the most common and practical methods for American companies to begin their forays into the international marketplace. U.S. companies vary in their approaches to selling abroad. Some companies initially "fall" into international sales by responding to an inquiry from an overseas sales agent or distributor, and others actively recruit an agent or a distributor after a great deal of market research and planning. In either case, many prospective exporters believe that there are few "downsides" (i.e., upfront costs or risks) to selling abroad through sales representatives. Unfortunately, this is not always true. The attorney representing an export-minded small or medium-sized business must be prepared to lead clients through the often substantially different business and legal requirements involved in selling in a foreign country.

This chapter provides a step by step guide to the negotiation and drafting of international sales agency and distribution agreements (together referred to hereafter as "representative agreements"). Part II explains some of the legal and business considerations involved in selling products overseas. Part III discusses the negotiation and drafting of the basic terms and provisions of a typical representative agreement and focuses primarily on those provisions that the client may consider to be "business" decisions. Part IV covers the negotiation and drafting of the "strictly legal" provisions of the agreement. The appendix includes a sample distribution agreement and a sample agency agreement; each incorporates many of the provisions recommended in this chapter.

A few preliminary comments are in order. First, a foreign representative agreement should not be entered into without consulting with an attorney licensed in the jurisdiction of the proposed sales territory.

Second, to thoroughly cover all the issues encountered in negotiating and drafting an agency or distribution agreement, it is highly recommended that this chapter be read in conjunction with the chapter in Part 3 of this book entitled *Sales Agency and Distribution Laws*, which describes the foreign laws and regulations pertinent to such agreements.

Third, as mentioned above, this chapter was written with the U.S. exporter in mind and therefore is structured to assist the attorney in negotiating an agreement which will benefit the exporter to the greatest extent possible. However, it is important to bear in mind that creating an agreement that is balanced and fair to both parties will increase the likelihood of a positive and profitable business relationship over the long term. Moreover, if a foreign court decides that the agreement is fair to both parties, it may be less likely to award substantial compensation payments to the representative (hereafter "representative" refers to both agents and distributors) upon early termination of the agreement.

II.   BUSINESS STRATEGIES IN SELLING ABROAD

Helping the Exporter Take the First Step

Assessing Whether Selling Abroad is Practicable For the Exporter

Because there are many business problems inherent in foreign sales, a commitment by the exporter's management to commence foreign sales with long term goals in mind is necessary for success. First, marketing in foreign cultures and supplying parts and services for the products sold will almost always require a great deal of planning and forethought. Second, entering into a relationship with a foreign business "partner" carries with it substantial legal risks, the greatest risk being the cost and time required (because of the pro-agent or pro-distributor legislation enacted by some foreign governments) to extricate the U.S. exporter from a relationship with an agent or a distributor that has not met the exporter's expectations. Lastly, in order to help the client determine whether the company is prepared to make this next important step in its business strategies, an attorney must also be aware of various non-legal elements which may strongly impact the transaction, such as the potential for political instability, local culture, labor issues and economic conditions.[2]

Market Research

In counseling the exporter, it is important for the attorney to be involved at the earliest stages of the exporter's plans. The attorney can suggest a number of resources which assist exporters in finding markets best suited for their products such as export management companies or the Department of Commerce U.S. and Foreign Commercial Service's (US & FCS) global network of commercial service officers. The US & FCS has district and branch offices in cities throughout the U.S. and Puerto Rico which will actively help the company conduct an in-depth market analysis to determine whether sufficient demand for the product in question exists in the proposed territory.[3]

At the same time, the exporter's attorney should conduct a survey of the laws of each country in which the exporter plans to enter to determine possible legal pitfalls. There are at least five issues that the attorney should research for each such country: 1) whether the exporter's trademarks, copyrights or patents will be protected once its products are sold in a foreign country; 2) whether there are representative registration requirements dictated by local laws and whether it is even possible to appoint a representative under local laws; 3) whether the country has protective legislation which will make it difficult to terminate a representative relationship; 4) whether there are product liability laws that will impact the exporter's product; and 5) whether the exporter's product can be sold in the territory without significantly altering the product to comply with local product standards.

Choosing a Representative

It is important for the attorney to discuss with the client at the outset the various vehicles through which the exporter can sell its goods in foreign countries. These vehicles include: 1) direct sales from the exporter to customers in a foreign country; 2) direct sales from the exporter in the U.S., but with the assistance of the exporter's foreign-based sales office; 3) joint ventures in which, for example, the U.S. company may cooperate with a foreign company to sell its product, with the U.S. company contributing technological know-how and financial strength and the foreign company contributing market access and business contacts; 4) branches or subsidiaries in which the U.S. company sets up a facility in the foreign territory to manufacture or repackage already manufactured product for sale in the territory; and 5) indirect sales through a representative such as an agent or distributor. Because the use of a representative may offer the most guidance and support in learning about the foreign market, together with the lowest financial commitment, most companies taking the first step into international sales will find an agency or distribution relationship to be the most attractive and logical choice.

Methods of Conducting a Search for a Representative

It is not unusual for U.S. exporters to make plans to sell abroad through an agent or distributor without having a clear idea of how to locate a reputable representative. In the absence of the exporter using its own business connections or those of its trade associations, the exporter may again turn to the U.S. Department of Commerce's US & FCS. Two programs that the US & FCS offers are: 1) the Agent/Distributor Service (ADS) which includes a custom-made search for representatives; and 2) the Department of Commerce Trade Fairs, which are designed to promote U.S. products and manufacturers worldwide.[4] Other resources available to the exporter are: international trade departments of state governments, local Chambers of Commerce, and the international departments of U.S. banks.

Selecting a Representative

Once the field has been narrowed to a few candidates, the exporter should be concerned with making sure the final contestants meet certain threshold requirements.

To be qualified, a representative must have, first and foremost, the financial ability to fully perform its obligations under the contract with the exporter. Financial capacity may be determined by working with the international department of a U.S. bank that has offices and experience in the proposed territory, by analyzing credit reports, and by reviewing the representative's own financial statements.

The exporter should also determine to what extent the candidate is currently selling products which are directly competitive or are complementary to those of the exporter, and if the overall quality of the representative's product line matches the quality of the exporter's products. The exporter should discover what percentage of the representative's business the exporter's products will represent in order to determine what level of attention the exporters's products will receive from the representative.

Further, the only realistic way to be certain that the prospective representative has the "tools" to perform the job, is for the exporter to visit the facilities and talk with the representative's personnel.

Finally, the exporter should take time to review the representative's sales record and analyze whether its sales growth has been consistent over the past five years and determine its future sales objectives.

Choosing Between an Agent and a Distributor

Once the exporter has made the decision to sell its products in a certain territory, it must choose whether it would be better to hire the representative as an agent or a distributor. The exporter's decision should be based on two criteria: 1) which type of representative will best serve the business objectives of the exporter and best fit into the existing sales structure of the exporter; and 2) whether agents or distributors are protected by restrictive local legislation.

A distributor is defined as an independent merchant that purchases goods for resale directly from the American exporter and that earns its profit by purchasing from the exporter at a discount and reselling at a higher price. A distributor assumes the risk of buying and warehousing goods in the local market and provides additional product support services. A distributor often extends credit to its customers and bears responsibility for local advertising and promotion. Sales made through a distributor create no contractual relationship between the exporter and the ultimate purchaser and the distributor may not legally obligate the exporter to third parties.[5]

An agent is defined as a company or individual who works on a commission basis, frequently for several manufacturers with complementary product lines. An agent generally does not take title to, or possession of, the goods it sells. It is common for an agent to be responsible for making business introductions, advising the exporter about market strategies for its assigned territory and assisting with general promotional activities. Because the exporter retains title to the goods in an agency relationship and the agent sells on its behalf, the exporter can exert more control over an agent than a distributor.[6]

After the exporter has made the choice between an agent or a distributor based on its business needs and legal restrictions, the representative agreement and subsequent communication should be consistent in referring to the representative by the chosen form. This is especially important when the distributor or agent operates in a country having legislation according either an agent or a distributor special protection, as courts in that country might bend over backward to interpret an agreement in a manner that offers the representative the greatest protection, regardless of the specific designation of the representative to the contrary.

III. BUSINESS CONSIDERATIONS IN NEGOTIATING AND DRAFTING REPRESENTATIVE AGREEMENTS

Exclusivity

One of the most important issues involved in negotiating a representative agreement is the question of exclusivity. In the context of the relationship between an exporter and a representative, exclusivity has three different meanings: 1) the exporter gives the representative the sole right to distribute the exporter's products in the assigned territory ("territorial exclusivity"); 2) the exporter agrees to refrain from appointing other representatives in the territory but reserves the right to sell in the territory itself; and 3) the representative agrees to sell the exporter's brand of goods to the exclusion of competing brands (i.e., agrees not to compete with the exporter).

Territorial Exclusivity

From a business perspective, it may be practical for an exporter to grant the representative territorial exclusivity in order to concentrate the exporter's sales activities and thereby lessen the need for the exporter to maintain numerous business relationships in the territory. In addition, offering a representative territorial exclusivity may be the only way in which an exporter new to the territory can penetrate a foreign market. [7]

The argument against granting territorial exclusivity is that it removes the advantages of lower prices and better customer service which often result from competition among several sellers of the exporter's product in a marketplace.[8]

When structuring the exclusivity provision, the drafting attorney should investigate local competition (antitrust) laws to determine whether exclusive territorial arrangements are permitted. Although each arrangement merits individual evaluation, appointment of an exclusive representative in a foreign country usually does not raise United States antitrust concerns.[9]

Exporter's Right to Sell in the Territory

It is often advisable for the attorney to reserve for the exporter the right to continue to sell in the territory, despite the grant of territorial exclusivity to the representative. One reason to reserve this right is that the exporter may have already established relationships with certain customers in the territory that it wishes to maintain. The reservation of the right to sell directly in the territory also gives the exporter the security of knowing that it can enter the territory at any time to service its customers or rectify any problems created by the representative.

Agreement Not to Compete

If the representative agrees not to sell brands competing with the exporter's products, this provision should be clearly drafted to delineate which goods are considered to be competitive brands, which other suppliers are considered to be the exporter's competitors, and whether the provision should survive the termination or expiration of the agreement. Although a representative will usually not expect to be able to promote products in direct competition with those of the exporter, it is likely that the representative will be active in the exporter's industry and will sell products that are marginally competitive with the exporter's products. An overly broad definition of what is considered to be competitive product will likely cause ongoing disagreements between the parties. If the dispute goes before a foreign court, such a provision will probably be regarded as overly restrictive to the representative and will not be upheld.[10]

As with territorial exclusivity, it is recommended to review antitrust laws with local counsel before drafting a non-compete provision in the agreement. Furthermore, United States antitrust laws should be examined in light of the facts of the agreement. There may be violations under United States antitrust laws if the provision forecloses U.S. competition from selling into a foreign market.[11]

Term and Termination of an Agreement

Perhaps the single greatest legal risk involved in the establishment of foreign agency or distribution agreements arises out of the plethora of "protective" laws that attempt to prevent exporters from terminating representatives in bad faith.

In certain countries, codes, statutory provisions, or judicially developed doctrines exist that essentially restrict freedom of contract with representatives of those countries.[12] In such countries, agreements may not be terminated or not renewed without payment of compensation to the representative, unless the representative is found to have committed certain statutorily defined breaches. Foreign courts may enforce such protective legislation regardless of the original agreement between the parties, the language of the contract, or the governing law chosen by the parties in the agreement itself.[13]

It is possible, however, to lessen or in some cases, eliminate, damages faced by an exporter under such legislation by carefully drafting the term (duration of the agreement) and termination provisions. The first step is to determine whether such restrictive legislation exists in the territory to which the representative is assigned. As mentioned in Part II, the exporter's decision regarding whether to use an agent or a distributor in a particular territory may be influenced by whether and to what extent the territory's legislation protects one type of representative.

After analyzing the applicable law, the attorney should then follow the steps below in negotiating the term and termination provisions of the agreement: 1) choose the representative wisely to avoid the need to prematurely terminate; 2) limit the term of the agreement and avoid the existence or the appearance of an "evergreen" contract; 3) choose a corporation or partnership over an individual so that the exporter's representative will not be designated as an employee under local labor laws; 4) make the termination provision reasonable and as "balanced" between the interests of the exporter and the representative as possible so that if a foreign court is called upon to review the agreement, the court will determine that the agreement was negotiated in good faith; 5) follow the statutorily required guidelines regarding the number of months for advance written notice (in the absence of clear rules, three months - a rough average of the statutorily prescribed notice time periods - prior to the proposed termination or decision not to renew is suggested); 6) set forth very specific and realistic criteria regarding what constitutes "just cause" for early termination; and 7) include a clause limiting compensation upon termination.

Length of Term

The term of the agreement between an exporter and its foreign representative may be negotiated in several ways: 1) as an agreement for unlimited duration; 2) as an agreement for an initial term of one or two years, with automatic renewals of the same amount of time; 3) as an agreement for an initial period of one or two years, which may be renewed by the exporter upon advance written notice to the representative conditioned upon the representative fulfilling certain specific requirements; and 4) as an agreement for a specific number of years with no renewal period.

If a representative contract has no specified expiration date, or if the term is automatically renewed, or, despite a specified expiration date which is passed, the parties continue to act under the contract, the agreement is considered to be an indefinite term contract. In many jurisdictions, such an indefinite term contract or "evergreen" contract would fall under protective legislation.[14] Therefore, an agreement with a fixed term (one or two years is preferred) which includes a provision that the parties will negotiate a renewal at the end of the term, may prevent the arrangement from falling under such protective legislation. In the alternative, the parties may agree to a fixed term contract with a renewal clause that sets forth performance criteria from which the exporter determines whether renewal is warranted.[15]

Choosing an Independent Representative

In order to minimize the risk of the application of local labor laws to the relationship between the exporter and representative, the exporter should appoint a corporation or partnership, not an individual. If an individual is appointed as an independent representative, the appointment should not contain terms that indicate, or could be construed as, terms of employment. Classification of a representative as an employee under local employment law may subject the exporter to obligations to pay the representative severance pay and to make social security and disability insurance contributions. An independent representative, whether an individual, corporation, or partnership, exercises control over its business; therefore, the agreement with an independent representative should not permit the exporter to determine the hours of the representatives's business or the proportion of time the representative must spend in servicing the exporter's products. Payment to an agent should not be in the form of salary, but rather in the form of a commission on the sales of the agent, without reimbursement for expenses.[16]

Just Cause for Termination

Before drafting the exporter's definition of what actions or omissions by the representative would constitute "just cause" for termination, the attorney should review the law of the applicable territory, with the assistance of local counsel, to determine what reasons for termination are acceptable. Some jurisdictions permit termination only for narrowly defined egregious acts of default, for example, the representative's conviction for a criminal offense. In general, most jurisdictions permit the parties to specify what constitutes "just cause" for termination if the terms are reasonable and the representative was not subject to a disproportionate negotiating disadvantage.[17] The list should distinguish those acts justifying immediate termination, from those for which the representative receives written notice of the problem and has, for example, 30 days, to cure. The list should be as exhaustive as possible.

Standard reasons for immediate termination may include: 1) bankruptcy or insolvency; 2) merger or change of a majority shareholder; 3) resignation of certain key managers; 4) death, if the representative is an individual; 5) material adverse changes in local law affecting the exporter's rights or obligations under the contract; and 6) the representative's loss of license or registration to do business in the territory. Other justifiable reasons for termination, for which an exporter may wish to give the representative notice and an opportunity to cure are: 1) failure to meet well-specified minimum sales quotas;[18] 2) carrying on activities for a competing enterprise; 3) repeated and gross negligence in the promotion and marketing of the exporter's products; 4) the appointment of sub-representatives (if such conduct has been prohibited); and 5) the refusal of the representative to comply with the exporter's reasonable and legitimate instructions.

All duties or obligations which an exporter considers essential to the performance of the agreement should be included in the reasons for just cause. Alternatively, the section of the agreement discussing duties may be prefaced with the representative acknowledging that each of the duties is essential to the proposed relationship and that any breach of the obligations will seriously harm the exporter's commercial reputation and good will and therefore may result in termination of the agreement.[19] When reviewing the contract with the client, the attorney should take the opportunity to advise the exporter that if premature termination becomes necessary, the exporter should create an extensive file, prior to termination, documenting the reasons for termination, in order to counter any claim that the termination was arbitrary or in bad faith.

Limiting Compensation Paid to the Representative Upon Termination

In those countries which have legislation which protects representatives in the event of termination by the exporter, it may be possible to limit, or eliminate compensation upon termination by: 1) carefully drafting language that defines how statutorily mandated indemnity amounts are to be calculated or drafting language which limits those amounts; or 2) negotiating with the representative to waive termination indemnification and consequential damages to which the representative may have a right under local law. It is important to note, however, that it is likely that foreign courts, in an effort to protect local representatives from what is perceived as unequal bargaining power with the U.S. exporter, will not be inclined to uphold waivers of this type.

If an agreement falls under the protective legislation described earlier in this section, compensation paid to a representative is usually lost profits. Although countries with protective legislation calculate this amount in a variety of ways, attorneys may expect calculations to involve the following factors: 1) average profits of the representative; 2) length of service; 3) the amount usually earned by the representative in the length of time equal to the statutorily-required notice period; and 4) the length of the unexpired term of contract. The following additional elements may be included: 1) the goodwill created by the representative for the exporter's goods; 2) capital expenditures by the representative to develop a market for the exporter's goods; 3) labor and warehousing costs incurred by the distributor pursuant to the execution of the agreement in question which cannot be recouped by use in some other manner or for some other party; or 4) the repurchase of the goods, parts or accessories currently in the distributor's inventory.[20] By understanding the factors taken into consideration by a particular country's legislation, the exporter's attorney may be able to draft a provision limiting the damages the exporter will have to pay upon premature termination.

Responsibilities of the Representative After Termination

The agreement with the representative should clearly delineate the representative's responsibilities following termination. Of primary importance, in the case of both agents and distributors, is the requirement that the representative return, within a specific time period, all customer lists and documents containing the exporter's trade secrets.

In distribution agreements, the distributor should be required to return or destroy all tools, tangible assets, advertisements, literature and business cards and business manuals originally supplied by the exporter. If the agreement stipulates that such items should be returned to the exporter, it is customary that the exporter cover the cost of shipment. The agreement should also require that the distributor agree to "de-register" itself as a representative. Agreements should also address: a) how unfilled orders will be handled; b) the appropriate method to settle accounts between the distributor and the exporter; c) equitable solutions regarding compensation for orders placed by the distributor prior to receipt of the termination notice and during the notice period; and d) reasonable arrangements for liquidation or repurchase by the exporter of inventory supplies once termination has become effective. In light of the possibility that a distributor may decide to order a large volume of product during the notice period, and then refuse to pay or flood the market with the product and sell the product at below cost so that the product is cheapened in the eyes of the consumer, it may also be prudent to include in the contract a provision limiting the distributor's options during the notice period. Such a provision could state that there will be a restriction on the volume of the product which the distributor may order during the notice period (e.g., 150% of the volume ordered in the immediately preceding period of the same length as the notice period).[21] Provision should also be made for the exporter or a new representative to accept responsibility for outstanding service contracts the distributor may have with respect to products in the hands of customers.[22]

Duties of the Representative

Describing the duties of a representative during the term of the agreement in detail has the benefit of ensuring that the parties have the same expectations of their relationship. This is an especially important part of the negotiation process because exporters and representatives often will only focus on the basic economic terms of the relationship without fully contemplating how the day-to-day operations of the relationship should be carried out. Furthermore, it is advisable to clearly delineate which duties are so important that their fulfillment merits a renewal or their neglect should give rise to a penalty (or termination).

By explicitly setting forth the duties and offering rewards and penalties, the representative will be more likely to be motivated to sell the exporter's products in a manner which helps the exporter reach its sales goals for the territory and in a manner which protects the exporter's reputation in the territory. However, it is important to maintain a balance between the exporter telling the representative what is expected and maintaining the independence required to avoid the appearances of an employer-employee relationship.

Marketing

Representative agreements frequently require the exporter to provide product support to the representative in the form of advertising, promotional literature (the representative may be required to provide translation) and technical training. The representative, in turn, will be obligated to make and provide the exporter with sales forecasts, market analysis, customer profiles, and reports on relevant technological, economic, legal, and political developments in the territory. The representative should also contractually agree to keep the exporter advised of competitors' activities in the territory.

Service and Support

Since it is assumed that the exporter has reviewed the facilities of the representative, whether it be a salesroom for an agent or a warehouse facility for a distributor, the representative should commit, under the terms of the agreement, to maintain the premises in a manner which will reflect well on the exporter and will adequately service local customers. The agreement should provide that the exporter will have periodic access to the premises for inspection and should include an obligation by the representative to promptly remedy any deficiency discovered by the exporter.

The sales team of the representative should likewise be fully staffed at all times and well versed in the exporter's product; the contract should state that following initial training by the exporter, the representative will accept the obligation to maintain that education.

If the product is of the type that requires service, the agreement should require that the representative (usually a distributor) provide inspection, maintenance and repair service (including warranty service). Along with that obligation, the representative may agree to purchase necessary tools, machinery and equipment. It is prudent to add a clause stating that if a representative offers a warranty to customers in excess of what the exporter knows to be commercially reasonable, the representative will agree to indemnify the exporter against third party liability for failure to honor the excess warranty terms.[23]

Finally, a distributor should agree, in the contract, to maintain adequate levels of the exporter's product on hand to properly service its customers in the territory.

Financial Reporting Requirements

In order to insure that the representative has the financial ability to fulfill its obligations under the agreement, (especially if the exporter has become a creditor of the distributor) the exporter should be advised to require in the agreement that the representative provide annual (or more frequent) financial reports as well as periodic sales reports. These reports can be used as a way to increase the level of communication between the parties and provide a basis for readjustment of the minimum sales goals discussed below.

Minimum Sales Performance

The minimum sales requirements go to the heart of the success of the agreement since they directly impact how the representative performs under the agreement and whether the exporter is able to extricate itself from the contract if the representative does not perform. The exporter and representative should work closely together to develop initial sales levels and periodic increases. They should also cooperate to determine at what point the exporter has the right to prematurely terminate the agreement if sales fall below the minimum requirement. The minimum sales level should be set forth in the contract so that both parties will have the same criteria against which to measure how their business relationship is faring and against which to make decisions regarding termination or renegotiation of a new minimum sales level.

Rewards and Penalties

Since omissions or failures to fulfill obligations do not necessarily require that an agreement be immediately terminated, the attorney may include provisions in the agreement that if certain requirements are not followed, the representative's territory will become non-exclusive or the distributor's discount will be reduced (or the agent's commission percentage lowered). Alternatively, if sales volumes exceed certain amounts, the contract could require that a commission or discount be increased or a new territory be awarded to the representative. Naturally, it should be emphasized that continued failure of the penalty measures to motivate the representative will lead to termination.

Specific Business Issues Related to Distributors

Terms of Sale to a Distributor

Price

A distributor is compensated by the difference between the price the distributor pays the exporter for the product and the price it receives from its customer. Although the exporter is free to determine the price it sells to the distributor, in many foreign countries, as in the United States, it is illegal to control the distributor's resale price. Care must be exercised to either state in the agreement that the prices may be changed at any time by the exporter, without notice to the distributor, or that the prices stated are guaranteed for a certain period (e.g., 60 days).

The agreement can be structured so that the price may be conveyed to the distributor via a quotation or, more commonly, a pro forma invoice. Pro forma invoices are quotations in an invoice format. The U.S. Department of Commerce recommends that pro forma invoices include information about the product, the price, the method of payment and delivery terms.[24] Distributors often use pro forma invoices to apply for an import license or to arrange for funds.[25]

Terms of Shipment and Passage of Title

Disputes over the interpretation of shipping terms are frequently litigated by exporters and distributors. A clearly drafted distributorship agreement should do more that list terms of trade (shipping terms) such as CIF or FOB; the parties should take pains to spell out exactly what they mean by such terms. Shipping terms govern which party has the risk of loss and which party is responsible for loading the goods onto the carrier, obtaining insurance, providing notice, etc. For example, as described in the International Chamber of Commerce's universally accepted rules for the interpretation of trade terms, INCOTERMS, the term CIF (cost, insurance and freight) means that the exporter contracts and pays for any applicable export licenses, for the carriage of goods to the named port of destination, and for cargo insurance so that the distributor is entitled to claim directly from the insurer. The exporter is relieved from any further risk once the goods have passed the ship's rails at the point of departure and is relieved of any further cost after contracting for carriage, handing over the goods to the carrier,and providing for insurance.[26] If the drafting attorney is certain that both parties fully comprehend the shipping term used, there should not be a problem with merely stating, "CIF (named port of destination) (Incoterms 1990)." However, if there is any doubt that the parties may not fully understand or agree, it is better spell out each party's precise obligations under the term used.

The point at which title passes is determined by the contract between the parties. The place where title passes is where the rights, title, and interest of the exporter in the goods are transferred from the exporter to the distributor. To determine where this takes place, courts typically look to where the parties intended to pass title and examine the shipping documents, insurance documents and other indicia of ownership. The question regarding where title passes is often an important U.S. federal tax issue for U.S. exporters. For federal tax reasons, the attorney may draft the representative agreement so that title passes abroad at the foreign port of shipment. If title passes abroad, the transaction becomes a "foreign sale". Generally, by creating a "foreign sale" the exporter attempts to maximize its foreign source income. In doing so, the exporter can take greater advantage of its foreign tax credits (U.S. companies' foreign tax credits are limited to the amount of their foreign source income).[27]

Sales Law Under the CISG and the UCC

As a direct purchaser of the U.S. exporter's products, the distributor enters into a sale of goods contract with the exporter. As part of the decision regarding choice of law (which will be discussed in greater detail in Part IV, section J), a drafting attorney must consider whether it is the best interest of the client to have the United Nations Convention for the International Sale of Goods ("CISG") or the Uniform Commercial Code ("UCC") apply to the ongoing sales to the distributor.

The CISG applies to contracts for the commercial sale of goods between a U.S. party and a party doing business in a foreign county which has adopted the CISG, or the CISG will apply if the parties have elected to have the CISG govern their agreement.[28] In the case where the CISG applies because both the U.S. exporter and the distributor have places of business in countries which have adopted the CISG, it is possible to opt out of the CISG in whole or in part.[29] Opting out of the CISG requires careful drafting; therefore, stating in a choice of law clause that the law of a particular U.S. state will govern the contract is not sufficient, since the CISG, as U.S. federal law, is also part of the law of every state. It is necessary to include a provision saying "the provisions of the Uniform Commercial Code as adopted in the State of X, and not the Convention for the International Sale of Goods apply."[30]

Some of the advantages to choosing the CISG are: 1) it is published in six different languages, including English; 2) it is a fairly balanced compromise between common law and civil law, thereby placing both parties on equal footing if the distributor has its place of business in a civil law country; 3) the rules are often similar to the UCC; and 4) the exporter may maximize its chances of having the choice of law provision honored by a foreign court which may regard the CISG as less "imperial" than an American state's UCC.[31] Some disadvantages of the CISG are that no body of established jurisprudence interprets the CISG and no authoritative forum ensures consistent interpretations worldwide.

Before deciding to opt out of the CISG, it is worthwhile to gain an understanding of how it differs from and is similar to the UCC. Generally, the rules of CISG have the effect of keeping a troubled contract moving forward to a greater extent than the UCC. The following is a brief overview of differences and similarities:

(1)   One of the most important differences is that the CISG does not contain a

Statute of Frauds, therefore any sales contract formed under the CISG may be oral.[32] The result may be that a contract may be formed earlier under the CISG than the UCC. For those attorneys concerned about a statute of frauds problem, the CISG permits the addition of a provision requiring all amendments to be in writing.

(2)　Another difference is that the CISG codifies the "mirror image" rule in the "battle of the forms." Under the CISG a reply to an offer with additional or different terms is a rejection and counter-offer. However, if the terms do not materially alter the offer, the acceptance is effective (unless the offeror objects either orally or in writing to the acceptance).[33] The UCC provides that when both parties are merchants and one party acknowledges the offer with a writing containing new or different non-material terms, the writing is an acceptance and the new terms are incorporated into the contract.[34]

(3)　The CISG and the UCC also differ because the CISG lacks the UCC's "perfect tender rule" which permits a distributor to reject goods or documents if they fail in any respect to conform to the contract.[35] Under the CISG, the distributor may reject goods only where the nonconformity amounts to a "fundamental breach" of the contract.[36] Given the lead times, shipping times, distances, costs, and complexities of payment arrangements which often accompany international sales transactions, the CISG is probably preferable to the exporter over the UCC perfect tender rule.[37]

(4)　The CISG and the UCC share fairly similar approaches to warranties. Article 35 of the CISG combines in one article the several warranties of the UCC, found in Sections 2-313 through 2-315. Although the CISG does not expressly address the issue of implied warranties of merchantability and fitness for a particular purpose, Article 35 of the CISG does state that goods will not be deemed to conform to the contract unless they are fit for the purpose for which they would normally be used; fit for any particular purpose of which the distributor informed the exporter, expressly or implicitly, at the time of contracting; like in kind and quality to any sample held out by the exporter to the distributor; and adequately packaged. Because the CISG does not adopt the UCC's language of implied warranties, standard disclaimers of implied warranties may be inadequate. Counsel should therefore consider modifying these disclaimers to reflect the language of Article 35.[38]

Deciding whether to use the CISG or opt out will depend on the facts surrounding the particular distributor agreement being negotiated. Given that it is more likely that a foreign court will honor the rules of the CISG over those of the UCC and that the two bodies of law are not substantially different, it may be advisable, for an attorney who understands the CISG, to refrain from opting out.

Payments by Distributor to Exporter

Methods of Payment

Payments from a distributor to its U.S. exporter involve substantially more risk than is involved in a domestic transaction of the same nature. One reason is that the domestic-currency value of a prospective foreign-currency payment depends on the exchange rate between the two currencies. A second reason is that the distributor may be unable to convert its country's currency into U.S. dollars because of exchange restrictions imposed by the distributor's government. A third reason is that the distributor will fail to pay the exporter (this risk, although present in domestic transactions, is higher with international payments because legal action against defaulting distributors in foreign countries is more costly, more time consuming, and often less successful than in domestic payments).[39]

U.S. exporters try to minimize inconvertibility and default risks by adapting the method of international payment to the facts related to the transaction, such as the relationship the exporter has with the distributor, the distributor's credit history, the size and frequency of the sales to the distributor, the competitive nature of the exporter's industry, political and economic factors, and the strength of the exporter's negotiating position.

(i) Open Account—If the exporter has a long-standing, successful relationship with its distributor, selling on an open account basis is the simplest method. The exporter grants the distributor credit to pay for the product a certain number of days after delivery; there are no letters of credit, bank documents, or bank charges involved. The drafting attorney should include a payment provision in the agreement instructing the distributor when the payment should be made (i.e., 10 days after receipt of the shipment of product) and by which method payment should be made (i.e., check or wire transfer). When drafting this provision, the attorney should bear in mind that the exporter bears all the risks of collection, which, as described in the preceding section, can be substantial.

(ii) Cash-in-Advance—Payment in advance is the best arrangement from the exporter's perspective and therefore the most difficult to actually obtain. It may be prudent for the attorney to include in the contract the demand for cash-in-advance if the credit standing of the distributor is very poor or if the risk of currency inconvertibility is very high.

(iii) Letter of Credit—In the event the attorney is unable to negotiate cash-in-advance and does not choose merely to accept the distributor's promise to pay, a documentary letter of credit is a widely accepted compromise in international sales transactions. A letter of credit in "irrevocable" form, issued by the distributor's bank and confirmed by a U.S. bank, virtually eliminates credit risk for the exporter and protects the distributor since the U.S. bank will only pay the exporter when the terms and conditions of the letter of credit are met.

A documentary letter of credit is an instrument issued by the distributor's bank that obligates that bank to honor drafts drawn against it by the exporter in accordance with specified terms. These terms include the amount of the credit, tenor of the draft (the tenor determines the time of the payment of the draft, i.e., sight or time), general description of the merchandise, documents required, and expiration date. The letter of credit becomes "confirmed" when the exporter's bank also promises to honor drafts drawn under it. In the alternative, the letter of credit could be "advised" if the exporter's bank merely takes the exporter's draft for collection and forwards it to the distributor's issuing bank. The exporter's bank will not confirm a letter of credit unless the distributor's issuing bank makes it "irrevocable" i.e., it cannot be cancelled or altered except with the agreement of all the parties. Revocable letters of credit can be revoked by the distributor's issuing bank at any time for any reason.[40]

There are two principles which govern the operation of the letters of credit: 1) the rule of independence and 2) the rule of strict compliance.[41] The rule of independence means that the letter of credit is a separate contract from the distributor agreement; parties to a letter of credit are bound to pay according to their obligations at set forth in the credit, regardless of any developments that have occurred in the underlying transaction. The rule of strict compliance means that when the distributor opens the letter of credit, the distributor must specify precisely to whom the credit should be paid and on what terms. This rule permits the issuing bank to only honor the credit if the documents presented by the exporter conform precisely with terms of the letter of credit.

In drafting the payment provision, the exporter's attorney should request an "irrevocable letter of credit confirmed by a bank acceptable to the exporter and located in the exporter's jurisdiction". So that the exporter is certain that it can comply with the terms of the letter of credit, the documentary requirements should be agreed to in advance by the parties and set forth in the distributor agreement.

(iv) Bank Guarantee—An alternative to documentary letters of credit is a bank guarantee, which is an undertaking by the bank to perform if the bank's customer fails to perform. A bank guarantee may be used to cover the obligations of the distributor to make payment. In the United States, standby letters of credit are used instead of bank guarantees.

The bank issuing a guarantee is unconcerned with the underlying agreement between the distributor and the exporter. The bank's obligation to pay may be conditioned only upon the presentation of a statement asserting that the distributor has failed to pay the exporter in accordance with their agreed terms. In some instances, the bank's obligation to pay may also be conditioned upon certification by independent third parties or evidence of an arbitral award or the judgment of a court to the effect that the distributor has breached its agreement with the exporter.[42]

If the exporter chooses to protect its right to payment by requesting a bank guarantee from its foreign distributor, it is in the exporter's best interest for the agreement to require that the exporter receive a "demand" guarantee, whereby the exporter is only required to demand payment by the bank in order to be paid; no documents are involved. If the exporter is willing to accept a conditional guarantee, then other documents evidencing the distributor's breach will be involved. The conditions of the guarantee should be included in the payment provision of the distributor agreement.

(v) Documentary Credits—In cases where the distributor is unwilling to carry the often high cost of a letter of credit and the distributor has a reasonably good payment history with the exporter, the contract should request that the distributor arrange for a documentary credit in the form of a sight draft (the distributor is required to pay upon presentation of the draft by the exporter) or a time draft (the distributor must pay on some future date after it has accepted the daft).

To receive payment under a documentary credit, the exporter takes shipping documents and its own draft to its U.S. bank. The U.S. bank then forwards the documents and draft to its correspondent bank in the distributor's country. The distributor can only claim the documents and title to the goods when it pays (under a sight draft) or accepts (under a time draft).

Under this method of payment, the exporter can lower the risk of not being paid by keeping title to the merchandise until the distributor either pays or becomes obligated to pay. This method is more risky than a letter of credit because it depends solely upon the distributor to pay. Therefore, even with a sight draft, the distributor may refuse shipment, leaving the exporter to incur the costs of disposing the merchandise located in a foreign country.

(vi) Export Insurance—Export insurance seeks to limit the risk of loss faced by an exporter in selling across national boundaries. In the United States, the Foreign Credit Insurance Association (FCIA), a private organization operating in cooperation with the Export-Import Bank (Eximbank), a U.S. government agency, works with U.S. exporters to insure repayment of exporters' loans to distributors. The FCIA will insure both the credit and political risks of the venture but will generally require the exporter to coinsure from five to 10 percent. If the distributor does not pay for reasons covered by the insurance, the exporter suffers only a small loss.[43]

Currency Fluctuations

The majority of U.S. exporters will prefer to quote prices in U.S. dollars and be to paid in U.S. dollars. If both parties are amenable, and it is permissible under the representative's local currency regulations, the agreement should provide for U.S. dollars as the currency of account and the currency of payment.

If a contract provides for the exporter to receive payment in a currency other than U.S. dollars, or when the currency of the contract and the currency of payment differ, the exporter should consider adding certain provisions to the agreement which would protect the value of the contract to the exporter. In one such provision, the exporter partially shifts the risk of currency fluctuations to the distributor by requesting that the distributor either make an advance payment at the time the agreement is signed or set up an escrow account in a third country in an acceptable currency from which payments will be made. Another option is for the exporter to estimate the probable cost of the foreign exchange risk and add the cost to the price. Finally, the exporter could fix the exchange rate on the invoice. The distributor would then be invoiced in the foreign exchange currency at the rate established on the invoice. If this last method is employed, the agreement would provide that in case of devaluation of the importing currency from the fixed rate, the price in the foreign currency would be increased to compensate the exporter.

Specific Issues Related to Agents

Terms of Sale

A key element of agency agreements is the clause describing how the commission will be determined and paid. The commission provision should set forth the payment to the agent in terms of a fixed percentage of the net sales price of the goods. The net sales price is frequently calculated by subtracting returns, discounts, shipping costs, taxes, customs duties, insurance, and similar factors, from the gross sales price. The agreement should state that upon collection of the purchase price (or at some other designated time), the exporter will accrue a commission account for the agent; the agent will then be paid at the end of the period agreed to by the parties. Local laws should be reviewed to determine whether the selected commission terms are permissible.

It is prudent to add a clause stating that if the customer does not pay the exporter, the exporter will not pay the agent. Another issue that should be raised during negotiations about the commission is whether the agent will receive commissions on sales that the agent does not participate in but that are made in the agent's territory. The parties' resolution of this question should be reflected in the agreement as well. If the exporter is extending any loans to the agent, it may be worthwhile to add a clause permitting the exporter to withhold any amounts from the commission payments that are due to the exporter from the agent. In addition, the parties should develop a mutually agreeable method of calculating the commissions on sales that are made by the agent prior to termination or expiration of the agreement, but which may have involved the effort of the exporter or another agent to conclude.

The best method for paying the agent is by check or wire transfer to a bank in the agent's territory, unless it is clear that payment elsewhere would not violate local exchange control regulations or income tax laws in the agents' territory.[44] Along with the method of payment, the currency of the commission payment should be included in the agreement. If the currency of the commission differs from the currency of payment by the customers, it is desirable to determine the mechanism by which the sales volume will be translated into the commission currency.[45]

Agent's Authority to Bind Exporter

In order to avoid any claim by an individual agent that he or she is an employee, and in order for the exporter to retain control over the sale of its goods, the agreement must spell out the prohibition against the agent having authority to bind the exporter and that the agent should refrain from conveying that it has such authority to customers in the agent's territory. Further, to clearly avoid the appearance of the agent's authority to bind the exporter, the agent should be prohibited, under the contract, from receiving payments on behalf of the exporter. For the same reason, the exporter should ultimately decide whether sales will be made to certain customers in the territory and whether orders made by customers in the agent's territory will be accepted or rejected.

IV.   LEGAL CONSIDERATIONS

United States Export Control Regulations

The United States encourages the development of U.S. companies' export business, but not at the expense of national security interests and foreign policy objectives. The

United States monitors and controls all products exported from the United States by requiring that all products leaving the U.S. do so under an export license. Generally, there are two types of export licenses[46]: 1) a general license, which is the authority to ship commodities to certain destinations without application for a license; and 2) a validated license, which must be applied for specifically, and is the authority from the U.S. Department of Commerce Bureau of Export Administration to ship a product to a destination.

The majority of exports leave the U.S. under a general license. Since the general license is not truly a license in that no government agency actually issues an official permit, the exporter is responsible for determining when particular transactions fall under this general permissive rule.[47] A validated license is required for: 1) the export of goods and technical data which are subject to foreign policy controls; 2) the export of goods which are strategic, or unpublished information relating to such goods; and 3) scarce goods.[48] The validated license permits only a specific transaction to take place, i.e., the export of a specific commodity, to a named purchaser, in a particular country, for a designated use, for a particular time.

The exporter may be able to apply for a special distributor export license (the necessity for this depends upon the commodities involved and the country of distribution).[49] Such a license, once obtained, eliminates the need to make repeated applications for individually validated licenses for the export of certain items. In order for the exporter to obtain such a license, the distributor or agent will have to agree that it will sell or distribute the goods pursuant to a contract with the exporter which effectively requires compliance with the U.S. Export Administration Regulation, including record keeping requirements.[50]

General record-keeping duties are placed on all exporters by the Export Regulations.[51] Apart from cases where a special distributors license is obtained, a clause should be included in the representative agreement requiring the representative to maintain books and records concerning the type of merchandise being sold, the pertinent dates and the countries in which the goods are being sold, and subject to local laws, also requiring the representative to make such books and records available to the exporter in order to assist the exporter in complying with the U.S. export regulations.[52]

It is important to note that U.S. export control laws cover the movement from one foreign country to another of commodities that originated in the U.S. and technical data or products containing parts that originated in the U.S.[53] In addition to the Department of Commerce, there are several other federal agencies that impose some form of export control, depending on the type of commodity being exported; therefore, exporters must consider which agencies have control over the specific sale.

Import documentation requirements and other import regulations imposed by foreign governments differ from country to country. It is critical that the exporter's attorney determine what regulations apply by checking with local counsel and consulting with the U.S. Department of Commerce or the appropriate foreign government embassy or consulate in the U.S.

When drafting the representative agreement, the exporter's attorney should include an admonition against the representative taking any action on the exporter's behalf which is in violation of U.S. export control laws. Finally, it may be advisable to include in the force majeure clause in a distribution agreement or on the invoice to the customer in the case of selling via an agent, a provision stating that if any sale cannot be concluded due to the exporter's inability to obtain export clearance, then the exporter is released from its responsibility to deliver the product, without any payment of damages to the distributor or customer.

United States Antiboycott Laws

While all U.S. companies must comply with any U.S.- sanctioned boycott, such as the one against Cuba, a U.S. exporter is prohibited from complying with another country's boycott that has not been sanctioned by the U.S. The U.S. has two antiboycott laws: 1) Section 8 of the Export Administration Act[54], administered by the Department of Commerce and 2) Section 999 of the Internal Revenue Code[55], administered by the Department of the Treasury.

Antiboycott issues arise most often as a result of Arab countries' boycott of Israel. Upon receipt of a questionnaire asking about a prospective seller's activities in Israel, a U.S. company must report receipt of such a request to the Department of Commerce's Office of Antiboycott Compliance. The exporter is permitted to respond to the questionnaire only in a manner approved by the Department of Commerce.[56]

A U.S. exporter could be held liable for actions taken by its foreign representative which contravene U.S. antiboycott laws.[57] U.S. companies are prevented from having a third person take actions that they are themselves prohibited from taking. The representative agreement should make clear that if the representative violates any U.S. antiboycott law, the exporter has the right to immediately terminate the agreement.[58]

Tax Impact of a Permanent Establishment

For an American exporter to be certain that it will not be subject to taxation in the foreign country based on its export sales, it is critical that the exporter not be deemed to have created a "permanent establishment" in the foreign country. Under many bilateral tax treaties into which the U.S. has entered, a U.S. company is considered to have a permanent establishment in the foreign country if its representative has, and habitually exercises, the authority to conclude contracts to sell the exporter's goods in the name of the exporter.[59] As mentioned earlier in this chapter, the representative agreement should clearly state that the representative is not authorized to bind the exporter. To avoid the creation of a permanent establishment in a agency relationship, the exporter should emphasize that the agent must take all orders subject to approval by the U.S. exporter.

If a permanent establishment is created, the exporter will be subject to taxation in the foreign country on the net income attributable to the activities of the permanent establishment.[60]

Confidentiality

During the course of the business relationship, the exporter may intend to disclose ideas which it considers to be confidential information (whether protected under intellectual property laws or not), to the representative. It is good practice to include a clause in the agreement that requires the representative to agree that neither the representative nor its employees will use the confidential information for their own benefit or otherwise disclose the ideas to a third party without the exporter's advance written consent. The definition of "confidential information" should be carefully worded to protect the exporter's interest in its proprietary information. However, it is realistic to also provide clear cut guidelines that identify which information the exporter considers to be confidential. A practical solution is to agree in the contract that written information considered to be confidential will be marked by the exporter as such and any confidential information orally conveyed will be put in writing by the exporter and marked confidential within ten days after it is given to the representative. The obligation to maintain the confidentiality of the proprietary information should continue for a reasonable time period (for example one or two years) after termination or expiration of the agreement. Furthermore, the confidentiality clause should be drafted to survive termination or expiration of the agreement.

Intellectual Property

Registration by the Exporter

One of the risks faced by an exporter at the beginning stages of its foray into international sales is the potential for loss of control over its intellectual property rights. As mentioned in Part II, before entering into serious negotiations with a representative, the exporter should determine whether the representative's territory has adopted effective intellectual property laws. Without laws protecting the owner of patents, trademarks, copyrights, trade secrets, and know-how, the exporter takes the chance of entering into a foreign market only to have its intellectual property rights usurped by the representative.

The first step, after ascertaining whether the proposed territory has effective intellectual property laws, is to confirm that the intellectual property associated with the product to be exported is registered in the United States. Copyrights[61], trademarks[62] and patents[63] may be registered in the United States.

Second, the exporter and its attorney should confer with local counsel to determine the best method of registering and/or protecting its intellectual property in the proposed territory. If registration is the solution, all registration should be made in the name of the exporter, not the representative.

Although registration of trademarks and patents must be handled on a country by country basis, it may be possible to take advantage of some of multi-lateral treaties to which the United States is a party in order to simplify the registration process if the exporter is registering in several countries at one time. For example, the International Convention for the Protection of Industrial Property (the "Paris Convention"), gives U.S. exporters "right of priority" when registering their marks in one of the member countries.[64] Right of priority means that an applicant for trademark registration is entitled to backdate an application for the same mark in other member countries to the date of the first application in a member country, so long as the application takes place within six months of the first application (twelve months for a patent). Under the Paris Convention, a U.S. exporter would also receive "national treatment" which means that a member country cannot discriminate against nationals of other member countries in granting trademark or patent protection.[65]

Third, the attorney should advise the exporter to establish an internal system of monitoring its intellectual property abroad in order to maintain its registrations and to monitor whether its intellectual property rights are being infringed by its representatives or third parties.

Protection and Respect of the Intellectual Property by the Representative

The agreement should require that the representative consistently use the exporter's trademark in connection with the sale of exporter's products, in order to increase recognition of the products and to increase goodwill toward the product in the foreign territory. It is advisable to limit the representative's use of the trademark in promotional materials. For example, the representative should only use the exporter's trademark in connection with the words, "exclusive representative for . . . ."[66]

In addition, the agreement should require the distributor to inform the exporter immediately upon learning that a third party is infringing the exporter's intellectual property rights and promptly inform the exporter of any claims of exporter's infringement of third parties' proprietary rights.[67] The exporter should prosecute the infringement of its trademarks in its own name, so as to leave no doubt as to who owns the intellectual property.[68]

Force Majeure

The representative agreement should contain a contract provision that attempts to limit the liability of the exporter in the event that some intervening and disruptive force beyond its control makes its performance under the contract more difficult than anticipated. The force majeure clauses should list specifically those events that would excuse the exporter from performing. Such events typically include war, blockades, fire, acts of governments, failure to obtain export licenses (as mentioned in Section A above), acts of God, failure of transportation, quarantine restrictions, strikes, labor slowdowns, and other events.[69] In practice, force majeure clauses do not usually excuse the exporter's performance entirely, but rather suspend performance for the duration of the force majeure.

Foreign Corrupt Practices Act

The United States was the first country in the world to outlaw bribes by its citizens to public officials in other countries. Enacted in 1977, the Foreign Corrupt Practices Act (FCPA) punishes bribery of foreign officials and establishes internal accounting mechanisms for publicly held companies that will prevent such bribery.[70] Specifically, the anti-bribery provisions prohibits a U.S. exporter from "corruptly" paying or offering to pay a foreign official for assistance in obtaining or retaining business or from paying a representative if the exporter knows that a portion of the payment will go to a public official for the same reason.[71] The accounting provisions of the FCPA were created to make it difficult for publicly held corporations to disguise or hide illegal payments. Publicly held corporations are required to refrain from knowingly failing to implement a system of internal accounting controls so that the company's financial records accurately reflect the transactions and dispositions of the assets of the company.[72] Violations of the FCPA carry with them very substantial criminal and civil penalties.[73]

An exception to the FCPA exists for facilitating or expediting payments (commonly called "grease payments") made to secure the performance of routine government actions. Such routine government actions may include the obtaining of licenses, processing of visas, or providing police, mail, basic utilities or transportation services. Unfortunately, it is not clear what types of government actions will be considered "routine" or which actions result in the obtaining or retaining of business. Therefore, the exporter and its attorney are forced to guess, with the wrong guess possibly resulting in jail for the exporter.[74]

In light of the risks involved, an exporter should employ reasonable care in connection with entering into new relationships with overseas agents and distributors. Diligent investigation into the reputation of the representative prior to signing the agreement may help avoid future problems under the FCPA. The exporter's employees should be advised to report to management any suspicious methods of doing business proposed by the exporter. In the agreement, the representative should agree not to make any payment to a government official which would constitute a corrupt payment under the FCPA.

Registration of Representative

It is good practice for American attorneys to consult local counsel about requirements or restrictions involving the necessity to register a representative before a representative is chosen. Some countries require agents or distributors to be registered with a local governmental body before the representative is allowed to commence selling the exporter's products in the territory. Additional restrictions may involve submitting the representative agreement to the local government for approval before the contract is considered to be enforceable. Finally, certain countries only permit the use of representatives who are nationals of the country.

In the event registration is required, the representative should be required in the contract to accept the cost and responsibility of handling all documents and procedures related to registration, including the cost of translating documents, as well as the responsibility for monitoring local laws and informing the exporter if regulations affecting registration change during the term of the agreement. The agreement should also include a provision that the representative will promptly inform the exporter if the local government alters or terminates the representative's registration.

Choice of Language

Although an American attorney and exporter would probably prefer the language of the contract to be in English, the laws of the representative's country may require that another language govern the agreement. If the agreement is drafted in more than one language, one language version should be designated as the controlling version. That choice should reflect the choice of forum, since the judicial or arbitral body reviewing the agreement should have a high comfort level with the language of the agreement. As a practical matter, the agreement should state that the governing language of the agreement should also govern communication between the parties so as to avoid potential misunderstandings.[75]

Governing Law and Choice of Forum

The governing law provision should not be overlooked as a matter of boilerplate. If it becomes necessary for the exporter to enforce its rights under the agreement, the skillfully drafted choice of law, forum and jurisdiction provision of the agreement may make the exporter more secure in the expectation that the agreement will be interpreted in a predictable manner.

Governing Law

The United States and most commercially-oriented foreign countries will honor the law chosen by the parties to govern their agreement.[76] The policy consideration behind this approach is that competent parties have a right to freely enter into contracts in such a manner as would best promote their respective business interests.[77] Furthermore, it has been generally accepted that parties may choose the law of one country to apply to the entire agreement or portions of different countries' laws to different sections of the agreement.[78]

In the United States, there is some disagreement among the courts as to whether, in addition to a very clear designation by the parties in the agreement as to the choice of law, there must also be "significant contacts" between the contract and the chosen law, or merely a "reasonable relationship" between the contract and the designated law in order for a choice of law provision to be honored.[79] Given the differing standards applied by U.S. courts, it is recommended that the American attorney determine whether sufficient contact exists between the contract and the chosen law to meet the standard employed by the chosen forum. To gain greater certainty about the outcome of a potential dispute, the drafting attorney may prefer to choose the law of the state in which he or she is licensed and where, presumably, the exporter carries on its principal business activities. As an alternative, the attorney may select the law of either New York[80] or Ohio[81] as the law governing the agreement, since both states have enacted legislation which enable any contracting party to choose that state's law, even if the contract does not have significant contacts or a reasonable relationship with that state. Finally, parties may wish to choose the law of a country other than the U.S. or the representative's country, so long as there are reasonable contacts between the contract and the law of the chosen country.[82]

One example of governing law language for a contract in which the parties intend for the law of one country (or state) to govern is: "this contract shall be deemed to have been made, executed, delivered in [specify state or country] and shall be governed by and enforced *exclusively* in accordance with the laws of [specify state or country]".[83]

Choice of Forum

Judicial Forum

In addition to assisting business planning by making the outcome of potential disputes easier to predict, a forum selection clause may make it more likely that a given dispute will be resolved in a single forum, thus reducing the risk of costly litigation in two or more courts.[84]

Several issues typically arise in a court's interpretation of a forum selection clause. The first issue is the distinction between an exclusive forum selection clause, which requires that any litigation of disputes take place only in the specified forum, and a nonexclusive clause, which permits litigation of disputes in a particular forum but does not preclude the parties from going forward in other courts that have jurisdiction over the parties and the dispute. Whether a particular clause will be found to be exclusive or nonexclusive turns largely on the wording of a particular provision.[85]

The second issue that arises in interpreting a forum selection clause involves the scope of the disputes covered by the clause. If the attorney wishes to ensure that all of the exporter's disputes with the representative, including any disputes relating to the parties' contractual relationship (regardless of whether such disputes involve tort or other public law claims) are covered, care should be taken to use language such as "all disputes relating to [as opposed to arising under] this agreement . . . ."[86]

Third, another important issue in interpreting a forum selection clause is whether the parties expressly submitted to the jurisdiction of the forum (which might otherwise lack personal jurisdiction).[87]

The following clause may be used in drafting a forum selection provision in the event that the parties intend to litigate all disputes exclusively in the specified forum and are willing to submit to jurisdiction of the forum: "all disputes relating to this agreement shall be decided exclusively by the courts of [specify forum] and both parties irrevocably waive all rights to bring any such action in any other courts. [Specify party] hereby designates [specify agent] as its agent for the purpose of accepting service of process within [specify forum]."[88]

United States courts have generally enforced forum selection clauses in both the interstate and international contexts.[89] In considering the selection of a judicial forum, the analysis of which forum to choose is similar to that for the choice of law clauses. Again, the best choice for the exporter should be the law of the state from which it does business. In the alternative, the parties may chose New York, Ohio or a foreign country that has a reasonable connection sufficient to sustain subject matter jurisdiction.[90] When choosing a forum, a key consideration will be the extent to which a final judgment will be recognized and enforced. There exists a network of bilateral agreements setting forth the conditions on which judgments of each country's courts will be enforced.

Arbitration

Since 1970, Chapter 2 of the Federal Arbitration Act has required American courts to enforce international arbitration agreements and to recognize arbitration awards.[91]

Many international practitioners believe that arbitration is preferable to litigation in the international setting because the process of meeting and exchanging documents in a place other than a court's combative atmosphere is more likely to produce an amicable settlement. Other positive aspects of arbitration are: in many cases it proceeds much more quickly and is less expensive than litigation; it can provide for discovery not available under civil law systems; the private nature of arbitration is better suited than litigation to cases dealing with sensitive trade secrets or computer software issues; the enforcement of the award is reliable, and arbitrator's awards are not subject to trial de novo or extensive appellate litigation (they are vacated only on the limited grounds designated in the applicable law).[92]

The decision concerning the choice of arbitration should be cleared with local counsel since some countries only permit domestic and not international arbitration. There is not a united international arbitration system. In the U.S., the American Arbitration Association (AAA) administers international arbitration cases. Other well-known agencies are: the International Chamber of Commerce (ICC), a non-governmental body in Paris; the Stockholm Chamber of Commerce; the National Chamber of Commerce in Vienna; the Japan Commercial Arbitration Association; and the London Court of International Arbitration.

In drafting the arbitration provision, counsel should include, in addition to the choice of law, whether the arbitration will decide all disputes between the parties or only certain disputes, the place of arbitration, the language in which the arbitration will be conducted, the number of arbitrators, how the arbitrators will be selected, and the rules of procedure. It is fairly common to incorporate arbitration clauses pre-drafted by, for example, AAA, the ICC, or the London Court of Arbitration. These organizations have preestablished rules and procedures to appoint the arbitrators and conduct the arbitration.

V. CONCLUSION

This chapter provides a brief overview of a few of the many legal and business issues which frequently arise in the course of negotiating and drafting international representative agreements. The drafting attorney is advised to research the provisions in greater detail, as they pertain to the facts of the particular representative relationship, before incorporating them into his or her agreement.

It bears repeating that a well-negotiated and drafted representative agreement not only plants the exporter's feet firmly in the international marketplace and contributes effectively to its foreign sales success, but also, if fairly negotiated, forms the foundation for a strong business relationship with the representative which may be developed into more closely cooperative relationships such as joint ventures or branch foreign operations.

Notes

[1] The author gratefully acknowledges the editorial assistance of Roger D. Billings, Jr., Associate Dean, Chase College of Law, Michael E. Solimine, Professor of Law, University of Cincinnati College of Law and John E. Gardner, Esq., Keating, Muething & Klekamp.

[2] Richard Schaffer, et al., *International Business Law and Its Environment* 15-35 (1990).

[3] U.S. Department of Commerce, *A Basic Guide to Exporting* 7-1 (1992).

[4] *Id.*

[5] *See* A.H. Puelinckx and H.A. Tielemans, *The Termination of Agency and Distributorship Agreements: A Comparative Survey,* 3-4 Nw. J. Int'l L. & Bus. 452, 454 (1981-82).

[6] *See* Roger D. Billings, 5 *Handling Business Opportunities in the European Community* 11-12 (1993).

[7] Nicholas Green, *Commercial Agreements and Competition Law* 435 (1986).

[8] *Id.*

[9] Andre M. Saltoun and Barbara S. Spudis, *International Distribution and Sales Agency Agreements: Practical Guidelines for U.S. Exporters*, 38 Bus. Law. 883, 899 (1982-83).

[10] *See* G. Gregory Letterman, 2 *Letterman's Law of Private International Business* 301 (1990).

[11] *See* Billings, *supra* note 6, at 11-4.

[12] Saltoun and Spudis, *supra* note 9, at 885.

[13] *Id.*

[14] 1 Paul H. Vishny, *Guide to International Commerce Law* 4-38 (1992).

[15] Karl G. Herold and David D. Knoll, *Negotiating and Drafting International Distribution, Agency and Representative Agreements: the United States Exporter's Perspective*, 21 Int'l Law. 939, 960 (1987). The authors propose initially entering into a "trial" agreement for a period of two years. In the trial contract, the parties should agree that the contract *may* form the basis for any future agreements so long as performance criteria is met in the appropriate time frame. *Id.*

[16] Letterman, *supra* note 10, at 307-308.

[17] *Id.* at 317.

[18] When drafting the minimum sales quota provision, it should be explained in the agreement that the quota is being increased over time in proportion to the anticipated growth in goodwill for the exporter's product and trademark. Either party should be permitted to approach the other for reasonable adjustments to the quota if special circumstances arise. The foreign representative should acknowledge that lost sales hurt the exporter's goodwill in the territory, and that if the representative is terminated because of failure to meet the quota, the representative will not be entitled to compensation, since the damage to the exporter's goodwill is likely to be at least as great as the losses the representative might incur as a result of the termination. Herold and Knoll, *supra* note 15, at 970-971.

[19] Saltoun and Spudis, *supra* note 9, at 893.

[20] *Id.* at 888-889.

[21] Letterman, *supra* note 10, at 313.

[22] *Id.*

[23] Herold and Knoll, *supra* note 15, at 963.

[24] U.S. Department of Commerce, *supra* note 3, at 10-2.

[25] *Id.*

[26] International Chamber of Commerce, *Incoterms 1990* 6 (1990).

[27] I.R.C. §904 (1992). *See generally* Vishny, *supra* note 14, at 8-72, 1S-234—1S-237.

[28] United Nations Convention on Contracts for the International Sale of Goods, U.N. Doc. A/Conf. 97/18 art 1 (1)(b) (1981) (hereinafter CISG). The United States exercised its right to exclude the section of this convention which states that the CISG applies when traditional choice of law rules dictate that the law of the country which has adopted the CISG should apply. *See* Section of International Law and Practice, ABA, *The Convention for the International Sale of Goods: A Handbook of Basic Materials* 17 (Daniel B. Magraw and Reed R. Kathrein eds., 2d ed. 1990). The previously cited book contains the official English text of the CISG (and the text in the five other official languages) and offers an analysis of the CISG and comparison of the CISG to the UCC.

[29] CISG, *supra* note 28, at art. 6.

[30] Billings, *supra* note 6, at 11-6.

[31] R.M. Lavers, *CISG To Use, or Not to Use?*, 21 Int'l Bus. Law. 10 and 13 (1993).

[32] CISG, *supra* note 28, at art. 11.

[33] CISG, *supra* note 28, at art. 19.

[34] U.C.C. § 2-207 (1977).

[35] U.C.C. § 2-601.

[36] CISG, *supra* note 28, at art. 49 (1)(a). A "fundamental breach" is one which substantially deprives the other party of what it is entitled to expect under the contract and the resulting deprivation or dissatisfaction is foreseen or foreseeable by the breaching party. *Id.* at art. 25.

[37] Lavers, *supra* note 31, at 12.

[38] Graham R. Taylor and Maria L. Crisera, *U.N. Pact Has Wide Application*, Nat'l L.J., Dec. 23, 1991, at 23, 26.

[39] Franklin R. Root, *International Trade and Investment* 281 (6th ed. 1990).

[40] *Id.* at 282-283.

[41] In the United States, the law governing letters of credit has been codified in Article 5 of the Uniform Commercial Code, however, the great majority of international letters of credit issued today state that they are to be interpreted according to the International Chamber of Commerce's Uniform Customs and Practices for Documentary Credits (1993 revision) publication 500 (UCP). The UCP sets standard rules for issuing and handling letters of credit; it is widely recognized by judges and appears in virtually every reported decision on international letters of credit. Schaffer, et al., *supra* note 2, at 158-159.

[42] Vishny, *supra* note 14, at 2-18.

[43] Don A. Evans, *The Legal Environment of International Business* 162 (1990).

[44] Saltoun and Spudis, *supra* note 9, at 893.

[45] *Id.*

[46] The primary U.S. export control laws are embodied in the Export Administration Act of 1979 as amended, 50 U.S.C. App. §§ 2401-2420 (1988 and Supp. 1991), and the Export Administration Regulations, 50 C.F.R. §§ 700-799 (1993). The Export Administration Regulations issued thereunder are promulgated by the Commerce Department Bureau of Export Administration.

[47] 15 C.F.R. § 771 (1993).

[48] 15 C.F.R. § 772 (1993).

[49] 15 C.F.R. § 773.3 (1993).

[50] *Id.*

[51] 15 C.F.R. § 787.13 (1993).

[52] Saltoun and Spudis, *supra* note 9, at 909.

[53] 15 C.F.R. § 774 (1993).

[54] 50 U.S.C. App. § 2402(5) and § 2407(a) (1988).

[55] 26 U.S.C. § 999 (1988).

[56] *See* 15 C.F.R. § 769.1 (1993).

[57] 15 C.F.R. § 769.4 (1993).

[58] *See* Homer E. Moyer, Jr. and William M. McGlone, *International Contracts: Avoiding Problems Under U.S. Antiboycott Law, Export Controls, and The Foreign Corrupt Practices Act, in Negotiating and Structuring International Commercial Transactions: Legal Analysis with Sample Agreements* 53, 54 (Shelly P. Battram and David N. Goldsweig eds. 1991).

[59] The 1977 U.S. Model Treaty is set forth in R. Rhoades and M. Langer, 5 *Income Taxation of Foreign Related Transactions* §§92.00 et seq. (1990) *noted in* Stephen C. Nelson, *Negotiating and Drafting Agency, Distribution and Franchise Agreements in Negotiating and Structuring International Commercial Transactions: Legal Analysis with Sample Agreements* 189, 235 fn.100 (Shelly P. Battram and David N. Goldsweig eds. 1991).

[60] Nelson, *supra* note 57, at 208.

[61] 17 U.S.C. § 408 (1988).

[62] 15 U.S.C. § 1051 (1988).

[63] 35 U.S.C. § 100 (1988).

[64] International Convention for the Protection of Industrial Property (1833), 25 Stat. 1372, TS No. 379 (current version in 212 UST 1583, TIAS No. 6923) (Paris Convention).

[65] *Id.*

[66] *See* Letterman, *supra* note 10, at 306.

[67] *Id.* at 305.

[68] Herold and Knoll, note *supra* 15, at 978.

[69] Schaffer, et al, *supra* note 2, at 118.

[70] *See* The Foreign Corrupt Practices Act of 1977, 15 U.S.C. § 78d d-1 to -2 (1988) and its amendments in the Omnibus Trade and Competitiveness Act of 1988, 15 U.S.C. §§78m(b), 78dd-1, 78dd-2 (1988). For a discussion of the amendments, see Adam Fremantle and Sherman Katz, *The Foreign Corrupt Practices Amendments of 1988*, 23 Int'l Law. 755 (1989).

[71] 15 U.S.C. § 78dd -1 and -2 (1988).

[72] 15 U.S.C. § 78 m(b)(4)-(7) (1988).

[73] 15 U.S.C. § 78ff (1988).

[74] Schaffer, et al, *supra* note 2, at 382.

[75] *See* Herold and Knoll, *supra* note 13, at 950.

[76] *See* Ved P. Nanda, *Forum Selection and Choice of Law Clauses in Transnational Contracts, in Transnational Contracts in the Law of Transnational Business Transactions*, 8-1, 8-80.2 (P. Nanda, ed. 1993) (*citing* Restatement (Second) Conflict of Laws §187 (1971) and European Communities: Convention on the Law Applicable to Contractual Obligations, opened for signature June 19, 1980, O.J. EUR. COMM. 23/1 266)).

[77] Restatement (Second) Conflict of Laws §187, comment e (1971).

[78] Michael Grunson, *Selected Issues of Choice of Law in International Commercial Agreements 1992*, 51, 63 (Practising Law Institute 1992).

[79] *See* Nanda, *supra* note 76, at 8-73.

[80] N. Y. Gen. Oblig. Law §5-1401 (McKinney Supp. 1992). Under New York law, New York courts must enforce the choice of New York law for substantial transactions, which means transactions greater than $250,000 in some cases and greater than $1,000,000 in other cases. *See also* Joseph D. Becker, *Choice-of-Law and Choice-of-Forum Clauses in New York,* 38 Int'l and Comp. Law Q. 167 (1989).

[81] Ohio Rev. Code Ann. §2307.39 (Page's 1992 Supp.).

[82] *See e.g.* Nanda, *supra* note 76, at 8-80.13.

[83] *Id.*

[84] Gary B. Born and David Westin, *International Civil Litigation in United States Courts* 172 (1st ed. 1988). *See also* Michael E. Solimine, *Forum-Selection Clauses and the Privatization of Procedure,* 25 Cornell Int'l L. J. 51 (1992); Michael Grunson, *Forum Selection Clauses in International and Interstate Commercial Agreements*, 1992 U. Ill. L. Rev. 133.

[85] Born and Westin, *supra* note 84, at 173.

[86] *Id.* at 175

[87] *Id.*

[88] *Id.* at 176.

[89] The leading modern U.S. case on forum selection clauses in the international context is *The Bremen v. Zapata Off-Shore Co.*, 407 U.S. 1 (1972).

[90] Solimine, *supra* note 84, at 65.

[91] Federal Arbitration Act, 9 U.S.C. §§201–208 (1988).

[92] Robert Coulson, *Resolving Disputes: The Arbitration Option*, Am. Law., November 1991 at 45, 46.

AGENCY AGREEMENT

This Agency Agreement _____ ("Agreement") made and entered into this _____ day of _____, 199__, by and between _____, a(n) _____corporation with its principal place of business at _____ ("Exporter") and _____, a(n) _____ corporation with its principal place of business at _____ ("Agent").

IN CONSIDERATION OF the mutual covenants set forth in this Agreement, Exporter and the Agent agree as follows:

1. *Appointment of Agent.* Subject to all of the terms and conditions of this Agreement, Exporter hereby agrees to utilize Agent's services, and Agent agrees to serve as the agent for Exporter in the Geographic Area (as defined in Section). Agent shall use its best efforts to promote the products of Exporter, as listed on the attached Schedule 1 hereto, and as amended from time to time by Exporter (the "Products").

2. *Term.* The engagement of Agent for Exporter shall commence on ("Effective Date") and shall continue thereafter until _____ ("Initial Term").

3. *Geographic Area.* Exporter hereby appoints Agent as the exclusive agent of the Products solely within _____ (the "Geographic Area").

4. *Duties of the Agent.* The Agent shall, at its own expense perform the following duties during the Initial Term of this Agreement:

4.1 The Agent shall (a) implement a sufficient sales and marketing program in the Geographic Area to sell the Products, (b) perform all necessary promotion and advertising of the Products in the Geographic Area, and (c) in general, utilize its diligent and best efforts to effect the maximum amount of gross sales of each of the Products in the Geographic Area.

4.2 The Agent shall provide and maintain a place of business with sales and service personnel and facilities deemed adequate by Exporter to provide all necessary services and support to the Agent's customers for the Products and to provide proper surroundings for the marketing and sale of the Products in the Geographic Area.

4.3 The Agent shall submit to Exporter, within Sixty (60) days after written request by Exporter, a written analysis of all competition for the Products in the Geographic Area. In no event shall such an analysis be required more than once during any calendar year.

4.4 The Agent shall defend, indemnify and hold harmless Exporter from any and all suits, claims, actions, and liability of any nature arising in any manner out of the Agent's actions hereunder or its relations with its customers, potential and actual, for the Products, including, without limitation, liability arising from problems of any nature in the use and operation of the Products and improper installation, repair or maintenance of the Products.

4.5 The Agent shall permit Exporter to inspect its facilities at any time during the Agent's normal business hours, upon one week's advance written notice.

4.6 The Agent shall furnish to Exporter, upon request by Exporter, such duly certified financial statements and other financial information as may be reasonably required by Exporter to establish the financial capability of the Agent to perform under this Agreement.

4.7 All Products sold by the Agent shall be sold by the Agent as Exporter products in accordance with all Exporter selling standards.

4.8 The Agent shall furnish Exporter from time to time, upon request, such information as the Agent may have available in its books and records with respect to sales of the Products and permit Exporter to audit and inspect all such books and records during normal business hours.

5. *Duties of Exporter.* Exporter shall, at its own expense and without remuneration from the Agent, perform the following duties during the Initial Term of this Agreement:

5.1 Exporter shall supply such Product documentation, sales promotion literature, installation instructions, maintenance manuals and operator manuals as deemed necessary by Exporter.

5.2 Exporter shall furnish reasonable marketing and maintenance support and advice in the form of answers to questions in such areas.

5.3 During the Initial Term of this Agreement, the Agent shall have the right to use the trade names and trademarks of Exporter applied to the Products by Exporter, in advertising and promotional literature solely in connection with the Agent's sale of the Products. The Agent shall prominently identify itself in such advertising and promotional literature as an agent of Exporter and shall identify that such trademarks and trade names are the exclusive property of Exporter. The Agent shall have no right to register any such trade names or trademarks in its own name or right, whether as owner, user or otherwise. The Agent shall release any rights it may have acquired in such trademarks and trade names of Exporter and shall execute any and all instruments Exporter may deem necessary or advisable from time to time to accomplish such release. Upon termination or expiration of this Agreement, the Agent shall immediately cease using all trademarks or trade names of Exporter, and shall not thereafter use any marks or names similar thereto either in connection with the Products or otherwise.

6. *Commission, Ordering and Shipment.* The following shall govern the ordering of Products by the Agent, the Agent's commission and their shipment by Exporter:

6.1 Sales prices for the Products shall be as quoted from time to time by Exporter upon the Agent's request, all on a CIF (point of destination) (Incoterms 1990) basis. Agent will be paid a commission in an amount equal to ____percent of the "net selling price" for Products sold by Agent on Exporter's behalf in the Geographic Area. Net selling price shall be defined as the equivalent in U.S. dollars at the commercial rate of exchange in effect on the date of receipt, received by Exporter for Products sold in the Geographic Area, less returns, discounts, shipping costs, taxes, custom duties, and insurance with respect to Products sold.

6.2 The Agent may order whatever Products it desires from time to time during the Initial Term of this Agreement by written order delivered to Exporter. Each such order shall refer to this Agreement and shall include the Products ordered, their quantity, and the desired delivery date. Exporter shall furnish Agent notice of acceptance or rejection of an order within Thirty (30) days of its receipt.

6.3 All Products ordered by the Agent from Exporter pursuant to this Agreement shall be subject solely to the provisions of this Agreement and any other provisions contained in any Agent order shall be null and void and of no force or effect.

7. Termination.

7.1 This Agreement may be terminated as follows:

7.1.1 *Financial Condition.* Exporter shall have the right to terminate this Agreement immediately upon written notice to the Agent in the event the Agent (a) files or has filed against it any bankruptcy or similar proceeding or enters into any form of arrangement with its creditors, (b) demonstrates a financial condition of such a nature that Exporter may reasonably believe that the Agent may not be capable of performing all of its obligations under this Agreement, or (c) undergoes a material change of control in its management.

7.1.2 *Performance.* Upon written notice Exporter shall have the right to terminate this notice to the Agent in the event the Agent's sales performance falls below an _____ level, in Exporter's sole and absolute discretion.

7.1.3 *Breach.* In the event either party commits a material breach of this Agreement, the non-breaching party shall provide written notice of such breach to the other party. In the event such other party does not cure such breach within a period of Thirty (30) days from the date of such notice, the non-breaching party shall have the right to terminate this Agreement immediately upon written notice to the other party. In addition, in the event either party commits Three (3) or more material breaches of this Agreement, even if they are cured, the other party shall have the right to terminate this Agreement immediately upon written notice to the breaching party.

7.1.4 *Advance Notice by Exporter.* Notwithstanding Sections 7.1.1, and 7.1.2 , either party may terminate this Agreement at any time by giving to the other party Ninety (90) days prior written notice.

7.2 *Orders After Termination or Expiration.* In addition, for a period of Ninety (90) days after the expiration or termination of this Agreement, except for a termination by Exporter in accordance with Subparagraph 7.1.4(3) of this Agreement, Exporter will accept orders for Products from the Agent in accordance with the provisions of this Agreement if such orders were obtained by the Agent during the Initial Term of this Agreement or are the direct result of negotiations undertaken by the Agent during the Initial Term of this Agreement. If Exporter accepts orders from the Agent within said Ninety (90) day period following expiration of this Agreement, relating obligations regarding the purchase and sale of such Products shall be in accordance with the terms and conditions specified in this Agreement. If Exporter accepts orders from the Agent within said Ninety (90) day period following expiration of this Agreement, any obligations regarding the purchase and sale of such Products shall be in accordance with the terms and conditions specified in this Agreement.

7.3 To the extent necessary to implement the foregoing provisions of this Article, each of the parties hereby waives any right or obligation it or the other party may now or hereafter have under any applicable law or regulation to request or obtain the approval, order, decision or judgment of any court or other authority to terminate or cancel this Agreement.

8. Warranty and Limitation of Warranty and Remedy.

8.1 Exporter warrants that at the point and time of delivery to the port of shipment, the Products will be free from defects in workmanship and materials. This warranty will continue for a period of Ninety (90) days after delivery to the port for shipment. If, during such warranty period, the Agent promptly provides Exporter written notice of the discovery of any defects in the Products, Exporter will, at its option and expense, at Exporter headquarters, repair all defects or replace portions of the Products where appropriate, provided Exporter's inspection of such Products demonstrates the existence of the defects asserted by the Agent. Transportation charges to and from Exporter shall be at the Agent's expense.

8.2 Exporter's obligations under this Agreement, and the sole remedy of the Agent, whether arising from breach of warranty or contract, tort (including negligence), or otherwise, shall be limited to the replacement or repair described in Subparagraph 8.1 of this Agreement.

9. *Limitation of Liability*. Exporter's total liability under this Agreement, whether for breach of warranty or contract, tort (including negligence), infringement or otherwise, shall in no event exceed the purchase price of the Product alleged to have caused damage to the Agent. In no event shall Exporter be liable for any special, punitive, incidental, indirect, or consequential damages.

10. *Covenant Not to Compete*. During the Initial Term of this Agreement, the Agent and its employees, officers, shareholders, directors, principals, parent, subsidiaries, affiliates, and related persons or entities of any nature shall not (i) act on behalf of, represent, be employed by, or affiliated in any manner, with any other person or entity in the business of marketing like Products or any items of a substantially similar nature to the Products, and (ii) market, advertise, promote, carry, sell or otherwise distribute products in the Geographic Area which compete in any manner with any of the Products.

11. *Licensing and Permits*. Agent hereby represents that it has obtained all registrations, licenses, permits, certificates, and other documentation necessary to permit it to perform its duties and obligations under this Agreement. Agent further represents that it is duly qualified to transact business in the Geographic Area to the full extent contemplated by this Agreement. Agent further represents and warrants that its performance of this Agreement will not violate or contravene any provision of the law of any locality or nation, nor any agreement to which Agent is a party.

12. *Independent Contractor*. The Agent shall not have any authority to commit or legally bind Exporter in any manner whatsoever including, without limitation, the acceptance of any order or the making of any agreement, representation or warranty.

13. *United States Export Administration Regulations*. The Agent shall fully comply with all provisions of the United States Export Administration Regulations (the "Regulations") as may be in effect from time to time during the Initial Term of this Agreement. The Agent acknowledges that it has read and is familiar with the Regulations and shall fully comply with all provisions of the Regulations including, without limitation, Sections 373.3(1), (3), and (4) and Section 387.13 concerning recordkeeping and shall permit representatives of Exporter and/or the United States Government to inspect all such records as may be required for a period of at least Two (2) years after the expiration or termination of this Agreement. The Agent shall also fully cooperate, at its own expense, in the preparation and execution of all documents required by the Regulations.

14. *Miscellaneous Provisions*.

14.1 *Notice*. Any notices under this Agreement shall be sent by first class airmail to the parties at their addresses set forth in the preamble of this Agreement, provided that either party may change such address by providing notice of same to the other party.

14.2 *Applicable Language*. All amendments of this Agreement, notices and communications between the parties and all material supplied under this Agreement by either party to the other shall be in the English language.

14.3 *No License - Confidentiality*. This Agreement is not to be construed as granting a license to the Agent to manufacture any of the Products from information supplied by Exporter to the Agent or otherwise. Such information is to be utilized by the Agent only for the purpose of selling and servicing Products in accordance with this Agreement and no other use or disclosure shall be made of any such information.

14.4 *Assignment*. This Agreement is personal to the Agent and is not assignable by the Agent in whole or in part without Exporter's prior written consent.

14.6 *Governing Law*. The State of _____, United States of America, shall be deemed the place of contracting hereunder, and the rights and obligations of the parties under this Agreement shall be exclusively governed by and construed in accordance with the laws of the State of _____, United States of America.

14.5 *Arbitration*. Any dispute, controversy, or claim arising out of or relating to this Agreement, whether breach, termination, or invalidity thereof, shall be exclusively settled by arbitration in accordance with the American Arbitration Association rules in force as of the date of breach. It is further agreed as follows:

(a) the appointing authority shall be the American Arbitration Association.

(b) the number of arbitrators shall be three (3).

(c) the place of the arbitration shall be United States of America.

(d) the language to be used in the arbitral proceeding shall be English.

(e) any such arbitration shall be administered by the American Arbitration Association. All communications between the parties and the arbitrators shall be made through the American Arbitration Association. All such communication shall be deemed received by the addressee when received by the American Arbitration Association.

14.6 *Severability*. If any provision of this Agreement shall be held or rendered invalid, then such invalidity shall not affect the remainder of this Agreement which shall remain in full force and effect.

14.7 *Compliance with Laws*. In all of their respective operations related to this Agreement, the parties shall exercise prudent and ethical business practices and shall comply with all applicable laws and regulations of the United States of America and the Geographic Area. Such compliance with laws shall include, without limitation, the United States Foreign Corrupt Practices Act and the Regulations described in Article 13 of this Agreement.

14.8 *Waiver*. No waiver by either party of any default or breach by the other party of any of the provisions hereof shall constitute a waiver of any prior or subsequent default or breach hereunder.

14.9 *Force Majeure*. The Exporter shall not be liable for failure or delay in performance of any obligation under this Agreement if such failure or delay is caused by circumstances beyond the control of the Exporter, including, without limitation, failures resulting from fires, accidents, labor stoppages, war, inability to secure materials or labor, government acts or regulations, inability to obtain appropriate export licenses, or acts of God.

14.10 *Entire Agreement.* This Agreement constitutes the entire agreement between the parties concerning its subject matter and supersedes any and all prior or contemporaneous understandings or agreements in connection with such subject matter. This Agreement may be amended, modified or revoked only by a written instrument executed by both the Agent and Exporter.

IN WITNESS WHEREOF, the parties have executed this Agreement under seal in duplicate originals as of the date first written above.

(EXPORTER)

BY: _____

Title: _____

(AGENT)

BY: _____

TITLE: _____

SCHEDULE 1

PRODUCTS

DISTRIBUTION AGREEMENT

THIS DISTRIBUTION AGREEMENT is made and entered into this _____ day of
_____ 199__, by and between _____, a corporation organized and
existing under the laws of the State of _____, and having its principal place of
business at _____, _____ (hereinafter called "Producer") and
_____, a business organized and existing under the laws of
_____ and having its principal place of business at _____,
(hereinafter called "Distributor").

WHEREAS, Producer manufactures, markets and sells in its own name in the
United States certain products; and

WHEREAS, Producer grants to others the right to distribute the above mentioned
products for market and sale outside the United States; and

WHEREAS, Distributor warrants and represents that it is authorized by law and
qualified to act as a distributor for Producer and offers means for distribution of the
above mentioned products in certain territories outside Producer's usual channel of trade
and now wishes to obtain certain distribution rights for the above mentioned products;

NOW, THEREFORE, the parties hereto agree as follows:

1. *Grant of Right.* Producer hereby grants to Distributor an [exclusive or
nonexclusive] right to distribute _____ as may be made available from time to
time, which are manufactured by or for Producer and which are not otherwise excluded
hereunder from availability for distribution (hereinafter called "Products"). [Note:
Exclusivity will have to be qualified, in accordance with European Commission
Regulation No. 1983/83 of 22 June 1983 on the application of Article 85(3) of the Treaty
of Rome to categories of exclusive distribution agreements if the territory is in the EC.]
This right shall extend only to the territory of _____ (hereinafter called
"Distribution Territory").

2. *Limitations on Distributors Exclusive Right to Distribute in Territory.*

(a) Producer expressly reserves to itself, its subsidiaries and affiliated companies, the
right in the Distribution Territory to manufacture, reproduce, market and sell the Products.
[delete following if nonexclusive]

(b) If Producer determines, in its sole reasonable discretion, that Distributor has
failed to perform any of its obligations under this Agreement in the Distribution
Territory, Producer reserves the right, by giving Distributor Official Notice, (as defined
in Paragraph 9 hereinafter) to immediately change the grant of exclusivity to
nonexclusivity in said territory. This provision does not preclude Producer from
exercising its right to terminate this Agreement pursuant to Paragraph 10.

3. *Term.* This Agreement shall commence on _____ and shall continue
through _____. The period from _____ to _____ during
the term shall be considered to be a Contract Year.

4. *Consideration.*

(a) The purchase price of the Products shall be pursuant to the terms of sale set forth in Schedule _____, which is attached hereto and made a part hereof, but as to which reasonable price changes may be made by Producer upon Sixty (60) days Official Notice to Distributor.

(b) All payments required to be made by Distributor to Producer pursuant to Subparagraph 4(a) shall be made by irrevocable letter of credit based upon pro forma invoice confirmed by [Producer's U.S. bank] and payable at sight against documents at Distributor's bank.

(c) If at the end of any Contract Year while this Agreement, or any renewal thereof, is in effect, the total amounts paid or payable to Producer for such Contract Year shall not have amounted to the minimum set forth below, Distributor agrees to pay to Producer the difference between the applicable minimum and the total amount paid to Producer for such Contract Year under Subparagraph 4(a) such payment to be made within Ninety (90) days from the end of the Contract Year by wire transfer to _____, _____, to_____ Account _____ in United States dollars:

Contract Year   Minimum

(d) Distributor shall also be responsible for all freight, insurance, cartage and other costs related to transport of the Products from the point of embarkation. All shipments by Producer, therefore, shall be F.O.B. Producer's United States distribution centers (Incoterms 1990). Risk of loss or damage to any Product shall be assumed by Distributor after Producer delivers the Product to the first carrier.

5. *Distributors Obligations.* Distributor shall distribute and sell the Products in the Distribution Territory in accordance with the following obligations. Distributor shall:

(a) obtain, pay all costs associated with, and be in possession of all official approvals, licenses, registrations, and permits required by virtue of any applicable law or regulation for the effective operation of its business and its performance under this Agreement;

(b) keep books, records and accounts of all transactions covered by this Agreement and permit Producer, its agents and representatives to examine the same and to have access at any reasonable time to Distributor's business and warehouses;

(c) commence sale and distribution of the Products as soon as reasonably practicable following execution of this Agreement;

(d) purchase Products exclusively from Producer;

(e) at all times during the term of this Agreement, use its best efforts to market and otherwise promote the sale of Products throughout the Distribution Territory;

(f) comply with Producer's instructions and act beneficially and loyally to Producer and not do anything to prevent the sale, or development of sales, of the Products in the Distribution Territory;

(g) obtain an adequate number of sufficiently qualified staff to enable Distributor to promptly and efficiently perform its obligations under this Agreement;

(h) keep Producer promptly informed of any complaint or dispute concerning the Products supplied by Producer to Distributor;

(i) keep sufficient stocks of the Products in the relevant Distribution Territory to meet expected requirements and report stock levels and movement to Producer as it requests;

(j) conduct Distributor's business in an efficient, responsible, and ethical manner so as to enhance and support the reputation and goodwill of the Products in the Distribution Territory;

(k) conduct Distributor's business in accordance with all laws applicable in the Distribution Territory. Distributor must immediately notify Producer in writing if any law or regulation of a relevant Distribution Territory prevents it from complying fully with the terms of this Agreement. Producer shall, in such circumstances, have the option of terminating this Agreement with immediate effect by Official Notice;

(l) maintain adequate working capital, pay and perform all financial obligations at the time they are due, and maintain distributorship on a sound financial basis; and

(m) refrain from manufacturing or selling any or all products which are, in Producer's judgment, directly competitive with Products.

6. *Products Promotion.* Producer will assist Distributor in promoting Products by providing point of sale promotional material at no cost to Distributor. Distributor will advise Producer of its requirements for such promotional material.

7. *Confidentiality.* Distributor agrees not to disclose or make available for use for any purpose other than for the sales of Products any of Producer's proprietary information, including but not limited to, information relating to Products or to the operations or business of Producer, and agrees to provide reasonable security measures to prevent unauthorized persons from obtaining any such information. Producer agrees to mark all information it considers to be confidential and proprietary with the word "Confidential" and, in the case of confidential information orally conveyed to Distributor, put such information in writing and mark it "Confidential" within ten (10) days after it is orally conveyed to Distributor. The provisions of this Paragraph 7 shall survive the termination of this Agreement.

8. *Proprietary Interest.* Distributor hereby recognizes Producer's absolute right, title and interest in all patents, trademarks, trade names, copyrights and all other proprietary interest incorporated as any part of either the Products or other material received from Producer. Distributor shall have the exclusive right to use trademarks and service marks owned by Producer solely in connection with Products sold in the Distribution Territory. Distributor agrees that it will cooperate fully with Producer, at Producer's expense, to protect Producer's interest in the property herein described.

9. *Official Notice.* Any official notice provided for herein shall be in writing and sent postage prepaid by registered or certified airmail, return receipt requested. Any such notice sent to Producer shall be sent to the address as first noted in this Agreement. Either party may change its address by official notice to the other. Any official notice shall be effective upon receipt by the party to whom it is addressed.

10. *Termination.* Either party may terminate this Agreement, with or without cause, upon Six (6) months Official Notice to the other party. Notwithstanding any other provisions hereof, Producer may terminate this Agreement by Official Notice to Distributor, effective immediately upon such notice, on the happening of any one or more of the following events:

(a) Distributor, in the sole opinion of Producer, fails to purchase the minimum net wholesale shipment of Products during the periods set forth in Subparagraph 4(c) of this Agreement or during any subsequent renewal term;

(b) Distributor is in default under any term or condition of this Agreement, other than the default described in Subparagraph 10(a) above; provided, however, that in the case of any such default capable of being cured, Producer shall not terminate this Agreement unless and until Distributor shall have failed to cure the same within Sixty (60) days after it has been served with notice of default in writing by Producer provided further, however, that Producer may terminate this Agreement if any such default shall occur on a recurring basis;

(c) The commencement of voluntary or involuntary proceedings under any bankruptcy, reorganization or similar laws of any jurisdiction by or against Distributor or any partner of Distributor or any shareholder owning 25 percent or more of the voting stock of Distributor, or if any order shall be made or any resolution passed for the winding up, liquidation or dissolution of Distributor, if a receiver be appointed for it or its property, or if any of its goods or properties shall be taken in execution;

(d) Distributor shall become the subsidiary of any other company or if control of Distributor (by ownership or by composition of its Board of Directors or otherwise) shall be substantially changed, or if this Agreement is assigned to any other person or entity;

(e) Distributor is not authorized by law and is disqualified to act as distributor for the purposes of this Agreement. In such case the Agreement will be terminated by force of law as of the date of such disqualification and Distributor shall immediately inform Producer of such disqualification and both parties shall arrange to conclude the relationship in a reasonably short time;

(f) the death, incapacity, or incompetency of Distributor if a natural person, or if a partnership, the death, incapacity, incompetency, or withdrawal of any partner.

The exercise by Producer of any rights under this section shall be without prejudice to any other rights Producer may have at law or in equity, under this Agreement or otherwise, and shall not give rise to any rights or claims for compensation or consequential damages, including loss of profits, goodwill or otherwise, by Distributor.

11. *Duties Upon Termination or Expiration.*

(a) Upon termination or expiration of this Agreement, Distributor shall make every effort to cooperate with Producer to ensure the prompt de-registration of this Agreement, and shall comply with all reasonable instructions of the Producer in respect of any appointment by the Producer of a new distributor in the Distribution Territory.

(b) Upon termination or expiration of this Agreement, Distributor shall promptly return to Producer, or otherwise dispose of, as Producer may instruct, all samples, pamphlets, catalogs, advertising material, and any other materials or documents whatsoever sent to Distributor and relating to this Agreement, excepting correspondence between the parties hereto.

(c) Upon termination or expiration of this Agreement, Distributor shall forthwith deliver to Producer, or dispose of as directed, the Products and any other property covered under this Agreement and which Distributor may have in its possession or under its control. Any Products Distributor is not permitted to sell by Producer shall be repurchased by Producer at Distributor's cost. The cost of carriage, insurance, duty, and charges incurred in any such return delivery or other disposal shall be borne by Producer.

(d) Notwithstanding the foregoing, if termination occurs as a result of Distributor's breach of this Agreement, then no further sales of the Products shall be permitted, and Producer shall have no repurchase obligation.

12. *Severability.* Any provision of this Agreement prohibited by applicable law or by court decree shall be ineffective to the extent of such prohibition without in any way invalidating or affecting the remaining provisions of the Agreement.

13. *Assignment.* This Agreement and all rights and duties hereunder are personal to Distributor and shall not, be assigned, transferred, mortgaged, or otherwise encumbered by Distributor or by operation of law.

14. *Independent Contractor.* Nothing herein contained shall be construed to place the parties in the relationship of partners, agents, legal representatives, or joint venturers. It is agreed that Distributor is an independent contractor and that this Agreement does not appoint Distributor as the agent or legal representative of Producer for any purpose whatsoever. Distributor is not granted any right or authority to assume or to create any obligation or responsibility, expressed or implied, on behalf of, or in the name of, Producer or to bind Producer in any manner or thing whatsoever.

15. *Distributor's Representations.*

(a) *Experience in the Industry.* Distributor represents and warrants that it is an experienced distributor of goods similar to the Products and requires no advice or assistance from Producer except for the advice and assistance agreed to by the parties under this Agreement.

(b) *Conflicts of Interest.* Distributor represents and warrants that it has informed Producer, in writing, of any conflicts of interest it may have in entering into this Agreement with Producer.

(c) *Obligations to Third Parties.* Distributor represents and warrants that by entering into this Agreement with Producer, it is not breaching any duty or obligation to any third party.

(d) *Distributor's Indemnification.* Distributor agrees to indemnify and hold harmless Producer from any and all claims, liabilities, judgments, penalties, losses, costs, damages, and expenses resulting from the same, including reasonable attorneys' fees made by third parties against Producer arising by reason of or in connection with any act by Distributor under or in violation of this Agreement, including, but not limited to, the promotion, distribution, exploitation, advertising, offering for sale, sale, or use of the Products except if such claims, liabilities, judgments, penalties, losses, costs, damages, and expenses are directly caused by Producer's negligence or willful misconduct or that result from Producer's product liability. Distributor shall have the right to defend any such action or proceeding with attorneys of its own selection provided that such counsel is reasonably acceptable to Producer. The foregoing indemnity shall remain operative and in full force and effect, regardless of any termination or expiration of this Agreement, and shall be in addition to any liability which Distributor may otherwise have to Producer.

(e) *Insurance.* Distributor further agrees that it has or will obtain at its own expense, comprehensive public liability insurance from a recognized insurance company providing protection in the amount of at least $1,000,000.00 combined single limit, and fire and casualty insurance covering Distributor's premises, inventory, and equipment in an amount sufficient to fully protect Distributor's and Producer's interests therein. Such policies shall be secured and maintained at Distributor's own expense, and shall name Producer as an additional insured. Within Ten (10) days from the date of the execution of this Agreement, Distributor shall furnish to Producer a copy of the same or an insurance certificate attesting to the issuance of the same, and certifying that Producer will be given Thirty (30) days written notice of any material change in or cancellation of such coverage.

16. *Improper Payments*. Distributor agrees that it has not made, or promised to make, any payment to a public official as defined by the United States Foreign Corrupt Practices Act or other applicable laws. Distributor represents that it is aware of the applicable United States governmental regulations governing bribery, agency, and government purchases and any other relevant regulations and agrees to comply with such rules and regulations. Distributor agrees to hold Producer harmless against the consequences of a violation of this provision.

17. *Export Regulations*. Distributor shall fully comply with all provisions of the United States Export Administration Regulations. Distributor acknowledges that it has read and is familiar with the Regulations and shall fully comply with all provisions of the Regulations including wihout limitation Section 373.3(1), (3) and (4) and Section 387.13 concerning record keeping and shall permit Producer's representatives and/or the U.S. government to inspect all such records as may be required for a period of at least Two (2) years after the expiration or termination of the Agreement.

18. *Waiver*. Any attempted or purported waiver by either party of any breach by the other party of any provisions of this Agreement shall have no effect unless such waiver is in writing and signed by the Corporate Secretary or Chief Executive Officer of the waiving party, and any such waiver shall be without prejudice to the rights of the waiving party with respect to any further breach.

19. *Force Majeure*. Producer shall not be liable for any failure to deliver, if such failure has been occasioned by fire, embargo, strike, war, failure to secure materials from usual source of supply, failure to obtain export control clearance on any product, or any circumstances beyond its reasonable control which shall prevent Producer from delivering product in the normal course of business.

20. *Governing Language*. All contracts, agreements, instruments, or other writings shall be furnished and provided to Producer in the English language, and same shall be a full, faithful, and accurate translation of that which it purports to reproduce and represent. If this Agreement is written in two or more languages, the English text thereof will be deemed to be the authoritative version and will be controlling for all purposes.

21. *Governing Law*. The terms and conditions of this Agreement, the interpretation thereof and the rights and obligations of the parties thereunder shall be interpreted and construed as though jointly written and shall be exclusively governed and determined by the laws of the State of _____, U.S.A., as such laws may from time to time exist.

22. *Arbitration*. Any disagreement or dispute which may arise with respect to the interpretation or applications of this Agreement, or the breach thereof, shall be

exclusively settled by arbitration in accordance with the Commercial Arbitration Rules of the American Arbitration Association. Said arbitration shall be held in _____, _____ U.S.A., and be conducted in the English language. Judgment upon the award rendered by the Arbitrator may be entered into in any court having jurisdiction thereof.

23. *Entire Agreement*. This Agreement comprises the entire understanding between the parties hereto, superseding any prior oral or written understandings or agreements. Any modification or amendment to this Agreement must be in writing signed by duly appointed representatives of both Distributor and Producer.

IN WITNESS WHEREOF, the parties hereto have caused this Agreement to be duly executed by their duly authorized officers on the date first above written.

PRODUCER

By: _____

Name: _____

Title: _____

DISTRIBUTOR

By: _____

Name: _____

Title: _____

INTERNATIONAL JOINT VENTURES

Alan S. Gutterman

I. GENERAL CONSIDERATIONS

Introduction

ONE OF THE MOST common forms of organizational strategic business relationship is the "joint venture." The joint venture utilizes a separate business entity, usually a corporation or partnership, to conduct the specified business activities. The use of a separate entity allows the parties to limit the liabilities associated with the relationship and, in fact, the structure may be required in order for the parties to avail themselves of incentives and concessions offered under any local foreign investment programs when the joint venture is used as a means for selling and distributing products and services into a foreign market.

Functional Types of Joint Venture Relationships

In General

Joint ventures can be classified by the various functions which may be performed by the enterprise. For example, a joint venture may be formed to conduct research and development work on new products or technical application, to manufacture or produce various products, to market and distribute products and services in a specified geographic area or to perform some combination of the aforementioned functions. The function of the joint venture will be linked to the overall objectives of the parties and will dictate to a large extent the substantive terms of the joint venture arrangement.

Research and Development

A research and development joint venture can be a useful structure for combining the creative resources and assets of two or more entities in order to facilitate technical exchange and, hopefully, reduce the amount of time that might otherwise have been required in order to complete the development work. "R&D" joint ventures usually involve technology licenses from one or both of the parties to the new enterprise, agreement regarding the scope and duration of the research plan, covenants from both parties regarding protection of the technology developed by the joint venture and, in most cases, some agreement regarding the use of the technology developed by the joint venture by each of the parties.

Manufacturing and Production

Manufacturing and production joint ventures are primarily dedicated to combining the resources of the parties in order to produce goods which would be available for use or sale by one or both of the parties. For example, one of the parties may wish to license certain production technology and trade secrets to a new joint venture enterprise, while the other party would contribute facilities, equipment and personnel to manufacture the products. The finished products could then be delivered to the technology licensor for sale or sold by the joint venture, perhaps under a distribution arrangement with the manufacturing party.

Marketing and Distribution

Marketing and distribution joint ventures are used for the purpose of distributing the goods and services of one or both of the parties in a given geographic area. For example, if a United States company is seeking to enter a new foreign market with the assistance of a local partner with substantial expertise in that market, a new joint venture company might be created and the United States company would contribute the products, as well as any trade secrets or trademarks, and the local partner would provide the capital, facilities and human resources required to fully exploit the products in the market. In addition, the local partner may be able to provide the joint venture with access to various marketing channels and scarce supplies and utilities.

Hybrid Joint Ventures

Hybrid joint venture relationships combine two or more of those basic product development and distribution functions which have been referred to above. A joint venture of this type is usually intended to serve as an integrated business enterprise, owning or controlling all of the assets and resources which might be required in order to develop and manufacture new products and market and distribute such products in specified markets. Each of the parties will contribute, either directly or through licensing or similar contractual arrangements, all the capital, technology, facilities and human resources required to fulfill the objectives of the joint venture's original business plan.

Motivations for Joint Venture Relationships

A joint venture carries with it a number of advantages and disadvantages. On the one hand, a joint venture can provide a party with access to resources and skills which are unavailable to it at any reasonable cost. However, on the other hand, use of a joint venture can be quite risky given the reliance that must be placed upon the ability and willingness of the other party to perform its obligations during the term of the arrangement. In considering whether or not to enter into a joint venture, notice should be taken of some of the following motivations which might drive a party toward such a relationship:

(1)   The party may not have sufficient financial resources to take on a particular project by itself and may seek a partner to assist in sharing the financial burden and other risks of the project. Projects which require a substantial amount of investment in development work and product testing may be good candidate for the joint venture structure. In some cases, a partner may even be willing to provide most, if not all, of the funding in exchange for gaining access to the intangible assets of the party.

(2)   The party may want to gain access to the technical resources and skills of another party. A joint venture which brings together managers and scientists from each party will facilitate the rapid exchange of information regarding existing and new technologies.

(3)   The party may seek a joint venture with a local party in a new foreign market as a means of accelerating the pace of market penetration. The local party should be able to provide the requisite knowledge of local tastes and customs and providing for equity involvement by the local partner will ensure that it will provide the best services to the joint venture. A joint venture may also be required in order to satisfy host country rules which require local participation.

(4)   The party may use a joint venture to decrease the costs associated with the manufacture of its products while retaining some control over the quality of the process and the technology used in the course of completing the manufacturing activities.

(5)   A party may choose a joint venture structure, rather than a network of contractual relationships, in order to ensure that it is in a position to directly manage the specific functional process, be it research work, manufacturing or distribution. Also, a joint venture may be appropriate when the party believes that it will need to provide personnel to facilitate the rapid transfer of trade secrets and other information for use in the collaborative venture.

II.   REGULATION OF JOINT VENTURE RELATIONSHIPS

The formation and operation of a joint venture generally raises many of the same legal issues as confront any other entity which is conducted in partnership or corporate form. The parties must always be mindful of the requirements imposed by relevant partnership and corporations laws. In addition, contributions to, or distributions from, the joint venture by the parties may be subject to specific rules under domestic and international tax laws. Joint ventures often involve an exchange of sensitive business information between the parties and raise a number of concerns with respect to the protection of intellectual property and related rights. Also, in the case of international joint ventures, the parties must consider the effect of foreign exchange controls, differences in language and culture, and other aspects of law and business particular to the area in which the venture is to be formed and operated.

Joint ventures also raise unique issues in the area of antitrust, as well as under specific laws and regulations that are designed to deal with joint venture operations. Developing countries, in particular, may provide for detailed review of the terms of a joint venture arrangement which involves any foreign party. Among the issues which might be need to be settled with regulators are the following:

(1) Antitrust and competition laws are always an area of concern whenever a joint venture is to be formed, since the consolidation of resources from two or more parties which might otherwise compete with other will always, by its very nature, raise questions about the effect of the joint venture on competitive conditions in the marketplace. The parties may need to make filings with antitrust regulators in one or more countries setting out various information about their current activities and the proposed business of the joint venture.

(2) With regard to international joint ventures, there may be a need to obtain approval from local regulators of an investment by a foreign party. The regulators may also review the amount and form of the contribution which is to be made by the foreign party, particularly if local currency, rather than hard currency, is to be used or the foreign party is making an "in-kind" contribution.

(3) If a foreign party is to obtain a license to use any of the technology developed by the joint venture, a review might be made of the royalties which are to be paid by the foreign party to ensure that the parties allow the local party to receive a reasonable return through its interest in the joint venture.

(4) In countries where hard currency is scarce, regulators may closely scrutinize any arrangement which permit a foreign party to repatriate joint venture profits in hard currency or receive payments from the venture for components or technology in hard currency.

(5) Many countries offer various incentives to induce foreign parties to invest in joint ventures with local partners. If the joint venture wishes to qualify for a tax holiday, low-cost government loans or other types of benefits, application may need to be made at the time the joint venture is formed.

III. BASIC STRUCTURAL COMPONENTS OF EQUITY JOINT VENTURES

Introduction

In forming and operating an equity joint venture, referred to hereafter simply as a "joint venture," the parties must take into account all of the same issues which are generally encountered with any new business enterprise. Each of the joint venture partners must agree upon the relative contributions which are to be made to the business, including not only financing, but also new products, technology, personnel, facilities, raw materials and experience in the areas of production, marketing and distribution. Contributions may take the form of direct investments in the joint venture or may be made available under one or more ancillary agreements between the venture and the providing party. In addition, the parties must agree on the management of the joint venture, both day-to-day and long-term, as well as procedures for distributions, withdrawal of one of the parties, and termination.

Contractual Structure of Equity Joint Ventures

Shareholders' Agreement

The key operating contract of an equity joint venture is, assuming that the corporate form is selected, the shareholders' agreement, which will govern the respective rights and obligations of the shareholder-venturers with respect to the operation of the joint venture. Among the issues covered in this agreement are: the initial capitalization of the venture, additional financing for the venture, management and control of the venture, the business and operational activities of the venture, transfers of shares, allocations and distributions of income and other assets, and the term and termination of the venture. In addition, the agreement will include various representations and warranties by each of the parties, agreements with respect to confidentiality of information exchanged in the course of the venture, procedures for resolution of disputes, and a description of any internal controls required to monitor the progress of the venture.[1]

Charter Documents

In addition to the shareholders' agreement, the parties will includes various terms regarding the joint venture in the so-called "charter documents," which include the articles or certificate of incorporation and the bylaws for the corporate entity. Provisions generally covered in the articles of incorporation include the number of authorized shares of the corporation, as well as the rights, preferences and privileges of any separate classes of stock which the may be used by the corporation. Each class of stock may differ as to the assets which will be received upon liquidation of the corporation, voting rights, distributions and redemption. The bylaws include the procedures to be followed with respect to such things as the election of directors and officers, voting rights, committees and financial reports. Proper filing of the articles of incorporation with appropriate regulatory authorities must be made before the corporation can come into existence.

Ancillary Agreements

In most cases, the shareholder-venturers will enter into one or more separate contractual agreements with the corporation. These agreements will cover any services to be provided to the entity by the parties, as well as agreements with respect to the purchase of products developed or manufactured by the venture or the use of the assets of the venture (e.g., technology) by the parties in activities that may, or may not, be related to the specific purpose of the venture. Among the various agreements which might be used are an administrative services agreement, a supply agreement, an equipment purchase agreement, one or more licenses with respect to technology or manufacturing rights, one or more distribution agreements and, in some cases, an agreement with respect to the lease, acquisition, or construction of facilities.

Key Issues in Forming and Operating Joint Ventures

In General

While the interdependence created by the use of a joint venture makes it difficult to generalize regarding the key issues in forming and operating a joint venture, it is usually the case that the parties will need to expend a good deal of time and effort on discussing the following areas: the functional and financial objectives of the joint venture, the contributions which each of the parties are to make to the joint venture, the capital structure of the joint venture corporation, management and control, operating the joint venture, restrictions on transfers of ownership, pre-termination withdrawals of either of the original venturers, and the term and termination of the joint venture.

Defining the Objectives of the Joint Venture

At the outset of every proposed joint venture, it is necessary for the parties arrive at some understanding of the basic objectives of the proposed enterprise. This includes an identification of the nature and scope of the proposed activities of the joint venture and a description of the expectations of each of the parties as to the ultimate financial and technical performance of the joint venture. The process of defining the basic objectives of the joint venture is usually facilitated by the preparation of a summary of the key business terms of the transaction, as well as a formal business plan.

In defining the objectives of the joint venture, it is necessary for the parties to take into account the scope of the joint venture business, the size of the joint venture, the way in which the parties will allocate management responsibility for the day-to-day operations of the joint venture, the decision-making process for major decisions regarding the venture, the terms of any ancillary agreements between the joint venture and either of the parties and the term of the joint venture and any events that might lead to an early termination of the business relationship.

Contributions to the Joint Venture

The planning and negotiation process prior to the actual formation of the joint venture should include an analysis of the financial, technical, and functional requirements of the venture throughout the proposed term of its existence. Although this type of analysis should initially be conducted without regard to the specific capabilities of the parties in each of these areas, it will ultimately be necessary for the parties to focus upon each of the specific contributions to be made by the parties.

Since the venturers are something more than passive investors in the joint venture, the range of possible contributions will be much broader than is normally the case. For example, not only will the venturers contribute cash and cash equivalents to finance the operations of the joint venture, they may also provide the venture with services, tangible property (e.g., equipment or facilities), intangible property rights, and specific functional expertise in such diverse areas as research and development, manufacturing and distribution. In addition, the venturers may be able to contribute their experience and contacts in dealing with local regulators and in obtaining supplies of scarce raw materials.

Capital Structure

Whatever form that the initial capital contribution might take, a corporate joint venture actually commences operations upon the sale and issuance of shares to the parties. The parties become the owners, as shareholders, of the corporation with such rights as may be created under the laws of the jurisdiction in which the corporation is organized, as well as any contractual agreements between the shareholders. The shares of capital stock to be issued to the parties carry a number of rights with respect to management and control of the enterprise as well as the manner in which the holder can expect to receive a return with respect to its invested capital.

Management and Control

Devising an appropriate structure for the management and control of the venture is one of the most important matters to be negotiated between the parties. Assuming that the choice is made to utilize the corporate form of business entity, the parties must consider various issues relating to the election of the board of directors, the selection of the officers and key managers, the respective voting rights of each of the parties on matters deemed to be material to the existence and operation of the enterprise and the specific duties of the board of directors, the officers and any committees created by the parties to manage one or more of the business functions of the enterprise. Also, while hopefully the parties will not reach a situation where they are unable to agree on a certain matter, the parties should agree upon a procedure for the orderly resolution of disputes.

Generally, each of the parties will have the right to designate one or more representatives to act as members of the board of directors or officers of the corporation. In addition, either as a matter of law or by contractual agreement, each of the parties will have various voting rights on matters of importance to the corporation. Also, it is not unusual for the corporation to contract with one or both of the parties for the conducting of one or more specific functions or services, including such things as basic research and development, manufacturing and distribution. As a result of these contractual arrangements, the party effectively assumes control over a material aspect of the operations of the venture, even though nominal authority remains in the board of directors and in the officer or manager selected to oversee the specific function or service.

The parties need to strike an appropriate balance between permitting the officers and managers of the joint venture to make appropriate decisions regarding the operation of the enterprise and reserving the right, as the owners of the venture, to review and approve certain matters. The matters which are subject to the "shared control" of the owners, thereby requiring approval of both joint venture partners, should be limited to those items that are material to the performance of the venture, since making numerous actions subject to a unanimous vote will diminish, or even eliminate, the ability of the venture to quickly respond to appropriate business opportunities and changes in competitive and other environmental conditions.

While there are seemingly endless possibilities for the listing of items which might require the unanimous consent of the shareholders, or a supermajority vote of the board of directors, the following matters are typically considered:

- Capital expenditures or indebtedness in excess of a specified dollar amount at any one time, other than as provided in the annual operating budget.

- Sale of asset the value of which exceeds a specified dollar amount at any one time or the aggregate value of which exceeds a specified dollar amount within any six month period.

- Creation of material liens, mortgages, encumbrances or other charges of any kind on any asset of the venture or guarantees of payment by or of performance of the obligations of any third party.

- Approval of the annual operating budget and annual capital expenditure budget of the joint venture, as well as any amendments thereto.

- Any commitment of the joint venture which either creates a liability in excess of a specified dollar amount or which obligates the joint venture to perform under any arrangement, contract or agreement which is not within the ordinary course of its business.

- Any amendment to the articles of incorporation or bylaws of the joint venture corporation.

- Any issuance of additional shares of the joint venture corporation, declaration of dividends or reinvestment of earnings at a time when the corporation is otherwise permitted by law to pay dividends.

- Any agreement or material transaction between the joint venture and either (1) a shareholder or any affiliate of a shareholder or (2) a director or executive officer of the joint venture.

- Adoption of or change in any major policy of the joint venture relating to operations, manufacture, sale of products, or changes in product lines.

- A dissolution, liquidation, merger, consolidation, other business combination or sale of substantially all the assets of the joint venture.

Operating the Joint Venture

Although a good deal of the emphasis during the period of negotiating the terms of the joint venture is placed on issues relating to capitalization and management, it is important for the parties to remember that the venture company will become an independent operating entity with a life of its own. As such, the joint venture documents should cover the key points relating to operation of the venture, including the responsibilities for the functional activities of the company (e.g., research and development, manufacturing and distribution); operational matters, such as legal compliance, insurance, staffing and other similar issues; accounting and financial reporting matters; and the allocation and distribution of joint venture income.

Restrictions on Transfers of Ownership

As a general rule, the parties will generally agree to a strict prohibition on any sale or transfer of the shares for a specified period of time, usually corresponding to the initial term of the venture. Precluded transfers will include not only an outright sale of the shares, but also any pledge or other encumbrance of the shares, although in some cases a party will be permitted to transfer the shares to a successor corporation or a wholly-owned subsidiary of the party. Waiver of the restriction on transfer would require the consent of the other party.

After the restriction period has ended, the parties will usually agree to a "right of first offer" or a "right of first refusal." The right of first offer obligates the party wishing to find a purchaser for its shares to first offer them to the other shareholder on the terms at which the potential seller would like to complete the transaction. If the other shareholder is unwilling to purchase the shares on those terms, the seller would them have a specified period of time to find a purchaser on terms no less favorable to the seller than those originally offered to the other shareholder. The right of first refusal is slightly different, since the selling shareholder must first have an offer to purchase the shares from a third party at the time the transaction is proposed to the other shareholder.

Pre-Termination Withdrawals of a Joint Venture Partner

There may be a variety of situations in which one of the joint venturers will be allowed, or required, to withdraw from the venture prior to the date upon which the parties originally contemplated that the relationship would terminate. For example, a fundamental change with respect to one of the parties, such as a change in ownership of the party, may cause a sufficient amount of uneasiness for the other, or "non-changing" party, to trigger a right in the hands of the non-changing party to purchase the shares of the other party. Another situation where withdrawal may be appropriate is when a party which is not actively involved in the management of the venture is dissatisfied with the level of performance which the venture has achieved in the hands of the other party and seeks to have its interest purchased by the party that is in control of the venture.

Withdrawal of one of the parties and continuation of the business by the other party is obviously an alternative to simply dissolving and liquidating the entity. In some cases, continuing the business without both of the original parties is simply not a viable alternative, particularly when the withdrawing party takes with it certain resources, technical or otherwise, which are of fundamental importance to the success of the venture. However, since dissolution and liquidation often diminishes the value of the interests of both parties, some effort will generally be made to establish equitable procedures for liquidating the interests of the parties without terminating the business itself.

Duration and Termination of the Joint Venture

The joint venture documents must include provisions which specify the duration of the enterprise, the events which may lead to the termination and dissolution of the joint venture and the manner in which the assets and resources of the entity will be redistributed to the parties upon liquidation. The duration, or "term," of the joint venture will depend upon the specific goals and objectives of the parties and the amount of time which will be needed in order to achieve the required investment return. Termination and dissolution may occur either at the end of the fixed term or upon the occurrence of specified events prior to the termination date otherwise specified in the venture documents. The process of liquidation is generally governed by applicable law, although the parties do have some freedom to specify how the remaining assets of the joint venture will be allocated between them after the claims of creditors have been satisfied.

IV. SPECIAL CONSIDERATIONS FOR INTERNATIONAL JOINT VENTURES

International joint ventures raise all of the issues considered above and in the attached checklists. Moreover, the process of negotiating the joint venture arrangement and insuring that the partnership works effectively following formation is complicated by the differences which generally exist between the parties with respect to cultural attitudes and business practice. In addition, international joint ventures are usually the subject of intense regulation by the host country under it regulations governing foreign investment. Counsel involving in negotiating an international joint venture should consult one of the many excellent and comprehensive texts on the subject[2] as a means for dealing with some of the following issues:

• Host country regulation and promotion of joint ventures and foreign investment.

- Financing international joint ventures.
- Political risk insurance.
- Labor and immigration issues.
- Negotiating supply agreements with local vendors and producers.
- Technology transfer and product liability regulations.
- Arbitration and dispute resolution procedures.

In addition, international joint ventures raise a number of issues in areas which are covered by other chapters in this book, including antitrust, export controls, foreign corrupt practices, and taxation.

Notes

[1] If the joint venture is organized and operated as a partnership, each of the various issues listed will be covered in a partnership agreement, which will be substantially identical to the shareholders' agreement.

[2] See, e.g., Goldsweig & Cummings (eds), *International Joint Ventures: A Practical Approach to Working with Foreign Investors in the U.S. and Abroad* (ABA Section of International Law and Practice: 1990).

GUIDELINES FOR INTERNATIONAL JOINT VENTURES

Prepared by Richard A. Reed and Anita L. Esslinger. Reprinted with Permission.)

Section I—Basic Issues
  A. Reasons for Forming a Joint Venture.
  B. Major Considerations in Every Joint Venture.
  C. Problems Encountered in Joint Ventures.
  D. Other Alternatives.

Section II—Selection of a Joint Venture Partner (Checklist).

Section III—Negotiating Joint Ventures.

Section IV—Model Joint Venture Agreement Table of Contents.

I. *Basic Issues*

A. *Reasons for Forming a Joint Venture*
  1. Compelled by local law—government restrictions on foreign ownership (e.g., PRC, India);
  2. Lack of investment capital—parent company unable or unwilling to raise the necessary capital;
  3. Lack of local national competence—need for local facilities, sales or distribution outlets, management or labor personnel, manufacturing skills, knowledge of local business practices, customs and culture, law, local identity, market knowledge, access to raw materials;
  4. Establishment of a substantial captive customer or supplier;
  5. More effective relationship with local government;
  6. Means of reducing investment risk;
  7. Access to strong operating partner;
  8. Superior recruitment of middle management;
  9. Acquisition of needed technology;
  10. Selling old technology;
  11. Disposing of a business activity; or
  12. Last ditch effort to serve a market or faster market penetration.

B. *Major Considerations in Every Joint Venture*
  1. A joint venture is the most complicated form or method of international business and should be approached *very carefully*! Be aware that joint ventures typically do not have long lives. Joint control of the major decisions is probably the most significant characteristic of joint ventures.
  2. The joint venture method of establishing an international business relationship is a last resort alternative to other forms of doing business. Examples of such forms would be licensing of technology; licensing with a management assistance

agreement; licensing with an option for the local or foreign firm to buy certain technology know-how; and contracting the right to manufacture with a reservation that the firm providing the right to manufacture would be the direct sales connection for export purposes.

3. A joint venture is a transitory vehicle for market entry into a foreign country. It may only serve to initiate hopefully a long term business relationship. It is stressed that unless there is a continuous reciprocal need for each other, a joint venture will not endure.

4. There are different types of joint ventures. There are research and development, production, marketing, distribution joint ventures, and combinations of the foregoing.

5. Joint ventures can be used for different products and at different stages of the development and production of a particular product. A joint venture can be limited to a special project which may be of a short or long duration.

6. There are equity and non-equity types of joint ventures.

7. There are negative factors to consider:
   a. Sharing in operating losses.
   b. Exposure to ethical issues of legal violations.
   c. Protracted legal disputes.
   d. Loss of flexibility to dispose of investment.
   e. Loss of investment.

C. *Problems Encountered in Joint Ventures*
   1. *The fundamental problem*—the partners rarely have congruent long-term objectives.
      a. Cash returns vs. market share.
      b. The government partner—a special case.
         —social and political objectives.
   2. *The next major problem*—loss of exclusive control and resultant management complexity.
   3. *The third major problem*—when one partner's contribution declines or ceases altogether.
   4. *Specific differences of opinion.*
      a. Management of philosophy and ethics.
      b. Employee relations approaches.
      c. Marketing philosophy.
      d. Product pricing.
      e. Transfer pricing.
      f. Reinvestment of earnings.
      g. Capital investment.
      h. Payments for technology.
      i. Export markets.
      j. Production rationalization.
      k. Product quality standards.

D. *Other Alternatives*
  1. *Licensing of Technology.*
    a. Minimizes financial risk.
    b. May improve return on investment.
    c. Reduces knowledge/control of activity.
      1. Reputation.
      2. Quality.
      3. Customer service.
    d. May create a competitor.
  2. *Licensing with a management assistance agreement.*
    a. Adds a degree of control.
    b. Requires local national competence.
  3. *Licensing with an option to buy.*
    a. May be the best solution if lack of local competence is a key factor.
    b. Defers final decision until risk is better understood.
  4. *Contract manufacturing but a direct sales presence.*
    a. May get past government.
    b. Maintains direct customer relationship.
    c. Provides output check on quality.

II. *Selection of a Joint Venture Partner: Checklist*

A. *Looking for a partner.*
  1. *Organizations—information.*
    a. U.S. Export Development Office or U.S. trade shows abroad.
    b. U.S. Department of Commerce.
    c. AMCHAM—Bilateral Chamber of Commerce.
    d. Local banks.
      • Government banks.
      • Private banks.
    e. U.S. banks.
    f. Local private sector organizations.
      • Chambers of industry.
      • Chambers of commerce.
      • Specific trade associations.
      • Umbrella organizations.
      • Others.
    g. Host government organizations.
      • Ministry of commerce.
      • Ministry of trade or industry.
      • Government foreign trade organization or bank.
  2. *Traditional partners.*
    a. Distributors/representatives.
    b. Licensees.

     c. Suppliers.

     d. Customers.

     e. The Prince or his brother.

     f. Government agency.

3. *What to look for.*

     a. Complementing organization.

- Manufacturing capability.
- Marketing organization.
- Human resources.
- Government contracts.
- Other factors—corporate personality, conflicts of interest, creating competitor.

     b. Large company vs. small company.

- The supergroups.
- Supergroup plus bank.
- Small company.
- Families (Royal and other).
- Forming your own group.

     c. Profiling your potential partner.

- Sales.
- Assets.
- Manufacturing facilities.
- Marketing organization.
- People.
  - —Management.
  - —Shop people.
  - —Marketing people.
- Composition of ownership.
- Financial position.

     d. Active vs. passive partners.

4. *Reduction to the "short list."*

5. *Define your own strategic objectives.*

     a. Strategic marketing plan.

- Normal customers, normal markets.
- New customers.
- New markets.

     b. Why particular country?

- Defensive.
- Offensive.

     c. Corporate commitment to foreign joint ventures.

- Management resources.
- Capital investments.

6. *Local import policy.*

     a. Product classification (duty schedule).

- Import licenses.

- Higher duties.
- Secretary of Commerce: industry/product committees.
- Importance of specificity in product identification.
  —Example: pumps; valves.

   b. *Government policy (preferences).*
- Local manufacturer.
- Local assembly.
- Not otherwise available locally.

B. *The commitment.*
   1. *Your time in country.*
      a. The first meeting.
      b. The second meeting.
      c. The third meeting.
      d. The truth.
   2. *Your local network of advisors.*
      a. Bankers.
      b. Auditors.
      c. Legal Counsel.
      d. Local consultants.
   3. *The importance of showing the flag (when to bring in the CEO).*

C. *Approach to making final partner decision.*
   1. *Discussing the hard questions up front.*
      a. Participation.
      b. Capital contribution.
      c. Technology and know-how.
   2. *The local management resources.*
      a. People at the top.
      b. Who's going to run the shop?
      c. Recruitment: their plans.
   3. *The bottom line.*
      a. Objectives—Short and long term.
      b. Ethics and business philosophy.
      c. Trust.
      d. Respective contributions—now and continuing.

III. *Negotiating Joint Ventures*

A. *Long-term (negotiation preparation) consideration.*
   1. *Long-term compatibility.*
      a. Mutual interest—technical, financial, political.
      b. Reciprocal or supplemental resources to contribute to objectives of project or company.
      c. Commitment to general objectives.
- Profit: but what about dividend philosophy?

        • Market share: conflict with partner's operations?

        • Others (e.g., technology transfer).

          —Creating competitors.

          —Know-how as a capital contribution.

2. *Response to Nationalism.*

    a. Government as "partner."

        • Protection against exploitation.

        • Control of productive sector: self-reliance.

    b. Local private enterprise as "partner": same as 1c plus politically prudent.

    c. Local Bank Plus 2a or 2b: active vs. passive investor.

3. *What does "shared management" mean?*

B. *Negotiating with governments.*

  1. *Directly.*

    a. Objectives of host government.

        • Import technology to meet development goals.

        • Preserve scarce foreign exchange reserves.

        • Adapt and diffuse benefits of technology.

        • Creation of jobs to absorb labor force.

        • Training: Upgrade skill levels.

        • Avoid foreign control.

        • Create indigenous technological capacity.

        • Avoid unsuitable or irrelevant technology.

        • Promote local R&D and technology adaptation.

        • Promote exports.

    b. Objectives of transnationals.

        • Receive fair return on investment or R&D or other allocation of resources.

        • Protect property rights.

        • Increase market share or new penetration.

        • Maintain reputation, competitive standing, quality control, and product or process standards.

        • Use as a doorway to other markets.

  2. *Indirectly—registration of agreements: renegotiation.*

  3. *Extortion and bribes.*

    a. Grease and gravy payments.

    b. Exercising due diligence.

C. *Negotiating with private (commercial) companies.*

  1. Equity.

  2. Contributions of capital.

  3. Technology as a capital contribution.

  4. Selection.

  5. Voting rights.

  6. Protection of minority interests.

  7. Financial reporting.

  8. Dividend policy.

     9. Loans and guarantees.
   10. Future capital requirements.
   11. Local marketing.
   12. International marketing.

D. *Looking ahead to future requirements.*
   1. Control: is it a misnomer?
   2. Goal achievement.
   3. Net gain for each party.

E. *Sharing of management: meaning.*
   1. Understanding and communication.
   2. Information requirements.

F. *Conflicts of Interest.*
   1. Corporate opportunity doctrine.
   2. Local business culture.
   3. The American way.

G. *Blocking Rights.*
   Structure shareholder rights carefully.
     Matters that should require joint approval:
- Changes in capital structure.
- Changes in classes of shares and their respective rights.
- Changes in pre-emptive rights of shares.
- Change of company name.
- Amendment of the by-laws.
- Merger or acquisition.
- Dissolution.
- Issuance of bonds or debentures.
- Appointment of auditors.
- Appointment and removal of the general manager.
- Change in composition of the board of directors.
- Approval of long-term plans.
- Annual budget approval.
- Dividend distribution.
- Export.
- Use of intellectual property.
- Dealing with company's assets.
- Key executive compensation.
- Creation of branches and/or subsidiaries.

H. *Establish a divorce procedure.*
   1. Do it up front—while everyone is friendly.
   2. Establish trigger mechanism.
   3. Define rights for puts and calls.
   4. Establish a clearly defined formula for share value.

PART TWO

DOMESTIC LAWS AND REGULATIONS AFFECTING INTERNATIONAL BUSINESS ACTIVITIES

U.S. EXPORT CONTROL LAWS

Daniel J. Plaine
Peter Lichtenbaum
Lee H. Hsu

I. INTRODUCTION

THE UNITED STATES maintains a comprehensive system of export controls comprising various statutes, regulations, and executive orders. In accordance with foreign policy and national security goals, these export restrictions form an integral part of an ongoing effort to curb the worldwide proliferation of "weapons of mass destruction" and to prevent certain countries from obtaining goods and technology that may contribute to their military potential. Accordingly, U.S. export controls apply to "inherently military" products as well as commercial items that may have military applications. Various U.S. agencies, including the Department of Commerce and the Department of State, have authority over the export of different types of products or technologies, and controlled items are subject to varying licensing requirements before they can be shipped from the U.S.

The exporter bears full responsibility for complying with U.S. export control laws. U.S. export controls apply to goods, technical data, software, and technologies: (1) of U.S. origin; (2) of non-U.S. origin but containing a certain amount of U.S. components or materials; or (3) of non-U.S. origin but produced using U.S.-origin technical data or technology containing U.S. know-how. Moreover, the U.S. government has begun to impose controls on the sale of goods and technologies by all "U.S. persons," which may include foreign branches of U.S. companies. Thus, even foreign-origin exports may be subject to U.S. export controls when shipped by such "U.S. persons."

Penalties for noncompliance with U.S. export control laws can be severe. Violations can lead to civil or criminal sanctions, and possibly a revocation of all export privileges. Exporters in the U.S. as well as "U.S. persons" in foreign countries should be thoroughly familiar with U.S. export control laws and take appropriate steps to comply with U.S. export licensing requirements.

This chapter provides a general overview of the U.S. export control regime, emphasizing the controls that apply to commercial products. Because of the complexity of U.S. export controls, prospective exporters should consult the applicable regulations or contact the appropriate agency for specific details or to determine the extent to which particular products are subject to export restrictions or licensing requirements.

II. MULTILATERAL CONTROLS: COCOM

As a member of the Coordinating Committee for Multilateral Export Controls (COCOM), the U.S. assumed important international obligations in maintaining an effective export control regime.[1] Since its inception in 1949, COCOM sought to restrict, for reasons of national security, the export to "proscribed countries" of goods and technologies that may enhance the military potential of these countries. As a result of the dissolution of the former Soviet bloc and the Soviet Union itself and at the urging of certain European countries, COCOM members substantially liberalized the COCOM export control regime, allowing for more expedited licensing procedures for shipments to the former Soviet bloc countries and the People's Republic of China as well as more unlicensed transactions in general.

COCOM recognized three categories of controlled exports: the International Munitions List, the Industrial List, and the International Atomic List. Although COCOM was merely an informal body that existed without a treaty, each of the seventeen participating countries implemented COCOM agreements by means of national legislation and regulations. Accordingly, the United States adopted export controls consisting of legislation, regulations, and executive orders which furthered U.S. policy goals while adhering to COCOM obligations.

COCOM was dismantled on April 1, 1994, due to concerns that its "Cold War" focus was outdated and unproductive. However, a similar organization will take its place and will focus on exports to countries developing nuclear, chemical, or biological weapons of mass destruction. The new organization will contain all COCOM member countries and others who share the weapons proliferation concern. The focus of the new organization will be commodities which may be used as nuclear, chemical, or biological weapons precursors (many of these items are dual use items).

III. U.S. EXPORT CONTROL LEGISLATION

U.S. legislation establishes a classification scheme in which different agencies may have some jurisdiction over a given type of export. For most U.S. businesses, the most important agencies in the U.S. export control regime are the Department of Commerce, which controls "dual-use" products and technology, and the Department of State, which controls purely military exports. The Department of Commerce has its authority pursuant to the Export Administration Act (EAA), and the Department of State has its authority under the Arms Export Control Act (AECA).

Commercial Exports Under the Export Administration Act

The Export Administration Act (EAA) authorizes the President of the United States to "prohibit or curtail the export of any goods or technology subject to the jurisdiction of the United States or exported by any person subject to the jurisdiction of the United States." Under the EAA, the President has the power to control exports for reasons involving national security, foreign policy, or domestic materials in short supply. In practice, U.S. export controls focus primarily on national security and foreign policy concerns, scrutinizing the overseas shipment of certain products and technologies that may contribute to the military potential of "proscribed countries."

In accordance with the EAA's objectives, the U.S. Department of Commerce controls the export of "dual-use" goods. Dual-use goods are commodities, software, and technology that are intended for commercial uses but may also have military applications. Within the Commerce Department, the Bureau of Export Administration (BXA) is responsible for administering export controls under the EAA. To that end, the BXA maintains and enforces the Export Administration Regulations (EAR), 15 C.F.R. Parts 730–799, which control exports of dual-use items through export restrictions and licensing requirements. In terms of level of control, the EAR distinguish between different types of goods as well as different export destinations and end use/users.

Proscribed Countries

Canada is the only country for which no commercial export license is required, except for very sensitive items such as those involving nuclear energy. Apart from Canada, the Commerce Department distinguishes between several different groups of countries for purposes of authorizing exports. U.S. export control laws revolve around the following country groups:[2]

Group Z: Cuba, and North Korea

Group Y: the countries of the former Soviet Union, Bulgaria, Cambodia, Estonia, Laos, Latvia, Lithuania, and the Mongolian People's Republic and Vietnam

Group W: Czech Republic, Poland and Slovak Republic

Group V: all countries not specified elsewhere, including People's Republic of China, Yugoslavia, Hungary, Afghanistan (PRC and Afghanistan are subject to special licensing requirements and restrictions in certain cases)

Group T: Latin America, Greenland, South America, North America, Central America, and Caribbean countries

Group S: Libya

Group Q: Romania

Other than Canada, which is almost unrestricted, exports to countries in groups T and V receive the most favorable export licensing treatment from the Commerce Department.

The Commerce Department also maintains "special country policies" for North Korea, Vietnam, Cuba, the countries comprised by the former Soviet Union and Eastern Europe (other than the former East Germany), Mongolia, Laos, Cambodia, South Africa, Iran, Libya, Syria, Iraq, the People's Republic of China, and Afghanistan. These policies are found in 15 C.F.R. Part 785, and in most instances they articulate specific, restrictive rules regarding particular types of products that may not be shipped to one or more of these countries. In some instances, the policy will explain liberalized treatment for certain shipments. To ensure compliance, exporters shipping goods to these countries should consult the corresponding special country policies before exporting.

In addition, an export is prohibited if an individual or entity involved in the transaction has been denied export privilges by the Commerce Department. A "Table of Serial Orders," listing such persons, is published periodically by the Federal Register, and must be consulted before entering into an export transaction.

Exporters should also be aware of potential diversions of U.S. technology. A diversion occurs whenever commodities or technical data are either exported without the required export license, or exported to a destination other than the ultimate destination authorized by the license. To assist exporters in discovering potential diversion, the Commerce Department has published a list of characteristics that commonly exist in diversions. The characteristics can be found at 15 C.F.R. §77.3(e)(ix).

Licensing Requirements for Commercial Goods Under the Commerce Control List

In addition to its country groupings, the Commerce Department's BXA distinguishes between different types of products as indicated in its Commerce Control List (CCL). The CCL is a comprehensive list of dual-use items which are controlled by the Commerce Department, including equipment, assemblies, components, materials software, technology, and production and test equipment.[3] Each controlled product or group of products is designated by a corresponding Export Control Classification Number (ECCN), which specifies the appropriate licensing requirements.

As a general rule, all exports require one of two kinds of U.S. export licenses: a "validated license" or a "general license." A validated license requires specific prior authorization for a particular export transaction or group of export transactions. A general license, on the other hand, authorizes exports without specific government approval of each shipment or transaction. Thus, the threshold question for all exporters is whether they must obtain a validated license for a given export transaction or whether the export is authorized by an existing general license.

Specific questions about product classifications or licensing requirements should be directed to the BXA's Export Counseling Division in Washington, D.C., at (202) 482–4811. Exporters are responsible for identifying the correct ECCN for their products, and an exporter that is unsure about a particular product's ECCN can request a determination by the Commerce Department's Office of Technology and Policy Analysis. Although verbal determinations are available, they are not binding. To avoid problems and possible penalties, exporters should obtain from the Commerce Department a formal, written determination of the proper ECCN.

Validated Licenses

The end user/usc and ECCN determines whether an exporter must have a "validated license" to export a given product. There are numerous types of validated licenses, which may authorize individual shipments or a series of export transactions within a specified time period. For individual shipments of controlled items, an individual validated license (IVL) requires the exporter to file a specific license application with the Commerce Department and wait for specific approval before shipping the product outside the U.S. Since processing can take several weeks, an exporter should allow some flexibility in its delivery schedule.

Other validated licenses allow multiple-transaction exports with a single validated license. A "distribution license," for example, authorizes unlimited shipment of certain products to approved distributors or customers in T and V countries (except Afghanistan, Iran, Iraq, Jordan, Lebanon, Syria, and the PRC), on the condition that the distributors resell only to responsible parties or retailers within their approved sales territories. If these parties want to resell outside of their approved sales territories, they must obtain a license for each individual sale. The distribution license may also be available, in some instances, for export to the former Soviet bloc countries.

Other multiple-transaction export licenses include the "project license" and the "service supply license," both of which authorize multiple exports that relate to an established or ongoing business enterprise. A "project license" authorizes the export of products for up to one year, with a possible two year renewal, for (1) establishing or expanding a significant industrial or commercial project abroad; (2) supplying maintenance, repair, or operating supplies to a facility abroad; or (3) supplying materials to be used in a production facility abroad. Similarly, a "service supply license" authorizes an exporter or manufacturer to export spare and replacement parts to T and V countries (except Afghanistan, Iran, Syria, and the PRC) to service equipment previously exported by the licensee or made by a foreign subsidiary. For the more restricted destinations of Afghanistan, the PRC, and Q, W, and Y countries, a service supply license may be available for only certain replacement parts.

General Licenses

If the product is not very sensitive, has beeen found readily available from foreign sources not subjected to similar export controls, or if the U.S. has good relations with the destination country, then a U.S. exporter may be able to forego a specific license application and instead rely on an existing general license. Most general licenses exist as a matter of law and permit exports without specific government authorization. General licenses are published and described in 15 C.F.R. § 771. Despite its name, a general license is not an actual document and merely acts as an exemption from a validated license requirement.

The general license known as G-DEST allows the exporter to export only items of low-sensitivity and minimum value to specified countries without having to apply for permission from the Commerce Department. Other general licenses are available for shipments of minimal value (GLV), for temporary exports that will be returned to the U.S. (G-TEMP), for return of products to non-U.S. countries from which they were temporarily imported (GTF-US), and for repair or replacement of defective parts (GLR).

Also, the general license GCT permits unrestricted trade between COCOM and "5K" countries[4] of certain products which normally would require a validated license.

Licensing Requirements for Technology and Technical Data

To augment its categorical controls on commodities, the Commerce Department also requires licenses for the "export" of technology and technical data. The U.S. government is extremely concerned about the dissemination of technology information, and exporters should proceed with particular caution in complying with export controls in this area. The Commerce Department has traditionally taken a very broad view of the term "technical data," which typically means a prototype, blueprint, operating manual, software, etc. In addition, the Commerce Department has a very broad concept of "export," particularly as applied to technical data. For example, verbal or visual releases (i.e., in a seminar, conference, or facility visit) to foreign nationals in the U.S. can constitute an "export." An exporter must consult the CCL and 15 C.F.R. Part 779 to determine whether a validated license is required. Certain technologies or technical data always require a validated license, even if only Canada or Canadian nationals are involved.

If a validated license is not required, an exporter may proceed under one of three general licenses for technical data: GTDA, GTDR, and GTDU. The general license known as GTDA (found in 15 C.F.R. § 779.3) allows U.S. exporters to disseminate, without requesting government approval, technical data that is publicly available (for example, through libraries), as well as scientific and educational data "not directly and significantly related to design, production, or utilization in industrial processes." For all destinations, General License GTDA authorizes exports of generally available information in which the exporter does not claim a proprietary interest.

The general licenses known as GTDR and GTDU (found in 15 C.F.R. § 779.4) allow exports of proprietary technical data to selected countries, usually only T or V countries, without prior governmental approval. Exports to S and Z countries are prohibited, and exports to country groups Q, W, Y and the People's Republic of China may require prior approval in the form of a Technical Data Individual Validated License unless the technical data is intended to support a marketing effort and does not otherwise disclose design, production, or utilization information, or it constitutes "operational" technical data associated with an already approved export of a product. General License GTDR is slightly more restrictive than General License GTDU, since GTDR requires that an exporter obtain from the customer a written assurance that the technical data will not be exported to any of the proscribed countries. General License GTDU does not require such written assurances, but it operates like GTDR in virtually all other respects.

Military Exports Under the Arms Export Control Act

Under the Arms Export Control Act (AECA), the U.S. Department of State controls the export of goods, services, technology, and technical data designed or modified for military use—i.e., items and technologies that are "inherently military" in character.

The International Traffic in Arms Regulations (ITAR), 22 C.F.R. (subchapter M) Parts 120–130, implement the AECA and are administered primarily by the State Department's Office of Defense Trade Controls (DTC), formerly known as the Office of Munitions Control (OMC).[5] In theory, the AECA regulatory regime controls these items to avoid contributing to an arms race, to reduce the possibility of armed conflicts, or to further the achievement of arms control arrangements. In practice, however, the DTC reviews applications primarily to determine whether the proposed export transactions comport with U.S. national security or foreign policy interests.

The ITAR contain the U.S. Munitions List, which designates specific articles, services, and related technical data as defense articles and defense services for the purposes of export controls. Unlike the Commerce Department's CCL, the Munitions List is written using broad descriptions of products and technologies and arguably gives DTC more discretion in determining export control coverage on a case-by-case basis. In addition, there often arises a question whether a product or technology falls under the CCL or the Munitions List (no product or technology can be controlled under both.) By regulation, DTC is the agency that has sole authority to determine the product or technology coverage in any export transaction, if needed.

IV. OTHER CONTROLS ON EXPORTS FROM THE U.S.

In addition to its statutory and regulatory authority under the EAA and the AECA, the U.S. government has other important channels for controlling the overseas shipment of goods or technology. In particular, the International Emergency Economic Powers Act (IEEPA) gives the President the power to prohibit exports to certain countries in time of declared national emergency, and the Enhanced Proliferation Control Initiative (EPCI) has emerged as a significant effort to combat the spread of chemical, biological, and missile weaponry.

Economic Sanctions Under the International Emergency Economic Powers Act

The International Emergency Economic Powers Act (IEEPA), along with the Trading with the Enemy Act (TWEA), vests the President with the power to administer economic embargoes against certain countries in the event of a declared national emergency. By executive order, the Department of Treasury's Office of Foreign Assets Control (OFAC) can implement highly restrictive "economic sanctions" against such countries. These sanctions often prohibit persons and companies subject to U.S. jurisdiction from doing almost any form of business with specified countries, certain nationals of those countries, or "specially designated nationals" of those countries. Specially designated nationals are specifically named individuals and companies that OFAC has determined are acting on behalf of the government of a sanctioned country.

As of April 1994, OFAC maintained some form of economic sanctions against Angola, Iraq, Cuba, Libya, North Korea, Iran, Haiti, and Yugoslavia (Serbia and Montenegro only). The relevant regulations are located in 31 C.F.R. Parts 500–590. For further details or up-to-date information regarding the Treasury Department's economic sanctions or embargoes, exporters can contact OFAC in Washington, D.C., at (202) 622-2500.

Chemical, Biological, and Missile Weaponry Under the Enhanced Proliferation Control Initiative

In response to growing concern with the spread of chemical, biological, and missile weaponry, the U.S. government has instituted a new program of export controls known as the Enhanced Proliferation Control Initiative (EPCI). The purpose of EPCI is to impose stricter controls on products and technologies that are related to the development of such weaponry. Thus, for example, chemical compounds and equipment used to make such compounds are now more carefully regulated.

The EPCI also seeks to prevent the export of any products to end-users that are known to be involved in the development or production of chemical, biological, or missile weaponry. The Commerce Department actively attempts to identify certain entities located abroad that are deemed to be involved in these activities. Exports by "U.S. persons" to these and other entities involved in similar activities must be conducted under Individual Validated Licenses even if the commodity normally qualifies for export under a general license. "U.S. persons" are defined to include U.S. companies' foreign branches, but not their foreign incorporated subsidies. It is the responsibility of each exporter to undertake reasonable efforts to ascertain whether any party to the export transaction may be involved in chemical, biological, or missile weaponry activities. If an end-user is identified or known to be so involved, an unlicensed export of any product is prohibited.

V. PENALTIES FOR VIOLATING EXPORT CONTROL LAWS

Violation of export control laws may lead to criminal prosecution, arrest, extradition, and severe monetary penalties. Notwithstanding the criminal sanctions applicable in the U.S. (ranging up to $1 million in fines), the company involved in a violation either as a principal offender or an accomplice may be:

- fined by Commerce up to $100,000 per violation involving national security and up to $10,000 per violation in other cases;
- denied, for a limited or unlimited period of time, the privilege to export and to obtain general export licenses (all destinations) or to obtain validated licenses;
- have its products and vessels involved in an unauthorized export transaction seized by government officials.

VI. SCREENING

The Commerce Department publishes guidelines for implementing Export Management Systems. These systems are procedures exporters should consider part of the effort to ensure that exports are conducted in accordance with the U.S. export control laws. While these procedures are not fool-proof, they are indicative of good practices and may, if carefully tailored to the specific circumstances, establish a good faith effort to comply with the export control laws. In addition, such systems enhance exporters' ability to meet their burden of proof that there was no "reason to know" of a diversion.

The following is a list of some issues that an exporter must consider on a transaction-specific basis. It is advisable for an exporter to establish a documented transaction screening mechanism (i.e., a transaction checklist) which considers, among other factors, all of the following:

(1) Does the ECCN indicate a validated license is required for the given commodity/destination?

(2) Does the applicable general license require any documentation (e.g., GCT and GTDR require letters of assurance)?

(3) Is any party to the transaction on the Commerce Department Table of Denial Orders? 15 C.F.R. §778 Supplements 1 & 2.

(4) Is any party to the transaction on the list of known Nuclear/Chemical/ Biological weapons end users? 15 C.F.R. §778 Supplement 6.

(5) Is any party to the transaction on the Treasury Department's list of specially Designated Nationals? 15 C.F.R. §778 Supplement 3.

(6) Is any party to the transaction on the list of South African Military and Policy Entities? 15 C.F.R. §775 Supplement 2.

(7) Is any party to the transaction on the Department of State's debarred parties list?

(8) Are any diversion characteristics present?

(9) Have any requests been made to comply with an unsanctioned international trade boycott?

VII. CONCLUSION

The U.S export control regime is based on a complex network of laws and regulations which serve as vital components of U.S. national security and foreign policy objectives. One or more U.S. agencies may control a particular product or export transaction, and exports must be shipped under some kind of license, whether a validated license or a general license. To avoid civil or criminal sanctions and to preserve export privileges, prospective exporters should place top priority on complying with export control laws and the corresponding export licensing requirements.

Despite repeated calls for a reform of U.S. export control laws, the current system has remained relatively stable and intact through recent years. With the new Administration and the prospective improvement of relations with former Soviet bloc countries, however, many American exporters are revitalizing their campaign for a liberalization of U.S. export control laws. Although past efforts have yielded relatively little changes in the U.S. export control regime, demands for a more multilateral approach to export controls have prompted a renewed debate over the propriety and effectiveness of the current system. With the Export Administration Act due to expire on June 30, 1994, the Administration has submitted legislation to revise the U.S. export control laws. Similar legislation has been introduced by Rep. Sam Geidenson (Connecticut). Whether or not changes are forthcoming in the immediate future, prospective exporters should anticipate a gradual shift toward a greater emphasis on multilateral controls through vehicles such as COCOM or other international organizations or agreements.

Notes

[1] COCOM's other members are Australia, Belgium, Canada, Denmark, France, Germany, Greece, Italy, Japan, Luxembourg, the Netherlands, Norway, Portugal, Spain, Turkey, and the United Kingdom.

[2] These are the Country Groups found at 15 C.F.R. § 770 Supplement 1 as we go to press. Country groups change in response to world events and exporters are encouraged to consult the EAR for specific transactions.

[3] The CCL is broken into the following categories: Materials; Materials Processing; Electronics; Computers; Telecommunications and Cryptography; Sensors; Avionics and Navigation; Marine Technology; Propulsion Systems and Transportation Equipment; and Miscellaneous Items.

[4] "5k" countries, named after a section of the EAA include Austria, Finland, Ireland, Sweden, Switzerland, Hong Kong, and New Zealand.

[5] The DTC can be reached at its offices in Rosslyn, Virginia, at (703) 875-6644.

U.S. ANTIBOYCOTT LAW

Daniel J. Plaine
K. Russell LaMotte

I. INTRODUCTION

FOR NEARLY three decades now companies with international operations have had to monitor and abide by antiboycott legislation in the United States. These laws, although aimed primarily at the Arab boycott against Israel, prohibit or penalize cooperation with all unauthorized foreign boycotts and embargoes. They also require companies to report most boycott-related requests, and impose a range of sanctions on violators.

Compliance with the antiboycott regulations has always been a significant responsibility of transnational businesses. In recent months, however, federal regulators have shown renewed vigor in enforcing the obligations. Last spring, for example, prosecutors from the Justice and Commerce Departments secured a $6.5 million settlement of civil and criminal charges against Baxter International, Inc. for violations of the antiboycott laws. The *Baxter* case may well signal a new trend in heightened antiboycott enforcement activity; at the very least, it suggests that companies must be aware of these regulations and the restrictions they impose. Toward that end, this chapter sets out the general framework of the U. S. antiboycott regulations and highlights some key issues and concerns for companies considering international operations.

The chapter provides only a general survey of the antiboycott legal landscape. For more detail on specific problems, readers should consult the regulations under the relevant statutes, which often include interpretive supplements and comments prepared by the regulators. In addition, firms with foreign operations or exports abroad—and particularly those firms dealing with the Middle East—should consider establishing a formal antiboycott compliance program to ensure that the various restrictions and reporting requirements are observed.

II. THE ARAB BOYCOTT OF ISRAEL

A brief review of the Arab boycott of Israel will help explain the legal framework discussed below. Beginning in 1946 with the creation of national boycott offices, the Arab boycott has been designed to punish Israel by obstructing its commercial relations. A coordinating body for the boycott, known as the Central Boycott Office, was established in Damascus in 1951. An Arab League resolution in 1954 then put forth a set of unified boycott principles. Those principles have since been incorporated, subject to local variations, into the national laws of Arab states.

The boycott consists of three levels of trade restrictions. The primary boycott forbids exports to and imports from Israel and Israeli companies. Exporters and importers must therefore certify that their goods do not originate from or arrive in Israel. The secondary boycott bans trade with those non-Israeli companies that are "blacklisted" for doing business with Israel. Blacklisting may result from a company's partnership with Israeli companies, its maintenance of offices or other facilities in Israel, or a variety of other commercial relationships with Israel or Israeli companies. The boycott's final level—the tertiary boycott—applies to those companies that do business with blacklisted companies; it prohibits all trade that might result in the products of blacklisted companies entering the Arab market. Other aspects of the boycott include a maritime blockade, travel restrictions, and embargoes of oil shipments to countries friendly with Israel. Boycotting states implement the boycott through various documentation requirements imposed in customs declarations, letters of credit, and other contractual clauses. Although the boycott is coordinated among various Arab countries, its administration occurs on a country-by-country basis; thus, the particular rules and restrictions will vary by country, as will the depth and intensity of enforcement.

III.   SOURCES OF U.S. ANTIBOYCOTT REGULATIONS

The United States has responded to the Arab boycott by passing its own legislation to prohibit cooperation with the boycott. Both the Export Administration Act ("EAA") and the Internal Revenue Code ("the Code") currently contain antiboycott provisions that, with certain exceptions, apply to U.S. residents, nationals, corporations and their agents in overseas operations. Both laws address boycotts generally, not just the Arab boycott of Israel: by their terms they apply to any unauthorized foreign boycott of a country friendly to the United States. (In the absence of any enforcement action in over fifteen years other than those arising from the Arab boycott, however, it is unclear whether U.S. enforcement agencies would seek to apply the laws more broadly.) In addition, antiboycott considerations may arise under other miscellaneous bodies of law, including federal antitrust laws and state antiboycott laws. The remainder of this chapter explores in more detail the regulatory burdens imposed by these statutes, beginning with the Export Administration Act.

The Export Administration Act

Since 1979, the EAA has been the main source of U.S. antiboycott regulations.[1] The EAA prohibits companies and individuals from refusing to do business for boycott reasons, furnishing certain boycott-related information, taking discriminatory acts for boycott reasons, and implementing letters of credit that contain boycott conditions. It also prohibits agreements to take any of these actions, and imposes a requirement to report boycott-related requests. Its provisions are administered and enforced by the Commerce Department's Office of Antiboycott Compliance.

Prohibited Activities

The EAA and its regulations ("EAA") prohibit U.S. persons or their agents from acting (or agreeing to act) with the intent to comply with an unauthorized foreign boycott. Provided that a boycott-related reason at least partially motivates a prohibited action, the actor will be subject to civil and criminal penalties. Under the regulations, an actor's knowledge that his action is required or requested for boycott-related reasons will establish the requisite intent for a finding that the EAA was violated.

The statute targets two main types of prohibited practices: (a) refusing or agreeing to refuse to do business for boycott-related reasons, and (b) furnishing information for boycott-related reasons. The first category of prohibited activities covers those actions and agreements that involve active boycott participation. The statute prohibits any U.S. person from refusing to do business (either expressly or implicitly) with any person pursuant to a request, requirement, or agreement from a boycotting country. This prohibition would apply to the use of a blacklist, whitelist, or a client's boycott-based supplier list, for example. It may also extend to the failure to pursue a business opportunity. Similarly, under the EAA no U.S. person may refuse to employ or otherwise discriminate against any U.S. person on the basis of race, religion, gender, or national origin. The statute also forbids U.S. persons from paying, honoring, or otherwise implementing a letter of credit that contains a condition or requirement prohibited by the U.S. antiboycott laws.

The second category of restrictions prohibits activities that facilitate the boycott by providing information to boycotting authorities. Under the EAA, no U.S. person may furnish, or knowingly agree to furnish, information about his or any other person's business relationships with boycotting countries. Specifically, the statute prohibits the furnishing of information about any business (a) with or in a boycotted country, (b) with any business concern, national, or resident of the boycotted country, or (c) with persons known or believed to be restricted from having any business relationship with a boycotting country. For example, a company may not certify that it has no offices or facilities in a boycotted country. U.S. persons also may not furnish information about the race, religion, national origin or gender of any U.S. person, or about any owner, director, or employee of a U.S. firm. And they may not furnish information about whether any person is associated with any charitable or fraternal organization that supports a boycotted country.

Finally, the statute forbids any action designed to evade the regulations. Changing a company's annual report to include a list of all the countries where it did business would constitute evasion, for example, if such a change were for boycott-related purposes and had no independent business justification. The evasion regulations also prevent the use of dummy corporations or the diversion of business orders through third-country affiliates in order to comply with boycott requirements. For example, the FAA prohibits a U.S. exporter from providing a negative certificate of origin to a boycotting country. Under the evasion provisions, a company could not arrange to transfer an order for goods to a third country affiliate so that the affiliate could provide the prohibited certificate. As with all the FAA's prohibitions against activities conducted for boycott-related reasons, the evasion regulations depend on fact-specific inquiries to determine whether an activity's purpose stemmed from boycott or business reasons.

Exceptions to the Prohibited Activities

The regulations provide several exceptions to the restrictions discussed above. In general, the exceptions permit compliance with a boycotting country's laws that relate to activities within its own borders. The statute therefore permits any U.S. person to comply with the following types of foreign country requirements:

- Import restrictions that prohibit importation of goods or services from the boycotted country, or that prohibit shipment of goods into the country on a boycotted country's carrier or by a certain route;

- Import and shipping documentation requirements that supply information about (a) the country of origin of the goods (in positive terms only), (b) the name and nationality of the carrier (in either positive or negative terms), (c) the route of shipment (in positive or negative terms), and (d) the name and residence of the supplier or service provider (in positive terms only);

- Export restrictions that prohibit shipment or trans-shipment of exports to a boycotted country or its nationals or residents;

- Selection requirements made by the boycotting buyer relating to the carrier, insurer, or supplier of goods and services, provided that the selection does not discriminate against any U.S. person on the basis of race, religion, gender or national origin; and

- Immigration and employment requirements (but employers cannot furnish information about their employees).

In addition, the regulations provide certain "local law" exceptions for U.S. persons who are "bona fide" residents of the foreign country. Bona fide residency depends on the length, substance, continuity, purpose and formality of the presence in the boycotting country. A bona fide resident may comply with local laws with respect to activities exclusively within the foreign country. These activities include: (a) entering into contracts which provide that local law governs; (b) employing residents of the host country; (c) retaining local contractors to perform work in the host country; (d) purchasing or selling goods or services from or to residents of the host country; and (e) furnishing information gathered solely from within the host country. U.S. persons who are bona fide residents of boycotting countries may also comply with local import laws when they import goods, provided that: (a) the goods are for the use of the U.S. person; (b) the goods are specifically identifiable as to their source or origin; and (c) the local laws do not require discrimination against any U.S. person on the basis of race, religion, gender, or national origin.

The Reporting Requirements

The FAA also imposes a reporting requirement on U.S. persons who receive requests to cooperate with unsanctioned boycotts. Generally, the reporting regulations embrace a broader range of activities than the FAA's prohibitions—many boycott-related requests will trigger the reporting requirement, for example, even if the requested action would not be illegal. The regulations require each U.S. person to report (on a quarterly basis) to the Commerce Department anytime he receives a request for information or action if he knows (or should know) that the request is designed to further an unauthorized boycott. He must also report whether he actually complied with the request. For example, if a company representative receives a boycott questionnaire from a boycotting country after he visits that country to explore possible new markets there, the company must report that request regardless of whether it sends a reply. Certain types of requests need not be reported, however: these include requests attached to unsolicited proposals, requests to follow certain shipping routes, and requests for importers to certify the origin of their goods.[2]

To Whom Does the Law Apply?

The FAA applies only to the activities of U.S. persons. The regulations define a U.S. person as a corporation or a individual who is a resident or national of the United States. This definition also includes foreign subsidiaries or affiliates a of U.S companies that are "controlled in fact" by the U.S. concern. Such control generally depends on whether the domestic company has the authority to set the policies and control the daily operations of the foreign affiliate. Criteria that indicate such control include (among others) the authority to appoint a majority of the affiliate's board of directors, control of 50 percent of voting stock, or an exclusive management contract to operate the foreign affiliate. In these cases, the foreign affiliate will be bound by the antiboycott laws, and its U.S. parent will be held responsible for any noncompliance.

In addition, U.S. persons are liable for the conduct of their agents. Agents (who need not be U.S. persons) include independent contractors, consultants, freight forwarders, and procurement companies. Agents have created liability for a domestic concern even when the domestic concern had no knowledge of the boycott activity. Companies should therefore ensure that their affiliates and agents conform to the U.S. regulatory duties.

To What Activities Does the Law Apply?

Only activities in interstate or foreign commerce will trigger the FAA's provisions. For U.S. persons located in the United States, the FAA will apply to all transactions involving the sale, purchase or transfer of goods and services within the United States or between the United States and a foreign country. Thus, all activities involving exports from and imports into the United States are subject to the Export Administration Act. For "controlled in fact" foreign affiliates, the FAA will cover any transaction between the affiliate and a person located in the United States. With some exceptions, the FAA will also apply to any transaction between the affiliate and a person located abroad if it involves goods or services acquired from the United States. Activities between foreign affiliates and persons outside the United States are not covered, therefore, if they do not involve goods or services originating from the United States.

Penalties for Noncompliance—The Baxter *Case*

The FAA provides both criminal and civil penalties forviolations of the antiboycott regulations. On the criminal side, a person who knowingly violates the FAA regulations may be (a) fined up to $50,000 or five times the value of the exports (whichever is greater); (b) imprisoned up to five years; or (c) both. Willful violations are subject to even greater penalties. Civil fines may reach $10,000 for each violation, and may involve a suspension or revocation of a violator's export license, as well as public disclosure of the enforcement action. Typically, enforcement actions are settled before the initiation of formal proceedings. Violations involving letters of credit usually trigger a $10,000 fine, while illegal provision of information typically results in a $2500 fine. Fines for reporting violations range from $500 to $1000. Voluntary disclosure of violations may result in a 50 percent reduction in the amount of fines. Because the terms of these penalties are made public, a negative publicity makes up a significant component of the FAA's deterrent effect.

Although criminal penalties have been rare in past years, recent enforcement actions may suggest a new willingness on the part of regulators to seek indictments for antiboycott violations. Last spring, for example, the Departments of Justice and Commerce brought coordinated criminal and civil actions against Baxter International, Inc. and company officers for multiple counts of illegal boycott activities. Baxter admitted to violating the regulations by furnishing information about its activities in Israel to Arab League officials in an effort to remove its name from the blacklist. The civil and criminal cases were settled for a total fine of $6.5 million, and Baxter's senior vice-president (and general counsel) was fined $101,000 for his part in the violations.

The Internal Revenue Code

The Internal Revenue Code also penalizes cooperation with unauthorized foreign boycotts. Administered by the Internal Revenue Service, the Code imposes adverse tax consequences on a U.S. taxpayers who participate or cooperate in such a boycott in the course of their operations with a boycotting country. In addition, taxpayers may suffer tax penalties for the conduct of their related parties. Related parties include foreign corporations in which the taxpayer owns at least 10 percent of the voting stock, other members of a "controlled group," partnerships in which the taxpayer is a partner, and trusts owned by the taxpayer.

Generally, only "agreements" to refrain from doing business are subject to tax penalties under the Code's antiboycott provisions. Penalized activities include agreements to (1) refrain from doing business with or in a boycotted country, or with the government, companies or nationals thereof, (2) refrain from doing business with a company engaged in trade with a boycotted country; (3) refrain from employing individuals of a particular race, nationality or religion, or from doing business with a company owned by individuals of a particular race, nationality or religion; and (4) refrain from shipping or insuring products on a carrier that does not cooperate with the international boycott.

Such an agreement may arise from an express understanding between the U.S. person and the boycotting party, or it may be inferred from an overall course of conduct. Thus, while furnishing boycott-related information will generally not trigger tax penalties on its own, an agreement to furnish certain information in the future could be penalized as an agreement not to engage in certain conduct. Regulators might interpret an agreement to furnish a "certificate of eligibility," for example, as an agreement not to engage in any activity which could lead to blacklisting. Unlike the Export Administration Act, the Internal Revenue Code does not include a "U.S. commerce" requirement; therefore, conduct may result in adverse tax consequences regardless of where it occurs. Like the FAA, however, the Code regulations do provide an exception for compliance with those laws in a boycotting country that prohibit either the export of its products to a boycotted country or the import of goods from a boycotted country.

Taxpayers who participate or cooperate in an unsanctioned boycott are subject to the following adverse tax consequences: (1) loss of foreign tax credits for taxes paid to foreign governments; (2) denial of tax deferral on unrepatriated foreign income; and (3) denial of tax deferral on export income earned by Foreign Sales Corporations. Unless the taxpayer can demonstrate that its boycott-related operations are "clearly separate and identifiable" from its other operations, the tax penalties will apply to all the operations of the taxpayer (and its related parties) in all boycotting countries. A taxpayer may then choose to calculate its loss of tax benefits by applying the "international boycott factor" to the tax benefits derived from all its operations. The international boycott factor is the ratio of a taxpayer's operations in boycotting operations to its total worldwide operations.

As with the FAA, the Code also imposes reporting requirements on U.S. taxpayers. Taxpayers must report annually on all their operations with a boycotting country. (The Treasury Department maintains a list—not exclusive—of boycotting countries for this purpose.) In addition, they must report whether they (or their related parties) have cooperated in an international boycott or have been requested to do so. These reports, submitted on IRS Form 5173, differ from reports required under the Export Administration Act, so compliance with the Department of Commerce regulations will not be sufficient. Willful failure to file such reports subjects the taxpayer to a fine (up to $25,000), imprisonment (for up to one year), or both.

Other Miscellaneous Antiboycott Considerations

This section briefly reviews the application of federal antitrust laws and state legislation to the antiboycott field. In addition to the considerations presented here, antiboycott operations might conceivably implicate other laws, such as federal civil rights laws (which prohibit discrimination on the grounds of religion or national origin) and federal securities laws (which impose disclosure and reporting requirements for "material facts" and might apply to boycott activities that prevent access to certain markets). Because their effect is of relatively minor significance, however, they are not discussed in this limited treatment.

Antitrust Laws

Attempts to apply the antitrust laws to boycott-related activities appear to have diminished in light of the antiboycott provisions in the FAA. Nevertheless, the Justice Department has taken the position that refusing to do business with blacklisted companies may constitute a violation of the Sherman Act's proscriptions against conspiracies in restraint of trade. In the late 1970s, for example, the Bechtel Corporation signed a consent decree with the Justice Department arising out of its alleged boycott-related business practices. In general, the antitrust implications of the boycott have been overshadowed by the detailed FAA regulations, however, and little effort has been made to extend the principles established in the Bechtel decree to the wider boycott landscape.

State Antiboycott Laws

Some states have passed their own legislation relating to unauthorized foreign boycotts. Because the federal antiboycott laws explicitly pre-empt state laws prohibiting boycott cooperation, most state laws in this area take the form of civil rights or antitrust provisions. In addition, California has passed a law that prohibits the investment of state funds (including pension funds) in companies that cooperate with unsanctioned boycotts. And both New York State and New York City forbid state contracts with companies found to violate U.S. antiboycott laws. These state laws often incorporate by reference the terms of the Export Administration Act. In effect they increase the deterrent effect of the FAA proscriptions, and they give special weight to the formal Commerce Department finding of violation. By and large, though, compliance with the various federal antiboycott restrictions will ensure that state law provisions are also observed.

Notes

[1] The antiboycott provisions of the Export Administration Act of 1979 are codified (as amended) at 50 U.S.C.A. App. 5 2407 (1991); the regulations governing antiboycott compliance appear at 15 C.F.R. 769.
[2] Several other exempted requests áre listed in the regulations at 15 C.F.R. § 769(a) (5).

REGULATION OF FOREIGN INVESTMENT IN THE UNITED STATES

Daniel J. Plaine
William Kunze

I. INTRODUCTION

THERE ARE TWO distinct, seemingly conflicting, but equally valid ways of viewing the regulation of foreign investments in the United States.

Historically, the United States has been open to, and slow to place controls upon, foreign investment. Much of the capital improvement accomplished in the first century of the United States' existence was financed with foreign money. The United States continues to maintain, in broad terms and in comparison with the rest of the world, an open and stable investment climate. This openness results in part from the United States' efforts to reduce foreign barriers to its own investments overseas.

American policy is basically one of nonintervention: the federal government, in large part, neither encourages nor discourages foreign investors, and does not routinely discriminate between domestic and foreign capital. The United States, unlike many other nations, maintains no comprehensive regime for the approval or registration of foreign investments; no U.S. industries are absolutely closed to private enterprise; there are no exchange controls, and capital and earnings can be freely repatriated, subject to taxation; and foreign interests may, in general, own 100 percent of a U.S. business.

But there are important exceptions to this inviting picture. To begin with, there are significant sectoral restrictions, amounting to exclusions in some cases. For many types of investment, particularly in areas such as defense-related industries, communications, energy and natural resources, and shipping and aviation, the U.S. is a protected, and even closed, market. Most of these restrictions have been enacted in this century.

The foreign investor must also take account of U.S. tax laws and of general U.S. economic regulations, such as those governing competition (antitrust), securities, consumer protection, environmental protection, intellectual property, and labor and social security. The latter regimes for the most part treat foreign- and domestic-owned enterprises in the U.S. identically, but they may nevertheless present serious obstacles to a given foreign investment. U.S. competition and securities laws, in particular, are much more intrusive than many investors will be used to in their home countries.

In recent years, as a result of political pressures generated by the rise in foreign investment in the U.S., the federal government has implemented regulations requiring many investments from abroad to be reported, for the purpose of gathering aggregate statistical information. Investments that are not subject to any sectoral restrictions, and are not prevented by any of the general regulations just referred to, may still fall under one or more of these reporting requirements, with significant penalties for failure to comply.

In addition to these various sets of regulations, the U.S. maintains with many countries bilateral treaties affecting investment, taxation, and related issues. Every investor with business connections to both the U.S. and another country needs to be aware of the relevant terms of any such treaties, as they will in many cases affect the rules governing citizens of that country in their dealings with the U.S.

The United States consists of more than fifty separate jurisdictions: the federal government, the fifty states, the federal District of Columbia, and related entities such as Puerto Rico, Guam, and the Northern Mariana Islands. It would be impossible in this chapter to detail the investment regulations of all of these jurisdictions. Partly for this reason, this chapter focuses on federal regulations—but also because it is the single most important source of law in the area, as well as the constant that an investor will face regardless of which state serves as the site of an investment. Anyone considering investing in the U.S. from abroad, however, must be thoroughly familiar with relevant state laws. In some areas, such as the ownership and exploitation of land, state laws may entirely forbid what the federal government otherwise permits.[1]

II. SECTORAL RESTRICTIONS[2]

Defense-Related Industries

Exon-Florio

In recent years, foreign interests have tried, sometimes successfully, to acquire U.S. defense contractors. In 1986, the attempt by Fujitsu Ltd. to acquire Fairchild Semiconductor led to concern that foreign ownership of the company would pose a threat to U.S. national security, because the U.S. semiconductor industry was considered to be vital to national defense. The proposed acquisition also led to calls for giving the President general authority to prevent foreign acquisitions of defense-related companies and the related flow of American technology to other countries.

In a significant departure from the basic policy of openness to foreign investment, the U.S. Congress in 1988 responded to these calls by passing the "Exon-Florio" provision.[3]

Named after its congressional sponsors, Exon-Florio provides the President with broad and essentially unreviewable discretionary power to block foreign investments in the U.S. that pose a threat to national security. The President has authority to suspend or prohibit any potential acquisition, merger, or takeover, by or with "foreign persons," that "could result in foreign control of persons engaged in interstate commerce in the United States." The President may also order the divestiture of any such investment that has been concluded. The statute and regulations provide for little or no judicial or administrative review.

President Ronald Reagan assigned the Secretary of the Treasury, as the head of the Committee on Foreign Investment in the United States ("CFIUS"), to carry out Exon-Florio. CFIUS is an interagency group created in 1975 and includes representatives from the U.S. Departments of Treasury, Commerce, State, Defense, and Justice, as well as the Office of Management and Budget, the Council of Economic Advisors, and the Office of the United States Trade Representative.

CFIUS had previously been little more than a study group, but under Exon-Florio it has become potentially very powerful. CFIUS is now charged with deciding, on the President's behalf, whether to investigate a proposed transaction, and, if so, with pursuing that investigation. The following procedure has been established: CFIUS has 30 days, after receiving written notice of the proposed investment, to decide whether to investigate; CFIUS subsequently has 45 days to investigate and decide whether to recommend that the President intervene; and the President subsequently has 15 days to decide whether to suspend or prohibit the transaction. As a result, a transaction may be held up for 90 days even if it is eventually allowed to proceed.

The President and CFIUS may consider the following in determining whether control by a foreign company would impair national security:

- the domestic production needed for projected national defense requirements;

- the ability of domestic industries to meet those requirements; and

- whether the control of domestic industries and commercial activities by foreign citizens affects the ability of the United States to meet those requirements.

Under these general guidelines, CFIUS examines factors such as the impact of the proposed acquisition or merger upon the readiness of U.S. military forces, defense procurement, new technology, and research and development. In addition, CFIUS considers whether a transaction could lead to unauthorized access to classified information or violation of U.S. export control laws.

The President can exercise his power to block or suspend a transaction only where he finds:

- that there is a threat to "national security," and

- that no other provisions of law are adequate to address the national security concern.

A notified transaction is formally cleared and may not subsequently be interfered with under Exon-Florio if:

- CFIUS decides not to investigate;

- after a formal investigation, CFIUS decides not to forward the matter to the President; or

- after CFIUS forwards the matter, the President decides not to intervene.

The Office of International Investment in the Treasury Department serves as the secretariat for CFIUS, and all official business with CFIUS is conducted through that office.

Aside from the above mechanics, the following are the most important things to know about Exon-Florio:

(1)   There is no definition of "national security" in the statute or the implementing regulations. Most concern has focused on defense contracts, technology transfers, protection of classified information, and industrial base preservation, but the President and CFIUS are left with tremendous latitude in deciding what sorts of investments are threats to the United States.

(2)   Under Exon-Florio, "foreign person" and "control" are defined so broadly that the regulations may apply even to what seems to be a foreign-foreign or U.S.-U.S. transaction, joint venture, or proxy contest. A "U.S. person" is defined by business location: "a person engaged in interstate commerce in the United States." A "foreign person" is defined by nationality of control: any foreign national or any entity controlled by a foreign national or government.

"Control," in turn, is defined not by a bright-line test of percentage of shares owned, but functionally: it is the power to make business decisions for the entity, whether through share ownership (majority or dominant minority interest), proxy voting, or contractual arrangement. Control may be present without a majority of voting shares, or even if no actual control has been exercised. For example, the right to appoint a majority of the directors is "control," even if the foreign interest never in fact exercises that right. A deal which brings the foreign investor 10 percent or less of the outstanding voting shares, however, may be excluded from Exon-Florio oversight if there is no intention to control business decisions.

Under these standards, a U.S. subsidiary or branch of a foreign company may be both a U.S. person (engaged in U.S. commerce) *and* a foreign person (controlled by a foreign interest), and foreign acquisition of either the U.S. affiliate or the foreign corporation is potentially subject to Exon-Florio—as is an acquisition of another U.S. company by that U.S. affiliate.

(3)   If the acquiring foreign interest is a foreign government or its entity or representative, a formal 45-day investigation of the transaction is mandatory.

(4)   Exon-Florio does not apply to start-up or "green field" investments involving new plants, personnel, and technology, even if the transaction is in the form of an acquisition of stock from a new U.S. subsidiary. The provision does apply to joint ventures, if a foreign interest thereby gains control of a U.S. business.

(5)   Notification is voluntary—there is no legal penalty for not notifying CFIUS of an impending transaction—and it may be made by either party to the transaction. Any member agency of CFIUS, but no other third party, may request review of a transaction as well.

(6)   There is, however, an enormous potential price to be paid for not notifying. If no notice is given to CFIUS and the transaction is finalized, and thereafter a CFIUS member agency determines that the transaction should be reviewed, CFIUS may conduct

an investigation and the President may order divestiture. Again, there is little hope of judicial review of such an order.

As a result, the Office of International Investment advises that investors should notify CFIUS if there is any direct or indirect relationship between a transaction and U.S. national security interests. That office will offer guidance to investors but issues no formal, binding, advisory opinions. Certainly, any transaction involving a foreign government, however indirectly, should be notified to CFIUS.

(7)   To date the hammer has fallen very infrequently. Between August 1988 and July 1992, CFIUS was notified of more than 720 transactions; CFIUS pursued investigations in only 13; and the President blocked only one. In that case, a corporation of the Chinese government (CATIC) attempted to acquire a small U.S. company that manufactures metal parts used in airplane production (MAMCO). MAMCO notified CFIUS of the proposed acquisition but concluded the deal before CFIUS completed its investigation. President Bush ordered CATIC to divest itself entirely of MAMCO, but he reiterated that, in general, "the United States welcomes foreign direct investment." The political climate after the events at Tien-Anmen in Beijing may have been the most important factor in this decision.

(8)   But the fact that only one proposed deal has been expressly blocked does not fully indicate the influence Exon-Florio has had on foreign investment in the U.S. In five of the thirteen transactions CFIUS investigated, all with some military implication, the political controversy stirred up by CFIUS review caused the acquiring foreign interests to back away from the investments altogether, before CFIUS or the President could take final action. There is no way to know how many other possible deals were not even attempted, in order to avoid such controversy. In still other transactions, CFIUS gave its approval only after the parties restructured the deal.

Three examples may help illustrate these points:

(a)   The event that brought about the enactment of Exon-Florio—the proposed purchase of Fairchild Semiconductor in 1986 by Fujitsu Ltd.—revealed how much political pressure could be martialed to block transactions even *before* Exon-Florio. Fujitsu's proposal generated a firestorm of opposition in Congress and the executive branch, because of concern about the U.S. semiconductor industry and resentment over Japanese trade policies. Fujitsu withdrew its proposal under this fire, but Congress subsequently passed Exon-Florio anyway.

(b)   The subject of CFIUS's first full-scale Exon-Florio investigation was the proposed purchase of Monsanto's silicon wafer division by Huels A.G. of Germany. Although the division in question was not a defense supplier, the sale was controversial because the division was the last major U.S. producer of certain silicon wafers and its technology was thought to be central to the next phase in the development of integrated circuits. CFIUS gave many strong indications that it would not approve the deal, until Huels offered a series of performance guarantees and thereby won approval for the purchase.

(c) Thomson-CSF, a French defense electronics company majority-owned by the French government, attempted to buy LTV Corp.'s Missile Division. The deal was very controversial in CFIUS and in the Congress, and Thomson eventually abandoned it amid rumors that President Bush would block it. Congress then enacted the amendment that made investigation mandatory when the investor is a foreign government.

(9) Furthermore, even if CFIUS or the President clears a transaction, there is a cost in time. A full proceeding (decision to investigate, investigation, Presidential consideration) may take up to 90 days, which may be sufficient delay to undermine a deal.

(10) Any one member agency can notify CFIUS of the transaction, or request a 45-day formal investigation, or insist that the results of the investigation be forwarded to the President for a final decision. As a result, an investing firm and its American affiliate may need to lobby a number of federal agencies with competing interests, either to head off agency notification or to get a favorable vote following CFIUS consideration. Interested third parties, who may not officially notify CFIUS of a transaction, may nevertheless lobby these agencies.

(11) Because of all of these factors, Exon-Florio is open for defensive use by targets of hostile takeover attempts. The target company may not need presidential intervention, just delay. The target:

- may itself notify CFIUS and trigger the initial 30-day consideration period;
- only needs to convince one member agency to call for the 45-day investigation period, which may be accomplished by invoking the aid of influential members of Congress; and
- only needs to convince one agency to send it on to the President for an additional 15 days' consideration.

As noted, the definition of "national security" is elastic enough to allow considerable political stretching by the target company and others sympathetic to it. The 90-day delay this makes possible may be enough to scuttle the deal. The target may be able to arrange for another buyer or generate enough political pressure to force the original investor to back off.[4]

Defense Industrial Security Program

One focus of CFIUS review under Exon-Florio is the extent to which a proposed acquisition would threaten classified information. Even if a particular transaction survives Exon-Florio scrutiny, however, it may still run into other hurdles surrounding classified information. Any company with classified contracts must obtain security clearances for its personnel and facilities, which are difficult to come by if foreign interests have significant involvement in the company. The danger to a foreign investor and its American affiliate is that, after acquisition, the affiliate may lose its classified contracts or be barred from future ones.

The Defense Industrial Security Program (DISP) is designed to safeguard classified information given to U.S. defense industries performing government contracts. DISP policies are implemented by the Industrial Security Regulation (ISR) and explained to industry in the Industrial Security Manual (ISM). DISP is overseen by the Assistant Secretary of Defense for Command, Control, Communications, and Intelligence, and ISR and ISM are administered by offices of the Defense Investigative Service (DIS) throughout the United States.

Under DISP, each installation of a U.S. company performing classified defense contracts must obtain a facility security clearance (FSC). Only facilities located in the U.S. and existing under U.S. law can get FSC's, and any facility which possesses an FSC must notify DIS of any change in circumstances that would result in foreign ownership, control, or influence (FOCI) over the American company. As a general rule a subsidiary can obtain an FSC at a particular level only if its parent has at least that much security clearance. As a practical matter, therefore, foreign participation in U.S. classified contracts is strictly limited.

FOCI is present when "foreign dominance over the management or operations of the facility may result in the compromise of classified information or impact adversely the performance of classified contracts." The factors considered in making a FOCI determination include:

- the extent of foreign ownership over the U.S. contractor;
- the extent of foreign control or influence over the officers, directors, or other executives of the U.S. firm;
- the extent of the U.S. firm's foreign indebtedness or other contracts;
- interlocking directorates between the U.S. firm and foreign interests; and
- access of foreign nationals to classified information held by the U.S. firm.

FOCI is assumed to be present if foreign interests own five percent or more of the U.S. firm's voting securities, or if the firm receives 10 percent or more of its income from foreign interests, or any level of income from a hostile country.

As it is often in the interest of all parties—the U.S. government, the U.S. contractor, and the foreign investor—that the contractor continue to have access to classified information, various mechanisms have been developed to insulate a U.S. contractor from its FOCI.

If the acquiring foreigner is a national of a country with which the U.S. has a bilateral reciprocal industrial security agreement, that nation can issue a security assurance for the acquiring firm. The U.S. has such agreements with the United Kingdom, Canada, and Germany.

For nationals of other countries, devices include voting trusts, proxy agreements, and board resolutions, all designed to exclude the foreign interest from access to classified information and from management of facilities with FSC's. Note, however, that where the foreign interest controls the U.S. affiliate, the FOCI exemption, if obtained at all, will not normally extend to the most highly classified information or material.

The process of negotiating a FOCI exemption with the Department of Defense can be very time-consuming, and delays caused by this process, as well as by Exon-Florio, can put pressure on foreign firms to agree under DISP to relinquish control over a U.S. firm they have just acquired, or to take themselves out of competition for future contracts. In practice, it is difficult for foreign-controlled corporations, except some subsidiaries of Canadian, British, and German companies, to obtain the necessary FSC's.

Export Controls

U.S. export controls cover the transfer of technical data, and under certain circumstances a discussion between representatives of a foreign company and a U.S. classified contractor could result in disclosure of classified information. However inadvertent such a disclosure, it may constitute an "export" and violate either the International Traffic in Arms Regulations (ITARs)[5] or the Export Administration Regulations.[6] Violators are subject to stiff criminal penalties and may also be prevented from future involvement in the relevant industry. For further information, see the chapter on Export Controls.

Government Procurement

The Buy American Act[7] and other federal legislation obligates U.S. Government agencies, with some exceptions, to purchase only items produced in the United States. In most cases, however, the disadvantage applies to goods produced overseas, not to goods produced in the U.S. by foreign-controlled U.S. companies.

There are also a large number of state and local "Buy American" laws.[8]

Communications

The Federal Communications Act of 1934[9] restricts the ability of foreign persons to operate communications facilities in the U.S. Foreign governments are barred from obtaining any license issued by the Federal Communications Commission (FCC), and foreign individuals and corporations are barred from obtaining the licenses that are required to operate radio broadcasting facilities. Also barred from radio licenses are domestic corporations with any foreign officers or directors, or with more than 20 percent of stock owned or voted by foreign individuals, corporations, governments, or their representatives. In addition, if the FCC finds that the action will serve the public interest, it may refuse a radio license to a U.S. corporation which is controlled by another corporation which has:

- any foreign officers;
- more than 25 percent foreign directors; or
- more than 25 percent of its voting stock in the hands of, or actually voted by, foreign individuals, corporations, governments, or their representatives.

The same rules apply to acquisition of control over an existing licensee. Trust arrangements have occasionally been approved to insulate the licensee from its foreign ownership.

For FCC purposes, "radio" includes conventional radio and television, as well as satellite-carried telephone transmissions. It does not, however, included cable television or fiber-optic or other wire-carried telephone transmissions, and the latter are generally open to foreign investment. Despite periodic calls to keep foreign capital out of these media, Congress has yet to apply to them the restrictions on radio transmissions. As a regulatory body, however, the FCC does look at foreign-owned systems more closely.

By its chartering statute,[10] foreign interests may not own more than 20 percent of the Communications Satellite Corporation (COMSAT), and all its directors and officers must be U.S. citizens.

There are no prohibitions against foreign investment in U.S. newspapers and magazines. However, the Foreign Agents Registration Act (see Section III-B below) may require registration by any U.S. newspaper or magazine publisher controlled or financed by a foreign entity, if it engages in activity intended to influence U.S. domestic or foreign policy or to promote the interests of a foreign government.

Energy, Land, and Other Natural Resources

Nuclear and Other Energy

Foreign participation in the U.S. nuclear energy industry is strictly limited. The Atomic Energy Act of 1954[11] requires the issuance of a license by the Nuclear Regulatory Commission to any facilities which produce or use nuclear materials. Section 103(d) of the Act bars any alien, or any entity known to be "owned, controlled, or dominated by an alien, a foreign corporation, or a foreign government," from receiving such a license. Similar restrictions apply to the issuance of licenses for medical and research purposes. The Nuclear Regulatory Commission has permitted foreign entities to hold substantial but not controlling interests in nuclear-licensed U.S. facilities, where the parties have made arrangements to prevent the foreign entity from acquiring control.

Facilities for generating hydroelectric power on navigable streams within the United States may, under the Federal Power Act,[12] be developed and operated only by U.S. citizens, whether individual or corporate. However, nothing prevents foreign control of such a U.S. corporation. Similar rules govern the generation of geothermal power, as stipulated by the Geothermal Steam Act of 1970.[13]

Mineral and Grazing Rights

Under the Mineral Lands Leasing Act of 1920,[14] the Secretary of the Interior may only lease deposits of coal, oil, oil shale, gas, and other nonfuel minerals, located on federal land, to U.S. citizens. Foreign persons may invest in U.S. lease-holding entities only if their home countries grant reciprocal lease-holding privileges to U.S. citizens. The rules for grazing and lumbering permits on U.S. lands are similar.

Regulations also limit foreign exploitation of deposits in the submerged lands of the continental shelf. Under the Outer Continental Shelf Lands Act,[15] foreigners may not directly hold any exploitation leases from the Department of the Interior but may own stock in a U.S. corporation that holds such a lease.

Land

There are few federal regulations on the direct ownership of real estate, primarily restrictions are on ownership by nationals of countries at war with the U.S. (under the Trading with the Enemy Act[16]), or against which the U.S. has placed travel and trade restrictions (under the Foreign Assets Control Regulations and Cuban Assets Control Regulations[17]).

Public lands, however, may only be transferred or leased to U.S. citizens or persons declaring the intention to become U.S. citizens, to a partnership with no foreign partners, or to a corporation organized under U.S. laws. So long as reciprocal rights are granted in the entity's home country, a foreign interest may hold 100 percent ownership in such a U.S. corporation. If no reciprocity exists, the foreign interest must be less than 50 percent .

The Foreign Investment in Real Property Tax Act[18] may require withholding and forwarding of taxes related to the purchase or sale by foreigners of real property in the U.S. (see chapter on Taxation).

More than half the states restrict ownership of land in some way, or at least have reporting requirements. Some states, like the federal government, bar the acquisition of public land by aliens. Others restrict the acquisition of agricultural land, or restrict the amount of acreage that aliens may acquire. A few states have general prohibitions on alien ownership of real property. Many states also require aliens or their entities to report their holdings so that the state can monitor the degree of foreign ownership in its jurisdiction. These rules vary greatly and change frequently, so it is best to check with the appropriate state and locality before acquiring real property.[19]

Fishing

Only vessels with U.S. documentation ("U.S.-flag vessels") may fish within the 12-mile U.S. territorial sea or land catches in U.S. ports, according to the Magnuson Act (Fishery Conservation and Management Act).[20] Foreign-flag ships operate in the 200-mile Fisheries Conservation Zone (FCZ) under quotas and must have permits from the Department of Commerce.

U.S. documentation is available only to boats owned by individual U.S. citizens, or by corporations chartered in the U.S. which satisfy these conditions:

- U.S. citizens own at least 50 percent of the outstanding voting stock;
- U.S. citizens serve as president and board chair; and
- foreigners hold fewer directorships than the minimum number necessary to form a quorum.

Partnerships owning vessels must have all U.S. partners in order to gain U.S. documentation.

Only U.S.-documented vessels with 75 percent U.S. ownership are eligible for certain loans and grants. There are also various state laws governing fishing within their territory.

Transportation

Shipping

Foreign involvement in U.S. shipping is regulated under two sets of rules, one for coastwise trade and one for foreign trade. The coastwise trade is that involving cargo or passengers loaded and unloaded in U.S. ports, regardless of how the ship sails between them. Any shipping between points in the U.S. or its territories is "coastwise," even if the passengers or goods on board travel via a foreign port and are thus temporarily outside U.S. territorial waters.

Coastwise trade must be done by vessels "built in and documented under the laws of the United States and owned by persons who are citizens of the United States," according to § 27 of the Merchant Marine Act.[21] U.S.-flag vessels engaged in foreign trade do not have to be built in the U.S., but foreign-built vessels are ineligible for most of the financial assistance programs of the federal government.

A vessel may obtain U.S. documentation, under the Shipping Act of 1916[22] and the Vessel Documentation Act of 1980,[23] only if it is owned by a U.S. citizen. If a partnership, all general partners must be U.S. citizens, and the controlling interest must be owned by U.S. citizens.

In the case of a corporation, it must be organized under U.S. law; the president or other chief executive officer and the chair of the board must be U.S. citizens; and less than a majority of a quorum of the board can be noncitizens. For the coastwise trade, U.S. owners must hold (and exercise real control through) 75 percent of the voting stock; for the foreign trade, 50 percent.

Benefits available to U.S.-flag ships include construction and operating differential subsidies, capital construction aid, loan guarantees, preference for military and other government cargoes, and favorable financial arrangements under the Ship Mortgage Act of 1920.[24]

The Secretary of Commerce must approve the sale or transfer to a foreign person of any vessel which is owned in whole or part by a U.S. citizen and registered in the U.S.; the same applies to such a vessel's re-registration under another flag.

Vessels engaged in towing, salvaging, and dredging must be U.S.-documented, under regimes similar to that outlined above.

Aviation

Commercial aviation has been heavily regulated by the federal government, and foreign ownership and control of companies engaged in air transportation within the

United States is restricted. In recent years, with substantial deregulation of the U.S. airline industry, it has become easier for foreign interests to invest in U.S. aviation, but the regulatory hurdles are still significant.

The Federal Aviation Act of 1958[25] limits domestic air passenger and cargo transport to domestically registered aircraft, and only a U.S. citizen or resident alien can register an aircraft in the U.S. (The U.S. also grants foreign aircraft the right to operate in the U.S., under reciprocal agreements with other countries.) Under the Act, a partnership must have all U.S. partners, and a company is a U.S. citizen only if:

- it is incorporated in the U.S.;

- its president and at least two-thirds of its directors and other officers are U.S. citizens not installed by the foreign investor(s);

- at least 75 percent of its voting stock is owned or controlled by U.S. citizens; and

- U.S. citizens effectively control the corporation.

Since 1991, the Department of Transportation has permitted foreign ownership of up to 49 percent of equity, so long as not more than 25 percent of the *voting* stock is in foreign hands. President Clinton's National Commission to Ensure a Strong Competitive Airline Industry has floated a proposal that would allow foreign ownership of 49 percent of the voting stock, subject to reciprocal privileges being made available to U.S. investors abroad. The new threshold would not be available to enterprises owned by foreign governments or to investments deemed not to be in the national interest. This change would require Congressional action.

A foreign investor may also enter the U.S. air market by acting as a tour operator or air freight forwarder.

Banking and Insurance

Insurance

Restrictions on foreign participation in the insurance market are primarily at the state level. Most states do not permit foreign directorship and operation of insurance companies.

Banking

Banking in the United States is regulated by both the federal and state governments, and foreign banks may own banks chartered and branches licensed under either federal or state law. Banks with federal charters are national banks and are primarily supervised by the U.S. Comptroller of the Currency and the Board of Governors of the Federal Reserve System (Federal Reserve Board). National banks are required to be members of the Federal Reserve System and to carry deposit insurance from the Federal Deposit Insurance Corporation (FDIC).

State banks, which are chartered and supervised by state agencies, may elect to become members of the Federal Reserve System, subject to supervision by the Federal Reserve Board. State banks which are not members of the Federal Reserve System but whose deposits are federally insured are also subject to supervision by the FDIC.

Under the International Banking Act of 1978 (IBA),[26] most U.S. operations of foreign banks are subject to federal regulation in a manner similar to domestic banks. Any U.S. branch or subsidiary of a foreign bank which takes domestic retail deposits must purchase insurance from the FDIC, is prohibited from engaging in securities underwriting, and must meet reserve requirements. Foreign banks must also submit various annual and quarterly reports to the Federal Reserve.

In addition, the National Bank Act of 1933[27] requires that all directors of a national bank be U.S. citizens, and that at least two-thirds of the directors be residents of the state where the bank is located (or within 100 miles of that location). The Comptroller of the Currency may waive these requirements for a minority of the directors of a national bank that is a subsidiary or affiliate of a foreign bank. Many states also have citizenship and residency requirements for banks chartered under their laws.

Acquisitions of control over all federal and most state banks require prior application to a federal bank regulatory agency, under either the Bank Merger Act[28] or the Change in Bank Control Act.[29] This requirement applies to an acquisition of more than five percent of voting stock, or all or substantially all the assets, of an existing bank. Acquisitions of control may also be subject to state law requirements.

Both federal and state laws significantly limit the ability of foreign entities to carry on banking in more than one state. Under the Bank Holding Company Act of 1956 (BHCA)[30] and the IBA, a foreign bank is barred from acquiring more than five percent of the voting stock, or all or substantially all of the assets, of a United States bank located outside of its home state (the state of its major U.S. operation), unless that second state expressly permits such a foreign acquisition. Only a handful of states permit branches of foreign banks to operate, and the foreign bank must agree to limit its deposits from U.S. residents. Branches may be licensed under either federal or state law, but a foreign bank may not have both a federally-licensed and a state-licensed branch in the same state.

With the approval of the Federal Reserve Board, foreign banks may also own, under the Edge Act,[31] U.S. corporations created to conduct international and foreign banking and financial activities. Such corporations, which must limit their domestic deposits, are not subject to the requirement that the directors be U.S. citizens. A foreign bank is authorized by the Act to establish an "Edge corporation" in any state, regardless of that state's rules about foreign branches, and there are no restrictions on how many Edge corporations may be created in "second states."

Foreign banks may also establish international banking facilities (IBF's). By segregating deposits and loans of non-U.S. residents and other IBF's, these facilities may exempt such deposits and loans from most U.S. banking regulations.

There are no restrictions on foreign investors' access to financing in the United States, nor on their ability to invest in government securities or debt instruments of U.S. companies.

III. REPORTING REQUIREMENTS

In addition to complying with sectoral exclusions and the general laws and regulations faced by all persons doing business in the United States, foreign investors may be required to provide the federal government with various data on their U.S. investments. Investments may be subject to reporting even if exempt from any other requirements discussed above and below.

Statistical Reporting Requirements

The International Investment and Trade in Services Survey Act of 1976 (IITSSA)[32] and the Agricultural Foreign Investment Disclosure Act of 1978 (AFIDA)[33] were passed by Congress during the recession of the 1970's, in reaction to perceived threats to the U.S. economy. IITSSA was adopted in response to significant increases in foreign investment in the U.S. during the early 1970s, following many decades of net U.S. capital export. AFIDA was enacted out of concern that foreign ownership of U.S. real estate was escalating the cost of U.S. farmland and thus threatening family farms and rural communities. Both regimes were designed to collect data to be used by the federal government in developing reports and statistics on international capital flows and foreign investment in the U.S., in order to aid economic policymaking.

IITSSA

Under IITSSA, reports may be required as a result of three types of U.S. investments by foreign persons (individuals or entities):

- "direct investments" in a new or existing U.S. business enterprise, which involve direct or indirect foreign ownership of at least ten percent of the U.S. enterprise,;
- "portfolio investments," with less than 10 percent foreign ownership; or
- ownership of U.S. real estate or other natural resources, which may be either direct or portfolio investments.

Direct Investments

A direct investment must be reported within 45 days to the Bureau of Economic Analysis (BEA) of the U.S. Department of Commerce, and in some instances to the U.S. Department of the Treasury. These agencies may only use the information gathered for analytical and statistical purposes, and may not generally share it with other government agencies or with individuals. Civil fines of up to $25,000 may be assessed for failure to report; criminal penalties, for intentional failure to report or for wilful violation of the confidentiality provisions, may reach a fine of $10,000 and one year's imprisonment.

A foreign investor and/or its U.S. affiliate may need to submit:

- initial reports, which describe the investor, its investments, and any U.S. intermediaries;

- quarterly reports covering transactions of the U.S. enterprise with its foreign owner(s);
- annual reports on the condition of the U.S. enterprise; and
- benchmark surveys, every fifth year.

There are also any number of more specialized reports, depending on the nature of the investment and the activities of the U.S. affiliate. Exemption from reporting may be available if the investment totals $1 million or less and does not involve purchase of 200 or more acres of land.

Portfolio Investments

Foreign portfolio investments are reported to the Treasury on a monthly basis by U.S. institutions and individuals, such as banks and brokers, who purchase or sell long-term securities from or to foreign persons. Exemptions are available where transactions involving foreign persons total less than $500,000 in a given month. The Treasury also conducts a survey of foreign portfolio investments in the U.S. at least every five years.

Real Estate and Natural Resources

A foreign investment in U.S. real estate or other natural resources may constitute a direct or portfolio investment requiring reporting to the BEA and Treasury. Exemptions are available on the same basis as described above, except that for the purposes of the 200-acre threshold all properties of a given foreign owner are aggregated. Purchase for personal use need not be reported.

AFIDA

If the real estate in question is agricultural—currently used, or used within the last five years, for farming, ranching, forestry, or timber production—a foreign person acquiring or disposing of an interest in the property must report the transaction within 90 days to the Agricultural Stabilization and Conservation Service (ASCS) of the Department of Agriculture. Changes in use of the land must also be reported. Security interests in land (such as mortgages), short-term leases, and various contingent and future interests need not be reported.

Under AFIDA, "foreign persons" include U.S. corporations or other entities in which a foreign person or combination of persons holds a "significant interest or substantial control," currently construed as a 10 percent or greater interest. If a combination is not acting in concert, the threshold is 50 percent.

The information reported under AFIDA is available to the public. For failure to report, fines increase weekly to a maximum of 25 percent of the fair market value of the property. The maximum fine is also imposed for knowing submission of an incomplete, false, or misleading report.

Many states also have their own laws requiring disclosure of foreign ownership of agricultural land, with some states restricting foreign ownership.

Foreign Agents Registration Act

Political, including public relations, activities of the employees or representatives of a foreign principal (government, private entity, or individual), or of a U.S. entity controlled by a foreign principal, may require registration under the Foreign Agents Registration Act of 1938 (FARA).[33]

FARA is meant to reveal foreign political influence in the United States. Registration under the Act is required from any individual who, within the U.S., works on behalf of, or under the direction or control of, a foreign principal, and:

- engages in political activities on behalf of the principal;
- acts as a public relations or political agent or consultant for the principal;
- solicits, collects, or distributes loans, money, or other things of value for or in the interest of the principal; or
- represents the interests of the principal before any agency or official of the U.S. government.

Failure to register may result in criminal sanctions.

Exemptions from registration are available for diplomatic, relief, and academic and cultural activities; to persons engaged solely in "private and nonpolitical activities in furtherance of the bona fide trade or commerce of [the] foreign principal"; and to legal representatives of a foreign principal before a U.S. court or government agency, provided that the representation does not include "attempts to influence or persuade agency personnel or officials other than in the course of established agency proceedings."

Caution is advised before deciding not to register under FARA, as the line between registrable and nonregistrable activities can be hard to discern. Foreign principals and their U.S. representatives and affiliates may find it helpful to seek advisory opinions from the U.S. Department of Justice about whether to register.

IV. OTHER ISSUES

Taxation

Foreign persons investing in the United States may be subject to filing federal and state tax returns. The United States taxes nonresident foreign persons (individuals and corporations) not engaged in a U.S. trade or business only on certain passive income generated in the U.S. Foreign persons engaged in a U.S. trade or business are taxed on income effectively connected with the conduct of that trade or business, as well as on passive income. Thus, a foreign investor's U.S. tax liability depends upon both the type and source of income earned and the level and nature of the investor's U.S. activities. Consult the chapter on Taxation for further guidance.

General Regulations

As mentioned at the beginning of this chapter, foreign investors must also comply with the full regime of economic regulation faced by anyone doing business in the U.S. This includes antitrust, securities, consumer protection, environmental protection, intellectual property, and labor and social security laws. In many cases these regulations are more extensive and intrusive than foreign investors will be used to in their home countries. Investors should carefully consider them when structuring any investment in the U.S. Antitrust and securities regulations are covered in separate chapters of this book.

Visas

Foreign persons wishing to visit or reside in the United States in connection with their investment activities will need to obtain appropriate visas. Where travel to the U.S. is necessary to put together a deal or supervise an operation, difficulty obtaining a visa may be as much a bar to a particular foreign investment as is a sectoral exclusion. It is advisable to contact immigration law counsel, as well as the Department of State or the U.S. consulate in the home country, well in advance to investigate visa options.

Treaties

The United States maintains, with many other countries, treaties addressing investment, trade, travel, taxation, and other related issues. Many bilateral investment treaties (BIT's), for example, contain provisions regarding the establishment of businesses in each other's country, international financial transactions, protection of patents, trademarks, and copyrights, and dispute resolution. In some cases, these treaties may modify the application of the regulations discussed above and below to nationals of those countries.

Emergency Regulation

Finally, a foreign investor should be aware that the President has, under the International Emergency Economic Powers Act (IEEPA),[34] the authority to suspend, block, freeze, and otherwise intervene in foreign investments in the U.S. In recent years, for example, the President has taken such action against Iranian assets, in the aftermath of the taking of hostages at the U.S. embassy in Teheran, and against Iraqi and Kuwaiti assets, after the Iraqi invasion of Kuwait.

Notes

[1] Some useful sources for locating relevant state laws are: *The European Institute, State Legislative and Regulatory Policies Affecting European Investment in the United States* (Price Waterhouse, 1991); *Doing Business in the United States of America: A Guide for the Foreign Investor*, 163–79 (Deloitte Haskins & Sells, 1985); G. Spinner, *State-by-State Survey of Limitations on Foreign Investment*, in J. Eugene Marans, ed., *Foreign Investment in the United States* (1980). *See also* J. Eugene Marans, et al., eds., *Manual of Foreign Investment in the United States* (1984).

[2] What follows is an introduction to the most important sectoral restrictions on foreign investments in the U.S. Foreign investors and their U.S. affiliates and agents can contact the U.S. Department of Commerce, Office of International Trade Administration, for the most current information, for advice about a proposed transaction, and for referral to other appropriate agencies of the federal government.

[3] 50 U.S.C.A. App. § 2170 (West 1991 & Supp. 1993); implementing regulations codified 31 C.F.R. § 800 (1992).

[4] For more detail on Exon-Florio, for instructions on how to notify CFIUS, and for discussion of other cases, *see* Review of Foreign Acquisitions Under the Exon-Florio Provision, ABA Section of Antitrust Law Working Papers (1992).

[5] 22 C.F.R. §§ 120–130 (1993), implementing the Arms Export Control Act of 1976, 22 U.S.C.A. §§ 2751 *et seq.* (West 1990 & Supp. 1993).

[6] 15 C.F.R. §§ 768 *et seq.* (1993), implementing the Export Administration Act, 50 U.S.C.A. App. §§ 2401 *et seq.* (West 1991 & Supp. 1993).

[7] 41 U.S.C.A. §§ 10a–10d (West 1987 & Supp. 1993).

[8] *See* Marans, et al., eds., *Manual of Foreign Investment in the United States,* 204–22.

[9] 47 U.S.C.A. §§ 151 *et seq.* (West 1991 & Supp. 1993).

[10] 47 U.S.C.A. §§ 701 *et seq.* (West 1991 & Supp. 1993).

[11] 42 U.S.C.A. §§ 2011 *et seq.* (West 1973 & Supp. 1993).

[12] 16 U.S.C.A. §§ 791 *et seq.* (West 1985 & Supp. 1993).

[13] 30 U.S.C.A. §§ 1001 *et seq.* (West 1986 & Supp. 1993).

[14] 30 U.S.C.A. generally (West 1986 & Supp. 1993).

[15] 43 U.S.C.A. §§ 1331 *et seq.* (West 1986 & Supp. 1993).

[16] 50 U.S.C.A. App. §§ 1 *et seq.* (West 1990 & Supp. 1993).

[17] 31 C.F.R. § 500 (1992); 31 C.F.R. § 515 (1992).

[18] 26 U.S.C.A. §§ 861(a)(5), 897, 6039C, and 6652(f) (West 1988, 1989 & Supp. 1992, 1993).

[19] See Marans, et al., eds., *Manual of Foreign Investment in the United States,* 508–36, for a survey of state laws.

Another resource is the Department of Agriculture, Resources and Technology Division (202/786–1455).

[20] 16 U.S.C.A. §§ 1801 *et seq.* (West 1985 & Supp. 1993).

[21] 46 U.S.C.A. §§ 861 *et seq.* (West 1975 & Supp. 1993).

[22] 46 U.S.C.A. §§ 801 *et seq.* (West 1975 & Supp. 1993).

[23] 46 U.S.C.A. §§ 12101 *et seq.* (West 1993); Coast Guard implementing regulations at 46 C.F.R. §§ 67, 68 (1992).

[24] 46 U.S.C.A. §§ 911 *et seq.* (West 1975 & Supp. 1993).

[25] 49 U.S.C.A. §§ 1301 *et seq.* (West 1976 & Supp. 1993).

[26] 12 U.S.C.A. *passim* (West 1989 & Supp. 1993).

[27] 12 U.S.C.A. §§ 21 *et seq.* (West 1989 & Supp. 1993).

[28] 12 U.S.C.A. § 1828 (West 1989 & Supp. 1993).

[29] 12 U.S.C.A. § 1817 (West 1989 & Supp. 1993).

[30] 12 U.S.C.A. §§ 1841 *et seq.* (West 1989 & Supp. 1993).

[31] 12 U.S.C.A. §§ 611 *et seq.* (West 1989 & Supp. 1993).

[32] 22 U.S.C.A. §§ 3101 *et seq.* (West 1990 & Supp. 1993).

[33] 7 U.S.C.A. §§ 3501–3508 (West 1988).

[34] 22 U.S.C.A. §§ 611 *et seq.* (West 1990 & Supp. 1993).

[35] 50 U.S.C.A. §§ 1701 *et seq.* (West 1991 & Supp. 1993).

TAX ASPECTS OF EXPORTING AND SETTING UP OVERSEAS

Albert S. Golbert
William K. Norman
David L. Dubrow

THE UNITED STATES has a system of global taxation. Whether a United States corporation derives income from activities within or without the United States, such income is currently subject to United States taxation. When a foreign corporation is owned by United States taxpayers, practical limits are placed on the worldwide reach of United States taxation and the tension inherent in the relationship between the taxpayer and the taxing authority naturally ensues. The entire system of United States taxation of the foreign operations and activities of "persons" subject, directly or indirectly, to its jurisdiction is a response to the separate corporate identity principle and underlies the elaborate efforts undertaken by this country to qualify it.

I. CHOICE OF ENTITY

Characterization as a Corporation for U.S. Tax Purposes

To be treated as a corporation for U.S. tax purposes, an entity must (a) have associates and (b) carry on a business enterprise and divide the profits among the "associates." In addition, it must possess at least three of the remaining characteristics set forth in IRC § 7701(a) and Treas. Reg. § 301.7701–2(a): *(i)* continuity of life; *(ii)* centralized management; *(iii)* liability for corporate debts limited to property held by the entity; and *(iv)* interests which are freely transferable.

Evaluation of Entities

To determine if an entity is a corporation or a "pass-through entity other than a corporation, the following distinctions may be useful: (a) as between a "trust" and a "corporation," do the "associates" share in the profits of the entity? and (b) as between a "corporation" and a "partnership," is there free transferability of interests? Liability for the debts? And continuity of life?

IRS Guidance re: Facts and Circumstances

In determining the status of a U.K. unlimited liability company which possessed the corporate characteristics of centralized management and continuity of life, but lacked the corporate characteristic of limited liability and a provision in its articles requiring unanimous consent for a transfer of interests, the IRS found that the company did not possess three of four corporate characteristics (in addition to conducting a profit motivated business with associates) and held it to be a partnership for tax purposes.[1] The IRS recently had occasion[2] to revise its so-called "single economic interest" theory derived from a Ruling[3] in which the Service determined that a limited liability company formed under German law (G.m.b.H.) with only the corporate characteristics of limited liability and centralized management, was nevertheless to be treated as an association and taxed as a corporation in disregard of the provisions in its memorandum regarding restriction on trans-ferability of interests and dissolution upon the happening of specified events, because its interests were held by two affiliated U.S. companies owned by a common parent. The Service concluded that the controlling parent would make all decisions regarding transfer and continuous life because there were no separate interests to compel dissolution. In its most recent evaluation of a German G.m.b.H. with the same characteristics, the Service determined that the G.m.b.H. should be taxable as a corporation despite the fact that the two equity holders were wholly-owned affiliates of a common parent. The IRS found that common ownership of the equity holders did not vitiate the G.m.b.H.'s lack of continuity of life, revising the position it took on this essential characteristic in 1977.[4]

II.   USE OF "S" CORPORATION TO CONDUCT FOREIGN OPERATIONS

In considering the legal structure to be used for foreign operations, a number of options are available. One often overlooked is the use of a foreign branch of a United States subchapter "S" corporation owned by the shareholders of the United States operating company, instead of a foreign, say, United Kingdom (U.K.) corporation owned by the United States operating company, or a foreign branch of a United States chapter "C" corporation (either the United States operating company or a wholly-owned subsidiary formed for the purpose). The first option may have significant tax advantages for a U.S. company: *(i)* it avoids U.S. corporate level tax on the "S" corporation's profits; *(ii)* it allows the U.S. shareholders of the S-Corporation to gain maximum benefit from the U.S. foreign tax credit resulting from the U.K. taxes paid by such entity; and *(iii)* it may allow U.S. shareholders of the "S" corporation to claim a U.S. tax deduction for operation losses incurred in the U.K.

"S" Corporation as U.K. Resident Taxpayer

If the "S" corporation qualifies as a U.K. "resident"[5] taxpayer, its U.K. profits distributed to its shareholders would be subject to a worldwide effective tax rate[6] of 34 percent.[7] To qualify as an "S" corporation, a corporation must be incorporated under the laws of a U.S. state, have no wholly-owned subsidiaries (see below) and have no more than 35 shareholders (generally, U.S. citizens or resident individuals). It must file a timely election with the IRS and its shareholders will become personally liable for its worldwide income. Typically, an "S" corporation offers its shareholders limited liability with the tax advantages of a partnership. But, it cannot own over 80 percent of another corporation, though it can of a partnership. This is an important distinction.[8] To qualify as a resident of the U.K. for U.K. tax purposes, it must establish its place of central management and control in the U.K.[9] In other words, decisions should be made in the U.K. and not in the U.S. Because the burden is on the taxpayer, documentary proof should be available in the form, *inter alia*, of carefully maintained minutes documenting that major decisions have been made there and not abroad. Because ACT is available to the corporation's U.S. shareholders only when a dividend is paid to them, dividends should be distributed annually before the end of the tax year to avoid an increase in effective global rates and the accumulation of excess foreign tax credits.[10]

U.K. Corporation

The effective worldwide tax rate on U.K. corporate profits distributed to U.S. individual shareholders would be 51 percent (48 percent , if subject to surtax).[11]

"C" Corporation as U.K. Resident Taxpayer

The distribution by a U.K. resident "C" corporation which distributes its profits to individual U.S. shareholders would be subject to an effective worldwide tax rate (ignoring state and local taxes) of 54 percent.[12]

III. FOREIGN ENTITIES

Public Entities

Most civil law countries have "public companies" denominated by shares which may or may not be publicly traded in the United States sense. The principal distinguishing feature from the so-called private (stock) company is that they are required to publish accounts annually, have, in addition to their own auditors and accountants, public auditors and are not considered pass-through entities for purposes of their own fiscal laws. Examples of such companies include: (a) **Aktiengesellschaft** or **A.G.** (Germany), literally, a "stock company;" (b) **Société Anonyme** (France, Switzerland, Belgium), **Societa Anonima** (Italy) or **Sociedad Anonima** (Spain, Mexico, Latin America, generally) or **S.A.** literally, "anonymous company;" (c) **Naamlooze Vennootschaap** or **N.V.** (Netherlands, Netherlands Antilles), literally, "anonymous (nameless) company;" (d) **Kabushiki Kaisha** or **K.K.** (Japan) a public company; and (e) **British PLC**, a publicly traded entity, typically on the London Stock Exchange. The use of such entities is often required by local law if the foreign shareholder is a publicly traded company in the country of its incorporation. Because the formation rules and provisions are typically mandatory and provide requirements along the lines of IRC § 7701(a) and Regs., it is doubtful that one could purposely form one of the foregoing entities in a manner which would not result in its being treated as a "corporation" for U.S. tax purposes.

"Private" Limited Liability or Stock Companies

Far more interesting from a tax planning standpoint is the use of various forms of private entities which may or not be used in concert with other foreign private or public entities in order to create a "corporation" for the purpose of their jurisdiction of organization, but, say, a partnership for U.S. purposes; or, vice versa: (a) **Gesellschaft mit beschränkte Haftung** or **G.m.b.H.** (Germany) provides limitation on equity holders' liability to the amount of their capital contributions. Equity interests are not represented by stock certificates or other security instruments and may be freely (or not) transferred by notarial deed. It is required to have but one "managing director" who may be required to act only under instructions of the equity holder(s). Because of the flexibility inherent in this entity, it is the prevailing form of limited liability entity used in Germany for both domestic and foreign investors;[13] (b) **Société à Responsabilité Limitée** or **SARL** (France, Swiss Romande, Belgium) has a maximum of 50, but no minimum number of shareholders. Either a sole individual or entity may incorporate a SARL which is then referred to as an **Entreprise Unipersonnelle à Responsabilité Limitée** or **EURL**. Laws relating to formation of the SARL are typically less flexible than those relating to the G.m.b.H., but there is still room to maneuver through the interstices of IRC § 7701(a) and Regs; (c) **Sociedad de Responsibilidad Limitada** or **S. de R.L.** (Mexico, Latin America, Spain) has characteristics of both a partnership and a corporation. The liability of the members (at least two) of an S. de R.L. (also often referred to as a **Limitada**) is limited to the amount of their contribution. Their equity interests may not be represented by negotiable security instruments nor may a member transfer an interest without the approval of the other members. Management may be by one or more managers chosen by the members or by all of the members in the capacity of managers; (d) **Besloten Vennootschaap met beperkte Aansprakeljkheid** or **B.V.** is the most common form of entity in the Netherlands and can be compared with the German G.m.b.H., the Mexican or Latin American S. de R.L. or Limitada or the S.A.R.L. Like its German counterpart, especially, the B.V. may be flexibly manipulated; (e) **Yugen Kaisha** or **Y.K.** are authorized under the Limited Company Law of Japan which incorporates many of the provisions of the Commercial Code applicable to the Kabushiki Kaisha or K.K. The Y.K. may or may not have perpetual life, as provided in its Articles, and investor liability is limited to the amount of invested capital. However, it typically has centralized management and while its shares are freely transferrable among members, transfer to a non-member must be approved by resolution adopted by a majority vote of a quorum of members holding at least one-half of all voting rights;[14] (f) **Limited Company** (U.K.) or **Pty Ltd.** (Australia) is a company with limited liability, but typically neither a pass-through entity nor one which easily fails the corporate test of IRC § 7701(a) and Regs. (although it is possible!).

Economic Interest Group (Groupement d'Intèrêt Economique)

An Economic Interest Group (**GIE**) may be formed in European Community (EC) countries between two or more individuals or corporate entities with a view to facilitating or developing the economic activity of its members, and improving or increasing the results of such activity (e.g., two or more manufacturers could form a GIE to conduct a common research or marketing operation). The object of a GIE is not to seek profits for its own account, but to be shared amongst its members. It may be constituted without capital and with wide discretionary powers. Its purpose may be civil or commercial provided only that it is connected with the economic activities of its members and have an "ancillary character" concerning such activities.

European Community GIE (Groupement d'Intèrêt Economique Européenne) or (GEIE)

A GEIE may be incorporated in France and a number of other EC countries with full capacity in all EC countries from its date of registration. It is similar to the GIE, but may not hold interests (shares) of its members, employ more than 500 salaried employees or be a member of another GEIE.

Limited Liability and Other Pass Through Entities

(a) **Kommanditgesellschaft** and **offene Handelsgesellschaft** refer, respectively, to the limited and general partnership entities under German law. There is also the **stillegesellschaft**, or so-called "silent partnership" which more closely resembles a creditor-debtor relationship.

(b) The Netherlands also has its general partnerships, **vennootschap onder firma** or **VOF**, and limited partnerships, **commanditaire vennootschap** or **CV**. The general partnership is the ordinary form of commercial partnership, all partners being liable, jointly and severally, for the debts of the partnership which, under Netherlands' law, is not a separate legal entity. Limited partners of the VOF are liable only to the extent of their capital contributions.

(c) Mexico's **Sociedad en Nombre Colectivo** is similar to a U.S. partnership in that it is a separate legal entity and each partner is jointly and severally liable for all entity obligations. It is rarely used even amongst Mexicans who show a slight preference for the **Sociedad en Comandita Simple** or **Sociedad en Comandita por Acciones**, limited liability partnerships differing in the way the partners' interests are represented. The latter entity's equity is reflected in shares which may, in the hands of the limited partners, be freely transferred without restriction. Transfer of general partners' shares require the two-thirds vote of the limited partners.

(d) France's **Société en Nom Collectif** or **SNC** is similar to a common law general partnership, however, the two (minimum) partners may be limited liability companies. The **Société en Commandite Simple** or **SCS** and the **Société en**

Commandite par Actions or **SCA**, are similar to the Mexican limited liability partnerships, the SCA being a limited partnership with shares;[15]

(e) The Japanese **Gomei Kaisha** is similar to a U.S. general partnership in that it has all the disadvantages of such entity, including joint and several liability and limitations on transferability and amendment. Unfortunately, it has none of the advantages which might make it worth considering. It is a separate legal entity for all purposes, including *corporate income taxes*! The limited commercial partnership company, **Goshi Kaisha**, is similar to the Gomei Kaisha except that there are partners of limited as well as unlimited liability and there must be at least one of each. But, because a limited partnership is also a separate taxable entity (i.e., profits and losses cannot pass through to the partners for Japanese tax purposes), it has little advantage over a corporation and is rarely used by foreign investors. There is also a "Civil Code Association" known as a **Kumiai** which, to some extent, is considered a separate commercial entity and may carry on business as such even though it is not recognized as a company under the Commercial Code. It is essentially a contractual relationship (there are no Articles of Incorporation or of Partnership nor is a Kumiai registered in the Commercial Registry (typically a feature of Commercial Law entities) amongst the members with respect to a common undertaking. Its similarity to a U.S. partnership does not end there. The Kumiai does not file tax returns.[16] For Japanese tax purposes, profits and losses flow through to the members in proportion to their interests and corporations may be members of the association. The Kumiai may be administered by one or more managers or through a majority vote of its members. Its flexibility is limited, essentially, only by the creativity of its scrivener and the will of its members;[17] and (f) "other" entities (strange ones indeed abound), for example, the **Anstalt** made famous by Liechtenstein or, perhaps, it was the other way around. This is a curious legal creature in that it resembles a cross between a trust and a corporation. It has centralized management (or a "trustee") and can be of limited or indefinite duration (rule against perpetuities?), but it has neither shareholders nor beneficiaries, *per se*. But does it have a "settlor"? Or was that person a "founder"? Perhaps he, she or it is the parent, owner or beneficial owner (and/or beneficiary?). Only the Internal Revenue Service will not be confused. It will treat this entity in the manner which will lead to the best possible result; but not for the taxpayer. The Service is free to treat this entity as a trust or association (taxed as a corporation) or otherwise, in its discretion. Hence, one would use such vehicle at one's own risk (and that, of course, of one's malpractice insuror, if any).

IV. OPERATING THROUGH A FOREIGN BRANCH

Most countries will permit foreign corporations and other juridical entities to operate in their territory provided that they respect their laws concerning registration, licensing, exchange controls and taxation. The benefits of operating through a foreign branch are that start-up losses pass-through and are deductible against United States tax liabilities, and all foreign income and withholding taxes on the branches income are creditable against the company's United States tax liability. Note, however, that there is no deferral of United States taxation of eventual income as it too passes through and is taxed currently.[18]

United Kingdom

The focus of the tax law is upon "Resident Companies." A Company incorporated outside the U.K. may be treated as a U.K. resident if it satisfies the case law test of residence which provides that the residence of a company is the country where the central management and control of its business abides. The case law test has been recently buttressed by statute providing that a company incorporated in the U.K. is regarded for the purposes of the Taxes Acts as resident there.[19]

Germany

A branch of a foreign corporation must be registered in the Commercial Register of the court in the jurisdiction of the branch office unless the activities of the foreign corporation are not such as to require registration, i.e., liaison type functions.

The Netherlands

If a foreign corporation operates through a local establishment, it is not considered a separate entity but a legally inseparable part of the foreign corporation. Contracts concluded by the branch office are considered done in the name and on behalf of the foreign entity.

France

The establishment of a branch or any new company by a foreign company qualifies as a direct investment in France, but is expressly exempted from the prior consent or declaration procedure applicable to certain forms of foreign investment in France. Within 15 days of establishment, the branch must be registered with the Commercial and Corporate Registry. A branch does not have a corporate existence separate from that of its head office and is governed by the law applicable to the latter.[20]

(e) Technically, foreign corporations can do business in Mexico in branch form if they obtain the necessary authorizations from the Ministry of Foreign Affairs and the National Commission of Foreign Investments. In practice, however, the Mexican authorities do not favor this form of business organization and approval is difficult to obtain. As a result, only a small number of foreign companies have branches in Mexico.

V. SPECIAL PLANNING ISSUES: JOINT VENTURES, OUTBOUND TRANSFERS, INTERCOMPANY PRICING, AND U.S. FOREIGN TAX CREDITS

Introduction

This section discusses some of the complex tax issues that arise when the decision is made to "go international" through a joint venture. It also provides an overview of various special tax planning issues not addressed elsewhere in this chapter, including: (a) the tax treatment of outbound transfers of property to a foreign entity;[21] (b) the intercompany pricing rules;[22] and (c) the U.S. foreign tax credit rules.[23] Although these topics are discussed principally in the context of joint ventures, issues concerning outbound transfers, intercompany pricing and the utilization of foreign tax credits arise whenever the decision is made to go international — whether through a wholly-owned or a jointly-owned venture; a U.S. or a foreign entity; or an entity classified as a corporation or as a partnership, for U.S. tax purposes.

Joint Ventures

There are often compelling reasons for a U.S. company to conduct cross-border sales, servicing or manufacturing operations through a joint venture. For example, the joint venture approach may permit the U.S. company to minimize its capital commitment, share risk, exploit intangible property, or utilize the expertise of a co-venturer with an established foreign presence. As described herein, cross-border joint ventures raise complex tax issues. Therefore, the selection of an appropriate joint venture entity, and the structuring of its operations, require careful consideration of the tax laws of each of the countries involved, including applicable treaties. Various forms of domestic and foreign entities are available for conducting a cross-border joint venture.[24] Experienced local counsel should be consulted to determine the treatment of such entities under foreign tax and other laws. The U.S. tax treatment of the joint venture depends principally on whether it is classified as a corporation or as a partnership, for U.S. tax purposes, and whether the entity is organized in the U.S. or in a foreign country.[25] There are advantages and disadvantages to each of the different types of joint venture entities, depending on the particular circumstances applicable to the venture and the co-venturers. Fortunately, absent business considerations which compel the use of a certain type of entity, the co-venturers generally have considerable flexibility in determining the U.S. tax treatment of their joint venture, through the selection of an appropriate entity and/or holding company structure.

Tax Planning Objectives

The principal tax planning objectives for a cross-border joint venture (indeed, for any venture) include: (a) avoiding U.S. tax on the formation and funding of the venture; (b) minimizing U.S. and foreign taxes on the income generated by the venture; and (c) minimizing U.S. and foreign taxes on repatriation of the venture's earnings.[26] Of course, these tax planning objectives must be addressed within the context of the co-venturers' overall business objectives and arrangements.

Taxation of Outbound Transfers: Overview

The formation and funding of a joint venture often involves the transfer of appreciated (fair market value in excess of tax basis) property. The transfer of such property in a tax efficient manner, especially in the case of technology and other intangible property, raises important business and tax planning issues. Property can be made available to a venture in a number of different ways (contribution, sale, license, etc.), each with its own tax, economic and legal consequences. As described below, property that will be used in the active conduct of a foreign trade or business of the venture often can be contributed on a tax-free basis. However, the contribution of intangible property directly to a foreign entity almost always should be avoided because of the so-called "super royalty" provision.[27]

Contributions to Corporate Ventures

Tax-free contributions of property to a corporation are, generally, permitted,[28] provided that the contributing shareholders (collectively) control 80 percent or more of the corporation's stock following the contribution.[29] However, contributions of appreciated property to a foreign corporation are tax-free only to the extent that they come within one of the exceptions provided in the Code[30] for certain types of property (e.g. property that will be used in the active conduct of a foreign trade or business, or stock in certain subsidiary corporations).[31] Inventory, intangible property, installment obligations, accounts receivable, foreign currency, or other property denominated in a foreign currency generally may not be transferred tax-free to a foreign corporation.[32] As previously noted, the contribution of intangible property directly to a foreign corporation almost always should be avoided because of the "super royalty" provision[33] which treats the contributing U.S. shareholder as having sold the property to the corporation in exchange for annual royalty payments (whether or not made) "commensurate with the income attributable to the intangible" over the life of the intangible. The deemed annual payments are treated as U.S. source income. This sourcing rule adds insult to injury. In addition to creating "phantom" royalty payments, it effectively precludes the U.S. contributing shareholder from offsetting the U.S. tax on the imputed royalty payments with foreign tax credits.[34]

Contributions to Partnership Ventures

Where the joint venture is organized as a partnership, tax-free contributions of property are generally permitted without regard to the degree of control exercised by the contributing partners.[35] However, the contribution of appreciated property to a foreign partnership may be subject to an excise tax equal to 35 percent of the appreciation inherent in the property at the time of contribution.[36] The excise tax can be avoided if the contributing partner: (a) elects to realize the gain inherent in the property at the time of the contribution;[37] or (b) elects to have the contribution governed by "principles similar to the principles of section 367."[38]

Sales and Licenses

Because of the prohibitive treatment of contributions of intangible property to a foreign entity,[39] consideration should be given to a sale or license of such property. A sale of the intangible property to the foreign entity for a fixed price will generate taxable gain that is deemed to be U.S. source, with relatively adverse foreign tax credit consequences, as previously described.[40] In contrast, a sale or license of the intangible property to the foreign entity in exchange for an actual stream of contingent payments will generate foreign source (general limitation basket) income that generally will permit the U.S. co-venturer to offset the U.S. tax on the royalty payments with foreign tax credits.[41] If neither a sale nor a license is feasible as a business matter, various alternative structures may be utilized to make the property available to the foreign entity.[42]

Intercompany Pricing

Even if the super royalty provision[43] is avoided through a sale or license of the intangible property, the same practical problems can arise should the IRS determine to re-allocate income or deductions arising from transactions between entities "owned or controlled directly or indirectly by the same interests" if it determines that an allocation is necessary in order to prevent evasion of taxes or to reflect clearly the income of the entities.[44] This is the same Code provision which contains the "commensurate with income" standard discussed above, with respect to intangible property, and the IRS takes the position that it can periodically make re-allocations thereunder by reference to the varying levels of income earned by the parties from time to time. The authority of the IRS under IRC § 482 is extremely broad and covers any situation in which the parties have not dealt at "arm's length" including sales of tangible property, use of intangible property, loans and performance of services. In general, an IRS determination under IRC § 482 will be upheld unless the taxpayer can establish that the allocation is arbitrary, unreasonable or capricious. Thus, taxpayers bear a heavier-than-normal burden of proof. The Treasury Regulations under IRC § 482 contain detailed rules for the application of the "arm's length" standard in various situations. The Omnibus Budget Reconciliation Act of 1993 ("OBRA") significantly increased the stakes to U.S. taxpayers of successful attacks by the IRS under IRC § 482 by reducing the thresholds at which the 20 percent and 40 percent valuation misstatement penalties are imposed with respect to IRC § 482 adjustments.[45]

Minimizing Taxation of the Venture's Income

Another important planning issue is minimizing the U.S. and foreign taxes imposed with respect to the income generated by the venture's operations. Assuming that the venture will be subject to tax in a foreign country, this planning generally focuses on minimizing foreign taxes and maximizing utilization of U.S. foreign tax credits. In the case of a foreign corporate venture, the planning also may attempt to achieve deferral of U.S. taxes.

A variety of techniques are available to minimize foreign taxes. For example, intercompany prices can be adjusted, royalties can be changed for intangible property, fees can be charged for management services and other technical support and services, and the capital structure of the foreign entity can be modified (*e.g.* by increasing its debt).

Fewer techniques are available for maximizing utilization of foreign tax credits, but planning for the utilization of such credits is nonetheless important to minimize the extent of double taxation of the venture's income. A U.S. corporate venture is subject to current U.S. taxation on its worldwide income, but may claim a credit for taxes paid to foreign countries with respect to foreign source income.[46]

In contrast, use of a foreign corporate venture generally permits deferral of U.S. taxation on the venture's income until distributions are made to the U.S. co-venturers. However, if the foreign corporation is classified as a CFC or is subject to any of the other anti-deferral provisions under U.S. law, the U.S. co-venturers may be subject to current U.S. taxation of their share of the venture's income, subject to available foreign tax credits.

In general the U.S. attempts to eliminate double taxation through a "direct" dollar-for-dollar credit against U.S. income tax liability for income taxes paid directly to a foreign country, *e.g.* income tax on a branch; withholding tax on dividends, interest and royalties; etc. The U.S. also allows a 10 percent or more shareholder of a foreign corporation to claim an "indirect" or "deemed paid" credit against U.S. income tax liability for post-1986 foreign income taxes paid by a foreign corporation with respect to a dividend out of its post-1986 undistributed earnings. The amount of allowable direct and indirect credits is limited by a formula which takes into account the extent to which the U.S. shareholder's U.S. tax on its worldwide income (before foreign tax credits) is attributable to foreign source taxable income. It is therefore important to maximize foreign source taxable income in order to increase the available foreign tax credit.

The use of license arrangements can help to increase the venture's foreign source income.[47] Detailed rules are set forth in the Treasury Regulations for the allocation and apportionment of expenses against foreign source gross income for purposes of the formula.[48]

Since 1986, various restrictions have been placed on the ability of U.S. corporations to use foreign tax credits. For example, taxpayers are required to apply the foreign tax credit limitation separately to certain categories or "baskets" of income. The most important baskets are the passive income basket and the general or "active" income basket.[49] The passive basket includes such income as interest, dividends, rents, royalties and gains from the sale or exchange of passive assets. The active basket includes any income which is not included in other separate limitation baskets. Active basket income ordinarily falls in the active basket. Under the so-called "look-thru" rules, dividends, interest, rents and royalties paid by a CFC are characterized for credit limitation purposes by reference to the income of the CFC. The separate limitation rules prevent a taxpayer from using excess foreign tax credits, which usually arise in the active basket, against its U.S. tax on passive basket income, which ordinarily is subject to low foreign income tax rates.

Careful consideration of the foreign tax credit limitation rules is required in connection with the decisions relating to the financing of a corporate venture. This is because interest expense must be allocated between foreign and domestic sources and among the various foreign tax credit baskets based upon the relative values of the assets generating income in the relative baskets. The allocation of substantial domestic interest expense to reduce foreign source income can cause double taxation through the loss of foreign tax credits.

In the foreign corporate joint venture context, a number of special rules apply for foreign tax credit purposes. If the U.S. co-venturers own more than 50 percent of the total combined voting power or value of the foreign corporate venture, the venture will be a CFC. Thus, the U.S. co-venturer's pro rata share of any subpart F income earned by the venture would be constructively taxed to the U.S. co-venturer,[50] and the U.S. co-venturer would be entitled to foreign tax credits[51] for any income taxes paid by the venture with respect to the included income. The income would be foreign source and generally would fall into the active basket for credit limitation purposes.

In contrast, if the U.S. co-venturer owns at least 10 percent but not more than 50 percent of the voting stock or value of the foreign corporate venture, the U.S. tax results to the co-venturer would be different in important respects than the results in the more-than-50 percent ownership situation discussed above. In this case, the venture would not be a CFC, and the income earned by the venture generally would not be includible in the U.S. co-venturer's income under the subpart F provisions. However, actual dividends paid by the venture would be taxable to the U.S. co-venturer, would be foreign source income and would carry with them foreign tax credits for foreign income taxes paid by the venture with regard to the distributed profits. However, it is important to note that because the U.S. co-venturer is not in control of the venture, the dividends will fall into a *separate* basket for credit limitation purposes. Thus, the U.S. co-venturer will not be able to utilize its excess credits, if any, with regard to those dividends except within the separate limitation basket.[52]

If the U.S. co-venturer owns less than 10 percent of the voting stock of a foreign corporate venture, dividends received from the venture will be taxable as foreign source income to the U.S. co-venturer. However, since the U.S. co-venturer would not meet the 10 percent ownership threshold,[53] it would not be entitled to indirect foreign tax credits with regard to the dividends. Of course, the U.S. co-venturer would be entitled to direct foreign tax credits for withholding taxes paid by it with respect to the dividends, which generally would fall in a passive basket for credit limitation purposes.[54]

The use of an entity that is classified as a partnership for U.S. income tax purposes will produce very different results under the foreign tax credit limitation rules. If a venture is characterized as a partnership, the U.S. co-venturer will include in income for U.S. income tax purposes its distributive share of the venture's income. The character of the distributive share would be determined as if realized directly by the U.S. co-venturer. The income, therefore, would be included as foreign source income in the active basket for credit limitation purposes.

Thus, for foreign tax credit purposes, a foreign joint venture entity generally should be structured as a partnership for U.S. tax purposes if the foreign joint venture is expected to incur even moderate amounts of foreign tax and any of its co-venturers is a U.S. individual, an S corporation, a partnership with U.S. individual partners or a U.S. corporation which owns less than 10 percent of the vote in the joint venture. Partnership characterization is desirable in these instances so that the U.S. co-venturers can qualify for a foreign tax credit for foreign taxes imposed on the joint venture income.

VI.   INCOME TAXATION OF CONTROLLED FOREIGN CORPORATIONS ("CFC")

The earnings of a foreign subsidiary of a U.S.-based business are generally not subject to U.S. Federal income tax until they are distributed. This general principle of U.S. tax deferral is subject to numerous exceptions described below. The most pervasive limitations are found in "Subpart F."[55] These limitations on U.S. tax deferral apply only to "controlled foreign corporations" or "CFC's." Other limitations apply to "foreign personal holding companies" and "passive foreign investment companies." A CFC may also be a "foreign personal holding company" and a "passive foreign investment company."

A "U.S. shareholder" which owns directly (or through one or more intervening foreign corporations) stock in a foreign corporation on the last day of a taxable year in which such corporation was a controlled foreign corporation ("CFC") for an uninterrupted period of 30 days or more is required to include in its gross income its pro rata share of such corporation's "Subpart F income." For income recognition purposes, the stock ownership must be direct or indirect through one or more intervening foreign corporations in a chain. Constructive ownership other than through a chain of corporations is ignored for income recognition purposes.

The Subpart F income is deemed distributed directly to the "United States shareholder" which is lowest in the chain of ownership leading to the subject CFC.[56] The United States shareholder's pro rata share is further limited to the amount of Subpart F income which is proportionate to the number of days of the given taxable year the foreign corporation is a CFC.[57] The amount included is deemed distributed as of the close of the taxable year of the United States shareholder in which or with which the taxable year of the foreign corporation ends.[58]

CFC is defined as a foreign corporation of which either more than 50 percent of the voting power *or* the total value is owned directly, indirectly or constructively by one or more United States shareholders.[59] A "United States shareholder" is essentially a "United States citizen, United States resident, or domestic corporation" which owns directly, indirectly or by attribution (i.e., constructively) 10 percent or more of the voting stock of the subject foreign corporation. For the purpose of determining CFC status and not income recognition, actual stock ownership and constructive stock ownership are considered. For CFC status determination purposes, constructive ownership rules apply.[60]

In certain instances. U.S. shareholder(s) which in the aggregate own only a minority of the voting shares will nevertheless be deemed to own a majority of the voting power for purposes of determining CFC status. This would be so if, for instance: *(i)* the U.S. shareholder(s) have the power to elect a majority of the Board of Directors; *(ii)* the U.S. shareholder(s) have just 50 percent of the voting power but also have the power to break deadlocks; or *(iii)* the majority shareholders who are not U.S. shareholders have no compelling economic interest to exercise their voting power, e.g., the return of their shares is fixed.[61]

For tax years beginning after July 10, 1989, a CFC is required to conform its tax year to the tax year of the U.S. shareholder who owns more than 50 percent of the total voting power or value of the outstanding stock that is owned by all U.S. shareholders on any day during the CFC's taxable year.[62] In addition, a CFC may elect to use a tax year-end that provides no more than one month of income deferral to the majority U.S. shareholder.[63]

There are nine classes of Subpart F Income. Only three of the classes are frequently encountered by a U.S. business "going international," namely, *(i)* foreign personal holding company income, *(ii)* foreign base company sales income, and *(iii)* foreign base company services income. Each of these three classes as Subpart F income are described below.[64]

Foreign Personal Holding Company Income

Certain types of passive income are treated as foreign personal holding company income. The legislative purpose of limiting deferral for this type of income is to discourage the establishment of companies in a jurisdiction solely for the purpose of accumulating low taxed passive income. Typical activities which may generate FPHC income include the following: software licensing, motion picture distribution, leasing of office machines, car rental, apartment or office building rental and oil drilling equipment rental. For CFC purposes, foreign personal holding company income is gross income which consists of:

(a) Dividends, interest, royalties and annuities;

(b) Gains from sale or exchange of stock or securities except in the case of dealers;

(c) Rents;

(d) The net gains from transactions in commodities except for net gains resulting from bona fide hedging transactions, necessary to the conduct of business or from active conduct, of a trade or business in commodities;

(e) Net foreign currency gains;

(f) Any income equivalent to interest; and

(g) The net gains from sales of any non-inventory property that gives rise to passive types of income or does not give rise to any income.[65]

An exclusion from foreign personal holding company income treatment is provided for rents derived from the active conduct of a trade or business. These rents may include rentals from (a) any property manufactured by the lessor, or to which substantial value was added by lessor; (b) personal property ordinarily used by the lessor in its business but temporarily leased out during a slack period; and (c) any property leased as a result of substantial marketing efforts in the country of organization of the CFC.

A limited exemption from the definition of FPHC income for certain export financing conducted by banks. An additional exception is provided for certain income known as "same country income" even though it is derived from a related person as follows: (a) dividends and interest received from a related person which *(i) percent is organized in the same country as the recipient CFC, and (ii)* has a substantial part of its assets used in a business location within such country; and (b) rents, royalties and similar amounts for the use of property within the same country in which the recipient CFC is organized. The exception for same country income is not available where the interest, rent or royalty reduces the payor's Subpart F income. Further, to qualify for the same country exclusion for taxable years beginning after September 30, 1993, the earnings distributed must have been accumulated while the CFC held the stock of the distributing corporation.

Foreign Base Company Sales Income

Four classes of sales income of a CFC known as "foreign base company sales income" are treated as Subpart F income as follows: *(i)* purchase of personal property from a related person and its sale to any person; *(ii)* sale of personal property to any person "on behalf of" a related person, *e.g.,* CFC acts as a commission sales agent for U.S. manufacturer; *(iii)* purchase of personal property from any person and its sale to a related person; and *(iv)* purchase of personal property from any person on behalf of a related person, *e.g.,* CFC acts as a commission purchasing agent. The form of profit is not relevant. *e.g.,* commissions, service, interest, fees earned from sale of personal property.[66]

The legislative purpose is to eliminate any Federal income tax incentive to use an intermediate sales company incorporated in a jurisdiction other than the country of manufacture or consumption of the product being sold. The subject personal property need not be inventory. However, personal property sold to an unrelated person after substantial use by the CFC in its business will not generate FBC sales income. There is no application to gains from personal property sold pursuant to the discontinuation of the business of the CFC as long as substantially all of the property is sold.

Sales income derived from property manufactured, produced, constructed, grown or extracted in country where the CFC is organized is excluded from foreign base company treatment. The determination of whether property has been manufactured or produced is often difficult. The Treasury Regulations define manufacture, production, or construction to be *(i)* a "substantial transformation" of the subject property, *e.g.,* wood pulp to paper, steel rods to screws and bolts, fresh tuna to canned tuna; *(ii)* any activity including "assembly" where the property conversion costs for direct labor and factory burden equals or exceeds 20 percent of the cost of the goods sold, or *(iii)* the subject activities are substantial in nature and generally considered to constitute manufacturing. However, packaging, repacking, labeling will not be treated as manufacturing.[67]

Generally there is no application to property manufactured by the CFC itself. However, the manufacturing or sales branch rules may nullify the exception by treating one or more branches of a CFC as if it were a separate corporation. For instance, if a sales branch of a CFC has the same tax effect as if it were a wholly owned subsidiary of the CFC, it will be so treated solely for purposes of determining the existence of FBC sales income, the application of the de minimis and full inclusion rules, and the application of the not availed of rule. The procedures for determining tax effect are as follows:

(a) Allocate the sales income earned by the branch from all transactions which would be FBC sales income if such branch were itself a CFC.

(b) Determine the actual effective rate of income tax imposed on such sales income.

(c) Determine hypothetically the effective rate of income tax that would have been imposed in the subject sales income by the country in which the CFC is organized under the following conditions: *(i)* all income of the CFC was derived from sources within the country of organization; *(ii)* all income was attributable to a permanent establishment located in such country; and *(iii)* the CFC is managed and controlled where the sales branch is located.

A sales branch is treated as separate subsidiary if the effective rate actually imposed on the sales income is less than 90 percent of, and at least five percentage points less, than the effective rate that would be imposed if such income were earned in the country in which the CFC is organized.[68]

If a manufacturing branch of a CFC has substantially the same tax effect as if the branch were a wholly-owned subsidiary corporation of the CFC, it will be so treated solely for the purposes of determining the existence of FBC sales income, the application of the de minimis and full inclusion rule and the application of the not availed of rule. Procedures to determine the tax effect are as follows:

(a) Allocate the sales income earned by the branch from all transactions which would be FBC sales income if such branch were itself a CFC;

(b) Determine the actual effective rate of income tax imposed on such sales income; and

(c) Determine hypothetically the effective rate of tax that would have been imposed on the subject sales income by the country where the manufacturing branch is located under the following conditions: *(i)* all the income was earned from sources within the country where the manufacturing branch is located; *(ii)* all the income was attributable to a permanent establishment located in such country, and *(iii)* the establishment was a corporation managed and controlled in the country where the manufacturing branch is located.

The manufacturing branch is treated as a separate subsidiary if sales income is actually taxed at a rate less than 90 percent of, and at least five percentage points less, than the effective rate that would have been imposed if such sales income were earned in the country where the manufacturing branch is located.[69] The branch rules are an attempt to limit the artificial use of branches to achieve low rates of tax on sales income only. If the CFC has more than one sales branch, each such branch is treated as if it were the only one. If the CFC has a manufacturing branch and several sales branches, treat each manufacturing branch and each sales branch respectively as if each such pair were the only branches of the CFC.

Where the operation of a branch of a CFC has substantially the same effect as if that branch were a wholly owned subsidiary of the CFC, the branch is treated as a wholly owned subsidiary for purposes of applying the FBC sales income rules.[70] The Treasury Regulations provide that where a branch is engaged in manufacturing, the branch will only be treated as a separate entity if the activities conducted by the rest of the controlled foreign corporation include purchase or sale activity of the manufactured product.[71]

The IRS was unsuccessful in a recent attempt to have an unrelated contract manufacturer considered a branch or "similar establishment."[72] As a result, the taxpayer was able to avoid having FBC sales income.[73]

Foreign Base Company Services Income

A CFC is treated as earning FBC services income if income is compensation, commission or fees for the performance of skilled services performed for or on behalf of a "related person" outside of the country in which the CFC is organized. The services will be treated as being provided "for or on behalf of a "related person" under any of the following conditions:

(a) CFC receives substantial financial benefit from the "related person" for performance of subject services;

(b) CFC performs services that the "related person" is or has been obligated to perform;

(c) CFC performs services with respect to property sold by "related persons" and services are a condition or material term of sale; or

(d) Related person provides "substantial assistance" to CFC in connection with the latter's performance of services. Substantial assistance by a related person includes *(i)* assistance furnished in the form of direction and supervision so long as: such skills are a principal element in earning the subject income, or the cost to the CFC of the relative party assistance equals 50 percent or more of the cost of the CFC to provide the subject services and *(ii)* financial assistance, equipment, machines and supplies, but only to the extent, if any, that such items are furnished at less than an arm's-length charge.

Even if the assistance mentioned above would not be treated as substantial when viewed separately, such assistance may nevertheless constitute substantial assistance when taken together. Examples of substantial assistance from the Treasury Regulations included a situation where the CFC performs installation services in connection with the sale of machines by a related person and where the CFC acts as factory authorized service organization for related person selling machines used by industrial organizations.

General Limitations and Escape Hatches from Subpart F

The amount of foreign base company income is reduced by deductions (including taxes) properly allocable to such income.[74] Essentially, separate baskets are established for accumulated deficits related to FBC shipping income, FBC oil-related income, Subpart F insurance income for insurance companies only and FPHC income for banking or financial institutions only. Other categories of Subpart F income may not be reduced by accumulated deficits. The separate limitations described above do not apply to current year deficits in earnings and profits.[75]

If a corporation reduces its income by a deficit in earnings and profits described above, any excess of earnings and profits over Subpart F income in any subsequent year is to be recharacterized as Subpart F income under rules similar to those for the recapture of an overall foreign loss subject to separate limitations for foreign tax credit purposes. The purpose is to simplify the separate limitation look through rules for CFC's by conforming them and the Subpart F rules more closely.[76]

Amount of earnings and profits of a CFC are reduced by blocked foreign income. Blocked income includes any income that cannot be distributed because of currency exchange regulations. Such restrictions must, according to the Treasury Regulations, be imposed throughout a 150-day period beginning 90 days before the close of the subject taxable year and ending 60 days after the close of such year. Restrictions are deemed to exist if either the ready conversion (directly or indirectly) into the U.S. dollars or property is prohibited, or the distribution of a dividend to the U.S. shareholder is prevented.[77]

If the amount of gross income of a CFC qualifying as foreign base company income (excluding oil related income) plus the amount of gross insurance income is less than the lesser of (1) 5 percent of gross income or (2) $1,000,000 then no part of the gross income of the CFC will be treated as foreign base company income or insurance company income.[78] However, if the sum of foreign base company income (excluding oil related income) plus the amount of gross insurance income exceeds 70 percent of gross income then the entire gross income of the CFC shall be treated as foreign base company income or insurance income.

Subpart F income does not include income that is received by a controlled foreign corporation if it is established that the income was subject to an *effective* rate of income tax in the foreign country of greater than 90 percent of the maximum U.S. corporate rate.[79] The special exception does not apply to foreign base company oil-related income. The rule is meant to apply with respect to each item of income although regulations may be issued permitting reasonable groupings of gross income. Insurance companies are also subject to the new "not availed of" exception.

Any item of gross income of a CFC which is effectively connected with the conduct of a U.S. trade or business will not be Subpart F income unless such item is exempt from taxation (or is subject to a reduced rate of tax) pursuant to a treaty obligation of the United States.[80]

Earnings Invested in U.S. Property

The amount (if any) by which a CFC's earnings invested in U.S. property at the end of a given taxable year exceed the CFC's earnings so invested at the beginning of the taxable year is included pro rata in the income of its qualifying U.S. shareholders (U.S. shareholders holding 10 percent or more of combined total voting power or value of stock).[81] For these purposes, U.S. property includes tangible property located in the United States, stock of a domestic corporation, and an obligation of a U.S. person. Generally, U.S. property does not include the following items:

(a) Obligations of the United States;

(b) Deposits with persons carrying on the banking business;

(c) Certain debts arising in the ordinary course of business from the sale or processing of property;

(d) Certain moveable property used in transporting persons or property in foreign commerce; and

(e) Shares of, and loans to, domestic corporations, less than 25 percent of the total voting power of which is owned by the CFC or by the 10 percent or more U.S. shareholders of the CFC.[82]

Earnings Invested in Excess Passive Assets

For taxable years beginning after September 30, 1993, the amount of a CFC's earnings invested in "excess passive assets" is deemed distributed to its "U.S. shareholders."[83] For this purpose, "excess passive assets" are defined as the amount of "passive assets" held by a CFC in excess of 25 percent of its total assets.[84] The determinations are made quarterly and are averaged for each year. With exceptions, a "passive asset" is one that generates "passive income" defined to include all classes of foreign personal holding company income.[85] See discussion above. The application of the provision is coordinated with the application of the investment in U.S. property provision discussed above.

Passive Foreign Investment Company

The shareholder in a passive foreign investment company ("PFIC") is required to pay U.S. federal income tax plus an interest charge based on the value of the tax deferral when it disposes of its stock in a PFIC and receive "excess distributions" of earnings.[86] A qualified PFIC may file an election with the IRS that will cause its shareholders to currently recognize gain on their share of the earnings and profits of a PFIC.[87] However, individual shareholders of a qualified electing PFIC may elect to defer U.S. tax, subject to an interest charge, on amounts included in income in excess of current distributions.[88]

A PFIC is defined as any foreign corporation in which 75 percent or more of the gross income is passive income or 50 percent or more of the adjusted basis of its assets produce or are held to produce passive income.[89] Certain look-through rules are provided for 25 percent subsidiaries of foreign corporations. For taxable years beginning after September 30, 1993, a deemed basis is given to certain research and experimental expenditures and licensing costs. A CFC may also be a PFIC. Thus, a CFC may avoid, successfully the application of Subpart F, but its shareholders still may be subject to the interest charge on any U.S. tax deferred earnings under the PFIC rules.[90]

Foreign Personal Holding Corporation

A U.S. shareholder of an FPHC must include in gross income a pro rata amount of undistributed FPHC income.[91] A foreign corporation is an FPHC if (a) more than 50 percent of the total combined voting power or value of its shares are owned directly or indirectly at any time during the taxable year by five or fewer individuals who are citizens or residents of the United States; and (b) 60 percent (50 percent after the first taxable year) or more of its gross income from whatever sources for the taxable year consists of items of FPHC income.[92]

FPHC income includes items of gross income derived from investment activities such as dividends, interest, royalties, annuities, gains from the sale or exchange of stock or securities, gains from futures transactions on any regulated commodities exchange, personal service compensation, income from the use of property by a 25 percent (or more) shareholder and rents (unless constituting 50 percent or more of the gross income). Computer software royalties derived by corporations actively engaged in the computer software business are excluded from the definition of royalties includable in personal holding company income and foreign personal holding company income. [93]

A foreign corporation may be both a "foreign personal holding company" ("FPHC") and a CFC. In such cases, the CFC rules "preempt" the FPHC rules. It should be noted that certain closely held foreign corporations owned by U.S. persons may be foreign personal holding companies whose U.S. shareholders are subject to adverse U.S. federal income tax treatment even though the company has no "Subpart F income."[94]

Corporate Level Taxes Imposed on a CFC

A CFC may itself also be subject to U.S. federal taxes. Personal holding company tax may be imposed with respect to its gross income from sources within the United States.[95] The accumulated earnings tax may be imposed with respect to unreasonable accumulations of U.S. source income.[96] Any of its income effectively connected with the conduct of a U.S. trade or business will be subject to tax.[97] Its fixed, determinable, annual or periodical income derived from sources with the United States will be subject to withholding.[98] Dividend equivalent amounts are interest paid by a U.S. trade or business and excess interest allocable to effectively connected income will be subject to the branch tax. [99]

Foreign Investment Company

A foreign investment company ("FIC") is a foreign corporation 50 percent of whose voting power or value is owned directly or indirectly by U.S. persons and which is either

(a) registered under the Investment Company Act of 1940 either as a management company or as a unit investment trust, or (b) is engaged primarily in the business of investing, reinvesting, or trading in securities or commodities.[100] Gain from the sale or exchange of stock in a FIC held for more than one year is treated as ordinary income to the extent of the taxpayer's ratable share of earnings and profits accumulated in taxable years beginning after December 31, 1962.[101] Ordinary income treatment may be avoided if the FIC makes a special election to distribute 90 percent of its net income currently.[102]

Re-characterization of Gain from the Sale or Exchange of Stock in a CFC as Dividend Income

Gains derived by a U.S. person from the sale or exchange of shares of a CFC are included in the gross income of the disposing person as a dividend to the extent of earnings or profits accumulated in taxable years beginning after December 31, 1962.[103] For this purpose, earnings previously subject to federal income tax (and certain others) are not part of the measure used to determine the amount of re-characterized gain from the sale of shares.[104]

Planning for Deferral

Planning for deferral from U.S. Federal income tax is often not practical. Because of the passive foreign investment company and excess passive asset provisions, earnings in a foreign corporation must be re-invested and used in an active business. Even if share ownership can be structured to avoid CFC status and, hence, the applicable of the excess passive asset inclusion, the foreign corporation may still be a PFIC. The interest charge imposed upon on the tax attributed to PFIC gains or distributions will largely eliminate the benefits of deferral. For these reasons, U.S. income tax deferral for the small business is often best achieved through the use of a Foreign Sales Corporation, Interest Charge Disc or a possessions corporation eligible for a credit. [105]

VII. FEDERAL INCOME TAX BENEFITS FOR EXPORTERS

U.S.-based businesses entering the foreign market place often begins first by exporting. Since 1971, the Federal Government has provided significant tax benefits for the U.S.-based exporter. At this time, the tax benefits are available only the use of a "Interest Charge Domestic International Sales Corporation" and a "Foreign Sales Corporation." For administrative and international trade law reasons, the corporate vehicles needed to qualify for incentive are, at least for the inexperienced, technically difficult to use.

Overview of FSCA

A Foreign Sales Corporation ("FSC") is able to qualify for a special federal income tax exemption on a portion of its net profits derived from the export of 50 percent or more U.S. content products.[106] An FSC is required to be incorporated in a qualified foreign country or U.S. possession.[107] It may be an independent trading company or a commission agent for a related grower, processor, or manufacturer. When acting for a related supplier, an FSC will have no economic function but serves only as a tax reduction vehicles. It must file a valid election and consent of its shareholders with the IRS.[108] Finally, certain requirements described in more detail below concerning office maintenance, board membership, and record keeping must be satisfied for it to qualify for the tax exemption benefit.[109]

If an FSC buys qualified products from independent suppliers (or acts as a commission representative with respect to such sales), it qualifies for an exemption from federal income taxation on 32 percent of its net income derived from its transactions with foreign customers. Generally, products to be qualified (known as "export property") must be manufactured in the United States and have at least 50 percent "U.S. content." Certain export related services will also qualify. [110] The exemption amount is 30 percent of export income in the case of an FSC acting as an independent trader or representative.[111]

When an FSC acts as a commission agent for a related supplier, the amount of its commission is determined under special administrative pricing rules. The commission amount is equal to the sum of (a) 23 percent of the export net profits of the supplier or 1.83 percent of export sales receipts of the supplier (whichever is greater) and (b) the amount of costs borne by the FSC is allocated to the FSC as its commission.[112] In turn, only a portion of the commission net income allocated to the FSC from its related supplier is exempt from Federal income tax, namely 16/23 (or 15/23 for any corporate shareholders) of the commission net income allocated to the FSC.[113] As the result, a FSC with a related supplier is able to claim a federal tax exemption on 15 percent to 30 percent of the combined export net profits of it and its related supplier, depending on the net profit margin. The percentage amount of tax exempt net income varies inversely with the net profit margin of the supplier for transactions with net profit margins of eight percent or less.

The computations of the allocation of income to a FSC related to its supplier and the resulting tax benefits are mechanically complex. First, the combined taxable income derived by the FSC and it related supplier from a transaction, or qualified group of transactions, is computed.[114] Second, one of two special administration pricing rules (either (a) 1.83 percent of gross receipts not to exceed 46 percent of the combined taxable income or (b) 23 percent of combined taxable income) is used to compute the amount of net profit from the export sales allocated to the FSC.[115] Third, costs borne by the FSC are added to the allowable profit to determine the commission earned by the FSC. Fourth, the FSC reports a part of the net commission income (7/23 or 8/23) as subject to tax. The remainder is exempt.[116] Fifth, all of the net income less taxes is then distributed by the FSC to its corporate shareholder, which may claim a 100 percent dividend receivable deduction.[117]

Qualification for FSC Treatment

The requirements for FSC status and qualification of its transactions for the above-described favorable tax treatment are numerous and technical, although generally in practice they may be inexpensively satisfied. To qualify for the special tax exemption, an FSC must incorporate and maintain an office in a possession of the U.S. (Samoa, Virgin Islands, Guam, or Northern Marianas), or a foreign country that has a tax treaty approved for this purpose by the IRS and meet certain entity and shareholder conditions, including:

- File an election with the IRS with the written consent of its shareholders;
- Maintain the same taxable year as that of its principal shareholders;
- Have no more than 25 shareholders;
- Issue only common shares;
- Regularly maintain its corporate books of account, including invoices and purchase orders, in an "office" located in a qualified foreign country or U.S. possession, with duplicate copies of certain accounting and tax records kept at a U.S. location; and
- Include in the membership of its Board of Directors at least one non-resident of the United States.

In addition, in order for its transactions to qualify for the beneficial tax treatment described above, an FSC, must be selling or leasing (or more typically, acting as a commission agent with respect to) qualified products or services and except a "Small FSC," meet certain additional "foreign presence" requirements generally known as foreign sales and economic processes as follows:

- Hold all actual meeting of its shareholders and directors outside the United States;
- Maintain all principal bank accounts in a qualified foreign country or U.S. possession;
- Disburse all cash dividends and payments of compensation to its officers and directors from a "principal" foreign bank account located in a qualified foreign country or U.S. possession;
- Participate with respect to its export transactions outside the United States in solicitation (other than advertising); negotiation; or the making of contracts with its export customers; and
- Incur itself, with respect to its export transactions, a certain portion of the direct costs in connection with the export sales in two or more of the following five activities outside the U.S.: (a) advertising and sales promotion; (b) processing orders and arranging delivery; (c) transportation; (d) billing and collection of customer accounts; (e) assumption of credit risk. [118]

Planning for Smaller Exporters

Generally, all of the above requirements mentioned for FSC treatment may be economically satisfied through the use of agents, appropriate contractual provisions, and special transactional grouping. Further, exporters with annual export sales under $5 million may claim FSC tax benefits without incurring the cost or inconvenience of the "foreign presence" requirements by electing to be a Small FSC.[119] A Small FSC still has to be incorporated in a qualified jurisdiction and satisfy all of the entity and shareholder requirements first mentioned above.[120]

A manufacturer with export sales of $2 million to $5 million and a net margin of 10 percent or more would generally find the use of the Small FSC attractive. Under these circumstances, $30,000 to $150,000 of export net income would be exempt from federal income tax. The out-of-pocket start-up costs for a Small FSC, including related professional planning and compliance consulting costs, are roughly $7,500. The yearly maintenance costs exclusive of tax return preparation costs are roughly $2,500. Consequently, under the assumed circumstances, annual cash savings would exceed $20,000. A Small FSC may have annual export sales of more than $5 million, but federal income tax benefits are available only with respect to its more profitable $5 million of export sales.

A small exporter may reduce the start-up costs of qualifying for export tax benefits through the use of a "Shared FSC." Special rules apply to a Shared FSC. See IRC §927(g). Twenty-five or fewer unrelated exporters may own and operate a Shared FSC, each owning a separate class of common stock. The shareholders are not involved in each other's business, do not know the other's customers, and are not at risk for one another's debts. Several trade associations and state government agencies are sponsoring Shared FSC's. Typically, the sponsor pays the start-up costs and the participating companies share the ongoing administrative, banking, accounting and legal costs. Companies with export sales of $250,000 or more with at least a 10 percent net profit margin should consider joining a Shared FSC.

The use of a FSC by an S corporation is generally not feasible. First, an S corporation may not own more than 80 percent of the shares of another corporation including the shares of a FSC.[121] Thus, at least 21 percent of the shares of the FSC would need to be owned by a person other than the S corporation. Further, an S corporation may not claim the benefit of a dividend received deduction.[122] Hence, the earnings of a FSC could not be distributed to an S corporation shareholder without the imposition of tax on the receipt of the distributions. With an S corporation supplier, the maintenance of deferral will require the FSC to invest its earnings or perhaps lend them to the S corporation. Since a portion of a FSC earnings are subject to tax, a measure of double taxation, albeit with a deferral, will result.

Overview of Interest-Charge DISC

In lieu of forming a FSC, an exporter may form an Interest-Charge Domestic International Sales Corporation ("IC DISC") under the laws of any state. In this case, the federal income tax benefit is available only with respect to the most profitable $10 million of the annual export sales of qualified property and services.[123] The definitions of qualified products and services for an IC DISC are virtually identical to those for a FSC.[124] The deferral for the IC DISC comes with a cost, namely, an "interest charge" imposed on its shareholders computed as percentage of the tax being deferred. An IC DISC is primarily designed for use by smaller firms which had been DISCs under the pre-1984 law change, but others are using the vehicle as well.

Initially, an IC DISC will provide significantly greater cash flow benefits to a related supplier than will the use of a FSC, roughly by a factor of three. The amount of export net income eligible for deferral will be 47 percent to 94 percent of the export net income of the supplier attributed to no more than $10 million of earned export sales.[125] The exact amount of income eligible for deferral is dependent on the net profit margin derived from export sales and whether or not related suppliers are used. The percentage amount of tax deferred earnings of an IC DISC with a related supplier varies inversely with the net profit margin of the exporter for transactions with net profit margins of eight percent or less.

Unlike an FSC, an IC DISC is, and must be a domestic corporation. Unless it is acting as an independent trader or commission, it will have no economic substance. Ninety-five percent or more of its annual gross receipts must consist of "qualified export receipts," essentially, sales receipts from the sale of U.S. manufactured products for use and consumption abroad. At the close of each year, 95 percent of its assets must be invested in "qualified export assets," typically, export accounts receivables or "producer's loans made to its supplier."[126] Further, to qualify for IC DISC benefits, it must be a domestic corporation and all of the following additional conditions must be satisfied:

- It must have no more than one class of stock;
- Its stock must have a par or stated value of at least $2,500 on each day of the year;
- It must elect to be treated as a DISC with the consent of all of shareholders; and
- No FSC may be a member of its "controlled group."

Interest is charged to the shareholders of the IC DISC on the federal income tax they would have otherwise had to pay on the undistributed and untaxed income of the IC DISC.[127] A favorable interest rate based on 52-week treasury bill yield is used, a rate well below normal borrowing rates for most small businesses. Essentially, the IC DISC is a tax deferral device for which its shareholder pay an annual interest charge a determined on the basis of the amount of federal income taxes deferred. The treatment for an IC DISC should be contrasted to the Federal income tax exemption provided for earnings a FSC either in the hands of the FSC or its corporate shareholders.

VIII. APPLICATION OF TREATIES TO FOREIGN INCOME AND TO THE REPATRIATION OF FOREIGN EARNINGS

Introduction

The United States has an extensive network of income tax treaties with both developed and developing countries.[128] A tax treaty is a bilateral agreement which modifies the application of the national tax laws of each of the treaty partners to transactions, persons and/or entities with contacts to both countries.[129] Although there is some uniformity in the provisions of the income tax treaties entered into by the U.S., each treaty is unique and must be examined separately when analyzing the tax treatment of a particular transaction.[130] This section provides a brief overview of the current U.S. Model Treaty. Although not adopted in all of its details between the United States and any country, the U.S. Model Treaty contains provisions which are representative of those contained in many U.S. treaties.

Purposes of Tax Treaties

Tax treaties facilitate international trade and investment by removing tax-related barriers. The principal purposes of a tax treaty include: (a) preventing or reducing double taxation of income; (b) preventing discriminatory tax treatment of a resident of a treaty country; (c) establishing tax dispute resolution (so-called "competent authority") procedures; and (d) providing for the exchange of tax information between the countries' tax authorities (in order to prevent tax avoidance and evasion). In practice, tax treaties often create incentives for U.S. residents to structure their foreign operations and earnings repatriation strategies so as to take full advantage of treaty-established exemptions from tax, reduced rates of tax, or tax credits for certain types of income realized by a U.S. resident. They also help to coordinate the treaty partners' respective "source" rules, which directly affect the utilization of U.S. foreign tax credits, among other things.

Availability of Treaty Benefits

The benefits of the U.S. Model Treaty are extended to a person or entity that is a "resident" of one or both of the treaty partners, *i.e.* a person or entity liable for tax in the U.S. and/or its treaty partner on the basis of domicile, residence, citizenship, place of management, place of incorporation, or any other criterion of a similar nature. For example, individuals and corporations subject to worldwide taxation under U.S. tax laws are deemed to be U.S. residents under the U.S. Model Treaty. In contrast, persons and entities liable for tax in the United States based upon the source of their income are not deemed to be U.S. residents. Partnerships, trusts and other conduit entities raise special issues concerning residency.[131] In order to discourage "treaty shopping" recent U.S. treaties contain "limitation of benefits" provisions which restrict the availability of treaty benefits in instances where a non-resident seeks indirectly to obtain the benefit of treaty provisions (*e.g.* by establishing an entity in one of the treaty countries and artificially shifting income to such entity).[132] Of course, the IRS may challenge attempts at treaty shopping even in the absence of a limitation of benefits provision.[133]

Taxation of Business Profits Attributable to a Permanent Establishment

The U.S. Model Treaty provides that the business profits of an enterprise which is resident in the U.S. can be taxed by the treaty partner only if those profits are attributable to a permanent establishment of that U.S. enterprise in the treaty partner. The term "business profits" includes the income derived from any trade or business. A U.S. "enterprise" generally includes any undertaking carried on by a U.S. resident, whether or not there is actual economic activity in the U.S. In determining the business profits "attributable" to a permanent establishment, the U.S. Model Treaty adopts an arms' length standard.[134] The concept of a "permanent establishment" is unique to tax treaties, and is defined in the U.S. Model Treaty as "a fixed place of business through which the business of an enterprise is wholly or partially carried on." Treaties generally provide examples of specific activities that will be deemed to constitute a permanent establishment and specific activities that will not.[135] There are circumstances under which a permanent establishment can arise as a result of the activities of others, *e.g.*, the activities of a dependent agent in the treaty country.[136] Likewise, the activities of a partnership or trust may be imputed to the partners (general or limited) or to the beneficiaries for purposes of determining whether there is a permanent establishment. The use of an independent agent generally will not cause a permanent establishment to be imputed.[137] Similarly, the mere ownership of stock in a company that is resident in a foreign country generally will not cause a permanent establishment to be imputed as regards a non-resident shareholder.[138] In summary, one of the most important functions of tax treaties, from the perspective of a U.S. resident, is to establish a threshold for determining when the business profits earned by the resident will be subject to taxation in a foreign country. As described above, the threshold is the earning of business profits attributable to a permanent establishment in the foreign country.[139]

Taxation of Investment Income and Repatriated Earnings

Another important function of income tax treaties, from the perspective of a U.S. resident, is to either exempt or reduce the rate of foreign tax imposed on dividends, interest, royalties and other types of investment income earned in the foreign country. In the absence of a treaty, dividends, interest and royalties paid by a foreign corporation to a U.S. resident typically are subject to a 30 percent withholding tax by the foreign country. Under many income tax treaties, the rate of withholding on dividends is reduced to 15 percent or five percent (depending upon the extent of ownership of the dividend paying corporation by the recipient).[140] Some treaties completely exempt interest and royalties earned by a U.S. resident from foreign taxation. Others provide for a reduced withholding rate.[141] Since the payment of dividends, interest and royalties are the most common methods of repatriating the earnings of a foreign entity, treaties have a significant impact on earnings repatriation strategies. Of course, these strategies also must be coordinated with the overall tax planning objectives for the entity. For example, where earnings are repatriated in the form of (nondeductible) dividends, the income of the dividend paying entity will not be reduced for purposes of determining either the foreign taxes imposed on the entity, or the foreign source income of the entity for U.S. foreign tax credit purposes. This should be contrasted with the tax consequences resulting where the earnings of the entity are repatriated in the form of (deductible) interest or royalty payments. The identification and implementation of these strategies — taking into account foreign tax laws, U.S. tax laws, treaties, and the unique factors presented by each business opportunity — are at the core of international tax planning.

IX.   TAXATION OF AMERICANS WORKING ABROAD

Lawyers advising on international transactions will often be asked for tax advice on overseas employment matters. Nothing matters more to a United States individual working overseas than his or her own personal tax liability. If the tax concerns of a U.S. expatriate employee are not addressed, the employee will not focus on the job at hand and work effectiveness will often be impaired.

General Overview

Pursuant to the Code,[142] an American working abroad ("expatriate") may elect to exclude from his or her annual gross taxable income $70,000 of compensation income received for working abroad. An expatriate may also elect to exclude an additional amount of foreign earned income for annual housing costs that exceed 16 percent of the salary of an upper middle level (GS-14, Level 1) U.S. government employee. This amount is $8,055 for 1991.[143] The base housing threshold amount will change as the pay scale changes. for reasons discussed below, an expatriate may not find the election favorable in many circumstances.

An American expatriate may revoke his annual exclusion elections. Once he revokes an election, he cannot elect the exclusion again for six years without IRS consent.[144] The expatriate may elect for a taxable year or part thereof only if *(i)* he maintains his tax home in one or more foreign countries and *(ii)* he qualifies under the 330 day physical presence test or the foreign resident test. [145]

The annual $70,000 and excess foreign housing amount exclusions are both pro-rated on the basis of days in the year on which the expatriate qualifies under either the 330 day or the foreign residence tests. For example, if an expatriate qualifies as a foreign resident on 295 days of a given taxable year, the $70,000 exclusion for that year is $56,575 (295/365 x $70,000). Once an expatriate qualifies for either exclusion, the exclusions are available on a pro-rated daily basis from the first day of his qualifying period in the taxable year.

Foreign Tax Home Requirement

To establish a tax home in one or more foreign countries, the American expatriate must demonstrate that he does not maintain his principal dwelling place or "abode" in the United States. Next, he must either demonstrate that *(i)* one foreign country is his regular place of business, *(ii)* if he has more than one regular place of business, one foreign country is his principal place of business, or *(iii)* if he has no regular or principal place of business, one foreign country is his regular place of business.[146]

To avoid the maintenance of an abode in the United States, the expatriate must satisfy at least one (1) of the following conditions:

(a) he does not maintain "work contacts" in the vicinity of his personal residence in the United States;

(b) he does not duplicate *his own* personal living costs both at his foreign base of operations and at his former personal residence in the United States; or

(c) his immediate family members do not continue to live in his former personal residence in the United States *and* he does not frequently use his personal residence in the United States.

An expatriate on foreign assignment would generally satisfy item "b)." above relating to no duplicate living costs for himself. An individual may maintain a dwelling in the United States used by his spouse or dependents and still be treated as not personally having an "abode" in the United States.[147]

As a practical matter, an expatriate without an abode in the United States will usually establish a "tax home" abroad if his assignment is expected to last more than one year. If the expatriate expects his employment to last less than one year, the tax home of the expatriate remains in the United States in the absence of special fact and circumstances. In most cases of assignment of less than one year, the expatriate would not be able to satisfy the foreign residence or the 330-day test. Usually, an expatriate living abroad and *not* regularly returning to the United States (say under a "28 days on, 28 days off" schedule) will satisfy the tax home requirement. In a recent case, the Tax Court rejected the Section 911 claim for an MIT professor travelling abroad on his sabbatical on the basis that his "tax home" remained in Massachusetts. The court felt it need not reach the matter of domicile.[148]

Alternative Requirement of 330 Days Abroad

Under the 330-day test, the expatriate must spend at least 330 days during a consecutive 12-month period in one or more foreign countries. Presence in a foreign country for the full 330-day period may be waived if the expatriate is required to leave a foreign country because of war or civil unrest. Presence in a foreign country during any part of a single day will count toward the 330 day requirement unless some part of the day is spent in the United States. Any day or part of a day of presence in the United States is not included in the 330-day period. Entire days spent outside the territorial limits of any country do not count toward satisfaction of the 330-day foreign country presence requirement. The 12 consecutive month period may begin on any given day of a month and end on the same in the twelfth succeeding month. The 12-month period may, and often does, include up to 35 days of presence in the United States.[149]

Alternative Foreign Residence Test

To qualify as a foreign resident of a foreign country, only foreign residence, not foreign domicile, is required. The expatriate need not treat a foreign country as his country of residence until death. The expatriate may fully intend to return to the United States at some indefinite future time. To qualify, the expatriate need only be a "resident" of one or more foreign countries for a period that *includes* an entire taxable year.

As under the 330-day test, the exclusion periods under the foreign residence test may begin on the first day of foreign residence in the year preceding the entire taxable year of residence. Days of foreign residence in the year following the entire year of residence may also be within the exclusion periods.[150]

Under the foreign residence test, all the facts and circumstances are considered. These include: location of immediate family of the expatriate; occupancy by his immediate family members of U.S. residential property owned by the expatriate; the length of his assignment; and membership in local (foreign) social and professional organizations. If the expatriate submits a statement of nonresidence to foreign authorities, he can not be a foreign resident.[151]

An expatriate generally finds it easier to qualify for the exclusions under foreign residence test than under the 330-day foreign country presence test. Days spent outside the claimed country of residence are not relevant under the foreign country residence test. Days of presence in the United States do not count against an expatriate for purposes of the foreign residence test.

For example, an executive, who moves with family to London on an assignment in indefinite duration of a year or more, should qualify as a foreign resident.[152] The executive must maintain his residence in the United Kingdom for a full taxable year to qualify. He may make business or vacation trips to the United States during that period so long as his residence is maintained abroad.

Limitations on Foreign Earned Income Exclusions

The annual amount of the exclusion available to an expatriate during a qualified period is limited to the lesser of *(i)* $70,000 or *(ii)* the amount of "foreign earned income." Foreign earned income means compensation attributable to the performance of services outside the United States. Thus, interest from a foreign bank, dividends from foreign corporations, gains from sales of property abroad do *not* qualify as "foreign earned income."

For an employee, "earned income" means all items of gross income constituting compensation. The items include bonuses, foreign service premiums, cost of living allowance, reimbursed moving expenses (special rules for foreign moves), the rental value of employer furnished housing, housing allowances, tax reimbursement payments, rental value of furnished automobiles and so forth.

"Earned income" also includes self-employment income, such as fees received by a professional working as a partner. Further, a self-employed individual carrying on a foreign business may treat the income attributable to personal efforts as "earned income." Where, however, capital is a material income producing factor in the business, "earned income" may not exceed 30 percent of an individual's share of net profits.

"Earned income" includes the products of individual efforts, such as income derived by artists and writers. For example, gains of an American painter living in Switzerland from the sale of his paintings made through a gallery in the United States qualifies as "earned income." **Income received after the close of the taxable year following the taxable year in which the services were performed do *not* qualify.** No exclusion is available for retirement income derived under a pension plan.

The "earned income" must be from "foreign sources." This means that the income must be received for the performance of personal services without the United States. If the compensation is for work outside the United States, it does not matter whether the employer is a foreign corporation or a U.S. corporation, or whether the pay checks of expatriate are deposited in a U.S. or a foreign bank account.

An expatriate who performs work both within and without the United States pro-rates (or directly allocates) his annual compensation on a daily basis to determine the amount of "foreign earned income." If an expatriate takes a United States business trip, he may still qualify for the exclusions. However, the income he earns for work performed in the United States will *not* qualify as "foreign earned income." Such income is not derived from foreign sources. Further, each day or part day he spends in the United States will count against an expatriate seeking qualification under the 330-day foreign presence test.[153]

The elective exclusion for foreign housing costs is limited to qualified costs incurred in excess of the base housing amount assigned to GS-14, Grade 1, for Federal Government employees. For 1991, this amount was $8,050. Housing costs include utilities other than telephones. Treasury Regulation Section 1.911–4. Without loss of tax benefit, an employer may furnish the housing directly to the expatriate or provide him with a housing allowance. Even if the expatriate employee pays all or part of his own housing costs, he is still eligible for the housing cost exclusion. The exclusion is based on rent paid; or, if the expatriate or an employer owns the house, the annual rental value (not its purchase price) of the housing used.

Self-employed persons may claim the excess foreign housing deduction to the extent their foreign source earned income exceeds the $70,000 annual exclusion. In a few instances, the value of employer-furnished housing and meals will not be subject to Federal income tax. This rule, however, generally applies only to "camp" situations.[154]

U.S. Credit for Foreign Taxes Paid

A U.S. taxpayer may claim credit for foreign income taxes paid and reduce his United States tax liability attributable to foreign service income. Under the credit calculation, the combined (foreign and U.S.) effective tax rate imposed on the expatriate's compensation will be the higher of the United States or foreign tax rate. If the expatriate also elects one or both annual exclusions under Section 911, the foreign taxes paid attributable to the foreign earned income are not allowed as credit. Further, deductions related to excluded earned income are similarly not allowed.[155]

Foreign tax credits, including carrybacks and carryforwards, may only be used to offset United States tax imposed on foreign source income in the same category ("basket") of income on which the foreign tax was levied.[156] For an individual, foreign income tax on earned income would generally reduce only the United States tax liability attributable to foreign earned income.

To increase utilization of credit, employers often delay the payment of items as a foreign tax reimbursement or bonuses. After return to the United States, an expatriate may use his foreign tax credit carryforward to reduce U.S. taxes on his earnings attributable to business trips made to foreign countries.

Decision to Elect an Exclusion

An expatriate working in a high (over 40 percent) tax rate foreign country should generally not elect the foreign earned income exclusions. Instead, he should elect to claim a credit for foreign taxes paid and entirely eliminate the federal income tax imposed on his foreign compensation. Any unused foreign tax credits may be carried back two and forward five years.

In a moderate (say, 30 percent) tax rate country, federal income tax on foreign compensation up to $70,000 may or may not be eliminated. In this case, an expatriate will need to make calculations to decide whether to elect the Section 911 exclusions. In low or nonon-tax countries, the election of the exclusion will result in tax savings for the expatriate.

Foreign Tax Laws

Most foreign countries impose taxes on the compensation income of persons working in their country. Often, foreign income tax rates are higher than U.S. income tax rates. Although foreign tax laws vary, the expatriate is generally treated as a resident for local tax purposes, if he is present in a country for half a year or more. Countries normally impose taxes on worldwide income of local residents without regard to their citizenship.

A few countries, particularly those located in the Arabian Gulf area, impose no tax at all on the income received by foreign (U.S.) nationals from local employment. Some countries, such as Belgium and the Netherlands, provide special tax concessions to foreign (U.S.) nationals working locally. Other foreign countries, including Ireland, Belgium, Singapore, and the United Kingdom, allow complete or partial exclusions for income earned from services performed outside the country.

Employer Foreign Tax Protection and Equalization Plans

An employer should either *(i)* enter into a contract with each of its expatriate employees or *(ii)* adopt a general expatriate compensation policy. An employer generally uses one of two plan designs in its separate contracts or plan. These are known as: "tax protection" and "tax equalization."

Under "tax protection," the employer pays an expatriate employee any excess of his foreign income tax liability over United States income tax liability. The tax protection plan is easy to administer and is suitable for implementation through separate contracts or a general policy.

Under tax equalization, the employer seeks to put his employee in the same after tax net cash position in which he would have been if he had remained working and living in the United States. Tax burdens are "equalized" between the United States and the country of assignment. This is done through reimbursement payments made by the employer to the employee and deduction for hypothetical tax from the employee's base compensation. The United States and foreign tax burdens are calculated on a hypothetical basis typically with assumed deductions for various annual salary levels. Further, foreign service incentives (usually a percentage of U.S. base compensation) are paid to the employee on a tax free basis, i.e., grossed up for the tax on the payment or reimbursement.

Tax Return and Other Compliance Requirements

Generally, a United States employer must withhold taxes on wages paid to an expatriate for work attributable to services performed outside the United States. U.S. Federal wage withholding is not required under two circumstances: (a) the applicable foreign tax law requires the employer to withhold foreign income tax from the wages, or (b) the expatriate furnishes the employer with Federal Form 673 claiming an exclusion under Section 911 for all or part of his wages. An employer may rely upon the claim made on a Form 673 unless he knows the expatriate does not qualify for the exclusion.

A U.S. citizen or resident living abroad files a Federal Form 1040 for personal income tax purposes. He claims foreign tax credits on Form 1116 and foreign earned income exclusions on Form 2555. An American living abroad uses Form 2350 to request an extension of time to file until he qualifies under the 330-day or foreign resident tests for the year. An expatriate who files his federal return before qualifying for the exclusions must report and pay tax on all of his income. Later, after meeting one of the qualifying tests, he may file a claim for refund claiming the exclusions. A married person and his or her spouse may each choose to exclude separately earned foreign earned income up to the permitted annual limit of $70,000 per taxpayer.

Notes

[1] Rev. Rul. 88–8, 1988–1 C.B. 403.

[2] *See* f.n. 3, *infra*.

[3] Rev. Rule 77–214, 1977–1 C.B. 408.

[4] Rev. Rul. 93–4, I.R.B. 1993–3, January 19, 1993 (overruling Rev. Rul. 77–214). *See* f.n. 8, *infra, and text.*

[5] Which essentially means that it has U.K. resident management.

[6] Ignoring state and local taxes.

[7] Or, 39 percent if subject to the surtax added by the Omnibus Budget Reconciliation Act of 1993 "OBRA." The U.K. rate is 33 percent less the Advance Corporation Tax ("ACT") rebate of 22 percent which leaves, effectively, 89 percent of the U.K. source income available for distribution subject to U.K. withholding taxes of 15 percent, netting 76 percent of the U.K. earnings to U.S. taxation at the share-holders' 34 percent base rate (39 percent with surtax), but providing them with foreign tax credits of 24 percent leaving an effective 10 percent (or, 14 percent) subject to U.S. taxation. In short, the shareholders would net $66.00 (or, $61) on every $100.00 of U.K. earnings for a global rate of 34 percent (or, 39 percent), of their effective U.S. rate.

[8] To the extent that the owners of an "S" corporation wish to operate abroad through a limited-liability entity formed under local law, it is now possible to use entities such as a Dutch "C.V." or a German "G.m.b.H." which may be treated by the U.S. (per IRC § 7701(a)) as either a corporation or a partnership, depending upon the terms of its formation. *See* text at f.n. 3, *supra*.

[9] A facts and circumstances test accomplished if all major policy decisions affecting the corporation are made in the U.K. Hence, directors meetings should be held in the U.K. and the managing director should be resident there.

[10] U.K. resident corporations are taxed on their global income. Accordingly, such an entity as above described should not be conducting business outside the U.K. A separate entity should be used for such purpose to avoid U.K. tax on the business of the U.S. shareholders derived from sources outside the U.K.

[11] The same 33 percent U.K. rate would apply as would the ACT refund (generally equal to 1/3 of the amount of the dividend paid by the U.K. corporation to U.S. Shareholders of a U.K. corporation or U.K. resident corporation. Art. 10(2) of the U.S./U.K. Income Tax Treaty.) and the 15 percent withholding tax.

But, the foreign tax credit would be limited to the foreign tax (withholding) paid by the shareholders (who cannot take credit for the imputed U.K. corporate tax). Ignoring state and local taxes on individuals, this would leave the U.S. shareholders roughly $51.00 (or, $48.00, if subject to surtax) of each $100.00 of U.K. source earnings, or, an effective 49 percent (52 percent, if surtaxable) global tax rate.

[12] Again, the U.K. corporate tax rate is the same, 33 percent, but it is subject to U.S. corporate tax at 34 percent rates after allowance for the foreign tax credit (17 per 100) and ACT; the corporate withholding tax rate is 10 percent and the U.S. foreign tax credit reduces the federal tax to "10". It leaves but 43 (40, if subject to surtax) to U.S. shareholders for an effective global rate of 57 percent (or 60 percent).

[13] The flexibility of the G.m.b.H. is both its good and bad feature. Following on Rev. Rul. 77–214 (at f.n. 2, *supra*), one well known German Fachanwalt für Steuerrecht (tax attorney) referred to this entity as a "Gesellschaft mit besheissene Holle" (a Company with shitty trousers).

[14] LCL, Art. 38–2.

[15] N.B. In the case of any of the above-described limited partnerships, the limited (or silent) partner may not take part in management without incurring the risk of being treated as an acting (general) partner with corresponding joint and several liability for the entity's obligations.

[16] U.S. partnerships file "information" returns, only.

[17] N.B. A creditor without knowledge of the liability assumed by each member at the time his claim accrues, may enforce such claim against each member in equal proportions. Civ. C. Art. 675.

[18] Neither can one enjoy the start up losses until the company turns a profit and then quickly incorporate the business of the branch in order to defer U. S. tax on its income. There is an IRC § 367 "toll charge" on the conversion which requires the recapture of the losses for U.S. tax purposes and their transfer to the new foreign entity for offset against future income.

[19] The Finance Act of 1988 § 66(1) applies effective 3/15/88. Certain exceptions exist for companies incorporated prior to that date and which were operating as "Non-Resident U.K. Companies" at the time of the Act.

[20] *N.B.* Treaty provisions allow a writ to be served on the French branch of a foreign company at its registered office about disputes relating to operations in France.

[21] Per IRC §§ 367 and 1491.

[22] Per IRC § 482.

[23] Per IRC §§ 901–908.

[24] See § 4 *supra*.

[25] The attributes which determine the classification of an entity as a corporation or a partnership for U.S tax purposes are described elsewhere in this chapter. *See* §§ 1.1 - 1.3, *supra*.

[26] *See* §§ 4 and 5, supra. Repatriation strategies are discussed in the section of this chapter which addresses treaties.

[27] See, IRC § 367(d).

[28] IRC § 351.

[29] In the joint venture context, the 80 percent control requirement under IRC § 351 may present a problem if the business plans call for non-contributing shareholders to control 20 percent or more of the venture.

[30] IRC § 367.

[31] A U.S. shareholder contributing appreciated property to a foreign corporation in a transaction that would otherwise qualify as tax-free exchange under IRC § 351 will be taxed on the appreciation inherent in the property unless (a) the property consists of stock in a corporation (and the criteria described in the Treasury Regulations issued under IRC § 367(a)(2) are satisfied); or (b) the property is to be used by the foreign corporation in the active conduct of a trade or business (and does not consist of certain types of excluded property). See IRC § 367(a)(3). The Treasury Regulations under IRC § 367(a)(2) generally permit tax-free contributions of stock of foreign subsidiaries if the U.S. transferring shareholder owns 10 percent or more of the transferee, the transferee is a CFC, and the U.S. shareholder enters into a 10-year gain recognition agreement. Tax-free contributions of the stock of a U.S. subsidiary generally are permitted if the U.S. transferring shareholder owns 50 percent or less of the transferee and the U.S. shareholder enters into a 10-year gain recognition agreement.

[32] IRC § 367(a)(3)(B).

[33] IRC § 367(d).

[34] *See*, IRC § 367(d)(2)(C).

[35] IRC § 721.

[36] IRC § 1491.

[37] IRC § 1057.

[38] IRC § 1492. *N.B.* The consequences of an election under IRC § 1492 are unclear.

[39] IRC § 367(d).

[40] *See*, IRC § 865(c)(1), (d)(4)(B).

[41] *See*, IRC § 904(d)(3).

[42] For example, the U.S. co-venturer can license the intangible property to a wholly-owned subsidiary corporation, which can then contribute the intangible property to the foreign joint venture corporation. Alternatively, the co-venturers can form a U.S. partnership to which the intangible property can be contributed tax-free. The partnership can then form a wholly-owned foreign subsidiary to which it licenses the intangible property.

[43] IRC § 367(d).

[44] IRC § 482.

[45] In general, a 20 percent substantial valuation misstatement penalty is imposed on net IRC § 482 adjustments over a $5 million threshold or if the net adjustments exceed 10 percent of the taxpayer's gross receipts for that year. The 40 percent gross valuation misstatement applies at a $20 million threshold or where the net IRC § 482 adjustments exceed 20 percent of the taxpayer's gross receipts. There are two safe harbor rules which can be relied upon to avoid the valuation misstatement penalties. The first of these rules applies if the taxpayer (a) used one of the specific transfer-pricing methods contained in the existing Treasury Regulations and (b) applied the method in a reasonable manner. The second applies if the taxpayer demonstrates (a) that it cannot use one of the methods sanctioned by the existing Treasury Regulations (because none of those methods would clearly reflect its income) and (b) that the use of another pricing method was likely to result in a price that clearly reflects the taxpayer's income. Under either safe harbor rule, the taxpayer must have specific and adequate documentation regarding the pricing methodology it used at the time of filing its return, and it must provide such contemporaneous documentation to the IRS within thirty days of a request for the same.

[46] IRC § 901.

[47] In some instances, it also may be possible to increase foreign source income derived from the manufacture of products in the U.S. and the sale of the products to customers outside the U.S., by passing title to products to customers outside the U.S. See IRC §§ 861(a)(6), 863(b) and 865(b).

[48] *See*, Treasury Reg. § 1.861–8.

[49] *See*, IRC § 904(d)(1)(A) and (I).

[50] IRC § 951(a)(1)(A)(i).

[51] IRC § 960.

[52] Several planning techniques are available to avoid the separate limitation basket problem described in the text. For example, in 50–50 ownership situations, the U.S. co-venturer can acquire one share of new non-voting preferred stock of the venture in order to qualify it as a CFC. Alternatively, stock options can be used to achieve CFC status. In some circumstances, a foreign holding company can be used partially to solve this problem. *See* IRC § 904(d)(3).

[53] Under IRC § 902(a).

[54] IRC § 901(a) and (b)(1).

[55] *See*, IRC § 951 through § 964.

[56] IRC § 951(a)(1).

[57] IRC § 951(a)(2).

[58] IRC § 951(a)(2).

[59] IRC § 957(a).

[60] IRC § 957(a).

[61] *See*, Treas. Reg. § 1.957–1(b).

[62] *See*, IRC § 898.

[63] *See*, Rev. Proc. 90–26, 1990–17 I.R.B. 16 for details regarding making of the election.

[64] IRC §§ 952(a) and 959(a).

[65] *See*, IRC §§ 954(c) and 553.

[66] *See*, Private Letter Ruling 85–360 07.

[67] *See*, Treas. Reg. §1.954–3(a)(4). *See also, Dave Fishbein Manufacturing Co. v. Comm'r*, 59 T.C. 338 (1972).

[68] *See*, Treas. Reg § 1.954–3(b)(1)(i).

[69] *See*, Treas. Reg. § 1.954–3(b)(1)(ii).

[70] IRC § 954(d)(2).

[71] Treas. Reg. § 1.954–3(b)(1)(ii).

[72] For purposes of IRC § 954(d)(2).

[73] *See*, Ashland Oil, Inc. v Comm'r, 95 T.C. No. 25 (September 27, 1990). *See also*, VETCO, Inc. et al. v. Comm'r, 95 T.C. No. 40 (November 29, 1990), where a related contract manufacturer was not considered a branch of another corporation that was a CFC.

[74] IRC § 954(b)(4) and Treas. Reg. § 1.952–1(b).

[75] *See*, IRC §952(c)(1).

[76] *See*, IRC § 952(c)(2).

[77] Treas. Reg. § 1.964–2(b)(2).

[78] IRC § 954(b)(3).

[79] IRC § 954(b)(4).

[80] IRC § 952(b).

[81] IRC § 956.

[82] IRC § 956(c)(2).

[83] IRC § 956A(a).

[84] IRC § 956A(c).

[85] IRC § 956A(c)(2).

[86] IRC § 1291(a).

[87] IRC § 1295(b).

[88] IRC § 1294.

[89] IRC § 1296.

[90] *See*, Rev. Rul. 87–90, 1987–2 C.B. 216, which involved a manufacturing company which was not subject to Subpart F but was nonetheless a PFIC.

[91] IRC § 551(c).

[92] IRC § 552.

[93] IRC § 553.

[94] IRC § 951(d).

[95] IRC §§ 542–547.

[96] IRC §§ 531–541.

[97] IRC § 882.

[98] IRC § 881.

[99] IRC § 884.

[100] IRC § 1246(b).

[101] IRC § 1246(a).

[102] IRC § 1247. IRC § 1246 will not apply to any gain to the extent it is treated as ordinary income under IRC § 1248 (determined without regard to IRC § 1248(g)(2)) as briefly described below. *See*, IRC § 1246(g).

[103] *See*, IRC § 1248.

[104] *See*, IRC § 1248(d).

[105] Per IRC § 936.

[106] IRC § 921(a).

[107] IRC § 922(a)(1)(A).

[108] IRC § 922(a)(2).

[109] IRC § 922(a)(1)(B), (C), (D), and (E).

[110] *See*, IRC § 993(a).

[111] IRC §§ 923(a)(2) and 291(a)(4)(A).

[112] IRC § 925(a)(1) and (2).

[113] IRC §§ 923(a)(3) and 291(a)(4)(B).

[114] *See*, Treas. Reg. § 1–925(a)-1T(c)(b).

[115] *See*, IRC § 925(a)(b) and (2).

[116] IRC § 923(a)(3).

[117] IRC § 245(c)(1)(A).

[118] IRC § 924(b), (c) and (d).

[119] IRC § 924(b)(2).

[120] IRC § 922(b).

[121] IRC § 1361(b)(c)(a).

[122] Joseph F. Naporano v. U.S. No. 93–106, (U.S. Dist. Ct. N.J. 1994).

[123] IRC § 995(b)(1)(E).

[124] *See*, IRC § 993(a) and (c).

[125] *See*, IRC § 994.

[126] IRC § 992(a)(1).

[127] IRC § 995(F).

[128] At last count, the U.S had 40 income tax treaties in force, with the following countries: Australia, Austria, Barbados, Belgium, Bermuda, Canada, China (People's Republic of), Cyprus, Denmark, Egypt, Finland, France, Germany, Greece, Hungary, Iceland, India, Indonesia, Ireland, Italy, Jamaica, Japan, Korea (Republic of), Luxembourg, Malta, Morocco, Netherlands, New Zealand, Norway, Pakistan, Phillipines, Poland, Romania, Spain, Sweden, Switzerland, Trinidad and Tobago, Tunisia, Union of Soviet Socialist Republics and United Kingdom. Treasury has indicated that the income tax treaty with the former Soviet Union remains in effect for Russia and the other republics that now form the Commonwealth of Independent States (other than the Baltic States). A variety of other treaties have been signed but not approved by the Senate, or have been signed and approved by the Senate, but are not in force (pending the exchange of appropriate ratification documents).

[129] Treaties are a source of independent law and have co-equal status with federal statutes under U.S. law. In the event of a conflict (in the absence of a specific indication of congressional intent), the one adopted last in time generally prevails.

[130] The specific provisions in each treaty reflect the relative economic strength and bargaining power of the U.S.and its treaty partner, the peculiarities of their respective national tax laws, and the habitual flow of commerce between the countries (exporter versus importer of capital and technology, etc.).

[131] For example, U.S. Model Treaty art. 4(1)(b) provides that a partnership or a trust is a resident in a particular country for treaty purposes only to the extent that the income derived by such partnership or trust is subject to tax in that country as the income of a resident, either in its hands or in the hands of its partners or beneficiaries.

[132] *See*, Canada Treaty art. 29(6); Proposed Netherlands Treaty art. 26.

[133] *See*, Aiken Industries, Inc., 56 T.C. 925 (1971).

[134] *See* U.S. Model Treaty art. 7(2), which provides: "[T]here shall . . . be attributed to that permanent establishment the business profits which it might be expected to make if it were a distinct and independent enterprise engaged in the same or similar activities under the same or similar conditions."

[135] Examples of permanent establishments include: a branch; an office; a factory; a workshop; a place of management; a mine; a building site; etc. See U.S. Model Treaty art. 5(2) and 5(3). Activities (or combinations thereof) that are specifically excluded from the definition of a permanent establishment include: the use of facilities solely for the purpose of storage, display, or delivery of goods; the maintenance of a stock of goods solely for the purpose of storage, display or delivery; the maintenance of a stock of goods solely for the purpose of processing by another enterprise; the maintenance of a fixed place of business solely for the purpose of purchasing goods, or of collecting information; and the maintenance of a fixed place of business solely for the purpose of carrying on any other activity of a preparatory or auxiliary character. See U.S. Model Treaty art. 5(4).

[136] A dependent agent is a local agent that has and habitually exercises authority to conclude contracts in the name of the enterprise in the foreign country. *See* U.S. Model Treaty art. 5(5).

[137] *See*, U.S. Model Treaty art. 5(6).

[138] *See*, U.S. Model Treaty art. 5(7).

[139] Although not discussed in the text, many income tax treaties also establish rules governing the taxation of income from personal services, pensions, annuities, social security payments, alimony and child support. Special rules may be provided for the taxation of income earned by artists, athletes, students, scholars, and those in government service.

[140] Similarly, where the national tax law of a treaty partner imposes a "branch profits tax" (as does the U.S.), a treaty will often reduce the rate of such tax or eliminate it entirely. A branch profits tax is a tax on business profits earned through a branch in the foreign country; it is similar in effect (but not in form) to a withholding tax on dividends.

[141] Since U.S. companies have been net exporters of capital and technology (at least historically), the U.S. generally has sought to negotiate treaties that provide for "residence" based taxation of the income derived from such property. Needless to say, countries that rely more heavily on imports of such property generally prefer to enter into treaties that provide for "source" based taxation of the income from such property. It remains to be seen whether the historical U.S. position with respect to "residence" or "source" based taxation of the income from capital and technology will be altered in future treaty negotiations.

[142] IRC § 911.

[143] IRC § 911(c).

[144] IRC § 911(e).

[145] IRC §§ 911(a)(1), 911(d)(1) and 911(d)(3).

[146] Treasury Regulation § 1.911–1(b).

[147] Treasury Regulation § 1.911–2(b).

[148] *Gaelhard*, TC Memo 1992–16.

[149] Treasury Regulation § 1.911–2(d)(1).

[150] Treasury Regulation § 1.911–2(d)(2).

[151] IRC § 911(d)(5).

[152] *See*, Treasury Regulation § 1.911–3(a), (6) and (c).

[153] Treasury Regulation § 1.911(d) and (e).

[154] *See*, IRC § 119.

[155] IRC § 911(d)(6).

[154] IRC §§ 904.

PART THREE

FOREIGN LAWS AND REGULATIONS AFFECTING INTERNATIONAL BUSINESS ACTIVITIES

INTERNATIONAL SALES LAW

Robert Lee
Robert Walker

I. INTRODUCTION

THERE ARE a number of problems in engaging in contracts for the sale of goods across legal borders. Export sales present a range of difficulties which are not encountered in domestic sale transactions. These include the decision as to which body of law will govern the transaction. If the contract is governed by the law of another jurisdiction, novel or unfamiliar problems may result.

The very process of exporting involves risk. Goods will have to travel much greater distances, with the incidental dangers of transit. A wide range of matters involving transportation, including such issues as warehousing, customer clearance, etc will need to be considered. These may involve the making of separate contractual arrangements. Finally, there may be risks involving dealings with particular countries. These may include political instability, or fluctuation in exchange rates. Local law may govern importation of goods, and require licences, or impose quotas. In the midst of all of this, it may be difficult to check on the standing or creditworthiness of other parties to the transaction. In view of all of this, it is wise both to consider insurance provision prior to export, and to put in place some system of ensuring the speedy resolution of disputes should they arise.

II. CHOICE OF LAW

The international sales contract can nominate a particular body of law which will apply to its provisions. It is wise for the parties to ensure that agreement on this issue is clearly stated in the contract. Courts will usually respect this wish but courts in certain jurisdictions will only do so if the agreement is in writing and signed by the parties. The way in which the choice of law is incorporated is important. The provisions of a law or code can be incorporated directly into the contract itself, such that the terms of the code become terms of the contract. On the other hand, a contract may state that it is to be governed by a particular body of law, so that the relevant law should be applied when interpreting the terms of the contract itself. This is an important distinction. Law changes over time, so a contract governed by English law for example, will be subject to a legal system which may itself change. This may affect the interpretation of the contract over time. It is advisable to seek detailed legal advice on such points of drafting.

Although courts will generally uphold the choice of law, even if that legal system has no obvious connection with the contract, there may be provisions within legal systems which will restrict choice of law in certain classes of case. These generally have to do with matters of public policy. These situations arise where the choice of law provision is in some way not bona fide, representing an attempt to evade legal provisions which ought to apply to the contract, or where a system of foreign law is introduced which is absolutely repugnant to the legal system in question. In general, however, most commercial decisions concerning choice of law within the contract will be upheld, whereas in the absence of such provision, it may be difficult to determine the intention of the parties. Lengthy and expensive inquiries as to which body of law is applicable may follow as a result. These may involve court actions on points of private international law under rules relating to the resolution of conflict of laws. Careful planning should avoid such difficulties.

Prior to entering into the contract, the parties ought also to consider the most convenient process for the settlement of disputes should the need arise. This is a separate issue to which body of law should apply to the contract. All disputes are costly, so consideration should be given to cheap and speedy solutions. It may prove difficult, in the event of a dispute, to agree a procedure, whereas it is generally far easier to predetermine that procedure and include it within the contract. Again, this has the advantage of binding the parties to the procedure chosen. Consideration should be given to the introduction of a conciliation clause by which process the parties commit initially to negotiate an amicable settlement in the event of dispute. Where there is a long-standing relationship between the parties, conciliation may be possible, since those parties will wish to maintain their relationship. Failing that, the choice will be between be arbitration or litigation. For many parties involved in international sales transactions, arbitration is preferable. This is because arbitration may seem a more neutral solution where parties from different countries are contracting, and may have the advantage of producing a sound commercial resolution without the glare of publicity of a court case. Some of these issues are considered in a later chapter on dispute resolution procedures.

III.   DELIVERY

For practical purposes, the terms of delivery for the intended trade are of equal high priority to the arrangements for payment (see below). Delivery of the goods must be distinguished from the passing of property in them, and delivery may be actual or constructive and in either case conditional. The important thing which the parties must agree at the outset is what will constitute an effective delivery of the goods under the contract.

The moment of delivery and time for payment need not coincide, and indeed the interests of seller and buyer could not diverge more than upon these issues in most cases. However, under certain national laws, such as English law, in the absence of specific agreement between the parties as to their obligations regarding delivery and payment, they are treated as concurrent obligations. Such a result would be wholly inappropriate to an international sale transaction and thus internationally recognized trade terms providing a demarcation of the point at which the exporter's responsibility ends and the importer's begins have been developed over the last 75 years by the International Chamber of Commerce. These terms are known as INCOTERMS.

When both parties specify that delivery shall be according to INCOTERMS, there need be no dispute arising from this aspect of the transaction. The latest version of INCOTERMS, INCOTERMS 1990, came into effect on July 1, 1990. They will usually only apply to an international sale contract if they are specifically incorporated. Specific reference to INCOTERMS 1990 in the contract is therefore strongly recommended, particularly where the parties are from different regions of the world. The ICC Guide to INCOTERMS 1990, which is published both in the USA and in France, is an indispensable tool for any organization engaged in international sales transactions.

INCOTERMS 1990 cover 13 different types of sale transaction and these are grouped into four categories known as Groups E, F, C and D. Group E covers delivery ex-works. Group F covers the situation where the main carriage is *not* paid by the seller, but the seller delivers *free* carrier, alongside ship or on board (the classic FOB contract). Group C covers those situations where the main carriage is paid by the seller. There are four such situations, the classic one being the CIF contract, where carriage, insurance and freight is paid by the seller. Finally Group D covers five situations where physical delivery will be substantially to the buyer's premises or the frontier or designated port of the country in which those premises are located.

Although primarily concerned with delivery, for each type of transaction INCOTERMS 1990 stipulate, if appropriate, the respective obligations of seller and buyer as regards matters such as arranging import/export licences, carriage and, which is most important to the question of insurance, transfer of risk. INCOTERMS do not provide at all for matters such as quality and quantity of the goods contracted for, applicable law, consequences of breach, place of resolving disputes, the passing of property and, perhaps most importantly, payment, including time and method of payment.

Finally, it should be noted that the Vienna Convention (or rather, the UN Convention on Contracts for the International Sale of Goods, to give it its full title) contains a number of provisions regarding the passing of risk as between seller and buyer. However, where the sales contract expressly incorporates a specific trade term, e.g. one which is stipulated by INCOTERMS, then the INCORTERMS rules on transfer of risk will prevail over those provided by the Vienna Convention (see below).

IV. PAYMENT

As foreshadowed, commercially this can create the greatest tension between the parties and/or their respective bankers. The terms of payment will generally reflect the extent to which the exporter requires a guarantee of payment before parting with control over the goods. The more creditworthy and trustworthy the importer, the less will be the need to have payment guaranteed. There are generally available four different terms of payment in deals which do not involve counter trade or set off. The four are: open account, documentary collection, documentary credit and payment in advance.

Open account terms mean that the exporter sends the goods to the buyer and at the same time invoices for payment. If there are any documents of title to or other forms of receipt for the goods, these are sent to the importer direct. This is the least secure means of trading as the exporter loses control of the goods as soon as they are dispatched. Nevertheless, and especially with trade within the EC, it is quite common. If this is the basis of the proposed trade in question, consideration should be given to supplementing the rights given under certain legal systems to an unpaid seller (e.g. such as rights of stoppage in transit) with retention of title clauses. The extent to which rights of retention of title will work as against the liquidator or trustee in bankruptcy of the importer may differ according to the insolvency laws of the country in which the importer resides or their relevant place of business is located. Detailed legal advice should be sought wherever appropriate.

Where the trade will involve the use of documents of title, the exporter should consider using the documentary collection procedures available from the banking system. The documents of title are sent by the exporter to their bank with appropriate instructions. The exporter's bank then sends the documents of title to the buyer's bank abroad with the instructions that the documents can only be released on payment or acceptance of term drafts/bills of exchange. In this way the exporter should retain control over the goods until payment is made or a legally binding undertaking to pay is provided. If the arrangements for carriage will not involve the issue of a document of title, as understood by most common law systems, and airway or seaway bills or CMR (i.e. international road transport) notes are to be used, the documents should, if agreement can be reached, show the importer's bank as the consignee. The importer should then only be able to obtain the goods from the airport, shipping line or road transporter if their bank first provides a delivery order in their favor and this will only be given if the exporter has been paid or the importer's bank has satisfied itself that adequate arrangements for payment under any counter security from the importer are in place.

The instructions from the exporter to their bank and in turn from their bank to the importer's bank may include store and insure provisions (in case the importer fails to take up the documents), requirements as to protest in the case of dishonor of the drafts sent with the documents for collection, details of the exporter's agent in case of need, a provision as to whether release should be against acceptance pour aval, and so on. Detailed advice on what provisions will be appropriate for inclusion in the collection order in any particular case usually will be provided by the exporter's bank. It should be noted that the ICC has published Uniform Rules for Collections which govern the rights and obligations of the exporter, his bank and the importer's bank under any documentary collection to which they are to be applied. Exporters should ensure that they familiarize themselves with these Rules.

Where the exporter prefers not to rely on the importer's integrity, but rather on the reputation and creditworthiness of its bank, the exportor should insist that the importer open a letter of credit through its bank as a precondition of shipment. A letter of credit or documentary credit is a guarantee of payment by the importer's bank provided that the exporter presents specified documents within a stipulated period and conforms to the terms of the credit. The documents which will need to be presented to the bank should be stipulated in the sales contract and the exporter should satisfy itself before finalizing the details that it will be able to obtain them including, if appropriate, the necessary certificates of origin, inspection certificates, etc. The exporter should ensure that the credit meets its requirements as soon as it is advised to it, for example, as regards the documents specified and importantly, for most cases, that it is irrevocable.

Documentary credits can eliminate problems associated with buyer risk and transit risk although country risk can remain a problem as the importer's Government may prevent the issuing bank from making payment and also banks in certain areas of the world are not as sound as they might be and can fail. To meet this the exporter should seek from the importer a credit which is confirmed by an acceptable bank in its own country. As with documentary collections, it should be noted that the ICC has published a Uniform Customs & Practice for Documentary Credits (UCP). Almost all banks will advise that the credit is subject to UCP, which will prevail except where the terms of the credit contradict or national laws conflict with their provisions. The current version of UCP is UCP 1983 (ICC Publication No. 400) which is soon to be replaced (January 1994) with UCP 500. Familiarity with this is advisable for all importers and exporters using documentary credits as their preferred method of payment.

Payment in advance means exactly what it says: that the exporter will be paid before they dispatch their goods. Unless it is a very strong seller's market, the importer will usually only agree a partial payment in advance. If this is the case, the exporter should consider the use of a documentary collection or documentary credit for the balance of the purchase price.

Involved in considerations as to securing payment and the time of payment will be the question of the place of payment as currency fluctuations/risks can seriously erode any profit in the intended trade. The Vienna Convention provides that the buyer must pay at the seller's place of business or at the place at which goods and documents will be handed over. This may not be appropriate. In order to avoid this result and better manage the risks involved, with or without hedging arrangements, the sales contract should stipulate both the currency and place of payment.

V.   THE UN CONVENTION ON CONTRACTS FOR THE INTERNATIONAL SALE OF GOODS

There have been various attempts over the last 60 years to regularize the position in respect of international sale of goods contracts. The most recent and most successful attempt to establish a uniform law of international sales has been the introduction of the Convention on Contracts for the International Sale of Goods (hereafter 'the Convention'). 34 countries have now ratified the Convention, including the United States. The Convention which embodies uniform rules of substantive law is designed to obviate the necessity of referring to national law and involving conflict of laws rules.

While the option remains open for contractual parties to adopt their own choice of law clauses, given the apparent success of the Convention and its widespread applicability, it offers an obvious framework for international sales contracts.

The Convention which was placed before the Vienna Conference was signed by the United States a month before the deadline for signature on August 31, 1981. Twenty other countries signed before this deadline and indicated their intention to ratify. At the time of writing, 35 countries have ratified the Convention. The United States ratified the Convention on December 11, 1986. However, a notable exception is the United Kingdom.

The text of the Convention bears a great resemblance to the Uniform Commercial Code. American businesses can now govern the rights and obligations under international sales contracts in a manner akin to that of the UCC, without foreign mandatory rules being invoked. This should reduce problems of proof in foreign law, and generally decrease legal costs in researching problems under foreign law. Moreover, in the drafting of agreements, it ought to be easier to gain the agreement of foreign parties, on issues such as choice of forum or applicable law (see above) by invoking the text of the Convention.

Application of the Convention

The Convention sets out rules governing the formation of international sales contracts, and determines the rights and obligations of each party to an international sales contract. It is important to note the concept of international transactions used. Article 1(1) provides that "the Convention applies to contracts of sale of goods between parties whose place of business are in different states."

Thus the international element of the contract for sale of goods is satisfied when the parties have their "places of business" in different contracting states. Since it is the place of business that is the trigger for this rule, nationality of the parties, as such, is irrelevant. A party may have more than one place of business. When considering whether the Convention applies the relevant place is that with the most appropriate relation to the contract and its performance. Thus although we have a useful working definition of an "international" contract, this rule is not of itself certain. However, the 'appropriate relation' test in the Convention is clearly borrowed from the 'reasonable relation' test in the UCC and may work in a similar fashion (UCC § 1-105(1)). Moreover Article 1(2) of the Convention restricts the application of the rule by stating that "the fact that the parties have their places of business in different states is to be disregarded whenever this fact does not appear either from the contract or from any dealings between, or from information disclosed by, the parties at any time before or at the conclusion of the contract."

The Convention does not apply to consumer sales, which are defined as "goods bought for personal, family, or household use" (Article 2(a)). Also excluded are transactions of which services are a preponderant part. Claims for death or personal injury caused by goods to any person are excluded. A final limiting factor is the emphasis placed, within the Convention, upon the wishes of the parties, and the factual context within which rights and obligations arise. Specifically the Convention authorizes parties to exclude, derogate from or vary all or part of the Convention.

The Convention will also apply where the rules of private international law dictate that the law of a contracting state is applicable. Thus the Convention may be more widely invoked than is first imagined, and could lead to the application of the Convention against the wishes of an unwary party. Article 6 allows parties the flexibility of excluding the Convention in its entirety. Thus parties can opt-out of the Convention and apply domestic law, but they must be express in their intentions (cf the UCC which would recognize an implied agreement).

In order to avoid the possibility of such traps for unwary parties, Article 95 allows a contracting state to derogate from Article 1(1)(b). Upon signing the Convention in 1981, the United States expressed the intention of filing a reservation to exclude the latter provision. Thus where the transaction takes place in the United States and at least one party to the transaction is from a non-contracting state, the UCC rather than the Convention will apply.

Interpretation of the Convention

Article 7 of the Convention contains a provision which states that questions arising under, but not expressly settled by, it should be decided in conformity with the principles upon which the Convention is based. Article 7(2) of the Convention allows that, in the absence of such general principles to guide interpretation, questions are to be determined in conformity with the law applicable under private international law.

The other major issue of interpretation concerns trade usages. Again the Convention resembles the UCC in providing that both general commercial practices and the previous dealings between the parties may be used as an aid to interpretation of contracts for the sale of goods. The status of trade usages is regulated primarily by Article 9 of the Convention. The parties are bound by agreed and established usage. Where parties knew, or ought to have known of a usage widely and regularly observed by parties to the type of contract involved in their particular trade, that usage will be implied in the contract. The parties can expressly agree to limit the operation of usages which might otherwise be implied. Thus both explicit and implicit agreements on usage are binding. Note that, according to the Commentary to the Convention, the constructive knowledge of the parties necessary for implication of usage may be inferred from proof of 'regular observance in the trade'. Trade in this context 'may be restricted to a certain product, region or set of trading partners'. This interpretation in the Commentary draws much nearer, than might a literal interpretation of the text, to accepting, as does the UCC, that local conditions may themselves establish a usage not necessarily evident in the trade as a whole. (UCC §§1-205).

Note that there is no formal hierarchy of terms within the Convention to assist the interpretation of a contract. One might expect that national courts would give priority to express terms over implied usages (see Article 55 of the Convention). However, it is unclear how, if the matter is left to national courts, the precise hierarchies of ranking between course of performance, course of dealing and trade usage will work.

By virtue of Article 4, issues which affect the validity of the contract, or any of its provisions, are to be decided in accordance with the application of national law. This provision will include the validity of any usage. In effect this means that although, as we have seen, parties can incorporate usages, expressly or impliedly, which will avoid the rules under the Convention, the choice of these usages is restricted to those recognized as valid under the national law dictated by private international law rules. Where such national law would rule a usage invalid, the usage cannot be given priority over the Convention itself.

Finally, as with the UCC, good faith is introduced as a guiding principle. Article 7(1) states that "in the interpretation of the Convention, regard is to be had . . . to the need to promote . . . the observance of good faith in international trade." According to the commentary this "applies to all aspects of the interpretation and application of this Convention". This may assist in overcoming too literal an application of the Convention, of which a party, having shown bad faith, might have taken advantage otherwise. Nonetheless this is a problematic provision. The Convention will depend upon uniformity of application, and Article 7(1) seeks generally to promote this. It would be unfortunate if too great a discretion in the name of 'good faith' was to detract from this.

Formation of the Contract

It should be noted that States can declare their unwillingness to adopt the provisions of both Part II of the Convention on Formation and Part III of the Convention on Obligations of the parties (see below for the 'Implementation' of the Convention).

The Convention does not require an international sales contract to be in writing, rather that the contract may be in any form and be proved by any means. Note that nothing in Article 11 bars the parties from imposing formal requirements so that, for example, the person seeking to sell could require written acceptance. However, centralized economies may demand strict formal requirements for the conclusion of contracts, and Article 96 allows a Contracting State "whose legislation requires contracts of sale to be in writing" to declare that Article 11 will not apply where a party has its place of business within that State.

The rules governing the formation of international contracts, as such, are included in Part II of the Convention. An offer must be addressed to either specific persons or to persons identifiable according to the procedure written into the offer. Article 14(2) begins with the premise that where proposals are not addressed to specific persons, they will be considered invitations only. An offer must be sufficiently definite, indicating the intention of the offeror to be bound, indicating the goods and providing for a quantity and price. This latter provision of Article 14(1) should be read subject to Article 55 which allows that where a contract is validly formulated, but does not expressly or impliedly fix a price, the parties can be bound by an implied term to incorporate the price generally charged at the conclusion of the contract for goods sold under comparable circumstances in the particular trade.

Articles 14 and 55 appear contradictory. At least implied indication of price is an essential element of all contracts according to Article 14, yet Article 55 offers a formula for regulating price where a valid contract is silent on this subject. Article 55 seems to be necessary to allow for the commercial reality of parties agreeing to ship goods (e.g., spare parts) urgently prior to the conclusion of all formalities, on the assumption of reasonable price. It does not sit easily alongside Article 14, however, and it may raise other problems. For example, although it fixes the time for calculating payment due, it does not fix the location within which the market price is to be determined.

The withdrawal, revocation and termination of offers are regulated by Articles 15–17. An offer becomes effective on reaching the offeree, but even an irrevocable offer may be withdrawn if the withdrawal reaches the offeree before the offer. Until the conclusion of the contract, an offer may be revoked prior to the offeree dispatching acceptance. An offer cannot be revoked if clearly irrevocable or if it was reasonable for the offeree to rely upon it as irrevocable and act accordingly. An offer, of any sort, is terminated upon a rejection reaching the offeror. The Convention does not appear to deal with certain other possibilities such as the offeror dying or losing legal capacity prior to acceptance. These would seem to become matters for the domestic courts.

As for acceptance, this may be inferred by conduct, though not by silence or inactivity. Acceptance is not effective until it reaches the offeror. Any acceptance containing material additions, limitations or modifications will constitute a counter-offer. Therefore, the significant issue is what is "material". This is defined by Article 19(3) to cover terms relating to "the price, payment, quality and quantity of the goods, place and time of delivery, extent of one party's liability to the other or the settlement of disputes which are considered to alter the terms of the offer materially". Time limits for acceptance are governed by Articles 20–21 and Article 22 allows for withdrawal of the acceptance where the withdrawal reaches the offeror prior to, or alongside, the acceptance.

In broadly reviewing these principles of offer and acceptance, much more weight seems to have been given to the common law rather than the civil law foundations of contract. For example, the common law presumption of revocability is incorporated rather than the civil law presumption that offers are taken to be irrevocable. Having said that, the usual rule of common law rule (the so-called "postal" rule) which states that acceptance becomes effective on dispatch is rejected. Acceptance will not be effective until it reaches the offeror. Nonetheless the most significant implication of the common law rule is incorporated within the Convention, namely that an offeror may not revoke an offer once an acceptance is dispatched. Taken as a whole, the Convention rules on offer and acceptance are quite stringent, and may lead to fewer, rather than more, concluded agreements. One particular point that will make this so, is that any "battle of the forms" will probably not lead to an enforceable contract, because of the rule in Article 19 that the terms of an acceptance must conform with those of the offer (bearing in mind what is said, above, about "material" changes).

Obligations of the Seller/Remedies of the Buyer

The seller must deliver the goods, hand over any documents relating to the goods and transfer the property in the goods. This general rule, under Article 30, is then amplified by Articles 31–34. These rules will apply in the absence of other, more specific provisions agreed in the sales contract governing the seller's obligations. In the absence of any nominated place of delivery, Article 31 will require the seller to hand over the goods to the first carrier for transmission to the buyer in the case of any contract which involves the carriage of goods. For other contracts, the seller will satisfy the requirements as to delivery by merely placing the goods at the disposal of the buyer. This can be at the seller's place of business. Similarly Article 33 governs time of delivery where no fixed date or period of time is specified in the contract. The Convention allows that the seller may deliver within a reasonable time following execution of the contract. Where a period of time is stipulated within the contract, the Convention works upon the assumption that delivery may be at any time within that period. However this assumption can be ousted where there are clear indications that it is for the buyer to nominate a date.

Article 35 requires the seller to deliver goods of the quality, quantity and description, and in the manner of containment or packaging required by the contract. Understandably, this is one of the most significant provisions of the Convention. This is particularly so as Article 35(2) states that goods will not be deemed to conform to the contract unless they satisfy certain required implied warranties. These are:

(i) fitness for purpose for which goods of the same description would ordinarily be used;

(ii) fitness for any particular purpose expressly or impliedly made known to the seller at the time of the conclusion of the contract (except where it is clear that the buyer did not rely on the seller's skill and judgment);

(iii) possession of the qualities which the seller held out to the buyer as a sample or model;

(iv) containment in a manner usual for such goods or in a manner adequate to preserve and protect such goods.

One problem with the Convention in relation to these warranties is the extent to which they can be excluded by disclaimer provisions in the sales contract. Since the Convention is silent on this point, it may be a question of what the relevant national law may permit or restrict in relation to such disclaimers.

Under Article 39, it is necessary for the buyer to give notice to the seller specifying any lack of conformity within a reasonable time following the time at which the defect was discovered or ought to have been discovered. This is subject to a long-stop provision that the buyer will need to give notice to the seller within a two year period from the date upon which the goods were actually handed over to the buyer. This period can be extended by contractual periods of guarantee. Note that this period is not of itself the limitation period, which may be governed by the parallel provisions of the UN Convention on the Limitation Periods in the International Sale of Goods (signed on June 14 1974). This limits to four years the period within which a buyer or seller can pursue a claim under an International Sales Contract.

In the event of a breach of contract by the seller, the buyer is likely to have four broad options by way of a remedy. These are to:

(i) compel performance; or

(ii) reject the goods and rescind the contract (available only for a fundamental breach) (see below); or

(iii) accept the goods and claim damages; or

(iv) seek a reduction in price.

Specific performance is generally available in the event of non-performance of the contract by the seller. However, such a right may be lost by a buyer who resorts to other remedies inconsistent with specific performance such as declaring the contract void. Nonetheless, the buyer need not elect a single remedy only, and can pursue damages in addition to specific performance where these would help compensate for loss caused by additional delay. All of this is subject to the provisions of Article 28 which states that a court is not bound to enter a judgment for specific performance unless the court would offer such a remedy under its own law. This is implicit recognition of the width of the remedy of specific performance under the Convention. The traditional common law rule is to refuse the remedy except where damages fail to provide adequate recompense. Article 28 will permit the domestic law of common law jurisdictions to apply.

As indicated above, the Convention restricts the rights of the buyer to avoid the contract. It does so by retaining the common law distinction between fundamental and non-fundamental breach. Article 25 defines "fundamental" breach in a more objective fashion than under the earlier ULIS definition, which was widely criticized for being too subjective in its approach. The definition of "fundamental" is by reference to the results of the breach, and imposes quite a strict test in practice. A breach will be fundamental if it results "in such detriment to the other party as substantially to deprive him of what he is entitled to expect under the contract, unless the party in breach did not foresee, and a reasonable person of the same kind in the same circumstances would not have foreseen, such a result". It will be clear from a consideration of the above definition, that the cases in which international sales contracts governed by the Convention can be avoided will be restricted. The definition of "fundamental" breach is crucial also to the remedy of the buyer to seek delivery of substitute goods under Article 46(2). Reliance upon a fundamental breach is subject to notice being given in accordance with Article 39 (discussed above).

Clearly one possibility of fundamental breach is late delivery by the seller. However, in this case, the buyer also has the option, under Article 47, to put the seller on notice that he should fulfill his obligations within an additional reasonable period of time. This is a remedy based on German law (and is commonly referred to as the Nachfrist notice). Certainly once this notice is served, and the seller still fails to deliver within that time period, the seller's failure will be deemed to be fundamental, allowing the buyer to avoid the contract. A buyer wishing to pursue such remedies should serve notice under Article 26 of the Convention declaring an intention to avoid the contract. The buyer is thereafter exempt from the performance of obligations under the contract so that goods could be rejected or returned, with the buyer recovering payments made over to the seller, in addition to claiming damages for breach.

Where damages are claimed, these can be calculated in accordance with Articles 74–76 of the Convention. Damages are defined as the sum equal to the loss. This can include loss of profit flowing directly from the breach. However, in an attempt to place the buyer in the position in which he would have been had the contract obligations been performed, damages are restricted. They may not exceed the loss which the seller in breach foresaw or ought to have foreseen as the possible consequences of the breach at the time that the contract was concluded.

There is a duty to mitigate under Article 77, and in the event of a failure to do so, a reduction in damages may be claimed by the party in breach. There is no provision within the Convention regulating liquidated damages clauses. Parties remain free to use such clauses in international sale agreements but where they do so, the validity of such a clause will be governed by the relevant applicable national law.

The final remedy is that, where goods do not conform with the contract, the buyer has the right to reduce the price of the goods. This reduction is fixed in accordance with the formula which seeks to assess a proportion of the value of the delivered goods as against the value which goods in conformity with the contract would have had at that time. This remedy is available whether or not the price has already been paid.

This ends, formally, the remedies open to the buyer but there is another option to remedy non-performance subject to the consent of the buyer. Under Article 48 the seller may remedy non-performance, after date of delivery, where this can be done without unreasonable delay or inconvenience to the buyer. If the buyer agrees, he will forgo remedies inconsistent with performance by the seller. The buyer remains in a position of strength, however, especially where the breach is of a fundamental nature, and can reject reasonable offers made under Article 48 by the seller who could now perform without delay or inconvenience.

Obligations of the Buyer/Remedies of the Seller

Having dealt with obligations of the seller to the buyer, we can deal with the essentially similar converse provisions. As one might expect, the major obligations of the buyer are to pay the price and take delivery of the goods in accordance with the contract terms and/or the provisions of the Convention.

In relation to price, the provisions of Article 55 again apply. These will fix a consideration for the goods in the absence of an express or implied term as to purchase price. The other major obligations in relation to price are likely to concern place of payment. International sales contracts will often govern the place of payment expressly in order to guard against currency risks, and in particular the difficulties in converting currency. Where, however, this is not so, the Convention states that the buyer must pay at the seller's place of business or at the place at which goods and documents will be handed over. Where time of payment is not specified, the buyer will become obliged to pay once the seller places the goods or documents at the disposal of the buyer. Except in the case of a contract for a documentary sale, however, the buyer will have the right to examine the goods prior to payment of the purchase price.

As to delivery, the buyer must do what is required under the contract in order to enable the seller to make delivery, and must in fact take the goods as required. In the event of failure of all or any of these duties, the seller will have remedies available. Primarily these consist of:

(i) compelling performance;

(ii) avoiding the contract (available for fundamental breaches only); and

(iii) claiming damages.

Much of the rules considered above in relation to buyer's remedies apply directly to the seller. In addition, the following further provisions apply. Under Article 62, the seller can compel the buyer to accept the goods in order to render him liable for the purchase price. Once again this is subject to the provisions of Article 28. Under Article 64, a seller may avoid the contract in the case of a fundamental breach, which clearly includes failure to pay the purchase price. However, the seller can also use the 'Nachfrist notice' and fix an additional period of time, of a reasonable length, within which the buyer must perform his obligations. Again failure to perform within this period will allow the seller to declare that the contract is void. As for damages, the principles upon which damages are based are discussed above, and these provisions avail the seller seeking damages in the same way as the buyer.

Anticipatory Breach

In addition to the remedies considered above, there are certain Articles of the Convention which relate to the suspension or avoidance of contractual obligations where it becomes apparent that one party will not perform a substantial part of the contractual obligations. These "anticipatory breach" provisions are primarily contained in Articles 71–73. Under Article 71, at any time including following the conclusion of the contract, a party can suspend the performance of his obligations on the grounds of anticipatory breach. The likely non-performance by the other party may result from either a serious deficiency in that party's ability to perform or in his credit-worthiness, or it may be deduced from his conduct to date in the performance of the contract. This ground of suspension requires immediate notice to the other party, and if that party provides adequate assurance of performance, then the party serving the notice is obliged to continue with his own performance of the contract.

In addition to this right of suspension, Article 72 provides for an additional remedy of declaring the contract void. This is available if, prior to the date of performance, it is clear that the other party will fall into fundamental breach of the contract. The principles of fundamental breach (Article 25) will apply here. As with other remedies for fundamental breach under the Convention, this is subject to the service of reasonable notice. Also, as with the suspension ground, reasonable assurances of performance will oblige the party serving notice to continue the performance of the contract.

Finally, Article 73 contains provisions relating to installment contracts. These are similar in both form and content to the UCC. They allow the failure of a party to perform an obligation, in respect of any installment, to be treated as a fundamental and/or anticipatory breach such that the contract may be declared void. There is a provision which will allow earlier, accepted deliveries by installment to be avoided where the chain of deliveries under the installment contract are so inter-dependent, that individual deliveries could not be used for the purpose contemplated by the parties at the time of conclusion of the contract.

These provisions on anticipatory breach were apparently the subject of considerable discussion and in particular Article 71(1) on rights of suspension was significantly modified. Nonetheless, the outcome will be familiar to lawyers dealing with the UCC. In the event, the anticipatory breach provisions are based largely on objective grounds rather than the subjective fears of a particular party. They would seem to require a fairly high degree of probability of non-performance before these remedies may be invoked.

Passing of Risk

The Convention does not concern itself with transfer of property in, or possession of, goods. Rather, these subjects are left to private international law. However, there are provisions relating to the passage of risk from seller to buyer. As we have seen, under Article 36, the seller is liable for any lack of conformity which exists at the time the risk passes to the buyer. It follows that it was necessary for the Convention to establish rules of passing of risk which would offer clear guidance. This is crucial as a matter of commercial practice for insurance cover, and the Convention implicitly recognizes this commercial reality by imposing a general principle that risk passes when goods are taken by the buyer. However, the Convention has to deal with the differing circumstances of carriage of goods in relation to sales contracts.

Article 67 provides that in the case of contracts of sale involving the carriage of goods, where the seller is not bound to hand them over at a particular place, the risk passes to the buyer when goods are handed over to the first carrier. Risk will not pass under this first carrier rule until the goods are clearly identified by marking on the goods, by shipping documents, or by a notice given to the buyer, by virtue of the qualifications contained within Article 67(2). If the seller is bound to hand the goods over to a carrier at a particular place, risk does not pass until the carrier is in receipt of goods at that place. Thus, by and large, transit risks are borne by the buyer, and this is so even if the seller is permitted to retain documents controlling the disposition of the goods. Once risk passes, then, as might be expected, loss or damage to the goods will not discharge the buyer from contractual obligations except in the case of a proven act or omission on the part of the seller.

These essential rules of passing of risk are modified in other circumstances. In respect of goods sold in transit, risk will pass to the buyer at the conclusion of the contract (Article 62). This rule can be displaced, however, where the language of the contract makes it clear that the risk is to be assumed by the buyer from the time that the goods are handed over to a carrier issuing documents embodying the contract of carriage. Article 69 allows that, in all other cases, risk will pass when the buyer takes the goods, or, in the event of his failure to do so in due time, risk will pass when goods are placed at the disposal of the buyer so that the buyer would breach the contract by failing to take delivery.

Where goods are lost or damaged at the time of the conclusion of the contract, and this was not disclosed to the buyer, such loss or damage is at the risk of the seller where he knew, or ought to have known, of the loss or damage to the goods. Where the seller did not know, or could not have known of such damage, risk will pass in accordance with the rules discussed in this section.

All of what is written above on the passage of risk is subject to an extremely important qualification. The sales contract itself may contain a specific trade term. If such a trade term is governed by INCOTERMS (as generally would be for FOB or CIF contracts), then the INCOTERMS rules on risk will apply. In practice, many international sales contracts will be governed by the INCOTERMS rules, Moreover, even those contracts which are not so governed may incorporate specific provisions as to the passing of risk within the terms of the contract itself. Thus Articles 6 and 9 of the Convention in allowing such rules to prevail over those in the Convention will have the effect that the Convention rules will be of limited applicability in this area.

Exemption of Liability

The use of disclaimers has already been considered earlier, but there is a significant exemption from liability open to a party who fails to perform obligations under the contract. Article 79(1) offers such exemption where the failure to meet a contractual obligation is due to circumstances beyond the control of the relevant party. Here the party must show that it was not reasonable to have anticipated these circumstances and taken them into account at the time that the contract was concluded. The party will need to show also that it was not possible to avoid or overcome these circumstances or their consequences. These are broad rules, and the circumstances likely to give rise to their application are neither listed nor defined. Presumably, however, a broad law of *force majeure* will develop under the Convention.

Under ULIS it had been possible for a temporary impediment to permanently relieve a party of obligations under the contract if that impediment had so radically changed performance that it amounted to a quite different obligation. However, Article 79 of the Convention offers exemption only for the period in which the impediment is in existence, so that a temporary difficulty will not necessarily relieve a party from contractual obligations. Parties facing conditions of *force majeure* must give notice in reasonable time, of the impediment and its likely effect.

There are particular rules contained in Article 79(2) where the failure to meet contractual obligations is due to the failure of a third party engaged to perform the whole or any part of a contract. Where this is so, a buyer or seller seeking exemption from liability can only do so if the exemption would be available to himself, and would have been available to the third party had the provisions of Article 79(1) applied to him.

It is most important to note the effect of an exemption under Article 79. It relieves the party in breach from liability in damages. It does not, however, excuse non-performance of contractual obligations. Thus it is possible that, even though the failure to perform is attributable to an impediment which neither party foresaw, the failure to perform can nonetheless constitute a fundamental breach, such that the party may avoid the contract (see grounds for avoidance under Articles 25, 47–49, 63,64, 72 and 73). We shall see in the following section that there would be broad rights to restitution, but that the aggrieved party would be unable to claim damages. The limited nature of this exemption may be overcome, of course, by the parties agreeing wider *force majeure* clauses which would prevail over inconsistent provisions in Article 79, and perhaps assist in bridging gaps within the Convention, for instance, in relation to frustration.

Restitution

Earlier sections have dealt with rights to avoid the contract, but it is necessary to understand the precise effects of avoidance under the Convention. This body of law is dealt with in Articles 81–84. In its usual self-deprecatory way the Convention rules on avoidance give way to any other dispute settlement provisions within the contract. Subject to this, the primary rule is that avoidance of the contract releases both parties from their obligations subject to the payment of damages. Where a party has performed the whole, or part of the contract, then that party may claim restitution. This restitution must be concurrent with that made by the other party where circumstances dictate that both parties are so bound. A party bound in restitution will be required to return goods or payments received, and to account to the other party for the benefits.

Article 82 of the Convention is a significant provision under which the buyer will lose the right to make restitution if it is impossible to return goods in the condition in which they were received. However, this principle does not apply in a number of situations:

"(a) if the impossibility of making restitution of the goods or of making restitution of the goods substantially in the condition in which the buyer received them is not due to his act or omission;

(b) if the goods or part of the goods have perished or deteriorated as a result of the examination provided for in Article 38; or

(c) if the goods or part of the goods have been sold in the normal course of business or have been consumed or transformed by the buyer in the course of normal use before he discovered or ought to have discovered the lack of conformity."

Article 83 retains all the other remedies under the contract and the Convention for the buyer who has lost the right to declare the contract void, or who cannot require the seller to deliver substitute goods. A number of remedies are preserved in such circumstances including the buyer's right to recover damages, to reduce the price, and to require the seller to repair any lack of conformity (see obligations of the seller). It will be seen that these rights of restitution are wider than those provided in the UCC and prima facie available to either party to the contract. Nothing in these avoidance provisions affects the party's duty to take steps to preserve the goods. Duties to preserve goods are governed by Article 85–88 of the Convention. Thus where the seller is in possession of goods, or can control their disposition, then, even if the buyer delays taking delivery, the seller must take reasonable steps in order to preserve them. The seller can then be reimbursed for the reasonable expenses in so doing. Again these provisions are not dissimilar to those of the UCC.

VI. CONCLUSION

As the list of Vienna Convention Contracting States grows, an organized regulation of sales contracts at an international level may begin to develop. This has obvious attractions as the business community across differing economic and political systems begins to speak the same legal language. One of the strengths of the Convention is that it is based upon accepted practices of international transactions and is ready to incorporate trade usages into its framework. Again it is strongly driven by a policy that the parties should be free to contract and is not overbearing in its regulation of international sales. This is a delicate balancing act, but the Convention seeks to achieve a form of *lex mercatoria* which sets the boundaries of commercial sales transactions in a clear, well-defined fashion leaving the parties to divide the middle ground. Indeed the autonomy of the parties is recognized in its final form by the Convention permitting the parties to exclude, in whole or part, the application of its provisions.

For larger enterprises, problems concerning conflict of laws in international sales contracts can be marginalized. Their bargaining power may allow them to impose their national law or other choice of law upon the other party in the great majority of cases. For less powerful commercial parties, however, the Convention offers a more independent format within which to contract. There is no necessity when two businesses from differing States contract that one will be forced to accept a body of law which is largely unfamiliar and unknown. There is now a text delineating the rights and duties of buyer and seller and setting out, in broad terms and in six official languages, the essential legal provisions which can govern the international contract into which they intend to enter.

INTERNATIONAL INTELLECTUAL PROPERTY LAWS

Leslie Bertagnoli
Alan S. Gutterman[1]

I. OVERVIEW

Emerging companies seeking to enter new foreign markets must bear in mind that the intellectual property laws which govern the use and protection of their products and technology in the United States extend only to the domestic borders. As such, whenever the emerging company markets it products and services in any foreign market, it is necessary to understand how the various intellectual property laws in that market will apply to the activity. In this chapter, a brief overview is provided of the intellectual property laws in foreign markets; however, due to the great disparities in the manner in which such laws are enforced, it is essential for the emerging company to seek expert advice from local counsel.[2]

II. PATENTS

The protection provided by the United States patent laws extends only to the United States border. The grant of a patent in the United States does not prevent a party in another country from making, using or selling the invention in that country. If the United States patent owner is interested in exploiting the invention in a foreign market, it must apply for and receive the patent rights covering the invention in the foreign market. As it is likely that overseas operations will reach two or even more countries, the prospect of multiple patent applications must be considered with almost every invention with broad market appeal.

The International Convention for the Protection of Industrial Property, originally enacted in Paris in 1883 (the "Paris Convention")[3], provides for equal treatment toward nationals among member states with respect to patent rights and establishes procedures to ease the process of filing multiple patent applications in different countries. However, the equal treatment provisions do not guarantee harmonization of all of the substantive provisions of the various national laws. For one thing, there are a number of different forms of patent rights recognized under foreign patent laws, including utility models, petty patents, inventors' certificates, patents of importation, certificates of addition and patents of improvement. Moreover, substantial variations exist with respect to eligible subject matter, the scope of patentable claims, term of protection, the persons entitled to protection, publication requirements, working requirements and enforcement procedures.

Eligible Subject Matter. Each country is free to establish its own definition of the types of products for which a patent may be granted. While the United States has argued that patent protection must be available for *all* products and processes which satisfy the criteria of novelty, utility, and nonobviousness, a number of countries have explicitly precluded patentability for products in specified areas, such as pharmaceuticals. Also, even if patent rights are available, the government may sometimes reserve the right to license the patented invention to others in the name of the "public interest," thereby undercutting the utility of the monopoly usually associated with patent rights.[4]

Scope of Patentable Claims. Even though an invention is fully described in the application, the scope of protection is determined by the claims which are allowed in the examination process. Thus, even in those cases where the scope of available subject matter protection is fairly broad, various administrative practices of the patent authority may force claims to be applied so narrowly that others can easily avoid claim coverage and obtain their own patents based on very slight variations of the original invention that lack true innovation.

Term of Protection. The term of patent protection around the world is not uniform. The United States and other developed countries seek a minimum term for patent protection of at least 20 years from the date that the patent application is filed. However, in many cases, the patent term in developing countries is far less than the norm in the developed countries, sometimes extending no longer than five years.

Persons Entitled to Patent Protection. While the United States issues patents to the "first inventor," assuming that the application has been filed in a timely fashion, almost all other countries give priority to the inventor who is the "first to file" an application, even if the another conceived the invention at an earlier date.

Publication of Patent Applications. United States patent applications are not published before the patent has been issued, thereby preserving the secrecy of the invention while the application is being reviewed. On the other hand, in many other countries, applications are published prior to the grant of the patent. For example, publication occurs 18 months after an application is filed in Japan. Therefore, since the patent review process remains quite lengthy in Japan, the information in published applications can be "copied" and used for commercial purposes far in advance of the actual patent grant.[5]

Working Requirements. Patent rights in some countries may be subject to early termination because the invention has not been used, or "worked," in the country during a specified period.[6] Alternatively, failure to work an invention may result in the grant of a license to third parties at low royalty rates without the consent of the patent holder.[7] In some developing countries, products covered by a patent may still be imported until the patent is actually worked in the country.

Enforcement. The ability of a patent holder to enforce the patent rights effectively varies substantially around the world. Among the factors that must be considered regarding the potential patent litigation in any foreign jurisdiction are the time limits for bringing an infringement action, how far back in time the patent owner can go in collecting past damages[8], whether or not injunctive relief is available, whether a bond must be posted by the plaintiff, the use of discovery proceedings, the amount of time that it takes to prosecute an infringement action and the attitude of local courts toward patent holders, particular when the patent is held by a foreigner.

III. COPYRIGHTS

The most important international treaty relating to the protection of works of authorship is The Berne Convention for the Protection of Literary and Artistic Works. As is the case with the Paris Convention, the Berne Convention is fundamentally based on the concept of "national treatment." In addition, the Berne Convention requires that member states adhere to certain minimum requirements in formulating their own national copyright laws, including copyright duration of the author plus 50 years and the recognition of the exclusive rights of translation, reproduction, performance, broadcasting, adaptation and arrangement.

The United States finally became a member of the Berne Convention in 1988 and, as such, United States nationals are now entitled to the benefits of "national treatment" in each of the member states. However, the United States remains unsatisfied with the content of foreign copyright laws as they relate to the scope of works eligible for protection, limitations which are imposed on the exclusive rights of the copyright owner, the term of copyright protection and enforcement procedures. Many of these problems are particularly acute in those countries which have yet to bring their copyright laws into compliance with even the minimum standards of the Berne Convention.

Eligible Works and Media Forms. Even though foreign copyright laws cover some types of works, they fail to cover others, such as sound recordings, computer programs, or other print or electronic compilations (e.g., data bases), or may not encompass certain media in which the work may now be embodied, such as videocassettes or computer programs in ROM.

Limitations on Exclusive Rights. Some foreign laws grant only a portion of the exclusive rights enjoyed by authors in the United States. For example, in some foreign countries, copyright owners may be denied exclusive rights to cable retransmissions, public performances or displays or electronic distribution. In other cases, the exclusive rights of the copyright owner may be subject to compulsory licensing or restricted by broad exceptions for public performances in hotels or film clips and educational photocopying.

Term of Copyright Protection. The term of copyright protection in foreign countries is often much shorter than in the major developed countries. For example, in some countries the basic term of a copyright may extend only for the life of the author and the term of protection for certain works, including sound recordings or computer programs, is set at a fixed number of years (e.g., 20 or 30 years) without regard to the life of the author.

Enforcement. The limitations placed upon the exclusive rights of the copyright owner in many foreign companies are often accompanied by perceived deficiencies in the enforcement of the remaining rights. In a number of countries, specifically where public performances of copyrighted works were permitted without permission of the foreign producers, enforcement efforts and sanctions were perceived to be ineffective. Also, United States firms have noted a considerable problem in many parts of Asia and Latin America with respect to piracy of records, tapes, motion pictures, videos, books and computer programs.

IV. TRADE SECRETS

Overview

In contrast to patents and copyrights, the legal protections for trade secrets, often referred to as "know-how," are far from uniform around the world. While trade secret protection is well established in several common law countries[9], trade secrets are not recognized in many countries and no international agreement exists with respect to the subject matter.[10] Even in those cases where trade secrets are recognized, the scope of protection offered to the creator or owner of the secret often varies significantly from that which exists in the United States. In large part, variations in the treatment of confidential information in foreign countries are a function of fundamental difference in cultural attitudes regarding ownership and use of valuable business information[11], as well as economic and political objectives of the local governments with respect to diffusion of technical information[12] and insuring free mobility of labor.[13]

A clear understanding of the various legal, cultural and business practices of, and the relative availability of protection for trade secrets in, any foreign country is of vital importance to domestic firms engaged in international operations. The potential benefits of any relationship with a foreign partner involving the transfer of technical information must be weighed against any significant risk that valuable trade secrets will, by operation of local law or otherwise, be disseminated to competitors who may use it to produce similar products which diminish the value of the rights. Moreover, the firm should be concerned as to whether or not disclosure of the information into the public domain in the foreign jurisdiction will impede its own ability to claim trade secret protection for the same information in the United States and other markets.

The lack of uniformity in the trade secrets area means that disclosure of proprietary information into any new foreign market must be proceded by a careful analysis of a number of factors. In particular, the trade secret owner must examine: *(i)* the statutory and, if relevant, case law relating to trade secrets in the foreign country; *(ii)* the restrictions which might be imposed on clauses which may be included in contractual agreements with respect to the use and protection of trade secrets; *(iii)* cultural factors which might lead to the unwanted dissemination of trade secrets; whether or not the disclosures are prescribed by local law; *(iv)* any other local government regulations impacting the technology transfer; and *(v)* the enforcement history in the country with respect to any laws which do exist regarding trade secret protection.

Legal Basis for Protection of Trade Secrets

A number of countries provide some form of statutory or common law protection for trade secrets and/or know-how, either as part of their intellectual property laws or as part of their overall scheme of regulation of unfair competitive practices.[14] However, while some countries have adopted statutes which track, to some degree, the provisions in the United States' Uniform Trade Secrets Act, most countries have drafted statutes that incorporate their own ideas regarding the scope of protectable subject matter, the persons who may be found liable for misappropriation of trade secrets, and the penalties which may be imposed for violation of a non-disclosure obligation.

Scope of Protectable Subject Matter

The scope of the subject matter which qualifies for trade secret protection may differ in foreign countries and care should be taken to review all statutes and common law standards relating to trade secrets and unfair competition in order to identify the scope of protectable information. For example, some countries do not include techniques which are of a non-industrial nature in the definition of trade secrets. In other cases, different levels of trade secret protection are provided for commercial information, such as customers lists, and manufacturing information.[15]

Trade Secrets and the Employment Relationship

In the United States, a properly worded assignment and non-disclosure agreement can be used to insure that trade secrets that are developed by employees are assigned to the employer and that the employee remains obligated not to disclose such trade secrets, or any other confidential information received during the term of his or her employment, after the employment relationship ends. However, the situation is far different in some foreign countries.

For example, while many countries recognize the validity of non-disclosure agreements, such an agreement may be set aside if its effect is to unreasonably restrict the employee's right to choose his future occupation[16] Moreover, certain countries provide that an employee's right to seek new employment includes the right to make use of business information learned during the course of his prior employment.

Duration of Trade Secret Protection

While trade secret protection can be extended indefinitely in the United States, many countries explicitly limit the period of time which a recipient of trade secret information can be required to maintain the secrecy of the information. For example, in Brazil, non-disclosure obligations cannot extend beyond five years after the delivery of the confidential information to the party to which the obligation is applicable. Restrictions on the duration of confidentiality agreements are generally imposed in the context of governmental review of technology transfer agreements. While a patent holder may be allowed to restrict the ability of a licensee to use the patent beyond the term of the license, assuming that the patent itself has not yet expired, a number of countries require that technical information be completely transferred to the local party by the end of the term of the agreement.

Rights Against Third Parties

In the United States, trade secret owners have a right of action against third parties who benefit from the breach or other circumvention of a confidentiality agreement. However, a number of countries do not permit trade secret owners to go after persons who are not in privity of contract with the owner. Therefore, a trade secret owner has no remedy against a third party that acquires the secret without authority or induces another to breach an agreement with respect to confidentiality of the trade secret.

Local Business Practices and Regulatory Policies

Local business practices and regulatory policies can have a significant impact on the potential for wide diffusion of trade secret information. For example, in those economies where corporate networking exists, such as in many parts of Asia, it is common practice for members of the same corporate family to share competitive information in a manner that would clearly violate antitrust restrictions in the United States. Also, in developing countries, government policies may tend to favor the distribution of technical information throughout the local business community rather than permitting a few firms to enjoy a material technical advantage.

Enforceability

Trade secret protection can arise as a matter of statute or pursuant to contractual provisions. However, the manner in which these restrictions will be enforced will vary around the work. For example, a number of countries have been criticized by United States trade officials over the years for inadequate civil and criminal penalties, the lack of injunctive relief, unreasonably slow, underfunded or inexperienced enforcement procedures and political corruption and anti-foreign bias within the enforcement agencies. In particular, problems with respect to trade secret protection have been noted not only among developing countries, but also with a number of the major trading partners of the United States, including Brazil, Mexico, Korea, India, Taiwan, and Japan.[17]

IV. TRADEMARKS

A common misconception of young businesses is that protection of their trade names and trademarks or servicemarks in the United States through use and registration automatically reserves the right to use those trade names and trademarks in other countries. Many businesses likewise assume that as they grow in the United States their rights to use the mark in foreign countries should they ever wish to do so becomes stronger. In fact the opposite is true. Use and registration of names and marks in the United States do not reserve the names or marks for use outside the United States. The more successful and better known a mark becomes in the United States, the more likely it is to be pirated or imitated unless the successful business takes the necessary steps to protect itself.

The surest way to protect marks is to register them in as many foreign countries as is affordable. Registration is the surest method because it is the only method of creating rights that are readily discoverable by anyone who is interested in the availability of a mark and rights that are easily and surely provable evidence of rights. Almost every country in the world has a system for registering trademarks. The system begins with an application and ends with a certificate of registration which lasts a term of years (usually ten) and is renewable. The certificate of registration shows the mark protected and lists the goods or services for which the registrant has registered that particular mark.

Each country's registration usually covers only that country. There is one unified register that covers three countries (Benelux). There is planned in the European Economic Community a unified register. There are also some systems which streamline the process of obtaining registrations in several countries by allowing a central filing which extends to several designated countries such as The "International Registration" system provided by The Madrid Convention. However, obtaining registrations in each individual country by filing separate applications in each country is still the predominant means of protecting marks throughout the world.

Despite the territorial nature of registrations, there is much uniformity in the process from one country to the next. Almost all countries have a trademark law pursuant to which registration can be obtained. These laws describe the kinds of words or designs which qualify for registration and those which do not. The laws also describe how conflicts are resolved if unrelated parties desire to register similar marks. These laws also describe the conditions under which registrations once obtained can be maintained. Finally, most trademark laws describe under what circumstances one party can seek to prevent the use of a similar mark by another party.

The main purpose of trademark laws is to protect the public from confusion and to insure that marks that are so similar that they are likely to create confusion are not used by unrelated companies. A secondary purpose is to keep anyone from unfairly appropriating words that everyone should be free to use. These words include generic terms, highly descriptive terms that all need to describe goods and services, and surnames which the laws in many countries do not consider to function as trademarks until perhaps the public has come to recognize them as such because of their long usage as marks for certain products.

The registration system established by most trademark laws is designed to prevent two companies from registering the same or very similar mark for the same goods or services. This is accomplished first by a system of priority. The date an application is filed becomes the priority date of the applicant. As between applications filed for the same mark for the same or similar goods, the first to file wins. Applications are in most countries reviewed by trademark office personnel for compliance with the standards set by law and for conflict with existing registrations. In many countries, any interested party has an opportunity to do their own examination by reading official gazettes where applications filed or already approved by the examiner or registered have been published. For a short time after publication, any interested party may oppose an application or seek to cancel a registration if it has in their opinion been improperly accepted or granted. Opposition terms usually last a month or two. Cancellation periods usually last from two to five years before action is barred.

Many thousands of applications are filed in every country each year because it is the safest method of protecting a trademark. Registrations last ten to twenty years once issued in most countries. There is no penalty for leaving a mark on the register until renewal and some expense in expressly abandoning it. As a result there is a lot of "deadwood" on the registers worldwide. There are means of removing this deadwood. Renewal requirements and fees are one method. Use requirements are another. In many countries marks which have not been used for a period of three to five years after registration can be removed by interested parties. Generally, the registrant bears the burden of proving use once the interested party files a petition for cancellation on the ground of non-use.

There is a general trend in trademark laws throughout the world to toughen user requirements to ensure that only those marks in regular commercial use can stay on the register indefinitely. Some countries have use affidavits due periodically at time prior to the regular renewal date to force a registrant to show evidence of continued use. Other countries require evidence of use on renewal. Others require no showing of use but allow cancellation for non-use by interested parties. The biggest step recently taken to encourage use is the amendment of laws in certain countries which remove the burden on the petitioner to prove non-use.

As can be seen the company interested in selling products and services in foreign countries using the valuable marks has to worry about early filing, monitoring the registers for similar marks, keeping evidence of use in foreign markets, and meeting renewal deadlines. But before reaching the problems of maintaining marks, a company has to secure its rights in the international marketplace. Doing so is difficult if the mark was not selected initially with a view to its ease of protection in the international marketplace.

How should a United States company select a mark for international business? First, a mark should be selected that avoids the common pitfalls that exist in all countries. Surnames, alphanumeric marks, descriptive and generic terms should be avoided. The best marks are invented words or words and devices that do not depict the actual goods or services or describe their geographic origin. KODAK is often given as an example. We all know of registered trademarks that fall into one of these categories and of strong marks that have become generic. The United States trademark examination is only of average strictness when it comes to enforcing the prohibitions on the registration of certain kinds of marks. It also recognizes that long exclusive use of a mark can strengthen its chances of registrability.

Once an appropriate mark is selected for use, it should be searched internationally to see if there is any obvious obstacle to registration in the form of another company's previously registered rights. A business that is not operating in foreign markets or is just beginning to do so may not be in a very good position to know just from its own knowledge of the competitive environment whether a mark is taken. Astute companies register marks they propose to use not just what they are already using. Use prior to filing is not a requirement for filing an application in most foreign countries.

The only sure way of knowing whether a mark is available in a particular country at any one time is to do a search. There are methods developed by search companies to inexpensively search the world by regions for marks which have been registered or published. This type of search, although it does not disclose unpublished applications, costs less than $1,000 for 200 countries and should disclose any well established mark. Full searches of pending applications and registration can be done on a country-by-country basis for an average of about $300-$400 per country. These searches disclose all the previously mentioned "deadwood" and a thorough search can require that investigations be done to determine if problem registrations can be cleared off with cancellation actions. If there are the same or similar marks registered and in force (not vulnerable to cancellation) in another country, use of a business' mark in that country may give rise to a cause of action for infringement whereby a business can be prevented from using its marks in that country. To gauge these risks, a business must often obtain legal opinions from several countries regarding whether the marks and the goods or services are similar enough to meet the test of infringement.

A U.S. business that adopts and builds up goodwill in the U.S. without regard to availability or protection of its marks abroad is a hostage to fortune. An investment of $3,000 can usually secure a registration in a foreign country. Resolution of a problem either in the nature of an infringement action, a purchase of blocking rights, or a cancellation action can cost several if not many times that.

A U.S. business' trademark rights are vulnerable as long as no action is taken to register the mark in foreign markets. may become vulnerable in other ways. U.S. trademarks are often known far beyond their borders because of the internationality of media. Nothing except a prior application in a foreign country by the U.S. business prevents a foreigner from filing an application to register that mark. Most foreign countries require no proof of use prior to filing. Some areas of the world have citizens known for registering the marks of foreign businesses with a view to selling them back to the true owner.

A U.S. business is often particularly vulnerable when it is first thinking of doing business in a foreign country. Typically it begins interviewing potential distributors or licensees. These potential distributors or licensees sometimes take advantage of the "first to file" system and file an application to register the mark. The motive may be to protect the owner from his own failure to file, but the effect is to give the potential distributor or licensee a significant bargaining chip in negotiations.

Certain doctrines have been developed or are developing in an effort to deal with the potential abuses in the first to file system. Bad faith filings by potential distributors or licensees can sometimes be expunged. If a mark is truly "well-known" throughout a good portion of the world, prior filings of others can be canceled on that basis. Ownership of existing registrations in a number of countries is almost a requirement for showing that a mark is "well-known."

Despite the importance of registering marks in foreign markets, few businesses just establishing themselves in the international arena can afford to register their marks in the nearly two hundred countries with trademark systems. The costs of registering can mount quickly.

The effect of the breakup of the Soviet Union and other ethnic conflicts throughout the world has been to create new countries, each with a separate trademark system. The effect of trade pressures on the Far East has been to secure amendments in the laws of several Far Eastern countries such as Japan and The People's Republic of China to recognize servicemarks. As a result, there are now more countries than ever in which a U.S. business may have to register its marks to insure protection.

Besides the cost of coordinating trademark protection through in-house or outside counsel familiar with the business as a whole and the protection needs and strategies, there is the cost of local counsel which is always required, government filing fees and costs for technical requirements such as legalization, drawings, and prints.

A business going international needs to develop some means for deciding where to file applications. The following are key determining factors:

(1)   What are the anticipated markets over the next five years?

(2)   What are the countries where potential licensees or distributors are likely to be located and what are their anticipated markets?

(3)   Are the goods susceptible to counterfeiting so that countries with histories in this regard should be covered even though these countries are not in the first tier of marketing?

(4)   Do the marks suffer from inherent weaknesses that justify a decision to defer filing in some countries where negotiation will be difficult before there has been a history of use?

(5)   Where are significant foreign competitors who may wish to simulate the mark located?

Protection of trademarks is a continuing effort, but basic protection can be accurately budgeted. An emerging business just entering the marketplace may wish to set an annual budget and consult trademark counsel on a year-by-year basis to determine what needs to be accomplished in the coming year. Projects can be terminated or marks abandoned with minimal expense if plans change quickly.

The good news for U.S. businesses is that the United States may soon alter its international treaty arrangements to allow U.S. businesses to take advantage of the central filing system of The Madrid Convention. This change should enable U.S. businesses to file applications in a number of European countries at somewhat lower cost than previously.

Notes

[1] The material on international trademark protection was prepared solely by Ms. Bertagnoli. The material on international patent, copyright and trade secret protection was prepared solely by Mr. Gutterman.

[2] The discussion in this chapter assumes that the reader is familiar with the basic concepts of domestic intellectual property law in each of the substantive areas. Readers are also advised to consult the chapters relating to technology transfer arrangements and foreign regulations relating to inbound technology transfers.

[3] The Paris Convention has been supplemented in some respects by the Patent Cooperation Treaty. The latest revisions of the Paris Convention appear at 21 U.S.T. 1629, 24 U.S.T. 2140, 828 U.N.T.S. 305. Several "regional" conventions have been created to facilitate filing procedures in multiple countries. For example, the Convention on the Grant of European Patents permits an inventor to obtain a bundle of national patents for European countries designated in the application after filing with, and review by, a central European Patent Office. An application under this procedure is published 18 months from the priority date. Patents issued under this procedure remain subject to rights established under the national laws and courts of each of the nations mentioned in the application.

[4] In other cases, the government may, in the "public interest," issue a new patent which infringes upon some of the claims of an existing patent.

[5] As opposed to the United States, where patent rights do not vest until the patent is granted, patent rights will generally vest upon publication in Japan. However, the rights will not be enforceable against third parties until the patent is granted.

[6] Importation of the patented goods may not be sufficient to satisfy the working requirements in some countries. In such cases, the patent holder must attempt to locate a local partner to manufacture the goods, which may not be practical in light of the local resources.

[7] Compulsory licensing and "working" requirements are not confined to developing countries. Such provisions exist in Japan, Canada and portions of Western Europe.

[8] Under some laws, no infringement action may be brought against persons who, in good faith, may have begun to produce or sell a patented article prior to the date that the patent application is published.

[9] For example, Great Britain has a substantial volume of common law dealing with proprietary business information (see Wise, 2 *Trade Secrets and Know-How Throughout the World* (1981)) and the law generally has been followed in other parts of the British Commonwealth, such as in Australia (see Wise, 1 *Trade Secrets and Know-How Throughout the World* § 301 (1981)).

[10] The Paris Union and the General Convention for Trade Marks Commercial Protection of Washington (1929) do contain some general language regarding protection of unfair competition by member states; however, neither multilateral agreement address trade secrets as they are currently conceived or provide for any specific protections of proprietary information.

[11] For example, in many Asian countries, employees do not expect to transfer to their employers ownership of inventions and new technical information which the employees might create during the term of their employment. Accordingly, assignment of inventions and non-disclosure agreements are rarely used in those countries.

[12] Countries which regulate the content of international technology transfer agreements will often object to clauses which unduly restrict the ability of the local recipient to use and disclose technical information acquired as part of the transaction. See fuller discussion below.

[13] For example, Brazil and Mexico both have provisions in their laws which specifically recognize the freedom of employees to choose their employment, including the right to use techniques and information learned while employed by another.

[14] *See* generally A. Wise, *Trade Secrets and Know-How Throughout the World* (1981).

[15] For example, Brazil permits prosecution of employees who disclose commercial information without authorization after the term of employment; however, no similar remedy is available for employee disclosures of technological information, such as manufacturing techniques. With respect to the various practices in developing nations relating to the definition of know-how, see Correa, *Legal Nature and Contractual Conditions in Know-How Transactions*, 11 Ga. J. Int'l & Comp. L. 449 (1981).

[16] In Japan, for example, see on this issue the case of *Yugen Kaisha Foreseco Japan, Ltd. v. Okuno and*

Diamatsu (Decision of the Nava District Court, October 23, 1970, 624 Hanre; Jiho 78) (employee non-competition clause which unreasonably restricted the employee's right to choose his occupation was against "public order and good morals" and therefore null and void).

[17] As part of its efforts to enhance international intellectual property protection during the Uruguay Round of the General Agreement on Tariffs and Trade ("GATT"), the United States intended make proposals with respect to *(i)* development of adequate standards for the protection of trade secrets, *(ii)* development of broader internal enforcement mechanisms, and *(iii)* provisions for use of GATT dispute resolution measures to ensure adoption and enforcement of the standard developed by GATT member countries. *See, e.g.,* Gutterman, *The North-South Debate Regarding the Protection of Intellectual Property Rights,* 28 Wake Forest L. Rev. 89, 108–111 (1993). The United States, through the office of the United States Trade Representative, has also initiated a variety of unilateral and bilateral initiatives in this area. *Ibid.,* 111–118.

ANTITRUST CONSIDERATIONS: THE TYPICAL CASE OF THE EUROPEAN MARKET

Patrick Thieffry

AMONG THE PRIMARY considerations of emerging companies seeking to enter foreign markets are those involving antitrust provisions. This is particularly true for businesses which consider entering the single European market,[1] the economic zone consolidated by 1986 legislation which seeks to eliminate any remaining barriers to the complete economic integration of the countries comprising the European Community.[2] The competition policy of the EC lies at the very heart of its objectives, as it is designed to eliminate practices which interfere with the integration of the separate economies of the Member States into a single European market.

EC competition regulations should be the primary focus of any U.S. business going international as, except in the United States, there is no other such advanced provisions. By conforming their practices with both U.S. and EC laws, businesses can ensure that specific adjustements required by any given country of the world, if any, would be only minimal. This will be even more true as EC antitrust laws will also apply in the newly created European Economic Area ("EEA") which includes the 12 EC Member States, and six countries of the European Free Trade Association: Austria, Finland, Iceland, Liechtenstein Norway and Sweden[3]. The EC's primary antitrust provisions are contained in Articles 85[4] and 86[5] of the Treaty of Rome.

Article 85(1) prohibits all agreements, decisions, or concerted practices that may prevent, restrict, or distort competition within the common market and which affect trade between member states. Article 85(2) automatically renders void any such agreement, decision or concerted practice.

Article 85(3) provides exemptions from the prohibition contained in Article 85(1). Exemptions may apply[6] where the conduct in question contributes to improving the production and distribution of goods or to the promotion of technical or economical progress. In order for an exemption to be granted, however, consumers must be allowed a fair share of the resulting benefits. In addition, the restrictions imposed must be indispensable to achieving those objectives and not eliminate competition in a substantial part of the EC.

Article 86 prohibits activities that constitute an abuse of a dominant position by one or more businesses where such conduct affects trade between Member States. Article 86 is therefore designed for the control of monopoly power. Apart from the substantive differences between Articles 85 and 86, the latter does not offer the possibility of seeking an exemption from its application.

Although Articles 85 and 86 are not without certain similarities with Sections 1 and 2 of the United States' Sherman Act, the policies underlying EC competition law involve social, political, and market integration considerations that differ considerably from those underlying U.S. antitrust law policy.[7]

I. AGREEMENTS IN RESTRAINT OF TRADE

The first step in assessing a transaction with regard to Article 85 is the determination of whether an agreement (or a decision or concerted practice), is of such magnitude as to trigger Article 85 application.

In its Notice of December 3, 1986 on so-called "Agreements of Minor Importance"[8] the Commission stated that it would not challenge agreements providing for the distribution of goods, provision of services, and certain cooperative efforts if *(i)* the goods or services of the participating companies do not represent more than 5 percent of the total market value of such goods or services in the area of the affected market, and *(ii)* the aggregate annual sales of the participating firms do not exceed 200 million ECU.[9]

The Commission has also issued similar notices within which it has set forth the terms and conditions under which it considers that the following other types of agreements would be exempt from the purview of Article 85 (1):

- exclusive sales agency agreements[10];
- agreements for cooperation between small and medium size enterprises[11]; and
- sub-contracting agreements.[12]

Where an agreement (i) falls within the scope of Article 85 (1), *(ii)* is of such size as to render it beyond the previously described "de minimis" exception, and *(iii)* does not fit within any of the other notices, the next inquiry is whether it is such as to benefit from an exemption pursuant to Article 85(3). As stated in that provision, the prohibition "may be declared inapplicable" to certain practices. There are two kinds of such exemptions: by way of the so-called "block exemption regulations" or by way of individual decision[13] granted by the Commission upon the parties' application in the form of a notification. When notifying an agreement, the parties may request the grant of an individual exemption. They may also ask the Commission, in the alternative, to issue a so-called "negative clearance" that is to say, to rule that the agreement does not meet the conditions for being prohibited.

Block exemptions, on the other hand, do not require any notification or other formal action.

Block Exemptions

Prior to considering the notification procedure, those seeking negative clearance or an exemption should examine whether or not the agreement, decision, or practice which they seek to implement fits within one of the EC's block exemption regulations. Agreements falling squarely within the regulations benefit from exemption without any need for notification or formal decision by the Commission.[14]

The EC's block exemption regulations were developed in response to the Commission's experience with certain categories of agreements which generally meet the four conditions specified in Article 85 (3). In other words, these are agreements, decisions, or practices which are deemed, as a general rule, to (1) improve the production or distribution of goods or to promote technical or economic progress, (2) allow consumers a fair share of the resulting benefit, (3) impose on the parties only those restrictions which are indispensable to the attainment of these objectives and (4) prevent such undertakings from eliminating competition with respect to a substantial part of the relevant market.[15]

Block exemption regulations set forth the clauses or restrictions that may (so-called "white list") and may not ("black list") appear in agreements in order for them to be granted exemption. Currently existing block exemption regulations apply to exclusive distribution agreements[16], exclusive purchasing agreements[17], specialization agreements[18], patent licensing agreements[19], motor vehicle distribution and servicing agreements[20], research and development agreements[21], franchise agreements[22], and know-how licensing agreements.[23]

The scope of some of these block exemption regulations has recently been extended to cover certain types of cooperative joint ventures.[24]

Exclusive Distribution (Regulation No. 1983/83)

The regulation concerning exclusive distribution agreements applies to "agreements to which two undertakings are parties whereby one party agrees with the other to supply certain goods for resale in the whole or a defined area of the Common Market only to that other".[25] The only other obligation that may be imposed on the supplier is to refrain from supplying the contract goods to users in the contract territory.[26]

Pursuant to this regulation, the exemption will apply even though the following restraints may be imposed on an exclusive distributor: (1) to refrain from manufacturing or distributing goods which compete with the contract goods; (2) to obtain the contract goods for resale only from the other party; and (3) to refrain from promoting the contract goods, seeking customers, or establishing any branch and/or distribution depot outside of the contract territory—i.e., "systematically prospect" in other areas.[27]

Distributors must remain free to set their own prices and sales conditions, and may not be constrained as to their choice of customers.[28] Additionally, manufacturers' warranties must be honored throughout the Community.

A reciprocal exclusive distribution agreement between competitors will not benefit from the block exemption, while a non-reciprocal distribution agreement will, provided at least one of the parties has a total annual turnover below 100,000,000 ECU.[29] Other agreements excluded from the scope of the block exemption include exclusive distribution agreements in markets where users are unable to obtain the contract goods from alternative sources, even outside the contract territory, and agreements to which the parties render it difficult for intermediaries or users to obtain contract goods from other dealers inside the common market, including through the exercise of industrial property rights.[30]

Exclusive Purchasing (Regulation No. 1984/83)

The exclusive purchasing agreement block exemption applies where the reseller agrees with the supplier "to purchase certain goods specified in the agreement for resale only from the supplier or from a connected business or from another source which the supplier has entrusted with the sale of its goods".[31]

This exemption applies only to agreements whose duration do not exceed five years.[32] In addition, no more than two firms must be involved.

The principal difference with exclusive distribution agreements is that the reseller is not provided with any exclusive distribution area. Similar to the exclusive distribution agreement block exemption, the exclusive purchasing agreement block exemption is not applicable to reciprocal exclusive purchasing agreements between manufacturers of identical or equivalent goods or to non-reciprocal exclusive purchasing agreements between manufacturers of such goods, unless one of them has a total annual turnover of no more 100,000,000 ECU.[33] This regulation also contains specific provisions applicable to petroleum and beer supply agreements.

Motor Vehicle Distribution and Servicing (Regulation No. 123/85)

The motor vehicle distribution agreement block exemption applies to agreements whereby one party agrees within a defined territory of the Common Market to supply products only to the other party and to specified third parties within a distribution system for the purposes of reselling certain motor vehicles.[34] The exemption will apply where suppliers undertake to refrain from selling goods or providing services for goods to final consumers in the dealer territory.[35]

It also permits contractual provisions that restrict dealers from manufacturing or selling vehicles or spare parts that compete with the contract goods, as well as maintaining branches or seeking customers beyond the contract territory.[36]

The Commission has recently published a Notice relating to intermediaries who purchase vehicles for the account of a principal,[37] a quite widely developed practice in the EC as a result of price differences between the Member States. The Notice sets forth the circumstances in which a manufacturer or distributor may properly refuse to sell to such intermediaries. Here again, the Commission's goal is to stimulate to the greatest extent possible "parallel imports"—what is called "grey market" in the US—between the EC Member States.

Specialization (Regulation No. 417/85)

Pursuant to this regulation, an exemption is provided for agreements whereby one party agrees not to manufacture certain products (or to have them manufactured), while the other party is charged with manufacturing the products or having them manufactured. The parties may also agree to manufacture the products jointly.[38]

Agreements falling under this block exemption may allow for exclusive distribution rights, may restrict the parties from entering into specialization agreements with third parties relating to similar products, and may allow for exclusive procurement arrangements involving the other contracting party or a joint venture for the manufacture of the product.

This exemption applies to companies which do not account for more than 20 percent of the market for such products in the Common Market or a substantial part thereof, and which have total annual sales not in excess of 1,000,000,000 ECU. Where the distribution of the products concerned is carried on by one of the contracting parties, a joint venture, or a commonly designated third party, the above market share limit is 10 percent.

Article 4 of the specialization agreement block exemption provides for an opposition procedure whereby undertakings exceeding the size limits provided by the regulation may notify their agreements to the Commission and thereby benefit from the exemption if not opposed by the Commission within a period of six (6) months after notification. In practice, however, the use of this procedure remains exceptional.

Research and Development (Regulation No. 2821/71)

Pursuant to this block exemption regulation, an exemption is available for agreements entered into between two firms for the purpose of joint research and development of products or processes and joint exploitation of the results of that research and development.

This block exemption does not apply where the parties are competing manufacturers and their combined market share of the products "capable of being improved or replaced by the contract" exceeds 20 percent in the common market or a substantial part thereof.[39] If the distribution of the products concerned is carried on by one of the contracting parties, a joint venture, or a commonly designated third party, the above market share limit amount is 10 percent.

Article 4 of the regulation allows for provisions which restrict research in related areas, agreements with third parties, purchases from non-parties, manufacturing contract products, and/or selling in territories reserved for the parties and sales in reserved territories for a period of five years.[40] Article 4 further permits restrictions relating to the exclusive grant of distribution rights to one of the parties, to a joint venture, or to a third party. Minimum quantity and quality provisions may also be included, along with confidentiality agreements and royalty distributions.[41]

Restrictions on independent research and development with third parties in connected fields, restrictions on challenging the validity of intellectual property that the parties hold in the Common Market, as well as restrictions relating to price, quantity, and customers are not permitted by this block exemption.

The previously described opposition procedure is available for the research and development block exemption as to all provisions not provided for in the regulation.

Know-How Licensing Block (Regulation No. 556/89)

This block exemption applies to: (1) agreements for the licensing of know-how; (2) mixed agreements involving know-how and patent licensing; and (3) pure or mixed agreements containing "ancillary provisions relating to trademarks and other intellectual property rights where there are no provisions restricting competition other than those also attached to know-how and exempted by the regulation."[42]

Article 2 of the know-how licensing block exemption lists the permitted restrictions, for example, (1) territorial protection against systematic prospecting between licensor and licensees, (2) imposed quality standards, (3) reciprocal and non-exclusive grant-back, (4) obligations to pay royalties after know-how has become public knowledge, (5) post-term use bans, (6) exclusive use of licensor's trademarks, (7) non-assignment clauses, and (8) secrecy clauses.[43] A maximum duration of 10 years is permitted for restrictions on actual sales and manufacturing, and five years for passive sales.[44]

The opposition procedure is also available under the know-how licensing block exemption.

Patent Licensing (Regulation No. 2349/84)

This block exemption covers agreements for the assignment, acquisition, licensing, and sub-licensing of patents.

Article 2 of the regulation identifies obligations that are not restrictive and are therefore exempt; however, they do not require notification. These include mandatory procurement with the licensor, minimum royalty and quantity provisions, non-assignment clauses, non-disclosure clauses, and restrictions on the use of the patent during and after expiration of the agreement.[45]

Also permitted by the block exemption are prohibitions on the licensor during the lifetime of the patent from (1) granting licenses to others in the licensed territory, and (2) from exploiting the licensed invention in the licensed territory.[46] As long as the licensed patent remains in force, licensees may be obliged (1) to not exploit the licensed invention in territories reserved for the licensor, (2) to not manufacture or use the licensed product or use patented processes or communicate know-how in territories within the EC to other licensees, (3) to not engage in systematic prospecting specifically aimed at territories of parallel licensees, and even (4) to not market the product in territories licensed to other licensees within the EC for a period not exceeding five years from the date when it was first put on the market within the EC.[47]

Provisions that automatically bar the agreement from exemption include clauses prohibiting licensees from challenging the validity of the patent, clauses automatically extending the duration of the licensing agreement beyond the life of the patent, non-competition clauses that go further than the restraints described above, provisions requiring the payment of royalties on non-patented products, and customer and price restrictions.[48]

The regulation provides for an opposition procedure whereby agreements not falling within the requirements of the block exemption may nonetheless be notified to the Commission and are treated as exempt unless the Commission opposes the exemption within six months.[49]

Franchising (Regulation No. 4087/88)

Franchise agreements are exempted pursuant to this regulation where a franchisor agrees to restrain from exploiting its own franchise, marketing the goods or services which are the subject matter of the franchise, supplying the goods to third parties, or granting the right to exploit all or part of the franchise to third parties.[50]

A master franchisee may be prohibited from concluding franchise agreements with third parties outside its contract territory.[51]

Additionally, a franchisee may be restricted from (1) exploiting the franchise beyond the contract premises, (2) seeking customers outside the contract territory for the goods or services which are the subject matter of the franchise, and (3) manufacturing, selling, or using goods that compete with the franchisor's goods in the course of the providing services.[52]

The regulation does not apply where competitors enter into franchising agreements, in the case of provisions that prevent franchisees from continuing to use licensed know-how after the termination of the agreement although it has become public, price fixing provisions, clauses which prohibit the franchisees from challenging the validity of the industrial or intellectual rights of the franchisor, or provisions which bar franchisees from supplying goods or services within the EC to end purchasers based solely on the latters' places of residence.[53]

As with several other block exemptions, the previously described opposition procedure is available to parties seeking exemption in cases where certain provisions are not expressly barred or prohibited by the regulation.[54]

Negative Clearances and Individual Exemptions

When an agreement, decision, or concerted practice falls within the scope of Article 85 (1) but does not meet the requirements of any of the above discussed block exemption regulations, the parties may seek an individual exemption from the Commission.

Exemption from the application of Article 85 (1) is issued by virtue of a Commission decision in which conditions or obligations may be attached so as to conform a transaction to the Community's competition provisions.[55] Exemptions are issued for specified periods, usually for 10 to 15-year renewable periods.[56] Exemptions take effect when they are notified to the parties.[57] Regulation 17 provides a detailed notification procedure whereby parties can apply for such an exemption.[58]

For the purposes of seeking an exemption under Article 85 (3) or negative clearance from Article 85 (1) or Article 86, notification must be made on a single form referred to as "Form A/B"[59] together with all relevant information requested by the form. In general, both negative clearance and an exemption are requested alternatively.

There are no time limits within which to notify, yet it is suggested that notification be made before agreements are executed—failure to notify will subject the agreement to penalties and voidability as well as injunctive relief.

Any and all parties to an agreement, decision, or concerted practice have the right to notify it to the Commission; those parties that do submit applications have a duty to inform all other parties to the agreement.[60] The notification must be submitted, along with thirteen (13) copies, to the Directorate General for Competition (D.G. IV) of the Commission. It must provide the full name and address of the party as well as a brief description of the firms involved in the transaction, a definition of the purpose of the submission, and a formal declaration as to the correctness of the information submitted.[61]

The A/B Form requires that notifying parties provide detailed information as to the arrangements for which they seek negative clearance or an exemption as well as the market structure and the parties involved. Additionally, parties are to state the reasons why they should be issued negative clearance or exemption. The form also provides a "catch-all" section where the parties may present additional information and arguments justifying the notified transaction.

It must be emphasized that only those parties who notify agreements may obtain an Article 85(3) individual exemption. The other principal benefit of notifying an agreement to the Commission is that the Commission is barred from imposing fines for acts having taken place after notification.[62] It should be noted, however, that application for a negative clearance does not confer immunity from fines. The primary benefit of seeking negative clearance of a transaction is that exemption from Article 85 (3) may be requested in the alternative.[63]

II. MONOPOLIZATION ("ABUSE OF DOMINANT POSITION")

Generally speaking, emerging companies seeking to enter the European market should not be overly concerned as to whether their activities will trigger the non-exemptible prohibitions contained in Article 86 of the Treaty against abuses of a dominant position. Due to their generally smaller size, it is unlikely that they will hold a "dominant position" in a substantial part of the EC. Notwithstanding this fact, however, the applicability of this provision should not be entirely discounted as even a company of a smaller size can be deemed to hold a dominant position. Indeed, such a situation is likely to arise in the case of an emerging company, if it introduces a new product which is deemed to have no substitutes.

A Dominant Position on the Relevant Market

In determining whether a particular transaction falls within the scope of Article 86, the Commission first decides whether there exists a "dominant position" in the EC or a substantial part thereof, and then whether an abuse of that dominant position has occurred.[64] As Article 86 does not define what is meant by a "dominant position" EC case law has stated that it is present where an entity can conduct its business while disregarding its competitors, suppliers, or customers.[65] Although the size of an entity plays a large role in making this determination, the test is one of market control in a substantial part of the EC. Therefore, the Commission considers not only the percentage of the relevant market that an enterprise may control, but also the relative strength of its competitors as well as their respective access to know-how, raw materials, and capital. Barriers to entry are also factors.

An emerging company could fall within the scope of Article 86 when it introduces a product onto the market for which there exists no significant alternatives.[66] In Chemio Terapico, the Commission ruled that an American chemical manufacturer which had introduced a new chemical product within the EC market did hold such a dominant position, notwithstanding the fact that some alternative products existed.

A dominant position may also be found to exist in limited markets, such as markets for replacement parts. In one case, the Commission sanctioned a cash register manufacturer for its refusal to sell spare parts for its goods to independent repair companies, and as such, deemed the relevant market to consist of the spare parts of a named manufacturer.[67] At least one U.S. manufacturer was subjected to the Commission's narrow market definition when the Commission stated that IBM's products constitute a relevant market in and of themselves. As such, the Commission challenged IBM's refusal to supply competitors with technical information that would allow them to manufacture compatible and competitive equipment. Despite the absence of a formal ruling against IBM, the Commission's stance suggests that Article 86 may be employed against a company which exercises a dominant position over its own products.[68]

An Abuse

If a firm holds a dominant position in a substantial part of the EC, it is prohibited from abusing therefrom. Specific instances of abuses include: (1) imposing unfair buying or selling prices or other trading commissions; (2) limiting markets, production, or technical development to the prejudice of consumers; (3) imposing tying arrangements, or (4) discriminating in commercial transactions that would lead to a competitive disadvantage over trading partners.

Perhaps of greater relevance is the fact that Article 86 may be used by emerging companies against established entities that have acted to hinder market access due to their abuse of a dominant position.[69] Companies may, for example, challenge dominant entities that refuse to supply a product,[70] that engage in predatory pricing,[71] and that are party to illegal tying arrangements.[72]

An example is the recent case of Tetra Pak. Tetra Pak was subjected to the largest fine ever imposed by the EC. Commission for a violation of EC antitrust rules, 75 million ECU. By exploiting its virtually monopolistic position on the liquid foodstuff packaging market, Tetra Pak, according to the Commission, committed a number of abuses contrary to Article 86, the most notable of which was the purchase of a competitor with the intention of appropriating competing technologies.[73]

III. MERGER CONTROL

Originally, the Commission was of the belief that the EC Treaty provisions on competition should not apply to mergers. As a consequence, Article 86 was applied only once to a merger.[74] In 1984, however, Article 85 was applied to the acquisition by one company of the shares of a competitor. The Court of Justice of the European Communities upheld the decision, ruling that such an acquisition might serve as a means of influencing the competitive behavior of the companies involved.[75]

Mergers with a "Community Dimension"

In light of the limited use of existing EC antitrust provisions against the growing merger and acquisition activity within the EC, the Council of the European Communities unanimously adopted on December 21, 1989, a merger control regulation[76], pursuant to which the Commission was granted the exclusive power to oppose or modify large scale mergers[77] likely to affect the EC market.

In a nutshell, the Commission will not approve mergers that create or reinforce a dominant position.

The application of the merger control regulation is triggered by a combined turnover threshold of at least five billion ECU, and an aggregate Community-wide turnover of at least two of the parties that exceeds 250 million ECU. In its current form, therefore, the EC merger control regulation will not be of much significance to companies emerging in the EC market. It must be noted, however, that these turnover thresholds may be revised by the Council of Ministers on the proposal of the Commission.

Where transactions fall within the scope of the merger control regulation, parties are required to notify within one week of the signing thereof. These agreements include the acquisition of controlling interests, certain joint ventures, and the announcement of takeover bids.[78] The Commission is given one month to notify the parties as to whether it will review the transaction. Upon deciding to do so, the Commission is granted an additional four (4) month period in which to clear or oppose the transaction.[79]

To date, only a handful of cases have required such "second stage proceedings"[80] and only one merger has been prohibited by the Commission.[81]

Mergers without a "Community Dimension"

In addition, the merger control regulation provides a procedure whereby Member State authorities may ask the Commission to investigate mergers involving businesses whose turnovers do not meet the thresholds, provided, however, that such mergers are likely to create or strengthen a dominant position within the Member States' markets.[82] By virtue of this provision, therefore, emerging companies penetrating the European market in Member States that do not have national merger control or that would rather have the EC. Commission examine a transaction may find certain transactions subject to the EC merger control.

Because the merger control regulation will not be applied to transactions of smaller dimensions, emerging companies seeking to operate within the EC by way of merger, acquisition, or certain joint venture arrangements may find such agreements subject to the operation of Articles 85 and 86. While the merger control regulation provides that Regulation 17 (the implementing regulation of Articles 85 and 86) shall not apply to operations deemed to constitute a "merger" it remains unclear whether Articles 85 and 86 could nevertheless be applied. The Commission has indicated separately that it would not apply the Community competition rules to mergers where the turnover is less than two billion ECU and where either of the concerned groups has a community-wide turnover of less than 100 million ECU. Thus, if these amounts are met but the five billion ECU and 250 Million ECU thresholds of the merger control regulation are not, the Commission could apply Articles 85 and 86, albeit through an ad hoc procedure not provided for by Regulation 17.

Even in the event that the Commission does not apply Articles 85 and 86 to mergers, these provisions nevertheless remain in force as far as they grant causes of action to Member State authorities and private rights of action to persons or entities. Similarly, in cases where the Commission chooses to exercise its control over mergers, it remains unclear whether national authorities would be prohibited from allowing individuals to exercise their rights granted under Articles 85 and 86. An example would be where competitors of one of the parties to a merger or minority shareholders of take-over targets seek to void a concentration based on private rights of action granted by Articles 85 and 86.

IV. ENFORCEMENT

The extraterritorial effect of the EC's competition provisions have been upheld by the European Court of Justice.[83] Even non-EC companies whose business practices have but a nominal effect in the EC may fall subject to the scrutiny of EC antitrust authorities for practices "affecting" the common market.

Despite the grant of supremacy treatment to EC competition rules, EC competition law exists in tandem with the domestic antitrust laws of the greater part of the EC member states. Due to this coexistence, Member States' antitrust authorities are generally not prohibited from proceeding under their respective national laws against parties where there is no violation of Article 85(1) or Article 86.[84] When it has been determined by the Commission that Article 85 or 86 of the Treaty has been violated, EC law prevails over conflicting national laws, but national antitrust authorities are not prohibited from imposing additional penalties pursuant to domestic laws.[85]

Member States' courts have jurisdiction to enforce Articles 85 and 86 by virtue of the direct effect of these provisions. Two different circumstances can arise. In cases where Member State authorities seek enforcement of Articles 85 and 86 through national courts, they are divested of such power if the Commission initiates proceedings. On the other hand, where national courts entertain suits by private parties invoking the direct applicability of Articles 85 and 86, the subsequent initiation of proceedings by the Commission imposes no obligation upon the national Courts to stay their proceedings pending the outcome before the EC institutions.[86]

Where a transaction meets the criteria of Article 85 (1), it will be subject to prohibition by the EC Commission or by Member State courts. By way of example, agreements to fix prices,[87] to impose export bans,[88] or to share markets[89] would be prohibited. The Commission has reacted on several occasions against American companies whose restrictive export practices in the Community have resulted in market division.[90]

Important strategic considerations will result from various opportunities given to businesses with respect to both the enforcement of the prohibition and the possibilities for exemption. There are many ways of enforcing Article 85, e.g. at the initiative of interested third parties directly affected by such practices. This right could be exercised by individuals excluded from distribution systems[91], distributors bound by export bans[92], traders unable to import due to export bans[93], licensees subject to overly restrictive provisions in licensing agreements[94], traders unable to penetrate markets where customers are tied to other suppliers[95], and even dealers subject to abusive discount structures[96].

Not only do prohibited practices subject the parties to attack by Member States' authorities, Community institutions, and interested third parties, parties to the actual agreements may also utilize Article 85 to challenge suspect practices. Given that such agreements or certain provisions contained within them may not be enforced and, since competition rules are capable of conferring direct rights on individuals, there is no need for a party to seek a decision from EC authorities in order to void violative provisions of an agreement, notwithstanding the fact that the contesting party has agreed to them.[97]

As for public enforcement, the Commission, by decision, may require a firm or firms to terminate infringement of EC competition rules. It is also empowered, by decision, to impose fines on businesses that "intentionally or negligently infringe Article 85 (1) or Article 86 of the Treaty".[98] These fines may range from 1,000 to 1,000,000 ECU or 10 percent of the turnover of the firms concerned, whichever is greater. Of particular importance to emerging companies is the fact that the Commission often takes into account the market share of infringing enterprises when determining the amount and duration of its fines.[99]

The Commission may also impose periodic penalty payments in the range of 50 to 1,000 ECU per day in order to terminate an infringement of articles 85 or 86.[100] The Commission will typically calculate the time between the issuance of a decision ordering the parties to take a specific action and the time when their non-compliance ends in order to determine the amount of the penalty.

It should also be noted that, beyond the mere imposition of fines and periodic penalty payments, case law has afforded the Commission the power to take interim measures that are "indispensable for the effective exercise of its functions"[101]. The Commission has in certain cases ordered parties to take specific measures to terminate infringing behavior, such as the granting of a license or the resumption of supplies.[102]

The Commission is granted broad fact finding powers, and as such may obtain information from companies by simple requests which are followed, if necessary, by decisions ordering parties to supply requested information.[103] Additionally, the Commission on its own account or through local authorities may make on-the-spot investigations and enter any premises so as to examine business records and interrogate concerned parties. During Commission investigations undertaken to determine whether an exemption should be granted, the Commission is empowered to request from the parties additional information and may by decision compel parties to produce information by way of fines.[104]

V. CONCLUSION

American companies seeking to penetrate the European market must familiarize themselves with the requirements of the EC's competition law. As outlined above, it is in many instances more cumbersome than U.S. procedure. In light of the differences in the policies that distinguish the EC's competition rules from their U.S. counterparts, these requirements must be considered when preparing transactions with EC companies or organizing activities for the EC market.

Parties who overlook these provisions could subject exemptible or permissible transactions to unnecessary delays and fines. Unlike the merger control regulation, the notification procedure provided by Regulation 17, for example, imposes no deadline for Commission action, and transactions may therefore be delayed prior to clearance or prohibition.[105] Oftentimes, however, the Commission will not make a formal decision on certain transactions, issuing instead informal, non-binding "comfort letters" that offer parties limited legal certainty, but do not require the entire procedure to be completed.

While the EC Treaty provides that recourse may be had to the Tribunal of First Instance to review the legality of acts of the Commission on grounds of lack of competence, infringement of an essential procedural right, infringement of the Treaty, infringement of any rule of law relating to Treaty application, or misuse of powers,[106] the threat of being subjected to a costly and time-consuming Commission investigation remains one of the most troublesome aspects of the EC's competition policy. In the case of a *notification*, however, this must be taken as the price to be paid for more safety than in the U.S., where no such general prior review of transactions exists.

Notes

[1] Completing the Internal Market, White Paper from the Commission to the European Council, COM(85) 310, at 4; Single European Act, Feb. 17, 1986, 29 O.J. EUR. COMM. (No. L 169) 1 (1987).

[2] Treaty Establishing the European Economic Community, Mar. 25, 1957, 298 U.N.T.S. 11. The 12 members of the EC are Belgium, Denmark, France, Ireland, Italy, Federal Republic of Germany, Greece, Luxembourg, The Netherlands, Portugal, Spain, and the United Kingdom. The EC relies for its operation on a number of institutional bodies: (1) the European Commission, which proposes and implements Community legislation; (2) the Council of Ministers, the Community's legislative branch; (3) the European Parliament, which enjoys budgetary and advisory rights; and (4) the European Court of Justice, which is empowered to interpret and enforce Community legislation against member states.

While the European Union Treaty, also known as the Treaty of Maastricht, has amended the 1957 Treaty, e.g., by changing its name to "Treaty instituting the European Community" so that it will be referred to hereafter as the "EC Treaty," the provisions on competition have not been altered.

[3] A watchdog authority has been created to monitor compliance by the EEA states (see 1992 Annual Commission Report on Competition Policy, at pg. 67).

[4] Article 85 of the EC Treaty provides :

1. The following shall be prohibited as incompatible with the Common Market: all agreements between undertakings, decisions by association of undertakings and concerted practices which may affect trade between member states and which have as their object or effect the prevention, restriction or distortion of competition within the Common Market, and in particular those which: (a) directly or indirectly fix purchase or selling prices or any other trading conditions; (b) limit or control production, markets, technical development or investment; (c) share markets or sources of supply; (d) apply dissimilar conditions to equivalent transactions with other trading parties, thereby placing them at a competitive disadvantage; (e) make the conclusion of contracts subject to acceptance by other parties of supplementary obligations which, by their nature or according to commercial usage, have no connection with the subject of such contracts.

2. Any agreements or decisions prohibited pursuant to this Article shall be automatically void.

3. The provision of paragraph 1 may, however, be declared inapplicable in the case of;

any agreement or category of agreements between undertakings;

any decision or category of decisions by associations of undertakings;

any concerted practice or category of concerted parties;

which contributes to improving the production and distribution of goods or to promoting technical or economic progress, while allowing consumers a fair share of the resulting benefit and which does not:

(a) impose on the undertakings concerned restrictions which are not indispensable to the attainment of these objectives;

(b) afford such undertakings the possibility of eliminating competition in respect of a substantial part of the products in question.

[5] Article 86 of the EC Treaty provides:

Any abuse by one or more undertakings of a dominant position within the common market or in a substantial part of it shall be prohibited as incompatible with the common market in so far as it may affect trade between member states.

Such abuse may, in particular, consist in:

(a) directly or indirectly imposing unfair purchase or selling prices or other trading conditions;

(b) limiting production, markets or technical development to the prejudice of consumers;

(c) applying dissimilar conditions to equivalent transactions with other trading parties, thereby placing them at a competitive disadvantage;

(d) making the conclusion of contracts subject to acceptance by the other parties of supplementary obligations which, by their nature or according to commercial usage, have no connection with the subject of such contracts.

[6] Council Regulation No. 17/62 of February 6, 1962, implementing Articles 85 and 86 of the Treaty, 5 O.J. EUR. COMM. (No. L 13) 24 (1962) (hereinafter, "Regulation No. 17").

[7] Patrick Thieffry, *L'Appréhension Des Systèmes de Distribution en Droit Américain et en Droit Européen de la Concurrence, Revue Trimestrielle de Droit Européen, Vol. 21, No. 4 (1985)*

[8] Commission Notice of December 3, 1986, on Agreements of Minor Importance, O.J. EUR. COMM. (No. C 231) 2 (1986) replacing Commission Notice of December 19, 1977, O.J. EUR. COMM. (No. C 31) 3 (1977), which in turn replaced the Commission Notice of May 27, 1970, O.J. EUR. COMM. (No. C 64) 1 (1970). A "notice" issued by an institution of the European Community is not binding on national courts or the European Court of Justice. Notices are designed for guidance purposes only, and the European Commission is not estopped from proceeding in spite of its terms. There is authority which suggests, however, that parties who fail to notify agreements when relying upon a notice should not be subject to fines. See Bellamy and Child, *Common Market Law of Competition* (3rd Edition) (1987), p.125.

[9] As of November 8, 1993, 1 European Currency Unit ("ECU") equaled 1.1367 U.S. dollars. When considering the turnover of the firms involved, EC law includes all companies belonging to the group.

[10] Notice on Exclusive Agency Contracts Made with Commercial Agents, O.J. EUR COMM. (No. C 2921) 62 (1962). This Notice is currently under revision by the Commission's Antitrust Division ("DG IV").

[11] Notice Concerning Agreements, Decisions, and Concerted Practices in the Field of Cooperation between Enterprises, O.J. EUR. COMM. (No. C 75) 3 (1968).

[12] Notice of 18 December 1978 Concerning the Commission's Assessment of Certain Sub-Contracting Agreements in Relation to Article 85 (1) of the EEC Treaty, O.J. EUR. COMM. (No. C 1) 2 (1979).

[13] Regulation No. 17, art. 9 (1) gives the Commission the power to grant such decisions under Article 85 (3).

[14] *SA Cadillon v. Firma Hoss, Maschinenbau KG,* no. 1 /71, E. Comm. Ct. J. 351 (1971). *See also* Kerse, pg. 14 and pp. 68–69. Certain block exemption regulations, however, such as those pertaining to patent licenses, know-how licenses, franchising agreements, and research and development and specialization agreements provide for a notification procedure commonly referred to as the "opposition procedure" pursuant to which certain provisions of notified agreements which are neither expressly permitted nor condemned by the regulation will be granted exemption. In such cases, however, the Commission retains the power to oppose the exemption within a period of six (6) months from the time the agreement is notified.

[15] EEC Treaty, art. 85 (3).

[16] Regulation No. 1983/83 on the Application of Article 85 (3) of the Treaty, to Certain Categories of Exclusive Distribution Agreements, O.J. EUR. COMM. (No. L 173) 1 (1983) as amended by O.J. EUR. COMM. (No. L 281) 24 (1983) [hereinafter Exclusive Distribution Agreement Block Exemption].

[17] Regulation No. 1984/83 on the Application of Article 85(3) of the Treaty to certain categories of Exclusive Purchasing agreements, O.J. EUR. COMM. (No. L, 173) 5 (1983) as amended by O.J. EUR. COMM. (No. L 281) 24 (1983) (hereinafter Exclusive Purchasing Agreement Block Exemption).

[18] Regulation No. 417/85 on the Application of Article 85 (3) of the Treaty, to Certain Categories of Specialization Agreements, O.J. EUR. COMM., (No. L 53) 1 (1985) [hereinafter Specialization Agreement Block Exemption]; as amended by Regulation No. 151/93, O.J. EUR. COMM. (No. L 21) 8 (1993).[19]

Regulation No. 2349/84, on the Application of Article 85 (3) to Certain Categories of Patent Licensing Agreements, O.J. EUR. COMM. (No. L 219) 15 (1984) [hereinafter Patent Licensing Block Exemption]. as amended by Regulation No. 151/93, O.J. EUR. COMM. (No. L 21) 8 (1993).

[20] Regulation No. 123/85 on the Application of Article 85 (3) of the Treaty to Certain Categories of Motor Vehicle Distribution and Servicing Agreements, O.J. EUR. COMM. (No. L 15) 16 (1985) [hereinafter Motor Vehicle and Servicing Agreement Block Exemption].

[21] Regulation No. 418/85 on the Application of Article 85 (3) of the Treaty to Certain Categories of Research and Development Agreements, O.J. EUR. COMM. (No. L 53) 5 (1985) [hereinafter Research and Development Block Exemption]; as amended by Regulation 151/93, O.J. EUR. COMM. (No. L 21) 8 (1993).

[22] Regulation No. 4087/88 on the Application of Article 85 (3) of the Treaty, to Certain Categories of Franchise Agreements, O.J. EUR. COMM. (No. L 359) 46 (1988) [hereinafter Franchise Agreement Block Exemption].

[23] Regulation No. 556/89 on the Application of Article 85 (3) of the Treaty to Certain Categories of Know-how Licensing Agreements, O.J. EUR. COMM. (No. L 61) 1 (1989) {hereinafter Know-how Licensing Agreement Block exemption]; as amended by Regulation No. 151/93 (No. L 21) 8 (1993).

[24] Regulation No. 151/193, O.J. EUR. COMM. (No. L 21) 8 (1993), and Commission Notice Relating to Cooperative Joint Ventures, O.J. EUR. COMM. (No. C 43) 2 (1993).

[25] Exclusive Distribution Agreement Block Exemption, art. 1. Note that the concept of undertaking is used in the EC law as a substitute for firm or business and should generally be understood to encompass all companies included in a group, i.e. within a single controlling power.

[26] *Id.* art. 2 (1).

[27] *Id.* art. 2 (2).

[28] Exclusive Distribution Agreement Block Exemption, 8th Recital.

[29] *Id.* art. 3 (a)(b).

[30] *Id.* art. 3 (c)(d).

[31] Exclusive Purchasing Agreements Block Exemption, art. 1.

[32] *Id.* art. 3 (d).

[33] Exclusive Purchasing Agreement Block Exemption, art. 3.

[34] Moor Vehicle Distribution Servicing Agreement Block Exemption, art. 1.

[35] *Id.* art. 2.

[36] *Id.* art. 3.

[37] O.J. EUR. COMM. (No. C 329) 20 (1991).

[38] Specialization Agreements Block Exemption, art. 1.

[39] *Id.* art. 3 (2).

[40] *Id.* art. 4.41

[41] *Id.* art. 5.

[42] Know-How Block Exemption, "Second whereas clause and art. 5. Regarding mixed agreements involving trademarks and know-how licensing, parties should beware that agreements that are primarily trademark licensing agreements will be denied the benefits of this block exemption regulation." Moosehead/Whitehead, O.J. EUR. COMM. (No. L 100) 32 (1990).

[43] *Id.* art. 2.

[44] *Id.* art. 1 (2).

[45] Patent Licensing Block Exemption, art. 2.

[46] *Id.* art. 1 (1); 1 (2).

[47] *Id.* art. 1 (3)—(7).

[48] *Id.* art. 3.

[49] *Id.* art. 4.

[50] Franchise Agreement Block Exemption, art. 2.

[51] *Id.* art. 2 (b).

[52] *Id.*

[53] *Id.* art. 5.

[54] *Id.* art. 6.

[55] *Id.* art. 8.

[56] *Id.* art. 8

[57] EC Treaty, art. 191.

[58] Regulation No. 17, arts. 4 & 5.

[59] Regulation No. 27, First Regulation Implementing Council Regulation 17 of February 6, 1962, O.J. EUR. COMM. (No. 35) 1118 (1962); as amended by Regulation 2526/85 of August 5, 1985, O.J. EUR. COMM. (No. L 240) 11 (1985).

[60] *Id.* art. 1 (1).

[61] Form A/B, Comm. Mkt Rep. (CCH) ¶ 2659.

[62] Regulation 17, art. 15 (5).

[63] *Id.* art. 4 (1).

[64] EEC Treaty, art. 86.

[65] *United Brands v. Commission,* no. 27/76, 1978 E. Comm. Ct. J. 207 (1978).

[66] *Instituto Chemio Terapico Italiano S.P.A. and Commercial Solvents v. Commission,* no. 7/73, 1974 Eur. Comm. Ct. J. 223 (1974).

[67] *Hugin v. Commission,* no. 22/79, 1979 E. Comm. Ct. J. 1869 (1979).

[68] 1985 Annual Commission Report on Competition Policy, pp. 94–95. While it would be unfair for emerging companies to compare their operations and products to those of IBM, it should be noted that the Commission's interpretation of Article 86's scope has been increasing in recent years and as such, emerging companies should not discount its potential application to their operations.

[69] For an interesting decision, see *Société MORS vs. Société LABINAL* Paris Court of Appeals, 1st Chamber, Section A, May 19, 1993, International Arbitration Report, July, 1993, Vol. 8, #7, Doc. #05–930726–104.

[70] Commercial Solvents v. Commission no. 6 & 7/73, 1974 E. Comm.Ct. J. 223 (1973).

[71] Ecs/Akzo, O.J. EUR. COMM. (No. L 374) 1 (1986); United Brands, O.J. EUR. COMM. (No. L 95) 1 (1976).

[72] Vaessen/Morris, O.J. EUR. COMM. (No. L 19) 82 (1979).

[73] Tetra Pak (first decision), O.J. EUR. COMM. (No. L 272) 27 (1988); Tetra Pak (second decision), O.J. EUR. COMM. (No. L 72) 1 (1992).

[74] *Europemballage Corp. and Continental Inc. v. Commission,* No. 6/172, 1973 E. Comm. Ct. J. 215 (1973).

[75] *British American Tobacco Co., Ltd. and R.J. Reynolds Industries., I. Inc. v. Commission* (Joined Cases) nos. 142 and 156/84, E. Comm. Ct. J. 4487 (1987).

[76] Council Regulation No. 4064/89 on the Control of Concentrations between Undertakings, O.J. EUR. COMM. (No. L 395) 1 (1989); as amended by O.J. EUR. COMM. (No. L 257) 13 (1990) [hereinafter the "Merger Control Regulation"]. Patrick Thieffry, *The New EC Merger Control Regulation*, 24 Int.'l Law. 543 (1990); Patrick Thieffry, Philip Van Doorn and Peter Nahmias, *Notifying Agreements Under The New EC Merger Control Regulation*, 25 Int'l Law. 615 (Fall, 1991).

[77] The Regulation utilizes the term "concentration," which encompasses not only the straightforward situation where two companies merge, but also where direct or indirect corporate control is acquired through stock or asset purchases, contractual relationships, or other means. *Id.* art. 3.

[78] *Id.* art. 4 (1).

[79] *Id.* art. 10.

[80] Alcatel/Telettra, O.J. EUR. COMM. (No. L 122) 48 (1991); Magnetti Marelli/CEAC, O.J. EUR. COMM. (No. L 222) 38 (1991); Tetra Pak/Alfa Laval, O.J. EUR. COMM. (No. L 290) 35 (1991); Varta/Bosch, O.J. EUR. COMM. (No. L 320) 26 (1991); Aérospatiale-Alenia/de Havilland, O.J. EUR. COMM. (No. L 334) 42 (1991); Accor/Wagon-Lits, O.J. EUR. COMM. (No. L 204) 1 (1992); Nestlé/Perrier, O.J. EUR. COMM. (No. L 356) 1 (1992); Du Pont/ICI, (No. L 7) 13 (1993); Mannesman/Hoesch, O.J. EUR. COMM. (No. L 114) 34 (1993); KNP-BT-VRG, O.J. EUR. COMM. (No. L 217) 35 (1993).

[81] Aerospace-Alenia/De Havilland, O.J. EUR. COMM. (No. L 334) 42 (1991).

[82] *Id.* art. 22 (3).

[83] *Wood Pulp Case* (involving several non-EC companies, including Bowater Inc., the International Pulp Sales Company, and Pulp Paper and Paperboard Export Association from the U.S.A.), No. 89, 104, 114, 116, 117, 125, 126, 127, 128, 129/85, 1988 E. Comm. Ct. J. 5193 (1988).

[84] Procureur de la République v. Giry and Guerlain, S.A., no. 253/78, 1980 E. Comm. Ct. J. 2327 (1980).

[85] Nungesser v. Commission, No. 258/78, 1982 E. Comm. Ct. J. 2015 (1983).

[86] See B.R.T v. S.A.B.A.M., No. 127/73, 1974 E. Comm. Ct. J. 51 (1974); *see also* Kerse, EEC Anti-trust Procedure (2d Ed. 1987), p. 306–307.

[87] ACF Chemiefarm v. Commission, No. 41/69, 1970 E. Comm. Ct. J. 661 (1970).

[88] Consten and Grundig v. Commission, No. 56 and 58/64, 1966 E. Comm. Ct. J. 299 (1966).

[89] Suiker Unie v. Commission, No. 40/73, 1975 E. Comm. Ct. J. 1663 (1975).

[90] John Deere Co., O.J. EUR. COMM. (No. L 35) 1 (1984); Fisher Price Co., O.J. EUR. COMM. (No. L 49) 19 (1988).

[91] Metro v. Commission, No. 26/76, 1977 E. Comm. Ct. J. 1875 (1977).

[92] Distillers Co, Ltd., O.J. EUR. COMM. (No. L 50) 16 (1978).

[93] Camera Care v. Commission, No. 792/79 ,. 1980 E. Comm. Ct. J. 119 (1980).

[94] Breeders' Rights/Roses, O.J. EUR. COMM. (No. L 369) 9 (1985).

[95] Vassen/Morris, O.J. EUR. COMM. (No. L 19) 82 (1979).

[96] Michelin v. Commission, No. 322/81, 1983 E. Comm. Ct. J. 3461 (1985).

[97] See Bellamy & Child, pg. 449.

[98] Regulation No. 17, art. 15 (2) (a).

[99] *See eg.* Siemens/Fanuc, O.J. EUR. COMM. (No. L 376) 29 (1985).

[100] Regulation No. 17, Art. 16 (1). Note, too, that periodic penalty payments may also be imposed in order to compel undertakings to (1) refrain from any act prohibited under Article 8 (3) of Regulation 17 in connection with an exemption from Article 85 (3), (2) to supply complete and correct information requested by a decision of the Commission under Article 11 (5) of Regulation 17, and (3) to submit to an investigation ordered by the Commission under Article 14 (3) of Regulation 17.

[101] *See e.g.*, Camera Care v. Commission, No. 792/79 R, 1980 E. Comm. Ct. J. 119 (1980).

[102] Cfr. Peugeot v Commission, No. T-23/90, E. Comm. Ct. J., II-653 (1991).

[103] Regulation No. 17, art. 11. Recent cases have held, however, that undertakings are under no obligation to incriminate themselves. Orkem v. Commission, No. 374/87, E. Comm. Ct. J. 3283 (1989) and Solvay v. Commission, No. 27/88, E. Comm. Ct. J. 3355 (1989).

[104] Thieffry, Van Doorn, and Arnold, *Les pouvoirs d'enquête de la Commission en droit de la concurrence*, Gazette du Palais, June 8–9, 1990, at pp. 7–11.

[105] DG IV has recently taken steps to expedite the notification procedures, and in particular, those involving cooperative joint ventures.

[106] EC Treaty, art. 173.

SALES AGENCY AND
DISTRIBUTION LAWS

Vincent Mercier
Drake D. McKenney[1]

I. INTRODUCTION

IT IS OFTEN necessary for manufacturers or suppliers wishing to distribute their products or services in a foreign market to resort to the use of foreign intermediaries. One must bear in mind, however, that the negotiation of contracts between parties of different nationalities and cultures can often lead to complex legal problems. It is therefore essential to reflect in the contract an appreciation of the commercial and cultural forces that may affect each party, and be fully familiar with all potentially applicable laws.

Sales agency and distribution contracts often reflect a significant imbalance of power between the respective parties, as the manufacturer or supplier (hereinafter, "principal") frequently enjoys a bargaining advantage vis-à-vis the sales agent or distributor (hereinafter, "intermediary"). Just as a franchisor or manager usually bargains from a position of strength vis-à-vis the franchisee or the employer, the principal is generally in a stronger position than the intermediary.

It is sometimes the case, however, that the principal is in an inferior position. A strong intermediary may be solicited by a principal who seeks to sell a product in a competitive market over which the intermediary exerts a strong grip. Other times, the principal will have provided financial backing to an intermediary, and come to discover that end purchasers are making their buying decisions not upon the basis of product origin or the product itself, but rather upon the intermediary's personal reputation. One cannot ignore these market forces when counseling the respective parties, as they help to explain the existence and purview of distribution laws. It must be emphasized, however, that these distribution laws almost always protect the intermediary, not the principal. As explained below, perhaps the most striking example is the myriad of laws that prevent principals from unilaterally terminating distribution agreements.

It is also important to distinguish the various types of intermediaries. The classic business intermediaries are the "distributor" and the "agent" each unique in its function and often unique in its treatment under the law. In a broad sense, the distributor engages in arbitrage, purchasing from the principal and reselling on a secondary market at a profit. The agent, on the other hand, attempts to secure sales contracts between the principal and down-the-line purchasers, taking a percentage of the sales contract price as a commission.[2] The definition of "agent" under European Community law is representative: in the EC, a "commercial agent" is an independent intermediary who is permanently charged with the sale or purchase of goods for the principal, or with the negotiation and finalization of such transactions in the name and on behalf of the principal.[3]

As for applicable law, distribution agreements involving foreign parties are potentially subject to international law, and most notably, bilateral treaties on taxation. There are a host of proposed or pending international laws that would directly affect these agreements, for example, the proposed Hague Convention Law on Distributors and Agents, the Geneva Convention Law on International Agents, and the Benelux Convention on International Agents. In the European Communities, distribution contracts must be carefully drafted to accord with EC antitrust provisions. For the most part, however, distribution agreements are regulated by national laws.

The determination of which national law will apply in the case of a contract involving parties from two or more jurisdictions will be determined either by the parties through a choice of law clause, or, via the conflict of laws provisions of the concerned states. Most countries look to the site of contract execution for determining choice of law questions where the contract in question involves distribution. Notwithstanding the parties' choice of law, however, a number of countries' agency and distribution laws are mandatory in their application, and may not be avoided through choice of law or choice of jurisdiction provisions in a contract. The inclusion within the contract of an arbitration clause will sometimes avoid this problem.

II. INTERMEDIARIES

Certain National Laws Require Citizenship for Intermediary Status or Impose Restrictions Upon the Distribution of Goods by Foreign Parties.

Depending upon the country, the legal definition of "intermediary" is often quite broad and can include any person other than a salaried employee who is charged with one or more duties in relation to the promotion or distribution of a product. Certain countries, for example, Algeria, prohibit the use of intermediaries as so defined, the result being that their use, either directly or indirectly, during the preparation, negotiation, conclusion, or execution of a sales contract is expressly prohibited.[4]

Certain countries require citizenship of entities wishing to act as intermediaries. One such country is Egypt, whose laws require inscription on a national register of commercial agents and intermediaries.[5] Eligibility for inscription is restricted to the following:

- those who have possessed Egyptian nationality for a minimum of ten years; or
- in the case of a company, those companies which maintain their corporate headquarters in Egypt, and, whose capital is held entirely by Egyptian citizens, each possessing Egyptian citizenship for a minimum of ten years.[6]

A number of other countries have similarly restricted intermediary status to their own citizens and nationals, for example, Honduras, Abu Dhabi, Saudi Arabia, Bahrain, Lebanon, Qatar, and Syria.[7] The United Arab Emirates enacted a sweeping law in 1981 which restricts intermediate status to U.A.I. subjects or companies whose capital is held solely by U.A.I. subjects; the law applies to all activities of distribution, sales, and marketing of products or services for which a fixed commission or benefit is received.[8]

Questions of nationality aside, a number of countries require compliance with a licensure procedure prior to the grant of intermediary status. In Austria, for example, an intermediary must meet educational requirements, spend time as an apprentice, and obtain yet additional professional experience prior to eligibility for licensure.[9] Austria furthermore prohibits the licensure of foreign legal persons (e.g., foreign corporations, partnerships, joint ventures, etc.) as intermediaries.[10]

Different Types of Intermediaries and Protective Statutes

A number of countries have enacted protective statutes for the benefit of intermediaries, statutes that are not unlike labor laws which provide workers with the right to a mandatory indemnity in the event of wrongful termination.

"Intermediaries"

Certain countries provide a broad statutory definition of agent/distributors, the result being the statutory "intermediary". One such country is Lebanon, whose law defines as an "intermediary" any agent or commercial representative who is not bound by a services contract and that, by virtue of its independent and habitual business activities, negotiates and concludes contracts for the purchase, sale, and rental of goods or provision of services on behalf of principals or other business entities.[11] Also included in this category are business entities that purchase goods and services and resell them by virtue of their status as exclusive agents or distributors. Entities functioning as such intermediaries must gain their status by virtue of written contract. Furthermore, such entities may enjoy "exclusive" intermediary status vis-à-vis third parties only where their exclusive status is notified to the appropriate government authority.

The contractual relationship between the principal and intermediary under Lebanese law is deemed to benefit both contracting parties. As a consequence, the unilateral termination of a contract without cause by the principal and without fault of the intermediary grants to the intermediary the right to an indemnity equal to its real damages. The right to an indemnity exists regardless of any contractual provisions to the contrary. Where the representative can prove that it was "manifestly successful" in launching the principal's trademark or increased the number of the principal's customers, and, where the representative will be prevented from benefitting from such success because the principal refuses to renew the contract, the intermediary will be entitled to an indemnity in an amount to be fixed by the courts. This right exists regardless of contractual provisions to the contrary, and even where the relationship is terminated because the contract period has expired.

The Lebanese protective statutes carry severe penalties for principals who fail to comply with their provisions. Any entity challenged under the protective statutes or against whom a judgment has been rendered will have its name published on a list at the Economic and Commercial Ministry. Most importantly, any entity that has failed to satisfy a judgment rendered against it may not be represented in Lebanon. Similar protections exist in other Middle Eastern countries, most notably, in Abu Dhabi, Saudi Arabia, and Kuwait.[12]

"Agent" Representatives: The European Community's Directive on
"Commercial Agents"

In certain countries, the "agent" is defined as a representative who is remunerated by commission and who is not deemed to be economically autonomous of the principal. Its status is not wholly unlike that of a salaried agent who benefits from protective labor laws, and as a result, these countries have developed protective statutes geared toward such agents.

Still other countries have legislation affecting independent agents. In Europe, for example, the drive toward harmonization of the EC member states' economies has necessitated a uniform law on the treatment of "commercial agents". This law took the form of a European Council directive[13] which defines "commercial agent" as an independent intermediary who is permanently charged with the sale or purchase of goods for the principal, or with the negotiation and finalization of such transactions in the name and on behalf of the principal.[14]

Certain parties are prohibited from acting as commercial agents as that term is defined by the Directive, specifically, members of partnerships, liquidators, receivers, and trustees in bankruptcy.[15] By its terms, the Directive does not apply to non-remunerated commercial agents, agents active on commercial or commodity exchanges, and United Kingdom "Crown Agents."[16]

As for the remuneration of such agents where there is no agreement between the principal and agent for commissions, the agent is to be remunerated at a level commensurate with the custom or practice in the agent's territory and industry.[17] In the absence of custom, remuneration must be "reasonable" in light of all relevant factors.[18] Furthermore, the Directive defines a "commission" as any remuneration which varies in accordance with the quantity of goods ordered and number of accounts generated by the agent.[19] Finally, EC member states remain free to regulate the remuneration of agents notwithstanding the terms of the Directive.[20]

The Directive contains a number of provisions that regulate the termination of agency contracts. Contracts for a specific term which continue to be performed by both parties after the expiration of that term are automatically renewed for an indefinite term.[21] Where the contract is for an indefinite term, the Directive clearly provides that either party may terminate the relationship unilaterally.[22] Such termination, however, is not effective absent the provision of proper notification to the non-terminating party.[23] A one month advance notice is required prior to termination of an agency contract that is in its first year, two months notice for an agreement in its second year, and three months for agreements in their third year. These periods may not be shortened by agreement of the parties.[24] Member states are free to mandate similar notice periods for the fourth, fifth, sixth, and following years of the agreement, and they are free to prohibit derogation by the parties from such notice periods.[25] Where the parties decide to set longer notification periods, the period must be equal for both principal and agent.[26] The notification periods mandated by the Directive are without affect upon member state laws that provide for termination upon the failure of a party to fulfill all or part of its contractual obligations, or, for termination in the event of "exceptional circumstances".[27]

The EC Directive mandates the payment of an indemnity to the agent upon termination of the agreement. Specifically, the directive provides member states with a choice between requiring the payment of an indemnity to the agent, or, requiring compensation of the agent for the damages it suffers as a result of termination.[28]

An agent has the right to an indemnity where it has obtained new clients for the principal or expanded sales with the principal's existing clientele, and the principal continues to derive the benefits of this business.[29] The amount of the indemnity is to be calculated in light of all relevant circumstances, including the value of commissions that the agent would be expected to lose from those clients.[30] The amount of the indemnity may be no more than the agent's average annual commission over the preceding five years, or, if the agency was for less than five years, no more than the agent's average annual commission over the period of the agency.[31] Importantly, a member state's choice of the indemnification remedy does not deprive the intermediary of its right to separately seek damages.[32]

A member state may choose instead the straight damages remedy. Such payment is due where termination of the contract has deprived the agent of commissions that it would have received but for the termination of the contract, and where the principal has received substantial benefits from the agent's activities.[33] Damages are also recoverable where the agent has not yet amortized the costs it incurred in performing the contract as requested by the principal.[34]

In the case of either indemnification or damages, the agent must submit its claim to the principal within one year of the termination of the contract.[35] The right to these remedies also exists upon the death of the agent.[36]

Payment of an indemnity or damages is not always due upon termination. Such is the case, for example, where the principal has terminated the contract in response to non-performance of the agent that is grounds for immediate termination pursuant to the law of a member state.[37] No indemnity or damages are due where the agent terminates the contract, unless such termination was attributable to the behavior of the principal, or, to the age, infirmity, or poor health of the agent whereby the agent could not be expected to perform in accordance with the contract.[38] Finally, no indemnification or damages are due where the agent, with the permission of the principal, assigns its rights and obligations under the contract to a third party.[39]

The provisions with respect to the payment of an indemnification or damages are mandatory, and may not be waived by agreement of the parties.[40]

Although subordinate to member state laws that regulate non-competition agreements, the EC Directive also provides that agency agreements may include a limited non-competition clause. Specifically, a non-competition clause will be deemed valid where it is in writing, is in effect for no more than two years after termination of the contract, and it restricts the agent's performance to the geographic territory where the agent performed pursuant to the agency agreement, or, restricts the agent's performance as to clients, goods, and geographic territories granted to the agent by the contract.[41]

EC member states are required to modify their respective national laws to comport with the terms of the EC Directive.[42] At the present, most EC member states have complied with this obligation. The United Kingdom and Ireland are not required to implement the directive until January 1, 1994, while Belgium and Luxembourg have failed to act as required. In a step perhaps designed to ease their potential entry into the European Community, three non-EC member states, Norway, Sweden, and Finland, have enacted legislation that mirrors the essential terms of the Directive.

Of equal importance to the requirement imposed upon member states to harmonize their laws with the EC Directive is the fact that the Directive will apply to all agreements in effect in the Community on or after January 1, 1994, regardless of whether such agreements were entered into prior to that date.[43]

Additional Protective Statutes In EC Member States

It is important to understand the state of the law in the various members states in the wake of the EC Directive. Prior to the Directive, certain EC member states had protective statutes or bodies of case law that affected commercial agency agreements within their respective national territories. Of course, these pre-Directive laws have now been harmonized or are slated to be harmonized with the EC Directive. In addition to the commercial agency situation, however, many member states also have laws that affect certain non-commercial agent distribution agreements. As their name suggests, these laws have been enacted to protect local distributors, and in some cases can be quite strict. These statutes can be likened to legislation protecting franchisees in American states which often impose heavy obligations on the franchisor.

Belgium

One of the most restrictive distribution laws is found in Belgium. It broadly defines a distribution agreement to be any agreement in which the principal grants to one or more distributors the right to sell, in the principal's name and on its behalf, products made or distributed by the principal.[44]

The following distributorship arrangements are subject to the law's purview (Article 1, ¶ 1):

• exclusive distributorships;

• quasi-exclusive distributorships pursuant to which the intermediary sells in the territory almost all of the products to which the distributorship applies; and

• agreements under which the principal imposes upon the intermediary heavy obligations in direct relation to the distributorship in case of termination of the agreement by the principal.

Proving exclusivity may be accomplished in several different ways. An distributor may be considered "exclusive" if the distributor is the only one authorized to sell the goods covered by the agreement in its sector of activity.[45] Also, exclusivity can be proven by the fact that the distributor was in fact the sole seller of the goods for an uninterrupted period of time.[46]

Upon termination of the contract, Belgian law provides the distributor with a series of remedies. Where the principal fails to supply reasonable notice of the decision to terminate, an indemnity must be paid to the distributor. Another scenario permits the principal who terminates the choice of paying an indemnity in lieu of providing notice. Where the principal has provided the distributor with "reasonable notice" of termination, then it is not liable for the payment of an indemnity. However, regardless of whether an indemnity is due as described in the previous instances or where reasonable notice has in fact been given, Belgian law provides that in all cases, payment of a "fair indemnity" is due where the distribution agreement is terminated by a principal for reasons other than "serious fault" of the distributor.

At the moment of conclusion of an agreement, both parties must agree to a notice period. If they fail to do so, the Belgian courts may intervene to determine a reasonable period. The Commercial Court of Brussels identified the criteria which are to be evaluated in determining the notice period:

- the duration of the distribution agreement;
- the extent of the exclusive territory;
- the difficulty for the distributor of finding a new and comparable distributorship;
- the net profit of the distributorship;
- the amount of advertising provided by the distributor;
- the reputation of the products; and
- the impact of termination on the distributor's overall business.[47]

If a principal fails to provide notice, the payment of an indemnity is obligatory. On the other hand, a party may choose to pay an indemnity in lieu of providing a reasonable notice period. Three factors are used in determining the amount:

- the net profit which the distributor could have obtained during the notice period and which was not realized due to the termination;
- the fixed costs of the distributor resulting from the distribution agreement; and
- the upward or downward trend of the gross sales of the distributor.

The courts have also considered that any inventory of products which have become obsolete and which would otherwise have been sold by the distributor during the notice period should be calculated into the total indemnity.

Finally, Article 3 of the Belgian law provides that the distributor may claim the payment of a fair indemnity where a distribution agreement is terminated by a principal for reasons other than serious fault on the part of the distributor. This indemnity is payable even where a reasonable notice period has been granted, and should be stipulated in the contract. The courts have considered the following criteria in determining this amount:

- whether there was an appreciable increase in clientele obtained by the distributor and which will accrue to the principal after termination of the agreement;
- the expenses incurred by the distributor in operating its distributorship and which will benefit the principal after termination of the contract; and
- the amount of compensation owed by the distributor to personnel which he must dismiss due to the termination of the distribution agreement.

This indemnity may be added to the other indemnity, the indemnity in lieu of notice. If the parties fail to agree upon the amount of this fair indemnity, the Belgian courts will settle the matter according to principles of equity.

Article 4, Paragraph 1, of the law provides that an distributor who has a claim for wrongful termination of a distribution agreement effecting all or part of Belgian territory can bring the principal before the Belgian courts. In such instances, Belgian courts have generally found in the favor of the distributor.[48]

There are several circumstances in which a contract concluded for a specific term will be automatically renewed for an indefinite term. One such circumstance is where the contract has been renewed three times; in such a case, renewal occurs regardless of whether the contract contains a clause governing tacit renewal and regardless of whether the original contract terms have been modified by the parties. An agreement will also be rendered indefinite in duration where the parties continue to execute the contract after the contract's expiration.

As for commercial agency agreements, Belgium is presently in violation of its duty to conform its national laws to the EC Directive on commercial agency.

Denmark

Danish law does not limit the ability of the parties to include a provision specifying the date of termination of the distribution agreement. However, if the parties do not arrive at an agreement concerning the termination date, the Danish courts have ruled that a principal is not free to terminate a distribution contract without first according reasonable notice to the distributor.

In determining the length of the notice period, the courts will take into account all of the circumstances surrounding the distribution arrangement. In particular, they will consider the duration of the relationship between the parties, and, whether the distributor performed its obligations in a satisfactory manner.

The Danish courts have suggested that compensation may be due a distributor for loss of goodwill in the case of termination of a distribution agreement. The circumstances where this remedy would be available, however, appear very limited. Specifically, the Danish Supreme Court ruled that compensation for loss of goodwill is generally unavailable for intermediaries upon termination by a principal under Danish law. However, where an distributor can prove that there has been no reasonable commercial basis for termination and where it can show that it has performed in good faith (for example, by investing in marketing), it may be appropriate for a court to grant compensation for loss of goodwill.[49]

As for agency agreements in Denmark, the EC Directive has been integrated into that country's national laws.[50] The remedy chosen for agents in the event of contract termination is the payment of an indemnity to the terminated agent. This law applies to all contracts in effect in Denmark on or after January 1, 1992.[51]

England

There is no protective statute for intermediaries under English law, and normal principles of contract law govern such relationships. It follows that there is no provision which would interfere with the parties' inclusion of a termination clause in their agreement for exclusive distribution.

Where the parties have not entered into a written agreement, the English courts attempt to determine the actual agreement of the parties regarding termination. Generally speaking, and with respect to either written or oral contracts, the English courts will infer that the parties intended termination to follow a period of reasonable notice.

Should the principal decide to terminate the contract upon notice which is considered to be unreasonably short, the distributor will have an action in breach of contract and be entitled to damages representing the loss sustained during the reasonable notice period.

England has yet to implement the EC Directive on commercial agents, having been granted a grace period that does not require harmonization until January 1, 1994.

France

French law does not afford special protection to distributors, and parties to a distribution agreement may include a clause which provides for the conditions of termination of the contract and which specifically denies payment of any indemnity upon termination. However, French case law frequently imposes, in accordance with industry custom, a duty upon the principal to provide reasonable notice of termination to the distributor.

French law does require principals to disclose certain information to commercial agents prior to signature of a distribution agreement.[52] The law is applicable to the case where a company allows a distributor to use its name, trademark, or logo, and requires that the distributor act exclusively or quasi-exclusively. Where such disclosure is required, the principal must state how long it has been in business and the nature of its business, as well disclose whether it is party to similar agency agreements. It must additionally provide the commercial agent with prospective information on the market in question. Finally, it must furnish a draft contract that specifies its duration, conditions for renewal, and conditions for its termination and assignment, as well as the scope of its exclusivity. Failure to supply the required document may be sanctioned by the imposition of fines.[53]

France has adopted the EC Directive applicable to commercial agency agreements.[54] The Directive will henceforth be applicable to all commercial agency agreements in effect in France on or after January 1, 1994.[55] As the commercial agent was the beneficiary of extensive protections in France under French law prior to the Community Directive, harmonization in accordance with the Directive has not materially affected the stature of commercial agents operating in France. For example, the fact that France chose the "damages" remedy for terminated commercial agents in accordance with Article 17, ¶3 of the Directive will likely not alter such party's pre-Directive right to damages in an amount equal to two times its average annual commission. One additional advantage of the new legal regime is that the agent is no longer required to register its "agent" status with government authorities in order to qualify for the right to an indemnity.

Germany

Generally, a German distributor does not benefit from any particular statutory provision protecting it against termination by a principal. A principal and a distributor are therefore free to determine the conditions of termination. However, where the parties have not provided for a notice period prior to the termination of the relationship, the German courts usually apply (reasoning by analogy) statutory provisions which protect sales representatives or agents from the immediate termination of their respective agreements.

To determine whether or not the rules on agency agreements are applicable to a given distribution agreement for purposes of the payment of an indemnity, it is necessary to analyze whether the economic situation of the distributor is similar to that of a sales representative or agent under Section 89b of the German Commercial Code (HGB). The German courts will evaluate four factors:

- the extent to which the distributor is incorporated into the distribution organization of the principal;
- the obligation of the distributor to report sales activities on a regular basis to the principal;
- the freedom of the distributor to enter into agreements with other principals; and
- whether the distributor has a contractual obligation to transmit to the principal, either during the life of the agreement or after its termination, the names of its customers.

There is some indication that the mere fact that the principal is aware of the names of the customers of the distributor will suffice to impose upon the principal the duty to indemnify its distributor upon termination.

If it is found that the distributor does benefit from German laws applicable to agents, then the following rules for notice periods as found in the HGB provide that:

- during the first year of the agreement, a one month notice period is required;

- during the second year of the agreement, a two month notice period is required;
- during the period from the third up to and including the fifth year of validity of the agreement, a three month notice period is required; and
- after five years, the notice period will increase to six months.

Any such notice must be given through the end of the calendar month.

Germany has implemented the EC Directive on commercial agency agreements into its national law.[56] Implementation of the Directive in Germany was relatively painless, as its provisions do not materially alter the rights of agents as they existed under German law prior to the Directive. In fact, the "indemnification" remedy of the EC Directive was based upon Article 89b of the German Commercial Code, the latter remaining unchanged by enactment of the Directive. Article 89b provides that commercial agents will have the right to receive an indemnity where the following criteria are fulfilled:

- the principal profits in a considerable fashion, even after termination of the contractual relationship, from sales made to customers which the agent had acquired;
- the agent loses potential commissions which it would have had under the contract had the distributorship relationship continued due to sales already concluded, or which are about to be concluded with customers it has acquired; and
- the payment of compensation is required by the principles of equity when taking all relevant circumstances into consideration.

The amount of the indemnity is typically fixed at an amount equal to one year of the agent's annual commission.

Greece

The Greek Civil Code provides that the parties to a distribution contract have the right to terminate their distributorship at any time and without obligation to pay damages to the distributor. This general rule, however, may not apply if the principal fails to give reasonable written notice and if the distributor or any third party suffers damages therefrom. In such a case, the parties may have a claim for damages.

Greece has implemented the EC Directive on commercial agents via presidential decree,[57] and opted for the "indemnification" remedy (Article 17, ¶2) for terminated agents.

Ireland

Irish law does not provide any statutory or other protection to the intermediary which would interfere with the rights of parties to a distribution agreement to provide for the termination of the agreement or for its non-renewal. The Irish courts would be called upon to resolve any disputes.

Like England, Ireland is not required to implement the EC Directive on commercial agents until January 1, 1994.

Italy

Italian law does not prevent parties from including a termination clause in a distribution contract. Where the duration of the agreement has not been set forth in the contract, either party may terminate the agreement if notice is given in accordance with industry custom, or, if this is unknown, within a time that is reasonable in view of the nature of the contract. The notice period cannot be replaced by the payment of an indemnity, and any party that terminates a contract without giving reasonable notice is subject to the payment of damages.

The Community's commercial agency Directive has been implemented in Italy via legislative decree.[58] Italy has adopted the "indemnification" remedy for terminated agents,[59] but not without material changes. Specifically, the right to indemnification exists where the agent has *either* increased the volume of business for the principal, *or*, where payment of an indemnity would be equitable in light of all the circumstances.[60] The indemnification remedy as adopted by the other EC member states requires that both of these elements be present.

Luxembourg

Luxembourg case law allows parties to a distribution agreement to provide for termination at any time upon giving proper prior notice.

Luxembourg is presently in violation of its duty to implement the EC Directive on commercial agency.

The Netherlands

No specific legislation exists regarding distribution agreements in the Netherlands, and as a consequence, the propriety of terminating a distribution agreement would be decided based upon Dutch case law and general principles of contract law.

Dutch law would permit early termination only in cases of serious breach of contract or in the case of unforeseen circumstances that are of such a nature that a party cannot reasonably be expected to continue the contractual relationship.

The Netherlands have implemented the Community Directive on commercial agents,[61] and it will be applicable to all commercial agency agreements existing on or after January 1, 1994. As for remedies in the event of termination, the Netherlands chose the "indemnification" remedy, Art. 17, ¶2.

There is one unique aspect of Dutch commercial agency law which bears examination. Where the agent represents only one principal on the Dutch market and employs no more than two persons, the agent is considered a salaried employee of the principal. It is very costly for the principal to terminate such agreements, and in certain circumstances, the agent has the right to claim a minimum salary.

Portugal

There is no protective statute for intermediaries under Portuguese law and thus general contract law principles apply. Parties to a distribution agreement are free to include clauses providing for termination of the contract, the conditions of its renewal, and contract duration.

Where there is no contract provision, however, determining what a reasonable notice period will be depends upon the circumstances in each particular case. Portuguese courts look to the law governing agency contracts in making this determination.

The law of agency provides for four types of termination:

- by mutual agreement;
- at the end of a stipulated term;
- termination following the fault of a party; and
- unilateral termination.

The fourth possibility, unilateral termination, is only permitted in contracts which do not specify a duration or the conditions of termination. The law provides that termination must be notified with:

- one month prior notice if the contract has been in force for at least six months;
- two months notice where a contract has lasted less than one year; and
- three to twelve months notice if the contract has been in effect for more than one year.

The expectations of each party and any other pertinent circumstances would also be considered by the Portuguese court. If the party wishing to terminate the agreement fails to give notice in accordance with the periods specified above, the other party may seek an indemnity or make a claim for damages caused by that fact, or in the alternative, seek an amount corresponding to the monthly profit of the distributor multiplied by the notice period that should have been given.

Portugal has implemented the EC Directive via a decree-law,[62] the principal elements of which are set forth in the preceding paragraphs. The remedy chosen in the event of termination is an indemnity in accordance with Art. 17, ¶2 of the Directive.

Spain

There is no specific protective statute for distributors under Spanish law; however, the termination of distribution agreements has been treated extensively by the Spanish Supreme Court.

Parties may freely include a clause in a distribution contract which allows either of the parties to unilaterally cancel the contract; in such a case, the principal will not be liable for wrongful termination or be forced to supply an indemnity. Generally speaking, in a contract of indefinite duration, either party may unilaterally terminate the agreement where the terminating party is not acting in bad faith.

Notwithstanding the fact that termination by the principal does not normally allow for a right to compensation, the Spanish Supreme Court will allow compensation of the distributor where a principal unilaterally terminates a distribution agreement and realizes an unjust gain by appropriating the clientele built up by the distributor. Where this is the case, the distributor is entitled to seek compensation from the principal. This compensation does not represent damages for breach of contract, but is considered to be a share of the profits which result from the collaboration by the parties.

Compensation shall not be due the distributor if any one of the following is true:

- cancellation was for just cause, for example, the absence of profits, a misunderstanding between the parties, or a contractual breach by the distributor; or
- there is good faith and no abuse of rights in canceling the agreement on the part of the principal.

In deciding whether or not compensation should be paid to the distributor and in what amount, the courts will examine the facts on a case-by-case basis and take into consideration the following elements: the duration of the contract; the conduct of the parties during the contractual relationship; the good or bad faith of the principal; any future benefits flowing to the principal resulting from its association with the distributor, such as the acquisition of customers; and, the reputation of the principal's trademark or products.

In sum, the case law attempts to prevent unilateral cancellation of a distribution arrangement by the principal where the principal seeks to unfairly appropriate business generated by the distributor during the life of the contract.

The courts will determine the amount of compensation where the parties are unable to agree on an amount. The Spanish Supreme Court has indicated that compensation shall not exceed one year's profits obtained by the distributor from the sale of the products which are the object of the exclusive distribution agreement. In general, the amount is calculated on the basis of the annual average of the profits obtained by the distributor during the last three to five years of the contract.

Where an exclusive distribution agreement is concluded for an indefinite period of time, a notice to terminate within a time limit of six months will indicate to the court that the principal is acting in good faith and with loyalty to the distributor, an important factor should a court be called upon to determine the amount of compensation due.

The Spanish have implemented the Community Directive in a timely fashion,[63] and have chosen the "indemnification" remedy for terminated agents. As is generally the case throughout the Community, the Directive will apply to all commercial agency agreements in effect in Spain on or after January 1, 1994.

II. THE DISTRIBUTION AGREEMENT AND COMPETITION LAW IN EUROPE[64]

The European Community: Article 85 and Competition Law Procedure

Article 85 of the Treaty of Rome prohibits agreements between parties that are injurious to competition within the Community. This provision has been supplemented with an official "communication" issued by the Commission,[65] however, which provides an exemption for commercial agency agreements, such agents being deemed mere auxiliaries of their principals and lacking decision making authority. As for exclusive distribution agreements, they are indeed subject to Article 85's provisions. Such agreements are thought to be restraints upon competition in that the product which is distributed pursuant to the agreement is available from only one party within the contract territory.

If the Distribution Agreement is One of "Minor Importance" Then EC Competition Rules Are Not Applicable

In analyzing of the impact of a given distribution agreement in relation to Article 85(1) of the Treaty, the parties should first determine whether their agreement is one that the Commission considers to be of minor importance or de minimus, and therefore outside the prohibition of Article 85(1), i.e., the parties involved are of such a size that they do not have a significant impact on trade between Member States.

The Commission will find that agreements between undertakings for the production or distribution of goods or services do not fall within the prohibition of Article 85(1) if:

- the goods or services which are the subject of the agreement, together with the participating companies' other goods or services which are considered by users to be "equivalent" in view of their characteristics, price, and intended use, do not represent more than 5 percent of the total market for such goods or services in the area of the Common Market affected by the agreement; and

- the aggregate annual turnover of the participating undertakings does not exceed 200 million ECUS.[66]

Concerning the market share criteria, the Commission analyzes the "relevant market" i.e., the relevant product and geographic market. The relevant product market includes the contract products and any other products which are identical or equivalent to them. The geographic market is the area within the EC where the agreement produces its effects.

As for the "aggregate turnover" factor, it includes the turnover of all goods and services in the last financial year by the participating undertaking.

The Commission is primarily concerned with prohibiting agreements that have a substantial impact on market conditions in that they appreciably alter the position of non-participating firms and consumers. The decisions of the Commission and the Court of Justice indicate that factors to be considered are the nature of the product, the quantity of product available, the position and size of the parties, the availability of substitute products, the question of whether the agreement stands alone or is one of a series of agreements, and, whether re-exports or parallel imports are permitted.

This de minimus rule is merely a guideline and the Commission maintains the right to pursue a firm even where its agreement is of minor importance. As a consequence, borderline undertakings are best advised to seek exemption from Article 85 scrutiny pursuant to the block exemption on exclusive distribution agreements (see below).

If the criteria of the de minimus rule are fulfilled, there will be no restriction on competition and there is no need for further enquiry into EC rules on competition. However, if an undertaking's agreement surpasses these limits, further steps are necessary.

The Block Exemption Relating to Exclusive Distribution Agreements

If a party wishes to avoid having to notify its exclusive distribution agreement to the Commission, avoid the uncertainty of being party to an agreement which could later be declared void, and escape possible fines, the agreement must satisfy Regulation N° 1983/83 of the Commission of June 22, 1983, Concerning the Application of Article 85 §3 of the Treaty to Categories of Agreements of Exclusive Distribution (hereinafter, "the Regulation").

As for the language of this Regulation, Article 1 provides:

> . . . *Article 85, § 1, of the above-mentioned Treaty is declared inapplicable to agreements to which only two undertakings participate and in which one of the parties undertakes to deliver only certain products to the other party in order to resell them within the entire, or only part of, the territory of the Common Market.*

In Article 2, §§ (1) and (2), the Regulation lists the only other contract provisions which may be included in an exclusive distribution agreement that will still benefit from the Article 85(3) exemption. They are:

- the obligation of the principal to not sell the product to any other end user in the territory;
- the obligation of the distributor to not manufacture or distribute competing products;
- the obligation of the distributor to purchase the products for resale only from the other party to the contract;
- The obligation of the distributor to not prospect (actively market, establish a subsidiary, or maintain a warehouse for the products outside of the contract territory);
- The obligation of the distributor to buy complete sets of the products or to buy minimum quantities of them;
- The obligation of the distributor to sell the subject products under the trademark or in the trade dress provided by the principal;
- The obligation of the distributor to undertake any promotional sales measures, and in particular:
  —to advertise;
  —to insure the maintenance of a sales network or an inventory;
  —to insure service to the clientele; and
  —to employ personnel which have specialized or technical training.

If the parties add any other contract provisions, the entire agreement will fall back within the scope of the Regulation and will require an individual exemption—in other words, it must be notified to the Commission for approval.

Distribution Agreements and Notification to the Commission

Parties which have entered into an agreement or are undertaking a practice which falls within the prohibition of Article 85(1) may notify their agreement to the Commission in an attempt to obtain a "negative clearance." This procedure results in a decision by the Commission that the agreement or practice is not prohibited by Article 85(1), and may continue in its current state. As soon as an agreement is notified, the parties will no longer face exposure to Commissions fines.

However, certain agreements or practices, even if they are unlawful under Article 85(2), qualify for an "individual exemption" under Article 85(3). In such a case, an exemption may be granted by the Commission where the parties can demonstrate that the agreement contributes to the improvement of the production or distribution of products, helps promote technical or economical progress, and a fair share of the resulting benefits inure to consumers. It must also be shown that the restrictions imposed are essential to achieve the aims of the agreement, and that competition will not be eliminated for a substantial part of the products involved.

In order to simplify notification requirements and to help alleviate the caseload for notifications, the Commission established the "block exemptions" discussed above.

National Competition Laws in Europe and Distribution Agreements

In addition to EC competition law, parties to distribution agreements in the European Communities must also comply with the competition law regimes of the various EC member states. Taking as an example France's competition laws, there are a host of provisions which have direct bearing on distribution agreements:

- a party cannot impose on its French distributor the obligation to engage in predatory pricing;
- a party cannot impose a minimum resale price, but it may advise its French distributor about recommended resale prices;
- a party cannot refuse to sell its own products;
- a party should treat all of its intermediaries fairly and avoid discriminatory practices (i.e., discounts, rebates, bonuses, or other conditions of sale should be accorded equally to all intermediaries).

III. TAXATION OF DISTRIBUTION AGREEMENTS

One cannot neglect taxation issues when considering the use of intermediaries in foreign markets, as it is entirely possible that the principal will be subject to taxation in the foreign market based upon the activities of such intermediaries. Typically based upon the O.E.C.D. model tax treaty, bilateral treaties aim to avoid double taxation of entities operating in two taxing jurisdictions, and include dispositions which define the types of entities which may be taxed within a given jurisdiction.

The "distributor" is deemed an independent taxable entity that is subject to taxation on the full range of its commercial activities. As for the "agent," its activities will generate tax liability for the principal in the jurisdiction in which it performs its activities, provided that the agent in question is regarded by local fiscal authorities as an O.E.C.D. "permanent establishment." A "permanent establishment" exists upon the fulfillment of three conditions: the agent must be the "permanent representative" of the principal, it must follow the directives of the principal, and it must possess free reign to conduct business.

As for the requisite "permanency" the agent must centralize its activities in the taxing jurisdiction (residing there is sufficient). In order to determine if the distributor "follows the directives" of the principal, the following factors must be examined: (1) whether the agent must have its activities approved by or follow the instructions of the principal; (2) whether it is remunerated by salary or is paid on commission; (3) whether the principal reimburses the agent for its expenses; (4) whether the principal provides working space for the agent at its offices; or (5) whether the principal provides the agent with personnel at its own expense to assist the agent with its activities. The presence of any one of these conditions satisfies the "dependency" element. The final element, the freedom to conduct business, does not require complete autonomy of the distributor vis-à-vis the principal, but is satisfied where the distributor merely possesses the power to conclude a specified category of contracts.

In addition to the agent described above that is empowered to negotiate and conclude contracts on behalf of its principal, tax liability will also be incurred by the principal where its agent habitually maintains an inventory of the goods to which its agency pertains.[67]

Additional Practice Pointers

It is crucial to distinguish the type of distributor and distribution contract that is at issue, whereupon the possible application of protective statutes, antitrust laws, and bi-lateral tax treaties can be evaluated. Precisely defining the type of product to be distributed is also important in order to eliminate the accidental conferral of "exclusive" status upon an undesirable intermediary.

"Exclusive distributor" status, while often imperative to the success of the distribution strategy, must be approached with great care as not to offend potentially applicable antitrust provisions. Attention must equally be paid to the use of a non-competition clause, which can also raise antitrust concerns.

Any contract clause regulating sales quotas must be linked to a contract cancellation option in order to afford the principal the option of severing its relationship with an unsuccessful intermediary. Furthermore, quotas which do not comport with market realities may be deemed unreasonable and thereby vitiated.

The terms of payment must be carefully drafted and compliance with those terms carefully monitored. The intermediary, for its part, must be certain that the late payment of commissions will be deemed a material breach that justifies unilateral termination of the contract.

Provision must be made for inventories in possession of the intermediary. If the intermediary is an agent in possession of inventory, there may be double taxation concerns. If the intermediary is a distributor, the principal must be careful to ensure through appropriate contract language the return of its inventories in the event of the intermediary's insolvency.

The length of time that the contract will be in force is an important consideration in view of protective statutes. Tacit renewal of the contract can be risky, as a series of tacit renewals may lead a court to conclude that the contract term is indefinite. On the other hand, it is dangerous to provide too lengthy a notice of cancellation, as market fluctuations during the notice period can cause significant losses. In general, the right to unilaterally cancel the contract must be accompanied by a reasonable notification period, and must only arise upon breach of a material condition.

Where the success of the agreement is in large part dependent upon the business reputation of one of the contracting parties, a clause intuitu personae should insist that the existence of the agreement is wholly dependent upon the unique identity of the contractant in question.

The inclusion in the contract of conditions precedent is critical in certain circumstances, for example, in countries where the intermediary has yet to obtain mandatory government licensure, or, where the product or service to be distributed is subject to government approval prior to distribution.

As with all commercial contracts, choice of law and choice of jurisdiction clauses are standard and essential features of the distribution agreement. Of course, each party should seek agreement to the law and choice of jurisdiction most favorable to its position.[68] Finally, the inclusion of an arbitration clause should always be considered.[69]

Notes

[1] The authors would like to express their gratitude to Jean Thieffry, senior partner, Thieffry & Associés, Paris, for his invaluable assistance with the preparation of these materials.

[2] J. Thieffry, *La Distribution des Produits à l'Étranger, Revue Trimestrielle de Droit Commercial et de Droit Économique*, 1984, p. 727–728.

[3] 29 J.O. COMM. EUR. (No. L 382) 17, Art. 1, ¶2 (1986).

[4] Law No. 78–2, Art. 9; cf. Christine Lécuyer-Thieffry and Patrick Thieffry, *la Réglementation algérienne du commerce extérieur. L'implantation de l'entreprise étrangère et la négotiation des marchés*, J.C.P. 1982. II. 13866; A. Keesee, *Commercial Laws of the Middle East*, Vol. 5 (Algeria), Oceana (1989 and Supplement).

[5] Law No. 120–1982, Art. 2; A. Keesee, *Commercial Laws of the Middle East*, Vol. 3 (Egypt), Oceana (1989 and Supplement).

[6] Law No. 120–1982, Art. 3.

[7] For an overview of sales agency and distribution laws in the Middle East, *see* K. Redden, *Modern Legal Systems Cyclopedia*, Vol. 5A (William S. Hein & Co., 1990 and Supplement).

[8] Federal Law No. 18, 1981 (Presidential Decree), as amended by Federal Law No. 14, 1988 (Presidential Decree).

[9] Austrian law also sets forth a citizenship requirement, but this is tempered by a number of bilateral accords which permit, under certain circumstances, citizens of countries that are party to those treaties to seek licensure as intermediaries. Regional government authorities in Austria are furthermore vested with the power to dispense with the licensure requirement in certain cases.

[10] For materials on Austria, *see* L. Nelson, *Digest of Commercial Laws of the World*, (Binder)* (Austria—Ch. 5, Agency and Representation), Oceana (1992 and Supplement).

[11] Decree Law No. 34, modified by Decree No. 9639, February 9, 1975, Art. 1.

[12] Art. 8 and 9, Federal Law No. 18 of the United Arab Emirates; Art. 13 of Royal Decree M32 of Sept. 23, 1980 of Saudi Arabia; Art. 281–283 of the Commercial Law of Kuwait; Columbia Commercial Code, Art. 1324; Decree No. 4684 of Dec. 4, 1970, Costa Rica; Decree-Law No. 549 of Dec. 7, 1977, of Honduras.

[13] 29 J.O. Comm. Eur. (No. L 382) 17 (1986).

[14] *Id.*

[15] *Id.* Art. 1, ¶3.

[16] *Id.* Art. 2, ¶1, 2.

[17] *Id.* Art. 6, ¶1.

[18] *Id.*

[19] *Id.* Art. 6, ¶2.

[20] *Id.* Art. 6, ¶1.

[21] *Id.* Art. 14.

[22] *Id.* Art. 15, ¶1.

[23] *Id.*

[24] *Id.* Art. 15, ¶2.

[25] *Id.* Art. 15, ¶3.

[26] *Id.* Art. 15, ¶4.

[27] *Id.* Art. 16.

[28] *Id.* Art. 17, ¶1.

[29] *Id.* Art. 17, ¶2a.

[30] *Id.*

[31] *Id.* Art. 17, ¶2b.

[32] *Id.* Art. 17, ¶2c. The "indemnity plus right to damages" remedy of ¶2 should not be confused with the straight "damages" remedy of ¶3 discussed below.

[33] *Id.* Article 17, ¶3.

[34] *Id.*

[35] *Id.* Art. 17, ¶5.

[36] *Id.* Art. 17, ¶4.

[37] *Id.* Art. 18a.

[38] *Id.* Art. 18b.

[39] *Id.* Art. 18c.

[40] *Id.* Art. 19.

[41] *Id.* Art. 20, ¶2, 3, 4.

[42] *Id.* Art. 22, ¶1.

[43] *Id.* Art. 22, ¶1.

[44] Law of July 27, 1961, as amended by the Law of April 13, 1971.

[45] Court of Cassation, March 11, 1971.

[46] Court of Appeal of Brussels, October 1, 1975; Commercial Court of Brussels, January 26, 1972.

[47] Decisions of May 9, 1985, and December 20, 1985.

[48] Fierens and Kileste, *La loi du 27 juillet 1961, relative à la résiliation unilatérale des concessions de vente exclusive à durée indéterminée* (1977–86), Journal des Tribunaux 1987, 693–700; Willemart, *Les concessions de vente en Belgique*, Brussels, 1988.

[49] U88983 H.

[50] Law No. 272 of May 2, 1990.

[51] Law No. 272 of May 2, 1990.

[52] Law No. 89–1008, Art. 1, of December 31, 1989 (this law is commonly known as the "loi Doubin").

[53] Decree of April 4, 1991, in application of Law No. 89–1008, Article 1.

[54] Law No. 91–593 of June 25, 1991.

[55] *Id.*

[56] Law of October 23, 1989.

[57] Presidential Decree No. 2319 of May 18, 1991.

[58] Legislative Decree No. 303 of September 10, 1991.

[59] Civil Code, Article 1751.

[60] *Id.*

[61] Law of July 5, 1989.

[62] Decree-Law No. 17886 of July 3, 1986.

[63] Law No. 121992 of June 27, 1992.

[64] For a more complete discussion of the European Community antitrust law regime, see PART THREE, *infra*.

[65] Commission Communication, O.J. EUR. COMM. (1962).

[66] *See* the Commission's Notice of September 3, 1986, Concerning Agreements of Minor Importance Which Do Not Fall Under Article 85(1) of the Treaty Establishing the European Economic Community (86C23102).

[67] For an in-depth treatment of international distribution and taxation issues, *see* W. Streng and J. Salacuse, *International Business Planning: Law and Taxation*, Vol. 3, Ch. 13 (Tax Planning for Branch Sales and Distributorships), Mathew Bender (1990 and Supplement).

[68] J. Thieffry, *La Distribution des Produits à l'Étranger, Revue Trimestrielle de Droit Commercial et de Droit Économique*, 1984, p. 735–736.

[69] For a periodically updated reference source on international sales agency and distribution laws, see P. Vishny, *Guide to International Commerce Law, Vol.* 1, Ch. 4 (Agents, Distributors, and Other Representatives), Shepard's McGraw-Hill (1990 and Supplement).

FOREIGN REGULATION OF INBOUND TECHNOLOGY TRANSFERS AND FOREIGN INVESTMENTS

Alan S. Gutterman

I. REGULATION OF TECHNOLOGY TRANSFER ARRANGEMENTS

In General

AS A SUPPLEMENT to antitrust regulations aimed at various *competitive* effects of technology transfers, many nations have enacted specific legislation regulating the content of technology transfer agreements in order to foster the development of local technical capabilities and, in many instances, monitor the use of foreign exchange and the level of foreign involvement in the local economy. Regulations of this type may take a variety of different forms and are typically focused upon the transfer of technology into the country, although some restrictions may also be imposed on technology "exports."

One of the first pieces of legislation relating to imports of technology was the adoption of the Andean Code in 1969[1], which was to serve as the model for technology statutes in a number of South American countries, including Argentina[2], Brazil[3], Colombia[4], Costa Rica[5], Cuba[6], Dominican Republic[7], Mexico[8], Peru[9] and Venezuela.[10] Among the African countries, technology transfer regulations were adopted in Ethiopia[11], Ghana[12], Nigeria[13], Sudan[14], the United Republic of Tanzania[15], Togo[16] and Zambia.[17] Asian countries with similar statutes have included China[18], North Korea[19], India[20], Iraq[21], Japan[22], Malaysia[23], Nepal[24], Pakistan[25], the Philippines[26], South Korea[27], and Sri Lanka.[28] In Europe, countries such as Greece[29], Portugal[30], and Spain[31] have regulated technology imports at some point in time.

As a general rule, technology transfer regulations operate by requiring the international technology agreement be submitted to, and approved by, a national administrative authority in order for the agreement to be enforceable. Governmental bodies charged with reviewing technology transfer agreements often refer to statutory lists of objectionable business practices which must be excised from any agreement as a condition of approval. Among the most common areas of concern are royalty rates and other forms of remuneration, the scope and content of controls that the technology provider seeks to impose on the local transferee, the nature of any implied representations and warranties regarding the quality and performance of the transferred technology, the term of the agreement, governing law, and dispute resolution procedures. Local regulators may also evaluate the terms of the agreement in light of its potential effect upon the development of the national economy.

Policy Objectives of Technology Transfer Regulations

Technology transfer regulations are intended to serve of a number disparate objectives, most of which are generally related to the overall economic development of the local country, although some statutes are also drafted in a manner which serves to protect the relative bargaining position of the transferee. For example, a survey of the various regulations regarding technology transfers which have been adopted in South America indicated the following principal objectives[32]:

- Increasing the bargaining power of the local transferees, such as by prohibiting the use of package licensing and other similar practices.

- Increasing the amount of information available to local parties with respect to possible sources of technology.

- Controlling the nature of imported technology and improving the quality and local assimilation of any new technology which is to be transferred.

- Protecting local innovation and technology.

- Regulating remuneration for transferred technology in order to protect and improve the balance of payments position of the local economy, control foreign exchange operations, and prevent tax avoidance.

- Limiting the protection of industrial property by restricting the prohibitions which might be imposed upon disclosure and use of such information.

- Promoting other local public policy goals, such as the use and training of local employees and protection of the environment.

A number of countries have attempted to structure their laws relating to technology transfers to encourage and promote imports of technology for use in specified industrial areas. For example, a country might provide that the general technology transfer rules will be modified in relation to certain technologies, such as by providing for expedited reviews, liberalizing restrictions on the level of foreign investment participation, creating incentives for local manufacturing, permitting components needed for use in local manufacturing to be imported at concessional rates, and authorizing development subsidies, tax credits and tariff protections.[33] Industry promotion may be accomplished by announcing areas in which incentives and concessions will be available or by the use of "lists" which identify the type of regulations and restrictions on foreign investment in industries specified thereon.[34]

Approval and Registration of Technology Transactions

A technology transfer agreement, which may be defined to include not only license agreements but also technical assistance and consultation agreements, may need to be registered with, and even approved by, specified local authorities, including banks. Such registration is sometimes a condition to the validity of the agreement or, at a minimum, is required in order for deductions to be taken for any royalty payments or for amounts to be repatriated from the country. In some countries, criminal sanctions can be imposed for failure to register a technology transfer agreement.

Although there is some variation in the types of technology transactions which may be subjected to the registration procedures, the most common areas for regulation are as follows:

- Agreements relating to the transfer, assignment, or licensing of the use or exploitation of patents or trademarks.

- Agreements covering the provision of technical know-how and information in the form of plans, specifications, diagrams, models, instructions, formulae, and personnel training.

- Agreements relating to technical consultancy services and assistance, regardless of the form in which the services or assistance is provided.[35]

Some countries (e.g., Venezuela) limit their regulatory activities to a narrower class of agreements or contracts, such as patent and trademark licenses.[36] Other countries use the type of technology as a basis for determining whether an agreement must be reviewed. For example, a country may choose to monitor only the importation of technology relating to computers and information.[37] In other cases, a generic list of agreements and contracts such as those set out above may be supplemented by a requirement that *all* agreements which relate to the import of specified technologies also must be reviewed.[38]

In contrast to the governmental offices in the developed countries vested with responsibility for reviewing applications for intellectual property protection (e.g., patent applications)[39], the regulatory authorities which administer technology transfer laws in developing countries are generally heavily involved in formulating national technological policy and, as such, are obligated to apply economic and related sociological criteria in examining agreements which are submitted for review.[40] Regulatory authorities in this area often evolve from technological research and advisory bodies originally formed to provide assistance to the government on broad policy issues.[41] However, in other cases, the governmental agency given control over technology transfer agreements began as part of an effort to monitor the flow of foreign currency into and out of the country.[42]

Today, in most cases, the regulatory authority which has responsibility for the review of international technology transfer agreements will also provide a number of other functions, such as the following:

- Providing advice to the government on national investment priorities.

- Collecting, analyzing, and disseminating information on investment opportunities and sources of capital which can be used to finance these opportunities.

- Proposing guidelines and formulating overall courses of action for technology transfer plans and strategies in the country.[43]

- Promoting cooperation among specialized sectoral bodies with a view toward improving methods for the acquisition and adaptation of technology.

- Providing technical advice in the field of the transfer and development of technology.

- Promoting the dissemination of modern technological know-how and stimulating increased awareness concerning its various uses.

- Recommending further legislation for the encouragement and facilitation of foreign investment and technology transfer.[44]

The administrative structure which has been established in Brazil for the review of technology transfer agreements illustrates the integration of this function with national technology policy. The Brazilian National Institute of Industrial Property ("INPI") was established in 1970 as autonomous federal body within that country's Ministry of Industry and Trade.[45] INPI not only has the responsibility for evaluating and registering technology transfer agreements, but also is involved in formulating relevant laws and advising on international instruments relating to intellectual property. The INPI has promulgated a series of laws which amount to a code of practice which is used in evaluating international technology agreements[46] and has established a number of *ad hoc* commissions which provide advice on the rules which should be applied in particular technological areas, such as computers, petrochemicals, and heavy engineering.[47]

In addition, the INPI has developed a number of programs and practices relating to technological development, including some of the following:

- Requirements that government instrumentalities submit to the INPI calls for tender which entail contracting for the acquisition of foreign technology. The INPI then is empowered to decide whether the importation of foreign technology is desirable and reviews the agreement prior to finalization.[48]

- Authority to condition the approval of foreign agreements on the implementation of an investment program in the technological infrastructure of the transferee.[49]

- Requirements that local firms seeking to import any technologies from overseas must provide the INPI with comparative data regarding similar technology in order to justify the need for the importation.

- Establishment of a program for evaluating the commercial and technological potential of local inventions and for providing financial assistance for the exploitation of promising inventions in areas of national priority.[50]

- Facilitating the access of small and medium-sized businesses to patent information and information on foreign technology through agreements which the INPI has with national organizations which deal with industry, technology, and science.

In most countries, the parties must submit executed agreements for review and approval; however, a few countries will accept draft forms of the agreement.[51] The agreement should be accompanied by an application form which includes information regarding the content of the agreement and the parties themselves. Also, the parties must submit supporting documentation, including items such as audited financial statements of the transferee and projections regarding financial performance of the transferee in the future, and proof of the transferor's ownership of any relevant industrial property rights.[52] If the technology transfer occurs as part of any transaction involving foreign investment, a certificate which sets forth approval of the foreign investment by the relevant authority may also be required.[53]

Once an agreement has been submitted for review, the governmental authority will carefully review the legal, economic, and technical terms thereof in light of its published policies and guidelines, as well as comments received from authorities at the central banking and any other ministry having jurisdiction over the subject matter of the agreement. In some cases, the parties will take an active role in convincing the reviewing authority of the need for specified terms. Once the evaluation has been completed, the authority will advise the parties as to whether the agreement has been approved or rejected and, if the agreement is rejected, an explanation will usually be given to the parties.[54] If a specific provision of the agreement is found to be offensive, the parties may be given the opportunity to amend or modify the provision in order for the agreement to be approved.

Agreements may sometimes be approved subject to certain conditions. If the relevant legislation permits the imposition of such conditions, procedures will generally be included to monitor compliance by the parties by requiring the submission of an annual report on matters of concern to the regulatory authorities. For example, in the Philippines, parties may be required to report on:

(1)   The benefits received by the transferee from the technology transfer, including new developments and improvements.

(2)   The implementation of training programs for local employees.

(3)   The steps which have been taken by the transferee to establish research and development facilities for the absorption of the transferred technology.

(4)   The steps which have been taken in order to adapt the transferred technology for local use.[55]

Once a technology transfer agreement has been approved, the parties are generally issued a certificate of registration and the particulars of the registration are entered on a public register. Amendments, renewals, and terminations of registered agreements must generally be notified to the administrative authority within the time periods specified by law. Amendments and modifications to any registered agreement usually must be reviewed in the same manner as new agreements.

Failure of the parties to obtain approval for a technology transfer agreement may result in a variety of sanctions, including the inability of the transferor to repatriate royalties and profits paid by the transferee under the terms of the agreement[56], the imposition of fines[57], and the unenforceability of the technology transfer agreement.[58] In turn, there may be a number of incentives for complying with the technology transfer regulations, including automatic approvals of agreements meeting certain conditions[59], the ability to deduct payments made under the agreement for tax purposes[60], and the right to participate in government schemes promoting the development of indigenous technology or the expansion of industries in designated areas of national priority.[61]

Regulation of Form and Content of Technology Agreements

The overall form and content of technology agreements may actually be specified in the relevant regulations. For example, Article 15 of the Law of Technology Contracts which is used in the People's Republic of China provides that technology contracts shall generally include the following:

(1) The name of the project.

(2) The content, scope, and requirements of the object of the contract.

(3) The plan, schedule, time limits, place, and manner of performance.

(4) The maintenance of confidentiality of technical information and materials.

(5) The bearing of liability for risks.

(6) The ownership and sharing of technological results.

(7) The standards and methods of testing and acceptance.

(8) The price and remuneration and means of payment.

(9) Breach of contract damages or methods for computing the amount of compensation for losses.

(10) Methods for dispute resolution.

(11) The interpretation of terms and technical expressions.[62]

In addition, the PRC's law makes it clear that background materials on the technology, feasibility analyses, technological evaluation reports, a statement of the project mission and statement of the plan, technological standards, technological norms, original design and documents on technical processes are all considered integral parts of a technology agreement, as are drawings, tables, data and photographs that are related to the performance of the agreement.[63]

Policy Guidelines in Reviewing Technology Agreements

Regulatory authorities generally review technology agreements to insure that the terms thereof are compatible with the overriding objectives of the nation's technology policy. With respect to the developing countries, technology policy is usually intended to facilitate the development of indigenous technology and efficient absorption and adaptation of imported technology considered to be appropriate to local priorities and resources. Specific goals and objectives may include the following:

• Attain technological competence and self-reliance, particularly in strategic areas, by making maximum use of indigenous resources.

• Provide the maximum amount of gainful and satisfying employment to all strata of the national society, with particular emphasis on the employment of women and weaker sections of society.

- Enhance the competitiveness of traditional skills and capabilities.
- Identify obsolete technology and arrange for acquisition of modern equipment and technology.
- Develop internationally competitive technologies which have the potential for creating exportable products.
- Rapidly improve production through greater efficiency and fuller utilization of existing capabilities, while also enhancing the quality and reliability of performance and output.[64]

Economic evaluation of a technology transfer agreement will focus upon the reasonableness of the consideration payable by the transferee. Technological evaluation of the agreement looks at alternative sources of supply, the possible obsolescence of the subject technology and the assimilability of the technology within the local technological environment. Developmental evaluation will take into account the effects of the transfer on local employment and worker skills, balance of payments considerations, and the impact of the technology on the environment.

In order to achieve the specific goals and objectives of the regulation of technology transfers, government authorities usually will prohibit certain provisions in technology agreements which might be characterized as restrictive business practices. Another method which might be used is for the legislation to require that agreements expressly negate specific business practices, such as when the transferor is required to agree that the transferee will continue to have the right to use the transferred technology after the agreement has expired.[65] In cases where the government wants to be sure that local transferees are not required to continue to make payments for obsolete technology, the regulations may restrict the term of the agreement and prohibit automatic renewals.

Compulsory Licensing and "Working" Requirements

In many developing countries, "compulsory licensing" laws impose an obligation upon a patent owner to exploit or "work" a patent in order to avoid the grant of a compulsory patent license to a third party. Even though the patent owner will generally be entitled to some form of compensation, such as royalties, from the holder of the compulsory license, the grant of such a right will usually seriously impair the goals and objectives of the patent owner in the specific country. "Working" requirements may often be satisfied through the grant of a license to a local party. If this is the case, the license should contain a provision which requires that the licensee utilize its best efforts to meet any requirements necessary to avoid the compulsory licensing laws.[66] In those cases where the licensee fails to fulfill its obligations, the licensee should indemnify the licensor against any resultant damages.

Regulation of Royalty Provisions

The amount of compensation which must be paid, in the form of royalties or otherwise, by the local party under a licensing or any other form of technology transfer agreement generally will be the subject of close examination. Regulators will want to be sure that the payments are reasonable in relation to the technology supplied and the value of the technology to the national economy. This is usually accomplished through the imposition of limitations on the royalty rate, as well as the duration of the obligation to remit royalties. Maximum royalty rates may be established by statute or determined by administrators.[67] Minimum royalty requirements tend to be disfavored, since they are unrelated to sales of products which actually result from the use of the technology. Guidelines may also prescribe the form that payments will take, as well as the type of documentation which must be authenticated before payments can be made.[68]

Restrictions on Licensing Practices

Even in those cases where the antitrust laws of the host country are rudimentary, or even non-existent, the rules governing technology transfers will generally prohibit various practices which might constitute patent misuse in, or violate the antitrust laws of, developed countries such as the United States. Among the terms that will be regulated are: tie-ins, restrictions on the right of the licensee to manufacture competing products, various restrictions on pricing, "no contest" clauses as to statutory rights, grant-back requirements[69], export restrictions, restrictions on the right of the licensee to sublicense the technology, volume restrictions, and royalty obligations which extend beyond the scope of the patent.

Related Company Transactions

Some countries impose special screening procedures upon any agreement between foreign parents and local subsidiaries[70] and, in some cases, express prohibitions are imposed on any payments in consideration for technology by a subsidiary to a foreign parent company.[71] Regulation of these "related company" transactions is designed to prevent foreign companies from avoiding fiscal and exchange controls by effecting profit remittances through intra-enterprise transfers. Those countries which permit transactions of this type generally do so only upon verifying that the agreements between the entities are in conformity with normal practice between independent entities and that the consideration is in proportion to the technology transferred.[72]

Miscellaneous Restrictions

Some countries will impose additional restrictions on the content of technology transfer agreements. Since these provisions will vary, it is important to carefully review applicable local law and, if necessary, engage a local expert for consultation regarding compliance with the technology transfer laws. For example, some countries will limit the duration of confidentiality provisions in a technology transfer agreement. In other cases, local regulators will block any attempt by the foreign party to include any dispute resolution mechanism that does not require the use of local law[73] or the courts of the host country.

II. FOREIGN REGULATION OF INBOUND INVESTMENT TRANSACTIONS

Most countries have some sort of "investment law" or an "investment code" which would apply to foreign investment in the country, including direct investment or a joint venture with one or more local partners. Foreign investment laws may regulate any type of foreign investment or may be limited to investment activity in a specified industry sector, such as tourism, agriculture, services or certain manufacturing areas. Foreign investment laws usually require review of the transaction by at least one, and sometimes more than one, governmental authority. While it is difficult to make generalizations regarding the form and content of the foreign investment regulations around the world, the following issues seem to arise on a consistent basis:

- *Does the proposed investment fall within a permitted economic sector of the local economy?* In many cases, the foreign investment law will restrict foreign investment in one or more specified areas on the basis of so-called "national security" concerns.[74]

- *In what form must the foreign investment be made?* Some countries will limit the percentage of an enterprise that may be owned by a foreign investor, thereby creating the need to form a joint venture with local partners.

- *What requirements will be placed upon the amount and type of capital which may be contributed by the foreign party?* Many developing countries will not approve any investment proposal without some assurance that the foreign party will contribute hard currency or technology that is capable of rapid absorption and use in the local market.

- *What, if any, performance requirements will be placed upon the enterprise in which the investment is going to be made?* Many countries place certain requirements on the manner in which a foreign-owned entity must operate. For example, the enterprise may be required to use a certain minimum amount of local content in the products or hire local personnel. In those cases where the host country is seeking to encourage the acquisition of hard currency through exports, the enterprise may be under an obligation to export a certain minimum amount of its production.

- *What incentives and guarantees will be provided for the foreign investment activity?* Many countries have used a wide range of incentives and guarantees to induce foreign investment. These include tax and fiscal incentives, customs duty exemptions, "free trade" zones, guarantees that similar foreign investments will not be approved for a certain period of time, and government subsidies for certain factors of production.

- *What other controls will be placed upon the investment activities?* A wide variety of controls may be placed on the foreign investment activity, including controls on foreign exchange and repatriation of hard currency, price controls on the sale of goods in the local market, and controls upon the use of local managers and employment of local personnel.

Foreign investment laws generally serve dual, and often conflicting, purposes: to *control* the inflow of foreign capital into the local economy and to *encourage* foreign investment in those areas in which local resources will not be sufficient to achieve the desiredeconomic goals and objectives of the government. The need for local governmental review of a proposed investment will often cause delays in the transaction and, in some cases, lead to substantial changes in the form of the transaction. As such, it is usually important to locate a local partner who has experience in dealing with regulators so that the approval process can flow more smoothly and the investor can take advantage of incentives which might be available from the government.

Notes

[1] *See* Decision 24 of the Cartagena Treaty (Agreement on Andean Subregional Integration, (1969) 8 ILM 910). *See also Radaway, Comparative Evolution of Technology Transfer Policies in Latin America: The Practical Realities,* 9 Denver J Intl L and Pol 197 (1980); Correa, *Transfer of Technology in Latin America: A Decade of Control,* JWTL 388 (1981).

[2] Law 22426 on The Transfer of Technology of March 12, 1981, and Resolution 264—Guidelines for the Transfer of Technology on April 10, 1981. *See* Cabanellas, *The Argentine Transfer of Technology Law: An Analysis and Commentary,* 3 Hastings Intl and Comp. L. Rev 29.

[3] Ato Normativo nos. 015/75/, 030/78, 019A/80, 129/81, 55/81, 60/82, 103/82, 64/183, 65/83, 68/84, 74/85. *See* Nattier, *Limitations on Marketing Foreign Technology in Brazil,* 11 Int'l Lawyer 437 (1977).

[4] Decree 444 relating to the international exchange regulations relating to the approval and registration of contracts for the transfer of technology, March 22, 1967; Decree 1,234 concerning the content of contracts for the transfer of technology and establishing criteria for the aproval of such contracts, July 18, 1972.

[5] Executive Decrees 14475-H and 14694 of May and July 1983 to be replaced by Ley de Transferencia de Techologia, when promulgated.

[6] Decree 63 on Inventions, Scientific Discoveries, Industrial Models, Marks and Appellations of Origin of May 14, 1983; Legislative Decree 50 on Economic Association between Cuban and Foreign Entities of February 15, 1982.

[7] Law 861 on foreign investment and the transfer of technology (title X), July 19, 1978.

[8] Mexico rescinded its technology transfer regulations in 1992. The regulations formerly appeared in The Law on the Control and Registration of the Transfer of Technology and the Use and Exploitation of Patents and Trade Marks of December 29, 1981. For comments on prior regulations, *see* Gutterman, *Changing Trends in the Content and Purpose of Mexico's Intellectual Property Right Regime,* 20 Geor J. of Intl and Comp. Law 515 (1990).

[9] The rules for establishing precise rights and obligations of the licensors and licensees of foreign technologies, marks and patents of October 23, 1981.

[10] Decree 656, gazetted June 20, 1985.

[11] Joint Venture Establishment Proclamation 235/1983, promulgated January 22, 1983.

[12] Investment Code Act 437, promulgated August 11, 1981.

[13] Nigerian Enterprises Promotion Act 1977. *See* Osunbor, *Law and Policy on the Registration of Technology Transfer Transactions in Nigeria,* 21 JWTL 13 (1987).

[14] Encouragement of Investment Act 1980.

[15] Law of April 16, 1986.

[16] Loi 85–02 Charte des Enterprises Togolaises; Loi 85–03 Portant reamenagement du Code des Invesissements, both January 29, 1986.

[17] Industrial Development Act 1977.

[18] Law on Technology Contracts, June 23, 1987.

[19] Law of Joint Venture, September 8, 1984.

[20] Statement of Industrial Policy of June 1980, and the Technology Policy Statement of January 1983.

[21] Ordinance 18 of 1984, containing the Statutes of the National Committee on the Transfer of Technology of August 22, 1984.

[22] *See* Ohara, *Japanese Regulation of Technology Imports*, 15 JWTL 83 (1981); Ohara, *Regulations on Transfer of Technology in Japan*, 15 IIC 121 (1984).

[23] Industrial Coordination Act 1975, Guidelines on Technology Transfer.

[24] Foreign Investment and Technology Act 1981 (Act 2038).

[25] Guidelines for Agreements on the Transfer of Technology in Pakistan, 1985.

[26] The Science and Technology Plan integrated into the National Development Plan 1983 to 1987. *See* Bautista, *Transfer of Technology Regulations in the Philippines*, UNCTAD doc. UNCTAD/TT/32 (October 1980).

[27] The Monopoly Regulation and Fair Trade Law 333230 of December 31, 1980; Public Notice 50 on the Scope and Standard of Unreasonable Concerted Activities and Unfair Concerted Activities and Unfair Trade Practices in International Contracts of July 18, 1981; Foreign Capital Inducement Act, promulgated December 31, 1983. See *West, Evolving Industrial Property Law and Transfer of Technology Law in the Republic of Korea*, 18 Texas Intl L J 127 (1983); Song, *Experience and Practice on Technology Transfer in the Republic of Korea*, 15 IPAP 58 (1986).

[28] Computer and Technology Council of Sri Lanka Act 1984.

[29] Law 1262/1982 concerning incentives to support the country's regional and economic development June 16, 1982 and development programme for research and technology 1983 to 1987.

[30] Decree Law 174/82 of May 12, 1982. See Ferreira, *The Implementation of Laws and Regulations on the Transfer of Technology*, UNCTAD doc. UNCTAD/TT/73 (February 1986).

[31] Order 18240 amending the regulation on the registration of contracts for the transfer of technology laid down in the Ministry Order of December 5, 1973 of July 30, 1981; Law on Scientific and Technical Research of May 13, 1985; Ministry of Energy Order 3531 of February 22, 1985.

[32] See G. Cabanellas, *Antitrust and Direct Regulation of International Transfer of Technology Transactions*, 30–47 (1984).

[33] Various developing countries have attempted to promote investment and technology transfer in the iron and steel sector (*see*, e.g., D.M. Castur, *Case Studies in the Transfer of Technology: Purchase of Capital Goods and Technology in the Iron and Steel Sector—The Case of Bokaro, India*, UNCTAD doc. TD/B/C.6/27 (June 1978)) , capital machinery production (*see, e.g.*, S. Patel, *Technology Issues in the Capital Goods Sector: A Case Study of Leading Machinery Producers in India*, UNCTAD doc. UNCTAD/TT/55 (September 1985)), petrochemicals (*see, e.g.*, L.B. Singh, *Technology Policies in the Petrochemical Sector in India*, UNCTAD doc. UNCTAD/TT/54 (July 1983)), energy (*see, e.g.*, Cameroon, Ivory Coast and Guinea-Bissau: UNCTAD doc. TD/B/C.6/117 and Corr.1 (August 1984)), food processing (see, e.g., Mexico: UNCTAD doc. TD/B/C.6/75 (March 1982)), and pharmaceuticals (*see, e.g.*, India: UNCTAD doc. TD/B/C.6/20 (October 1977); Costa Rica: UNCTAD doc. UNCTAD/TT/37 (May 1982); Cuba: UNCTAD doc. UNCTAD/TT/33 (December 1980); Ethiopia: UNCTAD doc. UNCTAD/TT/58 (February 1984); Philippines: UNCTAD doc. UNCTAD/TT/36 (October 1980); Sri Lanka: UNCTAD doc. UNCTAD doc. TD/B/C.6/21 (June 1977); Tanzania: UNCTAD doc. UNCTAD/TT/35 (October 1980); Venezuela: UNCTAD doc. UNCTAD/TT/25 (March 1982)).

[34] For example, South Korea originally used a "positive list system" which enumerated those industries in which foreign investment was permitted. *See* Foreign Capital Inducement Law, April 12, 1973. Subsequently, as the economy matured, South Korea changed to a "negative list system" under which all industries other than those on the "negative list" would be open to foreign investment. See Foreign Capital Inducement Law, effective July 1, 1984.

[35] *See, e.g.*, Philippines, Rules and Regulations To Implement the Intent and Provisions of Section 5P.D. 1520 (1978), Rule I, section 1(b).

[36] *See* G. Cabanellas, *Antitrust and Direct Regulation of International Transfer of Technology Transactions*, 16 (1984).

[37] *See* UNCTAD, Policies, Laws and Regulations on Transfer, Application and Development of Technology, Periodic Report 1986, *TD/B/C.6/133 (July 24, 1986)*, Paragraph 35 (Sri Lanka).

[38] For example, the technology transfer regulations of the former German Democratic Republic were supplemented by specific rules designed to cover the review of agreements covering the export and import of certain scientific and technical results (*e.g.*, solutions for industrial and scientific organization, and microbiological processes and results). *See* Third Regulation to the Decree Governing the Management and

Operation of Foreign Trade—Export and Import of Scientific Technical Results, January 7, 1981, Section (3), appearing in Compilation of Legal Material Dealing with Transfer and Development of Technology, UNCTAD doc. TC/B/C.6/81 (August 4, 1982), 65.

[39] Such offices limit their functions to assuring compliance with the procedural requirements of intellectual property statutes, such as examinations which are limited to issues of novelty, originality, utility and inventorship. Examiners have neither the competence, nor the interest, in evaluating the economic and developmental impact of the information contained in the documents which are reviewed.

[40] The relevant administrative authority is generally heavily involved with other relevant governmental departments and is often an instrumentality of a government ministry which has responsibility for trade, investment and technology. For example, the Technology Transfer Board of the Philippines was established within the Ministry of Industry, P.D. 1520, section 5 (see Compilation of Legal Material Dealing with Transfer and Development of Technology, UNCTAD doc. TC/B/C.6/81 (August 4, 1982), 142); the Centre for the Transfer and Development of Technology of the United Republic of Tanzania is within the Commission for Science and Technology (*see* UNCTAD, Policies, Laws and Regulations on Transfer Application and Development of Technology, Periodic Report 1986, UNCTAD doc. TD/B/C.6/133, (July 24, 1986), paragraph 45); and the Offices of the Superintendent of Foreign Investments of Venezuela is part of the Ministry of Finance, Decree 2442, November 8, 1977 (*see* Compilation of Legal Material Dealing with Transfer and Development of Technology, UNCTAD doc. TC/B/C.6/81 (August 4, 1982), 196–200). In some cases, the government ministries which are directly involved with the relevant technology will take on the task of approving foreign technology agreements. For example, see India, WIPO, *The Situation of Industrial Property in the Countries of Asia and the Pacific, 1974*, 159–163; Mongolia, *ibid.*, at 223; Nepal, *ibid.*, at 238; and Pakistan, *ibid.*, at 258.

[41] For example, the Madagascan National Centre of Industrial and Technological Research was formed in 1984 to provide advice to the government on national technological needs, including methods for encouraging importation of technology. See UNCTAD, Policies, Laws and Regulations on Transfer, Application and Development of Technology, UNCTAD doc. TD/B/C.6/133 (July 24, 1986), paragraph 14.

[42] For example, regulation of technology transfers in Brazil originally began with its exchange control law of 1962, which contained a number of provisions relating to the transfer of technology and established a "special service" within the Directorate of Currency and Credit for the registration of movements of foreign capital and financial transfers overseas. See Brazil: Law 4131 on foreign capital, in Compilation of Legal Material Dealing with Transfer and Development of Technology, UNCTAD doc. TC/B/C.6/81 (August 4, 1982), 16–20.

[43] A related function is, of course, the formulation of a code of practice governing technology transfer agreements and review, evaluation, approval and registration of such agreements.

[44] Among the national authorities which have been established to provide broad guidance on technology matters are the Nigerian National Office of Industrial Property (National Office of Industrial Property Decree, September 24, 1979, in Compilation of Legal Material Dealing with Transfer and Development of Technology, UNCTAD doc. TC/B/C.6/81 (August 4, 1982), 120), the Argentinian National Institute of Industrial Technology (Established by Res. No. 264, March 27, 1981, in Compilation of Legal Material Dealing with Transfer and Development of Technology, UNCTAD doc. TC/B/C.6/81 (August 4, 1982), 13–15), the Mexican Ministry of Patrimony and Industrial Development (Established by the Law on the Control and registration of the transfer of technology and the use and exploitation of patents and trademarks, January 11, 1982), the Nepalese Industrial Promotions Board (Established by the Industrial Enterprises Act 1981), the Peruvian National Commission for Investments and Foreign Technologies (Established by Decree 18900, 1981), the Iraqi National Committee on Transfer of Technology (Ordinance 18 of 1984), the Brazilian National Institute of Industrial Property (Law 5,648, December 11, 1970), and the Ghana Investments Centre (By the Investment Code of 1985, which replaced the Investment Code of 1981).

[45] Law 5,648, December 11, 1970.

[46] *See, e.g.*, Normative Act 015 establishing basic principles and norms for the registration of contracts involving the transfer of technology and related agreements, September 11, 1975; Normative Act 30, amended by Normative Act No. 60, March 24, 1982 (specialized technical services); Normative Act 32 (prior examination), May 5, 1978; Normative Acts 64 and 65, September 16, 1983; Normative Act 68, January 5, 1984.

[47] Normative Acts 19A/80 of January 25, 1980; 129/81 of October 20, 1981; 103/82 of November 22, 1982; 22/82 of December 2, 1982.

[48] Normative Acts 55/81 of August 20, 1981 and 60/82 of March 24, 1982.

[49] Normative Act 64/83 of September 16, 1983.

[50] *See* UNCTAD, Policies, Laws and Regulations on Transfer Application and Development of Technology, Periodic Report 1986, UNCTAD doc. TD/B/C.6/133 (July 24, 1986), paragraph 45.

[51] *E.g.*, draft agreements are acceptable under the laws of Brazil (Normative Act 032//78) and Venezuela (Decree 746, Article 7 (1975)).

[52] *E.g.*, Philippines, Rules and Regulations to Implement P.D. 1520, Rule III, in Compilation of Legal Material Dealing with Transfer and Development of Technology, UNCTAD doc. TC/B/C.6/81 (August 4, 1982), 143.

[53] *See, e.g.*, Spain: Ministry of Industry Order regulating the entry of contracts for the transfer of technology in the Register established by Decree 2343, December 5, 1973, Section 1.5 in Compilation of Legal Material Dealing with Transfer and Development of Technology, UNCTAD doc. TC/B/C.6/81 (August 4, 1982), 168.

[54] A decision of an administrative agency may be subject to reconsideration upon application to the agency, or review may be sought through the court system. In those cases where the decision is made by an instrumentality of a government ministry, it may be possible to petition for review by the relevant minister. See, *e.g.*, Portugal Decree Law 348/77, August 24, 1977, which provides that decisions of the Portuguese Institute of National Investment may be appealed to the Minister of Planning and Economic Coordination.

[55] Rules and Regulations, 1978, Rule VIII.

[56] *See, e.g.*, Brazil: Law 4131 1962, Article 3; Normative Act 015, September 11, 1975, section 1(a); Columbia: Decree 1234, July 18, 1972, Article 3; Dominican Republic: Law 861, July 19, 1978, Article 35; Nigeria: National Office of Industrial Property, Decree 70, September 24, 1979, section 7.

[57] *See, e.g.*, Mexico's former Law on the control and registration of trade marks, etc., January 11, 1982, Articles 19 to 23.

[58] *See, e.g.*, Portugal: Decree 53/77, August 24, 1977, Article 12; Thailand: Patents Act 1979, section 41.

[59] *See, e.g.*, South Korea: Foreign Capital Inducement Act of 1984 (automatic technology licensing approval for agreements of less than ten years where the royalty rates does not exceed a prescribed maximum).

[60] *See, e.g.*, Argentina: Law 22, 426, March 12, 1981, section 9.

[61] *See* UNCTAD, Promotion and Encouragement of Technological Innovation, A Selective Review of Policies and Instruments, UNCTAD doc. TD/B/C.6/139 (August 4, 1986). Among the benefits which might be available are direct financial assistance from government programs, priorities in government procurement, and fiscal incentives for specified functional activities, such as research and development, technological assistance and the adaptation and assimilation of technology. See Compilation of Legal Material Dealing with Transfer and Development of Technology, UNCTAD doc. TC/B/C.6/81 (August 4, 1982), 106–114.

[62] Adopted June 23, 1987.

[63] Adopted June 23, 1987.

[64] *See, e.g.*, Government of India, Technology Policy Statement, Delhi, 1983, paragraph 2.1.

[65] *See, e.g.*, Zambian Industrial Development Act 1977.

[66] *See, e.g.*, Brazil: Normative Act 015, Article 2.5.1(g), in Compilation of Legal Material Dealing with Transfer and Development of Technology, UNCTAD doc. TC/B/C.6/81 (August 4, 1982), 29 (technology transfer contracts must "establish that the licensee is required to make effective use of the patent").

[67] *See, e.g.*, Brazil: Normative Act 015, September 11, 1975, Article 2.2, in Compilation of Legal Material Dealing with Transfer and Development of Technology, UNCTAD doc. TC/B/C.6/81 (August 4, 1982), 27 (payments under patent licenses are based "on the type of product or sector of activity, depending on the degree of essentiality . . . and shall be directly linked to the sale of the product resulting from the use of the patent").

[68] *See, e.g.*, Brazil: Normative Act 015, September 11, 1975, Article 4.3, in Compilation of Legal Material Dealing with Transfer and Development of Technology, UNCTAD doc. TC/B/C.6/81 (August 4, 1982), 9.

[69] *See, e.g.*, Brazil: Normative Act 015, Article 2.5.1(d), in Compilation of Legal Material Dealing with Transfer and Development of Technology, UNCTAD doc. TC/B/C.6/81 (August 4, 1982), 29 (technology transfer contracts shall specify "that the licensee shall own the rights to improvements or advances incorporated by him in the product or process covered by the license").

[70] *See, e.g.*, Argentina: Law 22,426 on the transfer of technology, March 12, 1981, Article 2, in Compilation of Legal Material Dealing with Transfer and Development of Technology, UNCTAD doc. TC/B/C.6/81 (August 4, 1982), 9.

[71] *See, e.g.*, Andean Code, Article 21, in Compilation of Legal Material Dealing with Transfer and Development of Technology, UNCTAD doc. TC/B/C.6/81 (August 4, 1982), 230; Venezuela, Decree 2242, Article 68, in Compilation of Legal Material Dealing with Transfer and Development of Technology, UNCTAD doc. TC/B/C.6/81 (August 4, 1982), 199–200.

[72] *See, e.g.*, Argentina: Law 22,426 on the transfer of technology, March 12, 1981, Article 5, in Compilation of Legal Material Dealing with Transfer and Development of Technology, UNCTAD doc. TC/B/C.6/81 (August 4, 1982), 9.

[73] *See, e.g.*, Philippines Rules and Regulations, 1978, Rule V, section 1(d).

[74] Even the United States, which historically has exercised little control over foreign investment activity, has recently adopted laws and regulations which authorize the President of the United States to review certain purchases of a United States business by a foreign entity and, if necessary, permit the President to block the transaction, either prospectively or retroactively, for national security reasons. See Exon-Florio Amendment, which was originally enacted on August 23, 1988 as Section 5021 of the Omnibus Trade and Competitiveness Act of 1988 (Pub.L. 100–418, 102 Stat. 1107).

PART FOUR

Multilateral Initiatives and Government Programs Affecting International Business Activities

FEDERAL EXPORT ASSISTANCE PROGRAMS AND RESOURCES

Eleanor Roberts Lewis

I. INTRODUCTION

Many American companies limit their business to the U.S. domestic market or adopt a random approach to exporting because they lack the time, expertise or resources for extensive research, advertising, or overseas travel. However, the Federal government has extensive resources to provide general export counseling as well as specific information and assistance for potential, novice, and experienced exporters. These resources are available free or at cost and should be recommended by legal counsel to their business clients, especially small and medium-sized firms. The programs and resources described below are only a sampling of what is available.

II. GENERAL EXPORT COUNSELING

U. S. Department of Commerce

District Offices

The United States and Foreign Commercial Service (US & FCS) of the U.S. Department of Commerce (Commerce) has field offices in 68 cities within the territorial United States. (See p. 253 for list.) Companies interested in exporting should begin with a visit to one of these offices. In addition to providing general export counselling, Commerce trade specialists can help a company determine its readiness to export and make recommendations to help a company enhance its ability to export. These domestic field offices also provide local access to the Department of Commerce programs described below and to many customized services that are too numerous to describe. Although the introductory export counseling is free of charge, cost recovery fees are charged for many of the more specialized programs and services.

Overseas Posts

US & FCS has commercial officers in 70 countries worldwide, including all the major commercial markets for United States products. (See p. 257.) These overseas officers collect information about commercial trends and trade barriers in their countries and seek out trade opportunities to benefit U.S. firms. They also provide a range of services to exporters traveling abroad, including appointments with potential buyers and government officials, as well as access to the Commerce programs discussed below. For a fee, companies can get the US & FCS Gold Key Service (available in 57 countries) which includes appointments with business contacts, assistance in developing a market strategy, country and market orientation briefings, personal introduction to potential clients and distributors, and effective follow-up activities.

Country Desks

Commerce country desk officers and regional business information centers are located in Washington, D.C., but are easily reachable by telephone. (See p. 263 for list.) These specialists can analyze the exporting needs of an individual firm in the context of a foreign country's trade and economic policies including tariff regulations, business practices, market size and growth. Government publications that are geographically focused can be accessed through these contacts.

Industry Desks

Commerce industry specialists located in Washington, D.C. work with trade associations and individual firms to identify trade opportunities and remove trade obstacles by product, service or industry sector. (See p. 269 for list.) Government publications that are product or sector focused can be accessed through these contacts.

Export Licensing Assistance

The Commerce Department's Bureau of Export Administration is responsible for the licensing of exports. To receive a range of information by telephone through an automated system, try the Export Licensing Voice Information System (ELVIS), 202/482-4811. (Although automated, ELVIS allows the caller to access a licensing counsellor at any time during the connection.) The Commerce Department also provides many useful publications and training seminars on this topic. Export licenses may be submitted and issued via computer through the Export License Application and Information Network (ELAIN). Instant updates on the status of license applications may be obtained by telephone through the System for Tracking Export License Applications (STELA), 202/482-2752.

U.S. Small Business Administration (SBA)

The SBA provides basic export counseling for small firms in some of its district offices and Small Business Institutes and through other mechanisms. See p. 281 for a list of SBA district offices or call SBA's Office of International Trade, 202/205-6720.

U. S. Department of Agriculture

Trade Assistance and Promotion Office (TAPO)

TAPO is a single contact point within the Foreign Agricultural Service in Washington D.C. for agricultural exporters seeking counseling on foreign markets and foreign barriers to agricultural exports. This office can be reached at 202/720-7420.

Overseas Trade Offices

The Foreign Agricultural Service has 15 overseas agricultural trade offices to help exporters of U.S. farm and forest products in key overseas markets. To get more information, call 202/720-6343.

U.S. Department of State

Overseas Posts

State Department Foreign Service Officers stationed in overseas embassies and consulates are able to provide political and economic briefings for U.S. exporters travelling abroad. In addition, in 120 smaller foreign posts not covered by Commerce commercial officers, Foreign Service Officers perform the commercial functions of commerce commercial officers. To reach overseas political or economic officers in particular foreign countries, call the State Department Operator at 202/647-4000.

Country Desks

State Department country desk officers based in Washington, D.C., maintain regular contact with overseas posts and can provide country-specific political and economic briefings for companies in the United States. To reach a particular Foreign Service country desk officer, call the State Department Operator at 202/647-4000.

III. MARKET INFORMATION, TRADE LEADS & OTHER PROMOTION ACTIVITIES

U.S. Department of Commerce

Trade Missions, Trade Shows, & Catalog Exhibitions

Each of the many Commerce Department trade missions going overseas annually includes about 5-10 U.S. business executives in a particular industry or service sector plus one or more Commerce Department trade specialists. Matchmaker Trade Delegations specialize in helping new-to-export and new-to-market companies. Commerce provides participants with detailed foreign market information, advance planning and publicity, logistical support, and pre-arranged appointments with potential foreign buyers and distributors as well as government officials.

In addition to organizing a wide range of export promotion events in promising markets around the world, Commerce certifies numerous overseas trade fairs staged by private sector organizers, as well as trade missions organized by economic development agencies, industry associations, and other export-oriented groups. Events carrying a Commerce certification provide a well publicized opportunity to promote U.S. exports with on-site assistance for U.S. participants and assurance of reliable support from the approved show or mission organizer. Call 202/482-2525 for information on Commerce-certified trade fairs; 202/482-4908 for Commerce-certified trade missions; and 800/USA-TRADE for events directly organized by Commerce.

Commerce Department catalog exhibitions offer a very low-cost, low-risk way to generate leads, whether a company is looking for sales or for representation for its products or services. Overseas commercial officers in embassies throughout selected regions show a company's catalogs or brochures to targeted agents, distributors or buyers in selected world markets. For further information contact the local Commerce District Office or call 202/482-3973.

National Trade Data Bank (NTDB)

The NTDB is a CD-ROM source for international trade information from 17 U.S. government agencies. Updated each month and released on CD-ROM disk, the NTDB enables a user with an IBM-compatible personal computer equipped with a CD-ROM reader to access over 100,000 documents including the latest Census data on U.S. imports and exports, the complete CIA World Factbook, as well as country market research reports and lists of foreign importers from the U.S. & Foreign Commercial Service. The NTDB is available free at over 800 federal depository libraries nationwide. Contact the nearest Commerce District Office or call 800/USA-TRADE for the location of the nearest library. The NTDB can also be purchased on a monthly or annual basis. To subscribe, call 202/482-1986.

Economic Bulletin Board (EBB)

The EBB, a personal computer-based electronic bulletin board, is an on-line source for the latest trade leads and statistical releases from the Department of Commerce, the Department of Labor, the Federal Reserve Board and other Federal agencies. Subscribers, whose computers must be equipped with a modem, pay an annual registration fee and are billed quarterly for access time. To subscribe, call 202/482-1986. To test out the system as a guest user, dial 202/482-3870 with a computer modem and type in "guest" as the log-in name.

Agent/Distributor Service

Through the Agent/Distributor Service, the Commerce Department conducts a customized search to identify overseas agents and distributors for U.S. firms. A fee is charged for each country searched. Contact the nearest Commerce District Office or call 800/USA-TRADE.

Trade Opportunities Program (TOP)

The Commerce Department Trade Opportunities Program provides companies with current trade leads from foreign firms seeking to buy or represent specific products or services. In addition, there is information on other foreign opportunities such as foreign government tenders, project bids, licensing partners, and joint venture partnerships. TOP leads are printed daily in leading commercial newspapers and are distributed electronically through the Electronic Bulletin Board described above. For information about TOP, contact the nearest Commerce District Office or call 800/USA-TRADE. To subscribe to the Electronic Bulletin Board, call 202/482-1986.

Export Contact List Service

This database retrieval service provides U.S. exporters with names, addresses, and other relevant information on foreign firms interested in importing U.S. products and services. Similar information on U.S. exporters is provided to foreign firms seeking U.S. suppliers. The names are collected and maintained by the Commerce District Offices and the commercial officers in overseas posts who should be contacted for information (or call 800/USA-TRADE).

Foreign Buyer Program

This program provides special export-related support to selected, leading trade shows within the United States which feature U.S. products or services with high export potential. The Commerce Department works worldwide to recruit delegations of foreign buyers to attend the event and then assists U.S. firms in matching their products, marketing objectives, and geographic targets with the needs of the international business visitors. An International Business Center is set up at each show to provide interpreters, multilingual brochures, export counseling, and private meeting rooms. For more information, all 202/482-0481.

Business America

This magazine is published bi-weekly by the Commerce Department. Originally issued under another name by the State Department, it is the U.S. government's oldest continuously published periodical. However, its basic mission has remained unchanged: to help American subscribers sell their products and services overseas. Each issue contains "how to" articles for new exporters, news of U.S. government actions that may affect trade, special features on particular countries or regions, and a calendar of upcoming trade shows and seminars. To subscribe, call the U.S. Government Printing Office at 202/783-3238 and ask for Stock #703-011-00000-4. Sample copies may be picked up at Commerce District Offices.

Commercial News USA

This catalog-magazine is published 10 times yearly to promote U.S. products and services to overseas markets. U.S. firms can have their product or service described in this publication for a fee which varies with the size of the listing. Commerce overseas posts distribute *Commercial News USA* in hardcopy to over 125,000 foreign businesspersons and government officials. In addition, in some foreign countries it is available to subscribers to commercial electronic bulletin boards. To be included in the next edition, contact the nearest Commerce District Office or call 202/482-4918.

Census Bureau Data Bases

The Commerce Department Bureau of Census maintains worldwide export and import statistics which can be obtained for a fee by calling 301/763-7754. They also compile demographic and social information for most countries which can be purchased by calling 301/763-4811. Some of this information also appears on the National Trade Data Bank described above.

U.S. Small Business Administration

SBA's Export Information System contains data reports on specific products and services in our top 25 world markets with market growth trends for the past five years. To obtain them, contact the nearest SBA office or call 202/205-6720.

U. S. Department of Agriculture

Agriculture Trade & Marketing Information Centers

These centers, part of the National Agricultural Library, help locate relevant material from their large collection of agricultural trade and marketing information and provide copies of research and data from the AGRICOLA database. For more information, call 301/504-5414 or 504-5509.

Country Market Profiles

Among the many useful publications available from the Department of Agriculture are Country Market Profiles which are country specific descriptions of 40 overseas markets for high-value agriculture products. They provide market overviews, market trends, labeling and licensing requirements as well as information on U.S. market position and competition. Call 202/720-7937 to obtain information on this and other Agriculture Department publications.

AgExport Connections

Through this service, an agricultural exporter can obtain: an AgExport Action Kit telling U.S. exporters how to get in touch quickly and directly with foreign importers of food and other agricultural products; trade leads based on current inquiries from foreign buyers; listings in *Buyer Alert*, an overseas newsletter circulated to potential foreign buyers; and access to or listing of foreign buyer and U.S. supplier databases. To connect with this valuable service, call 202/720-7103.

Computerized Information Delivery Service (CIDS)

For a fee, CIDS provides on-line computer access to Department of Agriculture information within seconds of its release in Washington. This is especially useful for such time-sensitive information as trade leads, current market reports, and certain agricultural statistics. Contact 202/720-5505 to subscribe.

IV. FINANCE AND INSURANCE

Among the most important export assistance provided by the Federal government is assistance related to financing and insuring international sales transactions. This topic is covered in detail in another chapter of this book. So only the name of the agency with a very brief description and contact number is provided below.

U.S. Export-Import Bank (Eximbank)

Eximbank provides direct loans, loan guarantees (including working capital loan guarantees), and export credit insurance to help finance the sales of U.S. goods and services to credit-worthy buyers in foreign countries. Call toll free for more information: 800/424-5201.

U.S. Small Business Administration

SBA provides financial assistance to exporters through regular business loans, international trade loans, and export revolving line of credit loan guarantees. Call toll free for more information: 800/8-ASK-SBA.

Overseas Private Investment Corporation (OPIC)

OPIC provides direct loans, loan guarantees, and political risk insurance for overseas investment projects. Call toll-free if outside the Washington D.C. area (800/424-OPIC) or 202/336-8799.

U.S. Department of Agriculture

Bureaus of the Agriculture Department, such as the Foreign Agricultural Service and the Commodity Credit Corporation, offer export credit guarantees, foreign aid assistance programs, and export enhancement bonuses which help agricultural exporters with the financial aspects of their sales. For information call 202/720-3448.

Trade and Development Agency

The Trade and Development Agency finances consultancies and feasibility studies for major foreign projects. Call 703/875-4357.

V. LEGAL ADVICE

Every Federal executive branch agency discussed above has a legal office (usually called an Office of General Counsel) which can provide specific legal advice related to the agency's specialty. For example, the Department of Commerce Office of General Counsel (202/482-4772) can provide legal assistance on such topics as export licensing, anti-boycott requirements, marketing and distribution agreements, the Foreign Corrupt Practices Act, the Export Trading Companies Act, protection of intellectual property rights, international trade and commercial treaties and codes, etc. To reach an agency's legal office, just ask a program official at the agency (through one of the numbers given above) for his or her lawyer's telephone number.

VI. A "ONE-STOP SHOP"

The vast array of Federal assistance for exporters, which has only been touched on above, is confusing to many newcomers who don't know where to start. When in doubt, call the Trade Information Center toll-free number: 800/USA-TRADE (800/872-8723). The Center, located in Washington, has as its mission to guide businesses through the many export assistance programs available from 19 Federal agencies. In addition, the Federal government is considering the idea of placing several regional "one-stop shops" around the country. These offices may be walk-in centers combining the programs of the Commerce Department, the SBA, Eximbank and perhaps others.

U.S. DEPARTMENT OF COMMERCE
INTERNATIONAL TRADE ADMINISTRATION
U.S. AND FOREIGN COMMERCIAL SERVICE
DISTRICT OFFICE DIRECTORY
FEBRUARY 1, 1994

Charles A. Ford
Acting Assistant Secretary and
  Director General
U.S. and Foreign Commercial
  Service
HCHB 3130
14th & Constitution Avenue, N.W.
Washington, D.C. 20230
PHONE: (202) 482-6228, FAX:
  (202) 482-3159

Vacant
Principal Deputy Assistant
  Secretary
U.S. and Foreign Commercial
  Service
HCHB 3802
14th & Constitution Avenue, N.W.
Washington, D.C. 20230
PHONE: (202) 482-0725, FAX:
  (202) 482-5013

Daniel J. McLaughlin
Deputy Assistant Secretary,
  Domestic Operations
U.S. and Foreign Commercial
  Service
HCHB 3810
14th & Constitution Avenue, N.W.
Washington, D.C. 20230
PHONE: (202) 482-4767, FAX:
  (202) 482-0687

ALABAMA

BIRMINGHAM—Patrick T. Wall,
  Director
Room 302 Berry Building
2015 2nd Avenue North, ZIP: 35203
PHONE: (205) 731-1331, FAX:
  (205) 731-0076

ALASKA

ANCHORAGE—Charles Becker,
  Director
Suite 319, World Trade Center
  Alaska
4201 Tudor Centre Drive, ZIP:
  99508
PHONE: (907) 271-6237, FAX:
  (907) 271-6242

ARIZONA

PHOENIX—Donald W. Fry,
  Director
Phoenix Plaza, Suite 970
2901 N. Central Avenue, ZIP: 85012
PHONE: (602) 640-2513, FAX:
  (602) 640-2518

ARKANSAS

LITTLE ROCK—Lon J. Hardin,
  Director
TCBY Tower Building, Suite 700
425 West Capitol Avenue, ZIP:
  72201
PHONE: (501) 324-5794, FAX:
  (501) 324-7380

CALIFORNIA

LOS ANGELES—Stephen
  Arlinghaus, Director
11000 Wilshire Blvd., Room 9200,
  ZIP: 90024
PHONE: (310) 575-7104, FAX:
  (310) 575-7220

(*) NEWPORT BEACH
3300 Irvine Avenue, Suite 305, ZIP:
  92660
PHONE: (714) 660-1688, FAX:
  (714) 660-8039

(*) LONG BEACH USEAC—Joe
  Sachs, Director
One World Trade Center, Ste. 1670,
  ZIP: 90831
PHONE: (310) 980-4550, FAX:
  (310) 980-4561

SAN DIEGO—Vacant
6363 Greenwich Drive, Suite 230,
  ZIP: 92122
PHONE: (619) 557-5395, FAX:
  (619) 557-6176

SAN FRANCISCO—Betty Neuhart,
  Director
250 Montgomery St., 14th Floor,
  ZIP: 94104
PHONE: (415) 705-2300, FAX:
  (415) 705-2297

(*) SANTA CLARA
5201 Great American Pkwy., #456,
  ZIP: 95054

PHONE: (408) 291-7625, FAX:
  (408) 291-7626

COLORADO

DENVER—Neil Hesse, Director
1625 Broadway, Suite 680, ZIP:
  80202
PHONE: (303) 844-6622, FAX:
  (303) 844-5651

CONNECTICUT

HARTFORD—Carl Jacobsen, Acting
  Director
Room 610B, 450 Main Street, ZIP:
  06103
PHONE: (203) 240-3530, FAX:
  (203) 240-3473

DELAWARE

Served by the Philadelphia District
  Office

DISTRICT OF COLUMBIA

Served by the Gaithersburg Branch
  Office

FLORIDA

(*) MIAMI USEAC—Lewis Nixon,
  Acting Director
P.O. Box 590570, ZIP: 33159
5600 Northwest 36th St., Ste. 617,
  ZIP: 33166
PHONE: (305) 526-7425, FAX:
  (305) 526-7434

(*) CLEARWATER
128 North Osceola Avenue, ZIP:
  34615
PHONE: (813) 461-0011, FAX:
  (813) 449-2889

(*) ORLANDO
Eola Park Centre, Suite 695
200 E. Robinson Street, ZIP: 32801
PHONE: (407) 648-6235, FAX:
  (407) 648-6756

(*) TALLAHASSEE
107 West Gaines Street, Room
  366G, ZIP: 32399
PHONE: (904) 488-6469, FAX:
  (904) 487-1407

GEORGIA

ATLANTA—George T. Norton,
Director
Plaza Square North, Suite 310
4360 Chamblee Dunwoody Road,
ZIP: 30341
PHONE: (404) 452-9101, FAX:
(404) 452-9105

SAVANNAH—Barbara Prieto,
Director
120 Barnard Street, Room A-107,
ZIP: 31401
PHONE: (912) 652-4204, FAX:
(912) 652-4241

HAWAII

HONOLULU—George B. Dolan,
Director
P.O. Box 50026
300 Ala Moana Blvd., Room 4106,
ZIP: 96850
PHONE: (808) 541-1782, FAX:
(808) 541-3435

IDAHO

(*) BOISE—Portland District Office
700 West State Street, ZIP: 83720
PHONE: (208) 334-3857, FAX:
(208) 334-2783

ILLINOIS

(*) CHICAGO USEAC—Brad
Dunderman, Director
Xerox Center
55 West Monroe Street, Suite 2440,
ZIP: 60603
PHONE: (312) 353-8040, FAX:
(312) 353-8098

(*) WHEATON
c/o Illinois Institute of Technology
201 East Loop Road, ZIP: 60187
PHONE: (312) 353-4332, FAX:
(312) 353-4336

(*) ROCKFORD
P.O. Box 1747
515 North Court Street, ZIP: 61110
PHONE: (815) 987-4347, FAX:
(815) 987-8122

INDIANA

INDIANAPOLIS—Andrew Thress,
Director
Penwood One, Suite 106
11405 N. Pennsylvania Street
Carmel, IN. 46032
PHONE: (317) 582-2300, FAX:
(317) 582-2301

IOWA

DES MOINES—Randall J.
LaBounty, Director
Room 817, Federal Building
210 Walnut Street, ZIP: 50309
PHONE: (515) 284-4222, FAX:
(515) 284-4021

KANSAS

(*) WICHITA—Kansas City District
Office
151 N. Volutsia, ZIP: 67214
PHONE: (316) 269-6160, FAX:
(316) 683-7326

KENTUCKY

LOUISVILLE—John Autin, Director
Marmaduke Building, 3rd Floor
520 South 4th Street, ZIP: 40202
PHONE: (502) 582-5066, FAX:
(502) 582-6573

LOUISIANA

NEW ORLEANS—Paul L. Guidry,
Director
Hale Boggs Federal Building
501 Magazine Street, Room 1043,
ZIP: 70130
PHONE: (504) 589-6546, FAX:
(504) 589-2337

MAINE

(*) AUGUSTA—Boston District
Office
187 State Street, ZIP: 04333
PHONE: (207) 622-8249, FAX:
(207) 626-9156

MARYLAND

(*) BALTIMORE USEAC—Roger
Fortner, Director
World Trade Center, Suite 2432
401 Pratt Street, ZIP: 21202
PHONE: (410) 962-4539 FAX: (410)
962-4529

(*) GAITHERSBURG
c/o National Institute of Standards &
Technology
Room A102, Building 411, ZIP:
20899
PHONE: (301) 975-3904; FAX:
(301) 948-4360

MASSACHUSETTS

BOSTON—Frank J. O'Connor,
Director
164 Northern Avenue

World Trade Center, Suite 307, ZIP:
02210
PHONE: (617) 565-8563, FAX:
(617) 565-8530

MICHIGAN

DETROIT—Dean Peterson, Director
1140 McNamara Building
477 Michigan Avenue, ZIP: 48226
PHONE: (313) 226-3650, FAX:
(313) 226-3657

(*) GRAND RAPIDS
300 Monroe N.W., Room 409, ZIP:
49503
PHONE: (616) 456-2411, FAX:
(616) 456-2695

MINNESOTA

MINNEAPOLIS—Ronald E.
Kramer, Director
108 Federal Building
110 South 4th Street, ZIP: 55401
PHONE: (612) 348-1638, FAX:
(612) 348-1650

MISSISSIPPI

JACKSON—Mark E. Spinney,
Director
201 W. Capitol Street, Suite 310,
ZIP: 39201
PHONE: (601) 965-4388, FAX:
(601) 965-5386

MISSOURI

ST. LOUIS—Sandra Gerley,
Director
8182 Maryland Avenue, Suite 303,
ZIP: 63105
PHONE: (314) 425-3302, FAX:
(314) 425-3381

KANSAS CITY—John Steuber,
Director
601 East 12th Street, Room 635,
ZIP: 64106
PHONE: (816) 426-3141, FAX:
(816) 426-3140

MONTANA

Served by the Boise Branch Office

NEBRASKA

OMAHA—Vacant
11133 "O" Street, ZIP: 68137
PHONE: (402) 221-3664, FAX:
(402) 221-3668

NEVADA

RENO—James K. Hellwig, Director
1755 East Plumb Lane, Room 152,
ZIP: 89502
PHONE: (702) 784-5203, FAX:
(702) 784-5343

NEW HAMPSHIRE

(*) PORTSMOUTH—Boston District
Office
601 Spaulding Turnpike, Suite 29,
ZIP: 03801
PHONE: (603) 334-6074, FAX:
(603) 334-6110

NEW JERSEY

TRENTON—Rod Stuart, Acting
Director
3131 Princeton Pike, Bldg. #6,
Suite 100, ZIP: 08648
PHONE: (609) 989-2100, FAX:
(609) 989-2395

NEW MEXICO

(*) SANTA FE—Dallas District
Office
c/o New Mexico Dept. of Economic
Development
1100 St. Francis Drive, ZIP: 87503
PHONE: (505) 827-0350, FAX:
(505) 827-0263

NEW YORK

BUFFALO—George Buchanan,
Director
1312 Federal Building
111 West Huron Street, ZIP: 14202
PHONE: (716) 846-4191, FAX:
(716) 846-5290

(*) ROCHESTER
111 East Avenue, Suite 220, ZIP:
14604
PHONE: (716) 263-6480, FAX:
(716) 325-6505

NEW YORK—Joel W. Barkan,
Director
26 Federal Plaza, Room 3718, ZIP:
10278
PHONE: (212) 264-0634, FAX:
(212) 264-1356

NORTH CAROLINA

GREENSBORO—Samuel P. Troy,
Director
400 West Market Street, Suite 400,
ZIP: 27401
PHONE: (910) 333-5345, FAX:
(910) 333-5158

NORTH DAKOTA

Served by the Minneapolis District
Office

OHIO

CINCINNATI—Gordon Thomas,
Director
550 Main Street, Room 9504, ZIP:
45202
PHONE: (513) 684-2944, FAX:
(513) 684-3200

CLEVELAND—Toby T. Zettler,
Director
Bank One Center
600 Superior Avenue, Suite 700,
ZIP: 44114
PHONE: (216) 522-4750, FAX:
(216) 522-2235

OKLAHOMA

OKLAHOMA CITY—Ronald L.
Wilson, Director
6601 Broadway Extension, Rm. 200,
ZIP: 73116
PHONE: (405) 231-5302, FAX:
(405) 841-5245

(*) TULSA
440 South Houston Street, ZIP:
74127
PHONE: (918) 581-7650, FAX:
(918) 581-2844

OREGON

PORTLAND—William Schrage,
Director
One World Trade Center, Suite 242
121 SW Salmon, ZIP: 97204
PHONE: (503) 326-3001, FAX:
(503) 326-6351

PENNSYLVANIA

PHILADELPHIA—Robert E.
Kistler, Director
660 American Avenue, Suite 201
King of Prussia, PA. 19406
PHONE: (215) 962-4980, FAX:
(215) 962-4989

PITTSBURGH—John A.
McCartney, Director
2002 Federal Building
1000 Liberty Avenue, ZIP: 15222
PHONE: (412) 644-2850, FAX:
(412) 644-4875

PUERTO RICO

SAN JUAN (Hato Rey)—J. Enrique
Vilella, Director

Room G-55, Federal Building
Chardon Avenue, ZIP: 00918
PHONE: (809) 766-5555, FAX:
(809) 766-5692

RHODE ISLAND

(*) PROVIDENCE—Hartford
District Office
7 Jackson Walkway, ZIP: 02903
PHONE: (401) 528-5104, FAX:
(401) 528-5067

SOUTH CAROLINA

COLUMBIA—Edgar L. Rojas,
Director
Strom Thurmond Federal Bldg.,
Suite 172
1835 Assembly Street, ZIP: 29201
PHONE: (803) 765-5345, FAX:
(803) 253-3614

(*) CHARLESTON
c/o Trident Technical College
P.O. Box 118067, CE-P
66 Columbus Street, ZIP: 29423
PHONE: (803) 727-4051, FAX:
(803) 727-4052

SOUTH DAKOTA

Served by the Omaha District Office

TENNESSEE

NASHVILLE—Jim Charlet, Director
Parkway Towers, Suite 114
404 James Robertson Parkway, ZIP:
37219
PHONE: (615) 736-5161, FAX:
(615) 736-2454

(*) MEMPHIS
22 North Front Street, Suite 200,
ZIP: 38103
PHONE: (901) 544-4137, FAX:
(901) 575-3510

(*) KNOXVILLE
301 East Church Avenue, ZIP:
37915
PHONE: (615) 545-4637, FAX:
(615) 523-2071

TEXAS

DALLAS—Donald Schilke, Director
P.O. Box 58130
2050 N. Stemmons Fwy., Suite 170,
ZIP: 75258
PHONE: (214) 767-0542, FAX:
(214) 767-8240

(*) AUSTIN
P.O. Box 12728

410 E. 5th Street, Suite 414-A, ZIP: 78711
PHONE: (512) 482-5939, FAX: (512) 482-5940

HOUSTON—James D. Cook, Director
#1 Allen Center, Suite 1160
500 Dallas, ZIP: 77002
PHONE: (713) 229-2578, FAX: (713) 229-2203

UTAH

SALT LAKE CITY—Stephen P. Smoot, Director
324 S. State Street, Suite 105, ZIP: 84111
PHONE: (801) 524-5116, FAX: (801) 524-5886

VERMONT

(*) MONTPELIER
c/o Vermont Dept. of Economic Development
109 State Street, ZIP: 05609
PHONE: (802) 828-4508, FAX: (802) 828-4507

VIRGINIA

RICHMOND—Philip A. Ouzts, Director
700 Centre
704 East Franklin Street, Suite 550, ZIP: 23219
PHONE: (804) 771-2246, FAX: (804) 771-2390

WASHINGTON

SEATTLE—Lisa Kjaer, Director

3131 Elliott Avenue, Suite 290, ZIP: 98121
PHONE: (206) 553-5615, FAX: (206) 553-7253

(*) TRI-CITIES
320 North Johnson Street, Suite 350
Kennewick, WA. 99336
PHONE: (509) 735-2751, FAX: (509) 735-9385

WEST VIRGINIA

CHARLESTON—Vacant
405 Capitol Street, Suite 807, ZIP: 25301
PHONE: (304) 347-5123, FAX: (304) 347-5408

WISCONSIN

MILWAUKEE—Johnny Brown, Director
517 E. Wisconsin Avenue, Room 596, ZIP: 53202
PHONE: (414) 297-3473, FAX: (414) 297-3470

WYOMING

Served by the Denver District Office

REGIONAL OFFICES:

(***) REGION I, PHILADELPHIA
Carl Jacobsen, Acting Regional Director
660 American Avenue, Suite 202
King of Prussia, PA. 19406

PHONE: (215) 962-4990, FAX: (215) 962-1326

(***) REGION II, ATLANTA
LoRee Silloway, Regional Director
Plaza Square North, Suite 405
4360 Chamblee Dunwoody Road, 30341
PHONE: (404) 455-7860, FAX: (404) 455-7865

(***) REGION III, CINCINNATI
Gordon Thomas, Acting Regional Director
9504 Federal Building
550 Main Street, ZIP: 45202
PHONE: (513) 684-2947, FAX: (513) 684-3200

(***) REGION IV, ST. LOUIS
Donald R. Loso, Regional Director
8182 Maryland Avenue, Suite 305, ZIP: 63105
PHONE: (314) 425-3300, FAX: (314) 425-3375

(***) REGION V, SAN FRANCISCO
Michael Liikala, Regional Director
250 Montgomery St., 14th Floor, ZIP: 94104
PHONE: (415) 705-2310, FAX: (415) 705-2299

(*)—DENOTES TRADE SPECIALIST AT A BRANCH OFFICE

(*)—DENOTES A U.S. EXPORT ASSISTANCE CENTER

(***)—OFFICE WITH MANAGE-RIAL AND ADMINISTRATIVE OVER-SIGHT RESPONSIBILITIES (OFFERS NO DIRECT BUSINESS COUNSEL-ING)

INTERNATIONAL TRADE ADMINISTRATION

U.S. AND FOREIGN COMMERCIAL SERVICE OVERSEAS POSTS

ALGERIA
American Embassy
Algiers
SCO Andrew Tangalos
Tel: 011-213-2-603-973
Fax: 011-213-2-603-979
U.S. Dept of State (Algiers)
Washington, D.C. 20521-6030

ARGENTINA
American Embassy
Buenos Aires
SCO Arthur Alexander
Tel: 011-54-1-772-1041
Fax: 011-54-1-777-0673
Unit 4326
APO AA 34034

AUSTRALIA
American Consulate General
Sydney
SCO Michael Hand
Tel: 011-61-2-373-9200
Fax: 011-61-2-221-0573
Unit 11024
APO AP 96554-0002

American Consulate
Brisbane
FCSN (vacant)
Tel: 011-61-7-839-8955
Fax: 011-61-7-832-6247
Unit 11018
APO AP 96553-0002

American Consulate General
Melbourne
FCSO Daniel Young
Tel: 011-61-3-526-5923
Fax: 011-61-3-510-4660
Unit 11011
APO AP 96551-0002

American Consulate General
Perth
FCSN Marion Shingler
Tel: 011-61-9-231-9400
Fax: 011-61-9-231-9444
Unit 11021
APO AP 96553-0002

AUSTRIA
American Embassy
Vienna
SCO Benjamin Brown
Tel: 011-43-1-313-39
Fax: 011-43-1-310-6917
U.S. Dept. of State (Vienna)
Washington, D.C. 20521-9900

BELGIUM
American Embassy
Brussels
SCO Jerry Mitchell

Tel: 011-32-2-513-3830
Fax: 011-32-2-512-6653
PSC 82 Box 002
APO AE 09724-1015

U.S. Mission to the European
  Communities
Brussels
SCO John Bligh
Tel: 011-32-2-513-445
Fax: 011-32-2-513-1228
PSC 82 Box 002
APO AE 09724

BRAZIL
American Consulate General
Sao Paulo
SCO Richard Ades
Tel: 011-55-11-853-2011
Fax: 011-55-11-853-2744
Unit 3502
APO AA 34030

American Consular Agency
Belem
FCSN Raymundo Teixiera
Tel: 011-55-91-223-0413
Fax: 011-55-91-223-0413
Unit 3500
APO AA 34030

American Consular Agency
Belo Horizonte
FCSN Jose Mauricio de Vasconcelos
Tel: 011-55-31-335-3250
Fax: 011-55-31-335-3250
Unit 3505
APO AA 34030

American Embassy
Brasilia
FCSO Larry Farris
Tel: 011-55-61-321-7272
Fax: 011-55-61-225-3981
Unit 3502
APO AA 34030

American Consulate General
Rio De Janeiro
FCSO Dan Pribyl
Tel: 011-55-21-292-7117
Fax: 011-55-21-240-9738
APO AA 34030

BULGARIA
American Embassy
Sofia
SCO John Fogarasi
Unit 25402
Tel: 011-359-2-88-48-01
Fax: 011-359-2-80-38-50
APO AE 09213-5630

CANADA
American Embassy

Ottawa
SCO Robert Marro
Tel: 1-613-238-5335
Fax: 1-613-233-8511
P.O. Box 5000
Ogdensburg, N.Y. 13669

American Consulate General
Calgary
FCSO Ann Tull
Tel: 1-403-266-8962
Fax: 1-403-266-4743
615 Macleod Trail, SE., Suite 1050
Calgary, Alberta, Canada T2G 4T8

American Consulate General
Halifax
FCSN Richard Vinson
Tel: 1-902-429-2482
Fax: 1-902-423-6861
Suite 900, Cogswell Tower
Halifax, Nova Scotia, Canada B3J
  3K1

American Consulate General
Montreal
FCSO Ed Cannon
Tel: 1-514-398-9695
Fax: 1-514-398-0711
P.O. Box 847
Champlain, N.Y. 12919-0847

American Consulate General
Toronto
FCSO Dan Wilson
Tel: 1-416-595-5413
Fax: 1-416-595-5419
P.O. Box 135
Lewiston, N.Y. 14092

American Consulate General
Vancouver
FCSO Jere Dabbs
Tel: 1-604-685-3382
Fax: 1-604-687-6095
P.O. Box 5002
Point Roberts, Wash. 98281-5002

CHILE
American Embassy
Santiago
SCO Ricardo Villalobos
Tel: 011-56-2-671-0133
Fax: 011-56-2-697-2051
Unit 4111
APO AA 34033

CHINA
American Embassy
Beijing
SCO Mel Searls
Tel: 011-86-1-532-3831
Fax: 011-86-1-532-3297
PSC 461 Box 50
FPO AP 96521-0002

American Consulate General
Guangzhou
FCSO Dennis Barnes
Tel: 011-86-20-67-8742
Fax: 011-86-20-666-409
PSC 461 Box 100
FPO AP 96521-0002

American Consulate General
Shanghai
FCSO David Murphy
Tel: 011-86-21-433-2492
Fax: 011-86-21-433-1576
PSC 461 Box 200
FPO AP 96521-0002

American Consulate General
Shenyang
FCSO Jenifer Young
Tel: 011-86-24-220-057
Fax: 011-86-24-220-074
PSC 461 Box 45
FPO AP 96521-0002

COLOMBIA
American Embassy
Bogota
SCO Richard Lenahan
Tel: 011-57-1-232-6550
Fax: 011-57-1-320-7945
Unit 5120
APO AA 34038

COSTA RICA
American Embassy
San Jose
SCO Maria Galindo
Tel: 011-506-20-39-39
Fax: 011-506-31-47-83
Unit 2508
APO AA 34020

COTE D'IVOIRE
American Embassy
Abidjan
SCO Catherine Houghton
Tel: 011-225-21-4616
Fax: 011-225-22-3259
U.S. Dept of State (Abidjan)
Washington, D.C. 20521-2010

CROATIA
American Embassy
Zagreb
FCSN Danjan Bencic
Tel: 011-38-41-444-800
Fax: 011-38-41-440-235
APO AE 09213-5080

CZECH REPUBLIC
American Embassy
Prague
SCO Dan Harris
Tel: 011-42-2-2421-9844
Fax: 011-42-2-2421-9965
Unit 25402
APO AE 09213-5630

DENMARK
American Embassy
Copenhagen
SCO Richard Benson
Tel: 011-45-31-42-31-44
Fax: 011-45-31-42-01-75
U.S. Dept. of State (Copenhagen)
Washington, D.C. 20521-5280

DOMINICAN REPUBLIC
American Embassy
Santo Domingo
SCO Larry Eisenberg
Tel: 1-809-221-2171
Fax: 1-809-688-4838
Unit 5515
APO AA 34041

ECUADOR
American Embassy
Quito
SCO Ralph Griffin
Tel: 011-593-2-561-404
Fax: 011-593-2-504-550
Unit 5334
APO AA 34039-3420

American Consulate General
Guayaquil
FCSN Gloria Ron
Tel: 011-593-4-323-570
Fax: 011-593-4-324-558
APO AA 34039

EGYPT
American Embassy
Cairo
SCO Laron Jensen
Tel: 011-20-2-357-2330
Fax: 011-20-2-355-8368
Unit 64900 Box 11
FPO AE 09839-4900

U.S. Commercial Office
Alexandria
FCSN John Abdelnour
Tel: 011-20-3-482-1911
Fax: 011-20-3-482-9199
Unit 64904
APO AE 09839-4904

FINLAND
American Embassy
Helsinki
SCO Maria Andrews
Tel: 011-358-0-171-931
Fax: 011-358-0-635-332
APO AE 09723

FRANCE
American Embassy
Paris
SCO Peter Frederick
Tel: 011-33-1-4296-1202
Fax: 011-33-1-4266-4827
APO AE 09777
U.S. Mission to the OECD
Paris
SCO Robyn Layton
Tel: 011-33-1-4524-7437
Fax: 011-33-1-4524-7410
APO AE 09777

American Consulate General
Bordeaux
FCSN Valerie DeRousseau
Tel: 011-33-56-52-65-95
Fax: 011-33-56-51-60-42
APO AE 09777

U.S. Commercial Office
Lyon
FCSN (vacant)
Tel: 011-33-78-24-68-49
Fax: 011-33-78-41-71-81
APO AE 09777

American Consulate General
Marseille
FCSN Igor Lepine
Tel: 011-33-91-549-200
Fax: 011-33-91-550-947
APO AE 09777

U.S. Commercial Office
Nice
FCSN Reine Joguet
Tel: 011-33-93-88-89-55
Fax: 011-33-93-87-07-38
APO AE 09777

American Consulate General
Strasbourg
FCSN Jacqueline Munzlinger
Tel: 011-33-88-35-31-04
Fax: 011-33-88-24-0695
APO AE 09777

GERMANY
American Embassy
Bonn
SCO Robert Kohn
Tel: 011-49-228-339-2895
Fax: 011-49-228-334-649
Unit 21701 Box 370
APO AE 09080

U.S. Embassy Office
Berlin
FCSO James Joy
Tel: 011-49-30-251-2061
Fax: 011-49-30-238-6296
Unit 26738
APO AE 09235-5500

U.S. Commercial Office
Duesseldorf
FCSN Barbara Ernst

Tel: 011-49-211-596-798
Fax: 011-49-211-594-897
c/o AmEmbassy Bonn
Unit 21701 Box 370
APO AE 09080

American Consulate General
Frankfurt
FCSO Donald Businger
Tel: 011-49-69-7535-2453
Fax: 011-49-69-748-204
APO AE 09213

American Consulate General
Hamburg
FCSO Hans Amrhein
Tel: 011-49-40-4117-1304
Fax: 011-49-40-410-6598
U.S. Dept. of State (Hamburg)
Washington, D.C. 20521-5180

American Consulate General
Leipzig
FCSN Birgit Lehne
Tel: 011-37-41-211-7866
Fax: 011-37-41-211-7855
APO AE 09235-5100

American Consulate General
Munich
FCSO Stephen Helgesen
Tel: 011-49-89-2888-748
Fax: 011-49-89-285-261
Unit 24718
APO AE 09178

American Consulate General
Stuttgart
FCSO Camille Sailer
Tel: 011-49-711-214-5238
Fax: 011-49-711-236-4350
APO AE 09154

GREECE
American Embassy
Athens
SCO John Priamou
Tel: 011-30-1-723-9705
Fax: 011-30-1-721-8660
PSC 108 Box 30
APO AE 09842

GUATEMALA
American Embassy
Guatemala
SCO Henry Nicol
Tel: 011-502-2-348-479
Fax: 011-502-2-317-373
Unit 3306
APO AA 34024

HONDURAS
American Embassy
Tegucigalpa
SCO Michael McGee
Tel: 011-504-36-9320
Fax: 011-504-38-2888
Unit 2923
APO AA 34022

HONG KONG
American Consulate General
Hong Kong
SCO Thomas L. Boam
Tel: 011-852-521-1467
Fax: 011-852-845-9800
PSC 464 Box 30
FPO AP 96522-0002

HUNGARY
American Embassy
Budapest
SCO Patrick Hughes
Tel: 011-36-1-122-8600
Fax: 011-36-1-142-2529
APO AE 09213-5270

INDIA
American Embassy
New Delhi
SCO Jon Bensky
Tel: 011-91-11-600-651
Fax: 011-91-11-687-2391
U.S. Dept. of State (New Delhi)
Washington, D.C. 20521-9000

U.S. Commercial Office
Bangalore
FSO Leonard Roberts
Tel: 011-91-80-581-452
Fax: 011-91-80-583-630
c/o AmConsul Madras

American Consulate General
Bombay
FCSO John Wood
Tel: 011-91-22-262-4590
Fax: 011-91-22-262-3850
U.S. Dept. of State (Bombay)
Washington, D.C. 20521-6240

American Consulate General
Calcutta
FCSN Nargiz Chatterjee
Tel: 011-91-33-242-3611
Fax: 011-91-33-242-2335
U.S. Dept. of State (Calcutta)
Washington, D.C. 20521-6250

American Consulate General
Madras
FCSO Michael Keaveny
Tel: 011-91-44-827-3040
Fax: 011-91-44-825-0240
U.S. Dept. of State (Madras)
Washington, D.C. 20521-6260

INDONESIA
American Embassy
Jakarta
SCO Theodore Villinski
Tel: 011-62-21-360-360
Fax: 011-62-21-385-1632
Box 1
APO AP 96520

American Consulate General
Medan
FCSN Wagiman Tandum

Tel: 011-62-61-322-200
Fax: 011-62-61-518-711
APO AP 96520

American Consulate General
Surabaya
FCSN Midji Kwee
Tel: 011-62-31-67100
Fax: 011-62-31-574-492
APO AP 96520

IRELAND
American Embassy
Dublin
SCO Gene Harris
Tel: 011-353-1-668-7122
Fax: 011-353-1-668-2840
U.S. Dept. of State (Dublin)
Washington, D.C. 20521-5290
ISRAEL
American Embassy
Tel Aviv
SCO Judith Henderson
Tel: 011-972-3-517-6161
Fax: 011-972-3-510-7215
PSC 98 Box 100
APO AE 09830

ITALY
American Embassy
Rome
SCO Keith Bovetti
Tel: 011-39-6-4674-2202
Fax: 011-39-6-4674-2113
PSC 59
APO AE 09624

American Consulate General
Florence
FCSN Alessandra Gola
Tel: 011-39-55-211-676
Fax: 011-39-55-283-780
PSC 59 Box F
APO AE 09624

American Consulate General
Genoa
FCSN Erminia Lezzi
Tel: 011-39-10-247-1412
Fax: 011-39-10-290-027
PSC 59 Box G
APO AE 09624

American Consulate General
Milan
FCSO Peter Alois
Tel: 011-39-2-498-2241
Fax: 011-39-2-481-4161
PSC 59 Box M
APO AE 09624

American Consulate General
Naples
FCSN Christiano Sartorio
Tel: 011-39-81-761-1592
Fax: 011-39-81-761-1869
PSC 59 Box N
FPO AE 09624

JAPAN
American Embassy
Tokyo
SCO George Mu
Tel: 011-81-3-3224-5000
Fax: 011-81-3-3589-4235
Unit 45004 Box 204
APO AP 96337-0001

American Consulate
Fukuoka
FCSN Yoshihiro Yamamoto
Tel: 011-81-92-751-9331
Fax: 011-81-92-713-9222
Unit 45004, Box 242
APO AP 96337-0001

Representative Office
Nagoya
FCSO Todd Thurwachter
Tel: 011-81-52-203-4011
Fax: 011-81-52-201-4612
c/o U.S. Embassy Tokyo
Unit 45004, Box 280
APO AP 96337-0001

American Consulate General
Osaka-Kobe
FCSO Ira Kasoff
Tel: 011-81-6-315-5953
Fax: 011-81-6-361-5978
Unit 45004 Box 239
APO AP 96337

American Consulate General
Sapporo
FCSN Kenji Itaya
Tel: 011-81-11-641-1115
Fax: 011-81-11-643-0911
APO AP 96337-0003

KAZAKHSTAN
American Embassy
Almaty
FCSO Susan Weidner
Tel: 011-7-3272-631-770
Fax: 011-7-3272-633-883
U.S. Dept. of State (Almaty)
Washington, D.C. 20521-7030

KENYA
American Embassy
Nairobi
SCO (vacant)
Tel: 011-254-2-334-141
Fax: 011-254-2-216-648
Unit 64100 Box 51
APO AE 09831-4100

KOREA
American Embassy
Seoul
SCO Robert Connan
Tel: 011-82-2-732-2601
Fax: 011-82-2-739-1628
Unit 15550
APO AP 96205-0001

KUWAIT

American Embassy
Kuwait
SCO (vacant)
Tel: 011-965-242-4151 or 244-8073
Fax: 011-965-244-7692
Unit 69000 Box 10
APO AE 09880-9000

MALAYSIA
American Embassy
Kuala Lumpur
SCO Paul Walters
Tel: 011-60-3-248-9011
Fax: 011-60-3-242-1866
APO AP 96535-5000

MEXICO
American Embassy
Mexico City
SCO Carlos Poza
Tel: 011-52-5-211-0042
Fax: 011-52-5-207-8938
P.O. Box 3087
Laredo, Tex. 78044-3087

U.S. Trade Center
Mexico City
Dir. Robert Miller
Tel: 011-52-5-591-0155
Fax: 011-52-5-566-1115
P.O. Box 3087
Laredo, Tex. 78044-3087

American Consulate General
Guadalajara
FCSO W. Brian Smith
Tel: 011-52-36-25-0321
Fax: 011-52-36-26-3576
P.O. Box 3088
Laredo, Tex. 78044-3088

American Consulate General
Monterrey
FCSO John Harris
Tel: 011-52-83-452-120
Fax: 011-52-83-42-5172
P.O. Box 3098
Laredo, Tex. 78044-3098

MOROCCO
American Consulate General
Casablanca
SCO Frederic Gaynor
Tel: 011-212-26-45-50
Fax: 011-212-22-02-59
PSC 74 Box 024
APO AE 09718

American Embassy
Rabat
FCSN Karima Hammoud
Tel: 011-212-7-622-65
Fax: 011-212-7-656-61
APO AE 09718

NETHERLANDS
American Embassy
The Hague
SCO Rafael Fermoselle

Tel: 011-31-70-310-9417
Fax: 011-31-70-363-2985
PSC 71 Box 1000
APO AE 09715

American Consulate General
Amsterdam
FCSO Tapan Banerjee
Tel: 011-31-20-575-5351
Fax: 011-31-20-575-5350
APO AE 09159

NEW ZEALAND
American Consulate General
Auckland
SCO (vacant)
Tel: 011-64-9-303-2038
Fax: 011-64-9-366-0870
PSC 467 Box 99
FPO AP 96531-1099

American Embassy
Wellington
FCSN Janet Coulthart
Tel: 011-64-4-722-068
Fax: 011-64-4-781-701
PSC 467 Box 1
FPO AP 96531-1001

NIGERIA
American Embassy
Lagos
SCO Walter Hage
Tel: 011-234-1-616-477
Fax: 011-234-1-619-856
U.S. Dept. of State (Lagos)
Washington, D.C. 20521-8300

NORWAY
American Embassy
Oslo
SCO Scott Bozek
Tel: 011-47-22-44-85-50
Fax: 011-47-22-55-88-03
PSC 69 Box 0200
APO AE 09707

PAKISTAN
American Consulate General
Karachi
SCO Danny DeVito
Tel: 011-92-21-568-5170
Fax: 011-92-21-568-1381
Unit 62400 Box 137
APO AE 09814-2400

American Consulate General
Lahore
FCSN Shalla Malik
Tel: 011-92-42-870-221
Fax: 011-92-42-368-901
Unit 62216
APO AE 09812-2216

PANAMA
American Embassy
Panama
SCO Americo "Mack" Tadeu
Tel: 011-507-27-1777

Fax: 011-507-27-1713
Unit 0945
APO AA 34002

PERU
American Embassy
Lima
SCO Franklin D. Anderson
Tel: 011-51-14-33-0555
Fax: 011-51-14-33-4687
Unit 3780
APO AA 34031

PHILIPPINES
American Embassy
Manila
SCO August Maffry
Tel: 011-63-2-818-6674
Fax: 011-63-2-818-2684
APO AP 96440

POLAND
American Embassy
Warsaw
SCO Joan Edwards
Tel: 011-48-22-621-4216
Fax: 011-48-22-621-6327
APO AE 09213-5010

PORTUGAL
American Embassy
Lisbon
SCO Miguel Pardo de Zela
Tel: 011-351-1-726-6600
Fax: 011-351-1-726-8914
PSC 83 Box FCS
APO AE 09726

American Business Center
Oporto
FCSN Adolfo Coutinho
Tel: 011-351-2-606-3095
Fax: 011-351-2-600-2737
c/o Embassy
PSC 83 Box FCS
APO AE 09726

ROMANIA
American Embassy
Bucharest
SCO Craig Atkins
Tel: 011-40-0-10-40-40
Fax: 011-40-1-312-0395
APO AE 09213-5260

RUSSIA
American Embassy
Moscow
SCO Dale Slaght
Tel: 011-7-502-224-1105
Fax: 011-7-502-224-1106
PSC 77-FCS
APO AE 09721

American Consulate General
St. Petersburg
FCSO Karen Zens
Tel: 011-7-812-213-6537
Fax: 011-7-812-213-6962

APO AE 09723

American Consulate General
Vladivostok
FCSO Roy Peterson
Tel: 011-7-4232-26-84-58
Fax: 011-7-4232-26-84-45
U.S. Dept. of State (Vladivostok)
Washington, D.C. 20521-5880

U.S. Commercial Office
Khabarovsk
FCSN Anatoly Fomine
Tel: 011-7-4232-26-84-58
Fax: 011-7-4232-26-84-45
c/o Vladivostok
U.S. Dept. of State
Washington, D.C. 20521-5880

SAUDI ARABIA
American Embassy
Riyadh
SCO Kevin Brennan
Tel: 011-966-1-488-3800
Fax: 011-966-1-488-3237
Unit 61307
APO AE 09038-1307

American Consulate General
Dhahran
FCSO Tom Moore
Tel: 011-966-3-891-3200
Fax: 011-966-3-891-8332
Unit 66803
APO AE 09858-6803

American Consulate General
Jeddah
FCSO Renato Davia
Tel: 011-966-2-667-0040
Fax: 011-966-2-665-8106
Unit 62112
APO AE 09811-2112

SERBIA
American Embassy
Belgrade
FCSN Radmila Diklic
Tel: 011-38-11-645-655
Fax: 011-38-11-645-096
APO AE 09213-5070

SINGAPORE
American Embassy
Singapore
SCO Steve Craven
Tel: 011-65-338-9722
Fax: 011-65-338-5010
FPO AP 96534-0006

SLOVAK REPUBLIC
American Embassy
Bratislava
FCSN (vacant)
Box 5630, Unit 25402
Tel: 011-42-7-33-0861
Fax: 011-42-7-33-5439
APO AE 09213-5630

SOUTH AFRICA
American Consulate General
Johannesburg
SCO George Kachmar
Tel: 011-27-11-331-3937
Fax: 011-27-11-331-6178
U.S. Dept. of State (Johannesburg)
Washington, D.C. 20521-2500

American Consulate General
Cape Town
FCSN Sylvia Frowde
Tel: 011-27-21-21-4280
Fax: 011-27-21-254-151
U.S. Dept. of State (Cape Town)
Washington, D.C. 20521-2480

SPAIN
American Embassy
Madrid
SCO Emilio Iodice
Tel: 011-34-1-576-0602
Fax: 011-34-1-575-8655
PSC 61 Box 0021
APO AE 09642

American Consulate General
Barcelona
FCSO Dorothy Lutter
Tel: 011-34-3-280-2227
Fax: 011-34-3-205-7705
PSC 64
APO AE 09642

SWEDEN
American Embassy
Stockholm
SCO Barbara Slawecki
Tel: 011-46-8-783-5346
Fax: 011-46-8-660-9181
U.S. Dept. of State (Stockholm)
Washington, D.C. 20521-5750

SWITZERLAND
American Embassy
Bern
SCO Kay Kuhlman
Tel: 011-41-31-357-7011
Fax: 011-41-31-357-7336
U.S. Dept. of State (Bern)
Washington, D.C. 20521-5110

U.S. Mission to GATT
Geneva
SCO Andrew Grossman
Tel: 011-41-22-749-5281
Fax: 011-41-22-749-4885
U.S. Dept. of State (Geneva)
Washington, D.C. 20521-5120

American Consulate General
Zurich
FCSN Paul Frei
Tel: 011-41-1-552-070
Fax: 011-41-1-383-2655
U.S. Dept. of State (Zurich)
Washington, D.C. 20521-5130

THAILAND
American Embassy

Bangkok
SCO Carol Kim
Tel: 011-66-2-253-4920
Fax: 011-66-2-255-2915
APO AP 96546

TURKEY
American Embassy
Ankara
SCO Dave Katz
Tel: 011-90-312-468-6110
Fax: 011-90-312-467-1366
PSC 93 Box 5000
APO AE 09823

American Consulate General
Istanbul
FCSO John Muehlke
Tel: 011-90-1-151-3602
Fax: 011-90-1-252-2417
PSC 97 Box 0002
APO AE 09827-0002

U.S. Commercial Office
Izmir
FCSN Berrin Erturk
Tel: 011-90-232-441-2446
Fax: 011-90-232-489-0267
APO AE 09827

UKRAINE
American Embassy
Ukraine
FCSO Stephen Wasylko
Tel: 011-7-044-417-2669

Fax: 011-7-044-417-1419
U.S. Dept. of State
Washington, D.C. 20521-5850

UNITED ARAB EMIRATES
American Embassy
Abu Dhabi
FCSO Paul Scogna
Tel: 011-971-2-345-545
Fax: 011-971-2-331-374
U.S. Dept. of State (Abu Dhabi)
Washington, D.C. 20521-6010

American Consulate General
Dubai
SCO Terry Sorgi
Tel: 011-971-4-378-584
Fax: 011-971-4-313-121
U.S. Dept. of State (Dubai)
Washington, D.C. 20521-6020

UNITED KINGDOM
American Embassy
London
SCO Kenneth Moorefield
Tel: 011-44-71-499-9000
Fax: 011-44-71-491-4022
PSC 801 Box 33
FPO AE 09498-4033

UZBEKISTAN
American Embassy
Tashkent
Tel: 011-7-3712-771-407

Fax: 011-7-3712-776-953
U.S. Dept. of State (Tashkent)
Washington, D.C. 20521-7110

VENEZUELA
American Embassy
Caracas
SCO Edgar Fulton
Tel: 011-58-2-285-2222
Fax: 011-58-2-285-0336 or 285-2558
Unit 4958
APO AA 34037

TAIWAN
Unofficial, commercial, and other
relations with Taiwan are
conducted through an unofficial
instrumentality, the American
Institute in Taiwan (AIT), which
has offices in Taipei and
Kaoshiung. Contact AIT at
American Trade Center, Room
3207, International Trade
Building, Taipei World Trade
Center, 333 Keelung Road,
Section 1, Taipei 10548 Taiwan,
tel. 886-2-7201550, telex 23890
U.S. Trade, fax 886-2-7577162.
AIT also maintains a commercial
unit in Kaohsiung, Taiwan: 3rd
Floor, #2 Chung Cheng, 3rd
Road, Kaohsiung, Taiwan, tel.
011-886-7-224-0154,, fax
011-886-7-223-8237, mailing
address, c/o AIT, Taipei.

INTERNATIONAL ECONOMIC POLICY
Country Desk List

COUNTRY	DESK OFFICER	PHONE/202	ROOM
A			
Afghanistan	Timothy Gilman	482-2954	2308
Albania	Brian Toohey	482-4915	3413
Algeria	Christopher Cerone/	482-1860	2029B
	Claude Clement	482-5545	2033
Angola	Finn Holm-Olsen	482-4228	3317
Anguilla	Michelle Brooks	482-2527	2039
Argentina	Randy Mye	482-1548	3021
Aruba	Michelle Brooks	482-2527	2039
ASEAN	Karen Goddin	482-3877	2032
Antigua/Barbuda	Michelle Brooks	482-2527	2039
Armenia	Lynn Fabrizio	482-2354	3318
Australia	Gary Bouck/	482-4958	2471
	George Paine	482-2471	2036
Austria	Philip Combs	482-2920	3039
Azerbaijan	Lynn Fabrizio	482-2354	3318
B			
Bahamas	Mark Siegelman	482-5680	2039
Bahrain	Claude Clement/	482-5545	2033
	Christopher Cerone	482-1860	2029B
Balkan States	Ann Lien	482-2354	7412
Bangladesh	John Simmons	482-2954	2308
Barbados	Michelle Brooks	482-2527	2039
Belarus	Christine Lucyk	482-1104	3413
Belgium	Simon Bensimon	482-5401	3039
Belize	Michelle Brooks	482-2527	2039
Benin	Debra Henke	482-5149	3317
Bhutan	Timothy Gilman	482-2954	2308
Bolivia	Rebecca Hunt	482-2521	2037
Botswana	Finn Holm-Olsen	482-4228	3317
Brazil	Horace Jennings	482-3871	3019
Brunei	Raphael Cung	482-3877	2032
Bulgaria	Brian Toohey	482-4915	3413
Burkina Faso	Philip Michelini	482-4388	3317
Burma (Myanmar)	Hong-Pong B. Poe	482-3877	2032
Burundi	Philip Michelini	482-4388	3317
C			
Cambodia	Hong-Phong Pho	482-3877	2032
Cameroon	Debra Henke	482-5149	3317
Canada	Kathy Keim	482-3103	3033
Cape Verde	Philip Michelini	482-4388	3317
Cayman Islands	Mark Siegelman	482-5680	2039
Central Africa Republic	Philip Michelini	482-4388	3317
Chad	Philip Michelini	482-4388	3317
Chile	Roger Turner	482-1495	3021
Colombia	Paul Moore	482-1659	2037
Comoros	Chandra Watkins	482-4564	3317

COUNTRY	DESK OFFICER	PHONE/202	ROOM
Congo	Debra Henke	482-5149	3317
Costa Rica	Mark Siegelman	482-5680	2039
Cote d'Ivoire	Philip Michelini	482-4388	3317
Cuba	Mark Siegelman	482-5680	2039
Cyprus	Ann Corro	482-3945	3042
Czech Republic	Mark Mowrey	482-4915	3413
D			
Denmark	Maryanne Kendall	482-3254	3037
D'Jibouti	Chandra Watkins	482-4564	3317
Dominica	Michelle Brooks	482-2527	2039
Dominican Republic	Mark Siegelman	482-5680	2039
E			
Ecuador	Paul Moore	482-1659	2037
Egypt	Thomas Sams/	482-1860	2029B
	Corey Wright	482-5506	2033
El Salvador	Helen Lee	482-2528	2039
Equatorial Guinea	Philip Michelini	482-4388	3317
Estonia	Pam Green	482-4915	3413
Eritrea	Chandra Watkins	482-4564	3317
Ethiopia	Chandra Watkins	482-4564	3317
European Community	Charles Ludolph	482-5276	3036
F			
Finland	Maryanne Kendall	482-3254	3037
France	Elena Mikalis	482-6008	3042
G			
Gabon	Debra Henke	482-5149	3321
Gambia	Philip Michelini	482-4388	3317
Georgia	Lynn Fabrizio	482-0988	3318
Germany	Brenda Fisher/	482-2435	3409
	John Larsen	482-2434	3409
Ghana	Debra Henke	482-5149	3321
Greece	Ann Corro	482-3945	3042
Grenada	Michelle Brooks	482-2527	2039
Guatemala	Helen Lee	482-2528	2039
Guinea	Philip Michelini	483-4388	3317
Guinea-Bissau	Philip Michelini	482-4388	3317
Guyana	Michelle Brooks	482-2527	2039
H			
Haiti	Mark Siegelman	482-5680	2039
Honduras	Helen Lee	482-2528	2039
Hong Kong	Sheila Baker	482-3932	2317
Hungary	Brian Toohey	482-4915	3413
I			
Iceland	Maryanne Kendall	482-3254	3037
	John Crown		
India	John Simmons	482-2954	2308
	Timothy Gilman		
Indonesia	Karen Goddin	482-3877	2032

COUNTRY	DESK OFFICER	PHONE/202	ROOM
Iran	Paul Thanos	482-1860	2029B
Iraq	Thomas Sams/	482-1860	2029B
	Corey Wright	482-5506	2033
Ireland	Boyce Fitzpatrick	482-2177	3045
Israel	Paul Thanos	482-1860	2029B
Italy	Boyce Fitzpatrick	482-2177	3045
J			
Jamaica	Mark Siegelman	482-5680	2039
Japan	Ed Leslie/	482-2425	2320
	Eric Kennedy/		
	Cynthia Campbell/		
	Allan Christain		
Jordan	Paul Thanos	482-1860	2029B
K			
Kazakhstan	Pam Feodoroff	482-2354	3318
Kenya	Chandra Watkins	482-4564	3317
Korea	William Golike/	482-4390	2327
	Dan Duvall/		
	Jeffrey Donius		
Kuwait	Corey Wright/	482-5506	2033
	Thomas Sams	482-1860	2029B
Kyrgysztan	Pam Feodoroff	482-2354	3318
L			
Laos	Hong-Phong B. Pho	482-3877	2032
Latvia	Pam Green	482-4915	3413
Lebanon	Corey Wright/	482-5506	2033
	Thomas Sams	482-1860	2029B
Lesotho	Finn Holm-Olsen	482-4228	3317
Lithuania	Pam Green	482-4915	3413
Luxembourg	Simon Bensimon	482-5401	3039
Liberia	Philip Michelini	482-4388	3317
Libya	Claude Clement/	482-5545	2033
	Christopher Cerone	482-1860	2029B
M			
Macau	Sheila Baker	482-3932	2317
Madagascar	Chandra Watkins	482-4564	3317
Malawi	Finn Holm-Olsen	482-4228	3317
Malaysia	Raphael Cung	482-3877	2032
Maldives	John Simmons	482-2954	2308
Mali	Philip Michelini	482-4388	3317
Malta	Robert McLaughlin	482-3748	3045
Mauritania	Philip Michelini	482-4388	3317
Mauritius	Chandra Watkins	482-4564	3321
Mexico	Shawn Ricks	482-0300	3022
Moldova	Lynn Fabrizio	482-2354	3318
Mongolia	Sheila Baker	482-3932	2317
Montserrat	Michelle Brooks	482-2527	2039

COUNTRY	DESK OFFICER	PHONE/202	ROOM
Morocco	Claude Clement/	482-5545	2033
	Christopher Cerone	482-1860	2029B
Mozambique	Finn Holm-Olen	482-4228	3317
N			
Namibia	Finn Holm-Olsen	482-4228	3317
Nepal	Timothy Gilman	482-2954	2308
Netherlands	Simon Bensimon	482-5401	3039
Netherlands Antilles	Michelle Brooks	482-2527	2039
New Zealand	George Paine/	482-2471	2036
	Gary Bouck	482-4958	2036
Nicaragua	Mark Siegelman	482-5680	2039
Niger	Philip Michelini	482-4388	3317
Nigeria	Debra Henke	482-5149	3317
Norway	James Devlin	482-4414	3037
O			
Oman	Paul Thanos	482-1860	2029B
P			
Pacific Islands	George Paine/	482-2471	2032
	Gary Bouck	482-4958	2036
Pakistan	Timothy Gilman	482-2954	2308
Panama	Helen Lee	482-2528	3021
Paraguay	Randy Mye	482-1548	2039
People's Republic of China	Cheryl McQueen/	482-3932	2317
	Laura McCall	482-3583	2317
Peru	Rebecca Hunt	482-2521	2037
Philippines	George Paine	482-3877	2032
Poland	Audrey Zuck	482-4915	3413
Portugal	Mary Beth Double	482-4508	3045
Q			
Qatar	Paul Thanos	482-1860	2029B
R			
Romania	Pam Green	482-4915	3413
Russia	Lynn Fabrizio	482-2354	3318
Rwanda	Philip Michelini	482-4388	3317
S			
Sao Tome & Principe	Philip Michelini	482-4388	3317
Saudi Arabia	Christopher Cerone/	482-1860	2029B
	Claude Clement	482-5545	2033
Senegal	Philip Michelini	482-4388	3317
Seychelles	Chandra Watkins	482-4564	3317
Sierra Leone	Philip Michelini	482-4388	3317
Singapore	Raphael Cung	482-3877	2032
Slovak Republic	Mark Mowrey	482-4915	3413
Somalia	Chandra Watkins	482-4564	3317
South Africa	Emily Solomon	482-5148	3321
Spain	Mary Beth Double	482-4508	3045
Sri Lanka	John Simmons	482-2954	2308

COUNTRY	DESK OFFICER	PHONE/202	ROOM
St. Kitts-Nevis	Michelle Brooks	482-2527	2039
St. Lucia	Michelle Brooks	482-2527	2039
St. Martin	Michelle Brooks	482-2527	2039
St. Vincent Grenadines	Michelle Brooks	482-2527	2039
Sudan	Chandra Watkins	482-4564	3317
Suriname	Michelle Brooks	482-2527	2039
Swaziland	Finn Holm-Olsen	482-4228	3317
Sweden	James Devlin	482-4414	3037
Switzerland	Philip Combs	482-2920	3039
Syria	Corey Wright/	482-5506	2033
	Thomas Sams	482-1860	2029B
T			
Taiwan	Robert Chu/	482-4390	2327
	Dan Duvall		
Tajikistan	Pam Feodoroff	482-0360	3318
Tanzania	Finn Holm-Olsen	482-4228	3317
Thailand	Jean Kelly	482-3877	2032
Togo	Debra Henke	482-5149	3317
Trinidad & Tobago	Michelle Brooks	482-2527	2039
Tunisia	Corey Wright/	482-5506	2029B
	Thomas Sams	482-1860	2033
Turkey	Ann Corro	482-3945	3042
Turkmemistan	Pam Feodoroff	482-2354	3318
Turks/Caicos Islands	Mark Siegelman	482-5680	2039
U			
Ukraine	Chris Lucyk	482-2018	3413
Uganda	Chandra Watkins	482-4564	3317
United Arab Emirates	Claude Clement/	482-5545	2033
	Christopher Cerone	482-1860	2029B
United Kingdom	Robert McLaughlin	482-3748	3045
Uruguay	Roger Turner	482-1495	3021
Uzbekistan	Pam Feodoroff	482-2354	3318
V, W			
Venezuela	Laura	482-4303	2037
	Zeiger-Hatfield		
Vietnam	Hong-Phong B. Pho	482-3877	2032
Virgin Islands (UK)	Michelle Brooks	482-2527	2039
X, Y			
Yemen,	Paul Thanos	482-1860	2029B
Republic of			
Yugoslav Republics	Ann Lien	482-2354	7412
(former)			
Z			
Zaire	Philip Michelini	482-4388	3317
Zambia	Finn Holm-Olsen	482-4228	3317
Zimbabwe	Finn Holm-Olsen	482-4228	3317

"FLASH FACTS"—EXPORT INFORMATION FAXED INSTANTLY (5-30 MIN.)

[24-HOUR AUTOMATED FAX DELIVERY SYSTEM]

Simply dial number from your desk touch-tone phone, follow instructions, information will be automatically faxed to you!

	PHONE (202)
Business Information Services for the Newly Independent States (Central Asia/Russia/Ukraine)	482-3145
Eastern Europe Business Information Center (Albania/Balkan States/Bulgaria/Czech/Republic/Estonia/Hungary/Latvia/ Lithuania/Poland/Romania/Slovak Republic)	482-5745
Africa, Near East, and South Asia (Afghanistan/Algeria/Bahrain/Bangladesh/Bhutan/Egypt/India/Iran/Iraq/ Israel/Jordan/Kuwait/Lebanon/Maldives/Morocco/Nepal/Nigeria/Oman/ Pakistan/Qatar/Senegal/SaudiArabia/Sub-Saharan Africa/South Africa/Sri Lanka/Syria/Tunisia/UAE/Yemen/Zimbabwe)	482-1064
Office of Mexico	482-4464
	PHONE (202)
Office of Canada	482-3101
Office of the Pacific Basin	482-3875
	482-3646
(ASEAN/Australia/Cambodia/Indonesia/Korea/Laos/Malaysia/New Zealand/Philippines/Singapore/Taiwan/Thailand/Vietnam)	

ITA TRADE CENTERS

	PHONE (202)
Business Services for the Newly Independent State (BISNIS)	482-4655
Consortia of American Business in Eastern Europe (CABEE)	482-5131
Eastern Europe Business Information Center (EEBIC)	482-2645
Japan Export Information Center (JEIC)	482-2425
Latin American/Caribbean Business Development Center (LA/CBDC)	482-0841
Trade Information Center (TIC) (for general trade inquiries)	1-800-USA-TRADE 1-800-827-8723)

TRADE DEVELOPMENT INDUSTRY SPECIALISTS

Industry	TD Contact		Phone (202) 482-	Room	Sector
A					
Abrasive Products	Presbury	Graylin	5158	4035	BI
Accounting	Chittum	J Marc	0345	1112	SIF
Adhesives/Sealants	Prat	Raimundo	0128	4059	BI
Advanced Materials	Driscoll	George	4431	1012	TAI
Advertising	Elliott	Frederick	1134	1124	SIF
Aerospace Financing Issues	Jackson	Jeff	4222	2124	TAI
Aerospace Industry Analysis	Bender	Juliet	4222	2124	TAI
Aerospace Market Development	Largay	Tony	2835	2128	TAI
Aerospace Trade Policy	Bender	Juliet	4222	2124	TAI
Aerospace-Space Programs	Mowry	Clay	4222	2124	TAI
Agricultural Chemicals	Maxey	Francis P	0128	4053	BI
Agricultural Machinery	Wiening	Mary	4708	4327	BI
Air Conditioning Eqmt	Shaw	Bob	0132	4024	BI
Air Couriers	Elliott	Frederick	3734	1124	SIF
Air Pollution Control Eqmt	Jonkers	Loretta	0564	4321	BI
Air Traffic Control Eqmt	Pederson	Heather	1228	2128	TAI
Air Transport Services	Johnson	C William	5071	1120	SIF
Air, Gas Compressors	McDonald	Edward	0680	4327	BI
Air, Gas Compressors (Trade Promo)	Zanetakos	George	0552	4324	BI
Aircraft & Aircraft Engines	Smerkanich	Audrey	1228	2128	TAI
Aircraft Auxiliary Eqmt	Smerkanich	Audrey	1228	2128	TAI
Aircraft Parts (Market Support)	Smerkanich	Audrey	1228	2128	TAI
Aircraft Parts/Aux Eqmt (Trade Promo)	Largay	Tony	2835	2128	TAI
Airlines	Johnson	C William	5071	1120	SIF
Airport Eqmt	Pederson	Heather	1228	2128	TAI
Airport Eqmt (Trade Promo)	Largay	Tony	2835	2128	TAI
Airports (Major Proj)	Smith	Jay L	4642	4314	BI
Alcoholic Beverages	Kenney	Cornelius	2428	3015A	TACGI
Alum Forgings, Electro	Cammarota	David	5157	4035	BI
Alum Sheet, Plate/Foil	Cammarota	David	5157	4035	BI
Aluminum Extrud Alum Rolling	Cammarota	David	5157	4035	BI
Analytical & Scientific Instruments (Trade Promo)	Manzolillo	Franc	2991	1008	TAI
Analytical Instruments	Nealon	Marguerite	3411	1010	TAI
Apparel	Dulka	William J	4058	3119	TACGI
Apparel (Trade Promo)	Molnar	Ferenc	2043	3109	TACGI
Asbestos/Cement Prod	Pitcher	Charles B	0132	4022	BI
Audio Visual Services	Siegmund	John	4781	1114	SIF
Auto Industry (Trade Promo)	White	John C	0671	4028	BI
Auto Industry Affairs	Keitz	Stuart	0554	4036	BI
Auto Parts & Supplies	Reck	Robert O	1418	4044	BI

Industry	TD Contact		Phone (202) 482-	Room	Sector
Avionics Marketing	Pederson	Heather	1228	2128	TAI
B					
Bakery Products	Janis	William V	2250	3015A	TACGI
Ball Bearings	Reise	Richard	3489	4025	BI
Banking Services	Shuman	John	3050	1004	SIF
Basic Paper & Board Mfg	Stanley	Gary	0375	4016A	BI
Bauxite, Alumina, Prim Alum	Cammarota	David	5157	4035	BI
Beer	Kenney	Cornelius	2428	3015A	TACGI
Belting & Hose	Prat	Raimundo	0128	4059	BI
Beryllium	Males	Barbara	0606	4029B	BI
Beverages	Kenney	Cornelius	2428	3015A	TACGI
Bicycles	Vanderwolf	John	0348	3006	TACGI
Biomass Energy Eqmt	Garden	Les	0556	4312	BI
Biotechnology	Arakaki	Emily	0128	4051	BI
Boats, Pleasure	Vanderwolf	John	0348	3006	TACGI
Books	Lofquist	William S	0379	3015B	TACGI
Books (Export Promo)	Kimmel	Ed	3640	2007F	TACGI
Breakfast Cereal	Janis	William V	2250	3015A	TACGI
Bridges (Major Proj)	Smith	Jay L	4642	4314	BI
Broadcasting Eqmt	Rettig	Theresa	4466	1009	TAI
Brooms & Brushes	Harris	John M	1178	3006	TACGI
Building Materials & Construction	Pitcher	Charles B	0132	4022	BI
Business Forms	Bratland	Rose Marie	0380	3008	TACGI
C					
CAD/CAM/CAE/CASE/CAM	Swann	Vera	0396	2807	TAI
Canned Food Products	Janis	William V	2250	3015A	TACGI
Carbon Black	Prat	Raimundo	0128	4059	BI
Cellular Radio Telephone Eqmt	McCullough	Stephanie	4466	1009	TAI
Cement	Pitcher	Charles B	0132	4022	BI
Cement Plants (Major Proj)	Vacant		5226	4314	BI
Chemical Indust. Mach	Shaw	Eugene	3494	4021	BI
Chemical Plants (Major Proj)	Vacant		5226	4314	BI
Chemicals & Allied Products	Kelly	Michael	0128	4057	BI
Chinaware	Bratland	Rose Marie	0380	3008	TACGI
Civil Aircraft Agreement	Bender	Juliet	4222	2124	TAI
Civil Aviation Policy	Johnson	C William	5071	1120	SIF
Coal Exports	Rasmussen	John	1466	4413	BI
Cobalt	Presbury	Graylin	5158	4035	BI
Commercial Aircraft (Trade Policy)	Bender	Juliet	4222	2124	TAI
Commercial Lighting Fixtures	Bodson	John	0681	4029	BI
Commercial Printing	Lofquist	William S	0379	3015B	TACGI
Commercial/Indus Refrig Eqmt	Shaw	Bob	0132	4024	BI
Commercialization of Space (Market)	Mowry	Clay	4222	2124	TAI
Computer Consulting	Atkins	Robert G	4781	1112	SIF
Computer Software	Hijikata	Heidi	0569	2806	TAI

Industry	TD Contact		Phone (202) 482-	Room	Sector
Computer Systems	Miles	Timothy O	2990	2806	TAI
Computer and DP Services	Atkins	Robert G	4781	1112	SIF
Computer and DP Services	Inoussa	Mary C	5820	1114	SIF
Computers (Large Scale)	Streeter	Jonathan	0480	2803	TAI
Computers (Personal)	Woods	R Clay	3013	2805	TAI
Computers (Portable)	Hoffman	Heidi	0569	2806	TAI
Computers (Trade Promo)	Fogg	Judy A	4936	2132	TAI
Computers (Workstations)	Hoffman	Heidi	2053	2803	TAI
Confectionery Products	Kenney	Cornelius	2428	3015A	TACGI
Construction	MacAuley	Patrick	0132	4026	BI
Construction Machinery (Large, Off Road)	Heimowitz	Leonard	0558	4325	BI
Consumer Electronics	Fleming	Howard	5163	1014	TAI
Consumer Goods	Bodansky	Harry	5783	3013	TACGI
Containers & Packaging	Cosslett	Patrick	5125	4024	BI
Conveyors & Conveying Eqmt	Wiening	Mary	4708	4327	BI
Copper	Males	Barbara	0606	4029B	BI
Cosmetics (Export Promo)	Kimmel	Ed	3640	2107	TACGI
Countertrade Services	Mitchell	Paula	4471	1106	SIF
Countertrade Services	Verzariu	Pompiliu	4434	1106	SIF
Cutlery	Bratland	Rose Marie	0380	3008	TACGI
D					
Dairy Products	Janis	William V	2250	3015A	TACGI
Data Base Services	Inoussa	Mary C	5820	1114	SIF
Data Processing Services	Atkins	Robert G	4781	1112	SIF
Dental Eqmt	Eyring	Patricia	2846	1008	TAI
Dental Eqmt (Trade Promo)	Keen	George	2010	1006	TAI
Desalination (Major Projects)	Holroyd	William	6168	4314	BI
Desalination/Water Reuse	Wheeler	Frederica	3509	4321	BI
Direct Marketing	Elliott	Frederick	1134	1124	SIF
Disk Storage	Valverde	Daniel	0573	2808	TAI
Distilled Spirits	Kenney	Cornelius	2428	3015A	TACGI
Dolls	Hodgen	Donald	3346	3008	TACGI
Drugs	Hurt	William	0128	4057	BI
Durable Consumer Goods	Ellis	Kevin	1176	3004	TACGI
E					
Earthenware	Bratland	Rose Marie	0380	3008	TACGI
Education Facilities (Major Proj)	White	Barbara	4160	1120	SIF
Educational, Training	Chander-sekaran	Achamma	1316	1124	SIF
Elec, Power Gen, Transmission & Dist Eqmt (Trade Promo)	Kostalas	Anthony	2390	4318	BI
Electric Industrial Apparatus Nec	Bodson	John	0681	4029	BI
Electric Power Plants (Major Proj)	Dollison	Robert	2733	4314	BI

Industry	TD Contact		Phone (202) 482-	Room	Sector
Electrical Test & Measuring Instruments	Finn	Erin	2795	1012	TAI
Electricity	Sugg	William	1466	4413	BI
ElectroOptical Instruments	Nealon	Marguerite	3411	1010	TAI
ElectroOptical Instruments (Trade Promo)	Manzolillo	Franc	2991	1008	TAI
Electronic Components	Mussehl-Aziz	Judee	0429	1002	TAI
Electronic Components, Prod & Test Eqmt (Trade Promo)	Ruffin	Marlene	0570	1015	TAI
Electronic Database Services	Inoussa	Mary C	5820	1114	SIF
Elevators, Moving Stairways	Wiening	Mary	4708	4327	BI
Energy (Commodities)	Yancik	Joseph J	1466	4413	BI
Energy Services	Burroughs	Helen	1542	1124	SIF
Energy, Renewable	Garden	Les	0556	4312	BI
Entertainment Industries	Siegmund	John	4781	1114	SIF
Environment Trade Promotion	Mack	Mildred	0616	4321	BI
Environment Trade Promotion	Vial	Catherine P	0617	4321	BI
Explosives	Maxey	Francis P	0128	4053	BI
Export Trading Companies	Stow	Don	5131	1800	SIF
F					
Fabricated Metal Construction Materials	Williams	Franklin	0132	4026	BI
Factoring & Forfaiting	Ring	Mary Ann	4472	1106	SIF
Farm Machinery	Wiening	Mary	4708	4327	BI
Fasteners (Industrial)	Reise	Richard	3489	4025	BI
Fats and Oils	Janis	William V	2250	3015A	TACGI
Fencing (Metal)	MacAuley	Patrick	0132	4026	BI
Ferroalloys Products	Presbury	Graylin	5158	4035	BI
Ferrous Scrap	Bell	Charles	0608	4029B	BI
Fertilizer Plants Major Projects	Vacant		5226	4314	BI
Fertilizers	Maxey	Francis P	0128	4053	BI
Fiber Optics	Mocenigo	Anthony	4466	1009	TAI
Filters/Purifying Eqmt	Wheeler	Frederica	3509	4321	BI
Flat Panel Displays	Hoffman	Heidi M	2053	2803	TAI
Flexible Mftg Systems	Pilaroscia	Megan	0609	4027	BI
Floor Covering, Hard Surfaced	MacAuley	Patrick	0132	4026	BI
Flour	Janis	William V	2250	3015A	TACGI
Fluid Power	McDonald	Edward	0680	4327	BI
Food Products Machinery	Shaw	Eugene	3494	4021	BI
Food Retailing	Kenney	Cornelius	2428	3015A	TACGI
Footwear	Byron	James E	4034	3015B	TACGI
Foreign Sales Corporations	Burroughs	Helen	1542	1124	SIF
Forest Products	Stanley	Gary	0375	4016A	BI
Forgings Semifinished Steel	Bell	Charles	0608	4029B	BI
Fossil Fuel Power Generation (Major Proj)	Dollison	Robert	2733	4314	BI
Foundry Industry	Bell	Charles	0608	4029B	BI

Industry	TD Contact		Phone (202) 482-	Room	Sector
Frozen Foods Products	Janis	William V	2250	3015A	TACGI
Fruits	Janis	William V	2250	3015A	TACGI
Fur Goods	Byron	James E	4034	3015B	TACGI
Furniture	Hodgen	Donald	3346	3346	TACGI
G					
Gallium	Cammarota	David	5157	4035	BI
Games & Children's Vehicles	Hodgen	Donald	3346	3008	TACGI
Gaskets/Gasketing Materials	Reise	Richard	3489	4025	BI
General Aviation Aircraft	Green	Ron	4222	2124	TAI
Geothermal Energy Eqmt	Garden	Les	0556	4312	BI
Germanium	Cammarota	David	5157	4035	BI
Giftware (Trade Promo)	Beckham	Reginald	5478	2107	TACGI
Glass, Flat	Williams	Franklin	0132	4026	BI
Glassware	Bratland	Rose Marie	0380	3008	TACGI
Gloves (Work & Dress)	Byron	James E	4034	3015B	TAGCI
Grain Mill Products	Janis	William V	2250	3015A	TACGI
Greeting Cards	Bratland	Rose Marie	0380	3008	TACGI
Grocery Retailing	Kenney	Cornelius	2428	3015A	TACGI
Ground Water Exploration & Development	Wheeler	Frederica	3509	4321	BI
H					
Hand Saws, Saw Blades	Abrahams	Edward	0312	4025	BI
Hand/Edge Tools Ex Mach Tl/Saws	Abrahams	Edward	0312	4025	BI
Handbags	Byron	James E	4034	3015B	TACGI
Hardware (Export Promo)	Beckham	Reginald	5478	2107	TACGI
Health Care Services	Francis	Simon	2697	1112	SIF
Helicopters	Green	Ron	4222	2124	TAI
Helicopters (Market Support)	Smerkanich	Audrey	1228	2128	TAI
High Tech Trade, U.S. Competitiveness	Hatter	Victoria L	3895	2225	OTEA
Highways (Major Proj)	Smith	Jay L	4642	4314	BI
Hoists, Overhead Cranes	Wiening	Mary	4708	4327	BI
Hose & Belting	Prat	Raimundo	0128	4059	BI
Hospitals (Major Proj)	Haraguchi	Wallace	4877	4314	BI
Hotel & Restaurants/Eqmt (Export Promo)	Kimmel	Edward	3640	2107	TACGI
Hotels And Motels	Sousane	J Richard	4582	1120	SIF
Household Appliances	Harris	John M	1178	3006	TACGI
Household Appliances (Export Promo)	Beckham	Reginald	5478	2107	TACGI
Household Furniture	Hodgen	Donald	3346	3008	TACGI
Housewares (Export Promo)	Beckham	Reginald	5478	2107	TACGI
Housing Construction, Domestic	McAuley	Patrick	0132	4026	BI
Housing Construction, International	Cosslett	Patrick	5125	4024	BI

Industry	TD Contact		Phone (202) 482-	Room	Sector
Hydroelectric Power (Major Proj)	Dollison	Robert	2733	4314	BI
I					
Industrial Controls	Bodson	John	0681	4029	BI
Industrial Drives, Gears	Reise	Richard	3489	4025	BI
Industrial Organic Chemicals	Hurt	William	0128	4057	BI
Industrial Robots	Pilaroscia	Megan	0609	4027	BI
Industrial Trucks	Wiening	Mary	4608	4327	BI
Information Services	Inoussa	Mary C	5820	1114	SIF
Insulation	MacAuley	Patrick	0132	4026	BI
Insurance	McAdam	M Bruce	0346	1110	SIF
Insurance	Muir	S Cassin	0349	1110	SIF
Intellectual Property Rights (Services)	Siegmund	John E	4781	1114	SIF
Irrigation Equipment	Wiening	Mary	4608	4327	BI
J					
Jams & Jellies	Janis	William V	2250	3015A	TACGI
Jewelry	Harris	John M	1178	3006	TACGI
Jewelry (Trade Promo)	Beckham	Reginald	5478	2107	TACGI
Jute Products	D'Andrea	Maria	4058	3119	TACGI
K					
Kitchen Cabinets	Wise	Barbara	0375	4018	BI
L					
LNG Plants (Major Proj)	Vacant		5226	4314	BI
Laboratory Instruments	Nealon	Marguerite	3411	1010	TAI
Laboratory Instruments (Trade Promo)	Manzolillo	Franc	2991	1008	TAI
Lasers	Nealon	Marguerite	3411	1010	TAI
Lasers (Trade Promo)	Manzolillo	Franc	2991	1008	TAI
Lawn & Garden Eqmt	Hodgen	Donald	3346	3008	TACGI
Lead Products	Larrabee	David	0607	4029B	BI
Leasing (Eqmt)	Uzzelle	Elnora	4654	1004	SIF
Leather Products	Byron	James E	4034	3015B	TACGI
Leather Tanning	Byron	James E	4034	3015B	TACGI
Legal Services	Chittum	J Marc	0345	1112	SIF
Local Area Networks	Davin	Mary	0568	2809	TAI
Logs, Wood	Wise	Barabara	0375	4018	BI
Luggage	Byron	James E	4034	3015B	TACGI
Lumber	Wise	Barbara	0375	4018	BI
M					
Machine Tool Accessories	Abrahams	Edward	0312	4025	BI
Magazines	Bratland	Rose Marie	0380	3008	TACGI
Magnesium	Cammarota	David	5157	4035	BI
Management Consulting	Chittum	J Marc	0345	1112	SIF
Manifold Business Forms	Bratland	Rose Marie	0380	3008	TACGI
Manmade Fiber	Dulka	William J	4058	3119	TACGI
Margarine	Janis	William V	2250	3015A	TACGI

Industry	TD Contact		Phone (202) 482-	Room	Sector
Marine Insurance	Johnson	C William	5012	1120	SIF
Marine Recreational Eqmt (Trade Promo)	Beckham	Reginald	5478	2107	TACGI
Maritime Shipping	Johnson	C William	5012	1120	SIF
Mass Transit (Major Proj)	Smith	Jay L	4642	4314	BI
Mattresses & Bedding	Hodgen	Donald	3346	3008	TACGI
Meat Products	Janis	William V	2250	3015A	TACGI
Mech Power Transmission Eqmt	Reise	Richard	3489	4025	BI
Medical Eqmt	Edwards	Matthew	0550	1006	TAI
Medical Eqmt	Kader	Victoria	4073	1010	TAI
Medical Facilities (Major Proj)	Haraguchi	Wallace	4877	4314	BI
Medical Instruments & Eqmt (Trade Promo)	Keen	George B	2010	1006	TAI
Medical/Dental Eqmt (Special Proj)	Rathmell	Gregory	2796	1006	TAI
Metal Building Products	Williams	Franklin	0132	4026	BI
Metal Cookware	Bratland	Rose Marie	0380	3008	TACGI
Metal Cutting Machine Tools	Pilaroscia	Megan	0609	4027	BI
Metal Forming Machine Tools	Pilaroscia	Megan	0609	4027	BI
Metal Powders	Males	Barbara	0606	4029B	BI
Metals, Secondary	Cammarota	David	5157	4035	BI
Metalworking	Pilaroscia	Meagan	0609	4027	BI
Microelectronics	Donnelly	Margaret T	5466	1015	TAI
Microwave Communications	Neff	Carrie	4466	1009	TAI
Millwork	Williams	Franklin	0132	4026	BI
Mineral Based Const Mtrls (Clay/Concrete/Gypsum Asphalt/Stone)	Pitcher	Charles B	0132	4022	BI
Mining (Major Proj)	Vacant		5226	4314	BI
Mining Machinery	McDonald	Edward	0680	4327	BI
Mining Machinery (Trade Promo)	Zanetakos	George	0552	4324	BI
Miscellaneous Publishing	Lofquist	William S	0379	3015B	TACGI
Mobile Homes	Cosslett	Patrick	5125	4024	BI
Mobile Radios	Neff	Carrie	4466	1009	TAI
Molybdenum	Presbury	Graylin	5158	4035	BI
Monorails (Industrial)	Wiening	Mary	4708	4327	BI
Motion Pictures	Siegmund	John	4781	1112	SIF
Motor Vehicles	Warner	Albert T	0669	4317	BI
Motorcycles	Vanderwolf	John	0348	3006	TACGI
Motors, Electric	Bodson	John	0681	4029	BI
Music	Siegmund	John	4781	1112	SIF
Musical Instruments	Harris	John M	1178	3006	TACGI
Mutual Funds	Muir	S Cassin	0349	1110	SIF
N					
NATO	Kemper	Alexis	4466	1009	TAI
Natural Gas	Gillett	Tom	1466	4413	BI

Industry	TD Contact		Phone (202) 482-	Room	Sector
Natural, Synthetic Rubber	Prat	Raimundo	0128	4059	BI
Newspapers	Bratland	Rose Marie	0380	3008	TACGI
Nickel Products	Presbury	Graylin	5158	4035	BI
Non-alcoholic Beverages	Kenney	Cornelius	2428	3015A	TACGI
Noncurrent Carrying Wiring Devices	Bodson	John	0681	4029	BI
Nondurable Consumer Goods	Simon	Les	0341	3015	TACGI
Nonferrous Metals	Cammarota	David	5157	4035	BI
Nonresidential Constr	MacAuley	Patrick	0132	4026	BI
Nuclear Power Plants (Major Proj)	Dollison	Robert	2733	4314	BI
Numerical Controls For Mach Tools	Pilaroscia	Meagan	0609	4027	BI
Nuts, Bolts, Washers	Reise	Richard	3489	4025	BI
O					
Ocean Shipping	Johnson	C William	5012	1120	SIF
Office Buildings (Major Proj)	Haraguchi	Wallace	4877	4314	BI
Office Furniture	Hodgen	Donald	3346	3008	TACGI
Oil & Gas (Fuels Only)	Gillett	Tom	1466	4413	BI
Oil & Gas Development & Refining (Major Proj)	Vacant		5226	4314	BI
Oil/Gas Field Machinery	McDonald	Edward	0680	4327	BI
Oil/Gas Field Machinery (Trade Promo)	Miles	Max	0679	4329	BI
Outdoor Lighting Fixtures	Bodson	John	0681	4029	BI
Outdoor Power Eqmt	Hodgen	Donald	3346	3008	TACGI
P					
Packaging & Containers	Cosslett	Patrick	5125	4024	BI
Packaging Machinery	Shaw	Eugene	3494	4021	BI
Paints/Coatings	Prat	Raimundo	0128	4059	BI
Paper	Stanley	Gary	0375	4016A	BI
Paper & Board Packaging	Stanley	Gary	0375	4016A	BI
Paper Industries Machinery	Abrahams	Edward	0312	4025	BI
Pasta	Janis	William V	2250	3015A	TACGI
Paving Materials (Asphalt)	MacAuley	Patrick	0132	4026	BI
Paving Materials (Concrete)	Pitcher	Charles B	0132	4022	BI
Pens/Pencils, etc	Vanderwolf	John	0348	3006	TACGI
Periodicals	Bratland	Rose Marie	0380	3008	TACGI
Personal Communications	Gossack	Linda	4466	1009	TAI
Pet Food	Janis	William V	2250	3015A	TACGI
Pet Products (Trade Promo)	Kimmel	Ed	3640	2107	TACGI
Petrochemicals	Kelly	Michael	0128	4057	BI
Petrochemicals Plants (Major Proj)	Vacant		5226	4314	BI
Petroleum Refining Machinery	Shaw	Eugene	3494	4021	BI
Petroleum, Crude & Refined Products	Gillett	Tom	1466	4413	BI
Pharmaceuticals	Hurt	William	0128	4057	BI

Industry	TD Contact		Phone (202) 482-	Room	Sector
Photographic Eqmt & Supplies	Watson	Joyce	0574	2805	TAI
Pipelines (Major Proj)	Vacant		5226	4314	BI
Plastic Construction Products (Most)	Williams	Franklin	0132	4026	BI
Plastic Materials	Prat	Raimundo	0128	4059	BI
Plastic Products Machinery	Shaw	Robert M	5124	4024	BI
Platemaking Services	Lofquist	William S	0379	3015B	TACGI
Plumbing Fixtures & Fittings	Shaw	Robert M	5124	4024	BI
Plywood Panel Products	McNamara	Kathy	0375	4016A	BI
Point-Of-Use Water Treatment	Wheeler	Frederica	3509	4321	BI
Pollution Control Eqmt (Air)	Jonkers	Loretta	0564	4321	BI
Porcelain Electrical Supplies	Bodson	John	0681	4029	BI
Ports, Harbors (Major Proj)	Smith	Jay L	4642	4314	BI
Potato Chips	Janis	William V	2250	3015A	TACGI
Pottery	Bratland	Rose Marie	0380	3008	TACGI
Poultry Products	Janis	William V	2250	3015A	TACGI
Power Distribution & Transmission (Major Proj)	Dollison	Robert	2733	4314	BI
Power Generation & Distribution Eqmt (Trade Promo)	Kostalas	Anthony	2390	4318	BI
Power Hand Tools	Abrahams	Edward	0312	4025	BI
Precious Metal Jewelry	Harris	John M	1178	3006	TACGI
Prefabricated Buildings (Metal)	Williams	Franklin	0132	4026	BI
Prefabricated Buildings (Wood)	Cosslett	Patrick	5125	4024	BI
Prepared Meats	Janis	William V	2250	3015A	TACGI
Pretzels	Janis	William V	2250	3015A	TACGI
Printing & Publishing	Lofquist	William S	0379	3015B	TACGI
Printing Trade Services	Lofquist	William S	0379	3015B	TACGI
Printing Trades Mach/Eqmt	Shaw	Robert M	5124	4024	BI
Process Control Instruments	Nealon	Marguerite	3411	1010	TAI
Process Control Instruments (Trade Promo)	Manzolillo	Franc	2991	1008	TAI
Project Finance	Hinds	Michael	5131	1800A	SIF
Pulp And Paper Mills (Major Proj)	Vacant		5226	4314	BI
Pulpmills	Stanley	Gary	0375	4016A	BI
Pumps, Compressors (Trade Promo)	Zanetakos	George	0552	4324	BI
Pumps, Pumping Eqmt	McDonald	Edward	0680	4327	BI

R

Radio & TV Broadcasting Services	Siegmund	John	4781	1112	SIF
Radio Communications Eqmt	Gossack	Linda	4466	1009	TAI
Railroad Services	Sousane	J Richard	4581	1120	SIF
Railroads	Smith	Jay L	4642	4314	BI
Recorded Music	Siegmund	John	4781	1112	SIF

278 FEDERAL EXPORT ASSISTANCE

Industry	TD Contact		Phone (202) 482-	Room	Sector
Recreational Eqmt (Trade Promo)	Beckham	Reginald	5478	2107	TACGI
Recycling, Waste Management	Copperthite	Kimberly	0560	4321	BI
Refrigeration Eqmt	Shaw	Bob	0132	4024	BI
Renewable Energy Eqmt	Garden	Les	0556	4312	BI
Residential Lighting Fixtures	Bodson	John	0681	4029	BI
Retail Trade	Walsh	James	5131	1800A	SIF
Rice Milling	Janis	William V	2250	3015A	TACGI
Roads (Major Proj)	Smith	Jay L	4642	4314	BI
Robots	Pilaroscia	Megan	0609	4027	BI
Roller Bearings	Reise	Richard	3489	4025	BI
Roofing, Asphalt	Williams	Franklin	0132	4026	BI
Rubber and Rubber Products	Prat	Raimundo	0128	4059	BI
S					
Saddlery & Harness Products	Byron	James E	4034	3015B	TACGI
Safety & Security Eqmt (Trade Promo)	Umstead	Dwight	2410	1015	TAI
Satellite Communications Eqmt	Cooper	Patricia	4466	1003	TAI
Satellite Communications Services	Cooper	Patricia	4466	1003	TAI
Satellites & Space Vehicles (Marketing)	Mowry	Clay	4222	2124	TAI
Science & Electronics (Trade Promo)	Moose	Jake	4125	2800A	TAI
Science Policy	Shykind	Edwin B	4694	2800A	TAI
Scientific Instruments (Trade Promo)	Manzolillo	Franc	2991	1008	TAI
Scientific Measurement/Control Eqmt	Nealon	Marguerite	3411	1010	TAI
Screw Machine Products	Reise	Richard	3489	4025	BI
Screws, Washers	Reise	Richard	3489	4025	BI
Search & Navigation Eqmt	Kemper	Alexis	4466	1009	TAI
Securities	Muir	S Cassin	0349	1110	SIF
Semiconductor Materials	Blouin	Dorothea	1333	1012	TAI
Semiconductor Prod Eqmt	Finn	Erin	2795	1012	TAI
Semiconductors (except Japan)	Roark	Robin	3090	1012	TAI
Semiconductors, Japan	Scott	Robert	3360	1202	TAI
Services Data Base Development	Atkins	Robert G	4781	1112	SIF
Services, Telecom	Edwards	Daniel	4466	1009	TAI
Shingles (wood)	Wise	Barbara	0375	4018	BI
Shipping, Maritime	Johnson	C William	5012	1114	SIF
Shoes	Byron	James E	4034	3015B	TACGI
Silverware	Harris	John M	1178	3006	TACGI
Small Arms, Ammunition	Vanderwolf	John	0348	3006	TACGI
Snack food	Janis	William V	2250	3015A	TACGI
Soaps, Detergents, Cleaners	Hurt	William	0128	4057	BI
Softwar	Hijikata	Heidi	0569	2806	TAI

Industry	TD Contact		Phone (202) 482-	Room	Sector
Software (Trade Promo)	Fogg	Judy	4936	2132	TAI
Software, Packaged	Smolenski	Mary	0551	2809	TAI
Solar Cells/Photovoltaic Devices	Garden	Les	0556	4312	BI
Solar Eqmt	Garden	Les	0556	4312	BI
Soy Products	Janis	William V	2250	3015A	TACGI
Space Commercialization (Eqmt)	Mowry	Clay	4222	2124	TAI
Space Policy Development	Mowry	Clay	4222	2124	TAI
Space Vehicles (Marketing)	Mowry	Clay	4222	2124	TAI
Speed Changers	Reise	Richard	3489	4025	BI
Sporting & Athletic Goods	Vanderwolf	John	0348	3006	TACGI
Sporting Goods (Trade Promo)	Beckham	Reginald	5478	2107	TACGI
Steel Industry Products	Bell	Charles	0608	4029B	BI
Steel Mill Products	Bell	Charles	0608	4029B	BI
Steel Mills (Major Proj)	Vacant		5226	4314	BI
Storage Batteries	Larrabee	David	0607	4029B	BI
Supercomputers	Streeter	Jonathan	0480	2803	TAI
Superconductors	Chiarado	Roger	0402	1012	TAI
Switch Gear & Switchboard Apparatus	Bodson	John	0681	4029	BI
T					
Technology Affairs	Shykind	Edwin B	4694	2800A	TAI
Telecommunications (Customer Premises Eqmt)	Bien	William	4466	1009	TAI
Telecommunications (Major Proj)	Paddock	Richard	4466	1009	TAI
Telecommunications (Military Communications Eqmt)	Kemper	Alexis	4466	1009	TAI
Telecommunications (Network Eqmt)	Henry	John	4466	1009	TAI
Telecommunications (Services)	Edwards	Daniel	4466	1009	TAI
Telecommunications (Trade Promo)	Rettig	Theresa	2952	1009	TAI
Telecommunications (Wireless or Radio Eqmt & Services)	Gossack	Linda	4466	1009	TAI
Teletext Services	Inoussa	Mary C	5820	1114	SIF
Textile Production Machinery	McDonald	Edward	0680	4327	BI
Textile Production Machinery (Trade Promo)	Miles	Max	0679	4329	BI
Textiles	Dulka	William J	4058	3119	TACGI
Textiles (Trade Promo)	Molnar	Ferenc	2043	3109	TACGI
Timber Products (Tropical)	McNamara	Kathy	0375	4016A	BI
Tires	Prat	Raimundo	0128	4059	BI
Tools/Dies/Jigs/Fixtures	Pilaroscia	Megan	0609	4027	BI
Tourism Services	Sousane	J Richard	4582	1120	SIF
Toys	Hodgen	Donald	3346	3008	TACGI
Toys & Games (Export Promo)	Beckham	Reginald	5478	2107	TACGI
Trade Finance	Shuman	John	3050	1004	SIF

Industry	TD Contact		Phone (202) 482-	Room	Sector
Transborder Data Flows	Inoussa	Mary C	5820	1114	SIF
Transformers	Bodson	John	0681	4029	BI
Transportation Industries	Johnson	C William	5012	1114	SIF
Trucking Services	Sousane	J Richard	4581	1120	SIF
Trucks, Trailers, Buses (Trade Promotion)	White	John	0671	4028	BI
Tungsten Products	Cammarota	David	5157	4035	BI
Tunnels (Major Proj)	Smith	Jay L	4642	4314	BI
Typesetting	Lofquist	William S	0379	3015B	TACGI
U					
Uranium	Sugg	William	1466	4413	BI
Used Reconditioned Eqmt	Bodson	John	0681	4029	BI
V					
Value Added Telecommunications Services	Atkins	Robert G	4781	1112	SIF
Valves, Pipe Fittings (Except Brass)	Reise	Richard	3489	4025	BI
Vegetables	Janis	William V	2250	3015A	TACGI
Venture Capital	Hinds	Michael	5086	1800A	SIF
Videotex Services	Inoussa	Mary C	5820	1114	SIF
W					
Wallets, Billfolds, Flat Goods	Byron	James	4034	3015B	TACGI
Warm Air Heating Eqmt	Vacant		3509		
Wastepaper	Stanley	Gary	0375	4016A	BI
Watches	Harris	John M	1178	3006	TACGI
Water Resource Eqmt	Wheeler	Frederica	3509	4321	BI
Water Supply & Distribution	Wheeler	Frederica	3509	4321	BI
Water and Sewage Treatment Plants (Major Proj)	Holroyd	William	6168	4314	BI
Welding/Cutting Apparatus	Abrahams	Edward	0312	4025	BI
Wholesale Trade	Walsh	James	5131	1800A	SIF
Wind Energy Systems	Garden	Les	0556	4312	BI
Wine	Kenney	Cornelius	2428	3015B	TACGI
Wire & Wire Products	Bell	Charles	0608	4029B	BI
Wire Cloth	MacAuley	Patrick	0132	4026	BI
Wire Cloth, Industrial	Reise	Richard	3489	4025	BI
Wood Products	Wise	Barbara	0375	4018	BI
Wood Working Machinery	Abrahams	Edward	0312	4025	BI
Writing Instruments	Vanderwolf	John	0348	3015B	TACGI
Y					
Yarn	Dulka	William J	4058	3119	TACGI
Z					
Zinc	Larrabee	David	0607	4029B	BI

BI = Basic Industries; SIF = Service Industries and Finance; TACGI = Textiles, Apparel, and Consumer Goods Industries; TAI = Technology and Aerospace Industries

U.S. SMALL BUSINESS ADMINISTRATION
District and Branch Offices

ALABAMA
2121 Eighth Ave., N., Suite 200
Birmingham, AL 35203-2398
Telephone (205) 731-1344, TDD
(205) 731-2265

ALASKA
222 W. Eighth Ave., Room 67
Anchorage, AK 99513-7559
Telephone (907) 271-4022, TDD
()907) 271-4005

ARIZONA
2828 N. Central Ave., Suite 800
Phoenix, AZ 85004-1025
Telephone (602) 640-2316, TDD
()602) 640-2357

300 W. Congress St., Room 7-H
Tucson, AZ 85701-1319
Telephone (602) 670-4759, TDD
None Listed

ARKANSAS
2120 Riverfront Drive, Suite 100
Little Rock, AR 72202-1747
Telephone (501) 324-5871, TDD
()501) 324-7162

CALIFORNIA
2719 N. Air Fresno Drive,
  Suite 107
Fresno, CA 93727-1547
Telephone (209) 487-5189, TDD
()209) 487-5917

330 N. Brand Blvd., Suite 1200
Glendale, CA 91203-2304
Telephone (213) 894-2956, TDD
()213) 894-6338

880 Front St., Suite 4237
San Diego, CA 92101-8837
Telephone (619) 557-7252, TDD
()619) 557-6998

211 Main St., Fourth Floor
San Francisco, CA 94105-1988
Telephone (415) 744-6820, TDD
()415) 744-6778

901 Civic Center Drive W.,
  Suite 160
Santa Ana, CA 92703-2352
Telephone (714) 836-2494, TDD
()714) 836-2200

660 J St., Room 215
Sacramento, CA 95814-2413
Telephone (916) 551-1426, TDD
None Listed

6477 Telephone Road, Suite 10
Ventura, CA 93003-4459
Telephone (805) 642-1866, TDD
None Listed

COLORADO
721 19th St., Suite 426
Denver, CO 80202-2259
Telephone (303) 844-3984, TDD
()303) 844-5638

CONNECTICUT
330 Main St., Second Floor
Hartford, CT 06106
Telephone (203) 240-4700, TDD
()203) 524-1611

DISTRICT OF COLUMBIA
1110 Vermont Ave., N.W.,
  Ninth Floor
P.O. Box 34500
Washington, DC 20043-4500
Telephone (202) 606-4000, TDD
()202) 606-4240

DELAWARE
1 Rodney Square
920 N. King St., Suite 412
Wilmington, DE 19801
Telephone (302) 573-6295, TDD
()302) 573-6644

FLORIDA
1320 S. Dixie Highway, Suite 501
Coral Gables, FL 33146-2911
Telephone (305) 536-5521, TDD
()305) 536-7110

7825 Baymeadows Way,
  Suite 100-B
Jacksonville, FL 32256-7504
Telephone (904) 443-1900, TDD
()904) 443-1909
501 E. Polk St., Suite 104
Tampa, FL 33602-3945
Telephone (813) 228-2594, TDD
None Listed

5601 Corporate Way, Suite 402
West Palm Beach, FL 33407

Telephone (407) 689-3922, TDD
None Listed

GEORGIA
1720 Peachtree Road, NW,
  Suite 6000
Atlanta, GA 30309
Telephone (404) 347-4749, TDD
()404) 347-0107

52 N. Main St., Room 225
Statesboro, GA 30458
Telephone (912) 489-8719, TDD
None Listed

GUAM
238 Archbishop F.C. Flores St.,
  Room 508
Agana, GU 96910
Telephone (671) 472-7277, TDD
None Listed

HAWAII
300 Ala Moana Blvd., Room 2213
Honolulu, HI 96850-4981
Telephone (808) 541-2990, TDD
(808) 541-3650

IDAHO
1020 Main St., Suite 290
Boise, ID 83702-5745
Telephone (208) 334-1696, TDD
(208) 334-9637

ILLINOIS
500 W. Madison St., Room 1250
Chicago, IL 60661-2511
Telephone (312) 353-4528, TDD
(312) 886-5108

511 W. Capitol St., Suite 302
Springfield, IL 62704
Telephone (217) 492-4416, TDD
(217) 492-4418

INDIANA
429 N. Pennsylvania St., Suite 100
Indianapolis, IN 46204-1873
Telephone (317) 226-7272, TDD
(317) 226-5338

IOWA
373 Collins Road, N.E., Suite 100
Cedar Rapids, IA 52402-3147
Telephone (319) 393-8630, TDD
(319) 393-9610

210 Walnut St., Room 749
Des Moines, IA 50309
Telephone (515) 284-4422, TDD
()515) 284-4233

KANSAS
100 E. English St., Suite 510
Wichita, KS 67202
Telephone (316) 269-6616, TDD
()316) 269-6205

KENTUCKY
600 Dr. M.L. King Jr. Place, Room
188
Louisville, KY 40202
Telephone (502) 582-5971, TDD
(502) 582-6715

LOUISIANA
1661 Canal St., Suite 2000
New Orleans, LA 70112-2890
Telephone (504) 589-6685, TDD
(504) 589-2053

500 Fannin St., Room 8A-08
Shreveport, LA 71101
Telephone (318) 676-3196, TDD
None Listed

MAINE
40 Western Ave., Room 512
Augusta, ME 04330
Telephone (207) 622-8242, TDD
(207) 626-9147

MARYLAND
10 S. Howard St., Sixth Floor
Baltimore, MD 21201
Telephone (410) 962-4392, TDD
(410) 962-7458

MASSACHUSETTS
10 Causeway St., Room 265
Boston, MA 02222-1093
Telephone (617) 565-5590, TDD
(617) 565-5797

1550 Main St., Room 212
Springfield, MA 01103
Telephone (413) 785-0268, TDD
None Listed

MICHIGAN
477 Michigan Ave., Room 515
Detroit, MI 48226-2573
Telephone (313) 226-6075, TDD
(313) 226-2958

228 W. Washington St., Suite 11

Marquette, MI 49855
Telephone (906) 225-1108, TDD
(906) 225-4126

MINNESOTA
100 N. Sixth St., Suite 610-C
Minneapolis, MN 55403-1563
Telephone (612) 370-2324, TDD
(612) 777-2332

MISSISSIPPI
101 W. Capitol St., Suite 400
Jackson, MS 39201
Telephone (601) 965-4378, TDD
(601) 965-5328

1 Hancock Plaza, Suite 1001
14th Street
Gulfport, MS 39501-7758
Telephone (601) 863-4449, TDD
(601) 865-9926

MISSOURI
323 W. Eighth St., Suite 501
Kansas City, MO 64105
Telephone (816) 374-6708, TDD
(816) 374-6764

815 Olive St., Room 242
St. Louis, MO 63101
Telephone (314) 539-6600, TDD
(314) 539-6654

620 S. Glenstone St., Suite 110
Springfield, MO 65802-3200
Telephone (417) 864-7670, TDD
(417) 864-8855

MONTANA
301 S. Park, Room 528,
Drawer 10054
Helena, MT 59626-0054
Telephone (406) 449-5381, TDD
(406) 449-5053

NEBRASKA
11145 Mill Valley Road
Omaha, NE 68154
Telephone (402) 221-4691, TDD
(402) 498-3611

NEVADA
301 E. Stewart St., Room 301
Las Vegas, NV 89125-2527
Telephone (702) 388-6611, TDD
(702) 388-6653

50 S. Virginia St., Room 238
Reno, NV 89505-3216,

Telephone (702) 784-5268, TDD
None Listed

NEW HAMPSHIRE
Stewart Nelson Building, 143 N.
Main St., Suite 202
P.O. Box 1257
Concord, NH 03302-1257
Telephone (603) 225-1400, TDD
(603) 225-1462

NEW JERSEY
60 Park Place, Fourth Floor
Newark, NJ 07102
Telephone (201) 645-2434, TDD
(201) 645-4653

2600 Mt. Ephraim Ave.
Camden, NJ 08104
Telephone (609) 757-5183, TDD
None Listed

NEW MEXICO
625 Silver Ave., S.W., Suite 320
Albuquerque, NM 87102
Telephone (505) 766-1870, TDD
(505) 766-1339

NEW YORK
26 Federal Plaza, Room 3100
New York, NY 10278
Telephone (212) 264-4354, TDD
(212) 264-9147

100 S. Clinton St., Room 1071
P.O. Box 7317
Syracuse, NY 13261-7317
Telephone (315) 423-5383, TDD
(315) 423-5723

111 W. Huron St., Room 1311
Buffalo, NY 14202
Telephone (716) 846-4301, TDD
(716) 846-3248

333 E. Water St., Fourth Floor
Elmira, NY 14901
Telephone (607) 734-8130, TDD
(607) 734-0557

35 Pinelawn Road, Room 102E
Melville, NY 11747
Telephone (516) 454-0750, TDD
None Listed

100 State St., Room 410
Rochester, NY 14614
Telephone (716) 263-6700, TDD
(716) 263-3146

Leo W. O'Brian Federal Building,
   Room 815
Albany, NY 12207
Telephone (518) 472-6300, TDD
None Listed

NORTH CAROLINA
200 N. College St., Suite A 2015
Charlotte, NC 28202-2173
Telephone (704) 344-6563, TDD
   (704) 344-6640

NORTH DAKOTA
657 Second Ave., N., Room 218
Fargo, ND 58102
Telephone (701) 239-5131, TDD
   (701) 239-5657

OHIO
1111 Superior Ave., Suite 630
Cleveland, OH 44114-2507
Telephone (216) 522-4180, TDD
   (216) 522-8350

2 Nationwide Plaza, Suite 1400
Columbus, OH 43215-2542
Telephone (614) 469-6860, TDD
   (614) 469-6684

525 Vine St., Suite 870
Cincinnati, OH 45202
Telephone (513) 684-2814, TDD
   (513) 684-6920

OKLAHOMA
200 N.W. Fifth St., Suite 670
Oklahoma City, OK 73102
Telephone (405) 231-4301, TDD
None Listed

OREGON
222 S.W. Columbia St., Suite 500
Portland, OR 97201-6695
Telephone (503) 326-7251, TDD
   (503) 326-2501

PENNSYLVANIA
475 Allendale Road, Suite 201
King of Prussia, PA 19406
Telephone (215) 962-3819, TDD
   (215) 962-3806

960 Penn Ave., Fifth Floor
Pittsburgh, PA 15222
Telephone (412) 644-2780, TDD
   (412) 644-5143

100 Chestnut St., Room 309
Harrisburg, PA 17101

Telephone (717) 782-3840, TDD
   (717) 782-3477

20 N. Pennsylvania Ave.,
   Room 2327
Penn Place
Wilkes-Barre, PA 18701-3589
Telephone (717) 826-6497, TDD
   (717) 821-4174

PUERTO RICO
Carlos Chardon Ave., Room 691
Hato Rey, PR 0091-1729
Telephone (809) 766-5002, TDD
   (809) 766-5174

RHODE ISLAND
380 Westminster St., Fifth Floor
Providence, RI 02903
Telephone (401) 528-4561, TDD
   (401) 528-4690

SOUTH CAROLINA
1835 Assembly St., Room 358
Columbia, SC 29201
Telephone (803) 765-5376, TDD
   (803) 253-3364

SOUTH DAKOTA
110 S. Phillips Ave., Suite 200
Sioux Falls, SD 57102-1109
Telephone (605) 330-4231, TDD
   (605) 331-3527

TENNESSEE
50 Vantage Way, Suite 201
Nashville, TN 37228-1500
Telephone (615) 736-5881, TDD
   (615) 736-2499

TEXAS
4300 Amon Carter Blvd., Suite 114
Fort Worth, TX 76155
Telephone (817) 885-6500, From
Dallas (817) 355-1868
   TDD (817) 885-6552

10737 Gateway West, Suite 320
El Paso, TX 79935
Telephone (915) 540-5586, TDD
   (915) 540-5196

222 E. Van Buren St., Room 500
Harlingen, TX 78550
Telephone (210) 427-8533, TDD
   (210) 423-0691

9301 Southwest Freeway,
   Suite 550

Houston, TX 77074-1591
Telephone (713) 773-6500, TDD
   (713) 773-6568

1611 10th St., Suite 200
Lubbock, TX 79401,
Telephone (806) 743-7462, TDD
   (806) 743-7474

7400 Blanco Road, Suite 200
San Antonio, TX 78216-4300
Telephone (210) 229-4535, TDD
   (210) 229-4555

606 N. Carancahua, Suite 1200
Corpus Christi, TX 78476
Telephone (512) 888-3331, TDD
   (512) 888-3188

819 Taylor St., Room 8A-27
Ft. Worth, TX 76102
Telephone (817) 334-3613, TDD
None Listed

300 E. Eighth St., Room 520
Austin, TX 78701
Telephone (512) 482-5288, TDD
None Listed

505 E. Travis, Room 112
Marshall, TX 75670
Telephone (903) 935-5257, TDD
None Listed

UTAH
125 S. State St., Room 2237
Salt Lake City, UT 84138-1195
Telephone (801) 524-3209, TDD
   (801) 524-4040

VERMONT
87 State St., Room 205
P.O. Box 605
Montpelier, VT 05601-0605
Telephone (802) 828-4422, TDD
   (802) 828-4550

VIRGINIA
400 N. Eighth St., Room 3015
P.O. Box 10126
Richmond, VA 23240
Telephone (804) 771-2400, TDD
   (804) 771-8078

VIRGIN ISLANDS
4200 United Shopping Plaza,
   Suite 7
P.O. Box 4010
Christiansted, St. Croix, VI

00820-4487
Telephone (809) 778-5380, TDD
 (809) 766-5174

V.I. Maritime Building
Charlotte Amelie
St. Thomas, VI 00802
Telephone (809) 774-8530, TDD
 (809) 766-5174

WASHINGTON
915 Second Ave., Room 1792
Seattle, WA 98174-1088
Telephone (206) 220-6520, TDD
 (206) 553-6579

W. 601 First Ave., 10th Floor E.
Spokane, WA 99204-0317

Telephone (509) 353-2800, TDD
 (509) 353-2424

WEST VIRGINIA
168 W. Main St., Fifth Floor
P.O. Box 1608
Clarksburg, WV 26302-1608
Telephone (304) 623-5631, TDD
 (304) 623-5616

550 Eagan St., Room 309
Charleston, WV 25301
Telephone (304) 347-5220, TDD
 (304) 347-5438

WISCONSIN
212 E. Washington Ave.,
 Room 213
Madison, WI 53703

Telephone (608) 264-5261, TDD
 (608) 264-5333

310 W. Wisconsin Ave., Suite 400
Milwaukee, WI 53203
Telephone (414) 297-3941, TDD
 (414) 297-1095

WYOMING
100 E. B St., Room 4001
P.O. Box 2839
Casper, WY 82602-2839
Telephone (307) 261-5761, TDD
 (307) 261-5806

All of SBA's programs and services
are extended to the public on a
non-discriminatory basis.

STATE AND LOCAL GOVERNMENT ASSISTANCE PROGRAMS

Mark C. Hendricks

THERE IS an amazing wealth of resources available to parties who are willing to invest time and effort in locating and exploiting them. These resources are offered by a variety of organizations that have an interest in promoting international trade: state and local governments, professional and trade associations, financial and academic institutions. Because these organizations benefit from the success and growth of your client's business, they go to great lengths to offer their assistance.

The resources available from the United States Government are described in another chapter of this volume, and that would certainly be a good place to begin research. However, more localized agencies and organizations offer certain advantages. These organizations are typically more sensitive to local industry and business. They can often provide specialized knowledge of local programs and personnel. In many instances, these organizations are well-funded efforts to enhance the image and business climate of a particular geographic area. Very often, they are underutilized and therefore only too happy to be of service. In short, they provide a great source for more particularized and personal assistance.

The most important consideration when dealing with these organizations is that their missions are rarely defined in specifics. A common statement of mission would be "to promote the economic well being of the greater metropolitan area through assisting small and medium-sized businesses in export promotion." It may take a few telephone calls, and perhaps even a few visits to an office to determine what resources are available to accomplish this mission. In my experience, the time invested in exploring these resources is rarely wasted, and more often than not, leads to valuable contacts and information.

Some of the resources that might be found through the organizations listed in this chapter include:

Libraries of international trade publications, trade data, small business handbooks, etc.

Books and publications may be available free or for a nominal charge. Several state agencies produce excellent handbooks of international business. If your state does not, consider requesting one from another state. For example, the Maryland Guide to International Trade is an excellent volume.

Newsletters are particularly valuable because they disseminate *current* local information. Several newsletters also publish trade leads which may have come directly to the organization and are unavailable elsewhere (for example, "XYZ Company in Korea is looking for a supplier of seafood products . . . ").

Educational programs and seminars allow the local experts to share their expertise.

Networking/matchmaking services are perhaps the most helpful services provided. These organizations often serve as clearinghouses of all local interest in international topics. The camaraderie among locals can be valuable. Members are introduced when a common goal has been discovered, or members may share the benefit of their experience with non-local suppliers or customers.

Business referrals— If, for example, you make it clear that you are interested in supplying widgets for export from your local factory, the next inquiry that comes to the local organization for widgets may be referred to you.

Expert counseling may be available, although sometimes at a price. I would recommend exhausting the free-of-charge sources first (the Small Business Administration and SCORE, or the U.S. Department of Commerce), and through them, narrowing the issues for which you ultimately pay an expert.

Market research may be available, but it will often be based on Federal government data. It will, therefore, be more current if obtained directly from the Department of Commerce or other Federal source. However, look for special insights from organizations with foreign offices or personnel, especially overseas state trade offices.

Certificates of origin which may be required to comply with regulations or to take advantage of incentive programs are typically issued by chambers of commerce.

Trade missions— Many of these organizations provide excellent means of pooling resources for travel to target markets in order to present or demonstrate products, and to meet with local leaders and potential trading partners. By pooling groups of local business leaders, these organization often arrange for special treatment during the mission, and may open doors otherwise unaccessible to the individual businessperson. Also, there are several trade mission subsidy programs which may cover some of the costs of participation.

Interpreter services may be required for written correspondence and documentation, for telecommunications, or for visits from your foreign clients.

Export financing— While the Federal programs are more widely utilized, certain organizations are funded locally to promote local business, and may involve partial or complete financing packages, sometimes at terms more favorable than otherwise available.

It may take some detective work, but the resources available from state and local sources will undoubtedly save time and money, and reduce the possibility of costly mistakes. Experience has proven that a general inquiry such as, "What can you do to help me?" will elicit a general response. The more specific you can be, the greater the likelihood that you will be lead to a specific valuable resource.

STATE AND LOCAL RESOURCES

Alabama Development Office
International Marketing
State Capitol
401 Adams Ave
Montgomery AL 36130
(205) 242-0400

Alabama Export Council
2015 2nd Ave. North, Suite 302
Birmingham AL 35203
(205) 731-1331

Alabama International Trade Center
University of Alabama
P.O. Box 870396
Tuscaloosa AL 35487-0396
(205) 348-7621

Birmingham Chamber of Commerce
World Trade Association
2027 1st Avenue N.
P.O. Box 10127
Birmingham AL 35202
(205) 323-5461

Center for International Trade & Commerce
250 N. Water Street, Suite 131
Mobile AL 36602
(205) 433-1151

Madison County Commission
Madison County Courthouse, 7th Floor
Huntsville AL 35801
(205) 532-3505

N. Alabama International Trade Assoc.
1000 Glenn Hearn Blvd.
Huntsville AL 35824
(205) 461-1147

Tuscaloosa Chamber of Commerce
2200 University Boulevard
Tuscaloosa AL 35402
(205) 758-7588

Alaska Center for International Business
University of Alaska
3211 Providence Dr.
Anchorage AK 99508
(907) 786-4300

Alaska State Chamber of Commerce
217 2nd Street, Suite 201
Juneau AK 99801
(907) 586-2323

Anchorage Chamber of Commerce
441 W. Fifth Avenue, Suite 300
Anchorage AK 99501
(907) 272-2401

**Department of Commerce and
  Economic Development**
P.O. Box 110800
Juneau AK 99811-0800
(907) 465-2500

Fairbanks Chamber of Commerce
709 2nd Avenue
Fairbanks AK 99701
(907) 452-1105

State of Alaska
Office of International Trade
3601 C Street, Suite 798
Anchorage AK 99503
(907) 561-5855

World Trade Center
Anchorage
4201 Tudor Centre Drive, Suite 320
Anchorage AK 99508
(907) 561-1615

Arizona Department of Commerce
International Trade
3800 N. Central
Phoenix AZ 85012
(602) 280-1300

Arizona District Export Council
4617 E. Ocotillo Road
Paradise Valley AZ 85253
(602) 840-7439

Arizona World Trade Center
c/o Phoenix Chamber of Commerce
34 W. Monroe Street, Suite 900
Phoenix AZ 85003
(602) 495-6480

Phoenix Chamber of Commerce
34 W. Monroe Street, Suite 900
Phoenix AZ 85003
(602) 254-5521

Tucson Chamber of Commerce
465 W. St. Mary's Road
Tucson AZ 85702
(602) 792-2250

World Trade Center
Sunbelt Holdings, Inc.
426 N. 44th Street, Suite 375
Phoenix AZ 85008
(602) 244-1440

Arkansas Industrial Development Commission
International Marketing
1 State Capitol Mall
Little Rock AR 72201
(501) 682-1121

Arkansas International Center
University of Arkansas at Little Rock
33rd and University
Little Rock AR 72204
(501) 569-3782

Arkansas State Chamber of Commerce
410 S. Cross
Little Rock AR 72203
(501) 374-9225

Jonesboro State Chamber of Commerce
593 S. Madison
Jonesboro AR 72403
(501) 932-6691

World Trade Club
P.O. Box 25853
Little Rock AR 72221
(501) 225-5574

California Community College
Economic Development Network and International Trade
90 West Fir, Suite 204
Clovis CA 93611-0244
(800) 344-3812

California Council for International Trade
700 Montgomery Street, Suite 305
San Francisco CA 94111
(415) 788-4127

California Export Finance Office
6 Centerpointe Dr., Suite 760
La Palma CA 90623
(714) 562-5519

California Trade and Commerce Agency
One World Trade Center, Suite 990
Long Beach CA 90831
(310) 590-5965

California State Chamber of Commerce
1201 K Street, 12th Floor
P.O. Box 1736
Sacramento CA 95812
(916) 444-6670

California State World Trade Commission
1121 L Street, Suite 310
Sacramento CA 95814
(916) 324-5511

California Department of Commerce
801 K Street, Suite 1700
Sacramento CA 95814
(916) 322-1491

Export Small Business Development Center
110 East Ninth Street, Suite A669
Los Angeles CA 90079
(213) 892-1112

Foreign Credit Insurance Association
222 N. Sepulveda Boulevard, Suite 1515
El Segundo CA 90245
(310) 322-1152

Foreign Trade Association of Southern California
900 Wilshire, Suite 1434
Los Angeles CA 90017
(213) 627-0634

Greater Los Angeles World Trade Center Long Beach
100 W. Broadway, Suite 295
Long Beach CA 90831-0295
(310) 499-8181

Inland International Trade Association
1787 Tribute Road, Suite A
Sacramento CA 95815
(916) 920-7945

International Business Association of Southern California
Long Beach Area Chamber of Commerce
One World Trade Center, Suite 350
Long Beach CA 90831
(310) 436-1251

International Marketing Association of Orange County
Cal State Fullerton, Marketing Department
Fullerton CA 92634
(714) 773-2223

Los Angeles Area Chamber of Commerce
International Commerce Division
404 S. Bixel Street
Los Angeles CA 90051
(213) 629-0602

Los Angeles World Trade Center
350 S. Figueroa Street
Los Angeles CA 90071
(213) 617-1414

Northern California District Export Council
250 Montgomery, 14th Floor
San Francisco CA 94104
(415) 705-2300

Oakland Chamber of Commerce
475 14th Street
Oakland CA 94612
(510) 874-4800

Oakland World Trade Association
475 14th Street
Oakland CA 94612-1900
(510) 388-8829

San Diego Chamber of Commerce
402 W. Broadway, Suite 1000
San Diego CA 92101
(619) 232-0124

San Diego District Export Council
6363 Greenwich Drive, Suite 260
San Diego CA 92122
(619) 557-5395

San Francisco International Trade Center
465 California Street, 9th Floor
San Francisco CA 94104
(415) 392-4511

San Francisco World Trade Association
San Francisco Chamber of Commerce
465 California Street, 9th Floor
San Francisco CA 94104
(415) 392-4511

World Trade Association of Orange County
Santa Ana Chamber of Commerce
801 Civic Center Drive, Suite 110
Santa Ana CA 92701
(714) 724-9822

World Trade Association of San Diego
6363 Greenwich Drive, Suite 215
San Diego CA 92122
(619) 453-4605

World Trade Center Pomona
c/o Birtcher Urbanetics
276 LaPaz Road
Laguna Niguel CA 92677
(714) 831-8031

World Trade Council, San Mateo
951 Mariners Island Boulevard, Suite 260
San Mateo CA 94404
(415) 354-8300

Colorado Association of Commerce and Industry
1776 Lincoln Street, Suite 1200
Denver CO 80203
(303) 831-7411

Denver Chamber of Commerce
1445 Market Street
Denver CO 80202
(303) 894-8500

Colorado International Trade Office
Department of Commerce & Development
1625 Broadway, Suite 680
Denver CO 80202
(303) 892-3850

The Forum For World Affairs
5 Landmark Square
Stamford CT 06103
(203) 356-0340

Connecticut Business & Industry Association
370 Asylum Street
Hartford CT 06103
(203) 244-1900

Connecticut Foreign Trade Association
c/o Shawmut Bank
One Landmark Square
Stamford CT 06904
(203) 358-6175

Connecticut International Trade Association
c/o Sabo International
P.O. Box 270403
W. Hartford CT 06107
(203) 231-7800

Connecticut World Trade Association
177 State St., 4th Floor
Bridgeport CT 06604
(203) 336-5353

West Connecticut International Trade Association
P.O. Box 3063
Stamford CT 06905
(203) 324-5620

Connecticut Department of Economic Development
International Division
865 Brook Street
Rocky Hill CT 06067-3405
(203) 258-4256

Delaware State Chamber of Commerce
1207 King St.
P.O. Box 709
Wilmington DE 19899
(302) 656-7905

Delaware Division of Economic Development
630 State College Road
P.O. Box 1401
Dover DE 19901
(302) 736-4271

World Trade Center Delaware
P.O. Box 709
Wilmington DE 19899
(302) 656-7905

Florida Department of Commerce
Bureau of International Trade
107 W. Gaines St.
Tallahassee FL 32399-2000
(904) 488-6124

Florida State Chamber of Commerce
136 S. Bronough Street
Tallahassee FL 32302
(904) 425-1211

Foreign Credit Insurance Association
World Trade Center
80 SW 8th Street, Suite 1800
Miami FL 33130
(305) 372-8540

Greater Miami Chamber of Commerce
1601 Biscayne Boulevard
Miami FL 33132
(305) 350-7700

Greater Tampa Bay International Trade Council
P.O. Box 420
Tampa FL 33601
(813) 228-7777

Florida International Agricultural Trade Council
Mayo Building
Room 412
Tallahassee FL 32399-0800
(904) 488-4366

Orlando World Trade Association
c/o Greater Orlando Chamber of Commerce
P.O. Box 1234
Orlando FL 32802
(407) 425-1234

World Trade Center Orlando
122 E. Colonial Drive, Suite 102
Orlando FL 32801
(407) 649-1899

World Trade Center Miami
1 World Trade Plaza
80 SW 8th Street, Suite 1800
Miami FL 33130
(305) 579-0064

Atlanta Chamber of Commerce
235 International Boulevard, NW
Atlanta GA 30303
(404) 880-9000

Georgia Department of Agriculture
International Trade Division
330 Agricultural Building, Capitol Square
Atlanta GA 30334
(404) 656-3740

Georgia Department of Industry and Trade
285 Peachtree Center Avenue, Suite 1100
Atlanta GA 30303
(404) 656-3571

South Georgia Chamber of Commerce
213 E. Monroe Street
Thomasville GA 31799
(912) 228-1299

World Trade Club Atlanta
240 Peachtree Street, NE, Suite 2200
Atlanta GA 30303
(404) 525-4144

Economic Development Corporation of Honolulu
Pacific Tower
1001 Bishop Street, Suite 735
Honolulu HI 96813
(808) 545-4533

Hawaii Chamber of Commerce
World Trade Association
432 Bishop Street, Suite 200
Honolulu HI 96813
(808) 545-4300

Hawaii Department of Business & Economic Development
Trade and Industry Branch
201 Merchant St.
P.O. Box 2359, Suite 1510
Honolulu HI 96813
(808) 587-2797

Idaho District Export Council
700 W. State St., 2nd Floor
Boise ID 83720
(208) 334-2505

Idaho Department of Commerce
Division of International Business
700 W. State Street
Boise ID 83720-2700
(208) 334-2470

Twin Falls Area Chamber of Commerce
858 Blue Lakes Boulevard N
Twin Falls ID 83301
(208) 733-3974

World Trade Committee
Boise Area Chamber of Commerce
310 N. 6th Street
P.O. Box 2368
Boise ID 83701
(208) 344-5515

American Association of Exporters and Importers
7763 S. Kedzie Avenue
Chicago IL 60652
(312) 471-1958

Charleston Chamber of Commerce
501 Jackson Avenue
P.O. Box 77
Charleston IL 61920
(217) 345-7041

Chicagoland Chamber of Commerce
World Trade Division
200 N. LaSalle Street
Chicago IL 60601
(312) 580-6900

Foreign Credit Insurance Association
19 S. LaSalle Street, Suite 902
Chicago IL 60603
(312) 641-1915

Illinois Department of Agriculture
1010 Jorie Boulevard, Room 20
Oak Brook IL 60521
(312) 990-8256

Illinois Department of Commerce & Community Affairs
International Business Division
100 W. Randolph, Suite 3-400
Chicago IL 60601
(312) 814-7179

Illinois Export Council
321 N. Clark Street, Suite 550
Chicago IL 60610
(312) 793-1WTC

Illinois Manufacturers' Association
209 W. Jackson Boulevard, Suite 700
Chicago IL 60606
(312) 922-6575

Peoria Area Chamber of Commerce
124 SW Adams Street, Suite 300
Peoria IL 61602
(309) 676-0755

World Trade Council of Northern Illinois
515 N. Court
Rockford IL 61103
(815) 987-8100

Fort Wayne Chamber of Commerce
International Development Group
826 Ewing Street
Fort Wayne IN 46802
(219) 424-1435

Greater Lafayette Chamber of Commerce
224 Main Street
P.O. Box 348
Lafayette IN 47901
(317) 742-6276

Indiana Department of Commerce
International Trade
1 N. Capitol, Suite 700
Indianapolis IN 46204
(317) 232-8888

Indiana State Chamber of Commerce
Indiana Economic Development Council
1 N. Capitol Avenue, Suite 700
Indianapolis IN 46204-2288
(317) 232-8800

Indianapolis Chamber of Commerce
Development and World Trade
320 N. Meridian Street, Suite 928
Indianapolis IN 46204
(317) 464-2200

South Bend Chamber of Commerce
401 E. Colfax Avenue
P.O. Box 1677
South Bend IN 46634
(219) 234-0051

Tri-State World Trade Council
100 NW 2nd Street, Suite 202
Evansville IN 47708
(812) 425-8147

World Trade Club of Indiana
1 Capitol, Suite 200
Indianapolis IN 46204
(317) 264-6892

Cedar Rapids Area Chamber of Commerce
424 1st Avenue, NE
P.O Box 4860
Cedar Rapids IA 52407
(319) 398-5317

Iowa Department of Agriculture
International Marketing Division
Wallace Building
Des Moines IA 50319
(515) 242-6238

Iowa Department of Economic Development
International Marketing
200 E. Grand Avenue
Des Moines IA 50309
(515) 281-3251

Iowa-Illinois International Trade Association
112 E. 3rd Street
Davenport IA 52801
(319) 322-1706

Siouxland International Trade Association
Legislative & Agriculture Affairs
101 Pierce Street
Sioux City IA 51101
(712) 255-7903

Kansas City Kansas Chamber of Commerce
727 Minnesota Avenue
P.O. Box 171337
Kansas City KS 66101
(913) 371-3070

Kansas Chamber of Commerce & Industry
500 Bank IV Tower
Topeka KS 66603
(913) 357-6321

Kansas Department of Commerce
Trade Development Division
400 SW 8th Street, Suite 500
Topeka KS 66603-3957
(913) 296-4027

Mid-America World Trade Center
301 N. Main Street, Suite 1860
Wichita KS 67202
(800) 776-2982

Louisville Economic Development Cabinet
1 Riverfront Plaza
Louisville KY 40202
(502) 566-5041

Kentucky Cabinet For Economic Development
Office of International Trade Office
2100 Capital Plaza Tower
Frankfort KY 40601
(502) 564-2562

Louisiana Association of Business & Industry
3113 Valley Creek Drive
Baton Rouge LA 70898
(504) 928-5388

Louisiana Department of Economic Development
International Trade Division
P.O. Box 94185
Baton Rouge LA 70804-9185
(504) 342-3000

New Orleans & River Region
Chamber of Commerce
301 Camp Street
New Orleans LA 70190
(504) 527-6900

World Trade Club of Greater New Orleans
World Trade Center, Canal Street,
   Suite 1132
New Orleans LA 70130
(504) 525-7201

Greater Portland Chamber of Commerce
142 Free Street
Portland ME 04101
(207) 772-2811

Maine State Development Office
193 State Street, State House, Station 59
Augusta ME 04333
(207) 289-2656

Baltimore Economic Development Corporation
36 S. Charles Street, Suite 1600
Baltimore MD 21201
(301) 837-9305

Greater Baltimore Committee
111 S. Calvert Street, Suite 1500
Baltimore MD 21202
(301) 727-2820

Maryland Office of International Trade
World Trade Center, 7th Floor
401 E. Pratt Street
Baltimore MD 21202
(410) 333-8180

World Trade Center Baltimore
World Trade Center, Suite 1355
Baltimore MD 21202
(410) 576-0022

Associated Industries of Massachusetts
222 Berkeley St.
Boston MA 02117
(617) 262-1180

Central Berkshire Chamber of Commerce
66 W Street
Pittsfield MA 01201
(413) 499-4000

Fall River Area Chamber of Commerce
200 Pocasset Street
P.O. Box 1871
Fall River MA 02721
(508) 676-8226

Greater Boston Chamber of Commerce
600 Atlantic Avenue, 13th Floor
Boston MA 02210
(617) 227-4500

Greater Gardner Chamber of Commerce
55 Lake Street
Gardner MA 01440
(508) 632-1780

Greater Springfield Chamber of Commerce
1350 Main Street, 3rd Floor
Springfield MA 01103
(413) 787-1555

International Business Center of New England
World Trade Center, Boston, Suite 323
Boston MA 02210
(617) 439-5280

Massachusetts Department of Commerce & Development
100 Cambridge Street, 13th Floor
Boston MA 02202
(617) 727-3221

Massachusetts Department of Food & Agriculture
100 Cambridge Street
Boston MA 02202
(617) 727-3018

Massachusetts Office of International Trade
100 Cambridge Street, Room 902
Boston MA 02202
(617) 367-1830

New Bedford Area Chamber of Commerce
794 Purchase Street
P.O. Box G827
New Bedford MA 02742
(508) 999-5231

World Trade Center Boston
164 Northern Avenue
World Trade Center
Boston MA 02210-2004
(617) 439-5000

Ann Arbor Chamber of Commerce
211 E. Huron, Suite 1
Ann Arbor MI 48104
(313) 995-7283

Central Macomb County Chamber of Commerce
58 N Avenue
P.O. Box 855
Mt. Clemens MI 48043
(313) 463-1528

Detroit Chamber of Commerce
600 W. Lafayette Boulevard
Detroit MI 48226
(313) 964-4000

Detroit Community & Economic Development Department
150 Michigan Avenue, 7th Floor
Detroit MI 48226
(313) 224-6533

Flint Area Chamber of Commerce
316 W. Water Street
Flint MI 48503
(313) 232-7101

Greater Grand Rapids Chamber of Commerce
17 Fountain Street, NW
Grand Rapids MI 49503
(616) 771-0300

Kalamazoo Chamber of Commerce
128 N. Kalamazoo Mall
Kalamazoo MI 49005
(616) 381-4000

Michigan Department of Agriculture
Office of International Trade
525 W. Ottawa
P.O. Box 30225
Lansing MI 48909
(517) 373-1154

Michigan State Chamber of Commerce
600 S. Walnut Street
Lansing MI 48933
(517) 371-2100

Michigan State University
International Business Centers
6 Kellog Center
East Lansing MI 48824-1022
(517) 353-4336

Muskegon Area Chamber of Commerce
349 W. Webster
Muskegon MI 49443-1087
(616) 722-3751

Michigan Department of Commerce
Michigan International Office
P.O. Box 30105
Lansing MI 48909
(517) 373-1054

Twin Cities Area Chamber of Commerce
185 E. Main Street
P.O. Box 1208
Benton Harbor MI 49022
(616) 925-0044

West Michigan World Trade Club
99 Monroe, NW
Grand Rapids MI 49503
(616) 456-9622

Minnesota Export Finance Authority
1000 World Trade Center
30 E. 7th Street
St. Paul MN 55101-4902
(612) 297-4658

Minnesota State Chamber of Commerce
480 Cedar Street, Suite 500
St. Paul MN 55101
(612) 292-4650

Minnesota Trade Office
1000 World Trade Center
30 E. 7th Street
St. Paul MN 55101
(612) 297-4227

Minnesota World Trade Association
P.O. Box 24341
Apple Valley MN 55124
(612) 441-9261

Minnesota World Trade Center
400 Minnesota World Trade Center
30 E. 7th Street
St. Paul MN 55101
(612) 297-1580

St. Paul Area Chamber of Commerce
101 Norwest Center
55 E. 5th Street
St. Paul MN 55101
(612) 224-3278

International Trade Club of Mississippi, Inc.
P.O. Box 1249
Jackson MS 39215-1249
(601) 949-0245

Jackson Chamber of Commerce
201 S. President Street
P.O. Box 22548
Jackson MS 39225-2548
(601) 948-7575

Mississippi Department of Economic & Community Development
P.O. Box 849
Jackson MS 39205
(601) 359-3552

International Trade Club of Greater Kansas City
920 Main Street, Suite 600
Kansas City MO 64105
(816) 221-1462

Missouri Department of Agriculture
International Marketing Program
P.O. Box 630
Jefferson City MO 65102
(314) 751-2613

Missouri District Export Council
8182 Maryland Ave., Suite 303
St. Louis MO 63105
(314) 425-3305

Missouri Department of Economic Development
International Development Office
P.O. Box 118
Jefferson City MO 65102
(314) 751-4855

Missouri State Chamber of Commerce
428 E. Capitol Avenue
Jefferson City MO 65102
(314) 634-3511

Montana Department of Commerce
Business Development Division
1424 9th Avenue
Helena MT 59620
(406) 444-3494

Montana State Chamber of Commerce
2030 11th Avenue
Helena MT 59624
(406) 442-2405

Lincoln Chamber of Commerce
1221 North Street, Suite 320
Lincoln NE 68508
(402) 476-7511

Nebraska Department of Economic Development
International Division
301 Centennial Mall South
Lincoln NE 68509
(402) 471-4668

Omaha Chamber of Commerce
International Affairs
1301 Harney Street
Omaha NE 68102
(402) 346-5000

Economic Development Authority of Western Nevada
5190 Neil Road, Suite 111
Reno NV 89502
(702) 829-3700

Nevada Commission of Economic Development
Capitol Complex
Carson City NV 89710
(702) 687-4325

Nevada Commission on Economic Development
3770 Howard Hughes Pkwy., Suite 295
Las Vegas NV 89158
(702) 486-7282

Greater Manchester Chamber of Commerce
889 Elm Street
Manchester NH 03101
(603) 666-6600

State of New Hampshire
Office Of International Commerce
601 Spaulding Turnpike, Suite 29
P.O. Box 856
Portsmouth NH 03801-2833
(603) 334-6074

New Jersey Department of Commerce
Division of International Trade
153 Halsey Street, 5th Floor
Newark NJ 07102
(201) 648-3518

Metro Newark Chamber of Commerce
40 Clinton Street
Newark NJ 07102
(201) 242-6237

New Jersey State Chamber of Commerce
1 State Square
50 W State Street, Suite 1110
Trenton NJ 08608
(609) 989-7888

New Mexico Economic Development
and Tourism Department
International Trade Division
1100 St. Francis Drive
Santa Fe NM 87503
(505) 827-0569

Greater Albuquerque Chamber of Commerce
International Trade Committee
401 2nd Street, NW,
P.O. BOX 25100
Albuquerque NM 87125
(505) 764-3700

New Mexico Department of Agriculture
International Marketing Program
P.O. Box 30005, Dept. 5600
Las Cruces NM 88003-0005
(505) 646-4929

Albany-Colonie Regional Chamber of Commerce
518 Broadway
Albany NY 12207
(518) 434-1214

American Association of Importers & Exporters
11 W 42nd Street
New York NY 10036
(212) 944-2230

**Buffalo Area Chamber of Commerce & Economic
   Development**
107 Delaware Avenue
Buffalo NY 14202
(716) 852-7100

Buffalo World Trade Association
P.O. Box 39
Tonawanda NY 14150
(716) 877-1452

Canada-U.S. Trade Center/University of Buffalo
Department of Geography
Wilkenson Quad
Box 610023
Buffalo NY 14261-0023
(716) 636-2299

Foreign Credit Insurance Association
40 Rector Street, 11th Floor
New York NY 10006
(212) 306-5000

Long Island Association, Inc., World Trade Club
Legislative & Economic Affairs
80 Hauppauge Road
Commack NY 11725
(516) 499-4400

New York Chamber of Commerce & Industry
1 Battery Park Plaza
New York NY 10004-1405
(212) 493-7500

**New York State Department of Economic
   Development**
International Trade Division
1515 Broadway, 51st Floor
New York NY 10036
(212) 827-6220

Private Export Funding Corporation
280 Park Avenue
New York NY 10017
(212) 557-3100

**Rochester Area Chamber of Commerce World Trade
   Department**
International Trade & Transportation
55 St. Paul Street
Rochester NY 14604
(716) 454-2220

Tappan Zee International Trade Association
1 Blue Hill Plaza, Suite 812
Pearl River NY 10965
(914) 735-7040

Westchester County Association, Inc.
World Trade Club of Westchester
235 Mamaroneck Avenue
White Plains NY 10605
(914) 948-6444

Western New York International Trade Council
300 Main Place Tower
Buffalo NY 14202
(716) 852-7160

World Commerce Association of Central New York
572 S. Salina Street
Syracuse NY 13202
(315) 470-1343

World Trade Institute
1 World Trade Center, 55 West
New York NY 10048
(212) 435-4044

North Carolina Department of Agriculture
International Trade Office
P.O. Box 27647
Raleigh NC 27611
(919) 733-7912

North Carolina Department of Economic &
Community Development
International Division
430 N. Salisburg Street
Raleigh NC 28611
(919) 733-7193

Winston-Salem Chamber of Commerce
P.O. Box 1408
Winston-Salem NC 27102
(919) 725-2361

Fargo Chamber of Commerce
321 N. 4th Street
Fargo ND 58108
(701) 237-5678

North Dakota Dep't of Economic Development
International Trade Division
Liberty Memorial Building
604 East Boulevard
Bismarck ND 58505
(701) 221-5300

Akron Regional Development Board
International Business & Trade
One Cascade Plaza, Suite 800
Akron OH 44308
(216) 379-3157

Cleveland World Trade Association
200 Tower City Circle
Cleveland OH 44113
(216) 621-3300

Columbus Area Chamber of Commerce,
Economic Development
37 N. High Street
Columbus OH 43215
(614) 221-2747

Columbus Council on World Affairs
2 Nationwide Plaza, Suite 705
280 N. High Street
Columbus OH 43215
(614) 249-8450

Dayton Council on World Affairs
300 College Park
Dayton OH 45469
(513) 229-2390

Dayton Development Council
5th & Main Streets
Dayton OH 45402-2400
(513) 226-8222

Greater Cincinnati Chamber of Commerce
Export Development
300 Carew Tower
441 Vine Street
Cincinnati OH 45202
(513) 579-3100

Ohio Department of Agriculture
Ohio Department Building
65 S. Front Street, Room 607
Columbus OH 43215
(614) 466-2732

Ohio Department of Development
International Trade Division
77 S. High Street, 29th Floor
Columbus OH 43266
(614) 466-5017

Newark Area Chamber of Commerce
50 W. Locust Street,
P.O. Box 702
Newark OH 43055
(614) 345-9757

Springfield Area Chamber of Commerce
333 N. Limestone Street, Suite 201
Springfield OH 45503
(513) 325-7621

Toledo Area International Trade Association
218 Huron Street
Toledo OH 43604
(419) 243-8191

Youngstown-Warren Chamber of Commerce
World Trade
1200 Stambaugh Building
Youngstown OH 44503-1604
(216) 744-2131

Oklahoma City Chamber of Commerce
Economic and Community Development
1 Santa Fe Plaza
Oklahoma City OK 73102
(415) 278-8900

Oklahoma Department of Agriculture
Market Development Division
2800 N. Lincoln Boulevard
Oklahoma City OK 73105
(405) 521-3864

Oklahoma Department of Commerce
6601 Broadway Extension
Oklahoma City OK 73116
(405) 841-5217

Oklahoma District Export Council
6601 Broadway Extension
Oklahoma City OK 73116
(405) 231-5302

Oklahoma State Chamber of Commerce
4020 N. Lincoln Boulevard
Oklahoma City OK 73105
(405) 424-4003

Tulsa Chamber of Commerce
Economic Development Division
616 S. Boston Avenue
Tulsa OK 74119
(918) 585-1201

Tulsa World Trade Association
3148 S. 108 E Avenue, Suite 140
Tulsa OK 74146
(918) 665-6100

Willamette International Trade Center
1401 Willamette
Eugene OR 97440
(503) 686-0195

International Trade Institute
One World Trace Center
121 SW Salmon, Suite 230
Portland OR 97204
(503) 725-3246

National Association of Small Business
International Trade Educators (NASBITE)
P.O. Box 2427
Portland OR 97204
(503) 223-3896

Oregon Department of Agriculture
One World Trade Center
121 SW Salmon, Suite 240
Portland OR 97204
(503) 229-6734

Oregon Economic Development Department
International Trade Division
One World Trade Center
121 SW Salmon, Suite 300
Portland OR 97209
(503) 228-9411

Portland Chamber of Commerce
221 NW 2nd Avenue
Portland OR 97209
(503)228-9411

Small Business International Trade
Program (SBITP)
One World Trade Center
121 SW Salmon, Suite 210
Portland OR 97204
(503) 274-7482

Southern Oregon International Trade Council
Marie Morehead, Chair
P.O. Box 1762
Medford OR 97501
(503) 482-2021

Willamette International Trade Center
1059 Willamette Street
Eugene OR 97401-3171
(503) 686-0195

Western Wood Products Association
Yeon Building
522 SW 5th Street
Portland OR 97204
(503) 224-3930

World Trade Center Portland
One World Trade Center
121 SW Salmon, Suite 250
Portland OR 97204
(503) 464-8888

American Society of International Executives, Inc.
18 Sentry Parkway, Suite 1
Blue Bell PA 19422
(215) 540-2295

Pennsylvania Department of Agriculture
Bureau of Agriculture Development
2301 N. Cameron Street
Harrisburg PA 17110
(717) 783-8460

Pennsylvania Department of Commerce
Office of International Trade
464 Forum Building
Room 486
Harrisburg PA 17120
(717) 787-7190

Philadelphia Chamber of Commerce
1346 Chestnut Street, Suite 800
Philadelphia PA 19107
(215) 545-1234

Philadelphia Chamber
Municipal Services Building
Room 1660
Philadelphia PA 19104
(215) 686-3647

Pittsburgh Chamber of Commerce
Three Gateway Center, Suite 1400
Pittsburgh PA 15222
(412) 392-4500

**Southwestern Pennsylvania Economic Development
District**
12300 Perry Highway
Wexford PA 15090
(412) 935-6122

Western Pennsylvania District Export Council
1000 Liberty Avenue
Room 2002
Pittsburgh PA 15222
(412) 644-2850

World Trade Association of Philadelphia, Inc.
P.O. Box 58640
Philadelphia PA 19102
(215) 988-0711

Greater Providence Chamber of Commerce
30 Exchange Terrace
Greater Providence RI 02903
(401) 521-5000

Rhode Island Department of Economic Development
International Trade Division
7 Jackson Walkway
Providence RI 02903
(401) 277-2601

World Trade Center Rhode Island
Bryant College
1150 Douglas Pike
Smithfield RI 02917-1284
(401) 232-6400

Charleston Trident Chamber of Commerce
World Trade Center
P.O. Box 975
Charleston SC 29402
(803) 577-2510, ext. 3029

Midlands International Trade Association
1835 Assembly Street
Columbia SC 29201
(803) 767-5345

South Carolina District Export Council
Strom Thurmond Federal Building
Suite 172, 1835 Assembly Street
Columbia SC 29201
(803) 765-5345

South Carolina State Chamber of Commerce
1201 Main Street, Suite 1810
Columbia SC 29201
(803) 799-4601

South Carolina State Development Board
International Division
P.O. Box 927
Columbia SC 29202
(803) 737-0400

Rapid City Area Chamber of Commerce
444 Mt. Rushmore Road, N.
P.O. Box 747
Rapid City SD 57709
(605) 343-1774

Sioux Falls Chamber of Commerce
315 S. Philips Avenue
Sioux Falls SD 57101
(605) 336-1620

South Dakota Governor's Office of Economic Development
Export & Marketing Division
Capitol Lake Plaza
711 E. Wells Avenue
Pierre SD 57501
(605) 773-5032

World Trade Council
P.O. Box 1273
Chattanooga TN 37402
(615) 752-4302

Memphis Area Chamber of Commerce
World Trade Council
22 N. Front Street, Suite 200
P.O. Box 224
Memphis TN 38101
(901) 575-3500

Mid-South Exporters Roundtable
P.O. Box 3521
Memphis TN 38173
(901) 320-5811

Nashville Area Chamber of Commerce
World Trade Council
161 4th Avenue, N.
Nashville TN 37219
(615) 259-4755

Tennessee Department of Agriculture
Ellington Agricultural Center
P.O. Box 40627, Melrose Station
Nashville TN 37204
(615) 360-0160

Tennessee Department of Economic & Community Development
Export Office
320 6th Avenue N., 7th Floor
Nashville TN 37219
(615) 741-4815

Tennessee District Export Council
P.O. Box 2128
Brentwood TN 37024-2128
(615) 371-7350

Amarillo Chamber of Commerce
Amarillo Building, 1000 S. Polk Street
Amarillo TX 79105
(806) 692-1338

Dallas Council on World Affairs
P.O. Box 58232
Dallas TX 75258
(214) 748-5663

El Paso Chamber of Commerce
10 Civic Center Plaza
El Paso TX 79901
(915) 534-0500

Foreign Credit Insurance Association
1880 S. Dairy, Ashford II, Suite 585
Houston TX 77077
(713) 589-8182

Fort Worth Chamber of Commerce
777 Taylor Street, Suite 900
Fort Worth TX 76102
(817) 336-2491

Greater Dallas Chamber of Commerce
1201 Elm Street, Suite 2000
Dallas TX 75270
(214) 746-6600

Greater San Antonio Chamber of Commerce
602 E. Commerce
San Antonio TX 78296
(512) 229-2114

Houston Chamber of Commerce
1100 Milam Building, 25th Floor
Houston TX 77002
(713) 651-1313

**International Trade Association of Dallas/
  Fort Worth**
P.O. Box 5835
Dallas TX 75258
(214) 748-3777

Lubbock Chamber of Commerce
14th Street & Avenue K
P.O. Box 561
Lubbock TX 79408
(806) 763-4666

Odessa Chamber of Commerce
700 North Grant
P.O. Box 3626
Odessa TX 79760
(915) 332-9111

Texas Department of Agriculture
Export Services Division
1700 N. Congress
P.O. Box 12847, Capitol Station
Austin TX 78711
(512) 463-7624

Texas Department of Commerce
International Trade
816 Congress
Austin TX 78711
(512) 320-9439

Texas Economic Development Commission
International Trade Department
816 Congress Avenue
Austin TX 78701
(512) 472-5059

World Trade Center San Antonio
118 Broadway, Suite 621
P.O. Box 899
San Antonio TX 78205
(512) 225-5888

Salt Lake Area Chamber of Commerce
Export Development Committee
175 E. 400 Street, Suite 600
Salt Lake City UT 84111
(801) 364-3631

**Utah Department of Community & Economic
  Development**
International Division
324 S. State Street, Suite 200
Salt Lake City UT 84111
(801) 538-8737

Utah International Business Development Office
324 S. State Street, Fifth Floor
Salt Lake City UT 84114
(801) 538-8700

**Vermont Agency of Development & Community
  Affairs**
Pavilion Office Building
109 State Street
Montpelier VT 05609
(802) 828-3221

Vermont State Chamber of Commerce
Granger Road, P.O. Box 37
Montpelier VT 05601
(802) 223-3443

Federation of International Trade Associations
1851 Alexander Bell Drive
Reston VA 22091
(703) 620-1588

International Trade Association of West Virginia
P.O. Box 936
Lexington VA 24450
(703) 463-1095

Piedmont World Trade Council
P.O. Box 1374
Lynchburg VA 24505
(804) 384-3454

**Virginia Department of Agriculture & Consumer
  Affairs**
P.O. Box 1163
Richmond VA 23209
(804) 786-3501

**Virginia Department of Economic Development &
  International Trade**
1021 E. Carey Street, 14th Floor
Richmond VA 23219
(804) 786-3791

Virginia District Export Council
P.O. Box 10190
Richmond VA 23240
(804) 771-2246
Virginia State Chamber of Commerce
9 S. 5th Street
Richmond VA 23219
(804) 644-1607

Commencement Bay International Trade Council
Tacoma-Pierce County Chamber of Commerce
950 Pacific Ave., Suite 300
P.O. Box 1933
Tacoma WA 98401
(206) 627-2175

Greater Seattle Chamber of Commerce
1200 One Union Square
Seattle WA 98198
(206) 389-7200

Inland Empire World Trade Club
P.O. Box 3727
Spokane WA 99220
(509) 489-0500

Trade Development And Alliance Of Greater Seattle
600 University St., Suite 1200
Seattle WA 98101
(206) 389-7301

Washington Council on International Trade
2615 4th Avenue
Seattle WA 98121
(206) 443-3826

Washington State Department of Agriculture
Market Development Division
P.O. Box 42560
Olympia WA 98504-2560
(206) 753-5046

Washington State Department of Trade
Importing/Exporting Office
2001 6th Avenue, Suite 2300
Seattle WA 98121
(206) 464-7143

Washington State International Trade Fair
999 3rd Avenue, Suite 1020
First Interstate Center
Seattle WA 98104
(206) 682-6900

World Affairs Council
515 Madison Avenue, Suite 501
Seattle WA 98104
(206) 682-6986

World Trade Center Tacoma
3600 Port of Tacoma Road, Suite 309
Tacoma WA 98424
(206) 383-9474

Whitworth Institute For International Management
300 W. Hawthorne Rd.
Spokane WA 99251-1103
(509) 466-3742

Governor's Office of Community & Industrial Development
International Division
Building 6, Room 517
State Capitol Complex
Charleston WV 25305
(304) 348-2234

Institute for International Trade Development
1050 4th Avenue
Huntington WV 25755-2131
(304) 696-2451

West Virginia Manufacturers Association
405 Capitol Street,Suite 503
Charleston WV 25301
(304) 342-2123

Milwaukee Association of Commerce
756 N. Milwaukee Street
Milwaukee WI 53202
(414) 273-3000

Milwaukee World Trade Association
756 N. Milwaukee Street
Milwaukee WI 53202
(414) 287-4100

Small Business Development Center
432 N. Lake Street, Room 423
Madison WI 53706
(608) 263-7766

Wausau Area Chamber of Commerce
300 3rd Street, P.O. Box 6190
Wausau WI 54402
(715) 845-6231

Wisconsin Department of Development
123 W. Washington Avenue
Madison WI 53702
(608) 266-1018

Wisconsin World Trade Center
424 E. Wisconsin Avenue
Milwaukee WI 53202
(414) 274-3840

Cheyenne Chamber of Commerce
301 W. 16th Street
Cheyenne WY 82003
(307) 638-3388

Laramie Chamber of Commerce
P.O. Box 1166

Laramie WY 82070
(307) 754-3494

State of Wyoming
Office of the Governor
Capitol Building
Cheyenne WY 82002
(307) 777-6412

THE ROLE OF MULTILATERAL FINANCIAL INSTITUTIONS IN FINANCING INTERNATIONAL INVESTMENTS

James R. Silkenat

SMALLER COMPANIES in the United States, which already account for more than 20 percent of American exports, are increasingly taking the next step on the road to becoming global competitors: they are starting operations abroad, not just selling or shipping their goods overseas.

This is a definite "sea change" in the evolution of smaller companies in the United States. Overseas operations had previously been the domain of larger, dominant corporations, while smaller companies typically operated in a single city in the U.S., or at most in their own geographic region.

The reasons for this change are a combination of necessity and fear. Smaller companies are being forced into the international arena because they have no other financial choice.

While many smaller U.S. corporations are building their own factories abroad, most of them are taking much more measured steps by arranging joint ventures, licensing agreements or partnerships in foreign countries first. This is typically seen as a less risky arrangement because it gives the smaller U.S. firm a counterpart in the foreign jurisdiction that will presumably protect it from the most egregious of mistakes in this new foreign environment.

This chapter will focus in particular on the use of joint ventures and wholly owned operations abroad for small and medium-sized U.S. companies and on the multilateral financial institutions that are available to provide them with capital and technical assistance.

International joint ventures are not new, but in transactional legal practice their increased frequency of use is noteworthy. The proliferation of international joint ventures in recent years has been, surprisingly enough, at least in part a response to the unsettled economic conditions that have existed around the world.

In a sense, joint ventures have been viewed as a way of spreading the risk. Investments that might not have been considered prudent for one investor, either for financial or political reasons, become more realistic when the risk of such investment is shared with other parties. This is particularly true for investments abroad by smaller

American companies; the addition of a local joint venture partner is often a plus, in terms not only of added capital but of decreased political risk as well.[1]

In addition to the private sources of capital that are available for financing of international joint ventures, multilateral financial institutions have also become an important source of such funding, both with regard to equity and debt capital. Although they are by no means the only sources of such financing, the World Bank and its affiliated institutions alone provided over $20 billion in loans and credits for international project financing each year.[2]

The financial institutions which provide this type of financing can generally be divided into four categories. First, there is the World Bank group: that is, the International Bank for Reconstruction and Development (usually referred to as the World Bank), the International Development Association (the Bank's soft-loan window), and the International Finance Corporation (which makes loans and equity investments in the private sector).[3] A second grouping is composed of the regional development banks, such as the Asian Development Bank in Manila, the Inter-American Development Bank in Washington and the African Development Bank in the Ivory Coast.[4] There is also the newly formed European Bank for Reconstruction and Development (to be based in London) which will focus on Eastern Europe. Third, there are a variety of country-oriented development institutions, similar to AID and Eximbank, which provide project financing with regard to goods supplied from a particular country.[5] Finally, there traditionally have been the privately owned development institutions such as PICA, in Asia, and the ADELA Group, in Latin America. All of these institutions of course work with private commercial and investment banks in providing, or arranging for, loan funding for international joint ventures and other development projects. This paper will give particular attention to the project financing activities of the World Bank and IFC, and to their co-financing arrangements with commercial banks.

I. THE WORLD BANK

The World Bank and its sister institution, the International Monetary Fund,[6] were formed at the Bretton Woods Conference in 1944.[7] The Bank came into existence primarily for the purpose of helping reconstruct portions of Europe and Asia that had been destroyed during World War II.[8] It fairly quickly evolved, however, into a development institution where the emphasis has been on providing project financing in developing member countries. Such financing is generally made available for credit-worthy projects in the form of medium- and long-term loans when borrowing countries or companies are otherwise unable to obtain loans from private sources on reasonable terms.

The World Bank gets its funds from two principal sources: subscriptions to its capital stock from 140 some-odd member countries and borrowings by the Bank on international capital markets. With regard to subscribed capital,[9] only less than 10 percent of such amount is actually paid-in to the Bank. The remainder is on call but there has never been a call on subscribed capital. The bulk of the funds that the World Bank uses for lending to member countries is obtained from the sale of its own bonds or notes to private investors and, to a lesser extent, to governmental entities. Such borrowings during most recent years has amounted to the equivalent of $10–12 billion in various currencies, including Swiss Francs, Deutsche Mark, Japanese Yen and U.S. Dollars.[10] This amount includes borrowing through a variety of innovative financing techniques, including "COLTS" and swaps.[11] In the United States, World Bank bonds are rated AAA and are accorded the same general treatment as U.S. government and state and local bonds under the securities laws and are available for investment by the complete range of institutional investors. The funds for the International Development Association are raised separately from member countries.[12]

With minor exceptions, the Bank's lending activities are required to be for specific projects of "reconstruction and development."[13] This requirement is intended to make sure that the money is used for productive purposes: roads, farming, energy and similar activities. The Bank's loans typically cover the foreign exchange component of a particular project and have generally been in amounts ranging from as little as $2.5 million up to amounts in excess of $500 million.[14]

World Bank loans are made to governments of member countries or to public or private organizations with the guarantee of the member country in whose territory the project to be financed is located.[15] Such member countries currently include almost all nations other than the Soviet Union and certain of its aligned countries.[16] Although loans can be made by the World Bank to any member country, for over 25 years the focus has been almost exclusively on the less developed countries.

In 1982 there was a major change in the terms under which World Bank loans would be made. Effective July 1, 1982, the Bank essentially moved from fixed rate loans to a modified system of floating rate loans to its borrowers.[17] On each January 1 and July 1, a new rate is set for such loans based on the Bank's cost of funds for the preceding six month period. From an initial floating rate of 11.32% the rate has steadily declined to a rate in 1988 of 7.59%[18] and to a current rate based on the Bank's borrowing costs during any set period of time. Since the Bank borrows funds in a number of currencies, most with rates substantially below that of the U.S. dollar, the Bank's lending rates will, it is hoped, remain at a comparatively low level. Until July of 1982, the Bank had lent at fixed rates only. The most recently available annual rate for fixed-rate financing prior to this change had been 11.6 percent.

As mentioned previously, World Bank loans are normally medium-term or long-term. Typically there is a grace period of four or five years after which repayments of principal are made in approximately equal semi-annual installments over the life of the loan. The grace period is usually tied to the time at which the project will begin producing an economic return. Similarly, the amortization period is loosely tied to the estimated useful life of the project.

Since World Bank loans are disbursed in connection with the actual purchase of specific equipment, interest on loans from the Bank is charged only on that part of the loan which is actually disbursed. A commitment charge is made, however, on the undisbursed portion of the loan. This amount typically accrues from a date 60 days after the date of the loan agreement.

Increasingly important are the "soft" loans that the World Bank group makes. These come in the form of credits from the International Development Association and are typically repayable over 50 years with no interest charges and frequently with no commitment fee. These credits are made available only to the poorest developing countries, but are for projects that still meet all of the evaluation criteria applicable to projects considered for normal World Bank loans: that is, that they are economically and technically sound and that they will produce an adequate rate of return to the country on the investment made.[19]

Projects to be financed by World Bank loans or IDA credits are identified in a number of different ways. The most common method is for the country involved to make a proposal directly to the Bank staff. Often, however, the projects are brought to the Bank's attention by the United Nations, by investment banks or by World Bank missions to a particular country. Once a possible project is identified, an appraisal team will be sent by the Bank to examine the technical, financial and legal aspects of the transaction and to see whether the proposed project will provide a net economic and productive benefit to the country involved.

After the appraisal is completed, the details of the project are negotiated and draft loan and guarantee documentation is prepared by the Bank. Such documentation is in many ways similar to that involved in private loan transactions. The Bank's loan agreement, which is the principal document involved, also contains certain conditions of effectiveness, generally relating to government authorizations, that will need to be achieved before the Bank is obligated to disburse any funds. Such loan agreements are typically subject to international law and arbitration in the event of disputes. Bank loans are also normally unsecured, although a negative pledge is usually included, and such loans are made in a basket of currencies at the choice of the Bank. Upon execution, the loan and guarantee agreements are registered with the United Nations and published in the U.N. Treaty Series.

One element of the World Bank's lending arrangement that deserves some attention is the procurement process.[20] Most private lenders do not involve themselves in the actual purchase of equipment involved in the projects they finance. The Bank does. It does this because it is required by its Articles of Agreement to make sure that its loans are used with "due attention to considerations of economy and efficiency."[21] In practice this means that, with certain exceptions, the Bank will insist on international competitive bidding as a means of ensuring the integrity of the procurement process and to avoid discrimination among bidders because of their country of origin.

Among the items that it is necessary to keep in mind with regard to the procurement process in Bank-financed projects are: first, World Bank funds can only be paid to finance goods and services originating in countries that are members of the World Bank (plus Switzerland); second, the Bank procurement policy, by agreement, supersedes domestic law with regard to purchases of foreign goods; and, third, local tariffs are not always taken into consideration in evaluation of competing bids. Although the competitive bidding process is on occasion a complicating factor in some transactions, on balance it has proven to be the only realistic way of ensuring that scarce funding resources are not wasted or diverted from the projects for which they were intended.

Smaller U.S. companies will only occasionally be joint venture partners in projects being financed by the World Bank or IDA, since bank loans are made only to member governments or with member government guarantees. Much more likely will be the participation of smaller U.S. companies as suppliers or contractors on large projects financed by the Bank. An understanding of the Bank is crucial, however, for U.S. companies in securing and benefiting from these sorts of arrangements.

II. INTERNATIONAL FINANCE CORPORATION

The funding of private sector enterprises and projects within the world Bank group is mainly the responsibility of the International Finance Corporation.[22] IFC was formed in 1956 and has approximately the same country membership as the World Bank. It is a separate legal entity, however, and as a general matter has a separate staff, except for its President, Barber B. Conable, who holds the same position in the Bank.

While the World Bank is required to lend only to governments or with regard to projects which are covered by government guarantees, IFC is prohibited from accepting such guarantees or from lending directly to governments.[23] IFC's orientation is entirely toward the private sector. This explains, in part, why IFC's projects are structured so strictly along commercial lines. Another distinguishing feature is that IFC, almost alone among similar public institutions can and does make equity as well as loan investments.[24] IFC also acts as underwriter in the sale of debt and equity instruments or private sector companies, and frequently provides capital markets advice and assistance to public and private banking institutions in developing countries. Essentially, IFC acts as an investment banking firm in developing countries—that is, as a catalyst in putting together private sector projects and financings.

Since it operates in the private sector, IFC's appraisal and project identification procedures are much less complex than Bank's. For example, although considerable care is taken with regard to eventual disbursement of IFC loans and subscriptions, there is no requirement of competitive bidding.

To date IFC's operations have been on a more modest scale than the Bank's. Typical investments have been in the range of $15 million to $75 million, although several of the more recent loan approvals have been for considerably larger amounts (including loan financings of up to $500 million). IFC's investments also usually involve some, even if minor, element of local ownership and are made to help finance productive projects where adequate financing is not otherwise available on reasonable terms.[25] IFC has had investments in over 800 different companies[26] with sizable investments in energy, agribusiness, finance, tourism, and financial institutions, as well as in a wide variety of light and heavy industries.[27]

IFC's loans are provided on either a fixed or a floating-rate basis, are long-term and are available in a number of different currencies at the choice of the borrower. Interest rates are set on the basis of the cost of funds to IFC, the currency involved, and the particular circumstances of the project in question. Such interest rates are meant to approximate existing market rates. Borrowers are allowed the right to prepay IFC loans at any time without prepayment penalty.

IFC's equity investments are usually limited to no more than 25 percent of the equity of a corporation. As a matter of policy, IFC does not participate in the management of the companies in which it invests and typically will only vote its shares for quorum purposes. Only in development finance corporations will IFC normally accept a position on the board of directors of one of its companies.

IFC's loans and equity subscriptions are usually made through an investment agreement which contains the relevant disbursement and repayment arrangements for a particular project. On the loan transactions there will typically be a grace period of two to four years and a commitment fee for IFC on the undisbursed portion of the loan, beginning to accrue 30 days after approval of the investment by IFC's board of directors. A variety of innovative financing investments have been added to IFC's board of directors. A variety of innovative financing investments have been added to IFC's repertoire in recent years, including deferred rate-setting interest rate caps and fixed/floating-rate conversion features.

III. CO-FINANCINGS

One of the most important elements of IFC's operations, and increasingly so of the operations of the World Bank and other multilateral institutions, is the use of co-financings, or participations, by private banks in the loans being made. This idea has received a considerable amount of attention from the press[28] and, given the interest of private banks and the growing need for loan financing for joint venture projects, it would be useful to briefly describe what is involved.

For the World Bank, co-financing has traditionally referred to any arrangement whereby funds from the Bank are associated with funds provided by other sources outside the borrowing country in the financing of a particular project.[29] Typically, this has meant that private banks will, at the behest of the World Bank, negotiate a separate or parallel loan agreement with a borrower at the same time the Bank is negotiating with such borrower. With the consent of the borrower (and guarantor, if any), the Bank will provide the private lending institutions with detailed financial and technical information on the project and country involved. This is important because this is economic data that would generally not otherwise be available to private lenders or which would be available only at significant expense. Because of the World Bank's involvement, the private lending institutions are typically able to reduce the cost to the borrower of the loan package that is made available. The respective loan agreements are linked by optional cross-default clauses and various cross-reference provisions. In July 1988, such co-financing by private banks and official aid agencies totaled approximately $6.6 billion.[30]

IFC's participation arrangements operate somewhat differently. In this case the entire loan is made in the name of IFC and a portion of the loan is set aside, without recourse to IFC, for funding by private financial institutions pursuant to a Participation Agreement with IFC. The portion which is "participated-out" is usually made on a floating rate basis tied to six-month LIBOR and can be called by the participating financial institutions under certain conditions. In almost all cases such participating institutions are involved throughout the negotiation of the transaction and have a hand in shaping the terms being required of the borrower. Since IFC is exempt from withholding taxes in member countries and since all of the loan (both fixed-rate portion and floating rate portion) is in IFC's name, this benefit is passed along to the participating private financial institutions and eventually to the borrower. Over the years more than 260 commercial banks around the world have participated in IFC loans.

In both the World Bank and IFC situations the participating lending institutions and joint venture project sponsors see some element of protection against arbitrary government action because of the involvement of the Bank or IFC. A developing country may be willing to treat one private bank or group of banks unfairly, but it is generally thought that borrowing countries would be reluctant to act unfairly with regard to transactions in which the World Bank or IFC is directly involved. On the other hand, developing countries and their joint venture companies also see the Bank and IFC as moderating influences on the private lenders and foreign sponsors that are involved in any one transaction.

The different approaches of the Bank and IFC to co-financing have both been successful, but both need to be expanded to bring in additional project funding for developing countries and joint ventures in such countries. Several solutions to this problem are being tried. The World Bank for example has initiated several approaches intended to increase the participation of private financial institutions in the projects the Bank finances. The central element of the variety of schemes that have been approved for use since 1983 is that the Bank would participate directly in the separate loan being made to a borrower by private banks. Such participation by the World Bank would decrease, in the eyes of private lenders, the risks associated with lending to certain developing states. To the borrower such participation would have the advantage of increasing the availability of funds generally by increasing the number of private banks willing to lend to it.

The World Bank's traditional form of co-financing consisted largely of a memorandum of agreement between the Bank and private lenders with regard to exchanges of information and issues for consultation and with regard to the inclusion of optional cross default provisions in the parallel loan agreements of the Bank and the private lenders. Although the World Bank's co-financing activities with private banks have been of substantial size, they have been fairly modest in comparison to the volume of funding needed by borrowing countries. As a result of this financial shortfall, the World Bank at the beginning of 1983 initiated a new set of co-financing tools which would augment but not replace, its traditional co-financing approach. Continuing implementation of the program will depend on the size, number and timing of suitable projects that become available.[31]

Essentially three different types of co-financing approaches are being used in the new program. All three involve the World Bank taking a direct financial stake in a normal commercially-syndicated loan. As before, however, the co-financing involved will be parallel to a separate (and additional) loan made by the World Bank to the borrower in question. The first new type of co-financing vehicle involves direct financial participation by the Bank in the later maturities of a private bank syndication. In this case the Bank's loan would be of sufficient size (roughly 10 percent to 25 percent of the total syndication effort) to provide additional comfort to participating banks. The Bank's portion would also be large enough to extend the maturities of the syndication beyond what they would have been if only commercial banks had been involved.

A second type of co-financing that the World Bank now undertakes pursuant to this initiative, is to guarantee the later maturities of a private bank loan, rather than itself directly providing the financing. The World Bank's guarantee would be seen, in the circumstances in which it was used, as providing a positive incentive to private bank lenders to extend their loans for substantially longer periods of time than would otherwise have been the case.

Finally, a third new approach for the World Bank in its co-financing efforts has been for it to have a contingent participation in the last maturity of a private bank loan with a fixed aggregate payment of interest (at floating rates) and principal. Thus, if interest rates rose above the rate existing at the time the loan was made, the timing of the principal payments would be extended, with the World Bank accepting the obligation to finance the final repayment.

The mechanics for implementation of the above co-financing procedures are not overly complex. Essentially, the question of whether the Bank will participate in some way in the later maturities of a commercial syndication will be a joint decision of the World Bank and the borrower. Discussions will then be held with potential lead lenders concerning the structuring of the particular financing and the market strategy to be followed.

In establishing these new co-financing techniques, the World Bank was very careful to build into the system additional features to make such co-financing activities attractive to commercial banks (thus increasing the "additionality" of funding available to developing country borrowers). Among these features are that the commercial banks would get to take the lead role in drafting the documentation and that such banks would be able to assume fiduciary functions for the financing. The World Bank also has agreed to take less than a controlling position in the syndication; most major issues are expected to be decided by the participating banks on a majority vote basis.

Another element of the Bank's co-financing program is that procurement and disbursement procedures for the loan will be reviewed by the Bank. This attention to the details of the financing are required by the Bank's Articles of Agreement and should provide extra comfort to the private banks participating in the loan.

In the initial transactions under the World Bank's new co-financing program, the documentation specified that the Bank would take a direct financial participation in the later maturities of a private bank syndication. Although each transaction will be fitted to meet the needs of the participants involved, generally the principles are expected to remain the same. Among the provisions included in recent transactions were: *(i)* in light of the role played by the World Bank, an agreement by the participating banks not to reschedule the debt without the consent of the World Bank; *(ii)* an agreement that decision-making by the syndicate is to be on the basis of the vote of two-thirds of the loan outstanding; *(iii)* a reservation by the World Bank of its right to assign or sell some portion of the financing; and *(iv)* a reservation by the World Bank of its right to assign or sell some portion of its loan (up to a specified maximum).

IV.   FINANCING: AN EXAMPLE

Finally, in terms of gaining a practical perspective on how a particular financing by a multilateral development bank would operate, it would be useful to walk through at least one joint venture project sponsored and funded by one of these institutions. This will give some of the flavor of how these transactions are put together. Because of the private, rather than public, nature of this financing, certain facts may be glossed over in this example, but it would be possible for you to get a realistic picture of the interests involved.

In July 1980, shortly after Rhodesia became Zimbabwe, a large private sector coal company in Zimbabwe and the new government in Harare approached IFC about assisting in the financing of a $191 million open-cast coal mining project. Since this was the only coal and coke producer in the country and was a major source of Zimbabwe's electrical power, the project had considerable importance to the country. Since it was likely to be the first major external loan to the private sector in Zimbabwe in a long time, it was also likely to be a good barometer of whether capital was going to be available to assist private enterprise in this new country.

A project appraisal team from IFC visited Zimbabwe in September of 1980 and prepared an evaluation report on the financial and technical aspects of the transaction. Discussions were held with the foreign joint venture sponsors of the coal company and appropriate governmental officials who would have to approve the financing. A financial plan for the project was developed and commitments were made for the purchase of the necessary equipment. Draft loan documentation was then prepared in October. These documents included an investment agreement concerning the proposed IFC loan and a project funds agreement which obligated the largest shareholder of the coal company (in this case a foreign minerals company) to provide sufficient funding to complete the project if the financial plan proved inadequate.

In this transaction IFC undertook to make a loan of $38 million, with $20 million of such amount for its own account at fixed rates for 10 years. The remaining $18 million was to be provided by private bank participants in the form of a floating rate loan tied to LIBOR. Such participants were to be brought into the transaction by IFC and were also to take part in a parallel Eximbank loan of $43 million which was to be guaranteed by the Government of Zimbabwe. The participating lending institutions brought into the transaction included private banks in England, the U.S., France, Luxembourg, Holland and the State Bank of India.

From initial contact with the borrower to execution of the relevant loan agreements, the transaction took six months and four trips to Zimbabwe by IFC staff. Among other details in this transaction it was necessary to seek amendment of the usury law in Zimbabwe to bring the rate above the percentage limit that had existed previously for external loans. Since Rhodesia had been almost totally excluded from normal international capital markets for 15 years or so, it had not occurred to anyone that this might be a problem with regard to Eurodollar loans in Zimbabwe.

This financing could have been further augmented by an equity subscription or purchase of shares by IFC. This portion of the financing would have been made available by IFC for a number of reasons: to balance the interests of the other joint venture participants, to complete the financial package or to provide a more significant political umbrella for the project. In any case, IFC's shareholder role would typically be a passive one, except in jeopardy situations.

V. THE MULTILATERAL INVESTMENT GUARANTEE AGENCY

In addition to raising capital for joint ventures and other operations abroad by smaller U.S. companies, there is the important task of reducing the risk that the money invested will be lost other than for business reasons. The multilateral agency that has an important role here is the Multilateral Investment Guarantee Agency (MIGA).

MIGA was established by a Convention sponsored by World Bank to "encourage the flow of investment to and among developing countries by issuing guarantees against non-commercial risk and carrying out a wide range of promotional activities."[32]

MIGA's support is available to individual and corporate investors in its member countries which contribute to MIGA's capital. The MIGA Convention lists four broad categories of non-commercial risk:

(1) the risk of transfer resulting from host government restrictions on currency conversion and transfer;

(2) the risk of loss resulting from actions of the host government that eliminate or diminish the foreign investor's investment;

(3) the repudiation or breach of government contracts in the cases where the investor has no access or limited access to a competent judicial or arbitral forum; and

(4) the risk of armed conflict and civil disturbance.[33]

Eligible investments for MIGA guarantee contracts would be new and medium to long-term investments that are expected to contribute positively to development in the host country.

While the concept of MIGA has been around for several decades, it was only established officially in April of 1988 and only signed its first insurance contract at the beginning of 1990. Among MIGA's first projects are a copper mine in Indonesia, a gold mine in Ghana and a paper plant in Chile.

MIGA's coverage typically is in the range of $.041 to $1 a year for each $100 of insurance and can be provided for up to 20 years. It is designed to supplement both private insurers and the investment insurance agencies of national governments (such as OPIC). At present, MIGA's coverage is limited to $50 million per project.

As of the end of 1989, MIGA had 59 countries which had ratified its Convention (including the U.S.). These countries have subscribed $780 million in capital, of which 10 percent is paid-in. Under its charter, MIGA's total insurance exposure may be up to 150 percent of its subscribed capital.

VI. CONCLUSION

While the risks involved in foreign investment by smaller companies are considerable, institutions and methods have developed to lessen such risks to more manageable proportions. The task for the lawyer for a smaller U.S. company is to develop a list of the financing sources and risks that exist and then to use one or more of the available tools mentioned above to tap those resources and reduce those risks effectively.

Notes

[1] For an unusually precise discussion of these and related issues, *see,* G. Delaume, *Legal Aspects of International Lending and Economic Development Financing* (1967). *also see,* Silkenat, *Eurodollar Borrowings by Developing States: Terms and Negotiating Problems,* 20 Harv. Int'l. L.J. 89 (1979). Some of these issues are also discussed in a less technical fashion in A. Sampson, *The Money Lenders: Bankers and a World in Turmoil* (1981). *Also see,* Silkenat, *Book Review,* 14 L. & Policy in Int'l. Bus. 271 (1982).

[2] *See, The World Bank Annual Report 1988* at 9. This amount actually substantially underestimates the impact of World bank institutions on the development process. The Bank's role as catalyst is substantially greater. For an examination of the various economic elements involved in public multilateral financings, *see,* R. Mikesell, *Public International Lending for Development* (1966).

[3] *See,* generally, E. Mason and R. Asher, *The World Bank Since Bretton Woods* (1973); World Bank, *IDA in Retrospect: The First Two Decades of the International Development Association* (1982); and J. Baker, *The International Finance Corporation* (1968). *Also see,* J. Lewis and I. Kapur, *The World Bank Group, Multilateral Aid and the 1970's* (1973); L. Pearson, *Partners in Development* (1969); *The Independent Commission on International development Issues, North-South: A Program for Survival* (1980); and *U.S. Department of the Treasury, United States Participation in the Multilateral Development Banks in the 1980's* (1982).

[4] *See,* J. Syz, *International Development Banks* (1974); and S. Rubin (ed.) *Foreign Development Banks* (1971) at 94 to 180.

[5] *See,* Hornbostel, *Financing Exports: Government and Multinational Programs,* 11 Lawyer of the Americas 285 (1979); and Hoskins, *United States Technical Assistance for Legal Modernization,* 56 A.B.A.J. 1160 (1970). *Also see,* Lipman, *Overseas Private Investment Corporation: Current Authority and Programs,* 5 N.C.J. Int. L. & Com. Reg. 337 (1980).

[6] The most perceptive articles on the legal aspects of the International Monetary Fund have generally been those written by its former General Counsel, Sir Joseph Gold. *See, e.g.* Gold, *Political Bodies in the International Monetary Fund,* 11 J. Int'l & Econ. 237 (1977); and Gold, *Weighted Voting Power: Some Limits and Some Problems,* 68 Am. J. Int'l L. 687 (1974). *Also see,* K. Dam, *The Rules Of The Game: Reform and Evolution in the International Monetary System* (1982).

[7] To some extent the system of monetary stability and support that was created at Bretton Woods has been challenged by a call for a "New International Economic Order." *See,* Lillich, *Economic Coercion and the New International Economic Order: A Second Look at First Impressions,* 16 Va. J. Int. L. 233 (1976); and Brower & Tepe, *The Charter of Economic Rights and Duties of States: A Reflection or Rejection of International Law?,* 9 Int'l. Lawyer 295 (1975).

[8] Of the purposes of the Bank, the first to be listed is: "To assist in the reconstruction and development of territories of members by facilitating the investment of capital for productive purposes, including the restoration of economies destroyed or disrupted by war, the reconversion of productive facilities to peacetime needs and the encouragement of the development of productive facilities and resources in less developed countries." Article I(i) of the *Articles of Agreement of the International Bank for Reconstruction and Development* (hereinafter cited as the *Bank's Articles*).

[9] For the purposes of its own financial statements, the Bank since 1978 has expressed the value of its capital stock on the basis of special drawing rights (SDR's) in terms of United States dollars as computed by the International Monetary Fund. *See, The World Bank Annual Report 1988* at 171.

[10] *See e.g., The World Bank Annual Report 1988* at 48. On the World Bank's borrowing policies, *also see, When Rotberg Speaks*, Journal of Commerce, July 19, 1982, at 4a, col. 1; and Akant, *Managing a Multicurrency Borrowing Program*, The Bank's World, January 1984, at 2. *But see*, Johnson, *In Search of Max Headroom*, The Banker (UK), November 1987 at 117.

[11] *The World Bank Annual Report 1988* at 48–49.

[12] *See*, footnote 19 *infra*.

[13] *See*, footnote 8 *supra*.

[14] For a list of the projects financed by the World Bank in a typical year, *see, The World Bank Annual Report 1988* at 111–156.

[15] The guarantee element for loans not made directly to member countries is required by Article III, Section 4(i) of the *Bank's Articles*.

[16] For a discussion of the proposed membership of the Soviet Union in the Bank at the time of the Bretton Woods Conference, *see*, E. Mason and R. Asher, *The World Bank Since Bretton Woods* (1973) at 29. *Also see* Witcher, *Soviets Consider Joining IMF, World Bank*, Wall St. J., August 15, 1986, at 19.

[17] *World Bank Plans Variable Interest*, New York Times, July 4, 1982, at 6, col. 1.

[18] *The World Bank Annual Report 1988* at 49.

[19] IDA's positive impact on the development process in Third World countries is discussed in some depth in World Bank, *IDA in Retrospect: The First Two Decades of the International Development Association* (1982). *Also see* Clausen, *Address to the Board of Governors of September 1982* at 16–23. The funding of IDA has been the source of considerable controversy in recent years. The principal issues have been, first, the effect of delays in payment by member countries with regard to current commitments, and second, the amount of funding that would be required for future years. For a brief summary of these issues, *see, The Host Who Will Not Pay*, Financial Times, September 16, 1983, at 5; *Wild Pitch in Toronto*, Wall St. J., September 13, 1982, at 30, col. 1; Lubar, *Reaganizing the Third World*, Fortune, November 16, 1981, at 80; and *A Bank for All Seasons*, The Economist, September 4, 1982, at 75.

[20] *See*, Sasson *Monitoring the Procurement Process*, 2 Finance and Development 12 (1975).

[21] *Bank's Articles*, Art. III, Section 5(b). This Section also states that loans are to be made "without regard to political or other non-economic influences or considerations."

[22] *See*, Bayless, *Merchant Banker to the Third World*, Institutional Investor, September 1982 at 213; and Silkenat, *Public International Law Report: Activities of the International Finance Corporation*, 18 International Practitioner's Notebook 11 (1982). *But see*, Bovard, *World Bank's Leftist Love Affair Unabated*, Washington Times, August 30, 1988, at F1; and Bovard, *World Bank Unit's Lip Service to the Private Sector*, Wall St. J., June 21, 1988, at 38.

[23] Article III, Section 1 of the *Articles of Agreement of the International Finance Corporation* (hereinafter cited as *IFC's Articles*) provides that: "The Corporation may make investments of its funds in productive private enterprises in the territories of its members. The existence of a government or other public interest in such an enterprise shall not necessarily preclude the Corporation from making an investment therein."

[24] IFC was originally prohibited by its *Articles of Agreement* from making equity investments. This provision (Article III, Section 2 of *IFC's Articles*) was revised in 1961 so that the Corporation could "make investment of its funds in such form or forms as it may deem appropriate in the circumstances."

[25] As a result of this approach (Article III, Section 3(i) of IFC's Articles), IFC is not generally considered to be in direct competition with normal commercial banks. *But see*, Kraus, *A Private, Profitable Niche*, American Banker, September 21, 1988.

[26] *How to Invest in Development with IFC: A Guide for Canadian Business* at 1.

[27] For a summary of IFC's project and investment portfolio as of June 30, 1989, *see, International Finance Corporation Annual Report 1989*, at 76–88.

[28] *See, e.g. The Multilateral Development Banks: A U.S. Viewpoint*, Economic Impact, Vol. 4 of 1982,

at 36; Lukasiewicy, *Commercial Bank Involvement Is Pushed in Co-finance Deals*, The Globe and Mail (Toronto), September 6, 1982, at R11; and *Selling Africa to the Bankers*, Africa Now, September 1982, at 66.

[29] For a broad-brush analysis of the World Bank's co-financing arrangements during the past decade, see, World Bank, Co-Financing—World Bank Co-Financing with Private Financial Institutions (1980).

[30] *The World Bank Annual Report 1988* at 60.

[31] *See*, Morais, *World Bank Promotion of Private Investment Flows to Developing Countries Through Co-financing and Other Measures*, 3 ICSID Review—Foreign Investment Law Journal 1 (1988).

[32] Ibrahim F. I. Shihata, *"The Multilateral Investment Guarantee Agency,"* 20 Int'l Lawyer 485 (1986).

FEDERAL GOVERNMENT INTERNATIONAL FINANCING AND INSURANCE PROGRAMS

Robert B. Shanks

THE UNITED STATES GOVERNMENT maintains several programs that can provide vital assistance to emerging companies as they invest overseas or export their goods or services from the United States. Among these programs are the limited recourse financing and political risk insurance programs operated by the Overseas Private Investment Corporation (OPIC); the export credit guarantee and insurance programs of the Export-Import Bank (Eximbank); and the guarantee programs offered by the Small Business Administration (SBA).

I. OPIC

OPIC is a U.S. government agency created to encourage U.S. private investment in friendly, developing countries. Its programs currently operate in approximately 140 countries, including all of the major Central and Eastern European countries, the former Soviet Republics, and most developing countries in Asia, Central and South America, the Caribbean, the Middle East and Africa. As of the time this chapter was drafted, OPIC programs were suspended in China based on human rights concerns and were not yet available in Mexico, pending the outcome of the debate over the North American Free Trade Agreement (NAFTA). OPIC is a self-sustaining U.S. Government agency. All of OPIC's obligations are backed by the full faith and credit of the United States Government.

OPIC Financing

OPIC provides U.S. government-backed loan guarantees and direct loans for overseas investments by majority U.S.-owned companies. OPIC's lending programs have grown dramatically in recent years, most recently in response to the surge in demand for OPIC financing for projects in Central and Eastern Europe and the former Soviet Union. The Foreign Assistance Act for Fiscal Year 1994, provided OPIC with authority to issue approximately $1 billion in additional annual loan guarantees to support projects in the former Soviet Union. With this increase, OPIC currently has approximately $1.5 billion in annual lending resources. This represents more than a tribling in the size of OPIC's finance program in the past two years.

OPIC offers limited recourse "project" financing in the form of direct loans, loan guarantees and equity techniques that provide medium-to-long term financing for ventures involving significant equity and management participation by U.S. businesses. A project's cash flows must be adequate to cover all operational costs, service all debt and provide the owners with an adequate return on their investment. If these criteria are met, generally investors need not pledge their general credit once project completion is achieved.

All projects considered for financing by OPIC must be commercially and financially sound, and within the demonstrated competence of the proposed management, which must have a proven track record in the same or a similar business. Although OPIC will provide financing for a wide range of industries, there are statutory and policy restrictions that prevent it from supporting certain kinds of projects. Current examples include gambling facilities and projects producing munitions or alcoholic beverages. Additionally, OPIC is prohibited from supporting projects that will have a significant negative impact on the U.S. economy, such as "runaway plants" that are leaving the U.S. in search of cheaper labor, or projects in certain trade-sensitive industries that are likely to displace U.S. goods and workers.

Eligible borrowers include U.S.-based companies majority owned by U.S. citizens or nationals. Foreign subsidiaries of U.S. companies are also eligible provided they are at least 95 percent owned by U.S. citizens or nationals.

OPIC will finance both wholly-owned overseas investment and joint ventures with local companies. The U.S. investor must bear a significant portion of the risk, normally by contributing at least 25 percent of the project's equity. Generally, a majority of the voting shares must be held by private firms or persons, although projects with majority government ownership may qualify if management is contractually agreed to be in private hands.

Generally, OPIC requires a ratio of no more than approximately 60 percent debt to 40 percent equity for start-up projects, although it will permit up to 75 percent debt for expansions of existing projects, and higher leverage may be acceptable for certain kinds of projects, such as power projects, that typically are more highly leveraged in the U.S. OPIC may also invest up to 30 percent of the project's equity securities.

OPIC, like other project lenders, does not accept construction or completion risk. Sponsors are therefore required to agree to provide any funds necessary to complete the project and to provide adequate working capital until certain operating tests are met. Because OPIC was created as a development agency, projects must contribute to the economic and social development of the host country.

Direct Loans

OPIC provides financing for smaller projects through direct loans. These loans generally range from $500,000 (or less) to about $6 million. Direct loans may be used only for projects sponsored by small-to-medium sized businesses or cooperatives. Larger projects and companies can utilize OPIC's loan guarantee program.

Loan Guarantees

Larger projects and borrowers not eligible for the direct loan program are financed through OPIC's loan guarantee program. Small businesses and cooperatives may also use this program. Typical OPIC loan guarantees range from about $2 million to $25 million. Projects as large as $50 million are possible and, for major capital projects, a high-level government interagency group has recently recommended that OPIC provide loan guarantees up to $200 million per project. Political and credit risks are analyzed in the same manner as for direct loans.

Under the loan guarantee program, the borrower approaches OPIC to analyze and structure financing for the project. The guarantee, which is backed by the full faith and credit of the United States Government, may be utilized to obtain financing from any financial institution that is more than 50 percent beneficially owned by U.S. citizens, corporations or partnerships.

Terms for OPIC direct or guaranteed loans generally range from five to 12 years, depending upon the needs of the project. Terms may extend to 15 years for major capital projects.

Interest rates vary according to OPIC's assessment of the financial and political risks involved. Interest rates on OPIC guaranteed loans are comparable to those of other U.S. Government-guaranteed issues of similar maturities, and OPIC's guarantee fee averages about two percent per annum on the outstanding principal amount. In addition, OPIC charges commitment, facility, and cancellation fees in accordance with standard commercial lending practices.

Equity and Equity Participating Investments

In addition to providing debt capital, OPIC can provide equity through capital stock investments and purchase of a project's debentures. Because of the increased risk associated with equity investments, OPIC is very selective in its equity investment program. OPIC generally seeks only a relatively small minority position, does not play an active role in management, and limits its equity stake to the $250,000 to $2 million range.

OPIC Political Risk Insurance

Political risk insurance for investments is generally available to American investors from three sources: OPIC; the Multilateral Investment Guaranty Agency (MIGA), the World Bank Group's new political risk insurer, discussed in a previous section, above; and a relatively short list of private sector insurers, including Lloyds and American International Group ("AIG"). Among these sources, OPIC is the largest provider of insurance for investments and probably offers the most comprehensive coverage available for U.S. investors. MIGA is also an important source. Its coverages are very similar, but not identical in all respects. Private sector political risk insurance tends to focus on shorter term risks, such as trade credits. Private political risk insurance is also limited to one, two or, at most three years, renewable at the option of the insurer. Insurance against political violence is generally unavailable from private sector insurers, and private inconvertibility insurance is not available in many countries that are served by OPIC and MIGA.

OPIC provides political risk insurance and financing for new investments and significant expansions of existing investments in eligible countries. The agency's terms generally limit the maximum insurable amount to 90 percent of an investment's value for equity, up to a maximum of $100 million per risk, per project. This per project limit may be exceeded on a case-by-case basis. In the former Soviet Union, for example, OPIC has announced a willingness to offer larger packages in appropriate cases based on the U.S. Government's foreign policy interests. OPIC insurance coverage is long-term, up to 20 years. OPIC's insurance is backed by an excellent history of paying claims, by OPIC's substantial reserves and, ultimately, by the full faith and credit of the United States Government.

OPIC's policies insure against all three major categories of political risk: (1) confiscation, expropriation, or nationalization; (2) transfer risk (currency inconvertibility); and (3) damage to physical assets or lost income due to political violence, include war, revolution, insurrection and civil strife. The agency does not, however, insure against commercial risks.

OPIC insures against *de facto* or "creeping" expropriations, as well as outright nationalizations. However, OPIC expropriation insurance is "all or nothing" coverage. No compensation is available for a partial expropriation of the investor's business that merely diminishes its value.

OPIC's inconvertibility coverage is only available to the extent that a legal right to convert local currency into hard currency exists at the time of the policy's issuance. Thus, the agency insures the continuance of a foreign exchange right; inconvertibility insurance is not available to parties who invest in countries that do not maintain any right of conversion and repatriation. The risk that a currency may be devalued is not insurable through OPIC, as it is regarded as a commercial risk.

Generally, OPIC's political violence coverage can extend to damage or destruction of physical assets, or to lost income due to a period of downtime resulting from political violence. For institutional lenders, the agency has extended its policies to cover liability for principal and interest payments on loans or payments under technical assistance agreements where a form of political violence has caused a default. This coverage, like coverage for "creeping" expropriation, is subject to careful scrutiny as a result of the potential blurring of commercial and political forces. OPIC looks carefully to ensure that a failure to make payment is in fact attributable to a political event and not to commercial difficulties of the borrower or a contracting party.

It is important to emphasize several features of OPIC's coverage. First, as mentioned above, OPIC can cover only political risks, not commercial ones. Second, OPIC can insure only new investments, including expansions or modernizations of existing operations. Third, OPIC insurance is based on the underlying contractual relationship that the investor has negotiated. In other words, OPIC insures against the risk that the host government will unlawfully interfere with the terms of the underlying contract; it does not insure that the underlying agreement is a good one or that the investment will be profitable.

Eligibility Criteria

Because OPIC is a government agency, there are both statutory and policy restrictions affecting eligibility of investors and investments under OPIC's programs. The most significant of these limitations are set forth below.

(i) Eligible investors include U.S. citizens, entities incorporated in the U.S. (if more than 50 percent beneficially owned by U.S. citizens), and entities incorporated outside the U.S. if more than 95 percent beneficially owned by U.S. persons or nationals.

(ii) OPIC is restricted to providing coverage in "friendly developing countries." "Developing" countries are defined as those countries having an average per capital income of less than U.S. $3,887 (in 1983 dollars). OPIC currently operates in approximately 140 countries.

(iii) As a development institution, OPIC attempts to assist investments that would not go forward but for OPIC insurance. OPIC attempts to achieve this objective by issuing insurance only to investors who register their projects with OPIC prior to entering into an irrevocable commitment to invest. Investors who have not registered their projects may nevertheless be eligible for coverage if they can demonstrate that they would not have entered into the investment but for the expectation of obtaining OPIC insurance. For example, investors may satisfy this requirement by providing in their contracts that an investment is contingent upon obtaining political risk insurance from OPIC or some other appropriate source.

(iv) The project must involve new investment, including modernization or expansion of existing facilities or privatization of state assets.

(v) OPIC will cover only up to 90 percent of an equity investment, generally to a maximum of $100 million per risk, per project. There are case-by-case exceptions to this rule. In rare occasions, OPIC has agreed to exceed the $100 million figure, and OPIC is prepared to insure up to 100 percent of loans by lending institutions.

(vi) OPIC is required to enter into "satisfactory arrangements" with host country governments before it can offer its insurance programs. Bilateral agreements establish the basic relationship between OPIC and the countries in which it operates. Among other things, these agreements provide that the host government must approve projects to be insured by OPIC; that OPIC can be subrogated to the rights of an insured in the event that it pays a claim; that OPIC can dispose of local currency through U.S. Government channels in the host country; and that any disputes between OPIC and the

host government that cannot be resolved amicably are subject to international arbitration in accordance with international rules.

(vii) OPIC cannot assist any investment in a "runaway" plant or an investment that would result in a significant net loss of jobs in the U.S. OPIC is also required to be sensitive to the U.S. balance of payments in deciding whether to assist an investment.

(viii) OPIC screens projects for environmental risks and will not finance or insure any project that poses unreasonable risks to the host country's environment.

Coverages

(i) Expropriation: OPIC insures against losses caused by "expropriatory acts," including acts beyond the scope of a host government's legitimate regulatory authority, or outside its role as a commercial participant in the investment. For situations in which there is an inherent difficulty in distinguishing between commercial and political acts of a government participant in an investment, which will typically arise in centrally-planned economies, OPIC has devised a special coverage for noncompliance with the dispute resolution provisions of the underlying contract.

(ii) Inconvertibility: OPIC's insurance against inconvertibility of local currency assures that local currency will continue to be convertible on the terms in effect at the time the insurance was issued. In contrast to inconvertibility, currency devaluation is considered a commercial risk and is not insurable. To obtain OPIC insurance, an investor must establish that it has a legal right to convert the local currency into dollars. OPIC then insures the continuance of that right. If the right is subsequently abridged (through exchange controls, moratoria on conversion, transfer restrictions, or simple inability to honor a proper application to convert), or is substantially altered to the detriment of the insured, OPIC will exchange dollars with the investor for local currency at the prevailing rate of exchange.

OPIC's contract imposes a waiting period (usually 60 days) to permit the host government's central bank to act upon the investor's request to convert. This period may be longer for countries in which investors have been experiencing considerable delays. OPIC's inconvertibility insurance is not available in countries in which no legal right to convert exists and where, as a practical matter, foreign exchange is currently unavailable. The insured bears the risk of devaluation during the waiting period. Thereafter, the risk of devaluation shifts to OPIC.

(iii) Political Violence: For most investors, this insurance covers damage or destruction of physical assets or lost income caused by political violence. For institutional lenders, however, coverage extends to liability for payments, such as payments for principal and interest on loans or under technical assistance agreements, when events of war, revolution, insurrection, or civil strife cause a default.

Civil strife coverage was added to cover events that do not fit neatly within traditional definitions of war, revolution, or insurrection. Losses due primarily to labor or student disputes, however, are specifically excluded.

In addition to paying claims, OPIC has successfully negotiated resolution of expropriation claims between the host government and investor without payment by OPIC. Some disputes with host governments are resolved before claims are filed. OPIC has also utilized its authority to guarantee host government obligations offered as compensation for an expropriation in the context of a workout between the host government and the investor. Many investors believe, with good reason, that the mere existence of OPIC insurance can deter political interference by a host government both because of the host government's reluctance to interfere with a project "sponsored" by the U.S. Government and because of the potential for highly visible international arbitration pursuant to the OPIC bilateral agreement.

OPIC often cooperates with other political risk insurers through reinsurance or co-insurance arrangements to form larger insurance packages. In addition to cooperating with its counterpart political risk insurance agencies in other developed countries, OPIC has formed combined packages with MIGA and with a number of private political risk insurers.

II. EXIMBANK

The Export Import Bank of the United States (Eximbank) is the U.S. Government agency that facilitates export financing of U.S. goods and services. By neutralizing the effect of export credit subsidies from other governments and absorbing credit risks that the private sector will not accept, Eximbank enables U.S. exporters to compete more effectively in overseas markets.

Eximbank offers a wide range of financing support, including loans and loan guarantees, export credit insurance, and project financing.

Loans

Eximbank's loans provide fixed-interest rate financing for U.S. export sales facing foreign competition backed with subsidized official financing. Eximbank extends direct loans to foreign buyers of U.S. exports and intermediate loans to fund responsible parties that extend loans to foreign buyers.

Eximbank's direct loans and long-term loans to intermediaries carry the lowest interest rates permitted under the "OECD Arrangement," the agreement among the export credit agencies of the major developed countries, for the market and term of the loan.

Guarantees

Eximbank's guarantees provide repayment protection for private sector loans to creditworthy buyers of exported U.S.-goods and services. Eximbank guarantees are backed by the full faith and credit of the United States Government. Most guarantees provide comprehensive coverage of both political and commercial risks, although a guarantee covering only political risks is available for certain transactions, and is the only type of guarantee available where there is common ownership between the supplier (or exporter) and the foreign buyer (or guarantor), as in the case of exports to a foreign subsidiary. Covered political risks include war, cancellation of an existing export or import license, expropriation, confiscation of (or intervention in) the buyer's business, or transfer risk (failure of the appropriate government authorities to convert the foreign deposit into dollars). Losses due to currency devaluation are not considered a political risk. Commercial risks cover nonpayment for reasons other than specified political risks, including deterioration in the buyer's market, fluctuations in demand, unanticipated competition, shifts in tariffs, technological change, buyer insolvency, and natural disasters.

Bank-to-bank line of credit guarantees are available to cover multiple sales financed under a single line of credit provided by a U.S. bank to a foreign bank. Exim will also guarantee payments on cross-border leases structured as either operating or finance leases.

In recent years, Eximbank has modified its guarantee program in several significant ways in order to respond to the needs of financial institutions, especially investment banks, in providing competitive medium and long-term financing. For example, in contrast to its earlier policies, Eximbank will now guarantee 100 percent of the interest on the borrower's note to the lender, and banking and legal fees are eligible for financing. Eximbank will permit a special purpose corporation or a trust to be the guaranteed lender for securitized financing structures and commercial paper offerings, and will afford the lender of record the one-time option of switching the interest rate basis on amounts of outstanding principal of $10 million or more from a fixed rate to a floating rate at any time during the term of the guaranteed loan.

Working Capital Guarantee

Eximbank has designed a loan guarantee program to provide eligible exporters with access to working capital loans from commercial lenders. This program covers commercial lenders extending export-related working capital loans to creditworthy small and medium-sized businesses. Exporters may apply and then "shop" their preliminary commitments for a lender. The guarantee covers 100 percent of the loan's principal and interest, generally with a 12-month repayment period. This is a guarantee with recourse to the exporter, which must provide the lender with acceptable collateral. The guarantee can be for a single loan or a revolving line of credit.

Eximbank Insurance

Eximbank also offers various forms of export credit insurance—in effect, insurance that the buyer will pay.

The New-to-Export Insurance Policy provides a one-year blanket policy covering multibuyer short-term export credit sales. Applicants must qualify as small businesses, as defined by the Small Business Administration, with average annual sales volume of less than $2 million. This policy generally covers 100 percent of political risks and 95 percent of commercial risks, for loans with a maximum repayment period of 180 days (360 days for some agricultural commodities, consumer durables and capital goods).

Other policies available include the Umbrella Insurance Policy, providing one-year blanket coverage insuring multibuyer short-term export credit sales for small businesses; the Bank Letter of Credit Insurance Policy, providing a one-year blanket policy insuring commercial banks against losses on irrevocable letters of credit issued by foreign banks for U.S. exports; Short and Medium Term Policies for both Single and Multiple Buyers; and Lease Insurance Policies, covering either a stream of payments under an operating lease, plus the fair market value of lease products, or the total payments due under a finance lease.

Project Financing

In addition to these programs, Eximbank has recently inaugurated a project finance program, providing off-balance sheet financing for major capital projects. This program is effectively limited to large projects, such as energy or power generation. The minimum amount eligible for financing under this program is $50 million.

III. SMALL BUSINESS ADMINISTRATION

The Small Business Administration (SBA) also provides financial and business development assistance to small businesses attempting to develop export markets. Applicants must first attempt to obtain private bank financing, must invest a reasonable amount of their own capital, and must demonstrate that the SBA loan can be repaid from future earnings.

Various SBA programs are available, provided the SBA-guaranteed portion does not exceed $750,000, the Agency's statutory loan guarantee limit. These include, for example, the SBA's regular 7(a) business loan guarantee program, which provides loan guarantees for fix-asset acquisition, with a maximum maturity of 25 years and shorter term guarantees for working capital loans.

SBA also offers an Export Revolving Line of Credit Program, with a credit line of up to 36 months. Loans may be used to finance labor and materials for manufacturing or wholesale export, to develop foreign markets, or to finance foreign accounts receivable. Professional export marketing advice or services, foreign business travel, and participation in trade shows are among eligible uses.

SBA's International Trade Loan Program provides long-term financing to help small businesses compete more effectively and to develop or expand export markets. Proceeds may be used to purchase or upgrade facilities or equipment and to make other improvements that will be used to produce goods or services within the United States.

Applicants generally must have been in a business—not necessarily exporting—for at least 12 continuous months before applying for an SBA loan or guarantee. Maximum loan rates are 2.25 percent over prime. Guarantee fees are based on maturities. Personal guarantees or other appropriate collateral are required.

IV. CONCLUSION

As this chapter was being written, important changes were underway to expand and harmonize the various U.S. Government programs described above. The Clinton Administration's Trade Promotion Coordinating Committee recently released a Report to the United States Congress, "Toward A National Export Strategy" (September 30, 1993) (*TPCC Report*), which called for, among other things, harmonization of Eximbank and SBA export programs, toward the goal of creating a single working capital program combining the best features of each. For a trial period, SBA will be given exclusive jurisdiction for loans under $750,000 and Eximbank will have exclusive jurisdiction over that limit.

The TPCC report also recommended expansion of OPIC's loan guarantee program, finding that current authorization levels are not adequate to meet the increasing demand for OPIC assistance, particularly for major capital projects. The TPCC Report further recommended that the OPIC per-project loan guarantee limit be raised from the current $50 million to as much as $200 million. Meanwhile, Eximbank is developing a project finance program for major capital projects involving exports of U.S. capital equipment and services. Eximbank is also attempting to streamline its guarantee program to make it a more flexible financing vehicle and to substantially speed up its decision-making process.

For U.S. companies beginning to market or invest overseas, the programs described above offer important tools for financing export sales and cross-border investments and for managing unacceptable risks of doing business overseas. Because these programs are specifically designed for, and responsive to, U.S. companies, and because their minimum lending limits tend to be more in line with the needs of smaller companies than those of the major multilateral programs, these U.S. government programs deserve careful investigation by any emerging U.S. company in the process of "going international."

PART FIVE

PRACTICAL CONSIDERATIONS IN COUNSELING CLIENTS ON INTERNATIONAL BUSINESS ACTIVITIES

EVALUATING BUSINESS AND MARKET OPPORTUNITIES IN FOREIGN MARKETS

William A. Burck

EFFECTIVE EVALUATION of an international market and business opportunity is a formidable task. It involves a unique interplay of practical and theoretical concepts, and mixing the better elements of common sense with relatively sophisticated methodology from a variety of disciplines. It also requires the use of intellect. Simply stated, successful and thorough evaluation of an international opportunity requires deep knowledge and using it, sometimes in unexpected ways. To illuminate this process of evaluation, the writer will first show some results of evaluation (or failures to evaluate), and in the process examine attitudes and approaches to evaluation on an international scale, then comment on the negotiating skills one should use in exploring and concluding international market or business opportunities and evaluations thereof, and finally conclude with a section highlighting several of the critical points which in the writer's opinion need attention in every appropriate evaluation.

I. EXAMPLES AND APPROACHES: HAVING THE RIGHT ATTITUDE

One of the most critical attributes that a successful international business lawyer must have when engaging in an evaluation of a given market opportunity is well-developed knowledge of just what his company or client is, and should be "getting into," and the ability to be flexible in constructing the model that client will ultimately take and use to enter the given market.

In order to organize and prepare a sound and useful evaluation the effective international business lawyer must free himself from the litany of the lawbooks and related business school concepts and focus on the objectives of the business in that particular market and the controls needed to make those objectives realizable.

Examples of flexibility, of using hard-earned and deep knowledge to advantage, can be found throughout the multinational business world. Failures can also be found. Some examples:

329

Brazil—In years past, high-technology policy was decidedly in favor of local development and control. The government, however had carved out exceptions for joint-venture companies organized "traditionally." There were also specific laws which allowed for compensation on technical management and assistance which was not available to the classic foreign parent-local subsidiary relationship; moreover, there were specific laws which specifically extended protection (by requiring approval of two-thirds of the voting quotaholders) on important decisions to minority partners. The minority partner company, through the joint venture, gained an indefinite, PROTECTED market access and an opportunity to participate in any economic expansion of Brazil even if and when its own contributed venture technology became obsolete and other joint venture products (to be developed) more profitable. The vehicle also allowed for payback on the obsolete technology after the time in which other mechanisms would have cut such a stream. The alternative? Distribution through independent channels, to very limited markets and protracted delays with respect to import licenses and needed hard currency; or the parent-subsidiary route, again limited to very specific markets and bound to stringent exchange control remittances and significant withholdings; or pure technology licensing, subject to severe limits on royalties, and loss of control over output and quality with no chance for second-generation product, as well as shared ownership of the key technology after just a few years.

Chile and Australia—A U.S. company has an opportunity for a specific win on a specific transaction, brought to its attention through a complementary entrepreneurial local company. The U.S. company has not evaluated long-term market opportunities nor does it have the financial and personnel wherewithal to undertake that review prior to committing on the specific transaction and understandimg that local market potential for its product may be very limiting for the near and foreseeable future. Distances from Headquarters, Somewhere, U.S.A., are daunting in establishing and maintaining a distinct corporate vehicle for its operations. In a successful undertaking, the company "teams" with the local company on a single contract basis (with the contracting parties sharing in the risks and losses according to the contract only) for purposes of meeting local bid requirements of a single vendor with a local presence and a low budget target. Since neither party takes a prime contracting role (and corresponding risk for the other's input) neither party needs to mark-up the "outside vendor" material and services, thus keeping margins down and within purchaser's budget. An invaluable offshoot of this form of contract venture approach in Australia was the governmentally-required recognition of local"content" supplied by a local party. The opportunity for a win and a market was there AND the U.S. company preserved its options, putting only a first foot in without irrevocable or expensive decisions and processing for just the one win and the one market.

Belgium—A U.S. company had good success in selling from the U.S. to the Belgian government but was now faced with the prospect of losing a large bid because of lack of local content and a direct local presence. It had a long-term, de facto exclusive Belgian distributor with a superannuated contract (which could not be terminated or modified without substantial mandatory legal indemnification). In a flexible turn, the U.S. concern sold parts to the Belgian distributor, the latter acting as sub-contractor, which in turn sold them back to the U.S. company's subsidiary based in Belgium for the sole purpose of resale to Belgian governmental authorities. In meeting local content and presence, the U.S. company also retained its technology and basic business margins and an intact distribution scheme without financial fallout. The alternatives, of acquisition of the Belgian distributor, of indemnity buyout, or a full-scale subsidiary, or a shared pot of technology, to preserve the one market and the one piece of business, did not have to be utilized. All the alternatives would have presented overkill and accomplish nothing more than the short-term hubris of preservation of the one line of transactional sales at an extraordinarily high incremental cost.

Japan—In the Japan of fifteen years ago, local participation in the market was available effectively only through joint ventures. Two U.S. high-tech companies took different approaches to the same set of laws and opportunities and ended up with profoundly different results because of different levels of understanding of the Japanese "system" and how to implement ongoing management, manufacturing, and technology interchange.

One company set up its joint venture to take advantage immediately and directly of the recognized expertise of the Japanese partner in supplying the mechanical parts of the JV product, putting an expatriate U.S. team in to direct, limited interacting of the two distinct technologies with further assurance of early satisfactory levels of return and profit to the U.S. partner. The Japanese joint venturer, seeing the limits to the venture, parceled out the meaningful parts of the workproduct to the traditional, outside small Japanese supplier, thus limiting effective infrastructure and cultural development, and took its own indigenous, new developments to other sources for fruition. The JV began to shrink and grow stale. After the initial product had its technological and profit run, the U.S. partner necessarily sold out its interests for its marked-down book value with no permanent investment or marketing presence in Japan.

The other company looked to Japan as a long-term supplier for export of immediate as well as future, product requirements and as a developer of technology with local marketing strengths. The Japanese JV retained all characteristics of the local Japanese company, and product changes on both sides evolved naturally. This vehicle expected and incented internal technology interchanges of all forms, whether they were immediately implementable, or long-term in both structure and strategy. The result is that today the Japanese JV is a major supplier of niche-high-tech products as well as a seller of the full line of U.S. products of its U.S. partner with a strong Japanese input, market presence and profitable bottom line; and the outsider is "in."

Russia and Hungary—A computer company has a chance to enter these two formerly very restrictive markets. In Hungary the proposed associate company is comprised of relatively young engineers, small and focused in scope, and has been in a quasi-free market mode for several years, relying very little on any specific government contacts or contracts. Moreover, it has been assembling personal computers from foreign parts for several years and has established, through its entry at the lower end of the market, adequate service capabilities throughout Hungary. In Russia, the prospective associate company is a significant part of a large Ministry's output for engineering services and is well-established in an industrial city some 1000 miles distant from where it has received its orders and oversight management. It has been engaged in engineering and construction of large plants for the assembly of electronic parts, but not computers.

It contracts out warranty and related implementing services outside its region or province in accordance with the Ministry directives. Its employee population is highly-educated in great part. The Russian Ministry is willing to put its official imprimatur and concessions on this company to be formed with partial infusion from the U.S. computer company.

The same computer company joins up with both companies in exactly the same fashion, buying a minority interest through the infusion of equipment and training in both, leaving both to their local management and devices, but with sales training committed at critical levels throughout the company's endeavors. Five years later, the Hungarian company is generating revenues twenty times the investment directly for its computer company investor and the Russian partner, along with the computer company's investment, is out of business.

Peru—A U.S. company has been doing business steadily with small but foreseeable growth through an independent distributor who buys and resells for its own account for several years. Recently, however, the distributor has advised that it no longer has the capital to support the sophisticated needs of the maintenance operations, which require, because of distance and importation bureaucracy, considerable levels of spare inventories in-country at all times. The company determines to acquire the operations of the distributor, thus entering the market directly. After much heated negotiation it agrees to pay no more than invoice value for all inventory and other equipment held by the distributor, and hires the well-trained staff of the distributor for its new operations. The company now has a full-blown sales and service subsidiary operating in relatively uncharted waters. It finds that the labor laws of the country virtually prohibit termination of employment without extreme cause (and losses in business and redundancy are not good cause) with dissolution being virtually the only allowable escape. It also finds that many customers were in a transition mode to other types of equipment which the company can also supply but not with the inventory at hand, and it learns quickly that required handling of the importation bureaucracy to meet the customer's timely needs does not comply with the company's codes of conduct. Peru's economic turmoil has also led to a reduction in sales, with sales cycles not in keeping with corporate standards and the hard currency to pay for importation of goods is both expensive and scarce.

It must be acknowledged that a variety of options were available to the U.S. company in dealing with the distributor's capital shortfall in its maintenance business. It could have purchased all or a part of the maintenance operation, leaving sales with the distributor; it could have consigned spare parts to a tax and duty free bonded warehouse to be released and paid for when and if customers were in need of same. It could have done nothing more than lend specialized personnel on an ad-hoc basis when unusual maintenance operations were needed with direct maintenance contracts between itself and a select base of customers, feeding same through an "unpopulated" subsidiary organized for tax establishment purposes in Peru. It chose an "acceptable multinational" overblown and self-important route, which ended up miserably.

Puerto Rico—In a place often perceived incorrectly as an extension of the United States, a significant sales opportunity to a prestigious U.S.-based customer extending its franchise to Puerto Rico leads an anxious sales representative to appoint a good acquaintance of the customer as a distributor for Puerto Rico, as the customer demands a specific local contact for sales and also local maintenance support on the island. The Puerto Rican party demands exclusivity for undertaking the function and the Company "compromises" by agreeing not to appoint other parties in Puerto Rico so long as it is satisfied with the efforts of the distributor. Three years pass, and the distributor has a modicum of success in the market. New major opportunities arise which the now-established distributor cannot handle directly because of some significant commercial fallouts with the potential customers in previous years. The company appoints a second distributor. The first distributor sues for breach of contract under Puerto Rican Law no. 67 (protecting distributors from unlawful termination), wins, and collects a five-year income stream (based on gross margins). The company brings a case of constitutionality before the Supreme Court of Puerto Rico and then the U.S. Circuit Court of Appeals and loses that too. Other alternatives at the outset? Appointment of a U.S.-based distributor, use of a sales agency on a commission basis, establishment of a subsidiary, limited maintenance appointment for the specific customer base, and multiple distribution channels once the decision was made to enter the market, all after prophylactic review of Puerto Rican law in detail to forge an effective but not costly alliance with a localized Puerto Rican entity.

Two Southeast Asian Countries—In a move to produce a product for the cheapest price possible. the driving corporate guideline in a very competitive marketplace, a U.S. company was able to buy an existing factory at a significant discount and bundle into it numerous tax holidays and labor training incentives. The fact that the best form of communication was a telex on a line that might be available in a year was not mentioned by the developing country's development "spin-doctors" and not discovered by the cost-conscious manufacturer. In a country next door, while labor costs were 30 percent higher and only reductions in tax were available (highly-skilled labor was available in both. countries), there were advanced telecommunications networks available to manufacturers who needed them in order to monitor and direct quality and quantity changes in their fast-paced, exacting industry. Nevertheless, the U.S. company chose the first option because of the significant difference in initial capital outlay and ongoing labor costs. When civil turmoil occurred and no reliable telephone lines could be installed, the company first scaled down and then closed its operations. A competitor of this U.S. company had chosen the second, and conditioned its entrance on receiving a fair share of sales to the government sectors in return for its investment. It is still there, and its market share in-country has grown to over 25 percent even though its worldwide share is less than eight percent.

The Strange Tale of Unexpected Juncture—Israel and Yet Another Southeast Asian Country—A U.S. company had a significant position with an important customer in Israel; it also had significant requirements to find offsets, that is,purchases from Israeli sources to warrant increasing sales to the Israeli government. At the same time, this Israeli customer "owed" offsets to a Southeast Asian country where the customer had made significant sales. The U.S. company had invested heavily in plant and equipment in this Southeast Asian country for the purposes of assembling its lower-cost equipment. The country was now looking for higher value add and more sophisticated projects for its citizens. Through the vehicle of a joint venture, the U.S. company married its equipment with software designed by its Israeli customer which in turn was written (from the Israeli design and technology) by a Southeast Asian country partner affiliated to the government. The result, the U.S. company met its Israeli offset by purchasing packages of its software where it could sell the same to global markets, and the Israelis met their offset requirements with the purchase of services from the Southeast Asian company and "credit" of the U.S. company investment. Moreover, the U.S. company gained further access to Israel and the Southeast Asian country as well as new markets with a new global product.

From the above, one can draw several significant conclusions from what may appear to be an interesting, but random, gamut of international undertakings. These include:

(1) One prescription will not fit all cases, even where the symptoms are the same.

(2) What works one time, even if spectacular in its results, may never work again.

(3) Never take, or COUNT on, the easy way through the thicket.

(4) Avoid (or at the very least be extremely cautious in utilizing) the atavistic urge to replicate and regenerate the multinational company on a microcosm wherever the market may take you.

(5) Localized contacts, however important and prestigious, will never be sufficient to guarantee success in implementation; they must always be tempered by and measured with skills brought from experience elsewhere.

(6) Do not assume that the most expensive and expansive option is the best.

(7) Factor in political change and ferment into all decisions and count on them happening when least expected.

(8) Never try to apply even to an equal set of facts the same solution without first reviewing thoroughly all relevant legal principles in the assumed-to-be equivalent market.

(9) Do not try to be "devious" or intentionally ambiguous in a contract providing for the final approach to the market; ambiguities will most likely be construed against you in any event when you need that least.

(10) Think long-term even if you need results short-term.

(11) Resist the impulse to "change the world" or tilt romantically with windmills; it may lead you to forget that windmills had (and may still have) in fact a useful purpose and that aggressive, direct and honest approaches to a market, especially when steps are taken sequentially and logically and with a view to cost containment, will often lead to change in what needs to be changed in any event.

(12) Be inclined to think small where the market is small and underdeveloped; do not "oversell" your commitment before any interested party; or where it has many unknowns and few constants.

(13) People are always the most important resource you can have in reaching into any given market, but the people needed are not necessarily the most experienced or expensive ones available.

(14) Never rely on freedom from tax or extant significant investment incentives as

being the principal reason for choosing a market for production or even for sales. The market/location potential must stand on its own; it will often be belatedly found that those incentives and tax-free enticements are done because of poor infrastructure, poor potential, untrained labor, or an ill-informed consumer market, and other like items which will probably render the business opportunity in that market "inopportune."

(15) The smallest details, such as phone lines and ongoing communication links, may make or break success in the market; high concept and context must play a part but logistics must be given their due.

(16) Whatever the immediate objectives (such as manufacturing, sub-contracting, etc.) are for making an investment in an international location, do not lose sight of the location as a market for generating sales revenues or as a contributor to another revenue generating source and the potential for its growth and your place in that growth. The long-term objective of all companies must be revenues for its products and services, and that factor never changes.

(17) Never consider investment in or entering a given market until you are able to give the necessary time and resources, whether they are people or money, to the required IMPLEMENTATION of the course finally agreed upon and in a timely fashion.

(18) Always have a contingency plan if the first program and method of entering a market fails at the outset or in the very early stages, being either an alternative or an orderly exit therefrom.

(19) Evaluate a market from both a macro and micro point-of-view and prioritize it against other potentially worthwhile markets and evaluations, keeping in mind the physical and financial limitations of the client/company. It is better to do two projects well than three in a decidedly mediocre fashion.

(20) Never deny the value and utility, at any time in the process of evaluation, of detailed decision fees and checklists to cover all fronts and all forms of optimistic/pessimistic permutations/combinations. The number of items that can enter into a mix and affect the outcome of a decision is limited only by the human condition and is far greater than the number of countries on this globe.

(21) Regardless of what you are told, never believe that there is but one course available to you. It may be a mix of many formats and procedures, and sometimes an odd and inconsistent mix, but there are always alternatives available to understand, evaluate and then engage in a market.

(22) Do not diminish the use of "objective," somewhat homogenized, sources of information on the country and the market therein, such as may be available through the Chambers of Commerce, United States Commercial Service and the like. These are compendia offered by people who have spent time working in and studying the market and, being objective, will offer an insight different from those who are interested in your entry., i.e., local consultants, lawyers, potential partners, customers, competitors, etc.

(23) Never treat or consider an evaluation of a market in a vacuum—relate it to the

rest of the company's resources and needs and geographical layout and responsiveness, and consider the synergies of this market with any one or more of the other markets presently or potentially part of the strategic plans of the company.

(24) If possible, the ultimate team of evaluators must represent several different disciplines (legal, accounting(finance), personnel, sales/marketing) operating at the same time with the same data because each will have a different perspective on what is perceived and will be complementary to what the others are projecting and considering.

(25) Allow for and take into account emotional and visceral reactions and conclusions in whatever evaluations are being made, and by any member of the evaluating group or a subset thereof. Any "foreign" market offers some shock to a person disciplined and trained by a system different from that "foreign" market. Necessarily some form of unspoken even subliminal reaction (and, daresaid, bias whether positive or negative) will be part of the evaluation. These reactions are often as valuable as the expert, hard advice offered by the skilled, multinational hand. Such reactions do not have to be "discounted": they need to be understood because they may play a part in a later failure or in implementation.

(26) The evaluation team should give frequent, well-documented updates to all responsible management in order to gain insight into possibly new directions and to cover new subjects when they arise. Nothing is worse than a stale or misdirected evaluation for finding the right way to enter and maximize a market.

(27) Never neglect to factor into the evaluation the fact that, while the market being evaluated may have potential and offer some incremental value to the company, it also means that there is an opportunity elsewhere not being evaluated and gained. Moreover, to the extent that reaching for the new market utilizes existing resources which are otherwise productive in an existing market the opportunity cost becomes that much more significant and must always be factored in. Conversely, the extent to which one can create NEW value in and out of a market with minimal use of existing internal resources (whether capital or personnel), creates an intangible but very significant uptick to the intrinsic value of the new market opportunity.

(28) A market whose value lies exclusively in potential will probably stay that way for quite awhile. This must be recognized and dealt with at all stages of an evaluation. Nothing can be done without an adequate infrastructure and existing opportunity base to warrant the first entry, no matter how "exotic" and enticing the lure of "pioneerism."

(29) Do not overestimate or underestimate your own company or client's capacities to apply resources; adapt its own culture and effectively implement the final plan for entry into a market. Take whatever is there and extrapolate it honestly into what is being proposed as an investment or market entry. Whatever is possible may not be in fact achievable because of those limitations. Conversely, unusual strengths can make the unlikely or virtually impossible quite doable. An example recalled is of a company that made a significant investment because of special tax holidays. Only much later was it discovered that its loss positions in the United States and the intentional skewing of income to the U.S. to use up the losses made such tax holidays virtually meaningless. On

the other hand, another company (tiny in all respects) with a unique cost-saving approach to a particular high-tech objective in one country made that company, with virtually no capital or related leverage, capable of changing the investment law to permit its entry as a fully-owned, operating subsidiary of the parent with full control of its technology.

II. NEGOTIATING FOR BEST RESULTS AND EFFECTIVE EVALUATION

It should be evident that the blurbs and case studies recited above, in precis, contain some aspect of or allusion to many of the guidelines on the attitudes and tools one should bring to any evaluation of entry into a new international market or in making any form of investment in a new market.

It should also be made clear that all the tools and proper attitudes in approaching evaluation and reaching what should be right conclusions will mean little if the negotiation for a position in the market through sales or manufacturing or a combination of activities falls flat. Good negotiators and well-managed negotiations are absolute keys to evaluating fully and bringing the evaluation to its desired fruition. To perform effective negotiation for anything more significant than a one-time transaction or sale or disposition (that is, some permanent form of entry) the negotiators in the aggregate must have an understanding of:

(1) The history and culture of the market.

(2) The economic system within that market and the specifics of the industry targeted.

(3) The political system and likely developments and effect on the specifics of the targeted evaluation.

(4) The specifics of the business system and practices belonging to both the opportunity being evaluated and the industry in which it operates (if different).

(5) The fundamental geography of the market in the broader sense of that word and how it affects likely developments in the evaluation target.

This is not to suggest as a prerequisite an encyclopedic knowledge of the market. If that were the case, an evaluation would hardly be necessary; it would simply be gleaning from facts already at hand within the group of negotiators. Nevertheless, an intellectual and educated awareness of the "other" coupled with an emotional sense of the "other" is critical to success associated with long-lasting and effectively negotiated undertakings.

At the very least, the negotiators must understand that there is a vast difference between surface culture and deep culture in the market they are studying and evaluating. Surface culture is what one can see quickly as would any tourist, i.e., fads, styles, slang language, even verbal and nonverbal behavior. These identifiable symbols may have very little to do with fundamental expectations, assumptions, attitudes, business, and private norms and values, as well as perceptions held in the target market country, all of which represent manifestations of the deep culture. One is tempted to delve deeply into the surface culture, relying on it in communications to find commonality, believing that approach will lead to deeper connection and understanding. This is rarely the case, and the opposite often happens. Certainly, uses of and references to local color, slang, and humor which are not within the bounds of the deep culture's acceptance of the same, as well as improper use of words and grammatical errors can sink the best-planned negotiating strategy.

In addition to avoiding (participating at best passively and as an understanding spectator) the facile but dangerous "connection" through surface culture contact, the effective negotiator must meld the aggregate awareness of the macro-framework of the five areas of knowledge mentioned above into a positive strategy dealing with the specifics of the market and the "representatives" of the market with whom they are dealing. The writer keeps a handy list of "DO's" and "DON'Ts" which, at the risk of oversimplification, are worth repeating here:

(1) Have no fear of isolating the hard and perhaps embarrassing issues, bringing them up with the critical people only. Do not delay their introduction if at all possible. This will prevent unnecessary misunderstandings and incorrect communications and will get the answer when and where you need it most.

(2) One can praise, but it is not useful to engage in sycophantic behavior.

(3) Don't ignore rank, and know where rank and status are in a given group on the "other" side.

(4) While anathema to some lawyers, overlegalism and overbearing terms, or conscious insertion of complexity in order to delay understanding and tilt in one's favor, do not bear fruit. Clarity of purpose and expression and minimization of minor aspects, while emphasizing the points embodying the true overriding objectives, are far more important.

(5) Keep all doors open, except where there is literally no alternative. Extensions lead often to resolution.

(6) Be prepared to have the authority to commit and be willing to commit. The "I have no authority" routine rarely is beneficial.

(7) Explain and clarify the main objectives and be prepared to repeat them. When they are understood and accepted, confirm and verify them. Confirmation of the critical objectives will avoid misunderstandings later and will let the final " legalisms" into the agreement with much less difficulty.

(8) Emphasize (and explain in a forceful, but not condescending way) the strengths of each party in order to create an unmistakable ambience of a "mutual win" opportunity. Have no hesitation in accepting equivalents in performance and results if the first route, even if more direct, cannot be gained for whatever reason.

(9) Prepare for more time to be used than planned. Too much emphasis on speed and quick action will not be appreciated for anything but short-term results.

(10) Often it will be better to make proposals rather than submit final-looking plans

for approval. This will allow for modifications and action by the "other" side without confrontation and a direct negative.

(11) Strive to find consistency and agreement with stated and encountered positions and policies of both sides, and be prepared to re-emphasize those when the bumps in the negotiations are encountered.

(12) Rushing into negotiations without attention to etiquette (here surface culture often blends with deep culture) and the element of physical connection will lead to possibly insuperable barriers to final agreement.

(13) Never generalize the course of negotiations in relationship to, or compare the experience of entering the market with, another country (particularly not a neighboring one or one using the same language). Each target market truly stands on its own.

(14) Have no fear (and encourage) negotiations in a setting comfortable for the other side, i.e., their own turf. This will give your side an opportunity to view firsthand both the deep and surface cultures and their interplay and the other side will have confidence in facing issues upfront. A visit to your turf may be useful in the final and very early stages to surround the relationship established and offer a glimpse into what you have to offer; however, result-orientation suggests clearly that the primary focus should be where the international deal will have principal effect, i.e., the target market.

(15) Following on point (1) above, the contract documents should address all the known essential or hard issues. The philosophy of "postpone what might be unpleasant because it may never arise anyway" may be an effective negotiating tactic to concluding a transaction, but it will not be an effective negotiation because it will not conclude what needs to be in fact anticipated and concluded. For example, do not select an arbitration mechanism that is exceedingly difficult for one or more parties on the theory that this is a "soft" way of approaching something and promoting compromises before disputes arise. A realistic mechanism will give both parties an incentive to stay on a track to resolution because they both know the other has a way of resolving the dispute effectively. Another example is to leave the choice of law out, hoping to seize the initiative if and when you decide you have a dispute. It will probably not work out that way. Bluntly spoken, DO NOT THINK in the end that the other side has any different agenda from you or that you can transcend them in cleverness. Be aggressive, but fair; be ambitious, but not overreaching or arrogant.

International negotiations offer barriers not seen in the "domestic" arena. Things are simply complicated by the double set of standards against which to measure progress or failure, e.g., two sets of laws, governments and corresponding bureaucracies, different culture, multiple currencies, and policies with respect to same, varying ideology, just to name a few. But the barriers can be hurdled through systematic negotiations, with continuity of "ownership" contribution and personal commitment. It is also important that the continuity be perceived by the "other" side as such while always keeping in mind the fundamental objectives of the evaluation and the resulting decisions to be made.

III. EVALUATION OF THE OPPORTUNITY: WHAT TO LOOK FOR AND WHY

A business or market opportunity for a company "going international" can and MUST be considered as capable of taking several forms, including:

a. Specific sales opportunities, both near and long-term;

b. Strategic alliances for long-term development and technology, or in combination with sales or licensing;

c. Opportunities relying on service and support revenues;

d. Locations sought for manufacturing expertise and cost-efficiency, and simply taking advantage of the political and economic "geography"of the times;

e. Opportunities based on what is happening elsewhere both generally and then specifically with the company or client and how such other happenings can affect positively or negatively what might not otherwise be perceived as contributing to or diminishing (or even creating) an opportunity in the specific market being evaluated;

f. A combination of any or all of the above.

It is the intention of the writer to leave the clear message that no evaluation can be undertaken in a vacuum as a case study unto itself; it must be viewed from all possible angles from the very outset even if the immediate objectives are very limited or specific. This process is necessary to determine just what the breadth of the opportunity is and only then will it be understood and properly evaluated as an ongoing business and market opportunity. Fundamentally ANY business venture can end up taking a multitude of forms and points of entry and if all possible forms and points are addressed from the inception there will clearly be a better view of the aggregate of the evaluation, thus increasing the chances of a correct set of choices arising from the evaluation.

With this fundamental precept in mind, the properly-focused international business lawyer will stay alert to and work with the client/company to the end that the evaluation consider, several detailed sets of issues and elements within a business or market opportunity in the international arena. It is not the intention here to be exhaustive and each discipline and profession playing a part in the evaluation team and process will need to have their own answers to the specific questions that their experience tells them need to be asked. Nor does this essay purport to establish the forms and formulae that a client/company must use in assembling and assessing numerical and market data, meeting its profit margins, returns on investment, budget methodology and other specific company cultural pre-requisites. Furthermore, no assessment or distinction is made here on what variations in evaluating tools might be necessary depending on whether it is a service or a product that is the subject matter for the business or market opportunity but it does not appear that there would need to be much change in the approaches to be made.

It should also be noted that in the assessment of legal and other considerations it is certainly not a prerequisite to investment or marketing that all or even MOST answers be "positive" or not fraught with risk, but that all must be analyzed and weighed. Another important aspect of the resulting process is to compare the "negatives" to other countries where the market has already been tested and those same or similar negatives were evident but where success has come at some useful stage and in some useful form. What worked and how it worked may well work here again. Furthermore, only by full understanding can the target be truly be evaluated and the elements leading to imperfect or failed market and business entries minimized from the outset by preparing alternatives, or taking radically different steps than normally taken in any form of implementation, or perhaps by linking up further parties and countries to the venture to buttress the established order and apparent weakness.

With these caveats the following are many of the most important facets of a market which should be evaluated and considered:

Whether it be any one or more of the forms of opportunity described above, the following should be assessed:

1.   Does the venture proposed need assistance from any other entity, whether it be government or private? If so (and no venture is free-standing without vital assistance needed from at least one independent quarter), to what extent and when and where do these elements "kick" in?

a. In the case of government, consider each juncture when the obligation or need is required or advised; measure the government's responsiveness to each need and juncture. Weigh others' experience in this regard. Consider for yourself:

(i) Form and stability of government, depth of and transparency of law and administrative functions within government and the ability to rely on the government decision-making process;

(ii) Degree of class, economic, racial or ethnic antagonism in the country-market;

(iii) Relations with neighboring countries: is it in an economic bloc or moving away or toward one;

(iv) Professed and actual attitudes towards private entry into the market, in all the varieties and forms it might take, particularly private foreign ownership and corresponding investment;

(v) Economic and political policies and trends which indicate the shape of demonstrable government stimulus of the local market, protection of local vendors, manufacturers and related parties and how these policies might affect your proposed operation.

(vi) Degree of small groups' disproportionate political and/or economic power, if any;

(vii) Importance and any favoritism towards state industries, express and implied and;

(viii) Attitude towards corruption and size and weight of bureaucratic infrastructure.

b. In the case of private parties and alliances or cooperation therewith in any part of the opportunity being reviewed (this includes anything from a subcontractor refitting the premises to an independent sales channel to a full-blown joint venture partner in an ongoing sales and service operation), weigh all of the following:

(i) What kinds of structure can be used for the projected cooperation, i.e., contract, legal entity, independent ventures of distribution or agency, licensor-licensee and so forth, and in each case, what are the restrictions and limitations imposed by law and practice on the forms taken;

(ii) What kind of culture does the private party have in comparison to your own and how dependent is it on certain personnel;

(iii) Experience of the private party and its capacity and recognition as perceived by itself and others and also how it actually performs in the market being evaluated;

(iv) Capital position and strength of financial participants in the private party, and level of commitment to the venture being proposed;

(v) Other patterns of business previously practiced by the private party, measuring both successes and failures;

(vi) Flexibility of the private party in withstanding and absorbing sudden changes in law, regulations and economic climate;

(vii) Transparency in operations and practices and willingness and capacity to cooperate at each critical level with your client/company, including in reporting relationships, financial disclosures and forecasting;

(viii) Strengths and weaknesses of private party in direct relation to the products or services of your client/company; and

(ix) Apparent and potential flexibility of each and any such private parties in adapting and responding to any specific needs of your client/company.

2. In evaluating the market/business opportunity, what does the legal climate consist of with respect to at least the following:

a. System of law available:

(i) What principles govern access to the legal system; can it be used in tandem with diplomatic review and access; do foreign interests receive equal treatment in terms of access and enforcement;

(ii) What are the remedies available for breach, i.e., can one not only receive damages in an expeditious fashion, but can one stop unlawful activities through injunctive and related processes;

(iii) Competency (not in the abstract but related to how you and your

client/company need answers and action) of legal and related counsel in the specific market, status within the target market as a profession and of the particular persons chosen;

(iv) Transparency of laws and comprehensibility to "foreign" eyes and minds: any history of freedom from arbitrary government intervention or unreviewable governmental imposition of the latter's exercise of "discretion" and do the statutory law and framework rely on government "discretion" and specific particularized action to make the system work at all (one market studied by the author required a special bill signed by the President in order to apply for even a permit to run electricity to a plant; another market studied was marked by a plethora of exceptions to the rule and there was in fact no "regular" foreign investment);

(v) Is binding arbitration in a neutral venue available? In general, what treaties and conventions does the market country belong to relating to allowable forms and enforcement of arbitral awards as well as for agreements on intellectual property protection and rights; are there effective tax treaties extant between your client's host country and the target market or with other countries in the company/client family which can effectively assist in limiting tax exposure and seeking redress in the event of issues of double taxation or excessive extraterritorial tax exposure;

(vi) Further to (v) above, what are the forms and levels of protection accorded intellectual property rights and, in particular, is the concept of trade secrets recognized and to what degree; and what happens to and who can own and/or control technology after licensing the same in the target market;

(vii) Participation in, and adherence on the part of the target market country in world organizations and institutions promoting fair trade and lowering tariffs and diminishing or eliminating trade-related investment measures which disincent effective foreign investment and sales from foreign markets into the target market. Lawyers often underestimate the importance of this (although that is a real body of actual international law) but in the absence of military occupation and force and "cold war" issues, these economic and treaty frameworks will play an increasingly important part in the development of relations and the stability of investment, trade, and economic growth.

b. Types of legal entities available to the foreign investor and marketer, assessing further these aspects of such entities:

(i) Depending on the type of entity involved, what are the different tax and duty rates applicable; what kind of "edge" is gained in bidding for and participating in "national" undertakings of whatever form; what are the liabilities associated as a shareholder and as director; advantages and availability of local directors or quotaholders; limitations on authority of officers and directors; utility, receptiveness, and enforceability of shareholder and similar "side" agreements.

(ii) If participating with others in the venture, what minority rights are protected and how are they protected; is there an active local stock market, how is it managed and policed in terms of financial and other disclosures and can it be used to

fund growth or promote debt/equity in the market; is there local receptiveness to foreign participation and are the reasons for stock price fluctuations readily ascertainable and reasonably logical;

(iii) Rules on dividends, loans, capital repatriation and inpatriation, and fluidity allowed to movements between related companies, i.e. consolidation of results, offsets in receivables and payables; allowance for technical, administrative and management fees, expatriate charges, and tax allowances, etc.

(iv) If the entity chosen is an independent vehicle such as a distributor, representative, or agent, special care must be taken in both law and practice with respect to the operation of these agreements and any modification or termination thereof. There are often supervening laws which prevent freedom of contract with any or all of these forms. This does not mean that these are vehicles to be avoided, but planning ahead can mitigate their impact if and when such modification or termination must occur because of good business reasons. When and how to choose such independent channels for entering a market are a subject of a separate treatise and cannot be explored here. Nevertheless, these relationships bring special problems and opportunities and need special (often local) wisdom.

3.   In the course of the evaluation, financial and fiscal concerns which must be addressed include (but are obviously not limited to) the following:

Tax Issues

(i)   All Taxes of whatever nature, duties, stamp and conveyancing deed charges, and all fees associated with each level of the client/company enterprise as purchaser, supplier, purveyor, and owner/lessor/lessee, both actual and hidden (the latter can be as much as the former) and how they are administered and collected;

(ii)   All taxes and government fees, uses, deeds, stamps, etc. implicit in any form of arrangement with another party being undertaken INCLUDING those levied on entities with which one will be allied arising from or out of the relationship contemplated, i.e., consulting by certain professional groups often bears special taxes held as a form of withholding even in such "nearby" places as Mexico. These taxes will affect your operations and may also act as unexpected drags on expected and potential commerce - they may also represent an opportunity if your service or product is designed to cut such taxes or fees or allows them to be administered more efficiently;

(iii)   All tax and fiscal incentives for importing limitations (i.e., import substitution programs, domestic content rebates), attaining exporting objectives, or those relating to site selection and training of personnel.

Fiscal and Monetary Undertakings:

(i)   Foreign exchange stability, fungibility and availability; understanding of monetary policies in the country both historically and by way of projections; recognized

and available forms of nexi and documentation covering stages of both importation and exportation, analysis of allowed and practiced payment systems including letters of credit and other forms of payment, possible counter-trade mechanisms and likely agents (and products and services) for the same, modes of consignment, leasing, royalty conditions and related types of endeavors.

(ii) Local borrowing, historical and actual interest rates and trends in expansion and contraction of money supply; any and all exchange controls on each and every form of money movement;

(iii) Foreign funding and borrowing, restrictions and constraints on the same as well as favorable opportunities from tax treaty countries and ALL sources offering potential synergy (Think global in finance as well as in the formulation of objectives for, and the reasons to evaluate the target market); relationships and trends in relations with regional and transnational financial networks, and with world lending authorities, including drawing rights agreements (World Bank, IMF and IBRD for example).

4.   Other critical inputs in evaluation would at the minimum include assessment of the following factors:

Labor Availability and Quality

(i) Restrictions on employment and deployment of personnel, customary practices, termination and retirement rights, and indemnification provisions;

(ii) Level of union activities, focus of such activities, generally and to your client/company's specific industry, and the trends in the same;

(iii) Nature of training in accessible labor force, loyalty to the concern, and under what conditions is such loyalty extended.

General and Specific Business Climate Issues Include:

(i) Ethics of important business entities in the market and their (as well as the "public's") attitude towards business, including actual and professed compliance with existing laws and regulations affecting business;

(ii) Share of market and industry held by government both as a purchaser and as a supplier and what critical elements in the proposed enterprise depend on government supply or purchase;

(iii) Extent of government interaction with business and dependency of business on government approval or disapproval; elements of corruption and at what levels and amounts, and extent of likely or potential interference by government in all its forms, both official and unofficial, with the daily course of business conduct;

(iv) Extent of comfortable reliance on government and quasi-government

agencies and institutions for binding and non-political agreements, accurate information and precise rulings in the conduct of business;

(v) Strength and utility of private business organizations and trade associations as well as applicable Embassy and Consular personnel in support or rejection of host market proposals or activities; ability to exercise with relative impunity freedom of speech on business matters and reactions to government activities in the target market; visibility and reputation of the business press in the target market;

(vi) Patterns in government intervention in business matters, including expropriation and nationalization, disruption in internal trade and with competitive practices (whether through antitrust regulations or informal procedures and administrative guidance), price and wage controls, any exercise of draconian monetary and fiscal restrictions over critical elements of the economy.

Logistics, Infrastructure and Movement of Goods and People

(i) Transportation systems, both internal and external, adequacy of communications links and variations of communications technology available for use;

(ii) Adequacy of supply of utility needs, water resources, general state of self-sufficiency in the target market economy (the more self-sufficiency there is the less likelihood there should be for imposed import restrictions and other artificial constraints on needed imports and paying for the same in an internationally required fashion);

(iii) Availability of insurance for all aspects of transactions including credit risk, property damages, product and third-party liability, OPIC coverage and FCIA availability and under what terms, relationship to EXIMBANK and USAID programs (as well as similar programs offered by other countries, wherever your client/company might have some leverage) and the availability of sales incentives thereunder;

(iv) Customs treatment, fluidity and equality and internationalization of treatment—does the Customs system accept internationally recognized invoicing and documentation practices for determining value, for temporarily exporting and returning goods (is there duty drawback) what systems are available for emergency entry and consignment operations and warehouse (duty free) methods of controlling costs on inventory and disposition of products; level of bureaucracy and sophistication of customs systems in place in target market;

(v) Existence and extent of any export licensing and controls, both internal and imposed by the host government and/or externally applied by COCOM (or successor; or like multilateral organizations), United States Commerce or State Regulations, participation in, or the target of, any boycott or other trade imbalancing procedure impairing relatively free movement of goods in and out of target market for manufacture or sale both within and without the target market; actual and potential participation in any favored economic bloc (CBI, NAFTA-type, ASEAN, French West Africa, MERCO-

SUR, and so forth) or special favored relation to any other market where your company has or may have leverage or presence.

5. KNOW what your competition is doing, meaning both actual and potential competition in the target market. Knowing these elements does not necessarily mean following lock-step or acting to the contrary because it is your competition or because, perhaps, they have not been as successful as your client/company desires and believes can be done. In the end, it is the knowing the why and how of their status and positioning, and where they started and where they are and are likely to be that will offer necessary and important input into your own evaluation. In addition, do not be afraid to share confidence on "common" problems which do not entail the use of a commercial advantage belonging to either your client/company or the competitor(s).

Studying and Using Trends in the Evaluation Process

It is important to stress that none of the evaluating tools or approaches to evaluation should be done in the form of a snapshot or in stasis; because we live in a dynamic and changing universe it is equally important to take into full account those TRENDS and MOVEMENTS in or around (particularly in politically similar or geographically proximate markets) the market or business opportunity being evaluated as those trends relate to any item being evaluated. This necessarily lends more imprecision to the conclusions and results of any evaluation and may entail the use of probabilities and similar analytical tools that lawyers are not wont to use, but there is distinctly proven utility in the use of such models. Consideration of trends will buttress the open and creative mode that one must utilize in assessing the full view of the international market or business opportunity.

The use of trends will allow one (as was done) to detect, in one market whose system from all traditional vantage points had not changed in (and this is not unusual) 30 years and was firmly within the grip of a state-controlling mechanism, the embryo of a movement to open a specific form of trade to foreign investment or licensing. This detection, coupled with knowledge of covert permission given to certain local entrepreneurs to operate in a specific niche were sufficient "positives" to launch a small and controlled presence in the market with sales into that niche from places which had been politically friendly to the still-paranoid and repressive regime. When the trend became an open secret, there was natural evolution to an entire legal framework permitting what the foreign supplier had done and its position was firmly entrenched in a market now receptive to what it had anticipated. This is just one small example of how the trend-assessing process can help illuminate and evaluate markets.

It may also simply be a restatement of the existential lesson that nothing is exactly as it appears to be. Into all checklists and firm, number-filled, and quantified analyses must be factored the continuum of change and movement, whether they be "positive" or "negative," to the models of a good business or market opportunity, and we must be alert to both the mutations and possibilities arising from the changes. We can then connect those changes to what we have learned historically from other markets and help predict the success of the market or business opportunity being evaluated and how that success can be brought about.

Globalizing It All

A recent concept gaining popularity in the business community is that of the "global village" or the need and desire to "think globally, act locally." While like any popularized idea these phrases become overused and incorrectly applied there is a significant kernel of truth to its application in the evaluation process of taking a business into the international marketplace and arena. If an evaluator in the assessment process of an international opportunity believes that real differences in market opportunities are along geographic lines, then the evaluator will be forever reliant on pointing out and sticking to surface differences. If on the other hand the evaluator begins to look at differences on a world-resource basis and segments of the market wherever they manifest themselves in the world, the evaluator will begin to focus on global commonalities and find in those commonalities new approaches to international business and market opportunities.

Proper evaluation in this globalized view compels the evaluating team to have knowledge of lead and established markets (whether they are present in those markets or not) drawn from actual experience in those markets and a firm comprehension of how events or innovations in those lead markets can ripple throughout the world economy including the market being evaluated. Globalized evaluation, "done right," demands an objective view of all markets and trends; it also demands maintaining an equidistance to all parts of the world which, ironically, will allow for each of those to be viewed more carefully and free of the innate prejudices that (1) necessarily different levels of direct experience, and (2) simply concentrating on in just one part of the world tend to perpetuate.

Global evaluation means utilization of world resources and experiences, an understanding of the interrelationship between a particular history to global history, a singular economic system to a global economic system, and an individual business and political system to a global business and political system. Keeping one's collective and trained eye on these relationships will permit coordination between the specific and the general and promote a global networking of opportunities. There will perforce be more real opportunities from this approach, and results will not be tied to old standards of risk and results. Indeed, global evaluations utilizing and conceiving of all possibilities alleviate the inherent risk in being anchored in but one region of the world; that market position, being monolithic, is truly and fully at risk even if the market share is dominant. If market positions are anchored in many regions, and the positions are properly narrowed (because of thorough AND realistic evaluation) and are drawn on the peculiar resources from all regions with interdependence based on strengths, there is less aggregate risk and the opportunity for improved results for the long-term certainly enhanced.

The evaluation will draw on many, many elements, some seemingly far from the subject at hand, but by doing so the evaluators will have all the tools, the necessary approach and attitude, negotiating skills and fact-laden checklists to make an evaluation which one can truly say is an evaluation based on a global vision drawn to a particular market. As such, the evaluation will be one which has the best chance of being most useful, resistant to staleness and, of course, yielding the best results in any implementation of the recommendations from the evaluation rendered.

SELECTION AND USE OF FOREIGN COUNSEL

Patrick B. Fazzone

I. INTRODUCTION

UNLIKE the major accounting firms relatively few legal firms or corporate law departments have offices in all locations where legal issues might arise affecting their businesss or their clients' business. Nor, in general do most legal firms or corporate lawyers have expertise in the law of every jurisdiction in which their clients may do business. U.S. law firms, for example, have been selective in determining where to establish offices both in the United States and abroad. And, in general, most firms have been somewhat conservative in their decisionmaking. Unlike accounting firms, which have decided that they must extend their accounting and audit capability to track the activities of their multinational clients, the type of services rendered by legal firms often do not necessitate the establishment of a local office. And, where local presence is necessary law firms and corporate counsel can generally make effective use of local counsel.

Through the use of competent foreign counsel, U.S. lawyers effectively can build a worldwide network of legal capability. Particularly if effectively supervised, use of foreign counsel can be a very efficient way of providing international legal services.

In a true international practice, there is a symbiotic fit between the managers or supervisors of a legal matter, and local counsel.[1] The role of foreign counsel is often critical to the effective resolution of legal issues. There are a number of areas in which their assistance is key. These include:

- advising on issues of local law;
- dealing with foreign government officials, courts and agencies;
- advising on government policy, legislative, regulatory and other legal developments;
- advising on local cultural and business practices;
- serving as local counsel in litigation;
- assisting in negotiations and other dealings with other local nationals;
- advising on legality of local contracts;
- setting up local offices of an enterprises;

349

• comparing versions of a contract in two different languages for accuracy.

In other instances, the role of foreign counsel will be less important. In the structuring of international transactions, financing mechanisms, and in other similar areas it is those lawyers with a much broader perspective on the matter that will have the most effective role to play. Indeed, this specialized type of assistance and "transaction management" is typically the province of the so-called "international" rather than local lawyers.

This chapter explores why the use of foreign counsel is important, how to use foreign counsel most effectively, and how to select competent foreign counsel. Finally, this chapter will review certain other issues which should be considered in the selection and use of local counsel.

II. THE RESPECTIVE ROLES OF INTERNATIONAL AND FOREIGN COUNSEL

In matters with an international aspect, there is an important role for foreign counsel that is analogous in many respects to that of local counsel in litigation, government relations, and many types of commercial matters in the United States. What is perhaps less widely appreciated is the interrelationship that should exist between foreign counsel and those advisers with a broader, international perspective on the particular matter. The key to effective handling of matters with an international flavor may well be the establishment of a workable, efficient and cost effective division of labor and responsibility between these two sets of legal advisers.

The Role of the "International" Lawyer

In international matters there typically is one lawyer or group of lawyers that is responsible as the supervisor or manager of the overall project. Often, these attorneys are in-house lawyers. Other times they are lawyers in an outside firm that acts virtually as general counsel for the client, or that supervises and coordinates international or complex legal matters. These lawyers ideally are in the position of understanding the overall objectives and priorities of the client. They also are in a position, and are typically expected to coordinate, the various elements of an international project. A major role is to help ensure that what is done on a particular project will not have unintended adverse consequences for other aspects of the client's business.

At least a portion of these responsibilities could be called those of an "international" lawyer, to the extent that an "international" attorney is one who is competent to address and help resolve issues having international aspects. Whatever the terminology used, on most international projects there should be a lawyer involved with a broader perspective and expertise that can coordinate and supervise. Typical matters where this role is important include cross-border investments, joint ventures, infrastructure and other major projects; other international transactions and financing projects; multiforum litigation and alternative dispute resolution; and the international protection of intellectual property.

Beyond their supervising and coordinating roles, "international" lawyers serve other important functions. One is identifying the international, or transnational dimension in a particular matter and formulating an appropriate means of resolving issues that have been identified. An obvious example is the resolution of issues arising from the interface of two legal systems through the rules of private international law. Another example is the resolution of issues relating to the enforceability of foreign judgments.

International lawyers may also play a key role as virtual business advisers in structuring transactions and financing mechanisms, in addressing international tax planning questions and in handling other aspects of transnational business for their clients. Once again, it is because international lawyers are in a position to comprehend the larger issues in a matter while understanding the "micro" issues that need to be resolved by local counsel that they can serve effectively as overall supervisors of a matter. Indeed, it is the "international" adviser alone that will be in a position to ensure that the various aspects of an international project are properly coordinated and structured.

The Role of Foreign Counsel

In international matters, foreign counsel serves the key role of expert on local law and procedures as well as the principal contact with local officials and bodies. Foreign counsel is also in the best position to ensure compliance with local rules and requirements in litigation and other proceedings.

Because of greater familiarity with the local environmental, culture and language, local counsel is in a strong position to assist in the development of strategy and in formulating an appropriate approach for resolving local issues and accomplishing objectives. Local counsel presumably is also in the best position to assist in dealing with local governments and officials and business partners. Most importantly, foreign counsel must be relied upon to have critical day-to-day knowledge of how things work and how to "get things done" in the local jurisdiction.

The Cultural Dimension

It is extremely important not to underestimate the cultural aspects of using foreign counsel. Local counsel, if well selected, will be far better suited to identify unique aspects of the local business, legal and social culture, and the "local" dimensions of a problem. An experienced international lawyer can then interpret and synthesize these cultural differences.

It is often most effective to select foreign counsel who has had some experience with the culture of the international lawyer and/or the client. In a place like Taiwan, for example, this is relatively easy. Many Taiwanese lawyers have studied and/or worked in the United States. A lawyer with this type of background ideally will experience fewer difficulties in communicating with the international supervisor. A lawyer with this background may also have some appreciation for the requirements and priorities of the international lawyer and the client.

Similarly, it is extremely useful, but less important, if the international lawyer has had experience working in or dealing with the particular culture and legal system of the foreign counsel. Qualification in the local legal system could be invaluable (albeit rare) as it permits the international lawyer more critically to evaluate the advice coming from local counsel. At a minimum, the international lawyer should have had some exposure to and therefore some understanding of the culture and legal and business environment of the country. This helps prevent problems in communications, and misunderstandings among local counsel, the international adviser, and the client.

This "cultural sensitivity" can also aid in the drafting of instructions to which foreign counsel will respond. Foreign counsel performs best when provided specific, detailed instructions on what precisely is required. This is especially the case where English is not the first language of the foreign lawyer. Instructions which reflect some understanding of the business and legal environment and requirements of the local law and culture are naturally easier for the local lawyer to interpret and follow. Unfortunately, there are all too many instances of something being lost in translation between the client and/or the international supervisor and local counsel. Unless the client is assisted by an international lawyer with some "feel" for the local culture, there is no great assurance that the client's wishes will be successfully implemented.

The situation becomes even more compelling when a U.S. based lawyer is asked to supervise such matters as commercial negotiations or similar projects. A lack of sensitivity to the local culture and business environment can spell disaster. There are countless stories of failed negotiations or aborted discussions with government officials or potential business partners. Often, the cause is a "faux pas" by an American lawyer or client who "parachuted in" for the session with little or no cultural preparation. Examples of this range from using the term "acquisition" in negotiations with a potential Japanese business partner (almost always fatal to the deal), to insisting on filling every silent pause in negotiations with a client's prospective Chinese business partner (usually counterproductive at best).

Indeed, Americans are notorious for ill-considered acts of "cultural imperialism." The tendency of most of the international business world to deal in English can lull the ill-prepared American into a false sense of security, and mask real differences in culture, outlook, expectations, and the like. Moreover, the "insensitive" adviser may do more than miscommunicate. He or she may well incorrectly interpret local conditions, circumstances and requirements, more often than not interpreting them through American cultural goggles.

The ill-prepared adviser may also incorrectly assume that a U.S. lawyer's approach to problem solving is the only way of addressing a situation and "bulldoze" over the suggestions of local counsel. American lawyers tend to be far more exhaustive in their approach to drafting documents than lawyers in many other systems. This is undoubtedly due in part to the more comprehensive and sophisticated system of regulation and standards of professional liability in the United States than in most other countries. Nevertheless, a lawyer's resort to an American style approach in many less openly adversarial countries may be counterproductive and unnecessary.

Equally serious, the "culturally insensitive" lawyer often is completely unaware that something has gone wrong or that the American-style approach is doing more harm than good. The client invariably is left in the dark as well. Months later, the client and its

U.S.-based counsel still wonder why the deal fell apart or why the government contract was awarded to another firm.

Foreign counsel is there to be utilized. Working together with the international supervisors, a very effective team can be mobilized. But the most effective team members are those who also understand foreign counsel's perspective and the environment in which they must operate.

In sum, an effective and advisable approach to international practice is to use foreign counsel in each relevant jurisdiction supervised or managed by international advisers. In this way, both local and larger issues can be adequately addressed and coordinated. By combining the strengths of each, oversights and problems can be avoided.

III. EFFECTIVE SELECTION AND USE OF FOREIGN COUNSEL

Introduction

There are certain essential steps in selecting foreign counsel. The first is, of course, to identify the proper lawyer(s) for the job. Just as in the United States, certain firms are specialists or have more expertise in some areas than others. While the degree of specialization that has developed in the United States is still not the norm in many countries, it is invariably true that some lawyers are more expert or better informed than others. For example, in the East Asian countries, some lawyers specialize principally in assisting local companies and individuals. Generally these clients' needs are more local in nature and relatively unsophisticated. Other lawyers specialize in' representing overseas companies and multinationals. It is this latter group of lawyers that normally would be more suitable candidates for use as local counsel.

A second important step that is often overlooked is the importance of having developed a relationship with the foreign lawyer. It is generally far more effective to utilize counsel whom you have used before and with whom you have an ongoing relationship than simply to select a lawyer with whom you have no prior experience. This is important for several reasons. First, this approach helps ensure that the lawyer you select is in fact competent and qualified for the task. This, of course, is highly important if the matter is complex and presents difficult issues. Second, it also helps ensure that the foreign lawyer will be responsive and timely in completing all tasks. A request for action "yesterday" is more likely to be complied with by foreign counsel that views the international lawyer as a source of ongoing work and someone they know personally. Third, working with the same people helps increase accountability. You simply have more leverage over someone with whom there is an ongoing relationship than someone who views the relationship as a "one off" event.

It often furthers the objective of relationship building to establish an informal tie between the international firm and local counsel. As discussed more fully below, law firms have approached this from several different ways including merger, lawyer exchanges, and the like.

The last crucial step is effective management and supervision of local counsel. Again, there is an important role here for the international adviser. Through effective management and supervision, costs can be controlled far more effectively and the chances of satisfactory results enhanced.

Locating Competent Counsel

Locating the right lawyer can be somewhat tricky. A traditional approach has been through the use of international directories. Martindale Hubbell's international directory of lawyers is highly useful at least for identifying candidates from which to select counsel.

Word of mouth among international practitioners and business people is also very useful. Through international conventions of such bodies as the International Pacific Bar Association or the Section of International Law and Practice of the American Bar Association one can meet foreign practitioners and establish a potentially effective network of foreign lawyers. In some ways this process is a bit self-selecting as the most aggressive and network conscience lawyers are likely to be the ones attending the international conferences. Seeking local counsel who has worked with other international counsel that a client has engaged is also a good tool for selection.

Nevertheless, neither international directories nor networking ensures that international managers will always choose well. There really is no substitute for experience working with a particular foreign lawyer or firm. Again, international lawyers can add real value in instances where they have had experience using particular foreign lawyers and supervising them previously.

It sometimes can be very helpful if international counsel has had lawyers resident in the local firm. This helps international counsel develop a feel of how well the local firm operates and where its strengths and weaknesses are. Due to the creation of personal relationships, it also helps ensure responsiveness and accountability on the part of foreign counsel.

In selecting local counsel, clients and their lawyers often focus on individual lawyers rather than on their firms. This is often quite appropriate since in many jurisdictions firms tend to be smaller and centered around one or two key individuals. Moreover, as in the United States, firms typically will have certain areas of strength depending on the personnel involved.

Relationship Building

From my experience, relationship building is an important element in identifying and selecting foreign counsel. There is nothing like an established relationship to ensure quick feedback and prioritization of your matter. This is particularly important in "hot spots" like Hong Kong or China where there is burgeoning demand for quality local legal services. Indeed, relationships are heavily emphasized in certain areas of the world like Asia. Even though the profession generally is relatively sophisticated, relationships still count.

Relationships with foreign firms tend to start with relationships between individual lawyers. A logical next step is an interchange of lawyers at various levels and areas of practice. Obviously, it is the internationally-oriented lawyers who will have occasion and reason to do this.

Some sensible next steps include lawyer exchanges, joint seminars, joint publications and promotional efforts, joint meetings with clients and prospective clients, and residence programs. The April 1993 issue of the ABA Journal reported on various types of informal linkages between U.S. and British firms. These include:

Affiliation Agreements—Primarily formal or informal agreements to make reciprocal referrals.

Networks—Law firms in different jurisdictions will share information and training, and meet periodically to generate business. Networks can be open to new members or closed, and generally do not preclude a firm from entering other relationships.

Strategic Alliances—Arrangements designed to achieve a particular purpose, such as targeting a client or putting together a practice group.

All of these help foster trust and familiarity between the firms. They also help international counsel form a very clear judgment of the capabilities, and limitations, of foreign firms. Certain law firms, because of the nature of their practice, will tend to focus on certain geographic or substantive areas. In some countries, like Indonesia, many lawyers focus on providing political contacts in the government. Some lawyers there have better contacts than others. It is sometimes tempting to utilize the services of different firms depending on the nature of the project. Nevertheless, thought should also be given to whether identification with more than one firm—even on different matters—could adversely effect the local reputation of the international lawyer or of the client.

In addition to exchanges and joint activities, it may be advantageous in some instances to establish a formal relationship with a local firm if possible. One approach is to join together in an international legal group. There are a number of these types of groups operating. A major advantage of this approach is avoidance of the high overheads that can be associated with maintaining a foreign office. Predictably, however, there will still be issues of cost sharing, coordination of work, administration, and maintaining a fair balance of referrals. Invariably, some members of the group will be more active in referring work and an imbalance in referrals may cause some tension. Still, an international legal group can be a very effective way of maintaining a worldwide capability and ensuring responsiveness to the needs of clients.

A second approach adopted by a number of firms is joint venturing in the establishment of overseas offices. Under this approach, more than one firm from the same or different countries will enter into an arrangement to split the cost of establishing and maintaining a foreign office. The office may be staffed with lawyers from each firm and local lawyers hired as well. Again, this approach works where the interests are complementary and where all firms are contributing and benefiting more or less equally. One ongoing issue in a joint venture can be that of conflicts avoidance. Some proposed joint ventures may simply not be practicable where significant conflicts exist between each firm's client base. And in any event, reasonable procedures need to be worked out in advance for resolving conflicts issues that might arise.

A third approach as previously discussed, is to establish lawyer residency or exchange programs. One benefit of this approach is that it can help ensure responsiveness on the part of the local firm. It can also improve the service to clients as international counsel will be on location to work with local counsel on client matters.

A more comprehensive approach is a merger or similar arrangement with a local firm. This may not always be allowed under local laws. It also can involve considerable overhead and increased commitments for the international firm. Moreover, if the cultures of the local and international firm are significantly different, it can lead to major headaches. Cultural differences can undo the best laid plans. And a "divorce" later on can leave a bad taste in everyone's mouths and a tarnished reputation locally. Nevertheless, if the economics warrant such a commitment, this can be a very effective way of ensuring control and close supervision by the international firm. Once again, however, one must select a local partner carefully.

For most U.S. law firms, it is preferable to establish a close correspondent or "associate" relationship with local counsel. This gives the U.S.-based firm the flexibility to use other law firms—useful in case of conflicts or a gap in expertise. And, it avoids the substantial commitment of resources required in a merger with a local practice.

Selection

Actual selection of foreign counsel is, of course, critical. Once you have identified the need you then must identify what type of expertise you require. Often, local counsel will be selected based on a recommendation or information contained in an international directory. Increasingly, and particularly for large projects, clients may feel more comfortable in holding the international version of a "beauty pageant". International counsel may be asked to interview several firms to identify the most suitable counsel for a particular matter.

In cases where international counsel has an established and reliable relationship with a local firm it may be unnecessary to interview a range of firms. Nevertheless, a conflicts check is always an important step. And, on substantial matters, it is always advisable to interview the local firm prior to retaining them.

There are inevitably other details to be worked out with foreign counsel. Where the foreign lawyers are working jointly with international lawyers, the issue of how the client is to be billed will naturally arise. In some circumstances it may be more practicable and effective for the local firm to bill the client separately. On the other hand, the client may prefer to receive one invoice from the international lawyers listing the foreign counsel's invoice as a disbursement or separate item.

The lawyers must also identify with precision who their client is and who is therefore issuing instructions. This can be a tricky issue in some cases. One example is where there are a number of individuals or entities seeking to form a joint venture or partnership and all are in a position to request services from the legal advisers. Because of the nature of the ethical responsibility from lawyer to client, all counsel must be clear on who their actual client is. The consequences of taking instructions from someone who is not your client are such that great care should be exercised in this area.

Effective Management and Supervision

A final key aspect in the use of foreign counsel is effective management and supervision. There are certain important elements.

First, it is critical to provide clear instructions to foreign counsel detailing the assistance required. In my experience, it is most effective to provide intelligible written instructions, providing more detail than might normally be necessary if one were dealing with another U.S. firm or with lawyers within the same firm.

It is often very useful to follow up orally. This provides the opportunity to clarify the nature of the project and the precise assistance required.

As in the world of international commerce generally, English is the established *lingua franca* in business dealings. While it may be helpful to be able to communicate in the local lawyer's language, most lawyers with experience dealing with international clients invariably speak English well. The combination of written and oral communications helps minimize the chances of a misunderstanding as to what is required.

Foreign counsel's opinion or conclusions should also be rendered in writing. This generally is not a problem, as in most systems, local counsel are quite used to and may even prefer rendering written advice. It often is important, however, to follow up orally to clarify foreign counsel's findings and to discuss any issues that may seem somewhat ambiguous or unclear.

It is also critical not to analyze foreign counsel's opinion or findings from a Western or U.S. perspective. In many jurisdictions, familiar concepts are absent. In countries such as Vietnam, there is an absence of the rule of law. Counsel used to a legal system based on precedent and *stare decisis* may completely misapprehend the significance and import of an opinion rendered by local counsel in a jurisdiction where the rule of law does not apply. Unless local counsel has the sophistication to understand this important difference, the onus of interpretation falls squarely on the international lawyers.

Another problem in some countries is the absence of up-to-date statutory provisions. Indonesia, for example, is notorious in lacking "modern" provisions on corporate and commercial law—areas of the law vitally important to the conduct of international business.

In many jurisdictions, of course, there is no common law and therefore no consistent or discernible pattern of interpretation of the law. Another common problem from Western eyes is inconsistent or "inadequate" implementation or enforcement of the law. This is a particularly pressing issue in intellectual property protection in Asia and Latin America. International counsel would make a potentially catastrophic error by simply assuming that seemingly clear statutory law will be enforced in these countries in a manner similar to the United States.

Thus, an important role of international counsel is to analyze the foreign lawyer's opinion in the context of the overall project and client objectives. Essentially this is a process of issue and problem identification and risk assessment. And, equally important, international lawyers must be prepared to advise on how to deal with gaps in the local law and difficulties caused by differences from the home legal system. Where gaps in the law exist, the solution may be to develop suitable and all-encompassing contractual arrangements with reference to a jurisdiction where there is some meaningful chance of obtaining a remedy in the event of a dispute. Other times there may be commercial solutions which will work. Working closely with local counsel, the international adviser's role is to help find a way of resolving the difficulties occasioned by differences in the systems of law involved.

An important logistical issue is to decide how much should be disclosed to foreign counsel about the client and its objectives. Foreign counsel is likely to be more effective if it understands what the client's objectives and needs are in a particular matter.

Therefore it is probably preferable to err on the side of disclosure to local counsel. On the other hand, there is much information that local counsel simply does not need. Providing too much extraneous information could send local counsel on a "wild goose chase" or clutter his or her analysis with factors that are unimportant. A key role of the supervisor is to determine how much local counsel should be told in order to ensure that effective advice and assistance is rendered.

IV. OTHER ISSUES

There are various other issues that arise in connection with the selection and use of foreign counsel. Needless to say, it is important that all involved comply with their governing professional rules. Presumably, the client and its legal advisers will have a good feel for U.S. professional rules governing the rendering of advice and assistance in a particular matter. A grey area is whether and to what extent these rules have extraterritorial application. To be safe, the U.S.-based firm should probably ensure that its practice outside the country is in strict compliance with those ethical obligations imposed by the jurisdictions in which it operates in the United States.

Equally important is compliance with local professional and other rules. Indeed, the use of local counsel often is required by the foreign jurisdiction. A common requirement is that locally admitted counsel appear in any litigation. Moreover, in most countries only locally admitted lawyers can practice local law. (The precise definition of "practice" varies and can be fairly encompassing.) In many countries, only local lawyers can establish firms and hold themselves out as lawyers to the public. International counsel should be careful to avoid practicing local law if that is not allowed. Moreover, he or she should have some feel for local professional requirements in order effectively to manage foreign counsel.

An important consideration in this regard is that of professional liability. For a supervising firm an important self-help measure is to ensure that it has insurance coverage for malpractice in any matter under its supervision or management. This would include coverage for suit in other jurisdictions as well as in the United States. The policy should include coverage against liability in the event of suit for the international supervising lawyers' actions, as well as the actions of foreign counsel under its supervision.

Equally important is to verify local counsel's coverage. In some jurisdictions malpractice insurance may not be required. The extent of coverage will also vary. For the supervising lawyers, this is an important issue. If the local firm is inadequately covered, a plaintiff will have more incentive to proceed principally against the supervising firm in any malpractice action.

A final important issue is to clarify the respective roles and chain of command between foreign counsel and its supervisors. This is an important step in the effective management of foreign counsel and is critical to avoiding problems later on.

V. CONCLUSION

The selection and use of foreign counsel is not merely a matter of identifying a local firm through a directory or word of mouth, issuing instructions, and then waiting for the advice to come in. While some foreign firms are extremely sophisticated and can operate on this basis, experienced practitioners have found that there is no substitute for the active involvement of an international supervisor both before the matter arises and during the matter's pendency. The best results invariably occur where foreign counsel is brought in as a result of an established relationship and where international counsel plays an effective and ongoing role in managing and supervising the actions of all lawyers on a particular project. U.S. lawyers typically will do this in the United States when they bring in local counsel in matters such as litigation. There is no reason why it should be done differently when dealing overseas. Indeed, given the cultural pitfalls and risks the need for effective coordination and supervision is even more pressing.

Notes

[1] In this chapter, the terms "local counsel" and "foreign counsel" are used interchangeably.

INTERNATIONAL ARBITRATION PROVISIONS FOR EMERGING COMPANIES GOING INTERNATIONAL

Frederick Brown
Amy A. Meldrum

I. INTRODUCTION

INTERNATIONAL ARBITRATION is riding a strong wave of popularity. Approximately 40 percent of all requests filed with the International Chamber of Commerce in Paris ("ICC") since its founding in 1923 have been filed within the last 10 years. There were 747 arbitration cases pending before the ICC at the end of 1992.

During 1992, parties from 93 different countries were involved in new requests filed with the ICC. The issues presented are almost as diverse as the parties to international arbitrations. Claims in 1992 at the ICC involved foreign trade, agency transport or distributorship (41.0 percent), licensing, transfer of technology, high tech or technical assistance (23.6 percent), joint ventures or construction and engineering (13.7 percent), finance or management services (8.8 percent) and other (12.0 percent). (See Appendix A for a more detailed analysis of ICC filings.)

There has been a similar expansion of late in the number of arbitration fora which are available for international arbitrations. A partial listing of the larger associations appears at Appendix B. Individual states including California, Connecticut, Florida, Georgia, Hawaii and Texas have passed international arbitration statutes of their own, most following closely the UNCITRAL Amended Law on Commercial Arbitration (as adopted by the United Nations Commission on International Trade Law on June 21, 1985).

Established international arbitration groups are adopting their rules to the increasing number and complexity of international filings. For example, new rules for AAA international disputes were prepared by the AAA's World Arbitration Institute and were issued on March 1, 1991.

Even though international arbitration is popular, and increasingly so, serious and complex issues must be addressed before one should agree to an arbitration provision in an international agreement. Whether to agree to arbitration at all, of course, is the first question that must be carefully analyzed. The next, and equally important question, is what clauses should be included in an arbitration provision to best protect your client if arbitration is preferred to litigation. These questions are addressed in that order in this presentation.

II. INTERNATIONAL LITIGATION OR ARBITRATION: THE ANSWER IS NOT ALWAYS SO OBVIOUS

When drafting international business agreements, international business lawyers frequently assume that arbitration of international disputes is far preferable to resolving those disputes in court. While arbitration often does provide significant advantages over litigation, there are disadvantages, risks and complexities that must be analyzed on a transaction-by-transaction basis before advising a client to embrace international arbitration in an agreement, or to avoid it and to protect one's access to court. The purpose of this section is to examine the factors to be weighed in comparing international arbitration to litigation and to suggest that a rigorous analysis by counsel and client alike is mandated before an arbitration clause is agreed to in an international business agreement.[1]

Higher costs, clogged court calendars, procedural battles, publicity, the difficulty in enforcement of foreign judgments, abusive discovery, interminable pre-trial motions and the vagaries of judge and jury decision-making are often among the factors urged as the disadvantages of court proceedings and as compelling arbitration as the preferred method to resolve international disputes. An often unspoken but powerful factor is the business lawyer's understandable bias against resolution of disputes in court.

Often the assumed benefits of arbitration prove illusory. International arbitration may be as costly and lengthy as a court battle. The lack of firm evidentiary standards may prove problematic. The lack of appeal rights also may be a disadvantage. Proceeding with little or no discovery, depending on your client's likely position in the future dispute, also may be a negative consideration. The tendency of some arbitrators to issue compromise awards in lieu of applying the law may not be to your client's liking.

Some international business lawyers conclude that international arbitration's primary advantage is the lack of anything better. That conclusion and other considerations of international arbitration are examined from a litigator's viewpoint to see if the usual conclusion of the business lawyer favoring arbitration when drafting an international agreement ought to be re-thought and the analysis performed more thoroughly on a transaction-by-transaction basis.

General Considerations

Before analyzing the usually cited benefits of international arbitration, it is worthwhile to list some of the general considerations that should be reviewed before an arbitration provision is drafted for an international agreement:

- Who are the parties? Who is the likely claimant? In which jurisdiction will the claimant file in court?
- In what countries do the parties reside, conduct their business, or have assets?
- In what countries are the disputed goods or money?
- Where are the documents, evidence or witnesses, and who has greater access to them outside of discovery?
- Does security exist (*e.g.*, letters of credit or other guarantees)?
- What is the nature of the dispute? It is arbitrable at all?
- Do legal or factual issues predominate? Which issues are more important?
- What facts of the arbitration process favor your client's victory? What elements of litigation lean toward your client's prevailing?

Answers to these questions often have a strong influence on the answers to the questions that follow.

Is International Arbitration More Economical?

Traditional wisdom has it that international arbitration is significantly less expensive than litigation. From the avoidance of expensive discovery devices such as interrogatories and depositions if the case were litigated in the U.S., to the general lack of availability of pre-trial motions, many conclude that international arbitration generally is less expensive than litigation.

Litigation Discovery and Pre-trial Motions: A Double-Edged Sword

One must keep in mind, however, that discovery and pre-trial motions may narrow the issues for adjudication. Once the issues are more focused, the parties may be more likely to arrive at a reasonable settlement. Discovery often quickens the resolution of a dispute when embarrassing facts may have to be disclosed or when senior executives may have to devote their time answering oral questions under oath. Depositions of senior executives also sometimes draws the early attention of those executives to the dispute in ways not possible in the arbitration setting. Once those executives find out about the position urged by their juniors or their counsel, they sometimes inject more reason into their side's position which may lead to settlement, or at least a more reasonable approach.

In narrowing the issues, discovery and pre-trial motions also may shorten the time necessary for the trial. While litigation procedure generally is more time-consuming than arbitration when identical issues are presented, the trial of a single, focused issue may be far shorter than an arbitration hearing of a laundry list of issues not narrowed through discovery and pre-trial motions.

By winning a motion for summary judgment in court, a party may avoid an evidentiary hearing altogether. Nothing, of course, prevents parties from agreeing to summary judgment motions in an arbitration setting, but such a procedure is a rarity in arbitration.

Motions in limine in litigation also may shorten and thus render less expensive a trial. Such motions, generally not available in arbitrations where arbitrators tend to let almost all information be presented even if of a relatively low level of evidentiary value, may narrow the scope of permissible evidence and decrease the length of the trial.

Another advantage that litigation discovery and pre-trial motions have over arbitration procedures is that each side generally is able to learn the facts and the law relied upon by the opposition. That process encourages more realistic settlement evaluation. It also permits a more focused defense or offense at trial and sometimes a shorter proceeding than if arbitration proceedings were utilized. Going to arbitration prepared to defend against a myriad of unnarrowed claims based on undisclosed facts in reliance upon as yet unshared legal theories can be a very cumbersome and expensive process.

Arbitration and Counsel Fees: A Double or Triple Whammy

Adding significantly to the expense of arbitration is the expanding trend of paying the full hourly rates of seasoned professionals who serve as the arbitrator or arbitrators. Where a panel of three or more arbitrators is used, paying each decision-maker $250-$300 or more an hour can significantly increase the cost of the dispute. For example, an eight-week arbitration, with a panel of three arbitrators paid their usual hourly rate, was reported to have cost over $275,000 in arbitrators' fees alone. That sum could have been avoided if publicly-appointed judges or juries had been used.

If an administered arbitration is chosen, the fees of the arbitration agency, such as the ICC or the AAA also must be considered. Those fees can be quite high.

Counsel fees, too, can skyrocket in international arbitration if, because of the arbitrators' other commitments, consecutive sessions cannot be scheduled through the conclusion of the hearing and instead are held a day here, another there, two days here and so on, over many months. Not only does that require counsel to reorganize and reprepare for long separated sessions, but witness preparation, travel and the like may have to be repeated sending the costs yet higher and increasing the inconvenience. Moreover, long separated sessions stimulate repetitive presentations and the development of new facts and theories between sessions, suggesting more work and the higher costs which necessarily follow.

An Open Question

One cannot overlook the benefits of avoiding abusive discovery or interminable motions either. The expense of those litigation devices all too often outstrips any gains from their use and frequently compels the conclusion that arbitration is more economical. For some economically powerful parties, and even sometimes for those not so strong, the threat of expensive litigation may benefit one's litigation strategy and be seen as an advantage over the adversary. It is sufficient here to caution that what may be generally assumed true is not always so and the expense issue must be carefully analyzed each time one must choose between international arbitration and litigation.

Is International Arbitration More Expeditious?

Court calendars in many jurisdictions are overwhelmed with criminal trials, mass-tort claims and other matters such that it often takes years of waiting to be assigned a date for trial. In master calendar systems such as those prevalent in some state courts, litigants may be set for trial multiple times, each time counsel having to march to court with documents and witnesses fully prepared to proceed to trial, and each time being sent home after days of waiting for a judge to be assigned.

Overburdened Arbitration Fora

While similar experiences are generally avoidable in arbitration, it is not at all unusual to experience significant delays because of arbitration agencies being overburdened, the difficulties of scheduling experienced arbitrators most sought after by disputants, and the inevitable scheduling conflicts experienced if multiple arbitrators from multiple countries are used.

Unfocused Hearings, Language and Other Issues

Once started, international arbitration hearings may be longer than trials because no discovery or pre-trial motions are available to narrow or focus the issues. These matters are discussed above on the comparative costs of international arbitration and litigation. If the arbitration agreement provides for dual language proceedings this can add to the length and cost of the hearing. Even where one language is selected, but where multi-lingual arbitrators of different first languages are used, often counsels' presentations are slower paced so that the non-native speakers do not miss important nuances of the testimony, questions, or documents.

Who Wants a Quick Result?

Even if international arbitrations can be concluded more quickly, is that an advantage to your client? There are some situations when a prolonged decision-making process is a distinct advantage to your client and a dramatic disadvantage to your opponent. For example, if you represent a large, prosperous company, you may retain leverage over your less well-financed opponent if the threat of prolonged litigation is present.

A careful evaluation of whether international arbitration or litigation is faster and whether speed is an advantage or a detriment to your client is in order whenever you recommend one resolution process over the other.

Are International Arbitrators Better Equipped Than Judges or Juries to Decide Issues of Complicated, Commercial International Disputes?

An often cited advantage of international arbitration is that the parties can select experts familiar with the subject matter to decide their dispute. But these substantive experts are rarely experts at judging credibility, evaluating evidence, guaranteeing due process, or reigning in pugilistic counsel. Nor do they regularly exercise the myriad of other Solomon-like qualities only developed over a long judicial career, if ever.

Judges not familiar with technical areas of international finance, international intellectual property, or the like always have the opportunity to seek the advice of court appointed experts. *See*, *e.g.*, Rule 706, Federal Rules of Evidence. Also, special tribunals such as the U.S. Court of International Trade or at the appellate level, the Federal Circuit Court of Appeals, may provide sufficient substantive expertise.

Is This Dispute Better Decided by a Professional Judge?

Some disputes for some litigants are best decided before juries or judges. Issues of fairness or equity, bad faith, credibility, public policy and similar issues may, in some situations, best be decided for your client before a judge or jury rather than before a technical expert who may be more concerned with principles of engineering than with more fundamental human values. Also, if the potential dispute likely will involve important issues of law, perhaps a judge bound by precedent and trained in the application and interpretation of the law is the best choice.

Where truthfulness is at issue, an imposing federal or state court judge, or the eyes of multiple jurors, may be able to ferret out the truth far better than an arbitrator. Faced with the threat of perjury for false testimony, a witness may be more candid in an imposing courtroom setting than in a less formal conference room setting often used for international arbitrations.

How Important Is Neutrality?

The neutrality of the decision-maker generally is assumed in court, but the same presumption does not always operate in international arbitrations. Indeed, there is an ongoing debate on the meaning or need for "neutrality" in international arbitrations for party-appointed arbitrations. The American Bar Association's House of Delegates at its mid-Year Meeting in February 1990, for the first time approved amendments to the ABA-AAA Code of Ethics for Arbitrators in Commercial Disputes "to provide that, unless otherwise agreed, party appointed arbitrators in international commercial arbitrations should, to the extent practicable in the circumstances, serve as neutrals."

Ethics: A Troublesome Issue

General ethical considerations also may be new to some arbitrators in international arbitrations. That is not to say that they may be any less honorable than judges. They are simply not so accustomed to thinking about and reacting to issues that call for ethical considerations and actions. Recent debate and guidelines issued by international organizations do help in this regard. For example, the International Bar Association (IBA) issued in 1987 a document titled "Ethics for International Arbitrators" requiring arbitrators to be "impartial, independent, competent, diligent, and discreet." Those ethics guidelines also require that prospective arbitrators disclose any current business relationships with a party, any past relationships "if of more than a trivial nature," any substantial social relationships with a party or likely witness, and any prior service with a fellow arbitrator. The guidelines also prohibit *ex-parte* communication between an arbitrator and any party during the proceedings. Moreover, "[n]o arbitrator should accept any gift or substantial hospitality, directly or indirectly, from any party to the arbitration. Sole arbitrators and presiding arbitrators should be particularly meticulous in avoiding significant social or professional contacts with any party to the arbitration other than in the presence of the other parties."

Is Litigation Less Flexible Than Arbitration?

With litigation rules of procedure written for a broad array of cases from slip-and-fall to major antitrust cases, many have criticized litigation for its formula approach which sometimes does not fit the dispute at hand. One often discovers, however, how clever counsel can work the rules of evidence or civil procedure to accommodate the peculiarities of the issues presented. And these sometimes arcane rules, which can be utilized well by experienced trial counsel, give experienced counsel a decided advantage over the less prepared or less experienced advocate who sees rules only as roadblocks.

Because arbitration is a consensual matter frequently agreed to through detailed contractual clauses, the parties are free to, and often do, design custom procedures to fit their particular needs. Arbitration agencies such as the ICC also are active in creating novel approaches such as the ICC's "Pre-Arbitral Referee Procedure" designed for rapid, short notice intervention, generally mid-contract, by a referee empowered to order provisional remedies needed as a matter of urgency.

Can Your Client Select His Favorite Advocate to Represent Him in an International Arbitration?

In some jurisdictions, a lawyer who is not a member of a local bar may be prohibited by that country's laws to act as counsel. The inability for some clients to have their usual counsel represent them in the arbitration may be a disadvantage so overwhelming that the client would choose litigation in his home jurisdiction instead.

Some jurisdictions, in fact most, do not require that a lawyer represent a party. It necessarily follows that if a party in such a venue chooses to be represented by counsel, that choice is not limited to a lawyer admitted locally.

Sometimes a written power of attorney is required by local or arbitration rules, no matter what the representative's nationality or professional status may be. (*e.g.,* Argentina, Austria, Greece). The Netherlands, among others, requires such a document of non-lawyer representatives. The arbitrators in Italy, Denmark and in the London Court of International Arbitration may require such proof of legitimate representative status.

Arbitration associations, such as the Korean Commercial Arbitration Board, may decide a party's representative is not a proper one. Trade associations also may restrict a lawyer's access to representation.

Some countries require that parties be represented by lawyers but do not require admission to the local bar. Indonesia, Israel, Saudi Arabia and Spain have such laws.

Two countries stand out as the most restrictive on a party's right to select counsel, Japan and Singapore. Both require that locally admitted lawyers be representatives. This situation may be changing quickly and should be checked periodically.

The chart attached as Appendix D summarizes the restrictions in representation in a number of significant jurisdictions.

How Important Is the Right of Appeal?

Time and money may be saved in international arbitration where access to appellate court review generally is restricted. While saving time and money are laudable goals, those savings may be at a significant sacrifice. One only need experience a single errant arbitration award which ignores settled case law and imposes an award based on facts which do not exist, or at least were never presented as evidence at the arbitration hearing, to realize the time value of appellate review.

Without appellate court review, there is no guarantee that the arbitrators will pay any attention to settled law, the very law on which your client based his actions, and on which you founded your advice on the correct course of conduct. Arbitrators, except in limited situations, may not be constrained by the law. And for those arbitrators who issue no opinion explaining their award, there often is no sure way to understand whether they followed the law or simply ignored it.

With the increasing complexity of arbitration, the expanding reach of the issues subject to arbitration (RICO, securities, antitrust, for example) and the broadening of the types of damages awarded, including punitive damages in some jurisdictions, the right to appellate judicial review likewise may increase in importance.

A vital consideration in measuring the importance of appellate judicial review is whether facts or law may predominate in the expected dispute. Facts generally receive less judicial scrutiny, even where judicial review is guaranteed.

If legal issues are at the center of your client's expected case and conformity with legal procedure is important to your client, the savings in cost and time generally thought to accompany arbitration may be too high a price to pay to sacrifice appellate judicial review.

To Which Arbitration Forum are You Comparing Litigation? Litigation Where?

A critical element of any comparison of litigation and arbitration is the arbitration forum or rules against which you are measuring litigation. Several fora are, of course, available. Ad hoc arbitration, too, is an alternative. Appendix C attempts to summarize in chart form the salient features of some of the frequently used rules and fora for arbitration against which the advantages and disadvantages of litigation may be measured.

Of course, just as one must know the rules of the arbitration fora before a proper comparison may be made, one must also know the rules of the situs of litigation against which arbitration is being compared. One might come to a wholly different conclusion if the choice is the courts of Iraq rather than the federal courts in the United States. One of the many issues to consider here is whether the local jurisdiction follows the common law or civil law. Civil law countries, of course, allow little discovery, follow an inquisitorial method of examination at trial by the judge, empanel juries only in highly specialized circumstances, greatly limit the role of lawyers at hearings and proscribe third-party witness contact interviews outside of the courtroom.

Conclusion

Arbitration, especially in the context of international disputes, is a very productive way to resolve differences. There are situations, however, in which one party may give up significant strategic advantages if he were to waive his right to litigate and agree to arbitrate. The right decision for your client faced with choosing litigation or arbitration, as with so many other decisions, must be made on a transaction-by-transaction basis after a vigorous analysis of all factors.

III. DRAFTING THE BEST ARBITRATION PROVISION FOR YOUR CLIENT

Once the decision is made that international arbitration is appropriate for future disputes which may arise between your client and its international partner, what contract clauses should one negotiate to be included in the overall agreement? Sloppy drafting or insufficient consideration can lead to disaster. Unfortunately, too little consideration is given to the arbitration provisions. They often are inserted at the last minute without sufficient analysis and after the client's negotiating ammunition already is expended on seemingly more important business points. Who, after all, wants to talk about a possible divorce before the wedding takes place?

To make sure that all issues are fully analyzed from all perspectives, international business lawyers should involve litigators in formulating the international litigation or arbitration strategy and in determining which arbitration clauses in international agreements are necessary to best protect the client.

In drafting the international arbitration provisions one should address at least the following issues:

• scope of the arbitrator's authority

- place of the hearing
- language of the hearing
- selection of arbitration rules and arbitration forum
- number of arbitrators
- method of arbitrator selection
- governing substantive and procedural law
- discovery rights
- form, timing, and currency of the award
- interest, costs, and attorneys' fees
- judicial review
- enforcement of award
- waiver of sovereign immunity if a government is a party

Scope of Disputes Submitted

Parties have wide latitude in deciding which issues they wish to assign to arbitration. Some issues, of course, are not arbitrable in some jurisdictions because of statutory or public policy constraints. Putting those barred issues aside, the scope provisions may be as broad or as narrow as the parties design them to be.

Standard Clauses

Several arbitration groups have "standard" clauses which they recommend. The standard clause under the UNCITRAL Arbitration Rules is as follows:

"Any dispute, controversy, or claim arising out of or relating to this contract, or the breach, termination, or invalidity thereof, shall be settled by arbitration in accordance with the UNCITRAL Arbitration Rules in effect on the date of this contract. The appointing authority shall be the _____ (*e.g.*, the ICC, American Arbitration Association, the London Court of Arbitration, etc.)

(a) The number of arbitrators shall be _____ (one or three)

(b) The place of arbitration shall be _____.

(c) The language(s) to be used in the arbitral proceedings shall be _____.

(d) The law governing the contract shall be _____."

Other standard clauses recommended by the AAA, the ICC and others appear in Appendix C at C-1.

Reserved Disputes

If your client wants to reserve some potential disputes for the courts, those reserved disputes should be clearly set forth in the arbitration agreement. This is especially true since courts recently have taken a very expansive view of what disputes are covered in an arbitration provision. Disputes involving the nondisclosure of trade secrets or confidential information, or other disputes necessitating immediate judicial assistance in the form of a temporary restraining order or preliminary attachment may be included in a reserve provision. Consider, for example, the following:

> . . . except that: (1) disputes, claims and controversies concerning the breach or threatened breach of _____ Section concerning trade secrets and confidential information shall be decided by a court of competent jurisdiction in _____ ; and (2) no party is barred from seeking a temporary restraining order in jurisdiction involving _____. Where court action has been reserved, the parties irrevocably consent to the jurisdiction of the court of _____. The parties hereby appoint _____ as agent for service of process and waive the provisions of all international conventions on service of process (or other applicable service of process laws).

Extraordinary Powers

Sometimes parties may even want to provide for extraordinary powers to be granted by contract to the arbitrators. *Amiable compositeur* or *ex aqueo et bono* authority may be bestowed, although one should proceed in that direction only with great caution.

The Seat of the Arbitration

The seat of the arbitration is among the most important choices in drafting international arbitration provisions. Beyond the obvious significance for convenience of witnesses, access to evidence, and the like, lies the significance of the seat of the arbitration for enforcement of the award. Under the New York Convention on the Recognition and Enforcement of Foreign Arbitral Awards of 1958 (June 10, 1958, 330 U.N.T.S. 38), adopted by the U.S. and codified at 9 U.S.C.A. § 201 (Supp. 1988) (the "New York Convention"), the place or seat of the arbitration determines where it is enforceable, not the nationality of the parties. The seat is the formal situs of the hearing, and the first but not necessarily all hearings take place there. The arbitrators generally may conduct subsequent hearings where most convenient to the parties, witnesses, or themselves. The award is rendered at the seat.

Where the New York Convention does not apply, other treaties may, including the World Bank's Convention on the Settlement of Investment Disputes Between States and Nationals of Other States (March 18, 1975, 575 U.N.T.S. 159) ("ICSID Convention"), the U.S.-ratified Inter-American Convention on International Commercial Arbitration (Jan. 30, 1975, 42 O.A.S.T.S. 4) and the 17 or so bilateral Friendship, Commerce, and

Navigation ("FCN") treaties. Under the FCN treaties, the party seeking enforcement generally must satisfy three conditions: (1) the other party must be a national of the signatory country; (2) the award must be "final and enforceable" according to the local laws of the country of the seat of the arbitration; and (3) enforcement proceedings must be proper where filed. Usually these treaties provide that arbitration awards will not be discriminated against or rendered unenforceable because of their international aspects. While these treaties are not generally utilized in enforcement proceedings, U.S. courts have shown an inclination to interpret broadly their provisions in aid of enforcement. *See, e.g., Caneleggen v. Bayerische Hypotheken und Weschel Bank*, 357 F. Supp. 692 (S.D.N.Y. 1972).

Where no treaties apply, an award may be enforced by filing suit upon the award, *see e.g., Gilbert v. Burnstine*, 255 N.Y. 348, 174 N.E. 706 (1931), or upon a foreign court judgment confirming the award. California and fifteen other states have adopted a uniform act for summary enforcement of foreign country money judgments. *See, e.g.*, Cal. Code Civ. Proc. § 1713 *et seq.*

Procedural matters, too, may be influenced by the place of arbitration. Usually local law, in the absence of a contrary arbitration clause, governs compulsory process for third party witnesses, conflict of laws issues, appellate rights and access to the courts for provisional remedies such as temporary restraining orders or attachments. Whenever an unfamiliar jurisdiction is considered for selection as the seat of the arbitration, local counsel should be consulted to clarify local arbitration laws and customs.

A foreign lawyer's ability to represent his or her client in arbitration may be restricted by the laws of the chosen seat of arbitration. (See Appendix D).

Even selection of the neutral third arbitrator may be influenced by the seat of the arbitration. For example, ICC rules provide for recommendations from its national committees from the seat of the arbitration for selection of the neutral. That neutral's legal training — the common or civil law — may have a profound impact on the way the hearing is conducted and who wins.

Change of venue issues generally are not addressed in arbitration statutes and should be considered when drafting an arbitration clause. A sample clause follows:

> The seat of the arbitration shall be _____. If *force majeure* renders arbitration in _____ unreasonable in the discretion of the arbitrators, the arbitrators may for good cause transfer the seat of the arbitration to [or a neutral place of their choice.]

Change of venue clauses are usually reserved for situations where national disasters, war or civil strife make arbitration impossible at the chosen location.

Language of the Hearing

Choice of language is important for obvious reasons. The chosen language will influence the pool of available arbitrators. The ability of the arbitrators to understand the witnesses and documents without translation may be a central factor influencing who will prevail. Translation to one or more languages may be required, although it can add significant expense and complexity to the proceeding.

If the arbitration provision does not specify the language, the language of the contract or negotiations may be selected by the panel of arbitrators for the hearing. *See,* *e.g.*, AAA International Arbitration Rules, Art. 14; ICC Rules, Art. 15, ¶ 3; London Court of International Arbitration Rules, Art. 8, ¶ 1; UNCITRAL Rules, Art. 17.

Selection of Arbitration Rules and Arbitration Forum

Perhaps the most important choice to be made here is between an administered proceeding such as before the ICC, AAA or numerous other arbitration fora, and an *ad hoc* arbitration.

Ad hoc arbitrations generally are viewed as more flexible and less expensive but more difficult to design and conclude successfully. *Ad hoc* proceedings require more cooperation between the parties than do administered proceedings and thus should be selected with caution where great friction is likely. Of course, if one side is obstructionist in efforts to select the arbitrators or to initiate the hearings, a local court may be available to intervene to compel arbitration, assist with the selection of panelists, or to enforce the award after the hearing.

Detailed and thorough arbitration provisions are especially important in *ad hoc* proceedings because there are no agency or forum rules to fill in any gaps in the agreement. A thorough review of local rules is critical when *ad hoc* proceedings are contemplated because local courts may have to be used to assist in starting the proceedings or selecting the arbitrators.

If administered proceedings are preferred, the choice of fora is large and growing. A listing of selected agencies is attached as Appendix B. Among the more popular fora are the AAA, ICC and the LCIA. Each have their own detailed rules for proceedings and each act as an "appointing authority" under the UNCITRAL rules. (For a comparison of the salient rules of selected agencies, see Appendix C.)

Number of Arbitrators and Arbitration Selection

A single neutral arbitration or a panel of three arbitrators for more complicated cases usually are chosen. A single arbitrator usually means a less expensive, more expeditious and less complex proceeding. For large disputes, the single correct arbitrator may be impossible to agree upon and often a panel of three is preferred by the parties. AAA and ICC rules presume one arbitrator and UNCITRAL rules three arbitrators unless the parties agree otherwise. In the case of the ICC, the presumed number may be increased by the ICC if the dispute warrants three arbitrators.

In most cases with three arbitrators, the parties each choose a single arbitrator and these two choose the neutral third. Failing an agreement on the neutral third arbitrator, most agencies provide compulsory assistance in that selection. The ICC requests nominations of the neutral from the national committee at the seat of arbitration. AAA and UNCITRAL rules provide for the appointment by the administrative agency from a list previously sent to the parties from which they could have selected their own neutral third arbitrator.

If UNCITRAL rules are chosen, an "appointing authority" must be designated because UNCITRAL provides rules but no administrative functions. Often a court or an agency such as AAA or LCIA is selected in the contract as the "appointing authority" where UNCITRAL rules are referenced.

Where three arbitrators constitute the panel, final awards or other decisions generally are by majority vote. UNCITRAL and LCIA rules require awards by majority vote but permit some lesser procedural matters to be decided by the chair acting alone. Under ICC rules, the chair may issue the final award if no majority is possible. *See* ICC Rules, Art. 19.

Governing Substantive and Procedural Law

Arbitration rules such as UNCITRAL, AAA, and ICC allow the parties the freedom to select in their arbitration provisions the law which will govern their contract and resulting dispute. Such a choice of law provision should seldom, if ever, be left out of the arbitration provisions. The omission of a choice of law clause may add significant uncertainty and unpredictability to the outcome of a dispute, as the arbitrators must decide which law to apply before they decide the final result of the dispute.

U.S. parties often prefer U.S. law. Identification of a particular state's law (*e.g.*, California) is preferable where U.S. law is chosen. One might consider the following provision:

> The substantive, but not the procedural laws of the state of California shall govern except where a U.S. federal law would be applied by a California state court judge in which case that federal substantive law applies.

If U.S. law is not selected, most U.S. parties still prefer a common law based system where the legal concepts are somewhat similar to U.S. standards. Before any substantive law is chosen, especially a foreign law and most especially a foreign system based on civil law principles, local counsel should be asked to advise on a variety of dispute scenarios and their likely outcomes.

General principles apply as to when a choice of a particular law is allowable. Generally, there must be a sufficient connection between the parties, the contract or the dispute and the chosen law before the jurisdiction whose law is selected allows the application of its law despite the lack of connection.

As a result of a U.S. Supreme Court decision, *Volt Information Sciences* v. *Board of Trustees*, 109 S. Ct. 1248 (1989), it is important to make clear that only substantive not procedural laws are meant to be selected in the choice of law provision.

Discovery Rights

Discovery, as it is known to U.S. litigants, is not available in international arbitration unless it is guaranteed explicitly by the arbitration provisions. Foreign parties often are appalled by wide-ranging U.S. litigation-type discovery and a U.S. party may have a particularly difficult time negotiating what may seem to that party as basic discovery guarantees.

Under UNCITRAL rules, the arbitrators may require that the parties provide a summary of the documents and evidence to be used at the hearing to prove the issues asserted in the claim or the defense. At any time during the hearing, the UNCITRAL rules permit the arbitrators to require that documents or other evidence be shared. See UNCITRAL Rules, Art. 24. AAA rules also provide for disclosure of evidence. *See* AAA International Arbitration Rules, Art. 20.

AAA Rules require the parties to exchange witness lists and documents. AAA International Arbitration Rules, Arts. 16, 21. The ICC rules require submission of relevant documents with the claim or defense, but otherwise have no provision for discovery.

If your client is being asked to agree to an arbitration before the ICC or in a civil law jurisdiction where discovery is not the norm, strong consideration should be given to insisting upon a specific clause addressing discovery rights. A sample clause follows:

> For good cause shown, and after objections are considered, the arbitrators may compel: (1) the production of relevant, non-privileged documents or other evidence within the possession, custody or control of a party; (2) the inspection of any goods, real estate, samples or any other thing whatsoever if relevant and non-privileged; and (3) the disclosure of a list of witnesses who may testify at the hearing. The arbitrators may order the party seeking disclosure to pay the reasonable costs of the production of the information sought. Failure to abide by the arbitrators' production orders may lead to sanctions, monetary or otherwise, and if the disobedience substantially prejudices one side, the arbitrators may issue a total or partial award in favor of that party on the issue or issues to which that party was so prejudiced.

Form and Timing of Award

Written reasons explaining an award are not required of the arbitrators, unless the agency rules or the parties provide otherwise. AAA, UNCITRAL, and LCIA rules require the arbitrators to explain their reasons. ICC arbitrators generally issue written opinions so as to permit a more beneficial ICC Court review of awards, although opinions are not required under ICC rules.

The chances for a successful judicial challenge of an arbitration award are substantially decreased where an opinion explaining the award is absent. Also limited, however, is the opportunity for the parties to be counseled in their future conduct by an opinion planning their rights and obligations. Limited, as well, is the ability to make corrections to awards with computational or other errors.

The timing of the award also should be addressed in the arbitration provisions. If the parties desire an expeditious decision, a provision to that effect should be included so that unacceptable delays are avoided. If the parties desire to submit post-hearing briefs and a reasoned opinion is required. the time for decision should be linked to the receipt of the briefs (*e.g.*, a decision shall be issued within 30 days of the receipt of the parties' briefs).

Interest, Currency, Costs, and Fees

Interest, currency of award, costs, and fees should all be covered in the arbitration provisions. A lack of specification on these items may subject the parties to unexpected results. For example, outside of the United States, local law often provides for the losing party to pay the counsel fees of the prevailing party.

AAA and UNCITRAL rules permit the arbitral tribunal to fix costs and assess them as it deems appropriate, usually against the losing party. Attorney fees may be awarded against the losing party if a claim for those fees is made during the proceedings governed by the UNCITRAL rules. In ICC proceedings, reference is made to local law for award of fees and costs.

Judicial Review

For arbitrations governed by U.S. law, there is authority to support a contractual waiver of all judicial review of the arbitration proceeding if the waiver is clear and unequivocal. *See, e.g., Aerojet-General Corp.* v. *American Arbitration Ass'n*, 478 F.2d 248, 251-52 (9th Cir. 1973). There also is some authority that the parties can contract to grant greater judicial appellate review power than provided under the Federal Arbitration Act. *In re Fils et Cables d'Acier de Lens*, 584 F. Supp. 240 (S.D.N.Y. 1984).

If right to judicial review is not addressed in the contract, local law controls the extent and reasons for judicial review. In the United States, judicial review is limited under the Federal Arbitration Act, 9 U.S.C. § 1 *et seq.* Mere errors of law or mistakes of fact are not grounds for vacating an award. Rather, an award may be vacated on more narrow grounds, such as where the arbitrators exceeded their jurisdiction or engaged in misconduct by refusing to postpone a hearing upon sufficient cause shown.

If the arbitration is in England and one desires to exclude substantive judicial review, the following arbitration clause should be included in the agreement:

The parties hereto agree to exclude:

(a) The right of appeal under § 1 of the Arbitration Act of 1979 in relation to any award made by the arbitrators, and

(b) The right to apply to the High Court under § 2 of the Arbitration Act of 1979 for the determination of any question of law arising in the course of any reference to the arbitration.

For a more complete review of the scope of judicial review in a variety of jurisdictions, *see* Kolkey, *Attacking Arbitral Awards: Rights of Appeal and Review in International Arbitrations,* 22 International Lawyer 693 (1988).

Enforcement of Award

For any arbitration which may be subject to the Federal Arbitration Act a clause in the arbitration agreement should address enforcement of the award:

Judgment upon the award rendered in the arbitration may be entered in any court having jurisdiction thereof.

There is a split among the courts as to whether an enforcement provision is required to give a court jurisdiction to confirm the award under that Act, 9 U.S.C. § 9. *Compare Varley* v. *Tarrytown Assoc., Inc.*, 477 F.2d 208 (2d Cir. 1973) (judgment reversed where arbitral award confirmed because the court did not have jurisdiction to confirm the award where the parties failed to agree that a judgment of a court could be entered upon the award) *with Compania Chilena de Navegacio Interoceanica, S.A.* v. *Norton Lilly & Co.*, 652 F. Supp. 1512, 1515 (S.D.N.Y. 1987) (*Varley* called "highly questionable") *and Paley Assocs., Inc.* v. *Universal Woolens, Inc.*, 446 F. Supp. 212 (S.D.N.Y. 1978) (sufficient where AAA rules incorporated and contain enforcement provision).

For a more complete review of enforcement issues, *see* Mosk, *Enforcement of International Arbitration Awards*, Vol. 2, No. 1 California International Law Practitioner (1990).

Waiver of Sovereign Immunity

If the international agreement is with a government, issues of sovereign immunity should be addressed and waived for: (1) purposes of the arbitral proceeding; (2) enforcement of the award; and (3) execution of the award.

Alternative Dispute Resolution

ICC rules have conciliation rules which may be used by willing parties. Conciliation provisions also are provided in some state statutes which govern international arbitrations. *E.g.*, California Code of Civil Procedure § 1297.341 *et seq.*

Notes

[1] If there is a bias perceived in this section favoring litigation, that bias should be interpreted as that of a "devil's advocate" attempting to stimulate an active analysis of the issues in an area where current assumptions favor arbitration.

Appendix A
International Chamber of Commerce, Paris
Amount, Issues and Parties of ICC International Arbitration Claims

AMOUNT IN DISPUTES as stated in initial claims/counterclaims	1987	1988	1989	1990	1991	1992
(Percentages)						
Under U.S. $50,000	3.8	5.8	5.0	4.0		
U.S. $50,000–200,000	13.9	15.1	14.5	12.5		
U.S. $200,000–1 million	24.4	20.6	25.5	30.0		
U.S. $1 million–10 million	33.0	39.9	34.1	30.0		
Over U.S. $10 million	8.4	7.4	12.7	11.3		
Amount not specified	16.5	11.2	8.2	12.2		
NUMBER ON PANEL (Percentages)						
Cases submitted to 3 arbitrators	62.0	62.1	62.3	58.3	62.0	58.0
Cases involving 3 or more parties	19.0	22.6	17.8	21.0		
ORIGIN OF THE PARTIES (Percentages)						
Western Europe	56.4	57.1	56.2	59.8	63.8	58.4
Eastern Europe	3.7	4.2	2.2	2.3	5.3	6.4
Middle East	4.0	5.1	5.1	4.3	4.2	3.6
North Africa	6.2	4.3	4.4	3.0	2.0	2.8
Africa	4.0	5.5	5.5	2.2	2.1	2.6
North America & Canada	13.5	13.1	12.9	14.9	12.0	13.6
Latin America & Caribbean	3.8	4.1	4.4	2.3	3.3	4.4
Asia & Oceania	8.4	6.6	9.3	11.2	7.3	8.2

Appendix B
Selected International Arbitration Fora

1. Arbitration Centre of the Federal Economic Chamber (Vienna, Austria)
2. Arbitration Institute of the Stockholm Chamber of Commerce (Stockholm, Sweden)
3. Australian Commercial Disputes Centre Limited (Sydney, Australia)
4. British Columbia International Commercial Arbitration Centre (British Columbia, Canada)
5. Court of Arbitration of the International Chamber of Commerce (Paris, France)
6. Greek Arbitration Association (Athens, Greece)
7. Japan Commercial Arbitration Association (Tokyo, Japan)
8. Korea Commercial Arbitration Board (Seoul, Korea)
9. London Court of International Arbitration (London, England)
10. Netherlands Arbitration Institute (Rotterdam, Netherlands)
11. Quebec National and International Commercial Arbitration Centre (Quebec, Canada

Appendix C

AN OVERVIEW OVER THE BASIC RULES OF SELECTED INTERNATIONAL ARBITRATION FORA

Arbitration Rules: Issue:	American Arbitration Association (AAA)	California International Arbitration and Conciliation Code (CCP § 1297.11 et seq.)	UNCITRAL Rules	International Chamber of Commerce (ICC), Paris	Swiss International Arbitration Rules
Applicable Rules	International Arbitration Rules of the American Arbitration Association, effective May 1, 1992	California Code of Civil Procedure, Title 9.3, Arbitration and Conciliation of International Commercial Disputes, effective March 7, 1988	Uncitral Arbitration Rules, Report of the UN Commission on International Trade Law on the Work of its Ninth Session, 31 GAOR Supp. No. 17 (A/31/17, Chap. V., Sect. C (1976)	ICC Rules of Conciliation and Arbitration, in effect as of May 1993; Vol. 4, No. 1	International Arbitration Rules of the Zurich Chamber of Commerce in effect as of January 1, 1989
Standard Arbitration Clause	"Any controversy or claim arising out of or relating to this contract, or breach thereof, shall be determined by arbitration in accordance with the International Arbitration Rules of the American Arbitration Association." The parties may wish to consider adding: (a) The number of arbitrators shall be (one or three); (b) The place of arbitration shall be (city or country); (c) The language(s) of the arbitration shall be ____	"Any controversy or claim arising out of or relating to this contract, or breach thereof, shall be settled by arbitration in accordance with California's Arbitration and Conciliation of International Commercial Disputes Code, and judgment on the award rendered by the Arbitrator(s) may be entered in any Court having jurisdiction thereof."	"Any dispute, controversy or claim arising out of or relating to this contract, or the breach, termination or invalidity thereof, shall be settled by arbitration in accordance with the UNCITRAL Arbitration Rules in effect on the date of this contract." The appointing authority shall be the American Arbitration Association. The case shall be administered by the American Arbitration Association in accordance with its "Procedures for Cases under the UNCITRAL Arbitration Rules." Note-Parties may wish to consider adding: (a) The number of arbitrators shall be (one or three); (b) The place of arbitration shall be (town or country); (c) The language(s) to be used in the arbitral proceedings shall be ____	"All disputes arising in connection with the present contract shall be finally settled under the Rules of Conciliation and Arbitration of the International Chamber of Commerce by one or more arbitrators appointed in accordance with the said Rules."	"All disputes arising out of or in connection with the present agreement, including disputes on its conclusion, binding effect, amendment and termination, shall be resolved to the exclusion of ordinary courts by a three person Arbitral Tribunal in accordance with the International Arbitration Rules of the Zurich Chamber of Commerce." (Optional: "The decision of the Arbitral Tribunal shall be final, and the parties waive all challenge of the award in accordance with Art. 192 Private International Law Statute.")

(continued)

Appendix C (continued)

Arbitration Rules: Issue	American Arbitration Association (AAA)	California International Arbitration and Conciliation Code (CCP § 1297.11 et seq.)	UNCITRAL Rules	International Chamber of Commerce (ICC), Paris	Swiss International Arbitration Rules
Arbitration or litigation as a One-Party-Option		(As an additional paragraph to the chosen standard arbitration clause:) Instead of the provided arbitration, "X" may, at its own discretion, refer the dispute to the competent domestic courts. (Alternatively:) Instead of providing for arbitration, "X" may, at its own discretion, refer the dispute to the competent domestic courts *at its own domicile.*			
Number of arbitrators unless parties agree otherwise	1 arbitrator (Article 5)	1 arbitrator (§ 1297.101)	3 arbitrators (Article 5)	1 arbitrator unless it appears to the court that the dispute warrants three arbitrators. (Article 2 ¶ 5)	The President of the Zurich Chamber of Commerce decides whether 1 or 3 arbitrators are appointed. If the value in dispute exceeds SFr. 1'000'000. *or* it is a multi-party arbitration, there will be 3 arbitrators. (Article 10)
Place of Arbitration	AAA determines locale unless otherwise agreed or requested by one party without objection by the other. (Article 13)	Unless agreed otherwise: The arbitral tribunal determines the place of arbitration. Meetings and hearings may be held at any place the arbitral tribunal considers appropriate. (§ 1297.201-1297.203)	Unless agreed otherwise: the arbitral tribunal determines the place of arbitration. Meetings and hearings may be held at any place the tribunal deems appropriate. (Article 16)	Fixed by the Court unless agreed on by the parties. (Article 12)	Zurich, unless on motion of a party - the President of the Zurich Chamber of Commerce designates another place. Meetings and hearings of the Tribunal may be conducted in places other than the seat. (Article 6)
Applicable Substantive Law	The tribunal shall apply the substantive law or laws designated by the parties as applicable to the dispute. Failing such a designation by the parties, the tribunal shall apply such law or laws as it determines to be appropriate.	Unless agreed otherwise by the parties, the arbitral tribunal shall apply the rule of law it considers to be appropriate given all the circumstances surrounding the dispute. (§ 1297.281-1297.283)	Unless agreed otherwise by the parties, the arbitral tribunal shall apply the law determined by the conflict of laws rules which it considers applicable. (Article 33)	Unless agreed on otherwise by the parties, the the arbitrator decides which law is applicable. He must take into account the most appropriate law in view of the circumstances and bear in mind the provisions of the contract and the relevant trade usages. (Article 13 ¶ 3)	Unless agreed otherwise by the parties, Arbitral Tribunal decides the case based on the law applicable according to the rules of the Swiss Private International Law (PIL) Statute. If, however, application of the private international law of both (foreign) parties lead to a different substantive law, the case must be decided accordingly on motion of one of the parties. (Article 4)

(continued)

Appendix C (*continued*)

Arbitration Rules: Issue:	American Arbitration Association (AAA)	California International Arbitration and Conciliation Code (CCP § 1297.11 et seq.)	UNCITRAL Rules	International Chamber of Commerce (ICC), Paris	Swiss International Arbitration Rules
Applicable Procedural Law	Unless the parties or the AAA in its discretion determine otherwise, the cases in which a disclosed claim or counterclaim exceeds $25,000 shall be administered in accordance with Sections 1 through 52 of the Commercial Arbitration Rules.	Unless agreed otherwise by the parties, the arbitral tribunal may conduct the arbitration in the manner it considers appropriate. (§ 1297.191-1297.192)	Unless agreed otherwise by the parties or compelled by an applicable compulsory provision, the UNCITRAL Rules are applicable. Subject to these Rules, the arbitral tribunal may conduct the arbitration in such a manner as it considers appropriate, provided that the parties are treated with equality and are given a full opportunity to present their case. (Article 15)	Applicable are the ICC Rules and, where they are silent, any rules which the parties (or, failing them, the arbitrator) may settle, and whether or not reference is made to a municipal procedural law. (Article 11)	The procedure follows: a) The 12th chapter on international arbitration of the Swiss Federal Private International Law Statute of December 18, 1987 (PIL Statute); b) The International Arbitration Rules of Zurich Chamber of Commerce; c) The arbitration agreement and other agreements between the parties which are not contrary to the Statute and the International Arbitration Rules; d) The orders and decisions of the chairman and the Arbitral Tribunal applying the International Arbitration Rules.
Nomination of Arbitrator (general rule)	If the parties are unable or unwilling to select the arbitrator(s), the administrator shall appoint the arbitrator(s). (Article 6)	If the parties are unable or unwilling to select the arbitrators, appointment by the superior court. (§§ 1297.112 seq.)	If the parties are unable or unwilling to select the arbitrators, arbitrators are appointed by the agreed upon appointing authority. If no appointing authority has been agreed upon, either party may request the Secretary-General of the Permanent Court of Arbitration at The Hague to designate an appointing authority. (Article 6)	If the parties are unable or unwilling to select the arbitrator(s), the Court of Arbitration appoints or confirms the appointment of the arbitrator(s). (Article 2)	If the parties are unable or unwilling to select the arbitrator(s), the President of the Zurich Chamber of Commerce appoints the arbitrator(s) or the chairman from a permanent Arbitral Tribunal panel. (Article 11)
Costs:	Who Pays?	Who Pays?	Who Pays?	Who Pays?	Who Pays?

(continued)

Appendix C (continued)

Arbitration Rules: Issue:	American Arbitration Association (AAA)	California International Arbitration and Conciliation Code (CCP § 1297.11 et seq.)	UNCITRAL Rules	International Chamber of Commerce (ICC), Paris	Swiss International Arbitration Rules
Cost elements: -Administrative Costs		Unless agreed otherwise by the parties, the costs are at the discretion of the arbitral tribunal and may include-any administration fees, if any;	The arbitral tribunal fixes the costs with respect of all cost elements. The costs shall, in principle, be borne by the unsuccessful party. However, costs for legal presentation and assistance can only be awarded if such costs were claimed during the arbitral proceedings, and the tribunal remains free to determine which party shall bear such costs and whether the amount claimed is reasonable. (Article 38–40)	The arbitrator fixes the costs of the arbitration and decides which of the parties shall bear the costs or in what proportions the costs shall be borne by the parties with respect to all four cost elements. (Article 20) Unless the parties agree on a cost bearing mechanism, the arbitrators may - if provided in the Terms of Reference - rely on supplementary applicable municipal provisions of civil procedure or will base the decision on their civil law or common law background, *i.e.*, in the former case the losing party is likely to bear the costs in respect of all four cost elements, (including *court appointed* experts), whereas in the latter case the parties are likely to share the administrative costs and bear their own attorneys' and expert fees.	Unless the parties agree otherwise: "The costs of the proceedings are, as a rule, borne by the losing party. If no party wins totally, the costs are allocated proportionately. The Arbitral Tribunal may, for special reasons, depart from this rule, especially if the proceeding became without object or if a party caused unnecessary costs." (Article 56)
-Arbitrators' Fees and Personal Expenses	The arbitrators' fees are generally calculated per diem and unless agreed to by the parties, are subject to allocation by the arbitrator in the award;	-fees and expenses of the arbitrators;			

(continued)

Appendix C (*continued*)

Arbitration Rules: Issue:	American Arbitration Association (AAA)	California International Arbitration and Conciliation Code (CCP § 1297.11 et seq.)	UNCITRAL Rules	International Chamber of Commerce (ICC), Paris	Swiss International Arbitration Rules
-Attorneys' Fees	The parties pay their own legal fees independent of the outcome of the dispute unless agreed otherwise or a statute provides for fees to the prevailing party;	-legal fees and expenses;			
-Expert Fees	the parties pay their own appointed experts,	-fees and expenses of expert witnesses;			
-Cost of Witnesses, Translations, Etc.	parties pay their own witnesses and costs of translations, etc.	-any other expenses. And the arbitral tribunal may specify who bears the costs. (§ 1297.318).			
Procedural Systems Discovery and similar mechanisms	The AAA Commercial Arbitration Rules do not explicitly provide discovery devices. The Federal Arbitration Act or a state arbitration act control. At the request of any party, the AAA will make arrangements for the exchange of documentary evidence or lists of witnesses between the parties and for the arbitrator(s) to be provided with copies of the documents in advance of the first hearing. (Article 20)	The arbitration tribunal or a party with the approval of the tribunal, may request court assistance in taking evidence. Court subpoenas are available for witnesses. (§ 1297.271)	The arbitral tribunal may require a party to deliver to the tribunal and to the other party a summary of the documents and other evidence which the party intends to present in support of the facts at issue set out in the statement of claim or statement of defense. At any time during the arbitral proceedings, the arbitral tribunal may require the parties to produce documents, exhibits or other evidence. (Article 24).	The availability of pretrial discovery devices depends (1) on the parties' arbitral and other agreements; (2) on the legal system and whether it offers the judge sufficient flexibility; (3) on the willingness of the competent judge to make use of the flexibility that the law may offer.	The International Arbitration Rules do not provide any discovery devices. Unless excluded by the parties, the Arbitral Tribunal may order, on motion of a party, conservatory measures to secure evidence such as documents or witness testimony (if there is the danger that the evidence cannot be taken anymore in the ordinary course of the proceedings). (Article 28)

Appendix C (continued)

Arbitration Rules: Issue:	American Arbitration Association (AAA)	California International Arbitration and Conciliation Code (CCP § 1297.11 et seq.)	UNCITRAL Rules	International Chamber of Commerce (ICC), Paris	Swiss International Arbitration Rules
Evidence	The arbitrator shall be the judge of the relevance and materiality of the evidence offered. (Article 20)	The arbitral tribunal determines the admissibility, relevance, materiality, and weight of any evidence. (§ 1297.193)	The arbitral tribunal shall determine the admissibility, relevance, materiality and weight of the evidence offered. (Article 25)	The arbitrator decides whether to hear witnesses as well as the admissibility, relevance, materiality and weight of the evidence offered.	The Arbitral Tribunal is free in assessing the evidence. It takes into consideration the conduct of the parties during the proceedings, in particular a refusal to cooperate in the administration of proof. (Article 44).
Procedural Systems					
Discovery and similar mechanisms	The AAA Commercial Arbitration Rules do not explicitly provide discovery devices. The Federal Arbitration Act or a state arbitration act control. At the request of any party, the AAA will make arrangements for the exchange of documentary evidence or lists of witnesses between the parties and for the arbitrator(s) to be provided with copies of the documents in advance of the first hearing. (Article 20)	The arbitration tribunal or a party with the approval of the tribunal, may request court assistance in taking evidence. Court subpoenas are available for witnesses. (§ 1297.271)	The arbitral tribunal may require a party to deliver to the tribunal and to the other party a summary of the documents and other evidence which the party intends to present in support of the facts at issue set out in the statement of claim or statement of defense. At any time during the arbitral proceedings, the arbitral tribunal may require the parties to produce documents, exhibits or other evidence. (Article 24).	The availability of pretrial discovery devices depends (1) on the parties' arbitral and other agreements; (2) on the legal system and whether it offers the judge sufficient flexibility; (3) on the willingness of the competent judge to make use of the flexibility that the law may offer.	The International Arbitration Rules do not provide any discovery devices. Unless excluded by the parties, the Arbitral Tribunal may order, on motion of a party, conservatory measures to secure evidence such as documents or witness testimony (if there is the danger that the evidence cannot be taken anymore in the ordinary court of the proceedings). (Article 28)
Evidence	The arbitrator shall be the judge of the relevance and materiality of the evidence offered. (Article 20)	The arbitral tribunal determines the admissibility, relevance, materiality, and weight of any evidence. (§ 1297.193)	The arbitral tribunal shall determine the admissibility, relevance, materiality and weight of the evidence offered. (Article 25)	The arbitrator decides whether to hear witnesses as well as the admissibility, relevance, materiality and weight of the evidence offered.	The Arbitral Tribunal is free in assessing the evidence. It takes into consideration the conduct of the parties during the proceedings, in particular a refusal to cooperate in the administration of proof. (Article 44).

(continued)

Appendix C (continued)

Arbitration Rules: Issue:	American Arbitration Association (AAA)	California International Arbitration and Conciliation Code (CCP § 1297.11 et seq.)	UNCITRAL Rules	International Chamber of Commerce (ICC), Paris	Swiss International Arbitration Rules
Interim Measures: Court Ordered		It is not incompatible with an arbitration agreement for a party to request from a superior court, before or during arbitral proceedings, an interim measure of protection, or for the court to grant such a measure. (§ 1297.91)		The parties are free to apply to any competent judicial authority for interim measures.	Unless the parties have otherwise agreed, the Arbitral Tribunal may, on motion of one party, order provisional measures. If the party concerned does not voluntarily comply, the Arbitral Tribunal may request the assistance of the competent state judge; the judge shall apply the resident law of the state. (Art. 28 combined with Art. 183 Private International Law Statute).
OR Ordered by the Arbitral Tribunal	The arbitrator may issue such orders for interim relief as may be deemed necessary to safeguard the subject property that is the subject matter of the arbitration without prejudice to the rights of the parties or to the final determination of the dispute. (Article 22)	Unless otherwise agreed by the parties, the arbitral tribunal may, at the request of a party, take any interim measure of protection as the arbitral tribunal may consider necessary in respect of the subject matter of the dispute. (§ 1297.171)	A request for interim measures addressed by any party to a judicial authority shall not be deemed incompatible with the agreement to arbitrate. (Article 26)		

Appendix C (*continued*)

Arbitration Rules: Issue:	American Arbitration Association (AAA)	California International Arbitration and Conciliation Code (CCP § 1297.11 et seq.)	UNCITRAL Rules	International Chamber of Commerce (ICC), Paris	Swiss International Arbitration Rules
Language	Unless the parties agree otherwise, the language(s) of the arbitration shall be that of the documents containing the arbitration agreement, subject to the power of tribunal to determine otherwise based upon the contentions of the parties and the circumstances of the arbitration. The tribunal may order that any documents delivered in another language shall be accompanied by a translation into such language or languages. (Article 14)	Unless the parties agreed otherwise," the arbitral tribunal shall determine the language(s) to be used in the arbitral proceedings. (§ 1297.221-1297.222)	Subject to an agreement by the parties, the arbitral tribunal shall, promptly after its appointment, determine the language(s) to be used in the proceedings. (Article 17)	The arbitrator will determine the language(s) of the proceedings by taking into account all relevant circumstances such as the language of the parties and their Counsel and - in particular - that of the contract.	The Arbitral Tribunal determines the language(s) that must be used in written communications and in hearings. As a rule, the procedure is conducted in the language of the arbitration agreement. (Article 22)
Confidentiality	Unless otherwise agreed on by the parties, all matters relating to the arbitration or award shall be kept confidential.	Unless otherwise agreed by the parties, all hearings and meetings in arbitral proceedings shall be held in *camera*. (§ 1297.245)	Hearings shall be held in *camera* and the award may be made public only with the consent of both parties. (Article 25 and 32)	The proceedings before the arbitral tribunal and the Court of Arbitration are confidential.	All participants must keep the proceedings and the award confidential. Publications on individual arbitral proceedings by participants are possible only in neutralized form and with previous permission by the President of the Zurich Chamber of Commerce. (Article 51)

Appendix C (continued)

Arbitration Rules: Issue:	American Arbitration Association (AAA)	California International Arbitration and Conciliation Code (CCP § 1297.11 et seq.)	UNCITRAL Rules	International Chamber of Commerce (ICC), Paris	Swiss International Arbitration Rules
Conciliation/Mediation/Amicable Settlement	The Commercial Mediation Rules of the AAA provide the possibility and guidance for mediation.	Conciliation procedures are provided in Chapter 7 of the California International Arbitration and Conciliation Code. Note: "No person who has served as conciliator may be appointed as an arbitrator for, or take part in any arbitral or judicial proceedings in, the same dispute unless all parties manifest their consent to such participation or the rules adopted for conciliation or arbitration otherwise provide." (§ 1297.393) However, it is not incompatible for an arbitral tribunal to encourage settlement of the dispute and, *with the agreement of the parties*, the arbitral tribunal may use mediation, conciliation, or other procedures at any time during the arbitral proceedings to encourage settlement. (§ 1297.301)	The UNCITRAL Rules do not contain specific conciliation provisions.	The ICC Rules for Optional Conciliation provide for the appointment of Conciliation Committees to suggest terms of settlement to the parties. Note: In many civil law systems, participation as a conciliator does not necessarily exclude later participation in arbitration proceedings unless the parties have explicitly agreed otherwise.	With the agreement of the parties, the Arbitral Tribunal may, at any stage of the proceedings, seek an amicable settlement. If the parties have reached an amicable settlement, the Arbitral Tribunal, on motion of a party, issues an award embodying the settlement. If there is no such motion, the Tribunal issues a decision declaring the procedure closed through amicable settlement. Note: A motion for an award embodying the settlement is advisable for all enforcement purposes. (Article 45)

(continued)

Appendix C (*continued*)

Arbitration Rules: Issue:	American Arbitration Association (AAA)	California International Arbitration and Conciliation Code (CCP § 1297.11 et seq.)	UNCITRAL Rules	International Chamber of Commerce (ICC), Paris	Swiss International Arbitration Rules
Possibility of review	The award is final and there are only few grounds to vacate or modify arbitration awards in court. In general, there are three categories under which awards may be vacated: (1) arbitrator misconduct, such as corruption, fraud, or bias; (2) a showing that the arbitrators exceeded their authority; (3) the failure to meet statutory requirements of due process including awards that contravene public policy. (Article 28)	(1) A party may request the arbitral tribunal to correct any errors. (2) A party may, if agreed by the parties, request the arbitral tribunal to give an interpretation of a specific point or part of the award. (3) Unless otherwise agreed by the parties, a party may request the arbitral tribunal to make an additional award as to claims presented in the proceedings but omitted from the award. (§§ 1297.331/334)	Either party, with notice to the other party, may request - that the arbitral tribunal give an interpretation; - that the arbitral tribunal correct any errors; - that the arbitral tribunal make an additional award as to claims presented in the arbitral proceedings but omitted from the award. (Article 35-37)	The award is final and binding upon the parties. By submitting to ICC Arbitration, the parties have waived their right of appeal against the arbitral award insofar as this right may be waived by law. (Article 24)	The award may only be challenged: (a) When the Arbitral Tribunal was not properly constituted; (b) When the Arbitral Tribunal wrongly accepted or declined jurisdiction; (c) When the Arbitral Tribunal's decision went beyond the questions submitted to it, or failed to decide one of the items in the claim; (d) When the principle of equality of the parties or the right of the parties to be heard was breached; (d) When the award is contrary to public policy. Foreign parties may, by an express statement, waive fully or limit to one or several grounds their right of appeal (Article 49 combined with Article 190/2/3 Private International Law Statute).

Appendix D

Restrictions Against Use of Foreign Lawyers in International Arbitrations

	Counsel
1. No Restrictions	Argentina, Australia, Austria, Brazil, Bulgaria, Canada, Czechoslovakia, Denmark, England, Germany, France, Hong Kong, India, Italy, Korea, Netherlands, New Zealand, Norway, People's Republic of China, Poland, Sweden, Switzerland, Thailand, USA, USSR, Yugoslavia
2. Representative Must Be Lawyer Although Not Necessary To Be Admitted Locally	Belgium, Indonesia, ISrael, Japan, Nigeria, Peru, Saudi Arabia, Scotland, Singapore, South Africa, Spain
3. Must Be Member of Local Bar	Japan, Singapore

THE INTERNATIONAL CURRENCY OF ARBITRAL AWARDS: CHOOSING AN ARBITRAL SITUS

William W. Park

I. INTRODUCTION

THE CHOICE OF an arbitral situs that will enhance the international effectiveness of an arbitration award inevitably implicates a conflict between the parties' legitimate expectation that the arbitrators' award will be conclusive on the merits of the controversy, and a competing concern that judicial control mechanisms should be available to monitor the procedural integrity of the dispute resolution process. In the hope of attracting arbitrations that will generate income for local lawyers and arbitrators, the marketing strategy of some nations has included legislative reforms that create a more *laissez-faire* standard of review for arbitral awards.[1] The extent to which such reforms do in fact meet the needs of the international business community depends in large measure on whether national arbitration law preserves a right to challenge awards procured through fundamentally unfair proceedings.

As with so many matters of legal policy, finding the right level of judicial review requires a balance between finality and fairness. Just as business managers do not want re-litigation of questions of fact and law already decided by an arbitral tribunal, neither do they want a system of arbitral anarchy in which arbitrators are free to exceed their mission or to disregard basic norms of fundamental procedural fairness.

II. THE NEW YORK CONVENTION

The 1958 New York Arbitration Convention provides the basic legal framework that secures the binding character of international arbitration.[2] In its 90 contracting states, the Convention requires recognition of arbitration agreements and mandates enforcement of foreign arbitral awards. The Convention follows a territorial approach, covering awards rendered in a country other than the one in which enforcement is sought, regardless of the parties' nationalities.[3] Like many countries, the United States applies the Convention on the basis of geographical reciprocity only to awards rendered in another state adhering to the Convention.

A court of a Convention state may refuse recognition and enforcement of an award only on the grounds set forth in the limited litany of defenses enumerated in Article V of the Convention. These include several procedural defects that must be proven by the party resisting the award: *(i)* an invalid arbitration agreement; *(ii)* denial to a party of an opportunity to present its case; *(iii)* an excess of jurisdiction by an arbitrator in deciding matters beyond the scope of the arbitration submission; *(iv)* arbitral procedures not in accordance with the parties' agreement; and *(v)* annulment of the award under the law of the place where it was rendered. In addition, an arbitral award may be refused recognition by a court on its own motion if the subject matter of the dispute is not arbitrable, or if recognition and enforcement of the award would violate the enforcement forum's public policy. While the first five Convention defenses relate generally to safeguards against procedural injustice, the last two serve as an explicit catch-all for the forum's particular substantive public policy norms.

The Convention permits the forum in which enforcement is sought to deny recognition and enforcement to an award set aside by a court of "the country in which, or under the law of which, that award was made."[4] The Convention makes no distinction among the various grounds on which the award was set aside, whether for a matter as serious as arbitrator corruption or as parochial as an arbitrator's failure to state reasons.

The English version of Article V is permissive, stating that an annulled award "may" be refused recognition and enforcement. The equally authoritative French text is more forceful, leading some commentators to suggest that the French version prohibits enforcement of an award set aside where rendered.[5] While an annulled award might still be recognized under the enforcement forum's domestic law,[6] the New York Convention imposes no duty to enforce annulled awards.[7] To suggest an admittedly imperfect analogy from American Constitutional law, an arbitral award not protected by the New York Convention would be like a foreign judgment that did not benefit from "full faith and credit" under the Constitution, but might still be recognized on the discretionary basis of comity.

Convention defenses to recognition of foreign awards also may serve as grounds on which to withhold confirmation of awards rendered in the United States.[8] However, these grounds for non-recognition of foreign awards do not justify explicitly setting aside an award. This oft-ignored distinction between vacating an award and merely refusing to confirm an award is significant. The New York Convention permits refusal of recognition to awards expressly annulled where rendered, but not to awards that have only failed to receive court confirmation at the arbitral situs. For example, an award rendered in Boston might be refused confirmation there because it violates American "public policy," one ground of the defenses to recognition of awards under New York Convention Article V(2). However, the Boston court's failure to confirm the award does not uproot it internationally under the Convention, should its enforcement be sought abroad at a place where the loser has attachable assets. On the other hand, a court order vacating the award for fraud or some other basis for annulment under Section 10 of the Federal Arbitration Act would remove the award from the enforcement scheme of the New York Convention.

III.   THE ROLE OF THE ARBITRAL SEAT[9]

The New York Convention entrusts the place of arbitration with substantial power to enhance the global enforceability of awards rendered within its territory, giving them a worldwide presumptive validity sometimes referred to as an "international currency." An award will benefit from the Convention-imposed duty of enforcement only if the arbitral situs has not set the award aside. By the way it exercises its power to set awards aside, the arbitral situs can either uproot an award or vest it with presumptive international validity. In the view of many scholars and practitioners, this power either to enhance or to impair the international currency of an award carries with it an obligation to provide a judicial mechanism at the arbitral situs to control the arbitration's procedural integrity.

Judicial review of awards at the place where rendered traditionally has fallen into two categories: *(i)* full review on the legal merits, and *(ii)* limited review of basic procedural irregularities, including arbitrator fraud and excess of authority. The former model seeks to maximize legal certainty; the latter looks to ensure an arbitration's procedural fairness but not the correctness of its substantive merits. These two approaches will be discussed below in more detail as they apply in the major arbitral centers of England, France, Switzerland and the United States.

Recently a third paradigm for international arbitration has emerged, under which the arbitral situs does not provide any grounds at all on which an award may be set aside. Under such a total *laissez-faire* regime, even an arbitrator's fraud or excess of authority will not permit challenge of an award. In 1985 Belgium pushed arbitral autonomy to this limit with a provision that is mandatory for certain types of international arbitration.[10] Under Switzerland's conflict-of-laws code a similar exclusion of all judicial review is optional in some cases.

The Belgian measure is open to question. Awards rendered in Belgium continue to benefit from recognition and enforcement under the New York Convention. Therefore, winners of defective arbitral awards (for example, awards procured by a bribe) may try to enforce the awards wherever the loser has assets. Even if not ultimately successful, such enforcement attempts will cost the loser time and expense, and can hardly be reconciled with the fair operation of a private adjudicatory system. When the victim of procedural irregularities is the losing claimant, the results of arbitral autonomy are even more unfair. If denied the opportunity to have the award set aside where rendered, the unsuccessful claimant has no enforcement forum in which to contest the defective award, since there is nothing to enforce. Its only option will be court action or a second arbitration.

To illustrate, imagine that an entity which never signed the arbitration agreement was joined to an arbitration conducted in Brussels because of its relationship as parent company of the defendant. The parent will have no opportunity in Belgium to litigate the arbitrator's arrogation of jurisdiction. Nor could Belgian courts review errors on choice of law or arbitral rules. If the parties chose English law to govern the contract and UNCITRAL Rules to govern procedure, but the arbitrator nevertheless applied French law and I.C.C. rules, the loser would have to defend against enforcement of the award whenever and wherever it was later presented for enforcement.

IV. JUDICIAL REVIEW UNDER NATIONAL LAW

From the perspective of both the practitioner and the policy-maker, the goal of national arbitration law should be to provide safeguards for an arbitration's basic procedural integrity without permitting judicial meddling in the factual or legal merits of the dispute. Challenge of awards ought to be allowed on grounds of: *(i)* excess of authority by the arbitral tribunal; *(ii)* arbitrator bias, corruption or impartiality; and *(iii)* denial of one side's right to present its case. Each in its own way, the national arbitration régimes discussed below generally promote this policy of balanced judicial review by giving the victims of arbitrator unfairness a right to challenge in court an award rendered in a procedurally defective or irregular arbitration.[11]

England[12]

The parties to an international contract may conclude "exclusion agreements" that eliminate most judicial review of arbitration awards rendered in England, as well as interlocutory appeals on questions of law arising in the course of the arbitration. Absent an exclusion agreement, courts are empowered to hear appeals from an arbitrator's decision on matters of law.[13]

Even if the parties to an international arbitration conducted in England have agreed to exclude appeal, an award may still be set aside for arbitrator "misconduct".[14] English courts thereby have power to promote the basic integrity of the arbitral process. Court decisions have made clear that correcting arbitral misconduct will not serve as an excuse for back-door judicial tampering with the legal or factual merits of an arbitration,[15] in contrast to the practice before the 1979 arbitration law reforms, when the term "misconduct" was applied to a multitude of petty procedural omissions.

An exclusion agreement must be in writing. However, by reference to appropriate institutional arbitration rules parties may incorporate a valid exclusion agreement into the basic contract if such rules stipulate waiver of the right to appeal.[16] For example, arbitration rules of the International Chamber of Commerce (Article 24) and the London Court of International Arbitration (Article 16.8) both will operate as exclusion agreements.

Exclusion agreements concluded before an arbitration will not be valid when English law applies to the substantive merits of a dispute that relates to insurance, commodities, or admiralty matters. Parliament intended that commercial controversies should continue to fertilize the development of English law in areas in which it has long been pre-eminent. Nor will exclusion agreements be valid if all parties are residents or nationals of the United Kingdom, unless concluded after the dispute has arisen.

Under the supervision of the Department of Trade and Industry, the British government published a draft arbitration bill that would consolidate into a single statute the arbitration provisions now contained in several different acts.[17] The bill proposes nothing radically different from current law with respect to judicial review of awards. Agreements excluding appeal on questions of law would continue to be permitted in international arbitration, except for pre-arbitration exclusion agreements covering the "special category disputes" related to maritime, insurance, and commodities contracts governed by English law.[18] Notwithstanding an exclusion agreement, the High Court would still have power to set aside an award for arbitrator misconduct, which the bill now defines to include cases where "proceedings have been improperly conducted or a reference or award has been improperly procured."[19] The Court would not be authorized to set aside an award, however, if remission of the award to the arbitrators (a less drastic measure) would be appropriate.[20]

France

The French arbitration regime applicable to arbitrations that "implicate international commerce" is designed to promote the procedural integrity of arbitration but not to permit courts to second guess arbitrators on matters of law or fact. Article 1502 to the *Nouveau Code de Procédure Civile* permits an international award rendered in France to be annulled in the following cases:

(1)   the arbitrators decided in the absence of an arbitration agreement or on the basis of a void or expired agreement;

(2)   the arbitral tribunal was improperly constituted or the sole arbitrator irregularly appointed;

(3)   the arbitrators exceeded their mission;

(4)   the adversary principle (i.e., due process) was not complied with;

(5)   the recognition or enforcement of the award would be contrary to international public policy (*ordre public international*).[21]

Shortly after its promulgation the French decree was tested in a case in which a Hong Kong company had concluded a contract, signed by the Egyptian Minister of Tourism and the Egyptian General Organization for Tourism and Hotels, for a joint venture to develop a resort complex near the Pyramids.[22] It was uncertain whether the Minister of Tourism had bound Egypt as a party to the arbitration clause, or had intervened only in a supervisory and regulatory capacity. Opting for the first interpretation, the arbitrators rendered a $12 million award against the Republic of Egypt. The Paris Cour d'Appeal, affirmed by France's highest court, the Cour de Cassation, disagreed, and annulled the award as against Egypt on the ground that the arbitrator decided in the absence of a valid arbitration agreement.

There is nothing unusual about such court scrutiny of an award to determine whether the loser did in fact sign the arbitration agreement. What is less clear, however, is whether a judge should limit the judicial role to a minimal check on the arbitrators' possible distortion of the contract, or should engage in a full examination of all issues presented by a jurisdictional challenge.

Switzerland[23]

The Swiss federal conflict-of-laws code gives parties to international arbitration in Switzerland a choice between three regimes: (1) broad review for "violation of law or equity" under cantonal law; (2) complete autonomy, if the parties have concluded an explicit agreement to exclude court challenge;[24] or (3) limited court review for matters of procedural fairness under the federal conflict-of-laws code.[25]

If the parties neither elect cantonal procedure nor explicitly exclude judicial review, the code provides five grounds for challenge of awards: (1) irregular composition of the arbitral tribunal; (2) an erroneous decision by the arbitral tribunal with respect to its own jurisdiction; (3) an award beyond the issues submitted to the arbitrators, or the arbitrators' failure to decide claims within the request for arbitration; (4) failure to respect the principle of equal treatment of the parties or the right to adversarial proceedings (*"l'égalité des parties ou droit d'être entendu en procédure contradictore"*); and (5) incompatibility of the award with public policy (*ordre public*). Challenge to the award must be made before the Federal Supreme Court in Lausanne unless the parties have expressly agreed to substitute review by the cantonal court of the arbitral seat.

Review of awards may be excluded under article 192 of the code by an explicit agreement (*déclaration expresse*) if no party is a Swiss resident or has a Swiss permanent establishment. Because waiver of the right to judicial review of the award must be explicit, reference to institutional arbitration rules containing renunciation of appeal (such as those of the International Chamber of Commerce or the London Court of International Arbitration) will not be sufficient to exclude review. If the parties elect to apply cantonal rather than federal procedure, the Intercantonal Concordat permits judicial review of awards on grounds that include "arbitrariness," defined to encompass "clear violation of law or equity."[26]

The United States

A Federal District Court may vacate an award rendered in the United States on grounds that fall into three general categories: corruption, violation of procedural fairness, and excess of arbitral authority.[27] Contravention of public policy is *not* an enumerated ground on which a commercial arbitration award may be vacated under the U.S. Arbitration Act, notwithstanding the broad invocation of public policy in labor arbitration.[28] Section 10 of the Federal Arbitration Act permits vacatur of awards only as follows:

(a) where the award was procured by corruption, fraud or undue means;

(b) where there was evident partiality or corruption in the arbitrators;

(c) where the arbitrators were guilty of misconduct by refusing to postpone the hearing or in refusing to hear evidence pertinent and material to the controversy, or of any other misbehavior by which the rights of any party have been prejudiced; and

(d) where the arbitrators exceeded their powers, or so imperfectly executed them that a mutual, final, and definite award upon the subject matter submitted was not made.

The statute is drafted broadly enough to encompass arbitrator misconduct of the proceedings, for example by refusal to postpone hearings or to receive pertinent evidence. American courts can thereby annul awards when the bargained-for arbitral procedure was not followed by the arbitrators. The Uniform Arbitration Act generally parallels federal grounds for vacating an award, permitting vacatur only where an award was procured by fraud, or where arbitrators exceeded their authority, displayed partiality, or conducted the hearings so as to prejudice the parties' rights.[29]

In the United States as elsewhere, arbitrator excess of authority remains difficult to define. No bright line distinguishes clearly between an arbitrator's reviewable excess of authority and a simple arbitrator error which neither the parties nor the legislators intended should lead to re-litigation on the merits. A Supreme Court opinion handed down forty years ago contained dicta interpreting the U.S. Arbitration Act to include the right to challenge an award for "manifest disregard of the law."[30] A concept that is fuzzy at best, "manifest disregard of the law" clearly presupposes "something beyond and different from a mere error of the law of failure on the part of the arbitrators to understand and apply the law."[31] It might include an arbitrator's intentional disregard of the correct governing law, but not an honest mistake in contract interpretation. One federal appellate judge has suggested that manifest disregard of the law may be found only "where the arbitrators understood and correctly stated the law but proceeded to ignore it."[32]

The reluctance of American courts to set aside arbitral awards can be illustrated by a case involving arbitration under the rules of the International Chamber of Commerce arising out of a contract for exploration and production of petroleum in Indonesia.[33] Arbitrators sitting in New York prepared Terms of Reference stating that the arbitral tribunal would apply the 1975 version of the I.C.C. Rules.[34] One party had argued that the arbitrators were bound to apply the 1955 version of the Rules, which had been in force when the contract was signed and the arbitral proceedings commenced. The arbitrators concluded that the parties intended to refer to the Rules in effect from time to time, and issued an interlocutory award affirming the application of the 1975 Rules, which the New York State Appellate Division in turn confirmed. The Court reasoned that the arbitrators' result was rational, although it may not have been the result others would have reached. The court said it was for the arbitrators to determine which version of the I.C.C. Rules was intended by the parties.[35]

The final award ordering Mobil to pay royalties on gas and liquid hydrocarbons led to a federal court sequel in which the court was again called to distinguish between simple arbitrator error and reviewable excess of authority.[36] Mobil argued that the arbitrators had exceeded their power by essentially rewriting the contract between the parties. Although the contract provided for royalties on "crude oil," the arbitrators ordered Mobil to pay royalties payable on *all* hydrocarbons, despite the common sense meaning of the term "crude oil." The U.S. District Court for the Southern District of New York refused to vacate the award, finding it sufficient that the arbitrators' statement of reasons contained a "barely colorable" justification for the outcome.[37]

The UNCITRAL Model Law

The United Nations Commission on International Trade Law (UNCITRAL) has drafted a model law that strikes a balance between arbitral autonomy on the merits of the dispute, and court control of the arbitration's procedural fairness.[38] Adopted in 1985 for consideration by national legislatures, the Model Law on International Commercial Arbitration gives parties freedom to choose their procedural arbitration rules within a framework of judicial review inspired by the New York Arbitration Convention.

Article 34 of the Model Law permits annulment of an award for essentially the same reasons that an award may be refused recognition under the New York Convention. To secure annulment, the party making the application must furnish proof of one of the following defects:

(i) a party to the arbitration agreement was under some incapacity or the agreement is not valid under the law to which the parties have subjected it;

(ii) one party was not given proper notice of the appointment of an arbitrators or of the arbitral proceedings, or was otherwise unable to present its case;

(iii) the award deals with a dispute not falling within the terms of the submission to arbitration, or contains decisions on matters beyond the scope of the submission to arbitration; and

(iv) the composition of the arbitral tribunal or the arbitral procedure was not in accordance with the agreement of the parties.

Moreover, an award may be annulled at the place of arbitration if a court, even on its own motion, finds that the subject-matter of the dispute is not capable of settlement by arbitration or that the award conflicts with the forum's public policy.

V. CONCLUSION

From a legal perspective, the best place for arbitration is in a country whose judiciary will undertake to safeguard an arbitration's basic procedural integrity, but will not intervene to correct an arbitrator's honest mistake of law or fact. Finality in arbitration requires that the parties assume some risk that the arbitrators will render a bad award. This does not mean, however, that the losing party must accept an arbitrator's refusal to respect the terms of the arbitral mission, or that courts at the arbitral situs should ignore a fundamental discord between how the arbitrators were authorized to decide and how they in fact did decide.

The arbitral situs should be in a country that permits challenge of awards for; *(i)* excess of authority by the arbitral tribunal; *(ii)* arbitrator bias, corruption or impartiality; and *(iii)* denial of one side's right to present its case. Putting these basic principles into application, of course, can be problematic. For example, in an international dispute it is far from clear what it means to guarantee procedural fairness. Some aspects of the Anglo-American adversarial process, such as the right to cross-examine witnesses, probably should be considered an essential element to a fair arbitral hearing notwithstanding the divergence between different legal traditions.[39] On other procedural matters, however, the right approach is less clear. To the European business manager American-style discovery adds unfamiliar complication rather than comfort.[40] And to a merchant of any nationality, reference to malleable notions of public policy can raise uncertainty about how substantive legal norms are to be applied.[41]

As a matter of sound arbitration policy, judicial control at the arbitral situs should aim to promote the adjudicatory predictability necessary to permit informed decisions about the legal risks of commercial choices. The parties to a dispute as well as the public affected by an arbitration will be best served when private dispute resolution respects procedural safeguards designed to insure that arbitrators fulfill the shared expectations of those who entrusted them with their mission.

Notes

[1] The relationship between lawyers' fees and judicial review of awards does not yield to facile analysis. Appeals on the merits of an arbitration of course will provide work for some attorneys. On the other hand, a country's reputation for excessive court intervention in the arbitral process can scare away many arbitrations that would normally have required local counsel. During the Parliamentary debates in England before passage of the 1979 Arbitration Act, one member of the House of Lords estimated that this reform would bring England 500 million pounds sterling of "invisible exports," the euphemism for arbitrators' and lawyers' fees. 392 Parl. Deb. H.L. (5th ser.) 99 (1978). *See* William W. Park, *Judicial Supervision of Transactional Commercial Arbitration*, 21 Harvard International Law J. 87 (1980), at 89. *See generally* W. Craig, W. Park and J. Pamlsson, *INTERNATIONAL CHAMBER OF COMMERCE ARBITRATION* (2d ed., 1990), chapters 28 and 29.

[2] *See* generally A.J. van den Berg, THE 1958 NEW YORK ARBITRATION CONVENTION (1981). In addition, the United States and many Latin American countries have adhered to the 1975 Panama Arbitration Convention, which generally mirrors the terms of the New York Convention. European nations have also entered into the 1961 Geneva Convention for intra-European arbitration.

[3] As between American citizens, however, the United States will extend Convention coverage only to transactions with a foreign dimension. *See* 9 U.S.C. §202. The Convention's scope also extends to awards "not considered as domestic." One American case has interpreted "non-domestic" awards to include an award rendered in the United States in a dispute between foreign parties relating to a commercial transaction occurring principally outside the United States. Bergesen v. Joseph Muller Corp., 710 F.2d 928 (2d Cir. 1983).

[4] Convention Article V(1)(e). The somewhat ambiguous expression "the law under which the award was made" refers to procedural arbitration law, not the substantive law applicable to the merits of the dispute. *See* Bridas Sociedad Anonima Petrolera v. Int'l Standard Elective, 745 F. Supp. 172 (S.D.N.Y. 1990).

[5] The French text of Convention Article V(1)(e) states: "La reconnaissance et l'exécution de la sentence ne seront refusées . . . que si . . . la sentence . . . a été annulée ou suspendue . . . ." ("Recognition and enforcement will not be refused . . . unless . . . the award was annulled or suspended.").

[6] *See* Pabalk v. Norsolor, Judgment of Oct. 9, 1984, Cour de cassation, Cass. civ. Ire, Fr., 1985 REV. ARB. 431, with commentary by B. Goldman. *See also* 112 J. Dr. Int'l (CLUNET) 679 (1985), with commentary by Ph. Kahn. Austrian award based on *lex mercatoria* enforced in France notwithstanding annulment in Austria.

[7] Convention Article VII provides that its provision "shall not . . . deprive any interested party of any right he many have to avail himself of an arbitral award in the manner and to the extent allowed by the law or the treaties of the country where such award is sought to be relied upon."

[8] *See* 9 U.S.C. §207.

[9] Although not always co-extensive, the terms "arbitral seat," "place of the proceedings," "situs of the arbitration," and "place where the award is made" are often used interchangeably. The arbitrators may,

for convenience, hold hearings at places other than at the arbitral seat. For an intriguing English case on the arbitral seat, *see Hiscox v. Outhwaite, [1991] 3 Weekly L. Rep. 297, reprinted in 17* ICCA YEARBOOK OF COMMERCIAL ARBITRATION 599 (Van den Berg, ed., 1992); an award signed in Paris and deemed covered by the New York Convention was nevertheless held subject to English arbitration law.

[10] Law of March, 1985 enacting Code Judiciaire Art. 1717 provides:

Courts of Belgium may hear a request for annulment only if at least one of the parties to the dispute decided by the award is either a physical person having Belgian nationality or residence, or a legal entity created in Belgium or having a Belgian branch or other seat of operation.

The French text reads:

Les tribunaux belges ne peuvent connaître d'une demande en annulation que lorsqu'au moins une partie au différend tranché par la sentence arbitrale est soit une personne physique ayant la nationalité belge ou une résidence en Belgique, soit une personne morale constituée en Belgique ou y ayant une succursale ou un siège quelconque d'opération.

In cases where actions for annulment are permitted (*e.g.*, when a Belgian is a party to the arbitration), grounds for review include violation of public policy (*ordre public*), excess of jurisdiction, an award's lack of reasons, fraud, and violation of due process. *See Code judiciaire* art. 1704(2) (Laws of July 4 and August 8, 1972).

[11] As discussed *infra* at Section IV, however, the option granted under Switzerland's new conflict-of-laws code to exclude *all* recourse to courts at the place of arbitration is open to question.

[12] The provisions of the Arbitration Acts of 1950 and 1979 cover arbitral proceedings only in England and Wales. Scotland has its own arbitration regime, and has recently adopted the UNCITRAL Model Arbitration Law, discussed infra in Section IV-e. The Arbitration Act of 1975, giving effect to the New York Arbitration Convention, applies in Scotland and Northern Ireland as well as England and Wales.

As this chapter goes to press, the English are considering a new arbitration law, proposed by the British Department of Trade and Industry and discussed *infra* in text accompanying notes 17–20.

[13] *See* §1, Arbitration Act of 1979. On English arbitration law, *see generally* M. Mustill & S. Boyd, Commercial Arbitration (2d Edition); Adam Samuel, "Developments in English Arbitration Law," 5 J Int'l Arb., Sept. 1988, at 9.

[14] Arbitration Act of 1950, section 23.

[15] *See* Bank Mellat v. GAA Development & Constr. Co., [1988] 2 Lloyd's Rep. 44, 45 (Q.B.) (majority arbitrators refuse to convene further meetings at request of dissenter).

[16] Arab African Energy Corp. v. Olieprodukten Nederland B.V., [1983] Lloyd's Rep. 419 (Q.B.).

[17] Hereinafter "DTI 1994 Draft Arbiration Bill." The genesis of the Department of Trade and Industry bill can be traced to 1989, when the Departmental Advisory Committee on Arbitration Law (DAC), under the chairmanship of Lord Mustill, recommended that England not adopt the United Nations Committee on Trade Law (UNCITRAL) Model Arbitration Law, but instead adopt a new arbitration act of its own making. Subsequently a private working group (chaired by Mr. Arthur Marriott) and the Department of Trade and Industry, advised by the DAC (this time chaired by Lord Justice Steyn), produced a draft bill that was published in February of 1994.

[18] DTI 1994 Draft Arbitration Bill, § 33. In "special category disputes" exclusion agreements would be valid only if concluded after the beginning of the arbitration.

[19] DTI 1994 Draft Arbitration Bill, § 27(1)(b).

[20] The High Court's power to remit an award to the arbitrators is not circumscribed by any requirement that the Court find proceedings improperly conducted or an award improperly procured. Draft Bill Section 27(1)(a). In its commentary on the draft bill the DTI mentions the four traditional grounds for remission of awards (arbitrator misconduct, an arbitrator's request to correct admitted mistake, "procedural mishaps," and material fresh evidence discovered after the award), as well as recent cases evidencing what it terms a "retrograde" trend toward expanding the grounds for remission and thereby reducing the finality of awards. See Department of Trade and Industry Consultation Paper, pages III: 14–15.

[21] C. PR. Civ. art. 1502 (Fr.)

[22] Egypt v. Southern Pacific Properties, Ltd., Judgment of July 12, 1984, Cour d'appel, Paris 1987 J.D.I. (Clunet) 129; 1986 Rev. Arb. 75. *See* 23 I.L.M. 1048 (E. Gaillard trans. 1984). (Affirmed by Cour

de Cassation Judgment of Jan. 6, 1987), Cass. 1987 J.D.I. (Clunet) 469 (with commentary by Ph. Leboulanger), reprinted in 26 I.L.M. 1004 (E. Gaillard trans. 1987).

[23] *See generally* Marc Blessing, *The New International Arbitration Law in Switzerland, 5* J. Int'l. Arb. June 1988, *at 9;* Carlo Poncet & Emmanuel Gaillard, *Introductory Note and Translation to the Swiss LDIP,* 27 I.L.M. 37 (1988).

[24] Swiss Loi Federale de Droit Internationale Privé (L.D.I.P.) art. 192, permits exclusion of review only when both parties reside outside Switzerland. However, a party wrongfully joined to a Swiss arbitration on the basis of an agreement it never signed presumably would still be able to challenge the award under LDIP Article 192.

[25] Swiss L.D.I.P. Art. 190(2).

[26] Concordat Suisse sur l'Arbitrage, Article 36(f) permits an action for annulment of the arbitral award "where it is alleged . . . that the award is arbitrary in that it was based on findings which were manifestly contrary to the facts appearing on the file, or in that it constitutes a clear violation of law or equity." *See* Philippe Neyroud & William W. Park, *Predestination and Swiss Arbitration Law: Geneva's Application of the International Concordat*, 2 B.u. Int'l L.j. 1 (1983–84). On the *Concordat Suisse sur l'Arbitrage see* P. Jikusib, Commentaire Du Concordat Suisse Sur L'Arbitrage (1984).

[27] *See* 9 U.S.C. §10; U.A.A. §12; N.Y. C.P.L.R. §7511.

[28] The statutory foundation of labor arbitration lies in Section 301(a) of the Taft-Hatley Act rather than the Federal Arbitration Act. *See* 28 U.S.C. §185(a); Textile Workers v. Lincoln Mills 353 U.S. 448 (1957); United Paperworkers v. Misco, 484 U.S. 29 (1987); Michael Harper, *Limiting 301 Preemption*, 66 Chicago Kent L. Rev. 685 (1990).

[29] The grounds for vacating an award under the U.A.A., § 12 are as follows:

(1) the award was procured by corruption, fraud or under other means;

(2) there was evident partiality by an arbitrator appointed as a neutral, or corruption in any of the arbitrators, or misconduct prejudicing the rights of any party;

(3) the arbitrators exceeded their powers;

(4) the arbitrators refused to postpone the hearing upon sufficient cause being shown therefore or refused to hear evidence material to the controversy or otherwise so conducted the hearing, contrary to the provisions of section five, as to prejudice substantially the rights of a party; or

(5) there was no arbitration agreement and the issue was not adversely determined in proceedings under § 2 and the party did not participate in the arbitration hearing without raising the objection; but the fact that the relief was such that it could not or would note be granted by a court of law or equity is not ground for vacating or refusing to confirm the award.

[30] Wilko v. Swan, 346 U.S. at 436 (1953).

[31] Saxis S.S. Co. v. Multifacs Int'l Traders, Inc. 375 F2d 577, 582 (2d Cir. 1967) quoting San Martine Co. de Navigacion v. Saguenay Terminals, Ltd., 293 F.2d 796, 801 (9th Cir. 1961), the court refused to apply the concept of "manifest disregard." *See also* Amicizia Societa Navegazione v. Chilean Nitrate & Iodine Sales Corp., 274 F.2d 805, 808 (2d Cir. 1960). In one reported case, the court did strike down an award that did not "draw its essence" from the parties' agreement. *See also* Swift Indus. Inc. v. Botany Indus. Inc. 466 F2d. 1125 (3d Cir. 1972). In Sea Dragon v. Gebr. Van Weelde Scheepvaartkantoor, 574 F. Supp. 367 (S.D.N.Y. 1983) the court vacated an award that would have directed violation of a Dutch injunction ordering charterer not to pay debt to vessel owner.

[32] Merrill Lynch, Pierce, Fenner & Smith, Inc. v. Bobker, 808 F. 2d 903 (2d Cir. 1986).

[33] Mobil Oil Indonesia v. Asamera Oil Ltd., 487 F. Supp. 63 (S.D.N.Y. 1980). The New York state court decision is at 43 N.E. 2d 276, 372 N.E. 2d 21 (1977). Compare Inter City Gar Corp. v. Boise Cascade Corp., 845 F.2d 184 (8th Cir. 1988).

[34] Under the 1975 rules arbitrators clearly had power to order discovery apart from state or federal law.

[35] 56 A.D. 2d 339, 392 N.Y.S. 614, at 616 (1977); *rev'd on other grounds*, 43 N.Y. 2d 276, 372 N.E. 2d 21 (1977). Of course, one inclined to cavil might ask whether the parties' intent was as self-evident as the court suggested. If the Rules had been changed dramatically (for example, to permit the I.C.C. Court to modify the parties' stipulation of applicable substantive law) a reasonable person might conclude that the type of dispute resolution for which the parties had bargained was not being implemented.

[36] 487 F. Supp. 63 (S.D.N.Y. 1980).

[37] 487 F. Supp. 63, 65 (S.D.N.Y. 1980).

[38] *See generally* I. Dore, Arbitration and Conciliation Under the Uncitral Rules: A Textual Analysis (1986). The new Canadian federal legislation (which applies only to maritime matters and cases involving the federal government or a federal government agency) reproduces almost verbatim the UNCITRAL Model Law. *See* Commercial Arbitration Act, Act of June 17, 1986, 33–35 Eliz. II, Ch. 22.

[39] Continental legal systems generally provide for more "inquisitorial" proceedings than Americans are comfortable with. On cross-examination in arbitration, *see* N.Y. Arbitration Law § 7506(c) (McKinney 1980); Nestel v. Nestel, 38 A.D.2d 942–43, 331 N.Y.S.2d 241, 243 (App. Div. 1972).

[40] Foreign fears of extensive discovery may account for much reluctance to choose New York as an arbitral situs, even though courts in New York will ordinarily deny requests for discovery in arbitration. *See* cases cited in Stein & Wotman, The Arbitration Hearing, in International Commercial Arbitration in New York 86, 87–93 (J. McClendon & R. Goodman eds. 1986).

[41] In France and Switzerland violation of public policy (*ordre public*) is an explicit ground for annulling awards. However, both countries distinguish between policies applicable only to domestic disputes and policies relevant in international cases. While it seems clear in principle that parochial notions of public policy should be distinguished from broader norms applied to international transactions, there is little consensus on specific standards to distinguish these two types of policy. *See*, e.g., Northrop Corp. v. Triad Int'l Mktg., S.A. 811 F.2d 1265 (9th Cir.), cert. denied, 108 S. Ct. 261 (1987), confirming an award of allegedly illegal commissions for arms sales.

PART SIX

GOING INTERNATIONAL: AREA SPECIFIC SUMMARIES

GOING INTERNATIONAL IN CANADA

Edward J. Waitzer[1]

I. GOVERNMENT, LEGAL SYSTEM, AND BUSINESS ENVIRONMENT

Introduction

Canada is a federal state whereby legislative authority is constitutionally divided between the federal and provincial governments. Jurisdiction over some areas and activities is exclusively that of either the federal or provincial governments while jurisdiction over other areas will be shared. In addition, the provincial governments normally delegate specific powers to municipal governments. As a result, a business may be regulated at each of the three levels: federal, provincial and municipal.

In theory, Canada is a constitutional monarchy and the Queen of England is its official Head of State. In reality, however, it is a completely independent sovereign state having full international status. Governments are democratically elected at each of the federal, provincial and municipal levels and as the elections are independent, it is possible that the federal and provincial levels will be governed by different political parties. The major parties in Canada are, however, decidedly close to the political center and while it is reasonably common to have different parties in power at each level of government, this difference has not been particularly problematic. Canada is presently under the leadership of its first woman Prime Minister and a federal election is due to be held before the end of 1993.

With the exception of Quebec, all the provinces of Canada are common-law jurisdictions. Quebec is a civil law jurisdiction and derives its laws generally from the body of French law which led to the Napoleonic Code in France. Although the common, law provinces have strong historical ties to the British common law, American jurisprudence and legislative developments have also been influential with Canadian courts and legislators, particularly with respect to commercial matters.

In a referendum held on October 26, 1992, Canadians voted to reject a consensus reached by federal and provincial leaders which, among other things, dealt with the degree to which the Province of Quebec would be recognized politically and constitutionally as a distinct society, the process by which senate appointments would be made and the manner in which federal and provincial legislative powers should be divided. While public debate on these constitutional matters continues, federal and provincial political leaders have generally interpreted the rejection of the consensus as a mandate to put on hold the process of constitutional reform.

Canada has a stable political and economic environment and is rich in both natural and human resources, thereby providing an attractive forum for foreign investment. Foreign investors and businesses will find in Canada a highly developed industrial and mercantile environment accessible to and influenced by other industrialized markets.

As a result of the Canada-U.S. Free Trade Agreement ("FTA"), American businesses are provided with improved access to the Canadian marketplace and foreign investors in Canada will benefit from greater access to the U.S. market through their Canadian investments. The benefits of liberalized trade and investment may also be extended to include Mexico pursuant to a preliminary North American Free Trade Agreement ("NAFTA") reached between officials of Canada, the United States and Mexico on October 7, 1992. NAFTA is subject to legislative approval by all three countries and is scheduled to take effect on January 1, 1994. The FTA and NAFTA are discussed more fully at page 424.

Investment Canada Act

General

The Investment Canada Act (the "ICA") was passed in 1985, making the Canadian business environment more hospitable for non-residents. The Foreign Investment Review Act, the predecessor of the ICA, was based on a sentiment which favored Canadian economic nationalism and reflected the philosophy that no foreign investment should be permitted unless it could be shown that the investment would result in a "significant benefit to Canada". In contrast, the ICA significantly relaxes restrictions on foreign investment, encouraging any investment that produces a net benefit to Canada.

Reviewable Transactions

The ICA generally requires every "non-Canadian" investor to file an application with the Minister of Regional Industrial Expansion prior to making an investment if the investor proposes a direct acquisition of a Canadian business with assets valued in excess of Can. $5 million or an indirect acquisition of a Canadian business with assets exceeding Can. $50 million or assets valued between Can. $5 million and Can. $50 million if the Canadian assets acquired represent more than half of the assets acquired in the total deal. U.S. investors, however, are given substantially more freedom to invest in Canada by virtue of the FTA. For acquisitions made after 1992 by a U.S. person or a business controlled by a U.S. person, the FTA increased the threshold for review to Can. $150 million in constant 1992 dollars for direct acquisitions; indirect acquisitions ceased to be reviewable. The ICA amendments pursuant to the FTA also provide that the acquisition of a Canadian business under the control of a U.S. investor by an investor of a third country will be reviewed only if the higher thresholds applicable to U.S. investors are exceeded, making it significantly easier for U.S. investors to sell their Canadian businesses. The special rules for American investors will not apply, however, to investments which are termed "Sensitive Sector Investments" under the FTA, that is, investment in the development, production or ownership of proven reserves of oil or natural gas, the production of uranium or ownership of a uranium-producing property, or the operation of a financial service business, a transportation service business or a cultural business. The oil and gas industry is, however, opening up to foreign investment through industry reform unrelated to the FTA.

The ICA exempts from its application specific transactions involving securities dealers and venture capitalists acting in the ordinary course, government vendors, tax-exempt vendors, banks, the acquisition of government-owned or controlled businesses, involuntary acquisitions, the temporary acquisition of securities in connection with the facilitation of financing arrangements, the acquisition of a business in connection with the realization of security, corporate reorganizations, the acquisition of a business the revenue of which is generated from farming carried out on real property acquired in the same transaction and the acquisition of insurance company portfolios. Various other pieces of legislation may apply to transactions of these types.

A business is "acquired" under the ICA through the acquisition of control of that business. The ICA contains detailed rules for determining what constitutes a "business" when a new business has been established, when control of an existing business has been acquired and when an investor is "non-Canadian".

The ICA specifies several methods of acquiring control of a business; these are the only ways that control may be acquired for the purposes of the Act. Direct control of a business is acquired through the acquisition of all or substantially all of the assets used in carrying on the business in Canada or the direct or indirect acquisition of the voting shares of a Canadian corporation or the voting interests of a non-corporate entity carrying on business in Canada. Indirect control is acquired through the acquisition of the voting shares of a non-Canadian corporation or the voting interests of a non-Canadian non-corporate entity that controls directly or indirectly an entity or corporation that is carrying on business in Canada.

The ICA establishes certain deeming rules regarding acquisition of control. The acquisition of a majority of the voting interests of an entity, including a corporation, is deemed to be an acquisition of control. The acquisition of between one-third and one-half of the voting shares of a corporation is presumed to be an acquisition of control unless it can be shown that the investor has not in fact gained control of the corporation. The acquisition of less than one-third of the voting shares of a corporation is deemed not to be an acquisition of control. For entities other than corporations, such as partnerships, trusts or joint ventures, an acquisition of less than a majority of the voting shares is deemed not to be an acquisition of control. The acquisition of control may be the result of one transaction or event or a series of related or unrelated transactions or events.

Once the Minister has received an application for approval of a proposed transaction, a notice must be sent to the applicant within 45 days advising whether the Minister is satisfied that the investment will be of net benefit to Canada. If the Minister is unable to make a determination within the prescribed 45 day period, a 30 day extension may be granted. If the Minister fails to send notice in the prescribed time, he or she is deemed to be satisfied that the investment will be of net benefit to Canada.

In order for an investment to be found to be "likely to be of net benefit to Canada" it need only be demonstrated that, on balance, there is some benefit to Canada from the proposed investment. In making this determination, the Minister will take into account:

(1) the effect of the investment on the level and nature of economic activity in Canada;

(2) the degree and significance of participation by Canadians in the Canadian business and the relevant Canadian industry;

(3) the effect of the investment on productivity, industrial efficiency, technological development, product innovation and product variety in Canada;

(4) the effect of the investment on competition within any industry in Canada;

(5) the compatibility of the investment with national industrial, economic and cultural policies; and

(6) the effect of the investment on Canada's ability to compete in world markets.

The Minister will also consult with the government of any province likely to be affected by the proposed investment.

A decision by the Minister that he or she is not satisfied that a proposed investment is likely to be of net benefit to Canada may not be appealed. However, it remains open to the applicant to re-submit the application at a later time.

Notification

Investment Canada must be notified whenever a non-Canadian establishes a new Canadian business that is unrelated to any business already being carried on in Canada by that investor or acquires an existing Canadian business in a transaction that is not reviewable because it does not meet the thresholds discussed above. In such cases, the non-Canadian investor must give notice in the prescribed manner within 30 days of making the investment. The investment will then proceed without further government intervention unless it is in a prescribed type of business activity related to Canada's cultural heritage or national identity. There is no requirement for notice where the investment is simply an expansion of the non-Canadian's existing Canadian business or is related to a business already operated in Canada by the investor. A related business under ICA guidelines is generally a business the central purpose of which is the more effective operation of the existing business.

An investment in a business that is related to Canada's cultural heritage or national identity may be made subject to review on the order of the federal Cabinet notwithstanding that the normal thresholds for review have not been surpassed. The types of business activity which have been prescribed as relating to Canada's cultural heritage or national identity are:

(1) the publication, distribution or sale of books, magazines, periodicals, or newspaper in print or machine-readable form;

(2) the production, distribution, sale or exhibition of film or video products;

(3)   the production, distribution, sale or exhibition of audio or video music recordings; and

(4)   the publication, distribution or sale of music in print or machine-readable form.

The Cabinet has 21 days following notification of such an investment to decide whether to proceed with a review and to notify the investor if a review is to be conducted.

The ICA provides that where the Minister believes that a non-Canadian investor has acted contrary to the provisions of the Act, the Minister may send a demand requiring compliance. If the investor fails to comply with such demand, the Minister may seek court-imposed sanctions.

Immigration

General

While the federal government has primary jurisdiction over matters of immigration, the Constitution Act allows each provincial government to make laws in relation to immigration into that province to the extent that such laws are not repugnant to any federal legislation. To date, only Quebec has exercised this right.

Substantially all statutory matters relating to immigration are set forth in the Immigration Act and the Immigration Regulations. The Department of Employment and Immigration is the federal Ministry which is responsible for all Canadian employment, unemployment insurance, and immigration programs administered domestically or internationally. The Canada Employment and Immigration Commission is the administrative agency within the Department. The administrative relationship between employment and immigration services reflects one of the fundamental principles of Canadian immigration law: levels of immigration and the admission of foreign workers should not adversely affect labor market conditions within Canada.

Outside of Canada, the immigration program is administered through the International Services Group, a part of the Canada Employment and Immigration Commission, by visa officers located within most Canadian Embassies, High Commissions and Consulates in foreign capitals and other major centers throughout the world. An applicant is generally required to submit an application at the Canadian post abroad which is administratively charged with responsibility for processing applications from the applicant's country of residence. The time frame for processing depends on the country from which application is made. The waiting period for a standard immigration application submitted in the United States may be as little as six months.

Non-citizens and non-residents of Canada may be granted admission into Canada as visitors, immigrants, or persons present in Canada under the authority of a Minister's permit. The category of visitor includes anyone seeking admission for a temporary purpose. The provisions relating to visitors apply, therefore, to a non-resident wishing to come into Canada for a temporary period as an employee of a Canadian business enterprise, for example. The term "immigrant" refers to a person seeking admission for the purpose of establishing permanent residence. Minister's permits are used to grant admission in specific cases where the applicant would otherwise be inadmissible.

Temporary Entry

A visitor to Canada is required to obtain a visitor's visa prior to entry into Canada unless he or she is a national of one of the countries listed in the Regulations as being exempt from this requirement. There are more than 60 listed countries including, for example, the U.S., Mexico, and most of Europe. Whether or not a person is required to obtain a visitor's visa, however, every person who seeks admission as a visitor for the purpose of attending an academic institution or engaging in employment must make an application to a visa officer and obtain authorization to enter Canada for that purpose before appearing at a port of entry. There are a limited number of exceptions to the requirement of obtaining employment authorization. For example, a representative of a foreign business or government may enter Canada for the purpose of consulting with employees of a Canadian parent company, subsidiary or branch office, purchasing goods or services or selling goods other than to the general public without obtaining employment authorization.

Employment authorization must normally be applied for and obtained prior to appearing at a port of entry and the process can be time-consuming due to the requirement of obtaining Canada Employment Center approval. This process can, however, be abridged in certain circumstances. In particular, authorization will be granted readily at a port of entry and without Canada Employment Center approval where, in the opinion of an immigration officer, the employment of the applicant will create or maintain significant employment benefits or opportunities for Canadian citizens or permanent residents. This exception would apply, for example, to so-called "intra-corporate transferees" which are defined as:

> . . . persons in the senior, executive or managerial categories, carrying a letter from a company carrying on business in Canada, identifying the holder as an employee of the branch, subsidiary or parent of a company which is located outside of Canada and who seeks to enter Canada working at a senior, executive or managerial level as an intra-company transferee for a temporary period, for employment at a permanent and continuing establishment of that company in Canada.

In addition, the exception applies to self-employed persons who come to Canada temporarily to establish businesses for which Canadian citizens or permanent residents will be recruited or trained or whose temporary admission will result in significant benefits or opportunities accruing to Canada other than by way of direct employment.

Pursuant to the Canada-U.S. Free Trade Agreement ("FTA"), special procedures have been implemented to facilitate the entry of U.S. business persons into Canada. U.S. citizens who are categorized as "business visitors" "traders and investors" "professionals" or "intra-company transferees" can expect a more streamlined procedure for entry into Canada. Business visitors are defined as persons seeking to engage temporarily in the trade of goods or services or in investment activities within Canada as specified in the FTA. These visitors are either not required to obtain employment authorization or they may be eligible for "fast-track" procedures for obtaining authorization. A trader is a business person who is seeking entry temporarily to carry on substantial trade in goods and services between the U.S. and Canada and who will be employed in a supervisory or executive capacity; an investor is an individual who desires entry for the purpose of developing and directing Canadian operations of a business of a U.S. corporation in which he or she has invested or will invest significant amounts of capital. Professionals are individuals in specified fields who meet the education and experience qualifications appropriate to their professions as outlined in the FTA and who will continue to work in that profession while temporarily in Canada. Intra-company transferees, as noted above, are persons who have been employed by the same company for more than one year and who are coming temporarily to Canada to work as an executive or manager for that same employer or one of its subsidiaries or affiliates. Traders and investors, professionals, and intra-company transferees must obtain employment authorization but most prior approval procedures, petitions, labor certification tests and other similar procedures will be bypassed.

While the regulations respecting employment of non-residents in Canada apply equally to nationals of every country, they do permit citizens and permanent residents of the United States, Greenland and St. Pierre and Miquelon to apply for employment authorization at a port of entry rather than through a Canadian embassy or consulate abroad. In effect, this procedure reflects the frequency with which U.S. nationals come into Canada for employment purposes and the generally relaxed economic and social relationship which exists between Canada and her immediate neighbors. A resident of the U.S. who presents a valid "Confirmation of Offer of Employment" when appearing at a Canadian port of entry will generally be issued an employment authorization after standard questioning to establish medical and security clearance.

Permanent Residents

Individuals applying for Permanent Resident status in Canada are assessed according to selection standards which are designed to determine whether an immigrant will be able to become successfully established in Canada. Different selection criteria are prescribed for different classes and sub-classes of immigrants. The major classes of immigrants are the family class, the assisted-relatives class, the convention-refugee class and the independent immigrant class. The independent immigrant class may be further subdivided into entrepreneurs, investors, self-employed persons, and independent workers.

The Act requires that every prospective immigrant apply for and obtain an immigrant visa prior to appearing at a port of entry. The visa application procedure generally involves the completion of a pre-application questionnaire upon which a preliminary assessment is done. The applicant is then required to complete an "Application for Permanent Residence" form which is used to determine whether the applicant satisfies the admissions standards of the class in respect of which he or she is applying.

Upon the completion of the visa officer's assessment of the applicant, including a security investigation, a medical examination and a personal interview, the successful applicant and accompanying dependents (normally the applicant's spouse and children or grand-children who are under 19 years of age and unmarried) will be issued an immigrant visa valid for a specified period, usually up to six months from date of issue. Once the applicant arrives in Canada to take up permanent residence, landing will be granted if an immigration officer is satisfied at the required interview that the visa is valid, that circumstances regarding the individual have not changed since its issuance and that landing of the immigrant would not violate the Act or the Regulations. For those individuals who intend to immigrate to Quebec, the province requires that the applicant apply for a certificate of selection at either a foreign-based Quebec delegation or with the officer in charge of Quebec immigration at a Canadian consulate prior to consideration of the application by a federal visa officer.

The Regulations set out specific selection criteria for each class of applicant. The criteria are applied by way of a point system under which the applicant is awarded a number of units of assessment based on factors which are designed to measure both the short-term and long-term ability of the applicant to become successfully established in Canada. The factors upon which points are awarded include education, specific vocational training, work experience, occupational demand, degree of qualification and preparation for a designated occupation or pre-arranged employment, demographic factors, age, knowledge of the English and French languages and personal suitability. The manner of applying the point system and the number of points required differs for each class and sub-class of applicant. The Regulations provide for administrative discretion to deviate from the point system in appropriate cases.

An individual applying as a member of the family class must be sponsored by a qualifying Canadian citizen or permanent resident. Where such sponsorship is available, the point system is not used to assess the family class applicant. Included in the family class are the Canadian sponsor's spouse or fiancé, unmarried children who are under the age of 19 or who are in school or are mentally or physically handicapped and, in certain circumstances, other children, parents, grandparents and other relatives. The sponsor must provide an undertaking either to assist the family member and that person's dependents in becoming successfully established in Canada or to provide for their lodging, care and support. Siblings, children, grand-children, aunts, and uncles of a Canadian citizen or permanent resident who do not qualify as members of the family class may, in certain circumstances, be admitted into Canada as assisted relatives.

With respect to the independent immigrant class, the Regulations relating to entrepreneurs, investors and self-employed persons are designed to encourage the immigration of individuals who intend to establish business enterprises or otherwise invest in Canada. The admission of entrepreneurs into Canada will be conditional on the establishment of a business within two years and the admission of investors conditional on the maintenance of their investment for at least five years.

To qualify as an entrepreneur the applicant must have the financial ability and proven expertise to become involved in a Canadian business enterprise which will create or maintain employment and contribute to the Canadian economy and must intend to actively participate in the management of that business. While such an applicant is assessed under a modified version of the point system, the success or failure of his or her application will depend primarily upon the viability of the business proposal which the applicant submits in conjunction with the application. The entrepreneurial applicant must generally have sufficient economic resources to make an initial capital investment of at least $150,000 unless the business being proposed requires unusually low initial capitalization.

The business proposal which accompanies the entrepreneurial application is a substantial and comprehensive document containing a wide variety of information concerning the background, training and financial resources of the applicant. It must also describe in detail the nature of the business to be undertaken and the business and professional relationships to be established in furtherance thereof.

The completed business proposal is transmitted by the visa officer to the appropriate department of the province in which the business will be established or directly to federal officials, depending on the province of destination. The proposal will be reviewed and a determination made as to its viability. While the final decision as to the acceptability of the proposal remains with the federal immigration officials, approval generally requires a positive recommendation from provincial authorities. A visa will then be issued on a two-year conditional basis.

An "investor" is defined as an immigrant who (a) has operated, controlled or directed a financially successful business or commercial undertaking, (b) has by his or her own endeavor accumulated a net worth of a prescribed amount of either Can. $500,000 or Can. $700,000 depending on the nature of the proposed investment, and (c) has made a minimum investment since applying for an immigrant visa that will contribute to the creation or continuation of employment opportunities for Canadian citizens or permanent residents other than the immigrant or the immigrant's dependants. The prescribed minimum investment is Can. $250,000, $350,000 or $500,000 depending on the province of destination, whether the investment is subject to a guarantee by a third party and whether investment property of a fixed value is pledged as collateral.

The investment may, and generally will, be required to be irrevocable for five years and it must be made in an "eligible business or commercial venture" a privately-administered investment syndicate approved by the province in which the investment is made or a government-administered venture capital fund. An "eligible business or commercial investment" must be operated in Canada and have total assets not exceeding Can. $35 million.

The investor must submit a detailed application for permanent residence, along with documentation such as a curriculum vitae and statement of resources and business intentions. The application must be supported by the province of destination. The principal difference between the entrepreneur and the investor, however, is that the latter does not have to take an active role in the management of his or her investment.

The "self-employed" immigrant is defined as an immigrant who has the intention and the ability to establish or purchase a business in Canada that will create an employment opportunity for himself or herself and make a significant contribution to the economy or the cultural or artistic life of Canada. This category of immigrant generally includes professionals such as doctors and engineers, farmers, artists, sports personalities, consultants and operators of small businesses.

In most cases, the self-employed person will be required to submit a business proposal similar to, but less extensive than, that required from the entrepreneurial applicant. Generally, an initial capital investment of Can. $50,000 to Can. $150,000 will be required. The approval process does not usually involve a review or recommendation by provincial authorities although local licensing requirements will apply. A professional who applies as a self-employed person must be qualified to practice his or her profession in Canada at the time of the application.

Taxation

General

Taxes on income and capital gains are imposed by the federal and provincial governments based on the taxpayer's residency. Although each province has enacted taxation legislation, only Alberta, Quebec and Ontario administer their own provincial corporate income taxes, and only Quebec administers its own individual income taxes. Other jurisdictions rely upon the federal government to collect taxes on their behalf. The federal Income Tax Act ("ITA") is therefore the principal legislation in the field.

Taxpayers resident in Canada at any time in a taxable year are liable for tax in Canada on their world-wide income for that year, including employment income and business and property income. Capitals gains are also included in income to the extent that three-quarters of the taxpayer's capital gains exceeds three-quarters of that person's capital losses and are taxed at ordinary rates. Personal tax rates are progressive and are indexed annually for inflation; corporate rates are essentially flat, with certain exceptions. The Canadian tax system provides for preferential tax treatment in certain situations based on the nature of the taxpayer and/or the nature of the income being earned. In particular, the ITA contains a number of fiscal incentive regimes designed to encourage investment in particular sectors of the Canadian economy, including certain scientific and experimental development and oil and gas exploration, and in specific geographic regions.

The manner in which liability under the ITA is assessed depends on whether a person is resident in Canada at any time during a taxable year. As a general rule, an individual is considered to reside at the place where the individual keeps his or her home and to which he or she returns regularly. In addition, an individual is deemed to be resident in Canada throughout the year if he or she "sojourns" in Canada for more than 183 days of the year. A corporation is deemed to be resident in Canada if it was incorporated in Canada after April 26, 1965. In addition, a corporation incorporated outside Canada will be a Canadian resident for income tax purposes if its central management and control is exercised in Canada, a test which is normally satisfied if the board of directors meets in Canada. Proposed amendments to the Act state that a continued corporation will be treated as having been incorporated in the jurisdiction into which it is continued and not in the jurisdiction of original incorporation. Thus, a corporation continued from Canada into a foreign jurisdiction will cease to be resident in Canada, subject to the central management and control test, and will be liable for Canadian tax only as a non-resident. Conversely, a corporation continued into Canada will be a Canadian resident for tax purposes.

The effect of the application of deeming provisions may be to find a particular taxpayer to be resident in more than one country under the domestic tax laws of those countries. Absent treaty provisions, this dual residency would likely result in double taxation. Canada has concluded a reasonably comprehensive network of double taxation conventions with nearly all of its major trading partners which seek to eliminate double taxation by allocating jurisdiction to tax. In the event that a corporation is resident in two countries under domestic law, most tax treaties provide that the corporation will be resident in only one country for tax purposes. The Canada-U.S. Tax Convention, for example, resolves the dual residency question in favor of the country under the laws of which the corporation was created, if those laws are of either Canada or the United States. Tax treaties also generally solve the problem of double taxation resulting from the dual residency of individuals.

The establishment of Canadian operations may involve the international movement of personnel or even a relocation of corporate headquarters. Tax consequences will follow whenever a taxpayer, whether a corporation or an individual, becomes or ceases to be resident in Canada. A taxpayer who becomes resident in Canada is deemed to acquire each capital property owned by the taxpayer at that time, other than taxable Canadian property, for a cost equal to its fair market value. This cost adjustment will apply only for the purposes of calculating future capital gains and losses. Under proposed amendments to the Act, this deemed acquisition rule will apply to all property, with limited exceptions such as taxable Canadian property, and for all Canadian tax purposes.

An individual who ceases to be resident in Canada will be liable for tax on accrued net gains on capital property held by the taxpayer at the time of departure; a corporation will be liable for tax on all accrued net income and capital gains. An individual is deemed to dispose of each capital property, other than taxable Canadian property, at the time the individual ceases to be resident in Canada for its fair market value. This deemed disposition again only applies for the purposes of calculating capital gains and losses. The proposed amendments will deem a disposition of all property with limited exceptions and the deemed disposition will apply for all purposes of the Act. An exemption is available, however, in the case of an individual who is resident in Canada for less than five years during the 10-year period preceding departure. Furthermore, individuals may elect, in certain circumstances, to have specific properties excluded from the deemed disposition rules.

Corporations that are continued outside of Canada or that cease to be resident in Canada are deemed to dispose of each property, without restriction to capital property, for its fair market value at that time. The deemed disposition applies for all purposes of the Act. The proposed amendments to the Act will not significantly change the corporate deemed disposition rules but will amend the rules regarding residency as discussed above.

With respect to corporations, an important distinction is made between private corporations and public corporations. Preferential treatment afforded to private corporations is largely designed to achieve an integration of tax at the corporate and individual shareholder levels. In addition, Canadian-controlled private corporations are eligible for a small business tax credit on the first $200,000 of Canadian active business income.

In determining its "taxable income" for a taxation year, a corporation may deduct expenses reasonably related to the earning of that income. Certain other items may be deducted from net income including, subject to certain exceptions, taxable dividends received from a taxable Canadian corporation, all or part of dividends received from a non-resident corporation (other than a foreign affiliate) carrying on business in Canada through a permanent establishment and specified amounts in respect of dividends received from foreign affiliates. Deductions may also be made with respect to loss carry-overs. Net business and other non-capital losses sustained by the corporation in a given taxable year may be carried back three years and forward seven years to reduce taxable income in those years. Net capital losses for a taxation year may generally be carried back three years and forward indefinitely but may only be applied against taxable capital gains. These loss carry-overs will be extinguished if there is a change of control of a corporate taxpayer.

Taxable dividends distributed to an individual shareholder by a taxable Canadian corporation are included in income in an amount equal to the actual amount of the dividend plus a gross-up amount equal to one-quarter of the dividend received. The shareholder then receives a federal dividend tax credit equal to two-thirds of the amount of the gross-up and a provincial credit equal to the other one-third. Dividends received by individuals resident in Canada on shares of corporations not resident in Canada, including any foreign withholding tax deducted at the source, are included in income without gross-up and no credit is available with the exception of a credit for foreign withholding tax limited to 15 percent; any excess withholding tax paid and not credited is deductible in computing income.

Non residents are subject to Canadian tax on employment income earned in Canada, Canadian-source business and property income (unless it is excepted by treaty) and capital gains from the disposition of "taxable Canadian property." Taxable Canadian property includes real property situate in Canada, capital property used in carrying on business in Canada and shares of Canadian private corporations. Provincial taxes will be payable by a non-resident on taxable income earned in a province where the non-resident carries on business through a permanent establishment in that province.

Amounts paid by a resident of Canada to a non-resident with respect to most forms of passive income such as management or administration fees, interest, income from a trust, rents, royalties, pensions, annuities and dividends are generally subject to withholding tax. The standard rate of Canadian non-resident withholding tax is 25 percent, subject to reduction pursuant to a tax treaty between Canada and the country of residence of the recipient. The basic withholding tax rate is normally reduced by treaty to 15 percent and in some cases to 10 percent. The Canada-U.S. tax treaty, for example, limits Canadian withholding tax on dividends paid by a corporation resident in Canada to a resident of the U.S. which holds directly at least 10 percent of the voting shares of the payor corporation to 10 percent of the gross amount of the dividend. Proposed changes in the Canada-U.S. tax treaty would reduce the rate of withholding tax imposed on dividends in these circumstances from 10 percent to five percent; this reduction would be phased in over a five year period on a reciprocal basis.

An important exception to the withholding tax requirement is for interest payable by a corporation resident in Canada to an arm's length non-resident lender on an obligation in respect of which no more than 25 percent of the principal amount is repayable to the lender within five years of the date of issue of the obligation. Other important exceptions deal with government guaranteed bonds or similar obligations and foreign currency deposits with certain financial institutions, arm's length management fees and certain rents, royalties and similar payments.

Non-residents carrying on business in Canada are subject to Canadian tax on income from that business. Where a non-resident corporation is resident in a nation with which Canada has a bilateral income tax convention, Canada may generally tax the non-resident's business profits only if the non-resident carries on business in Canada through a permanent establishment. "Permanent establishment" is defined broadly such that any office or facility in Canada will generally constitute a Canadian permanent establishment. Non-residents who derive business income from the disposition of Canadian real estate are deemed to be carrying on business in Canada and are subject to Canadian tax in respect of their gains. In addition, non-resident corporations carrying on business in Canada through unincorporated branches are subject to a "branch tax" intended to take the place of the withholding tax that would apply to dividends paid to a non-resident parent corporation by a Canadian subsidiary.

Branch or Subsidiary

A non-resident corporation carrying on business in Canada through an unincorporated branch is not only liable for normal income tax on its Canadian-source business income, but is also liable for a branch profits tax of 25 percent of the amount that is approximately equal to the after-tax earnings of the branch less an allowance for capital invested in Canada. Branch tax is generally imposed at a rate of 25 percent but this rate is normally reduced by treaty to 15 percent or 10 percent. Under the Canada-U.S. tax treaty, for example, branch tax is limited to 10 percent with an exemption for the first Can. $500,000 of after-tax branch profits. A Canadian incorporated subsidiary of a non-resident corporation is liable as any other Canadian corporation for tax on its world-wide income. In addition, payments in respect of passive income, such as dividends, interest, management fees or royalties, made by the subsidiary to the parent will be subject to withholding tax as discussed above.

There are a number of important considerations to be weighed by a non-resident corporation in making the choice whether to do business in Canada through an unincorporated branch or through a subsidiary Canadian company.

In both cases, the profits of the Canadian operation will be subject to tax. If the business is carried on through a branch, there will also be the branch tax to consider, whereas if a subsidiary is used, withholding tax may be imposed. An important difference between the branch tax and the withholding tax is that withholding tax applies only if and when a dividend is paid or credited to the non-resident shareholder while branch tax is paid regardless of whether profits are remitted to the non-resident corporation. However, profits can flow freely between the branch and the head office without being subject to withholding tax.

The thin-capitalization rule must also be considered. This rule is designed to discourage non-residents from investing in a Canadian resident corporation such that virtually all of the investment is by way of loan and as little as possible by way of shares, thereby maximizing the amount that can be returned to the non-resident in deductible interest payments. A Canadian subsidiary generally may not deduct interest paid by it to specified non-residents to the extent that the relevant loans exceed three times the company's equity. A specified non-resident is defined as any non-resident who alone or in combination with other persons with whom it does not deal at arm's length owns 25 percent or more of the voting shares or of the fair market value of all issued shares of the subsidiary. The thin-capitalization rule does not apply to a branch operating in Canada.

A further distinction arises with respect to withholding tax on interest paid to foreign lenders by a Canadian branch or subsidiary. This tax must be withheld by a branch where the business of the non-resident is carried on principally in Canada, that business consists of manufacturing or purchasing goods in Canada or certain other activities and the interest is deductible by it in computing its taxable income earned in Canada or where the loan is secured by real property situated in Canada. A subsidiary must normally withhold Canadian tax on all interest paid to non-residents, but, as it is a corporation resident in Canada, it may benefit from the exemption on medium to long-term arm's length borrowings described above.

Where the non-resident taxpayer is protected by treaty from Canadian tax on any gain from a disposition of shares in Canadian subsidiaries, the non-resident may prefer, from a Canadian tax perspective, to hold each Canadian subsidiary directly rather than through a Canadian holding company or a vertical chain of Canadian companies. Direct holdings will allow for one subsidiary to be sold independently of the others without liability for Canadian tax on a resulting capital gain.

There are a number of other fiscal matters to be considered when deciding whether a Canadian branch or a Canadian subsidiary should be used. For example, if a new Canadian venture is expected to operate at a loss in its initial stage, it may be preferable to establish a branch of the non-resident enterprise so as to permit the latter to deduct the loss in computing its own tax liability.

Transfer Pricing

Under the ITA, companies carrying on business in Canada which purchase goods or services from or sell goods and services to a non-resident parent or related company at a price different from that which would have been reasonable in the circumstances if the parties had been at arm's length are deemed, for the purposes of computing their income, to have paid or received the reasonable amount rather than the price actually paid or received. An annual information return must be filed by branches or subsidiaries that engage in certain transactions with related non-residents. These transactions generally include the purchase or sale of goods or services, the payment of rent, royalties, dividends and interest and the lending of money between the related parties.

Non-Resident Partners

A partnership that includes one or more non-resident partners will be deemed to be a non-resident. Payments by a Canadian resident to such a partnership with respect to passive income will therefore be subject to withholding tax. In addition, tax will be levied on the non-resident partners' share of partnership income if the income is of a type which is normally taxable in Canada when earned by a non-resident, such as income from carrying on a business in Canada.

Corporate Capital Tax

The federal government and several of the provinces impose corporate capital tax on corporations resident in Canada and non-resident corporations carrying on business through a Canadian permanent establishment. The tax is calculated as a percentage of the corporation's "taxable capital employed in Canada" in excess of a specified dollar threshold. Taxable capital employed in Canada of a corporation resident in Canada, including a Canadian subsidiary of a non-resident parent corporation, will be approximately equal to its paid-up capital, retained earnings, contributed and other surpluses, undeducted reserves and certain debt capital or obligations less the carrying cost of certain investment assets. Capital tax will be imposed on the amount of this taxable capital in excess of Can. $10 million. A non-resident corporation with a Canadian permanent establishment will be liable for capital tax with respect to that branch based on the aggregate carrying value of the corporation's Canadian assets in excess of Can. $10 million less the deductions in computing taxable capital that would be allowed to a resident corporation.

Commodity Taxes

Customs duties, federal goods and services tax and provincial sales tax may be levied with respect to the import and export of goods into and out of Canada or the manufacturing or selling of goods in Canada. Additional excise taxes and duties may be payable on products such as alcohol and tobacco. In certain circumstances, however, importers may benefit from a reduction, refund, drawback or possible elimination of customs duties. For example, the Canada-U.S. Free Trade Agreement will eliminate all tariffs between Canada and the U.S. affecting goods originating in either country over a ten year period which began on January 1, 1989.

The comprehensive seven percent Federal Goods and Services Tax ("GST") is levied with respect to a broad range of goods and services and applies at each stage of production. This tax is payable by the purchaser on the amount paid for the goods or service. However, if the purchaser is involved in a commercial activity and has registered with the federal government to collect the tax, it is entitled to claim credits for all GST paid on goods and services used in the course of its commercial activity. GST on imported goods and services will be payable by the importer while exported goods and services will not be subject to GST. Any non-residents engaging in commercial activities in Canada must charge and collect GST. Such activities involve carrying on a business in Canada or receiving income from commercial real property located in Canada.

Retail sales tax at various rates from six percent to 12 percent is imposed by all provinces except Alberta.

Import-Export

General

Importers and traders of goods are subject to numerous regulations. Customs legislation imposes a variety of administrative requirements regarding the reporting and entry of goods into Canada. Other import regulations are designed to implement government policies on international trade, to protect Canadian industry from injurious imports, to collect revenue or to regulate importation of certain classes of goods such as food, drugs and agricultural products. Export controls include export formalities for statistical and customs purposes, the permit system governed by the Export and Import Permits Act and specific export controls applicable to certain products, such as energy and agricultural products.

Import Regulations

Most statutes regulating the importation of goods into Canada are administered in conjunction with the federal Customs Act. Under the Act, persons bringing goods into Canada must report to Canadian custom officials, make due entry of the goods and pay any duties and tax owing upon importation. Where imported goods are subject to import controls under legislation other than the Customs Act, customs officers have the authority to enforce such regulations at the time of importation. A wide range of enforcement provisions are available to Canadian customs officials, including criminal sanctions and civil penalties which may involve the seizure and forfeiture of goods and the imposition of fines. Customs officials also have substantial audit powers to ensure compliance with import controls and importers are required to keep extensive books and records.

The Customs Tariff Act imposes duties on a wide range of goods. Rates of duty depend on the country of origin and the nature of the product being imported. The country of origin is determined under a series of rules found in the Customs Tariff or the FTA and will indicate which of six tariff regimes presently in use in Canada is applicable. The classification of a product is determined under the Harmonized Commodity Description and Coding System which is also used in the U.S. and most countries of Europe and Asia. The Canadian system for determining the value of goods for duty purposes is based on the international Customs Valuation Code pursuant to the General Agreement on Tariffs and Trade.

Excise taxes and duties may also be levied with respect to certain goods. Excise taxes are levied on a limited number of goods imported into Canada, including certain clocks, jewellery, automobiles, air conditioners, gasoline products and tobacco products. Excise duties are imposed on spirits, Canadian brandy, beer or malt liquor, and tobacco, cigars, and cigarettes produced or manufactured in Canada and the Customs Tariff provides for an additional customs duty to be levied on these goods when they are imported into Canada in an amount equal to the excise duties that would have been imposed had they been manufactured in Canada.

Duty relief in the form of drawbacks or exemptions may be available where goods are imported and subsequently exported, used in the manufacture of products which are ultimately exported, used in the production of goods sold in Canada if an equal amount of a similar Canadian material is used to make the product for export or used in Canada for prescribed purposes or in specified industries. Duty relief may also be available where certain imported machinery is not available in Canada.

Much of the legislation affecting the importation of goods into Canada relates to product standards or is designed to prevent unfair marketing practices and address potential health and safety concerns. The Consumer Packaging and Labelling Act applies, with some limited exceptions, to all pre-packaged consumer products imported into Canada. A label containing a declaration of net quantity must be applied to the product and must be clearly and prominently displayed, easily legible, and in distinct contrast to any other information on the label. The label must also show the identity and principal place of business of the person by or for whom the product was manufactured, the identity of the product in terms of its generic name or in terms of its function, and such information respecting the nature, quality, age, size, material content, composition, geographic ordering, performance, use and method of manufacture or production of the product as may be prescribed. The Regulations outline further requirements regarding bilingual labelling, the application of a label and the part of the label on which the information is to be shown. In addition, the Marketing of Imported Goods Order made under the Customs Tariff lists products that must be legibly marked, stamped, branded or labelled to indicate the country of origin. If the Order is not complied with, the goods will not be released until marked under Customs supervision at the expense of the importer.

The Textile Labelling Act and accompanying Regulations state that any consumer textile article imported into Canada must have a label affixed thereto containing prescribed information. The label must show the textile content of the article and the name and postal address of the dealer by or for whom the article is made in both English and French. The Regulations also prescribe the manner in which a trademark or descriptive form may be shown.

The Food and Drug Act protects consumers from fraud, injury and deceptive practices by imposing labelling and packaging standards for imported foods, drugs, cosmetics and medical devices. The Regulations made pursuant to the Act stipulate which foods and drugs must carry a label when offered for sale. "Food" includes any article sold or represented for use as food or drink and "drug" includes any substance sold or represented for use in the treatment or prevention of disease, the restoration or correction of organic functions or the disinfection of premises in which food is manufactured or kept.

The Regulations with respect to food set out requirements with respect to labelling, food additives, compulsory ingredients for some foods and freezing. More particularly, the name of the food, the identity of the manufacturer, the durable life of the product, special storage instructions, and all the ingredients of the product must be shown on the packaged food labels.

Narcotics and controlled and restricted drugs may only be imported by a pharmaceutical manufacturer or a distributor or other person licensed by the Minister of National Health and Welfare. Package information must include the name of the drug, the identity and location of the manufacturer, a quantitative list of the ingredients, the lot number of the drugs, instructions for its use, and the net amount of the drug in the container.

The Hazardous Products Act contains lists of products which may not be advertised, sold or imported into Canada as well as those products which may only be imported if authorized by the Regulations. The Act does not apply to materials regulated by the Explosives Act, the Food and Drug Act, the Pest Control Act or the Atomic Energy Control Act. The Controlled Products Regulations prescribe the information that must be contained on labels and material safety data sheets by suppliers of specified hazardous controlled products destined for use in the workplace. Included among the labelling requirements are applicable product and supplier identifiers, hazard symbols and appropriate information respecting risk and precautionary and first aid measures.

There are also various legislative controls imposed on the importation of agricultural products, specific food products, wheat, oats and barley, alcoholic beverages, radiation emitting devices, offensive weapons and oil and gas. Legislation that further touches on and regulates the import and labelling of many products includes environmental protection legislation and language legislation.

The entry of certain goods into Canada may be quantitatively limited if the goods appear on the Import Control List. The majority of the items on the List may be classified as clothing, footwear, textiles, fabrics, yarns or animal and agricultural produce. The List may be added to if an inquiry by the Canadian International Trade Tribunal reveals that goods are being imported or are likely to be imported in such quantities and under such conditions as to pose serious injury to Canadian producers of like or directly competitive goods. Importers wishing to import goods which have been placed on the Import Control List are required to apply to the Special Trade Relations Bureau for a permit to import such goods. Although only Canadian residents may apply for import permits, a person is permitted to apply for an import permit on behalf of another person who will actually import the goods.

Special import measures will apply where importation practices have adverse effects on the development and expansion of Canadian industry. These measures are designed to protect Canadian producers from competition from foreign goods priced artificially low due to dumping, unfair subsidization of foreign imports and surges in importations threatening injury to Canadian producers. For example, an anti-dumping duty is imposed where it has been demonstrated that the dumping of goods has caused or is threatening to cause material injury to a domestic industry; countervailing duties may be imposed where goods have been subsidized by a foreign government to the detriment of Canadian producers.

Export Regulations

Exporters must submit to Customs an Export Declaration or Entry in prescribed form detailing the product to be exported from Canada. This declaration is primarily used for statistical purposes.

Pursuant to the Export and Import Permits Act, goods which are subject to export control are placed on an Export Control List. Goods may be listed for a number of reasons including the control of the exportation of arms or similar products the eventual use of which may be detrimental to Canada, of natural resources where further processing of these resources is to be promoted in Canada and of certain non-agricultural products in circumstances of surplus supply and depressed prices, the implementation of international agreements and the assurance of adequate supply of articles required for Canada's defense or other needs. The products found on the list generally include animal and agricultural products, wood and wood products, certain industrial machinery and electronic devices, transportation equipment, metals, minerals and other manufactured products, chemicals, metalloid and petroleum products, arms, munitions and military, naval or air stores and atomic energy materials and equipment along with other miscellaneous goods and materials. Exports to certain countries may also be restricted by virtue of the Area Control List.

Where goods are included on the Export Control List, an exporter is required to apply to the Export Controls Division of the Special Trade Relations Bureau for an export permit prior to exportation. Only Canadian residents may apply for such permits. If a permit is issued, goods may be exported only in such quantity or quality, by such persons, to such places or persons and according to such other terms and conditions as described in the permit or regulations. The U.S., however, has special status by virtue of the FTA and many of the items on the List may be exported to the U.S. without a permit.

The export of energy products including oil, natural gas, and electricity is controlled by requiring that exporters obtain export licenses or orders from the National Energy Board. The importation and the domestic distribution of energy goods are also regulated by the National Energy Board.

Government Programs

There are a number of programs which have originated with the Canadian government to provide services to importers and exporters. The Export Development Corporation ("EDC") was established by the federal Export Development Act to facilitate and develop trade between Canada and other countries by providing financial services to Canadian exporters and foreign buyers. The principal services offered by the EDC are insurance, guarantees and export financing. The Program for Export Market Development is designed to improve Canada's international trade performance by offering financial assistance to Canadian businesses seeking to participate in various trade promotion and export activities. Trade Commissioners operating out of Canadian embassies, consulates and High Commissions assist Canadian companies seeking export markets by collecting and analyzing information on legislation, commercial practices and business opportunities abroad and intervening on behalf of exporters with local authorities. The Business Opportunities Sourcing System is a computerized data base on Canadian companies, their products and the markets they serve which is available through Canadian international trade offices abroad and federal and provincial departments of industry across Canada. The World Information System for Exports is used by the Department of External Affairs Trade Commissioners to match Canadian sources of supply of goods and services with foreign customers. The federal Canadian Commercial Corporation assists in the development of trade between Canada and other nations on a government-to-government basis and generally assists Canadians in the import and export of goods and commodities. In addition, all of the provincial governments have export-related promotion program ranging from loans and insurance programs to incentives for participation in trade fairs overseas.

Canada-U.S. Free Trade Agreement and North American Free Trade Agreement

The stated objectives of the Canada-U.S. Free Trade Agreement ("FTA") which came into effect on January 1, 1989 are to:

(1)   eliminate barriers to trade in goods and services;

(2)   facilitate conditions of fair competition;

(3)   significantly liberalize conditions for investment;

(4)   establish effective procedures for the joint administration of the FTA and the resolution of disputes; and

(5)   lay the foundation for further bilateral and multilateral cooperation to expand and enhance the benefits of the FTA.

The FTA is very broad in scope and touches upon virtually every aspect of the Canadian and U.S. economies.

In general, the FTA deals with tariffs, customs, quantitative trade restrictions, government procurement, trade, goods, services, financial services, investment, energy, automotive trade, agriculture, wine and distilled spirits and temporary entry for business purposes. There are also provisions dealing with dispute settlement that create the Canada-U.S. Trade Commission and the Bi-National Panel to deal with anti-dumping and countervailing duty cases.

Of significant importance is the intention that all existing tariffs will be completely eliminated over a maximum period of ten years. Tariff elimination is dealt with in three categories to provide time for transition and adjustment in what are perceived to be the most vulnerable sectors of the economy. Some tariff elimination occurred immediately upon implementation of the FTA, a second category over a five-year period, and a third category over a 10-year period. Prescribed "rules of origin" will govern which goods qualify for duty-free treatment. Essentially a good must originate in either Canada or the U.S. to benefit from tariff elimination. The tariff elimination provisions refer to all customs and import duties including surtaxes and surcharges with certain exceptions which are consistent with various provisions of the FTA, including charges equivalent to internal taxes on like domestic goods, such as Canadian sales and excise taxes, anti-dumping and countervailing duties and certain other fees and charges.

After January 1, 1994 Canadian producers will no longer be able to recover duty paid on products imported from third countries when the good is exported to the U.S., as duty drawbacks on U.S.-bound exports will be eliminated as of that date.

The FTA relaxed or eliminated certain trade restrictions between both Canada and the U.S., including those with respect to used cars, grains, and grain products, eggs and poultry, sugar and meat. Other trade restrictions, such as those with respect to dairy products, logs, fish and beer, are unaffected.

The FTA eliminated export taxes and imposes conditions in cases where either country relies on certain General Agreement on Tariffs and Trade exceptions under which export restrictions can be justified.

On October 7, 1992 officials of Canada, the United States and Mexico agreed on the text of NAFTA. Subject to legislative approval in all three countries, NAFTA may be implemented on January 1, 1994.

NAFTA embodies many of the general principles of FTA in advancing its specific objective of strengthening and liberalizing Canadian and American access to the Mexican market. In particular, NAFTA proposes to eliminate tariffs on goods moving between Canada, the U.S. and Mexico in stages that will see some goods become tariff-free immediately while other tariffs will be phased out over five, 10 or 15 year periods, although the Canada-U.S. FTA will continue to reduce tariffs in accordance with its terms. It would also eliminate Mexican import licensing requirements for goods, provide for greater access by Canadian and American businesses to Mexican Government procurement contracts and generally open Mexico's investment regime to Canadians and Americans by removing or reducing restrictions on foreign ownership in most industries.

II. ESTABLISHING A BUSINESS

Types of Business Organizations

Sole Proprietorships

Although the sole proprietorship is free from most government regulations that apply to business corporations, certain registration requirements must be complied with in the jurisdiction in which the business is to be carried on. A sole proprietor who uses as his or her business style a name or designation other than his or her own is required to register the name under applicable provincial legislation.

A non-resident who establishes a business, whether as a sole proprietorship or otherwise, must notify the Canadian government pursuant to the Investment Canada Act but need not submit to the review process.

Partnerships and Joint Ventures

Partnership law in Canada is a matter of provincial jurisdiction. While a partnership is generally formed under the laws of a particular province, partnerships carrying on business in more than one province will be required to comply with the law of, and may be required to register in, each such province. In the absence of an agreement to the contrary, the rights and obligations of partners are those found in the governing provincial legislation. There is no specific joint venture legislation and parties entering into a joint venture must make it clear that they do not intend to be associated in partnership.

Limited partnerships are established by the filing of a declaration with the appropriate provincial Registrar, signed by all of the partners, stating the partnership name, the name and address of each partner, the general nature of the business, the value of money and other property contributed or to be contributed by each limited partner, the principal place of business of the partnership and such other information as may be required. The declaration generally expires a specified number of years after its filing unless cancelled earlier by the filing of a declaration of dissolution or renewed by the filing of a new declaration prior to expiration. The only filing normally required with respect to a general partnership is a registration of the business name where the partners are not using their own names.

Corporations

Both the federal and provincial governments have enacted legislation providing for the incorporation and the regulation of corporations. A corporation incorporated under provincial law may carry on business as of right in the province of its incorporation and also has the capacity to carry on business beyond the limits of that province. A federal corporation is subject to provincial laws of general application, although it has the basic right to carry on business in any province. Most provinces require corporations incorporated in other jurisdictions to register or be licensed therein before commencing to do business in that jurisdiction and to file initial and annual returns and notices reporting certain basic corporate changes. Failure to comply with the rules governing extra-provincial corporations can prevent a corporation from holding land in the subject jurisdiction, from maintaining an action before the courts and, in certain cases, from enforcing an otherwise valid agreement.

Certain types of business corporations such as banks, trust and loan companies, credit unions, or associations, and insurance companies are subject to specific legislation and are not governed by the general federal or provincial corporate statutes.

Although the requirements, formalities, and restrictions of the federal and provincial corporations statutes are essentially the same, the decision of whether to incorporate federally or provincially will depend upon such factors as the ease and timeliness of incorporation, the flexibility in carrying out corporate proceedings, licensing requirements, fees and taxes, the extent of financial and continuous disclosure requirements, the ease and timeliness of obtaining a desired corporate name and any requirement as to the residence of directors. Often a non-resident wishing to incorporate in Canada will prefer to incorporate federally given that, as a matter of practice although not as a matter of law, federal corporations are more readily recognized and accepted outside of Canada than are provincially incorporated companies. In addition, several of the corporations statutes require a minimum number or percentage of resident directors.

Franchising and Licensing

Franchising and licensing arrangements may be considered as alternatives to the types of business organizations discussed above. Both are governed by the applicable law of contracts.

Federally, the Competition Act prohibits certain practices relating to promotional allowances, resale price maintenance, pyramid selling, referral selling and advertising. In addition, the Act subjects certain trade practices to review including refusals to deal, consignment selling, exclusive dealing, tied selling, and market restriction. Other relevant federal legislation may include the Trade Marks Act and the Patent Act.

Certain provinces have enacted specific legislation with respect to franchising. Others have enacted legislation with respect to consumer protection, fair trade practices, pyramid selling, referral selling, advertising, and securities laws which may affect certain franchise arrangements.

Competition Act

Competition law is principally the subject of federal regulation under the Competition Act which was enacted in 1986. The substantial revisions to previous legislation contained in the Act and its enforcement since the date of its adoption reflect the increasing sensitivity of the Canadian government to the potential anti-competitive effects of mergers and other business practices. Under the revised legislation, the regulation of mergers and monopolies has been transferred from a cumbersome and largely ineffective criminal law framework to a civil law framework. While conspiracies, bid-rigging, and certain other offenses continue to be dealt with as criminal matters, responsibility for merger review, the regulation of "dominant" firms and other reviewable trade practices, such as refusals to deal, exclusive dealing, tied selling and market restriction, has been transferred to a specialized quasi-judicial body, the Competition Tribunal. These matters are dealt with on applications brought before the Tribunal by the Director of Investigation and Research. The Director is charged with the administration of the Act and principally responsible for the investigation of mergers and other anti-competitive business practices.

The principal substantive test under the Act with respect to mergers is whether an actual or proposed action or activity "would or would be likely to prevent or lessen competition substantially" in a market. This test applies both to the administrative decision of the Director to initiate an application to the Tribunal and the Tribunal's adjudication of the application. In making such a determination, the Director and the Tribunal will consider the extent and effectiveness of foreign competition, whether the business of a party to the merger has failed or is likely to fail, the extent and availability of acceptable substitutes for products supplied by the parties, current barriers to entry into the market, whether the transaction would result in the removal of a vigorous and effective competitor, the extent to which effective competition would remain following the transaction and the nature and extent of change and innovation in the relevant market. The analytical framework which has been adopted employs legal and economic criteria similar to those found in American anti-trust jurisprudence. In April 1991, the Director released Merger Enforcement Guidelines designed to provide guidance concerning the administration of the merger review provisions of the Act which are modelled on similar guidelines recently adopted by the United States Department of Justice.

Mergers are broadly defined under the Act to include the direct or indirect acquisition by one or more persons, whether by purchase or lease of shares or assets, by amalgamation or by combination or otherwise, of control over or a significant interest in all or part of the business of a competitor, supplier, customer or other person. If, on an application brought by the Director, the Tribunal determines that a merger or proposed merger prevents or lessens, or would be likely to prevent or lessen competition substantially in a market, then the Tribunal has broad discretionary authority to make orders remedying the anti-competitive effects of the merger, including prohibiting a proposed merger or requiring a dissolution or divestiture in the case of a completed merger. The Director is entitled to bring such an application at any time within three years of the completion of the merger.

The Act has also introduced an advance notification filing requirement for certain large transactions. Where notification is required, the parties are not permitted to complete the transaction until the review period has expired. Pre-notification filings are required in connection with a proposed acquisition of assets or shares or an amalgamation or other combination to establish a business in Canada where thresholds relating to the size of the transaction and the size of the parties are exceeded. If the parties to a transaction, together with their respective affiliates, have total assets in Canada or total gross annual revenues from sales in, from or into Canada of more than Can.$400 million, the Director must be notified of: (a) an acquisition of assets with a value in excess of Can.$35 million; (b) the formation of an unincorporated business combination with gross revenues from sales in or from Canada in excess of Can.$35 million; and (c) an acquisition of voting shares of a corporation which, together with all other corporations controlled by it, has assets or annual gross revenues from sales in or from Canada in excess of Can.$35 million. Notification of the latter type of transaction will only be required if as a result of such acquisition the acquiring corporation and its affiliates hold voting shares in excess of:

(a)   20 percent, in the case of the initial acquisition of shares of a public company,

(b)   35 percent, in the case of the initial acquisition of shares of a private company, or

(c)   50 percent, in the case of a subsequent acquisition of shares of either type of company by a person that has previously surpassed the threshold set out in (a) or (b).

Where these thresholds are met, and unless a specific statutory exception applies, a pre-notification filing obligation is triggered and the parties to the transaction must complete either a "short form" or "long form" filing in the prescribed form. The Director generally has seven days in the case of a short form filing and 21 days in the case of a long form filing within which to review the proposed transaction to determine if it would result or be likely to result in a substantial lessening of competition. Notification provisions also apply in the case of an amalgamation where an amalgamating corporation carries on business in Canada or controls a corporation that carries on business in Canada and the continuing corporation will own assets with a value exceeding Can.$70 million or will have gross annual revenues from sales in or from Canada in excess of Can.$70 million.

The Act also establishes an advance ruling process through which parties to a proposed merger transaction may seek an advance ruling certificate from the Director confirming that, on the basis of a review of the facts they have represented in their application, the Director will not challenge the proposed merger.

In addition to the administration of the merger review process under the Act the Director has the power to:

(1) inquire into reviewable trade practices including refusals to deal, refusal to sell, consignment selling, exclusive dealing, tied selling, market restrictions and delivered pricing;

(2) prosecute certain criminal offenses including bid-rigging, conspiracy in restraint of trade, price discrimination, predatory pricing, promotional allowances, misleading advertising, pyramid and referral selling, resale price maintenance and "bait and switch selling"; and

(3) initiate civil proceedings in relation to matters reviewable by the Competition Tribunal.

Employment Legislation

Legislative jurisdiction over labor and employment is shared by the provincial and federal governments. However, legislation in this area falls mainly within the provincial domain.

Minimum Standards Legislation

Each province and the federal government has enacted legislation regulating basic terms and conditions of employment, although the content and extent of such legislation varies. The legislation guarantees employees minimum rights with respect to the terms and conditions of their employment. These terms and conditions cannot be contracted out of, either by way of an individual contract of employment or through a collective agreement. The contract of employment may, however, provide for terms more favorable to the employee than those provided for in the minimum standards legislation and such terms shall become binding upon the employer. Terms and conditions established by legislation include but are not limited to minimum wage, hours of work, overtime pay, daily and weekly rest periods, vacations, statutory holidays, pregnancy leave, equal pay for work of equal value, and minimum periods of notice of termination or termination pay.

In Ontario, the Employment Standards Act also provides that where a sale of a business or part of a business has taken place and the purchaser hires employees of the vendor, the employees' length of service with the vendor is treated as service with the purchaser for the purposes of public holidays, vacation with pay, pregnancy and parental leave and termination of employment.

Workers' Compensation

Unlike the traditional common law approach, workers' compensation legislation establishes entitlement to compensation with respect to injuries occurring in the workplace as a matter of right, notwithstanding the presence or absence of any negligence on the part of the employer, the employee or other employees. This system is designed to replace the right of an employee to sue an employer for losses arising out of an accident in the workplace by providing the employee with the right to claim compensation from a statutorily established accident fund. Employers are required to contribute to the fund and compensation and medical expenses for injured workers are paid by an administrative tribunal out of the fund. No contribution to the fund by employees, either directly or indirectly, is permitted. In Ontario the statute provides for the mandatory reinstatement of injured workers in certain circumstances.

Human Rights Legislation

Human rights legislation in Canada has had a profound impact on the employer/employee relationship. The most significant right guaranteed with respect to the employment relationship is the right to equal treatment and the corresponding prohibition against discrimination in employment. Generally speaking, the prohibited grounds of discrimination include race, ethnic origin, culture, religion, sex, marital status, handicap and age. The specific grounds differ somewhat from province to province and within the federal sphere.

In addition to federal and provincial Human Rights Statutes, the Canadian Charter of Rights and Freedoms, which applies to both federal and provincial legislation, has had a major effect on labor relations and will continue to do so in the future.

Labor Law

The basic policy of both federal and provincial labor laws is to grant to employees the right to form or join a union of their choice. In addition, the labor laws place an obligation on the employer to bargain in good faith and give to the union exclusive bargaining rights with respect to the bargaining unit. Legislation in each jurisdiction provides for employee and employer protection against unfair labor practices, both on the part of the union and the employer. The legislation also provides for a system of certification of trade unions as bargaining agents, compulsory collective bargaining, compulsory postponement of strikes and lockouts during the bargaining process, government intervention by way of a conciliation process in situations where the parties have been unable to negotiate a collective agreement, the right of employees to strike and the right of employers to lockout. Each jurisdiction also provides for the imposition of a collective agreement by way of arbitration and recent amendments to the Ontario Labor Relations Act provide for first contract arbitration where parties have been unable to negotiate an agreement and have been in a lawful strike or lockout position for more than 30 days. The Ontario and Quebec legislation provides that replacement workers may not be hired during a strike or lockout.

Where there is a sale of all or part of a business and the vendor's employees are represented by a trade union, the bargaining rights held by that trade union will in almost all circumstances be preserved and extended to a corresponding unit of the purchaser's employees and the purchaser will be bound the vendor's collective agreement.

Currently, the most heavily unionized provinces are Ontario, Quebec and British Columbia; the most heavily unionized industries are manufacturing, public administration, transportation, and communications.

Miscellaneous

Both employers and employees are required to contribute to the Unemployment Insurance Fund and the Canada Pension Plan. Such contributions may be deducted by the employer for tax purposes. Ontario has also established a system of employer health tax whereby employers who have a permanent establishment in the province must pay an annual tax at a graduated rate depending on the total annual remuneration paid to employees.

Environmental Legislation

Environmental law is a fast growing area of law and regulation in Canada the boundaries of which are not yet fixed. A regulatory regime comprised mainly of environmental assessment and review procedures and a system of approvals, licenses, and permits has been adopted by the federal government and each of the provinces as the primary method of exerting control over activities affecting the environment. The central piece of federal environmental legislation is the Canadian Environmental Protection Act which regulates the manufacture, import, use, handling, release and disposal of toxic substances. The provinces have generally enacted similar legislation.

In most jurisdictions, the initiator or proponent of a development project has the responsibility for undertaking an environmental assessment of the proposed activity. Small projects with no substantial or significant impact are screened out and are allowed to proceed without any environmental assessment statement. However, projects which may have significant adverse environmental impact are usually submitted to an administrative agency for a structured review which may lead to the issuance of guidelines or general or specific directions. Major projects are also generally subject to public review by an independent board or panel.

The prescribed content and form of the environmental impact statement are similar in most jurisdictions. The statement will ordinarily contain a description of the project, a statement of the need for the project and possible alternatives, an analysis and prediction of how the project will impact on the environment, a presentation of proposed mitigating measures and a statement of residual adverse effects.

Each of the federal and provincial governments has enacted environmental protection legislation to regulate air and water pollution, the transportation and storage of dangerous goods and hazardous wastes, pesticides, contaminates, and radiation. The statutes dealing with such matters are generally enforced by criminal sanctions and give courts the power to strip profits, order license suspensions, and issue restoration and restraining orders.

There are also significant considerations with respect to the potential liability of directors and lenders for environmental problems. Directors may be held personally liable for the environmental consequences of a corporation's activities, particularly where the director is an inside director, that is, an officer or employee of the corporation or a major shareholder. The most recent targets of the enlargement of environmental responsibility, however, are lenders. Depending on the degree of financial control exercised by a lender and the lender's ability to control the behavior of the borrower, lenders are potentially liable for the environmental offenses committed by their borrowers. This issue is often raised in the context of receivership, where control is obvious.

Consumer Protection Legislation

The federal and provincial governments have enacted a wide variety of legislation designed to protect consumers. Fundamental to consumer protection law as it has developed in Canada is the requirement that the cost of credit in consumer transactions be fully disclosed. In addition, a consumer's right to be protected from negligent or erroneous credit reporting and to avoid liability for unsolicited credit cards or goods have been firmly established. Other regulated activities include direct sales, misleading advertising and certain other trade practices.

Many types of businesses must be registered or licensed under provincial consumer protection legislation, including collection agencies, real estate agents, motor vehicle dealers, direct sellers, consumer reporting agencies and private investigators, mortgage brokers, lenders, pyramid franchisers, dealers and sellers of farm machinery, travel agents, suppliers of pre-arranged funeral services, mobile home dealers, income tax discounters, hearing aid dealers, employment agents, conditional sellers, operators of physical fitness studios and paperback book dealers.

All of the provinces, with the exception of Quebec, have sale of goods legislation which defines the terms of contractual relations where there is a sale of personal property and where the agreement between the parties is silent. Such legislation is not directed specifically at consumer transactions but rather covers all sales transactions involving "goods".

Government Disclosure

As discussed above, while the Investment Canada Act provides for governmental review only in the case of significant foreign investment, non-Canadians must file a notice regarding all non-reviewable acquisitions or the establishment of new Canadian businesses. The information that is obtained in the course of the administration of the Act is considered to be privileged and confidential.

Other federal information returns include those filed pursuant to the Income Tax Act, Unemployment Insurance Act and the Canada Pension Plan. In addition, financial and other information is collected under the Corporation's and Labor Unions Returns Act from certain corporations, primarily to enable the government to evaluate the extent and effects of non-resident ownership and control of corporations in Canada. Corporations incorporated under the Canada Business Corporations Act are required to file an annual return in prescribed form as well as financial statements and other notices in certain circumstances.

Provincial incorporation or corporate information statutes generally require the filing of an annual or other return by all corporations doing business in the province. The information required to be disclosed may vary depending on whether the corporation is incorporated under the laws of the province or is merely registered to do business there.

All corporations which are "reporting issuers" or which distribute their securities to the public within the definitions contained in provincial securities laws may be required to make regular filings, including the filing of their financial statements and copies of materials sent to security holders.

Language Legislation

Canada is officially a bilingual country. Approximately 25 percent of its population is French-speaking. A majority of the francophones in Canada reside in Quebec. When doing business in Canada, a non-resident must therefore take into account a series of federal and Quebec laws and regulations which are designed to protect language rights and promote the survival of the French language and culture.

For example, the federal Consumer Packaging and Labelling Act provides for labelling and packaging in both English and French in equivalent form. The requirements apply to all consumer products marketed and sold in Canada, whether locally manufactured or imported. Goods marketed or sold in contravention of such requirements are subject to seizure and potential destruction by federal authorities.

When doing business in Quebec, it is necessary to consider the requirements of the Charter of the French Language. This legislation is designed to make French the everyday language of work, instruction, communication, commerce and business in Quebec. In general, the Charter requires every inscription on or related to a product to be in French. Instructions for use and warranty certificates must also be in French. A translation may accompany the French inscription but it may not be given greater prominence than the French version. The regulations specify certain exceptions to the French language labelling requirements including, for example, products intended solely for a market outside Quebec and greeting cards, calendars and agendas not for purposes of advertising. The Charter also requires all public signs, posters, and commercial advertising in Quebec to be in French although certain exceptions are permitted.

The name of firms doing business in Quebec are required to be French unless the statute under which they are incorporated does not permit it. Only the French firm name may be used in Quebec. Certain non-French elements may, however, be permitted to appear as part of the name and a version of the name in another language may also be shown on products that are offered for sale both in and outside of Quebec. Signs on commercial establishments are generally required to be in French only, with certain exceptions for small businesses.

Under the Charter, it is mandatory for business firms with 50 or more employees in Quebec to obtain a francization certificate in respect of their Quebec operations stating that it has properly applied and implemented a francization program at each level of the organization.

A non-Quebec corporation which does business in Quebec will be required to comply with many of the provisions of the Charter such as those relating to labelling of products and communicating with consumers in French.

III. FINANCING

Securities Legislation

Businesses whose operations are to be financed through the issuance and sale of securities will be subject to the securities laws enacted by each of the provinces; there is no federal securities law or federal securities commission in Canada. Regulatory standards imposed by the provincial securities administrators and the Canadian stock exchanges are generally comparable and are similar to U.S. standards.

The securities laws of most provinces prohibit any person or company from trading, underwriting or advising on securities unless that person or company is registered or comes within one of the exemptions from the registration requirements. Ontario and Newfoundland have adopted universal dealer/advisor registration regimes, including new categories of registration for "international dealers" and "non-resident advisers" who restrict their activities to certain types of clients and securities.

Provincial securities laws generally require that, absent a statutory or discretionary exemption, a prospectus be filed for any "distribution" of securities, such that no person or company may "trade" in a security unless a prospectus has been filed or the securities are those of a "reporting issuer" and have been held for a specified period of time.

The securities legislation of most provinces provides for similar exemptions from both dealer registration and prospectus requirements. Among the statutory prospectus exemptions are those available for distributions of securities made: *(i)* to "prescribed institutions" which generally include chartered banks, loan corporations, trust companies, insurance companies and various levels of government in Canada; *(ii)* to "exempt purchasers" which are generally persons with substantial pools of capital, sophisticated investment advisers and professionally managed pension or mutual funds who seek and obtain such status from regulators; and *(iii)* pursuant to the private placement exemption which is available where the purchaser purchases as principal and the trade is in a security which has an aggregate acquisition cost of not less than a specified amount (the prescribed amount in a number of provinces is Can. $150,000). Dealers who wish to promote secondary trading in privately placed securities may seek approval, which is often made subject to conditions, from the Canadian Dealing Network Inc. to quote a market in such securities on the over-the-counter market known as the CDN.

Trades made in reliance upon the statutory prospectus exemptions generally give rise to a requirement to make certain filings with provincial securities regulators. In some cases, an offering memorandum must be prepared and filed. An offering memorandum must generally give the purchaser a contractual right of action against the issuer in rescission or damages where the document contains a misrepresentation.

A prospectus must be prepared in accordance with the regulations of the applicable province and must contain "full, true and plain disclosure of all material facts relating to the securities offered". The preliminary prospectus will be reviewed and commented on by the relevant Securities Commissions; shelf prospectus rules and prompt-offering qualification rules may shorten the time periods for review for certain issuers. After filing the final prospectus, the issuer will become a "reporting issuer" and will be subject to rules regarding continuous disclosure and ongoing reporting requirements including those regarding timely disclosure of material changes, preparation of certain financial information for delivery to securityholders, solicitation of proxies, preparation of information circulars and insider reporting.

The rules governing secondary trading applied in the Canadian provinces take one of two forms, the "closed system" and the "investment intent system". In the closed system, every trade by an issuer of its own securities requires the filing of a prospectus or a ruling from the relevant provincial Securities Commission allowing the sale unless a statutory prospectus exemption is available. Securities distributed by way of a prospectus exemption must be resold either by way of a prospectus or reliance on a further exemption or pursuant to a set of resale restrictions. Under those restrictions, the issuer of securities must be a "reporting issuer" not in default, no unusual effort may be made to prepare the market for the securities being sold and the person proposing to sell the securities must have held them for a minimum hold period ranging from six to 18 months. Sales of securities by "a control person" are by definition a distribution, and therefore must be made pursuant to a prospectus, a prospectus exemption or resale rules similar to those relating to securities acquired pursuant to a prospectus exemption. A control person is indirectly defined under securities law as a holder of sufficient securities of an issuer to materially affect control of the issuer and includes, in the absence of evidence to the contrary, a holder of 20 percent or more of outstanding voting securities. The "investment intent system" generally permits the resale without a prospectus of securities which have been privately placed.

Provincial securities laws, as well as the Canada Business Corporations Act and certain provincial corporations laws, regulate the conduct of take-over bids made to securityholders within the relevant jurisdiction. The procedural requirements of such bids relate to such matters as the minimum period of time the bid must remain open, the conditions of the bid, the effect of pre-bid and post-bid purchases and the requirement to prepare and deliver to securityholders an information circular. On achieving ownership of 10 percent or more of the outstanding voting shares of any class, and for each additional two percent acquired, an acquiror must file a report with regulators and make public disclosure by way of a press release. Where related parties are participants to the transaction, these transactions as well as going private transactions and significant asset transactions may trigger additional procedural and substantive requirements. Exemptions from take-over bid rules are available where the bid is made through the facilities of and in accordance with the policies of certain Canadian stock exchanges, is a private agreement purchase or is in respect of a nominal amount of outstanding securities. Bids made by issuers to purchase their own shares are generally subject to disclosure and timing requirements similar to those of take-over bids.

Insider trading and tipping are statutory offenses carrying criminal penalties. Civil remedies are also available to a purchaser and seller of securities where the trade involves such activity.

As a result of a recent move to internationalize the regulation of capital markets, Canadian regulators and the U.S. Securities and Exchange Commission now permit distributions and rights offerings in Canada to be made by certain U.S. issuers on the basis of disclosure documents prepared in accordance with U.S. Securities Act of 1933 and Securities Exchange Act of 1934 rather than requiring compliance with Canadian provincial securities legislation. These new rules apply to certain rights and exchange offers, take-over bids, issuer bids and business combinations and extend to recognition of certain home jurisdiction continuous reporting obligations.

Personal Property Security

Where security is granted for a loan, registration of the secured interest is governed by provincial law. In this regard, Ontario, Manitoba, Saskatchewan, Alberta and British Columbia have adopted personal property security legislation modelled after Article 9 of the U.S. Uniform Commercial Code. Such legislation may or may not require the filing of financing statements within a specified time after execution of the underlying security instrument. The legislation provides for perfection of security interests and outlines the priority scheme to be applied if a lender seeks to realize on its security.

Each of the other provinces and territories, with the exception of Quebec, have a system of registration established pursuant to conditional sales legislation or similar provisions. Quebec's system of personal property security is found principally in its Civil Code, which states that personal property, labelled "movables" may not be hypothecated. While various forms of security have been developed, there remains no registration system which allows for a simple determination of priorities. This is normally dealt with through agreed covenants and representations.

The federal government has passed legislation dealing with personal property security in limited areas of federal authority, such as shipping and certain security taken by banks.

IV.   GENERAL PRIVATE AND COMMERCIAL LAW

Real Estate

The sale and development of real estate is under the jurisdiction of the provincial governments. In every province except Prince Edward Island, a non-resident is generally entitled to take, acquire, hold and dispose of real property in the same manner as a Canadian citizen or resident. Prince Edward Island, however, has enacted the Lands Protection Act which significantly restricts the amount of land that may be held by persons not resident in the province. In addition, provincial licensing or registration requirements imposed upon extra-provincial corporations carrying on business in the province must be complied with if the corporation is to hold land in some provinces.

Although provincial governments are responsible for land-use planning, a variety of planning functions are delegated to the municipalities. In Ontario, Quebec, British Columbia and New Brunswick, municipal powers are extensive and provincial supervision is minimal while the degree of control exercised by the other provincial governments over municipal action is considerably tighter. Much of the regulation of real property is in the form of zoning by-laws and building by-laws. Zoning by-laws regulate virtually all aspects of the use of land, the nature of buildings and structures thereon, the size of parcels of land and the permissible development of land among other things. Building by-laws, including building permit requirements and building code standards, govern such matters as building materials, heating and ventilation systems, electrical systems, sewage and water systems, access, and inspection. The National Building Code of Canada has been adopted in whole or in part by the municipalities of most provinces, resulting in a trend toward national uniformity in building regulation.

Other provincial legislation to be considered in appropriate circumstances includes environmental legislation, particularly with respect to potentially environmentally-sensitive properties, residential rent control legislation, and legislation regulating real estate brokers, which generally requires brokers to be resident in the province in which they are registered.

Each province administers a system for the registration of interests in land, both with respect to title to land and encumbrances thereon. The two major systems in use in Canada are the Registry System in the Maritime provinces and parts of Ontario and Manitoba and the Land Titles or "Torrens" System in British Columbia, Alberta, Saskatchewan, most of Manitoba and a substantial and increasing part of Ontario. The Registry System is a "registration of deeds" system which provides for the public registration of instruments affecting land but does not make any qualitative statement as to the status of title. The Land Titles System. however, provides for more than simply the registration of documents and title is, subject to certain exceptions, effectively guaranteed by the state.

Taxes on real property constitute a major source of revenue in Canada. The majority of these taxes are levied at the municipal level and used to provide municipal services. Some provinces also levy taxes on the purchase of land and impose various other taxes on mines, timber property and similar properties. Federal involvement in this area is limited to income taxes on rentals and the proceeds from sales of real property.

In several jurisdictions, the purchaser of lands is required to pay provincial and/or municipal land transfer tax or property purchase tax. The specifics of the legislation will differ significantly from province to province but they do not generally differentiate between transactions involving only Canadians and those involving non-residents. Under the Ontario Land Transfer Tax Act, however, non-residents of Canada who purchase land which is not zoned, assessed, or lawfully used for commercial, industrial, or residential purposes or which is assessed or actually used as farm or agricultural land, woodlands, recreation land, or an orchard are taxed at a significantly higher rate than Canadian residents. Quebec also levies considerably higher taxes on purchase by non-resident of certain agricultural and recreational lands.

Income taxes are normally payable on profits or gains from the disposition of land. Where the vendor of Canadian real property is not resident in Canada, the purchaser will generally require the vendor to provide a clearance certificate from the Receiver General of Canada prior to closing. If the vendor fails to provide such a certificate, the purchaser is required to withhold one third of the purchase price and remit it to the Receiver General on the vendor's behalf. In addition to these taxes, GST will be imposed on the sale or lease of real property with exceptions for prescribed property, such as previously inhabited residential property.

The imposition of other taxes will differ from one jurisdiction to another. For example, a recently-imposed Ontario tax, known as the commercial concentration tax, is imposed annually at a rate of $1 per square foot on commercial projects in the Greater Metropolitan Toronto Area having more than 200,000 square feet of floor space and on all parking lots.

Intellectual Property

Patent Law

Patent law in Canada has been greatly influenced by the legal systems of Great Britain and the United States. Amendments which became effective in 1989 brought the Patent Act into substantial conformity with the equivalent legislation of the other members of the Patent Cooperation Treaty of 1970. Under the Act, an inventor is granted the exclusive right to make, construct, use, and sell an invention, which is defined as "any new and useful art, process, machine, manufacture, or composition of matter" and any new and useful improvement thereof. The exclusive rights conferred under the Act are limited to Canada; a person who makes or sells the invention outside of Canada does not breach the Canadian patent.

A patent will be granted to an inventor who is first to file an application under the Act, and is valid for 17 years from the date granted for applications filed prior to October 1, 1989 and for 20 years from the date of filing for applications filed on or after October 1, 1989. Damages or an accounting of profits and injunctive relief are available where a patent has been infringed. Infringement includes the unauthorized use, sale, import, or export of the patented invention or a substantial equivalent thereof.

The requirement of "absolute novelty" must be met for a patent to be granted. Therefore, any invention that is disclosed or made available to the public before a patent application is filed in Canada or that is described in any patent application previously filed in Canada or elsewhere, in certain circumstances, will not be patentable. If the invention is disclosed to the public by the applicant or a person who gained knowledge of the invention through the applicant, a patent may still be granted unless such disclosure occurs more than one year before the filing of the application. Computer software *per se*, mere scientific principles, and abstract theories are not patentable under Canadian law.

The Patent Act Amendment Act came into force in 1993 and effectively abolished compulsory licensing of "drugs" as well as modifying the scheme for the pricing of patented inventions relating to medicine which are defined as inventions intended or capable of being used for medicine or for the preparation or production of medicine. Patentees of such inventions may be required to disclose to the Patented Medicine Prices Review Board prescribed information including the price at which the medicine is being or has been sold in Canada or elsewhere and the costs of making and marketing the medicine as well as, where requested, information as to the prices at which medicines of the same class are being or have been sold in Canada or elsewhere. Where the Board determines that prices are or have been excessive, it can order the reduction of the price of the medicine or of other medicines being sold by the patentee or order payment to the Crown such as to offset the amount of the excess revenue derived from the sale of the medicine at an excessive price or, where the Board finds that there was a policy of excessive pricing, double the amount of the excess revenues. In determining whether a price is excessive, the Board shall consider, among other things, the prices at which the medicine and similar medicines have sold in the relevant market and abroad, the cost of making and marketing the medicine and changes in the Consumer Price Index.

Copyright

The federal Copyright Act grants the owner of copyright the right to prevent the copying or commercial exploitation of original literary, dramatic, musical, and artistic works and performances. Amendments to the Act in 1988 provided explicit protection for computer programs and established a system for the determination and collection of cable re-transmissions royalties. Copyright is automatically granted to all authors who are citizens or subjects of the U.K., the U.S., or any member country of the Berne Convention, which includes almost all countries of the world. The Intellectual Property Law Improvement Act, which came into force in 1993, extends the provisions of the Copyright Act with respect to exclusivity of rights to all countries which are signatories to the Universal Copyright Convention. Canada had previously extended protection to some but not all Convention signatories.

The Act also provides for registration in the Copyright Office if desired by the owner of the copyright. Registration is optional, as copyright arises at the moment of creation alone, but it does confer benefits. Certain remedies provided for by the Act may only be available in the absence of registration if the author can prove actual knowledge on the part of the infringing party of the existence of the copyright. Actual knowledge is deemed to exist by statute if registration has been effected. Infringement includes the production or reproduction of a copyrighted work or any substantial part thereof and the knowing distribution or offering of the same to the public. A copyright owner also has the right to restrain any distortion, mutilation, misattribution, or other modification of the work which is prejudicial to the author's reputation. Remedies for infringement include damages, an accounting of profits, delivery up of any infringing material and injunctive relief. Criminal sanctions are also available.

Subject to exceptions set out in the Act, the term of protection of a copyrighted work is the life of the author and 50 years after his or her death.

Trademarks

A trademark must serve to distinguish the source of a particular product or service. While registration of a trademark under the federal Trade Marks Act is not mandatory, the extent of protection available to the owner of an unregistered trademark may be limited geographically to the area in which the trademark enjoys some notoriety. In respect of a registered trademark, there is exclusive protection across Canada. In addition, broader remedies are available where there has been an improper use of a registered trademark as opposed to an unregistered one.

In order to be registrable a trademark must be neither clearly descriptive nor deceptively misdescriptive of the character or quality of the goods or services, of the persons employed in their production or of their place of origin, simply the name of the ware or service in another language, primarily merely the name or surname of an individual who is living or who has died within the past 30 years, or likely to cause confusion with a trademark enjoying prior rights. In order to register a trademark, the applicant must claim to have used or made known the trademark in Canada, have registered and used the trademark in another country adhering to the Paris Convention, or propose to use the trademark in Canada.

A trademark is registered for 15 years subject to renewal every 15 years indefinitely. Infringement of a trademark, which may lead to both civil and criminal liability, occurs when there is a sale, distribution or advertisement of wares or services in association with a confusing trademark or trade name. Infringement also occurs where a person uses a registered mark in a manner likely to have the effect of depreciating the goodwill attached thereto.

A trademark registration will be invalid if at the time proceedings questioning the validity of the trade mark are commenced the mark has lost its distinctiveness and thus cannot be said to identify in the minds of the public the particular source of the goods or service. The most common means of losing distinctiveness has generally been the licensing of the trademark without registering such license. The new Intellectual Property Law Improvement Act has, however, abolished the requirement for the registration of licensed users of marks. Under the new regime the licensor/owner of the mark is obliged to maintain direct or indirect control over the character or quality of the wares or services in respect of which the mark is licensed.

Industrial Designs

The federal Industrial Designs Act grants exclusive rights with respect to a registered industrial design within Canada for the duration of its registration. Industrial design is defined as "features of shape, configuration, pattern or ornament and any combination of those features that, in a finished article, appeal to and are judged solely by the eye."

Registration requires the filing of a description and drawing or photograph of the design and a declaration that the design was not being used and had not been used, to the applicant's knowledge, by any other person at the time that the applicant adopted it. A valid registration requires absolute novelty, namely the design should neither be found to be identical with some other design already registered nor to so closely resemble some other design as to be confused therewith. Initial application must be made within one year of the publication of the design in Canada and may be made by the author, the author's successor in title or the person for whom the author created the work.

The exclusive rights conveyed by the registration of an industrial design are valid for five years and may be renewed for a further period of five years, to a limit of 10 years in total. The infringement of a registered industrial design may give rise to both civil and penal remedies. In the absence of marking of the object with the notice provided by statute only injunctive relief is available. Infringement includes the unauthorized use of an exact copy, an obvious imitation, or a fraudulent imitation, the application of the design or an imitation thereof to another article for purposes of sale, exposure for sale or use of the article and the publishing, selling, or exposing for sale or use of any such article. It is not, however, an infringement to apply a design similar or identical to that which has been registered to a substantially different article or in a new or novel manner.

Semi-Conductor Chips

The Integrated Circuit Topography Act was proclaimed in force in 1993 and gives registrants a 10 year exclusive term of protection for the design or topography of integrated circuits, that is, semi-conductor chips. Registration is available to creators of topographies who are nationals of Canada, legal entities who create topographies or manufacture circuit products in Canada, and nationals and residents of foreign countries who offer sufficient protection to Canadian topographies or who are parties to treaties or conventions respecting the protection of topographies to which Canada is also a party.

The application for registration must be filed in Canada within two years of the first commercial exploitation of the topography anywhere in the world. Registration gives the exclusive right to reproduce, manufacture, import, or commercially exploit the topography and any integrated circuit which incorporates the topography or a substantial part thereof. Reverse engineering is lawful for the purposes of evaluation, research, or teaching, but not for commercial purposes.

Bankruptcy Law

The new Bankruptcy and Insolvency Act became effective in 1992. The significant amendments to the former Bankruptcy Act are modelled after Chapter 11 of the Bankruptcy Code of the United States and mark a significant shift in Canadian bankruptcy law away from liquidation to reorganization and workouts of financially troubled companies.

The new Act addresses and substantially reforms commercial reorganizations, consumer arrangements and bankruptcies, Crown claims and priorities, and the protection of unpaid suppliers, among other things. Under the Act, a company may give notice of intention to file a proposal which effects a 30-day stay period against the government and against secured and unsecured creditors, other than any secured creditors who have taken possession of their security or given notice of their intention to enforce their security at least ten days before the first filing of a notice or proposal. During the stay period the business is monitored by a trustee while the debtor attempts to negotiate an acceptable proposal with its creditors. The debtor may seek extensions of the stay period to a maximum of six months in order to formulate a viable proposal. If a proposal is not filed within the allowed time, the debtor will be deemed to have made an assignment in bankruptcy.

The proposal may be made to unsecured creditors only, or to both secured and unsecured creditors. Creditors with proven claims are entitled to vote on the proposal and are divided into classes based on commonality of interest, with all of the unsecured creditors normally comprising one class. The approval of a proposal by a particular class requires a favorable vote by creditors representing a majority in number and two-thirds in value of those voting. The approved proposal will then be binding on all members of that class. A significant difference between the Canadian law and the U.S. Chapter 11 regime is the absence of a full-scale "cram down" to force a reorganization scheme on classes of dissenting secured creditors. The creditors of a class which votes to reject the proposal have all of their rights revived with respect to their security while the classes that vote to accept will be subject to the proposal. If any class of unsecured creditors rejects the proposal, the proposal dies and the debtor is deemed to have made an assignment in bankruptcy. If the unsecured creditors accept the proposal, it is submitted to the court for approval.

There are a number of other reforms under the new Act. Except for source deductions for income tax, unemployment insurance, and Canada Pension Plan contributions, the new Act generally treats government claims as ordinary unsecured claims. The Act also provides that contractual terms providing for the termination, amendment or acceleration of payment under a contract simply by reason that a person is insolvent or has filed a notice of intention or a proposal will be unenforceable. Similar clauses in leases of real property or licensing agreements which are triggered by the non-payment or rent or royalties will also be unenforceable. Any further supply of goods and services may, however, be on a cash basis and unsecured unpaid suppliers are given the right, in certain circumstances, to reclaim goods within 30 days of delivering them to a bankrupt or insolvent company.

Like the new Bankruptcy and Insolvency Act, the Companies' Creditors Arrangement Act may, in certain circumstances, permit a financially troubled company to continue its business through a reorganization by providing for a stay in proceedings against secured and unsecured creditors during a reorganization period. There are several differences between the Acts and an insolvent company has the option of proceeding under either one.

Conflicts

Each of the provinces and territories is a separate territorial entity with its own conflicts of law system. In addition, there is a federal system with respect to matters within federal legislative competence which encompasses the country as a whole. The rules of the common law provinces are similar though not identical, and there are significant differences between the civil law rules of Quebec and the common law regimes of each of the other jurisdictions. On the international level, Canada is a member of the Hague Conference on Private International Law.

It is trite law that matters of substance are governed by the *lex causae*, that is, the chosen law while matters of procedure are governed by the *lex fori*, the law of the forum. It thus becomes crucial to determine whether a given law or statute is procedural or substantive.

The laws of evidence and admissibility are, for the most part, governed by the *lex fori*. This rule is subject to the general qualification that it is not everything which the domestic law would consider as part of the law of evidence that is classified as procedural for conflict of laws purposes, but only provisions of a technical or procedural character. It is also established that questions of the priority of creditors are matters for the forum in relation to bankruptcies, windings-up and administration of insolvent estates.

The matter of the proper parties to an action is generally held to be one of procedure. However, the existence of the right and thus the status to sue is substantive and a matter for the *lex causae*. It is now generally accepted that questions as to the remoteness of damages are substantive and thus for the *lex causae*, whereas issues of the measure and quantification are procedural.

The general rule is that unless foreign law is pleaded and proven, the court applies the law of the forum. In most Canadian courts foreign law is proven:

(1) through provincial evidence statutes that provide for the proof of foreign law or the contents of foreign statues;

(2) through the testimony of duly qualified experts; and

(3) in that the Supreme Court of Canada hearing an appeal from a provincial appellate court will take judicial notice of the laws of another province or territory.

Generally speaking, a Canadian court will not apply a foreign law that deals with the recovery of foreign taxes or the enforcement of foreign penal laws. In addition, a Canadian court will not enforce or recognize a foreign law or judgment or a right, power, capacity or legal relationship arising under a foreign law that is repugnant to the private international law sense of public policy.

One must look to the case law in order to determine which laws a Canadian court will apply in specific situations regarding contracts, torts, and property where multiple jurisdictions are involved.

V. REGULATED SECTORS

There are several sectors of the Canadian economy which are strictly regulated due to their perceived importance to national economic policy including financial services, communications and energy.

Financial Services

The main types of entities providing financial services in Canada are banks, loan and trust companies, insurance companies, cooperative credit associations and securities dealers. These institutions are variously regulated at both the federal and provincial levels.

In 1992 a new framework of federal legislation governing these institutions, the result of a reform process which began in 1985, took effect. The Bank Act, the Trust and Loan Companies Act, the Insurance Companies Act and the Cooperative Credit Associations Act introduced changes which, among other things, were designed to broaden competition among financial institutions and to increase their lending and investment powers, all within the context of enhanced consumer protection. This new legislation has also revised the rules of ownership and acquisitions of Canadian financial institutions.

Banks are classified under the Bank Act as Schedule I banks, Schedule II banks, and foreign banks. Where any person beneficially owns directly or indirectly more than 10 percent of any class of shares of a bank, the bank will fall within Schedule II; where there is no such person, the bank will be classified in Schedule I. A Schedule II bank is referred to as a "foreign bank subsidiary" if it is controlled *de jure* by one foreign bank. A foreign bank is broadly defined under the Act to include any foreign entity that carries on a business that would be considered a banking activity if carried on in Canada and any affiliate of that entity. Notwithstanding the FTA and the special treatment afforded to U.S. residents elsewhere in the Act, a U.S. bank is still considered a foreign bank.

Foreign banks are not empowered to undertake any aspect of banking business in Canada except as expressly permitted by the Bank Act. A foreign bank may perform banking activities in Canada only through a foreign bank subsidiary, one or more non-bank affiliates, or one or more registered representative offices. The restrictions placed on the non-bank affiliates of a foreign bank, however, effectively preclude such affiliates from carrying on many core banking activities, including loaning money, accepting deposit liabilities and, in certain circumstances, borrowing money and issuing bonds, debentures, or other securities evidencing such borrowing. Representative offices are only permitted to promote the services of the foreign bank and act as a liaison between the foreign bank and its clients. Foreign bank subsidiaries generally have all the rights and privileges of other banks and are subject to most of the same restrictions and limitations. The major limitations on the incorporation of foreign bank subsidiaries in Canada are the requirements that the total domestic assets of foreign bank subsidiaries as a group not exceed 12 percent of the total domestic assets of the Canadian banking system and that there be favorable treatment for Canadian banks in the jurisdiction in which the foreign bank principally carries on business. All of the rules respecting foreign bank subsidiaries will also govern Schedule II banks controlled by statutorily-defined "eligible foreign institutions."

There are rules under the Bank Act governing the ownership of shares of banks operating in Canada which are designed to prevent any one shareholder or related group of shareholders from acquiring control of a Schedule I bank, to maintain a significant degree of Canadian ownership of banks and to restrict transfers of shares of foreign bank subsidiaries. Each of the other statutes refers to also addresses the share ownership of the relevant financial institutions. Canadian and U.S. residents, the latter generally being treated as Canadian residents under these statutes, are subject to a 10 percent limit on ownership of any class of shares of Schedule I banks and a 65 percent limit on ownership of the voting rights attached to shares of other large financial institutions. A Schedule II bank may be closely-held by Canadians or Americans for the first 10 years of its existence or until its consolidated capital reaches $750 million. After that time, no person may hold more than 10 percent of any class of shares, subject to the exception which permits a foreign bank or an eligible domestic or foreign financial institution to hold a Schedule II bank as its subsidiary indefinitely. As with Schedule II banks, trust, loan and stock insurance companies may be closely-held subject to a limit of 65 percent of voting rights in the case of companies with consolidated capital of $750 million or more. When consolidated capital reaches that level, shares carrying 35 percent of the voting rights attached to all issued shares must be beneficially owned by persons who do not own in excess of 10 percent of any class of shares and must be listed on a Canadian stock exchange. Non-residents other than U.S. residents, may generally not own more than 10 percent of any class of shares of any bank or 10 percent of the voting rights attached to issued shares of any other financial institution; non-resident investment in any financial institution is limited in the aggregate to 25 percent of total voting rights. These "10/25" rules do not apply to financial institutions, including foreign bank subsidiaries, which are under the *de juré* control of a non-resident.

Approval will be required to acquire more than 10 percent of any class of shares of a financial institution and to acquire additional shares where the person acquiring the shares already holds 10 percent of the shares of any class. The criteria which will be considered in granting approval include the nature and sufficiency of the applicant's financial resources, the existence of a sound and feasible business plan, the business record and experience of the applicant, the assurance of responsible operation by competent and experienced persons, the size of the acquiror and the institution to be acquired and the best interests of the Canadian financial system. The Competition Act and the Investment Canada Act will continue to apply to acquisitions in most cases.

In addition to the federal legislation mentioned above, trust companies, loan companies and insurance companies are subject to provincial legislation which varies from province to province. Most provinces impose a licensing or registration regime for each of these types of companies which must be complied with in order for such a company to operate in the province.

The new legislation reserves to the Cabinet and the responsible Minister and regulators substantial discretion to make regulations and to issue orders or directions respecting the activities of financial institutions.

Quebec and British Columbia, with the cooperation of the federal government, have each enacted legislation creating "International Financial Centers" in Montreal and Vancouver and providing tax and other advantages to foreign corporations, and in the case of Quebec, Canadian-owned corporations, and their employees where their activities consist of certain international financial transactions.

Communications

The field of communications has become increasingly subject to the legislative authority of the federal government. The federal government has exclusive jurisdiction over broadcasting, cable television and telecommunications except to the extent that telecommunications services are of a purely intra-provincial nature. The Canadian Radio-Television and Telecommunications Act ("CRTC Act") established the Canadian Radio-Television and Telecommunications Commission ("the CRTC") which is the primary regulatory body in the areas of broadcasting and telecommunications.

The principal federal legislative provisions governing broadcasting, both the technical "hardware" aspects and the content aspects, are the CRTC Act, the Broadcasting Act and the Radio Communication Act. The Minister of Communications is given the power under the Radio Act to regulate the technical aspects of broadcasting undertakings and the authority to license radio stations and radio apparatus other than broadcasting undertakings. The CRTC is charged under the Broadcasting Act with regulating and supervising all aspects of the Canadian broadcasting system with a view to implementing the policy enunciated in that Act, a key element of which is the declaration that

> . . . the Canadian broadcasting system should be effectively owned and controlled by Canadians so as to safeguard, enrich and strengthen the cultural, political, social and economic fabric in Canada.

The CRTC is empowered under the Act to issue, attach conditions to, amend, renew, suspend and revoke licenses, establish rules of procedure, make regulations and carry out and support research. The CRTC has enacted extensive regulations under the Act governing radio stations, television, information returns and license fees. The Broadcasting Act also provides for Cabinet to make directions to the CRTC regarding licensing, among other things, and a direction has been issued prohibiting the issuance and the granting of renewals of licenses to governments other than the government of Canada and to persons who are not Canadian citizens or "eligible Canadian corporations."

The Telecommunications Act became effective in 1993. There had previously been substantial confusion regarding the question of which level of government had jurisdiction over telecommunications and the result was a poor mix of federal and provincial legislation. The Telecommunications Act responds to recent judicial statements placing jurisdiction over the principal telecommunications carriers in Canada with the federal government.

The Act is administered by the CRTC which is bound by the terms of the statute to implement enunciated policy objectives when exercising its powers and performing its duties. The Act states that telecommunications perform an essential role in the maintenance of Canada's identity and sovereignty and lists a number of policy objectives including the promotion of Canadian ownership and control of telecommunications carriers operating or providing services in Canada, the enhancement of the efficiency and national and international competitiveness of Canadian telecommunications, the stimulation of Canadian research and development, and innovation in the field and the provision of services at reasonable rates in light of market forces.

The new licensing regime under the Act requires telecommunications carriers to be Canadian owned and controlled corporations incorporated or continued under Canadian laws. In order to be considered to be Canadian owned and controlled, not less than 80 percent of the board of directors must be Canadian and not less than 80 percent of the voting shares of the corporation must be beneficially owned by Canadians. Provisions are made, however, for the protection of the existing rights of non-Canadian owners so long as the present level of Canadian ownership is maintained.

The provision of telecommunications services by a carrier will be subject to such conditions as may be imposed by the CRTC or included in a tariff approved by the CRTC. Every carrier must file with and have approved by the CRTC a tariff specifying the rate or rates to be charged, which rates must be found by the CRTC to be just and reasonable and may not be discriminatory. The Act gives the CRTC the power to refrain from exercising its normal regulatory powers where it deems there is sufficient competition to ensure reasonable rates and prevent discriminatory practices. Finally, advance rulings from the CRTC will be available to entrepreneurs planing to provide telecommunications services in Canada.

The CRTC is given broad inspection. investigation, and enforcement powers and contravention of the Act may result in civil and criminal liability carrying fines of up to one million dollars in some situations.

The impact of the Canada-U.S. FTA on the communications field has been in the area of "enhanced" or value-added telecommunications services; the FTA does not apply to basic point-to-point telecommunications or to broadcasting. Each country must accord to carriers or providers of enhanced telecommunications services of the other country treatment no less favorable than that accorded to carriers of its own country in like circumstances. "Enhanced" services are similarly defined by the CRTC and the American Federal Communications Commission to include voice or data storage and retrieval, store and forward and computer applications of point-to-point services. The ultimate determination of whether a particular service is "enhanced" will, however, remain the decision of the regulatory body of each country and the FTA does not require them to adopt the same interpretation.

Energy and Natural Resources

Responsibility for the regulation of energy and natural resources in Canada is shared by the federal and provincial governments. The principal federal regulatory body is the National Energy Board (the "NEB") created by the National Energy Board Act. In addition, there are numerous provincial bodies whose statutory mandates relate to energy and natural resources. The determination of which level of government has jurisdiction over a particular matter depends on a number of factors including the scope of the undertaking, the nature of the energy development, and the national importance of the energy resource. The federal government will normally be the relevant authority regarding energy issues of interprovincial or international significance.

The general responsibility of the NEB is to regulate defined aspects of the interprovincial and international movement of oil, gas, and electricity in the public interest. The NEB has the power to grant certificates of public convenience and necessity for the construction of pipelines and power lines, to issue licenses for exports of oil, gas, or electricity and for imports of oil or gas and to approve tolls and tariffs for interprovincial and international pipelines. The NEB also has the authority to hold inquiries into any aspect of energy matters under its jurisdiction and to issue reports for the information of the government and the general public. The NEB does not regulate hydrocarbon exploration, drilling or exploitation, the generation of electric power for use in Canada, or the construction or operation of pipelines that do not cross provincial or national boundaries.

Many of the decisions of the NEB will require federal Cabinet approval. Such decisions include the issuance of certificates for pipelines and of licenses for the long term export of oil and gas, the long-term export of electricity and the construction of international power lines.

NEB approval is required for the establishment of interprovincial and international pipelines and power lines. The approval process normally includes a public hearing and will involve consideration of the technical and financial feasibility and the environmental and socio-economical impact of the proposed project. The long or short term export of oil, gas, or power will also require NEB approval. The Board will have to be satisfied that there will be an adequate supply of energy for Canadian requirements following the export of the proposed quantity, among other things. The market-based procedure used in the approval of export proposals involves a Complaint Procedure which gives Canadian users an opportunity to object on the grounds that they are not able to obtain supplies on similar terms and conditions, the required filing of an Export Impact Assessment to allow the NEB to determine whether the proposed export is likely to cause Canadians difficulty in meeting their energy requirements at fair prices and a Public Interest Determination which allows the NEB to consider virtually any other factors it considers relevant.

The Canada-U.S. FTA will have a significant impact on the energy trade between those countries. As a starting point, the FTA confirms that trade in electricity and other energy goods will be subject to GATT rights and obligations as well as to the provisions of the Agreement. The tariff elimination provisions of the Agreement eliminates existing duties on energy imports and exports and ensure that no new tariffs will be instituted. Canada is also exempt from any U.S. oil import fees. Both governments agree to lift most restrictions on energy imports and exports, subject to the existing GATT reasons for which such restrictions may be imposed, including short supply, conservation of an exhaustible resource, national security or the imposition of price controls. No taxes, duties, or charges on the export of any energy good from the U.S. to Canada or vice versa will be imposed unless they are also imposed on such energy goods when destined for domestic consumption. Amendments to the NEB Act pursuant to the FTA require the NEB to give effect to that Agreement when exercising its functions.

The Atomic Energy Control Board controls the development, application and use of atomic energy in Canada. The Board may, with federal Cabinet approval, make regulations relating to nuclear research, controlling and licensing the production, application and use of atomic energy, and controlling the import, export, use, and sale of uranium, thorium, plutonium, neptunium, deuterium, and derivatives.

Provincial governments have the basic responsibility for energy and natural resources within their own boundaries and, in most cases, are the owners of the resources. The role of the provincial governments in energy and natural resources is, therefore, fundamental. In addition, the provinces regulate energy transportation and marketing.

Notes

[1] Prepared as of July, 1993 by Edward J. Waitzer, formerly of Stikeman, Elliott (Toronto). Edward J. Waitzer is currently Chairman of the Ontario Securities Commission. Readers are referred to Stikeman, Elliott, *Doing Business in Canada* (New York: Matthew Bender) for a more detailed consideration of the Canadian legal environment and should consult Canadian counsel with specific inquiries.

GOING INTERNATIONAL IN LATIN AMERICA

Andrew J. Markus

THIS CHAPTER will seek to give the reader an overview of the major methods of doing business in Latin America other than Mexico. It will also attempt to alert the reader to the major trade blocks and treaties in effect in the region; however, it will not deal with the North American Free Trade Agreement, which now overlays most of the trading between U.S. and Mexican firms.

Latin America (not including Mexico but including Central America) consists of 17 countries with a total cumulative population of approximately 400 million people. It is a vibrant, thriving market which previously was often governed in a non-democratic fashion and which utilized, as its economic models, statism and import substitution. Beginning in the 1980's and as of today, Latin America has made a remarkable and profound change. No longer do totalitarian governments rule in any Latin American country. Trade has been freed or in some cases greatly liberalized. Inflation has been tamed almost everywhere. Debt agreements have been renegotiated and payments stabilized. Government companies have been privatized and capital inflows into Latin American countries have increased substantially. Latin America's potential as a market is slowly becoming realized.

By the same token, laws relating to foreign investment continue to be modernized. The influence of the Andean Pact model of market protection is slowly waning. At the same time dislocations in the markets and increasing unemployment is the result of market modernization. The next few years will tell whether the direction of liberalized trade and open markets will be permanent.

I. RESTRICTIONS ON FOREIGN INVESTMENT AND OWNERSHIP

It seems appropriate to begin this chapter with an indication of those areas in which trade is restricted. They are few in number. Businesses looking to do business in Latin America in some or all of these sectors will need to have specialized know-how in order to participate.

The Effect of Latin American Constitutions on Trade Restrictions

Latin American constitutions by and large contain certain restrictions on trade. The primary restriction is the concept of *patrimonio nacional*. This concept means that certain areas of investment are considered property of the state and therefore restricted to citizens of that state. For instance, in most countries in Latin America, non-citizens may not own land within a certain number of kilometers from the border. In Bolivia and Peru this restriction is 50 kilometers. Likewise, non-citizens may not explore and extract mineral resources in frontier zones. Often the oil industry is restricted to nationals. Before now, many state monopolies existed such as hydro-electric, electric, telephone, oil, and other strategic industries. Many of these industries have been privatized and made available to foreign investment, although sometimes only if such foreign investment is made through a national company. A potential investor must obtain advice concerning the type of business that the investor wishes to do in order to insure that it is available for foreign participation.

Public Policy

One other restriction on trade and investment is the pervasive use of the doctrine of public policy by Latin American lawmakers and courts. A number of common restrictions to freedom of contract are justified on this basis. Latin American lawmakers and courts use the public policy argument as a way of evening out what they see as the weak economic bargaining position of their constituency. For example, the ability to freely terminate agents or distributors is restricted in some Latin American countries and requires "just cause" and often indemnification payments. The modification of these restrictions by contract is prohibited and is viewed as contrary to public policy. Likewise, the extension of patent protection to pharmaceuticals has been denied pursuant to a similar public policy analysis. It is said that the provision of pharmaceutical products to the general population is a matter which should not be restricted in order to safeguard the health of the nation including those who might not be able to afford such medicines if they were subject to "monopoly" pricing. Accordingly, the granting of the patent, which could give the patent holder the right to restrict access to the product, is denied. Finally, another example of the public policy restriction is the refusal of certain Latin American countries courts to enforce clauses providing for the use of foreign law in the interpretation of contracts or for the exclusive jurisdiction of foreign courts in the enforcement of contractual provisions.

II.   DOING BUSINESS IN LATIN AMERICA: THE AGENCY/DISTRIBUTION RELATIONSHIP

The initial approach to going international in Latin American is often focused on supplying goods to purchasers in Latin America without the establishment of manufacturing facilities or other more permanent facilities. For this type of relationship, companies typically turn to agents or distributors. A distributor is defined as one who buys or sells for his or her own account and thereafter resells the goods, and receives compensation based on a mark-up. A distributor is independent from the manufacturer and bears the credit risk associated with the sale of the goods. An agent, however, does not buy for his or her own account. The agent sells products supplied by and at the risk of the manufacturer, making thereby a commission on each sale. There is a substantial difference between the two in most countries in Latin America. As a general rule, if a manufacturer has a choice between appointing an agent or a distributor, the manufacturer will appoint a distributor. This is appropriate for several reasons, including the avoidance of taxation, the avoidance of jurisdiction for suit, the avoidance of the applicability of local labor laws and ease of termination.

Labor Laws

Most Latin American countries have laws that protect and grant certain benefits to employees. A distributor is not generally considered an employee. Upon termination of the distributor relationship, the distributor would not be permitted to claim the benefit of employment termination indemnities. Manufacturers who wish to employ agents may contract with a corporation instead of an individual. This often avoids the application of local labor laws since the definition of employee under most Latin American laws includes physical persons but not juridical entities.

Taxes

The manufacturer who appoints an agent may be deemed to have established a branch or other permanent establishment within the applicable country. Doing business through independent distributors who work in their own names often avoids this problem.

Jurisdiction

A distributorship agreement can often be subject to foreign law. This gives the manufacturer the ability to make its distribution agreements consistent and avoid unfavorable local treatment. Agency contracts on the other hand are often required to be subject to local law based upon a contacts analysis.

Termination

In many Latin American countries, distributorship and agency contracts may be terminated freely at the expiration of the term of the agreement. This is true in Argentina, Chile, Peru and Venezuela, for example. It is appropriate not to provide for a renewal option. In these countries, termination is generally honored except if a contract has been renewed numerous times giving rise to a presumption that the contract is of indefinite duration. Another problem arises if a court considers that an abuse of rights has occurred. Such abuse of rights occurs when the manufacturer leads the distributor to believe that renewal will occur. This is the equivalent of an estoppel argument and has been upheld by at least one Latin American court.

Other countries in Latin America have much more protective legislation for distributors. These countries, including Costa Rica, the Dominican Republic, Ecuador, Honduras and Panama, typically require "just cause" for a distributorship contract to be terminated. Under these countries legislation, "just cause" typically requires either breach of contract by the distributor, fraud or abuse of confidence by the distributor, ineptitude or negligence, a continued decrease of sales of the product for reasons attributable to the distributor, improper disclosure of confidential information, or damage to the reputation of the manufacturer or its products or to the sale or distribution of the products. Andean Pact countries also delineate "just cause" as bankruptcy of the distributor. The manufacturer has the burden of proof and this burden is often difficult to establish. Therefore, contracts for distributors should contain specific enumerations of duties and not just best efforts or other vague standards. A manufacturer should consider placing in the contract a definite quota of sales, payment requirements, reporting requirements, trademark protection, and policing requirements and other specific duties. These provisions should be enforced and when specific acts occur and are not deemed "just cause" for termination, specific written waivers should be delivered.

Termination Payments and Indemnities

Certain countries in Latin America provide for more freedom of contract than others. In certain countries, notably Argentina, Bolivia, Chile, Peru, and Venezuela, no indemnification or compensation is required to be paid other than as provided by the contract. Agents in most of these countries are required to receive notice of termination and compensation under the labor laws. In other countries, distributors are much more protected. For instance, in Brazil, although indemnification for termination may be agreed upon by contract, such indemnification may not be less than five percent of the total compensation earned during the term of the agreement. In other countries such as Colombia, Costa Rica, the Dominican Republic, Ecuador, El Salvador and other Central American countries, indemnification is generally required to be paid. Such indemnification takes into account the distributor's investment, the value of physical assets used in the business with no alternative use, the value of inventories and credit extended by the dealer, as well as average yearly *gross* profits. Some egregious termination rights apply in countries such as the Dominican Republic where the manufacturer may have to pay, in addition to the value of the above items, an amount equal to the total *gross* profits of the distributor for the previous five years or five times the average annual profit of the distributor during the term of the contract if the contract is less than five years in duration. In Panama, a contract in place less than five years requires an indemnity equal to the average yearly gross profit of the distributor. If the contract has been in existence in excess of five years but no more than ten years, the indemnity amount is two times the average yearly gross profit; for contracts of 10 to 15 years, three times; for contracts of 15 to 20 years, four times; and for contracts over 20 years, five times.

In addition to the above termination indemnities, often agents are entitled to notice and compensation under a country's labor laws. In Venezuela, for example, an agent may be eligible for unjust dismissal compensation under the labor laws. This equals one half a month's salary (based on current salary) for each year of employment plus 15 days wages for each year of employment not to exceed a total of eight months' wages. In Argentina, an agent who is unjustly dismissed is entitled to one month's compensation for each year of service.

Other Potential Pitfalls

In most Latin American countries, a distributor or an agent is presumed to be exclusive unless the contract specifically provides for non-exclusivity. The burden of proof is on the manufacturer (i.e., the person appointing the agent/distributor). Accordingly, a failure to specify in the contract may restrict the manufacturer from supplying goods through others in the market and may also require the manufacturer to pay a commission to the distributor notwithstanding the fact that the manufacturer may have sold the products itself in the market.

It is difficult to supervise sub-distributors in many Latin American countries. The manufacturer will often want control over the quality of the product, representations made concerning the product, pricing, and standards for sales performance such as sales quotas. In the event that sub-distributors are utilized, the manufacturer should specifically require its distributor to supervise and police the performance of sub-distributors.

In all contracts where the application of law other than the law of the nation in which the distributor/agent operates is desired, the applicable law should be specified. Many countries will recognize the laws of the manufacturer's own country. Those that do not, will simply disregard the clause. In any event, it is appropriate for all such contracts to be reviewed by local counsel and to be harmonized with local law where possible.

III. FORM OF BUSINESS ENTERPRISE

Companies may wish to do business on a more concentrated basis in Latin America than merely by selling through an agent or a distributor. Obvious reasons for such establishment include manufacturing to supply a market or a group of markets (i.e., the Mercosur countries), the ability to take advantage of labor rates that are significantly less than those in the United States, or the ability to meet local content rules required to take advantage of free trade areas. The analysis will essentially consist of whether the company should organize a branch or a subsidiary in a specific country.

Branch Operation

Many companies utilize a branch organization in Latin America. Its advantage is that it is organized along centralized lines in a country whose laws the company understands. It can be utilized to allow the company to do business in many different countries in Latin America without having to deal with many different laws. Stockholder and board meetings may be held in one centralized location and major decisions may be taken by one board of directors. Legal requirements are vastly simplified. The company thereby saves considerable time and expense. Typically for the constitution of a branch, the parent company must provide documentation properly legalized indicating:

(i) That the company is duly constituted and in good standing under the laws of the jurisdiction in which it is formed;

(ii) That the company is authorized to constitute a branch and that the particular branch has been duly authorized by all requisite corporate action;

(iii) That the company has established a representative in the country for which the branch is to be established;

(iv) That the company has sufficient capital to fund its operations in the country. Some countries require that minimum capital be stated (i.e., Guatemala–U.S. $10,000; Honduras–U.S. $12,500 and El Salvador–U.S. $40,000 for a branch engaged in industrial activities and U.S. $80,000 for a branch engaged in commercial activities). In Brazil, a branch authorized to do business in Brazil also is mandated to maintain a certain level of capital. Chile and Colombia require only that the branch maintain sufficient assets to render it solvent and able to respond to its obligations.

(v) That the purpose for which the branch is constituted is lawful under the laws of the company's place of incorporation; and

(vi) That the branch recognizes the laws of the country in which it is being established as the law applicable to its operations.

All documentation must be submitted in the language of the country in which the branch is being established and legalized by the applicable consulate. Once submitted, registration requires from three to nine months, depending on the country. Changes in representatives or changes in stated capital must be also registered on a timely basis. Certain countries require corporate financial statements to be filed annually with the Registrar of Companies.

Subsidiary Companies

The use of a subsidiary company requires the creation of a company in the nation in which the subsidiary will operate. A board of directors separate from the parent company must be constituted. Local legal regulations must be followed in the constitution of the subsidiary company. A list of shareholders and minutes of meetings must often be filed in a public registry. Share transfers must also be registered. Often shareholder and directors meetings must be held in the country of origin (with the exception of Panama, Costa Rica, and the Bahamas). Unlike the United States, most companies require for their establishment no less than two shareholders. Certain countries, such as Uruguay and Nicaragua, require three shareholders, and other countries such as Ecuador require five shareholders. Shareholders are required to hold an annual meeting to approve the financial statements of the company for the previous year and appoint new directors. One distinguishing feature of some Latin American countries' companies is a surveillance committee which represents the shareholders and supervises the accounting functions of the company and the activities of the board of directors. Dividends are typically declared by the shareholders and not the board of directors. It is important to note that because the legal systems of Latin America are not uniform, certain influences make the operation of the companies different in different countries. Panama has typically had the most progressive corporate law in Latin America. Its corporate law is very much modeled on U.S. law with of course, Latin American influences. The British influence is very common in certain parts of the Caribbean. Other countries' laws are influenced by French and Spanish civil law, as well as the Dutch law.

Additional Types of Entities and Structures

It is not the attempt of this chapter to exhaustively describe each type of corporate and other structure utilized in Latin America. However, the major ones and some of their major attributes are:

(i) Company with Variable Capital (Sociedad de Capital Variable). This is a company structured pursuant to its charter with minimal capital which may be increased up to certain limits established in the Articles of Incorporation, without the requirement of amending the articles. Companies with variable capital may be established only in Mexico, Honduras and El Salvador. Other countries do not recognize this concept.

(ii) Limited Liability Company (Sociedad de Responsabilidad Limitada). The limited liability company, which is now becoming more generally in use in the United States, has long been utilized in Latin America. Only Puerto Rico and the Dominican Republic do not utilize this concept. The SRL's liability is limited to the capital of the company. No shares are issued and in some countries, notably Colombia, Ecuador, Chile, and Argentina, the number of owners of the company is limited. One manager or a committee of managers oversees the functioning of the company (and not a board of directors). The exposure of individual owners is limited to their contribution to the SRL. Unlike partnerships, the death or bankruptcy of a partner does not terminate the SRL.

(iii) General Partnership (Sociedad Colectiva). A partnership is a juridical entity in Latin America. It requires a registered partnership agreement notarized by a notary public. All partners have unlimited and joint liability. All partners have a right to a voice in the business of the partnership. Partnership meetings must be kept in writing and registered with the applicable government or judicial authority. Foreign investment is not usually carried out through a Sociedad Colectiva.

(iv) Limited Partnership with Shares (Sociedad Colectiva por Acciones). This entity is akin to a U.S. limited partnership. Laws of Latin America require at least two general partners with unlimited and joint liability. Other partners, known as *socios comanditarios* are limited partners with limited liability. Corporation laws apply to the responsibilities and obligations of the limited partners. General partnership laws apply to the responsibilities and liabilities of the general partners.

(v) Joint Ventures. Joint ventures in most Latin American countries are governed by the form in which the venture is accomplished. Ecuador, Bolivia and Colombia have created special corporate vehicles for joint ventures between foreign investors and the government or government agencies.

IV. TECHNOLOGY TRANSFER AND INTELLECTUAL PROPERTY PROTECTION

In order for most U.S. and foreign companies to do business in Latin America, given the state of technological advances in their respective countries compared to those in the applicable Latin American country, the foreign company will need to make an analysis of the laws of the country applicable to technology transfer and intellectual property protection. This portion of this chapter will not undertake an exhaustive review of such laws but will attempt to underline some of the highlights.

Historical Influences

It is important to understand some of the history of Latin America. The early history of Latin America was dominated by colonization from developed nations. This colonization was accomplished through military means. As the nations of Latin America broke away from this domination and began to stand on their own feet, a different type of "colonization" occurred. While the nations became politically independent, foreign companies exerted great influence as they began the process of developing the nation's resources. In fact, Latin American nations had no capital resources to be able to develop their resources at the time, but the legacy of the developed industrial sector left a bitter taste in the mouth of Latin American nations. These nations felt powerless to determine their own destinies.

Beginning with the 1950's and coinciding with the resurgence of the military in the political arena, Latin American countries determined to take their destiny more into their own hands. In what might be considered by some to have been an over-reaction to the perceived dominance of foreign powers, Latin American countries began to close their borders, expropriate properties, and attempt to build their economies based on models of import substitution and statism. High tariff barriers were enacted. Many sectors of their economies were deemed off limits to foreign participation. In Brazil, for example, computer hardware and software imports were greatly restricted or entirely curtailed.

Beginning in the 1980's there was a growing recognition that the import substitution model was not working. The debt positions of most Latin American countries was critical, these countries having failed to attract foreign investment as a result of their restrictive policies. Accordingly, these countries began to open up their markets to foreign presence and innovation. That is the present posture of governments in Latin America.

The Intellectual Property Laws of Latin America

The intellectual property laws of Latin America are by and large based on European models. For instance, the earliest Argentinean patent law was enacted in 1864. Latin American copyright laws are not based on U.S. law, which essentially has its roots in the British Licensing Act of 1692 enacted by the Stationers Guild. This Act and its successors protected the rights of the publisher of material as opposed to the author of material. Latin American copyright laws generally protect authors' rights. The concept of moral rights for authors is also one that has currency in French law. Authors' rights, which are inalienable and therefore cannot be assigned by contract, include rights in derivative works. Thus, a license of a right to create derivative works such as translations gives the licensee the right to own the copyright in the translation. Any assignment of the licensee's interest in the derivative work, if permissible at all, would be a transfer of technology as opposed to a copyright assignment and subject to technology transfer rules.

Copyrights

The major countries in Latin America have similar copyright protection. What varies is the amount of time that the registration has validity. All of the copyright protection provisions protect the copyright for the lifetime of the author plus a certain number of years. In Argentina that period is 50 years; in Brazil it is 60 years. Most major Latin American countries also are signatories of some or all of the major copyright conventions. These conventions and their signatories are:

(i) Universal Copyright Convention. Argentina, Brazil, Chile, Colombia, Ecuador, Mexico, Peru and Venezuela. To claim protection under the UCC, the UCC notice (*i.e.*, "Copyright 19____ [Name of Author]") must be prominently affixed to the work.

(ii) Berne Convention. All UCC members (except Colombia, Ecuador and Peru) and Uruguay. Berne will prevail where a country is signatory to both the Berne Convention and the UCC.

(iii) Buenos Aires/Interamerican Convention. Argentina, Bolivia, Brazil, Chile, Colombia, Ecuador, Paraguay, Peru and Uruguay. To claim protection under this treaty, the work should include the legend "All Rights Reserved."

As a result of these conventions, copyright registration is not formally required. However, copyright registration is generally recommended as a way to provide proof of prior ownership. In addition, without local registry, remedies for unauthorized use may be difficult to obtain. In Argentina, registry is accomplished with the National Copyright Registry. Once registered, the trademark has a 30-day challenge period. In Brazil, depending on the nature of the copyright, registration is effected with the National Library, the National Music Academy, the Academy of Fine Arts, or the National Institute of Industrial Property. Foreign works are afforded different treatment from locally produced works. In Argentina, for example, if the copyright period in the country of origin is shorter, then the shorter copyright period governs. In Brazil, the registration of a copyright is subject to a reciprocity requirement.

Trademarks

Trademarks are somewhat different than copyrights. In Latin America, the first registration of a trademark governs the ownership of the trademark. There is no "use in commerce" requirement for trademarks, unlike the United States. Thus, a trademark may be registered even though it has not been used and may belong to the registree.

Trademark registration periods are similar. In Argentina, for example, a trademark is registered for 10 years and is renewable if the trademark was used within the last five years of the registration period. In Brazil, a trademark has a registration period of 10 years. Any trademark transfer requires a registration of the document of assignment. For foreign trademarks, a trademark registered pursuant to the Paris Convention has a six-month priority period after which it must be registered or it will have no priority.

Technology Transfer

The area of technology transfer is the area that has historically had the most protection from Latin American governments. This is a result of the unequal bargaining power inherent in the history of Latin America and the notable lack of innovation which arguably may have been caused by the import substitution models utilized by Latin American governments. Prior to the mid 1980's the system of technology transfer operated as a system of forced transfer of technology. That mentality is changing so that licensing, and not forced transfer, is generally the rule today. In addition, Latin American governments typically limited the amount of royalties that were payable and required registration and approval of any license. Some vestiges of this remain.

It is also important to understand what the definition of "technology" is for the purpose of technology transfer laws. In Argentina, for example, technology refers only to patents, trademarks, industrial models, and designs. In Brazil, technology transfer encompasses supplying industrial technology, technical industry cooperation, and special technical services. Patents, trademarks, and industrial designs are not included as "technology." In Argentina, technology transfer contracts formerly required the approval of the National Institute of Industrial Technology. This Institute now merely keeps track of technology transfers. Registration is required for informational purposes only. Approval is not required unless a parent-subsidiary relationship exists between the licensor and the licensee. Such approval is limited to consideration of transfer pricing issues and national defense issues. In the event of noncompliance with the requirement, the license is not invalid, but royalties are not tax deductible to the licensee.

In Brazil, the government has recently abolished many of its controls over technology transfer. However, the government does still review and approve licenses. This is accomplished by two entities, the Directorate for Technology Transfer Contracts, a department of the National Institute of Intellectual Property, and the Department of Fiscalization and Registration of Foreign Capital of the Central Bank. Royalties are not restricted nor is transferability.

In Colombia, prior approval of the Royalty Committee was required for the payment of royalties under technology transfer agreements. Such approval is no longer necessary, having been replaced by the filing of the agreement with the Services and Technology Committee of the Colombian Institute of Foreign Trade (INCOMEX). Certain provisions are restricted in such contracts. These include the assignor's right to determine the price at which the products are sold, the volume of products to be produced, or the structure of production, the obligation of the assignee to transfer any inventions or innovations which it develops to the assignor, and any export limitations. The same types of restrictions and approvals are applicable in Venezuela.

V. THE FOREIGN INVESTMENT LAWS OF LATIN AMERICA

Latin American nations have very liberalized considerably concerning the scope of their foreign investment laws. This portion of the chapter will discuss some of the major foreign investment laws in effect in Latin America.

Andean Pact Decision 291

The Andean Pact, above all of the other investment laws, reflects the trend from closed markets to open markets in Latin America. The Andean Pact countries include Venezuela, Colombia, Peru, Ecuador and Bolivia. The initial decision of the Andean Pact concerning foreign investment, Decision 24 of December 31, 1970, was considered the most restrictive legislation concerning foreign investment in Latin America. This decision essentially permitted only "national companies" the right to trade in the Andean Pact nations. Decision 24 was superseded by Decision 220 of May 11, 1987 and finally by Decision 291 of March 21, 1991. Decision 291 denominates three types of ownership: a "national company," being a local company in which national investors have more than 80 percent ownership and more than 80 percent technical, financial, administrative and commercial control; a "mixed company," a local company in which national investors own a majority of the company and control a majority of the company, and a "foreign company," a local or foreign corporation in which national investors own less than 51 percent or control less than the majority of the technical, financial, administrative, and commercial aspects of the company.

As opposed to Decisions 24 and 220, Decision 291 eliminated most of the restrictions on foreign investors. Except for those areas restricted to foreign investment in countries (primarily areas of *patrimonio nacional*), foreign investors are accorded the same rights as national investors. Under Decisions 24 and 220, foreign enterprises were required to become mixed enterprises in order to obtain the benefit of duty free status in the Andean Pact. Decision 291 eliminates this restriction and permits foreign enterprises to obtain duty free trade benefits.

Under Decision 220, the Andean Pact regulated the rights of foreign investors to transfer profits and dividends. Decision 291 now provides that each country is free to regulate the remittance of profits or dividends as it wishes. In Venezuela and Colombia, profits and dividends are freely remittable. Colombia requires capital to have been registered in order for profits and dividends to be freely remittable. Ecuador permits the remittance of up to 30 percent of the registered capital of the foreign investor (40 percent for some export industries).

Chile

Chile first adopted its foreign investment statute, referred to as Decree Law 600, in 1974. Thus, Chile was one of the first and most progressive nations in Latin America for foreign investment. Chile accepts the principle of national treatment for foreign investors and attempts to intervene in business activities in a minimal way. There are no restrictions on foreign ownership of local enterprises or on foreign participation in joint ventures. DL-600 provides that investments may be made by non-Chilean persons or entities through the medium of an investment contract signed between the investor and the Chilean Foreign Investment Committee. The contract is a public document. It must state the period within which the investor is to bring in capital (such period not to exceed eight years extendable to 12 years for mining investments and three years for all others). Profits are freely remittable at any time. Capital can be remitted at any time after one year from the date of investment. A deposit of 10 percent of capital, known as *encaje* is required of the foreign investor. The U.S. government has expressed reservations concerning the *encaje* and it will certainly be discussed in any free trade negotiations. Technology may be used as capital and is ascribed a value by the Foreign Investment Committee. Technology which is utilized as capital is not amortizable or depreciable and cannot be transferred separate from the entity in which it is placed.

The most interesting part of DL-600 is that it allows an investor to choose the investor's tax rate at the beginning of the investment. Investors have a right to choose at the beginning in their contract to be taxed at a fixed overall effective income tax rate of 42 percent for a ten-year period beginning at the date of start up. If they do not choose this rate, they are taxable at the normal corporate income tax rates applicable from time to time in Chile. One time during the period of the investment, the investor can choose to renounce the fixed rate if it has chosen the fixed rate or to renounce the applicability of general tax law and opt for the fixed 42 percent tax rate.

Finally, certain types of investments require the approval of the Foreign Investment Committee. They are: investments with a total value exceeding $5 million, activities in the nature of public utility services, activities related to communications and media, and foreign-state-owned enterprises.

Argentina

Effective April 1, 1991, the Argentine Peso replaced the old currency, the Austral, and was made convertible on a one-to-one relationship with the U.S. dollar. This has led to a stabilization of inflation in Argentina. Foreign investment is welcome and is virtually unrestricted. The foreign investment law of 1976 has become increasingly liberalized. Argentina subscribes to the principle of national treatment for investors. No approvals or formalities are required for foreign investment. Capital and profits are freely remittable at any time. There is no withholding tax on the remittance of profits or dividends.

In Argentina only two areas are still off limits to foreign investment, broadcasting and atomic energy. These sectors may, however, be liberalized shortly. There are certain sectors that are restricted but not closed to foreign investment. The main areas are mining, oil, gas, and natural resources. These sectors are considered part of the *patrimonio nacional*. The state owns all mineral deposits below the surface of property in Argentina. However, anyone who discovers mineral deposits and decides to exploit them, must be granted a mining license by the state provided that they meet the requirements for such license (essentially payment of an annual fee, investment of a certain minimum capital and continuous exploitation). Large mining area exploration and exploitation has a limit of 36 years (five years for exploration, one to consider exploitation, and 30 for exploitation).

Oil and gas are much more restricted. The state owns the oil and gas deposits and exploits them through the national company, YPF. Lately, YPF has been granting concessions to non-Argentine companies to exploit, in a joint venture fashion, various oil and gas reserves. Some of the less profitable oil and gas reserves are able to be exploited on a concession basis without the necessity of a joint venture.

Finally, Argentina has had one of the most aggressive privatization programs in Latin America. Beginning with the highly publicized ENTEL privatization, Argentina has also privatized its national airline, certain television and radio stations, many power and light facilities, and gas and other companies. In addition, as discussed above, Argentina has granted large concessions and joint venture contracts in petroleum, oil, the operation of ports, the operation of water and sewage disposal facilities and other areas. Finally, Argentina has enacted a law, Decree 2284–91, known as the Deregulation Decree, which attempts to eliminate the requirement for government approvals, permits and other bureaucratic bottle necks for doing business. Argentina is in the process of enacting implementing decrees for this law and appears to be willing to continue to do so for the future. Likewise, Argentina is beginning to review its constitution with an eye toward amending it in order to further liberalize the atmosphere for doing business.

VI. LATIN AMERICAN INTEGRATION MOVEMENTS PRE-MERCOSUR

LAFTA

The idea of regional economic cooperation is not new in Latin America. Initially, Latin American nations created, by the Treaty of Montevideo of 1960, the Latin American Free Trade Association ("LAFTA"). Its purpose was to establish a free trade area within a period of 12 years along the lines of a common market. Its integration mechanism was an annual bilateral negotiation system for trade concessions on an item by item basis. A common set of products were to be duty-free forever. LAFTA did not succeed in its goals. What it did succeed in doing was to allow Latin America to rethink its views on economic integration in general.

ALADI

The Latin American Integration Association ("ALADI") was formed as a result of the thought generated by the failure of LAFTA. The Treaty of Montevideo of 1980 which formed ALADI entered into force on March 18, 1981. ALADI's members to date are Argentina, Bolivia, Brazil, Colombia, Chile, Ecuador, Mexico, Paraguay, Peru, Uruguay, and Venezuela. Its goal is not to create a free-trade zone but to seek gradual and progressive integration efforts and cooperation among the countries of Latin America ultimately resulting , by the cooperative actions of the countries themselves, in a common market for Latin America. It has no fixed time tables and is much more flexible than LAFTA. ALADI seeks to create a system of trade preferences by means of three mechanisms: Regional Tariff Preferences, Agreements of Regional Scope, and

Agreements of Partial Scope. Regional Tariff Preferences are granted among member states on a reciprocal basis in relation to the level of tariffs applicable to third countries. Agreements of Regional Scope are those in which all member states participate and may involve specific tariff reductions, cooperative efforts or other types of economic integration activities. Partial Agreements can be bilateral or multilateral and affect specific industries or various sectors. They grant tariff concessions in the form of percentage reductions of duties applicable to third countries. ALADI seeks to extend these agreements from partial scope into multilateral full scope agreements at some later date. States can enter into different agreements with different states, which then allows more developed states to be more equal and lesser developed states to have better preferences and protect their economies while they grow.

ALADI has, for its governing bodies, three organizational entities. A Council of Foreign Ministers is the highest executive authority with responsibility for decision-making over basic policy issues. A Committee of Representatives is the permanent body of ALADI which meets at least once per year to negotiate region wide agreements on tariff reductions and adopt other measures pursuant to the Treaty. Each member nation has one permanent representative. The third body is the Conference for Valuation and Convergence, which meets every three years to review and evaluate the program and to promote measures for achieving increasing levels of free trade. ALADI is extremely flexible and is meant to encompass all bilateral and multilateral economic agreements in the area, including Mercosur.

Mercosur

Overview

Less well known and less understood than NAFTA for North Americans is the Southern Cone Common Market ("Mercosur"). Mercosur was established by the Treaty of Asuncion on March 26, 1991. The signatories to Mercosur are Argentina, Brazil, Paraguay and Uruguay. This Treaty attempts to establish a true common market, a customs union with a common external tariff and no internal tariffs, together with free movement of goods, but also harmonized laws and policies. Mercosur contains a phase-in process which is intended to allow it to take effect for most goods and services by January 1, 1995.

Mercosur Goals

Mercosur's primary objective is to further the process of economic integration among Argentina, Brazil, Uruguay, and Paraguay, countries with combined gross national products of $400 billion, by promoting efficient use of resources, the preservation of the environment, and coordination of macro economic policies and complementary programs. The Treaty proposes to eliminate duties and non-tariff barriers among the nations, establish a common external tariff and a common trade policy, coordinate macroeconomic and sectoral policies and harmonize domestic legislation.

Mercosur Governance

The governing bodies for Mercosur are two: the Council of the Common Market and The Common Market Group. The Council is the highest authority and is composed of the foreign ministers and economic ministers of each country. It meets from time to time as it deems necessary. The Common Market Group is the executive body composed of four high ranking officials from each country, representing the Foreign Ministries, Economic Ministries and Central Banks. Working subgroups are in the process of being formed to coordinate macroeconomic and sectoral policies. Each will specialize in a particular area such as customs, technical specifications, monetary policy, transportation and energy policy. The Administrative Secretariat of Mercosur is located in Montevideo. A Joint Parliamentary Commission is also to be established.

Newer Developments in Mercosur

The first declaration of the Foreign Ministers of Mercosur indicated that Mercosur is intended to be consistent with the objectives of ALADI. Other nations are presently interested in joining into Mercosur, notably Bolivia. The second declaration of the foreign Ministers of Mercosur indicated the desire of Mercosur to explore the possibility of Bolivia's entry. Declaration 3 of the Ministers indicated that Mercosur has an interest in integrating Chile into Mercosur. For the moment, however, Chile will not be a member of Mercosur.

Within the framework of ALADI, other bilateral efforts are under way to integrate the nations. Uruguay and Argentina have an economic cooperation agreement established in 1973, which is still in force. Argentina and Brazil signed an Economic Integration Agreement in 1987 to attempt to more closely integrate their economies. These countries have established a joint integration committee to coordinate these efforts. The Agreement is most advanced in the automotive sector since the formation of AutoLatina and the operation of AutoLatina in both countries. Other prior projects that will benefit from Mercosur will be the hydro-electric project at Itaipu and the maintenance and dredging of the Paraguay Parana waterways, which will allow transportation from Paraguay and Bolivia to Argentina and over land to ports. This will also help Brazil by offering an alternative to land transportation for products from the Mato Grosso area.

Mercosur is just beginning to be a reality. Problems which arise seem to be projected to be solved politically at the ministerial level. The harmonization of legislation can do nothing but liberalize the legislation in effect in the applicable countries for transfer of technology and investment, the mainstays upon which the electronics industry subsists. The effect of Mercosur cannot be gauged at this time. As rules are developed for various sectors and laws are harmonized, one can expect that acquisitions of well-placed industries inside Mercosur will allow non-Mercosur companies access to one of the hemisphere's most promising markets.

Andean Pact

Overview

The Andean Pact was originally conceived as a protective, statist, import substitution oriented vehicle to allow the economies of Colombia, Venezuela, Ecuador, Peru and Bolivia to develop. After some years following the execution of the Cartagena Agreement establishing the Pact, it became clear to these governments that import substitution models of economic growth were ineffective to allow the growth of internal economies or competition by these countries with the outside world.

Andean Pact Liberalization

The Andean Pact was built around an import substitution model and was typified by Decision 24, which established severe restrictions on foreign investment in the region and Decision 85 which essentially disallowed foreign intellectual property protection. Indeed, these decisions essentially halted the flow of investment into the Andean Pact. After some attempts at liberalization that did not go far enough, the Commission of the Andean Pact issued Decision No. 291 in March, 1991. Its most important features are:

(a) That it creates a general framework based on the principle that foreign investors have the same rights and obligations as local investors, unless otherwise provided in member country legislation;

(b) That prior approval of investments is eliminated;

(c) That governments of member countries may set their own policies concerning issues such as the remittance of profits, reinvestment requirements, and restricted sectors of investment;

(d) That intellectual property protection is liberalized and transfer of technology contracts are no longer subject to prior government approval; and

(e) That "foreign companies" (i.e., local companies controlled by foreign investors) are entitled to access to the benefits and advantages of trade liberalization programs of the Andean Pact, provided that certain rules of origin are fulfilled.

Regulations have been issued by all countries implementing Decision 291. Colombia, for example, eliminated all prior governmental approvals and restrictions, except foreign investment in oil, gas, mining, public utilities, communications, and financial institutions. The Colombian government further struck any limitations on the repatriation of profits. Venezuela eliminated the five percent cap on intercompany royalties for technical assistance and transfer of technology, and struck any requirement for registration of foreign loan agreements. The Venezuelan government also eliminated security services as a restricted sector for foreign investment.

One of the tenets of the Andean Pact was to attempt to foster cross border investments within the region. Two basic mechanisms were put in place:

(a) Investments made by national investors from one country were given reciprocal rights in the other countries of the region; and

(b) The Andean Multinational Company ("EMA") would be able to operate without restriction throughout the region.

Unfortunately, the first attempt to regulate EMA's proved too restrictive and EMA's were not formed. Decision 292 of the Commission, however, established a new framework for EMA's to attempt to encourage their formation. Under Decision 292, an EMA must fulfill certain less restrictive formal requirements. The most important of these are that:

(a) The company must have its principal domicile in one of the member countries;

(b) All shares must have equal rights and obligations;

(c) National investors from at least two member countries must own at least sixty (60) percent of the company; and

(d) The marketing, technical, administrative, and financial management of the EMA must reflect the country makeup of the investors in the opinion of the country of nationality's competent authorities.

This decision allows EMA's to operate all over the Andean Pact Region by establishing branches in any country. It also prohibits currency control restrictions on capital destined for the operations of an EMA. It further allows contributions in kind to be exported and imported without tax or tariff, allows EMA's to have access to special import and export incentives, and allows EMA's to be subject to special double tax rules.

Another important development concerns intellectual property. Decision 313 abrogates Decision 85, which was one of the most controversial acts of the Andean Pact. Decision 85 did not allow intellectual property protection for foreign investors. Decision 313 allows patents to be granted to creations which are the subject of industrial application, as long as they are novel. It abrogates the prior prohibition of granting patents to pharmaceutical products, other than those that are included in the World Health Organization's list of essential medicines. The term of validity of a patent is 15 years extendable for an additional five years. Decision 313 allows utility model patents for a term of 10 years, but such patents cannot be extended. Industrial designs may be registered for a term of eight years, not extendable. Trademarks may be registered for 10 years from the date of the official act permitting the trademark registration, renewable for an additional 10 years. Use of the trademark is no longer required as a condition for renewal. Finally, commercial slogans may be registered as an adjunct to a trademark.

New Developments

In connection with trade, in December of 1991, the Presidents of the member countries met at Cartagena and agreed by means of a document called the Minutes of Barahona, to implement a free trade zone as of January 1, 1992, for all countries except Ecuador and Peru, and for those countries, as of July 1, 1992. Minimum external tariffs were agreed to be implemented at one of four levels, either five, 10, 15 or 20 percent. Certain sectors would be subject to exceptional tariff protection, such as the auto industry and agricultural products. The governments of Bolivia, Ecuador and Peru, however, were unable to agree upon methods of implementation of the minimum external tariff. Accordingly, the governments of Venezuela and Colombia decided to create a customs zone between their two countries and to implement their own minimum external tariff, which is that which was to be adopted by the Andean Pact countries. The minimum external tariff is now effective in both countries. However, apparently, there are certain sectors which are still subject to negotiations between the governments. The minimum external tariff negotiations for all of the Andean Pact countries were scheduled to occur in April of 1992 in Peru, but given the chain of events in Peru, these negotiations have been postponed indefinitely.

The Andean Region is still a difficult region for trade. Those countries that are ripe for investment and American products at this time are Colombia and perhaps Venezuela. Notwithstanding the difficult political era in Venezuela, it continues to be one of the most dynamic of all Latin American countries. Venezuela still has substantial oil resources and has signed a framework agreement with the United States, making it a candidate for Enterprise of the Americas treatment, and ultimately, if desired, a free trade agreement. Venezuela also imports over $6 billion more from the United States than it exports to the United States. Colombia, likewise, imports a substantial amount from the United States, having a negative balance of trade of over $1 billion with the United States. Both of these countries are interested in U.S. investment and of course, both of these countries have political problems, making investment therein less attractive than the Mercosur countries.

VII. CONCLUSION

Latin America is a dynamic and growing market. Latin America is multicultural and is impossible to understand if viewed as a monolithic market. The countries of Latin America are in various stages of development toward free market economies. There are many more facets to doing business in Latin America than have been discussed in this brief chapter. Hopefully the chapter has nonetheless given the reader a background which will help the reader learn more about this emerging market of the future.

GOING INTERNATIONAL IN THE EUROPEAN COMMUNITY

Philip Wareham

I. INTRODUCTION

What is the European Community? The Founding Treaties

THIS CHAPTER examines the basic legal structure of the European Community, the functions of the principal Community institutions and the main areas of Community law which are likely to have an impact upon any company wishing to establish itself in the Community or even simply trade with it.

The European Community is a community of twelve Member States which together represent one of the U.S.'s major trading partners. Originally known as the European Economic Community, it was created by the Treaty of Rome of March 25, 1957, and then had six members (Belgium, France, Italy, Luxembourg, the Netherlands and West Germany). The Treaty has undergone two major amendments as a result of the Single European Act of February 1986 (the "SEA") and the Treaty of Maastricht of February 1992 (the Treaty on European Union or "TEU"): The TEU, reflecting what was already common practice, has officially changed the name of the European Economic Community (EEC) to the European Community (EC). [*Note*: The TEU will enter into force as soon as it has been ratified by Germany, which is expected to be in late October 1993.]

The 12 EC Member States are also members of two other Communities, namely the European Coal and Steel Community (or ECSC, which will become part of the European Community in 2004) and the European Atomic Energy Community (or Euratom). The former was established by the Treaty of Paris in 1951 and the latter by the Treaty of Rome, signed simultaneously with the original EEC Treaty in 1957. They are together known as the European Communities. The twelve Member States are Belgium, Denmark, Germany, Ireland, Spain, France, Greece, Italy, Luxembourg, the Netherlands, Portugal and the United Kingdom.

European Union

The TEU has also established a European Union consisting of three "pillars" namely, (1) the three European Communities, (2) a common foreign and security policy and (3) a system of cooperation in the fields of justice and home affairs (the last two being systems of intergovernmental cooperation and policy coordination outside the framework of the Communities, but utilizing some of the Community institutions).

European Economic Area

The EC Member States have also, since the entry into force of the EEA Agreement [likely to be November 1, 1993], become members of a much larger free trade area known as the European Economic Area, which comprises the European Community and its members and the members of the European Free Trade Association (EFTA) (with the exception of Switzerland and, for the time being, Liechtenstein). Several of the EFTA states have also applied for full EC membership. The EC is currently negotiating entry terms with Austria, Finland, Norway, and Sweden, and it is expected that they will become members on January 1, 1995.

International Agreements

The Community is quite separate from the Council of Europe, a 26-member grouping created on May 5, 1949, and including all 12 EC Member States. The aim of the Council of Europe is to promote cooperation between its members in all fields (other than defence) and the preparation of conventions, the principal one being the European Convention for the Protection of Human Rights and Fundamental Freedoms (ECHR), which came into force in 1953. The ECHR established a Commission and a Court of Human Rights, with a right of appeal for individuals whose rights are infringed. These institutions are distinct from the institutions of the Community described below, although the similar names sometimes lead to confusion.

In the area of defense, some or all the Member States belong to various international organizations, with sometimes overlapping responsibilities, including the North Atlantic Treaty Organisation (NATO), the Western European Union (WEU), the Conference on Security and Cooperation in Europe (CSCE) and the Organisation for Economic Cooperation and Development (OECD), which are beyond the scope of this chapter.

At the international level, the Community has a number of bilateral and multilateral agreements and arrangements with third countries, including favorable trading arrangements with 69 African, Caribbean and Pacific (ACP) countries (through the Lomé IV Convention); association agreements with close trading partners (e.g. Cyprus, Turkey, Malta); and a recent series of bilateral free trade and association agreements (known as "European Agreements") with certain ex-Soviet bloc states (Poland, the Czech Republic, and Hungary).

Fundamental Aims of the Community: Internal Market and Economic Integration

This chapter concentrates on the European Community, which is the most important of the three Communities and covers all economic sectors except the coal, steel, and nuclear industries.

The EC Treaty has as its fundamental aim to create a harmonious single internal market free of internal trading barriers and to bring the economies of its various Member States closer together (with the eventual establishment of an economic and monetary union). The original Treaty of Rome established a common market (which was basically a customs union providing for the abolition of customs duties and quotas at the Community's internal borders and the creation of a common commercial policy governing trade into and out of the Community's external borders). Its original aims were similar to the currently proposed North American Free Trade Association. In addition the Treaty established common policies in various sectors, including the important common agricultural policy.

The creation of a common market and the rules on free movement were given added impetus by the Single European Act of 1986, described in more detail below. When the SEA was adopted, restrictions on cross-border trade were still rife (particularly indirect restrictions caused by disparate legal and technical rules in each Member State) and it was decided to launch an active program of Community legislation to ensure that the integration process was completed. The SEA laid down a specific deadline of December 31, 1992 for the introduction of legislation designed to complete the unification of the market.

In a White Paper published in 1985 the European Commission listed some 282 measures which it considered to be necessary to complete the internal market (*the 1992 program*). The vast majority of the 1992 program has now been adopted, although some of it is not due to enter into force until a later date (e.g., the common insurance market is only due to be completed in July, 1994 and, in the aviation sector, the rules governing internal domestic flights have been delayed until April, 1997).

These specific legislative measures are reinforced by the rules already existing in the Treaty designed to prevent market partitioning, whether by state legislation or other forms of state intervention, or by private agreements between commercial undertakings. These rules include the prohibition against all forms of discrimination on grounds of nationality, the principles of free movement of goods, persons, services and capital (the so-called four fundamental freedoms) and the competition rules which prohibit market sharing agreements and abuses of market power, as well as unauthorized state aids.

Future Developments

The TEU has made certain amendments to the EC Treaty which, as well as extending the scope of EC activity in such areas as the environment, transport and communications, and labor relations, aim to advance economic activity, particularly by seeking to establish a common currency regulated by a European Central Bank. These developments are considered below. As already indicated, the TEU also marks a transition towards a common EC foreign/security policy and a common justice/home affairs policy (being two of the three pillars supporting the European Union). However, the Treaty specifically provides for these to take the form of intergovernmental agreements and they therefore exist formally outside of the institutional framework of the Community and represent only very preliminary steps towards a fuller political union.

Once the process of market integration has been completed, it is hoped that the

Community will become an even more unified and harmonised single market than the United States. As yet, however, the Community is far from being a federation on the United States model. The TEU deliberately stops short of using the word "federal" but is stated to mark "a new stage in the process of creating an ever closer union among the peoples of Europe". Quite how far the European Community should go down the road of federalism is a matter of fierce current debate. The TEU provides for the establishment of an intergovernmental conference in 1996 to discuss ways in which the integration process can be continued. The ratification of the TEU itself has proved quite controversial, and although the Treaty was signed by representatives of the Member States on February 7, 1992, final ratification was not expected until October 1993. The delay was caused by political and constitutional disputes and legal challenges (particularly in Denmark, Germany and the UK) and the need for referenda (in Denmark, France, and Ireland). Any attempts at further integration of the Community's economic, monetary, and fiscal policies are likely to meet similar resistance.

It is in the areas covered by the TEU that there is greatest room for dispute between those Member States which would welcome a more federal structure for Europe and those which would restrict the ambit of the EC to the economic arena. Nonetheless, what is clear is that the Community is becoming an increasingly unified place in which to do business, both in terms of its legal systems, its business practices and ethos and in terms of its economies, tax policies and even currencies.

The next section explains the important steps which have already been taken to create a unified system of Community law and highlights the main features of that system which any non-EC businessman wanting to do business in the Community needs to know.

II. COMMUNITY LAW

Community and National Law

The European Community consists of 12 sovereign Member States operating under common rules of law set out in the EC Treaty and administered by the Court of Justice of the European Communities (CJEC). Each Member State, however, retains its own national systems of law, its ministries of justice, separate court systems and separate criminal and civil procedures. There is therefore no single Community law jurisdiction, but separate jurisdictions in each of the Member States (and in certain cases, as in the United Kingdom, separate jurisdictions within a Member State). This means, for instance, that the legal rules and procedures for setting up a company, for sacking a distributor, or registering a trademark license will differ from one Member State to another. For this reason it is generally necessary to ensure that appropriate advice is taken regarding the country in which one intends to do business. The differences may in certain cases be quite substantial, particularly as between common law (English and Irish) and civil law jurisdictions.

The differences are gradually being eroded through the process of harmonization. Harmonization, however, may only remove the major differences and in general creates only a minimum Community legal framework which can still differ in detail from one state to another. The process has also been slowed by the principle of "subsidiarity" (or delegation of power), enshrined in the EC Treaty by the TEU, which requires the Community to take action only where the relevant objectives cannot be sufficiently achieved by the Member States and can therefore be better achieved at Community level. Several initiatives which had already been put forward by the European Commission have had to be withdrawn as a result.

The position under the EC Treaty is to be contrasted with the position under the two other Treaties which, within their respective product sectors, have transferred sovereignty to the European Commission for specified purposes, so creating a supranational legal order.

Sources of Community Law

Community law is based on the Treaties themselves and subsidiary legislation enacted by the Community's law-making institutions, the Council of Ministers and the Commission of the European Communities (or European Commission). The system is usually that the European Commission (the Community's civil service) *proposes* legislation and the Council of Ministers (which comprises ministers from the relevant ministries of all 12 Member States—each with a set number of votes) is ultimately responsible for passing it. In certain areas the Council of Ministers has delegated law-making powers to the European Commission. Two other bodies, the European Parliament and the Economic and Social Committee, are also closely involved in the legislative process: The European Parliament, for instance, enjoys certain powers of "co-decision" with the Council, which allows it in certain cases to veto legislation agreed by the Council.

Supremacy of Community Law

Community law sits above but forms an integral part of what one may loosely call "national" law, e.g., English law. The principle of supremacy of Community law ensures that where there is a conflict, Community law always prevails. The principle of "direct effect" ensures that Community law provisions which are sufficiently clear and precise, and unconditional, may be relied on by individuals as against Member States and public bodies dependent on the state and must be given effect by the courts of the Member States even when they have not been implemented into national law or would appear to contradict national law. Treaty provisions satisfying the relevant conditions may also be *directly effective* against third parties.

A good example of how these principles operate in practice is provided by the *Factortame* cases (C-213/89, C-221/89 and C-246/89), in which the European Court of Justice confirmed that certain Spanish fishermen who had been operating under the British flag in order to take advantage of British fish quotas could continue to do so despite being in clear breach of the relevant provisions of the U.K. Merchant Shipping Act which defined which ships could fly the British flag. English law was contrary to one of the fundamental principles of the EC Treaty which prohibits discrimination on grounds of nationality. The European Court confirmed that the English courts could disapply the

U.K. provisions, even though as a matter of English law and procedure the courts had no means of disapplying statutory provisions which were clear and unambiguous. The European Court also decided in the cases of *Francovich* and *Bonifaci* (Cases C-6 & C-9/90) that a Member State which has failed to implement Community law by the due date may be liable to a citizen who suffers loss as a result of the unavailability of the rights conferred by Community law even in circumstances where the relevant Community law is not directly effective.

Secondary Legislation

Community law is therefore both a body of law in its own right (creating its own rights and obligations) and a system of law superimposed upon national law and integral to it. Community law consists of *primary* legislation (i.e. provisions in the Treaties) and *secondary* legislation. The main types of secondary legislation under the EC Treaty are regulations, directives and decisions. *Regulations* are *directly applicable*, i.e. apply without the need for any intervening national legislation. By contrast, much Community legislation (including virtually all the 1992 legislation) is in the form of *directives*. These lay down the basic minimum legal provisions which must be enacted, through national legislation, by each Member State by a given deadline. This gives Member States time to adapt their legislation and some flexibility in the way they choose to do so. They can cover such diverse matters as the types of company that can be set up, minimum capital requirements, accounting requirements, the terms on which commercial agents can be appointed and sacked, product standards, recognition of professional qualifications and authorization and licensing requirements in many industries ranging from pharmaceuticals to banking to transport. The legislation may cover both legal and technical aspects. Finally, *decisions* are usually addressed to one or more specific persons and in principle will be binding only on those to whom they are addressed. They include, for instance, decisions of the European Commission imposing fines for breach of the EC competition rules (see below). The EC Treaty provides for two further categories of act (*recommendations* and *opinions*) which have no binding legal force. The Council of Ministers may also adopt *resolutions*, particularly in relation to international conventions to which the individual Member States are signatories (and not the Community itself).

Level Playing Field

The EC Treaty and the legislation adopted under it have therefore, in the legal sense, created a level playing field. Although details of the legal framework will differ depending on where one decides to establish, and the basic dichotomy between common law and civil law jurisdictions remains, there is increasing harmonization and a system of law which ensures that Member States must give effect to their Treaty obligations (including the principle of non-discrimination). Thus the choice of business location should be primarily a commercial and not a legal one.

Diversity of Cultures

There are also certain non-commercial factors which may be important in deciding where to market or where to locate in the Community. Each Member State retains its own national characteristics and cultures and technical preferences. The cultural diversity of Europe is well known and it is as well to be aware of the differences in advance. The United Kingdom offers a culture which Americans may find more familiar than the rest of Europe, which may explain its favored status for U.S. investment. London's position as the leading financial center and the ready access to competitive financing may also assist.

Language and Business Practice

As well as purely cultural differences, there remain important linguistic barriers within Europe, although these are becoming increasingly eroded with the growth of English as the international language of trade and business. Business practices also differ widely between different parts of the Community and this may be an important factor in determining how and where to establish in Europe. Business acquisition may prove considerably easier within the U.K.

Regional Grants and Incentives

Lastly, it is worth mentioning the possibility of regional grants and tax breaks. Although in general Member States are not permitted to grant state aids or subsidies (whether direct or indirect) without prior Commission approval, there is a limited number of circumstances in which aid may be approved. In particular, approval is usually given to regional aid designed to promote the economic development of an area where the standard of living is abnormally low or where there is serious under-employment. Thus, most Member States are able to offer attractive financial incentives for companies willing to establish in designated areas. Certain Member States may also offer tax incentives to companies setting up in their country or in a particular region (e.g., Belgium offers special tax treatment for "coordination centers" making it attractive for U.S. companies to locate their European headquarters in that country). There have been several examples recently of Japanese manufacturers setting up plants in the United Kingdom under favorable conditions in order to take advantage of the opportunities offered by the European single market.

III. ACHIEVING A SINGLE MARKET

This section examines in more detail how the single market is being achieved through the 1992 program, and explains the fundamental role played by the rules on free movement of goods and the rules on competition in the process of market integration.

A Single Market : 1992

From the beginning, the EEC Treaty attempted to create a common market, involving a customs union, certain common policies (e.g., agricultural, transport), common external trade policies, and the abolition of internal customs duties and quotas and "measures having equivalent effect". This already enabled the removal of many indirect, as well as direct, trading barriers. Nevertheless, the driving force behind the single market came with the adoption in 1986 of the Single European Act (SEA), which entered into force in 1987, and was the first major revision of the EEC Treaty since its original signature in 1957. The SEA provided that by December 31, 1992 all necessary measures had to be in place to create a single internal market within which goods, services, people and capital could move freely. The European Commission proposed more than 280 separate items of legislation covering a whole range of subjects and industries which together constitute the "Single Market" or "1992" program. They included measures for abolishing physical border controls, harmonizing technical standards and harmonizing tax laws, with the aim eventually of creating a single trading bloc of 345 million people and removing all the visible and invisible barriers to internal trade within the Community.

Small and medium-sized undertakings, or SMEs, as they are known, were targeted as the principal beneficiaries of the single market. In practice, however, surveys in the various Member States have found that smaller companies have so far failed to take great advantage of the opportunities offered by the single market by promoting themselves outside their own borders and extending their market outside their traditional home base. It has tended to be larger European corporations and non-EC corporations who have seized upon the single market. Investment in the single market is clearly more attractive now that the internal trade barriers are coming down, so reducing the cost of moving goods within the Community and offering greater economies of scale. The basic principle of the single market is that a company should not be discriminated against according to where it is established in the Community and that a product meeting legal and technical standards in one Member State should be freely marketable in every other Member State. A company from Scotland and a company from Greece should be able to compete equally for customers and government contracts in each other's countries regardless of their nationality or place of establishment and regardless of the particular composition, design or specification of their products.

Riccardo Perissich, the Director General in charge of industrial affairs at the European Commission, has commented as follows on the Single Market Program:

Far from perpetuating the myth of a fortress Europe, the 1992 project is proving a catalyst outside Europe. On banking, as on industrial standards and public procurement, the Community is establishing an internal market which is more open and transparent than most. Indeed, the Americans have recognised that they have lessons to learn from our efforts—for example, in their major reform proposals on banking and investment banking and their attempts to grapple with their fragmented standards, testing and certification systems." (*Economist*; August 3, 1991).

Economic Benefits of Integration

The Commission (in its White Paper on Completing the Internal Market) classified the measures within the Single Market Program under three headings, as follows:

— Part 1, the removal of physical barriers;

— Part 2, the removal of technical barriers; and

— Part 3, the removal of fiscal barriers.

The potential gains to be made from a single market have been estimated at between 4.3 and 6.4 percent of Community GDP (or in value terms at least 200,000 million ECU (ca.US$225,000m) at 1993 prices). These were the conclusions of the Cecchini Report in which a research team of economists examined the problem of a fragmented European market. Elimination of customs duties, harmonization of standards, opening up of public procurement policies and economies of scale resulting from the larger market all play a part in this growth. The benefits will clearly differ from market to market and from product to product. Although the Cecchini estimates should be treated with caution and have been seriously distorted by the world recession which since 1990 has dramatically slowed growth throughout Europe, they do, nevertheless, give a useful indication of the potential long term impact of the 1992 program.

Another effect of the 1992 Program has been to facilitate pan-European investment decisions and in certain cases enable rationalization of production and distribution facilities within the Community. Well publicized cases have included the decision by the Hoover vacuum cleaner manufacturer to move production from Dijon, France to Glasgow, Scotland; and, in reverse, the decision by the confectionery manufacturers Nestlé Rowntree to switch some of their production from the U.K. to France. Such decisions will be based on numerous legal and commercial factors including labor and production costs, regional assistance, ease of transport, availability of raw materials etc. Costs still vary enormously from one Member State to another. A U.K.-based packaging group has estimated its average employment costs in Germany to be up to 70 percent higher than those in the U.K.

"Fortress Europe"

Fears have been expressed of a Fortress Europe, replacing the weak barriers which existed between the Member States by a ring fence between Europe and the rest of the world. However, the Community and its Member States are active members of the GATT and are bound by the GATT non-discrimination rules. Moreover, the cost savings from the lowering of trade barriers and the economies of scale which result from a single market are benefits which are open not only to existing Community businesses, but also to investors from outside the Community. There are only a few examples of Community legislation which contain reciprocity provisions: Examples are the Second Banking Co-ordination Directive, providing a bank from any one Member State with a license to do business throughout the Community; the Topography Rights Directive which allows the Member States to extend Community protection for semi-conductor chips on a bilateral basis to non-EEC nationals; and the EC Merger Control Regulation governing concentrations. The most controversial reciprocity provisions were contained in the EC Utilities Services Directive, governing public procurement, *inter alia*, in the telecommunications industry, which resulted in a bilateral agreement between the Community and the U.S. on May 10, 1993.

Scope of the Legislation

The Single Market program contained both detailed legislation affecting only specific product areas (e.g., provision of motor liability insurance or common rules on the pedigree of porcine animals or weights and dimensions of tractors) *and* general proposals for legislative reform with a potentially wider impact (e.g., mergers and take-overs legislation, company law harmonization, public tendering for services, harmonized trademarks legislation, new legislation on copyright and the protection of computer software). Banking, telecommunications and information technology have also been the targets of a number of specific proposals. As at July 1993, a total of 282 separate proposals had been tabled by the Commission to the Council of Ministers, of which 263 had been adopted. Of the remainder, the Council had "adopted a common position" on one of these (i.e., had reached the final stage of the legislative process), leaving only 18 measures outstanding. However, only some 101 of the 263 measures are in force in all Member States—emphasizing the difficulty in implementing Community legislation at the national level.

Follow-up Action

Political and economic difficulties in the latter half of 1992 had a profound impact on the Community's public perception and led to a more low-key approach by the Commission: The fanfare which might have been expected to greet the opening of the single market on January 1, 1993 was consequently somewhat muted. The Commission did, however, publish a report at the end of 1992, known as the Sutherland Report, which examined the practical implementation of the 1992 program and made various recommendations for follow-up actions. These include a greater "transparency" on the part of the Commission in publicising its legislative proposals and establishing the likely costs to industry before new laws are passed. Action to ensure that single market legislation is effectively and evenly enforced across all Member States is also proposed, including the imposition of fines against Member States who default (made possible by new provisions introduced by the TEU), as well as measures to encourage greater dialog and cooperation between the relevant health and safety authorities in each Member State.

Flanking Policies

The process of harmonization of laws, exemplified by the 1992 program, is, however, but one of the ways in which the single market is being achieved. Occupying a central place in the EC Treaty are two other policies which have a crucial part to play in the integration process, namely:

the "four freedoms" and the competition rules.

The Four Freedoms

The four fundamental freedoms guaranteed by the EC Treaty are:

— free movement of goods (Articles 30–36);

— freedom to provide services (i.e., from one's home Member State) (Articles 59–66);

— right of establishment or the right to locate a business in another Member State (Article 52–58); and

— finally, free movement of capital (Article 67–73).

The provisions governing free movement of goods are the most important and are considered in section 5 below. They basically reflect two principles: the principle of *mutual recognition* under which, in general, imports cannot be stopped if they meet all the legal requirements of the place where they were manufactured; and the principle that *import restrictions* (including any direct *or indirect* trading barriers) are *unlawful* and unenforceable unless justified by reference either to a *mandatory legal requirement* recognized by Community law (e.g. labelling requirements necessary for the protection of consumers) or by reference to one of a number of *specific public policy criteria* listed in the Treaty (e.g. the protection of industrial and commercial property).

Competition Rules and Rules on State Aids

The *competition rules* in Articles 85–90 of the EC Treaty are of direct relevance to any business operating in the Community. They even have extra-territorial effect in that they would, for instance, apply to a restrictive agreement between non-EC parties designed to be implemented in the Community (as recently confirmed by the European Court in the *Wood Pulp* cases: Cases 89, 104, 114, 116–7, 125–9/85). For instance if a group of American exporters agreed prices and quantities of goods for export to the Community this might qualify as a Webb-Pomerene export agreement under US rules but would be strictly prohibited by the Community competition rules.

The most important of the rules are:

— *Article 85*, an anti-cartel provision prohibiting anti-competitive agreements which have the object or effect of preventing, restricting or distorting competition within the Community; and

— *Article 86*, which is an anti-monopoly provision prohibiting companies with dominant positions from abusing their market power;

— *Article 90*, which applies to public undertakings, undertakings granted special or exclusive rights and certain state monopolies; and

— *Articles 92–93*, which in principle prohibits all forms of state aid and subsidy, unless specifically authorized.

Mergers and acquisitions (including certain types of joint venture) have, since

September 21, 1990 been covered by a separate regime set up by Regulation 4064/89 under which "concentrations" with a Community dimension come under the exclusive and direct jurisdiction of the European Commission, whereas all other concentrations remain under separate national jurisdictions (with their different procedures).

The most significant aspect of the Community's competition rules (in contrast with U.S. anti-trust rules) is that they place considerable emphasis on the single market objective of the EC Treaty and so treat more strictly than equivalent U.S. legislation any agreement (whether between competitors or between a company and its distributors, agents or licensees) which might tend to interfere with that overriding objective. Consequently the granting of territorial distribution or licensing rights (and other vertical restraints) needs to be handled with extreme care. A more detailed analysis of these rules appears below.

Harmonization of Laws

Many of the invisible barriers to trade are caused by discrepancies between the laws of the Member States. As already stated, the Community is far from being a unified legal market. This affects rules and regulations governing the safety of products, technical aspects, dimensions and performance of machinery, consumer protection legislation, intellectual property legislation, labelling and packaging law and regulations, and so on. Community rules tackle this problem in two ways:

(1)   by bringing national laws into line with each other by means of directives aimed at harmonization; and

(2)   pending harmonization, by applying the free movement rules in the Treaty to ensure as far as possible mutual recognition of standards and the elimination of legislation which might unfairly discriminate against imported products.

Under the old Article 100 of the EEC Treaty harmonization was a painfully slow process requiring the *unanimity* of all Member States. For instance, it took 17 years to agree uniform qualifications for architects. Since the Single European Act added a new *Article 100a*, only a *qualified majority* (calculated under a weighted voting system and equivalent to 75 percent) is required for most legislation. In practice, because the weighted voting gives Member States between two and 10 votes out of a total of 76 depending on their size, it now requires the votes of two large Member States and one small one to block proposals. Thanks to this revised legislative process, most 1992 legislation has been passed on time.

The speed of new legislation has also been helped by the so called "new approach" whereby directives no longer aim to harmonize every detailed rule, but only lay down minimum legal principles which have to be observed by the Member States in their national legislation. For instance, the Toy Safety Directive adopted in May 1988 simply specifies the minimum safety criteria which all toys have to comply with and leaves it to Member States to produce detailed legislation and certification procedures. However if a manufacturer satisfies one set of national rules, he is entitled to put the 'EC' certification mark on his products and they must be free to circulate in other Member States even if their specific local rules are different. There could theoretically be an advantage in establishing in a country where the legal requirements are laxer and therefore the compliance costs lower, giving a competitive advantage over companies established in countries with stricter regulations.

The Directive system (coupled with the rules on mutual recognition and free competition) do, however, ensure to a large extent that there is a level competitive playing field throughout the Community.

Specific Treaty Provisions

The text of the key Treaty provisions governing the single market, freedom of movement for goods and competition is reproduced at the end of this chapter. They include:

— Article 7a EC and Article 100a;
— Articles 30–36;
— Articles 85 and 86.

VI. COMMUNITY INSTITUTIONS; CREATING COMMUNITY LAW; ROLE OF THE COMMUNITY COURTS

Who's Who?

The principal institutions and bodies set up by the EC Treaty are as follows:
- The Council of Ministers*
- The European Council
- The Commission of the European Communities*
- The European Parliament*
- The Economic and Social Committee
- The Court of Justice*
- The European Court of First Instance
- The Court of Auditors*
- The Committee of the Regions

(* There are officially five institutions; in addition the proposed new Eurpoean Central Bank will have the same rights and obligations as an institution, without institutional status.)

The Council of Ministers

The Council of Ministers (or Council) consists of the 12 Member States and is the principal decision-making body of the Community. The Council is composed of government ministers from each Member State. They may either be from specific ministries or government departments dealing with particular sectors (e.g., the environment, finance, agriculture, trade) or, for general legislation, from the ministries of Foreign Affairs. In the latter case it is known as the General Council.

Each Member State takes it in turn to "preside" over the Council for a six month period and the country which has the presidency at any one time has considerable power to set the political agenda and to lay down the priorities for particular issues during its term of office. This has a considerable influence on Community legislation. In certain cases (particularly in the area of foreign policy) the immediate past and future presidents join the incumbent president to form a "troika" so as to maintain greater continuity of policy and to ensure a smoother handover of business from one presidency to the next.

The Council of Ministers carries out most of its day to day work through a number of working groups and advisory committees and in particular through COREPER (the Committee of Permanent Representatives or ambassadors from the 12 Member States). The U.K. permanent representation in Brussels (U.K.Rep) and its counterparts from each of the other Member States are therefore key players on the Community stage. The key stage in the Community law making process is when the Council "adopts a common position" at which stage legislation can only be blocked following an adverse opinion from the European Parliament (under the "co-operation procedure" referred to below).

Since the Single European Act a large number of measures (particularly those dealing with the completion of the single market and forming part of the 1992 program) have required only a qualified majority. A qualified majority is 54 votes out of 76, the main Member States (France, Germany, Italy and the United Kingdom) having 10 votes each, and the other Member States having a decreasing number of votes, down to two for Luxembourg. It therefore requires at least three Member States to block any piece of legislation where a qualified majority is necessary.

Under the so-called Luxembourg Compromise of January 1966, the French government settled a major dispute on agricultural policy on the basis that if in the future any Member State declared that one of its vital interests was at stake, the other Member States would not press the issue to a vote. The Luxembourg Compromise was never formally accepted by the other Member States and has no legal basis. However, it was never formally rescinded by the Single European Act and might, therefore, still be invoked.

In practice, none of the single market measures so far have had to be passed on a majority vote: A measure will only be put to the vote once there is a consensus in favor of it. There is a great deal of behind-the-scenes horse trading and and support for a measure can usually be secured by trading of one Member State's interest against another's.

Not surprisingly the resulting legislation tends to reflect these political compromises and is not always as well drafted or as effective as it might be under a more federal structure. For example, the Merger Control Regulation, which gives the Commission power to control mergers in the Community, only applies to the very largest of mergers where the parties have worldwide turnover of more than 5,000 million ECU and therefore only catches some 50 to 60 mergers a year rather than the 200 or so which the Commission had originally hoped would come within its jurisdiction. The high threshold for the application of this regulation was the price that had to be paid to ensure that the regulation was adopted. There are many other such examples that could be found.

European Council

The European Council was institutionalized by the Single European Act and is the name given to the summit of Heads of State or Government of the various Member States, accompanied by their foreign ministers, the President of the Commission and another Commissioner. There is usually at least one European Council meeting in the course of each presidency, so there are usually two European Council meetings a year. It is an occasion when the government leaders can resolve major political difficulties and can agree future policy objectives. The TEU states that it should "provide the Union with the necessary impetus for its development and shall define the general political guidelines thereof".

European Commission

The European Commission combines three functions: Civil service, executive, and legislative. The Commission itself is a collegiate body made up of 17 Commissioners (a number which may be reduced from 1995) appointed generally every five years by the Member States. It employs a total full-time staff of over 12,000, augmented by a very large number of "experts" and others seconded from Member goverments and third parties. The Commission is based in Brussels. The large Member States appoint two Commissioners each. Each Commissioner is given a specific portfolio. The Commission is organised into separate Directorates General (similar to ministries or departments of state), divided into directorates and units.

Business is most likely to come into day to day contact with DGIV (in charge of competition) which is headed by a Belgian, Mr Karel Van Miert. The other crucial Directorate General is DGIII (headed by a German, Mr Martin Bangemann) which is charge of industrial affairs. US companies may also encounter DGI which is in charge of external economic relations, including anti-dumping policy. Other important Directorates General are DGXI for the Environment; DGXII for Science, Research and Development; DGXIII for Telecommunications, Information, Industry and Innovations and DGXV which ensures the implementation of Single Market measures.

Most Community legislation is initiated by the Commission. The Commission is responsible for submitting a formal draft proposal to the Council, but before that stage is reached, the Commission generally circulates its proposals in draft to interested circles (Member Governments, industry and usually lawyers) to obtain initial views and fine tune the proposals. Major new proposals will usually be the subject of a public hearing, organised by the Commission in Brussels, to which interested parties are invited.

The Commission is also responsible for re-submitting amended proposals reflecting comments of the Council of Ministers, European Parliament and Economic and Social Committee at the various stages of the legislative procedure.

In addition to its legislative function, the Commission is responsible for ensuring that the provisions of the EC Treaty and of secondary EC legislation (e.g., the competition rules) are properly observed both by Member States and by private parties. Its role in enforcing the competition rules is a crucial one and brings it into day to day contact with business and industry. The Commission can, for instance, impose fines for breach of competition rules and, at the same time, it has exclusive powers to authorize anti-competitive agreements (covering the whole gamut of commercial agreements including distribution, agency, licensing, co-operation and joint venture agreements) under certain conditions. The Commission also has exclusive powers to vet large scale mergers and acquisitions within the Community where the turnovers of the parties involved fall above certain thresholds.

European Parliament

The European Parliament currently has 518 members voted by electors throughout the Community (to be increased to 557 members in 1994). The Parliament meets in Strasbourg (France), although its secretariat is largely based in Luxembourg and a great deal of its day to day work (particularly committee work and lobbying related work) is carried out in Brussels. Britain, France, Germany and Italy currently all have 81 directly elected members (known as MEPs) (to be increased to 99 for Germany and 87 for the other three). Smaller Member States have seats broadly in accordance with their population. There are 11 political groups. As already stated, the European Parliament is generally consulted on legislation before it can be adopted by the Council. Although on paper, the European Parliament's real powers are limited compared with a more traditional parliamentary democracy, in practice it has been able to exert important influence on Community legislation and its proposals are usually very carefully considered by the Commission. Its powers have also been considerably strengthened by the TEU, which introduced a "co-decision procedure". Where this applies, the Parliament will, provided it can muster an absolute majority of its members, reject a proposal on which the Council has adopted a common position (subject to going through a conciliation procedure first). The co-decision procedure applies for the time being in only a limited number of cases but there is provision in Article 189b(8) for the procedure to be extended to other areas in due course, so further strengthening the power and influence of the Parliament. Even under the co-operation procedure (which applies to most single market legislation) an absolute majority of the Parliament's members can reject a measure on which the Council has taken a common position, and when the measure is then referred back to the Council for a second reading it can only be adopted by unanimity. Although in theory, therefore, the Parliament could be overridden, an opponent of the measure would only need to persuade one Member State to vote against it to achieve stalemate.

The Parliament's formal powers are strongest in the area of budgets. Within the certain fixed limits, it can insist on increasing expenditure on non-agricultural policies through the annual budget and if the budget as a whole does not meet with its approval it can reject it entirely. It also has draconian powers to dismiss the whole of the Commission, powers so draconian they have never been exercised. Under the TEU it has furthermore acquired a positive right to approve new Commission members *en bloc* on their nomination by the Member States and will therefore wield some influence at the appointment stage as well.

Ecosoc

Ecosoc is the Economic and Social Committee made up of representatives from employers organizations, trade unions and other Community-wide social and economic groups, including consumer groups. It is formally consulted on policy and legislation and delivers formal opinions on draft legislation which can be influential in shaping the Commission's views.

Court of Justice of the European Communities

The CJEC (which sits in Luxembourg) handles appeals against Commission decisions and other acts of the institutions, actions for damages for non-contractual (i.e. negligent) liability on the part of Community institutions, cases between the institutions (and/or the Member States) and references for preliminary rulings on Community law from national courts as well as staff cases and cases arising under certain conventions such as the Brussels Convention on jurisdiction and the Rome convention on choice of law. The system of *preliminary rulings* (under article 177 EC) is crucial to the proper functioning of the Community: It is designed to ensure that when the national courts of the Member States apply Community law they do so in a uniform and consistent manner. The judgments of the Court of Justice are final and binding on Community institutions, governments, companies and individuals and in case of conflict with national law, Community law always takes precedence. The 13 judges of the Court are assisted by six Advocates General whose opinions provide useful non-binding guidance to the judges in each case. The Court usually hears cases as a chamber of three or five.

Some features of the Court may be unusual to those familiar with the US and English style of courts. In the first place, judgments are unitary with no dissenting opinions. The Court is also assisted by an Advocate General, who has a similar funtion to the *amicus curiae*, and delivers an opinion on which the Court generally bases its own judgment; the Advocate General's opinion is, however, only of persuasive authority and need not be followed by the Court. The Court of First Instance has no Advocates General, but can appoint one of their number to fulfil that function in appropriate cases. The system of Advocates General certainly goes some way to compensating for the lack of dissenting judgments. Cases are managed by a Juge Rapporteur who writes the initial drafts of judgments and is generally responsible for conducting the case, including the oral hearing. Oral hearings are an interesting part of the procedure although legal proceedings in the Community are essentially written. One particular feature of oral hearings before the Court of Justice is that submissions have to be simultaneously interpreted into the various official Community languages, giving some scope for judicial misunderstanding.

Court of First Instance

Since 1989 some of the Court's powers have been devolved to a newly created lower court, known as the Court of First Instance, made up of 12 judges. Originally it only handled appeals against decisions in competition cases (other than anti-dumping), as well as the vast number of disputes involving Community employees. Its jurisdiction has since been extended to all direct actions brought by national or legal persons: i.e. not including inter-institutional disputes, Member States or preliminary references. The exception for anti-dumping cases has been retained for the time being. Judgments of the Court of First Instance can be appealed, on points of law only, to the main Court of Justice.

Court of Auditors

The Court of Auditors is a corporate body of 12 members, one from each Member State, appointed for a renewable six-year term by the Council after consultation with the European Parliament. It is based in Luxembourg. It audits the accounts of all revenue and expenditure of the Communities and advises on the drafting of Community financial and budgetary legislation.

The Committee of the Regions

The Committee of the Regions is an important new advisory body set up by the TEU to represent regional and local interests in the Community. It has 189 members and assists the Council and the Commission in a consultative capacity in a similar way to the Economic and Social Committee.

European Council

The European Council was institutionalized by the Single European Act and is a summit of Heads of State or Government of the various Member States, together with their foreign ministers, the President of the Commission and another Commissioner. There is usually at least one European Council meeting in the course of each presidency. It is an occasion when the government leaders can resolve major political difficulties and can agree future policy objectives. The TEU States that it should "provide the Union with the necessary impetus for its development and shall define the general political guidelines thereof."

V. FREE MOVEMENT OF GOODS

Ambit of Articles 30–36

The rules governing free movement of goods are contained in Articles 30–36 of the EEC Treaty. They prohibit Member States from introducing or maintaining any direct or indirect barriers to trade within the Community. The effect of the rules is, however, more far reaching than might at first appear. The main impact of the rules is on product specifications, packaging and labelling, as well as health and safety and product registration requirements for food products, pharmaceuticals and agro-chemicals and other industrial products: they also have a direct impact on the enforceability of intellectual property rights, e.g., patents and trademarks. Business and company policy will need to take account of the rules in deciding such issues as the location of new plants, the structure of a distribution network, the licensing policy to adopt and so on.

The two fundamental principles underlying the rules on free movement of goods are the principle of "non-discrimination" and that of "mutual recognition" meaning that a product which is authorized for sale in one Member State must be free to be sold in all other Member States. Alongside these is the principle of "exhaustion of rights" applicable to intellectual property rights; once the owner of an intellectual property right has allowed his product to be sold in one Member State, he cannot generally rely on intellectual property rights subsisting in that product elsewhere in the Community to prevent that product from being sold on through licensees, wholesalers or other traders in other markets. The owner will therefore be unable to enforce those rights either to obtain an injunction against import or damages for infringement. These rules intermesh closely with the competition rules (see below) whereby any agreement which has the object or effect of restricting cross-frontier trade within the Community is unlawful and is not only unenforceable but will be likely to attract heavy fines.

The actual text of Article 30 prohibits quantitative restrictions on imports, and all measures having equivalent effect. It reads:

> Quantitative restrictions on imports and all measures having equivalent effect shall, without prejudice to the following provisions, be prohibited between Member States.

These words are, however, wide enough to catch any legislation which, although not on its face discriminatory, makes it more expensive or onerous for importers than for domestic producers: Such legislation is prohibited unless the Member State can show that it satisfies a general public interest need (known as a "mandatory requirement") and is not more restrictive than necessary. Mandatory requirements recognized by the Court of Justice include consumer protection, protection against unfair competition and environmental protection.

In addition, there is a number of specific derogations from Article 30, set out in Article 36. If a measure can be justified on any of the grounds set out in Article 36 it is allowed, provided it is not used as a means of arbitrary discrimination or a disguised restriction on trade between Member States. Article 36 lists the following grounds:

- public morality;
- public policy or public security;
- the protection of health and the life of humans, animals, or plants;
- the protection of national treasures possessing artistic, historic and archaeological value; and
- the protection of industrial and commercial property.

Health and Safety and Border Controls

A great number of cases have involved health and safety legislation, in particular relating to the composition and labelling of products, which *prima facie* are justified under Article 36 on grounds of protection of health. The European Court, although prepared to acknowledge this defense, has consistently held that "national rules restricting imports are compatible with the Treaty only insofar as they are necessary for the effective protection of human life and health and only if that objective cannot be achieved by measures less restrictive of intra-Community trade."

Case law on border controls makes it clear that health checks, etc. are in principle allowed but only provided that they are *proportionate* to the public health objective, i.e., going no further than reasonably necessary to achieve that objective, and do not duplicate tests already carried out in the Member State of export. Goods may still be subjected to a system of "light" controls sufficient to allow the country of import to satisfy itself that the health controls have been carried out. Border controls for goods have therefore now largely disappeared and a parallel simplification of the value added tax legislation has meant that most of the paperwork which had to be supplied at frontiers can now be dealt with on final delivery. Border controls for persons remain in place for the time being, although by 1994 most Member States will participate in the Schengen Accord, which will abolish most frontier checks on persons moving between those states.

Intellectual Property Rights

The effect of the free movement rules on intellectual property rights can be summarized as follows:

(i) many rights granted to owners of intellectual property under national law may be incompatible with Article 30 and may, therefore, be unenforceable. This applies, in particular, to the right to an injunction to stop imports: If the imported goods have first been put on the market elsewhere in the Community, a court may not grant injunctive relief, even where, as far as the domestic law is concerned, the act of importation would constitute an infringing act. Although Article 222 of the EC Treaty provides that the Treaty should not interfere with national systems of property ownership, this has been side-stepped by the European Court which has held that the *exercise* of such rights may nevertheless be incompatible with the Treaty.

(ii) any provision of national law which is discriminatory as between domestic and imported goods is unenforceable. This applies to all trading rules (for instance a rule obliging all manufacturers to indicate a country of origin on all goods, other than domestic goods). This can also catch discriminatory provisions in inteectual property legislation. For instance, in *Allen & Hanburys Ltd v Generics (U.K.)* (Case 434/85), the provisions in the U.K. Patents Act 1977 concerning the grant of an automatic patent license under the license of right provisions were less favorable for generic producers intending to manufacture the products under license outside the United Kingdom. Those provisions were discriminatory and thus incompatible with Article 30 and could not be justified under Article 36.

When applying for a patent or trademark in the Community, therefore, it is essential to bear in mind the possible effect of the EC free movement rules as these rights may not give as much protection as they appear to. The free movement rules (in combination with the competition rules described below) therefore have a crucial effect on a company's licensing policy and its policy for dealing with infringements.

(iii) In certain cases, intellectual property rights can be enforced against imported goods, in particular where these goods are infringing products manufactured and sold without the right owner's consent and without the consent of any associated company or licensee. If a product is patented in some but not all Member States (as is usually the case), a competing manufacturer establishing a manufacturing plant in an unprotected territory without a license would not be entitled to market its products throughout the Community. The patentee would be able to enforce its rights against unlicensed imports. Rights may also be enforceable as against imports where there are discrepancies in the laws of the Member States. For instance, so long as periods of copyright differ from one Member State to another, the copyright owner may still be able to rely on copyright to prevent imports of products from a country where the copyright has expired. From a manufacturer's point of view, there is therefore potentially some advantage in locating one's manufacturing base where the rights available are more extensive, or have longer duration, or can be more easily obtained and enforced. The opportunity for companies to take advantage of such discrepancies in the law will become rarer as the Community's harmonization program continues to develop.

(iv) Another area where companies need to be aware of the free movement rules is where they are disposing of intellectual property rights in the Community. The consequences will differ according to whether the rights are sold in their entirety to one third party or are divided up among one or two assignees in the Community. If all Community rights are assigned to one party, that party can enforce them against the original non-EC owner, since the rules on free movement of goods do not apply to imports from outside the Community (as confirmed in *EMI Records v CBS (U.K.) Ltd* (Case 51/75). If, on the other hand, the rights become split within the Community, the owners might be prevented by the free movement rules from enforcing the rights against each other.

(v) The exhaustion of rights principle has major commercial implications for patented products sold in countries where there is no patent protection. As the law currently stands, a patent owner who allows its products to be put on the market (either by direct sale, or sale through a subsidiary or distributor, or under license) in a part of the Community where the product does not enjoy any is no patent protection takes the risk that those products may be imported into other parts of the Community where there is patent protection. Since the price of the products in countries where there is no patent protection is likely to be lower, the temptation for parallel traders to exploit that price difference will be strong, particularly for high priced products such as pharmaceuticals. Under the present law, the only way in which a manufacturer can secure a degree of protection from such parallel imports is either by not authorizing the products to be sold in unprotected countries or doing so only through licensees with properly drafted license

agreements complying with the relevant competition rules. The application of the competition rules to licensing is described in section X below.

VI. OTHER FREEDOMS

Companies involved in service industries (e.g., telecommunications, computers, travel agency, financial services, and insurance) enjoy similar rights to provide their services across frontiers in other Member States on an equal footing with service companies already established there. There must be no discrimination based on nationality or place of incorporation within the Community. In order to benefit from the rules, one must have a basic establishment in one Member State.

The rules on freedom of establishment allow the pursuit of economic activity across borders through the setting up of companies or branches or subsidiaries without restriction. Similar rights apply to self-employed persons, and the rules governing the free movement of workers allow recruitment, secondment or transfer of personnel within the Community. Work permits are not necessary, although certain registration requirements may remain. For some professionals, certification may be required, but slowly the market is moving towards mutual recognition of "equivalent" qualifications for a number of professions.

In the case of financial services (banking, investment services and insurance), the Community has introduced the concept of the single "Community passport," avoiding the need for companies to comply with authorization requirements in more than one Member State. A company authorized to carry out certain activities in its home Member State will automatically be entitled to provide such services, either directly or through the establishment of a local branch in other Member States (the host state) with only minimal notification requirements. Once all the legislation is in place, it will represent a considerable advance. Any non-EC company wanting to take advantage of the rules, however, needs first to establish a subsidiary and obtain relevant authorizations in at least one Member State. Branches of non-EC entities still require separate authorization in each state.

VII. COMPETITION RULES: BASIC PRINCIPLES APPLYING TO COMMERCIAL AGREEMENTS

Introduction

As already stated, Article 85 prohibits anti-competitive agreements and Article 86 prohibits abuses of a dominant position. Article 85 is the provision which is most likely to affect a US business deciding to establish or sell in Europe for the first time. Before explaining how Article 85 applies to specific types of agreement (distribution, agency, licensing and joint ventures), it is necessary to understand some of the basic principles.

Article 85(1): The Basic Prohibition

Article 85(1) prohibits as incompatible with the common market "all agreements between undertakings, decisions by associations of undertakings and concerted practices which may affect trade between Member States [*to an appreciable extent*] and which have as their object or effect the prevention, restriction or distortion of competition within the common market [*to an appreciable extent*]."

Article 85(1) applies to both *horizontal* agreements (e.g. cartels, joint ventures affecting principally interbrand competition) and to *vertical* agreements (e.g. exclusive distribution and licensing agreements affecting interbrand competition). The Treaty gives as illustrative examples of anti-competitive agreements ones which:

(a) directly or indirectly fix purchase or selling prices or any other trading conditions (*price-fixing and resale price maintenance*);

(b) limit or control production, markets, technical development, or investment (*non-competition covenants and exclusive agreements*);

(c) share markets or sources of supply (*cartels, joint purchasing agreements, quota arrangements*);

(d) apply dissimilar conditions to equivalent transactions with other trading parties, thereby placing them at a competitive disadvantage (*cartels applying discriminatory terms to non-members*);

(e) make the conclusion of contracts subject to the acceptance of supplementary obligations which, by their nature or according to commercial usage, have no connection with the subject of such contracts (*tying arrangements*)." (Words in parentheses added).

Nullity

Article 85(2) provides that agreements or decisions prohibited under Article 85(1) are automatically void. The European Court has confirmed that Article 85(2) invalidates an agreement only to the extent of its restrictive provisions and that the validity of the remainder of the agreement must be determined in accordance with the applicable law of the contract.

Exemption

Article 85(1) does not, however, apply to agreements which are exempted pursuant to Article 85(3). In order to be eligible for exemption an agreement must satisfy two positive conditions and one negative condition, as follows:

- it must contribute to the improvement of production or distribution of goods or to the promotion of technical progress;
- it must allow consumers a fair share of the resulting benefit;
- it must not impose on its parties restrictions which are not indispensable to the attainment of such beneficial objectives; and
- it must not give the parties an opportunity substantially to eliminate interbrand competition in the relevant product market.

The Court has confirmed that Article 85(1) is subject to a *de minimis* rule and will not apply if it can be shown that the effect on interstate trade or the effect on competition is insignificant. In this regard the Commission has published a Notice on Agreements of Minor Importance ([1986] OJC 231/2): In general an agreement will be considered unimportant if the aggregate turnover of the parties concerned does not exceed ECU 200 million (US$ 224 million) *and* if their combined market share is under five percent.

The system of exemptions is an important feature of the EC competition law system and distinguishes it in particular from U.S. anti-trust law. An exemption may only be granted by the European Commission either on an individual application (known as a *notification*) pursuant to Article 4 of Regulation 17/62 (or a specific sectoral regulation) or by virtue of block exemption. *Block exemption* is automatically granted to defined categories of agreement set out in a series of regulations issued by the Commission under powers delegated to it by the Council. Such regulations cover the sorts of agreements which are commonly entered into by companies with distributors, licensees and competitors and which in general are beneficial to competition and not overly restrictive. Not *all* restrictions, however, are automatically permitted by such regulations: Agreements containing restrictions which do not comply with the relevant conditions for block exemption may require individual notification. Where parties are uncertain whether their agreement complies with Article 85(1) or 86 they may apply to the Commission for *negative clearance*, i.e., a formal declaration that an agreement or practice is compatible with the competition rules.

Dominant Companies

Clearly, once a company, US or otherwise, has acquired a high market share in the Community as a whole or in one of its constituent markets, there is a risk that it could be treated as dominant (i.e., enjoying a position of economic strength such that it is able to behave, to an appreciable extent, largely independently of its competitors and ultimately of consumers). Dominance may also arise where a company has strong patent or trademark protection giving it a significant market advantage over its competitors. Article 86 does not prohibit dominance or monopolies *per se*, but prohibits a dominant company from abusing its privileged market position through abusive behavior. Such behavior may either be exploitative (e.g., charging disproportionately high prices, or refusing to supply a product for which there is consumer demand) or exclusionary (e.g., predatory pricing, discriminatory discounts, tie-ins, exclusive purchasing or distribution, discriminatory conditions of sale or purchase). The relevant provisions are as follows:

> Any abuse by one or more undertakings of a dominant position within the common market or in a substantial part of it shall be prohibited as incompatible with the common market in so far as it may affect trade between Member States.

> Such abuse may, in particular, consist in:

> (a) directly or indirectly imposing unfair purchase or selling prices or other unfair trading conditions;

(b) limiting production, markets or technical development to the prejudice of consumers;

(c) applying dissimilar conditions to equivalent transactions with other trading parties, thereby placing them at a competitive disadvantage;

(d) making the conclusion of contracts subject to acceptance by the other parties of supplementary obligations which, by their nature or according to commercial usage, have no connection with the subject of such contracts.

Article 86 has on numerous occasions been applied to multinational corporations outside the Community. Examples include IBM in the computer industry, the Swedish-Swiss group Tetra Pak in the packaging industry, United Brands in the banana market, and Commercial Solvents in the nitropropane and aminobutanol markets: All are examples of non-EC companies which have been victims of the Community's rules on dominant companies. Dominant companies are also at a major disadvantage in not being able to rely on the system of block exemptions (under Article 85(3)).

Article 85 : Unenforceability and Fines

Article 85 is of crucial commercial importance as it affects the enforceability of ordinary contracts, even where one or more of the contracting parties are outside the Community. The consequences of infringing Article 85(1) are potentially threefold:

- First, provisions may be struck out of the contract by the courts, with the obvious commercial implications which that entails.

- Secondly, agreements infringing Article 85(1) are prohibited by law and, under powers delegated to it by the Council of Ministers, the European Commission has power to impose fines on parties to such agreements. The level of fines can in principle be up to 10 percent of the total turnover of each party to the contract and all other associated companies in the same group, regardless of whether they operate in the same market. While in practice this level of fines is never reached, the size of fines can be quite considerable: In July 1991, Tetra Pak was fined ECU 75 million (almost U.S. $90 million) for abusive pricing practices and the chemical companies ICI and Solvay were fined ECU 17 million and 30 million (US$19 million and 34 million) respectively in 1990 for price-fixing agreements.

- Thirdly, third parties may claim damages from the parties to an unlawful agreement for the losses caused to them as a consequence of that unlawful agreement.

Enforcement of Competition Rules

The Commission is responsible under various Regulations (principally Regulation 17/62) for enforcing the competition rules. It may act on its own initiative or at the request of a third party (a complainant): It has a limited discretion in deciding how to prioritize its cases and has indicated that it will tend to give priority to cases raising important issues of principle or a novel point of law. A decision to reject a complaint may be appealed to the Court of First Instance. The Commission has wide-ranging powers (*inter alia*) to seek out suspected infringements, to search premises with or without prior notice, to demand information and to take copies of any documents relevant to its enquiries, to impose fines in respect of breaches of the procedural regulations, to issue cease and desist orders requiring parties to put an end to infringements, to impose periodic penalty payments (i.e., daily fines) for non-implementation, and to require parties to submit periodic reports to ensure future compliance. Regulations govern the procedure to be followed in competition cases, rights of defense, oral hearings, business secrets, notifications etc. Although in each of the transport sectors separate procedural regulations exist, these are in most cases similar to the general regulations. The provisions of Articles 85 and 86 are directly effective, meaning that they are binding on individuals and can be relied on by individuals before national courts. This has the following effects:

(1)   national courts are under a duty not to give effect to contractual provisions or agreements which infringe Articles 85(1) or 86;

(2)   any person suffering loss as a result of a breach of Articles 85(1) and 86 is entitled to claim damages and/or an injunction as against the infringing party, and national courts are obliged to grant appropriate relief;

(3)   since national courts do not have the power to grant exemption, they may be required to stay proceedings where an agreement which is the subject of litigation has been notified to the Commission; on the other hand, national courts can interpret, and indeed have a duty to apply, block exemption regulations, whenever relevant;

(4)   under the system of preliminary references under Article 177 EC Treaty a national court which is uncertain of the correct interpretation of a relevant Community provision may request clarification from the CJEC.

The European Commission and the national courts must work together to enforce all Community law, including competition law. The European Commission, in an effort to assist national courts in that duty, issued a Notice on Cooperation between National Courts and the Commission in applying Articles 85 and 86 of the EEC Treaty in February 1993 (OJ C39/6) providing some useful guidance on the division of responsibilities and the correct approach to be taken by a national court when faced with a claim on a defense based on Community law.

Contrast with U.S. Law

U.S. corporations will be familiar with the U.S. anti-trust rules and their strict application to all types of collusive conduct between competitors and even to certain distribution and licensing arrangements. Although Article 85 covers similar ground, it does not always operate in the same way.

There are four main differences between Article 85 and the equivalent provisions in Section 1 of the Sherman Act in the U.S.:

(i) there is no rule of reason: an agreement (or decision of a trade association or concerted practice) only escapes Article 85(1) if its effect on competition is "not appreciable"—this is a *de minimis* test designed to exclude small agreements with only local effects;

(ii) by contrast, however, there is a system of *exemptions*: the Commission has the power under Article 85(3) to exempt, i.e., to authorize, agreements whose benefits outweigh their anti-competitive effects. The exemption system is even more generous than the American rule of reason doctrine, but has the disadvantage that only the Commission can apply it and not the national courts before whom a contract dispute is being heard: furthermore, agreements must be individually notified to the Commission unless they comply with a block exemption (as explained below);

(iii) thirdly, there is a system of fines, administered by the Commission: although, as mentioned, the fines can be heavy, they are not criminal in nature, are imposed on the companies, not officers or sales managers, and would only affect individuals to the extent that those individuals are independent economic operators (e.g., sole traders, architects, inventors, authors or artists);

(iv) Article 85 does not specifically provide for civil remedies, but any company suffering loss as a result of an anti-competitive agreement would have the right under the relevant national law to recover damages from the parties to the unlawful agreement. Unlike the U.S. with its system of triple damages, those damages would only compensate the plaintiff for actual loss suffered: the precise calculation of damages and the evidence required to prove the claim will differ from one Member State to another and in the U.K. at least actions for recovery of damages are rare.

National Competition Legislation

Article 85 applies only where the agreement, decision or practice has, or is capable of having, an appreciable effect on trade between Member States, a test which is applied so broadly that only highly localized agreements or networks of agreements can be certain of escaping the Community rules. However, double jeopardy applies: Whether or not they are caught by Article 85, anti-competitive agreements may be subject to the competition laws of the Member States. In the U.K., restrictive agreements may require filing with the Office of Fair Trading under the Restrictive Trade Practices Act 1976, even if they benefit from exemption under Article 85(3). A number of the Member States have competition rules based on Articles 85 and 86; the U.K. system is entirely different, although the U.K. government intends in due course to introduce legislation modelled on Article 85.

VIII. APPROACHING ARTICLE 85 IN PRACTICE

Strategies for Avoiding Article 85

It is useful to stress the basic purpose of complying with Article 85, which is twofold:

- to ensure that one's agreement can be enforced in court; and
- to avoid fines.

There are, however, in practice various ways of dealing with Article 85(1) depending on the type of agreement, the market positions of the parties, their relevant size and their commercial objectives. The following three approaches are considered:

(i) relying on block exemptions;

(ii) submitting an individual notification; or

(iii) drafting the agreement in such a way that the agreement could if necessary be notified and would be unlikely to attract fines.

The third possibility may often be commercially the most sensible route, although it requires careful legal advice and a full awareness of the legal and commercial dangers it could lead to.

Block Exemptions

The drafting of agreements in the Community is heavily influenced by the system of block exemptions. Block exemptions, in the form of regulations issued by the Commission, automatically authorize a given category of agreement (e.g., distribution, patent licensing, know-how licensing, and co-operation agreements).

An exclusive distribution agreement can, for instance, escape Article 85(1) if it complies with the relevant regulation (Regulation 1983/83). However, it may only contain the restrictions allowed by the regulation. As explained in Section IX below, these include restrictions on the distributor actively promoting the products outside his exclusive territory, handling competing products or re-packaging the products before re-sale. However, if the supplier were to include any restrictions of competition which were not authorized by the regulation (e.g., prohibiting the distributor from supplying a customer who intended to export the products outside the territory into other parts of the Community, or fixing the distributor's re-sale prices or credit terms), automatic block exemption is lost altogether and all the restrictions in the agreement are potentially void and unenforceable. It would then be up to the parties to argue in court what the relevant market was, whether the restrictions restricted competition in that market and whether they did so to an appreciable extent.

Block exemptions are also available for patent and know-how licenses (Regulations 2349/84 and 556/89). These regulations exempt various provisions relating to exclusive territorial protection (e.g., preventing the licensee from exploiting the technology in parts of the Community where the licensor wants to exploit it and restrictions on the licensee from actively promoting products manufactured by it in other licensees' territories). However, if the agreement provides that the licensee cannot supply a customer who orders products from it if the customer is based in another licensee's territory, that is a restriction which the regulation does not normally allow. If the licensor includes such a restriction in the license agreement, it will make the *whole* license agreement potentially void and unenforceable. This even affects restrictions which would otherwise be authorized under the relevant regulation. It is also to be remembered that any restriction on cross-border trade within the Community which is not specifically authorized by the regulation will be treated very seriously and will almost undoubtedly attract fines if the Commission finds out about it. Since free movement of goods lies at the heart of the EC Treaty, the Commission (and the European Court) would view with particular disfavor any attempt by private parties to restrict it by contractual arrangements.

Since the important decision of the Commission against Tetra Pak (decision of 26th July 1988, confirmed by the Court of First Instance on July 10, 1990 in case T-51/89) it is clear that any company with a dominant position in the relevant market in the Community cannot safely rely on the system of block exemptions. This is because Article 86 (which prohibits abuse of a dominant position) overrides block exemptions. The case concerned a license agreement under which Tetra Pak had exclusive rights to technology relating to the aseptic filling of cartons. Since Tetra Pak was the market leader in the underlying carton market, the exclusive license made it virtually impossible for any competitor to break into that market. Where this situation arises a dominant company cannot hope to rely on block exemption and would be unlikely to obtain an individual exemption either. Unless it notified its agreement it would moreover be at risk of being fined.

Any deal involving a dominant company therefore has to be thought about very carefully. In that particular case, Tetra Pak would have been in a stronger position if the technology had been assigned and Tetra Pak had from the start been prepared to grant licenses to any competitors on reasonable royalty terms. As it was, the Commission insisted on the agreements being made non-exclusive and Tetra Pak was thus deprived of any licensing income.

Individual Notification

As well as the system of block exemptions, there is a system of individual exemptions. These are granted individually under Article 85(3), but can only be granted by the European Commission and in almost all cases a formal notification to the European Commission is legally necessary (e.g., it is not a prerequisite for agreements between parties from the same Member State provided that they do not relate to imports or exports). From the moment of notification the parties can no longer be fined. Notifying an agreement to the Commission involves filling in a form known as Form A/B, which requires many details about the parties, their market shares, information about their competitors and about the relevant products and a detailed analysis of the restrictions in the agreement and the reasons why the parties consider they should be exempted.

If the notification is successful the Commission publishes a notice of intention to exempt followed by a formal decision. Both the notice and the decision appear in the Community's Official Journal. This is published in all Community languages and available to the general public on subscription. The exemption procedure is, however, discretionary and there is never any guarantee that the Commission will at the end of the day grant an exemption. Exemption may also be conditional: e.g., granted on condition that the parties must modify certain terms of the agreement or provide the Commission with regular market reports. If the Commission refuses to exempt a notified agreement, there is in principle a right of appeal to the European Court of First Instance. There is no time limit on when an agreement can be notified, but exemption can only be back-dated to the date of notification and the parties remain at risk of fines until the form is submitted.

Commercially, however, there are two problems with the notification system. First it requires a great deal of effort on the part of the companies involved and their legal advisers in preparing and submitting the notification, and sometimes negotiating a satisfactory decision. (The power of the Commission to grant exemption only if certain clauses are amended means that the parties will often have little option but to comply with the Commission's recommendations.) Secondly, there is the time element: Not only the time involved in preparing the notification, but the enormous length of time which can elapse between submitting the notification and receiving the Commission's answer. The Commission has at times had thousands of similar agreements and is unable to reach formal decisions on more than a handful per year (the number can range between fifteen and thirty across all types of agreement).

This logjam has to an extent been resolved by the system of "comfort letters" which are informal letters of an administrative nature (which are *not legally binding*). In a comfort letter the Commission states that having considered the notification it would be likely to issue a favorable decision and is prepared to close its file. Sometimes (but rarely) a comfort letter is private and simply addressed to the parties. Sometimes the Commission publishes a notice in the Official Journal of the European Communities of its intention to issue a favorable decision, but without following it up with a formal decision, and in either case the Commission may or may not report the informal decision in its monthly Bulletin and/or its Annual Report on Competition Policy. Although comfort letters are not legally of any validity, many parties may prefer to have a comfort letter sooner, rather than waiting for a full decision. If necessary (e.g. if there is a court case) a full decision could be requested later. In its guidance Notice on Cooperation with National Courts published on February 13, 1993 (OJ C39/8) the European Commission states that the opinion expressed in such a letter constitutes a factor which a national court may take into account. In practice the Commission is unlikely to change its mind unless facts were concealed or the market situation has significantly altered. For many agreements, particularly research and development agreements and joint ventures, this is a useful method of dealing with any potential competition problems.

The notification system (whether resulting in a formal decision or an informal comfort letter) is nevertheless somewhat of a lottery, in that one can never know what priority the Commission will give to one's agreement and what the eventual outcome will be. It will be obvious that, in most cases, there is a strong commercial incentive (as well as a legal incentive) to ensure compliance with the relevant block exemption. Whilst this sometimes imposes a commercial straitjacket on the negotiating freedom of the parties, for the majority of commercial arrangements the benefits outweigh the disadvantages. However, it is crucial for the parties to analyze the position carefully.

One should also be aware that in deciding which individual notifications to deal with first, the Commission will tend to give priority to important new categories (e.g., franchising agreements, or rate-fixing agreements in the insurance industry). The purpose is in the long term to acquire enough experience of those categories to be able to introduce a block exemption in due course. This has in fact happened in the last few years to both franchising agreements and insurance contracts. Software licenses (and possibly trademark licenses) are likely to be considered at some stage in the future. Priority will also be given to agreements which are being litigated, where the parties need to know whether their agreements are exempt or not in order to know if they are enforceable. In its Notice on Cooperation with National Courts the Commission states its intention to accord priority to "notifications, complaints and own-intitiative proceedings having particular political, economic or legal significance for the Community."

Notices

As well as issuing block exemptions, the Commission also issues guidance from time to time on the application of Article 85(1) to certain types of agreement, in the form of Notices. The most important of these are:

— The Notice on Minor Agreements (OJ C231/2 of September 12, 1986) which provides that where the parties to the agreement have less than five percent of the relevant market and do not have combined worldwide group turnover of more than 200 million ECU (U.S. $225 million), Article 85(1) will in principle not apply because competition is unlikely to be affected to an appreciable extent. This is clearly of great practical significance for small or medium-sized US companies starting up in Europe (although the need to take worldwide sales of all affiliated companies into account limits the utility of the Notice).

— Notice on Sub-Contracting Agreements (OJ C1/2 of January 31, 1979): this provides a useful exception to the rules on licensing, allowing sub-contracting of research and development or component manufacture to a third party, with considerable scope for imposing restrictions on the sub-contractor's activities.

— Notice on Exclusive Agency Agreements: this is shortly to be re-issued.

Various other notices explain how the block exemptions work. For instance there is a useful notice on the regulations governing exclusive distribution and purchasing agreements and on the rules applying to agreements between motor manufacturers and their dealers.

Significance of Black Clauses

All the block exemption regulations list the restrictions which must not be included if the agreement is to benefit from automatic exemption pursuant to the regulation. These are known as black clauses. As already explained, an agreement could still in theory be the subject of an individual exemption if it were properly notified. However, if an agreement contains such restrictions and is not notified, block exemption is not available and all the restrictions which have an appreciable effect on competition are void and unenforceable. A national court called upon to enforce the agreement would then have to apply its own rules on severance and it may be that having severed all the void provisions from the agreement there will be no agreement at all left to enforce; i.e., the effect of including just one black clause may be to make the whole agreement void. This could, for instance, not only affect the ability of a licensor to restrain a licensee from committing a breach of the contract (e.g. enforcing a clause prohibiting the licensee from selling outside the exclusive territory) but could also make it difficult for the licensor even to recover royalties. Alternatively, a licensee who had been granted exclusive selling rights under a patent license might still be required to pay the same rate of royalty if a court finds that the exclusive grant is contrary to Article 85(1) and severs it from the remainder of the agreement.

There may also be certain restrictions on competition which are neither expressly authorized by the regulations (i.e. not in the white list) and not expressly prohibited (i.e., not in the black list either). These "grey-listed" clauses present similar problems to black clauses, although the chance of obtaining an individual exemption is usually higher, reducing the risk of a fine.

In practical terms, it is important to avoid black clauses because the risk of fines is that much greater and the Commission is in any event likely to refuse exemption even if the parties take the precaution of notifying their agreement.

Risk/Benefit of Not Notifying

Apart from relying on a block exemption or individual notification, there is a third, practical, option which may need to be considered for agreements where there is no block exemption available, or if there is one where it would involve too many commercial compromises to bring an agreement within it. In such case, there is the option of not notifying the agreement. If there are no black clauses and if there is a reasonable chance that the agreement would benefit from individual exemption if notified, the parties may consider it unnecessary to notify at the initial stage, particularly since fines would be highly unlikely. At the back of their minds, may be the thought that if litigation arises, the plaintiff could always unilaterally notify the agreement to the Commission (with a reasonable prospect of obtaining exemption) and this will at least ensure that the plaintiff will be able to obtain an injunction to enforce the agreement. Recovering damages for breach of the agreement before it was notified will be more difficult, because before it was actually notified it was in a legal state of limbo and the restrictions were technically unenforceable. It is not, however, advisable to enter into agreements containing *black clauses* without notifying the agreement, in view of the risk of fines: Moreover the Commission is not entitled to impose fines in respect of notified agreements from the date of notification until either: (a) it adopts a specific decision suspending immunity from fines; or (b) it adopts a final decision refusing exemption.

This is an area which will always require careful advice from EC lawyers and a fine balancing of the parties' commercial objectives against the various legal factors involved.

Summary of the Various Considerations

In the simplest of cases it is worth remembering that the easiest route will usually be to bring an agreement into line with a relevant block exemption. The advantages can be summarized as follows:

(1)   This ensures automatic validity and enforceability of the restrictions;

(2)   It ensures immunity from fines;

(3)   If there is a legal dispute, a national court has the power to interpret the relevant block exemption regulation (in contrast with individual exemptions which only the Commission can grant);

(4)   It follows that it is easier to obtain an injunction and there is less risk of the proceedings being stayed (as would happen if the court had to await a Commission decision);

(5)   Parties negotiating agreements in the Community need to be aware that block exemptions can be used as negotiating tools, particularly by distributors, licensees, and franchisees, who will be unwilling to accept black or even grey clauses;

(6)   The effect of not complying could involve the parties in considerable legal costs as the courts have to grapple with complicated legal and economic issues to decide whether Article 85(1) applies at all;

(7)   Finally, the black lists have a subsidiary function in signalling the clauses which are (a) most likely to attract fines and (b) unlikely to be individually exempted; and so in drafting an agreement in the Community it is generally preferable to avoid such clauses (at least without taking the precaution of notifying).

IX.   DISTRIBUTION AND AGENCY

The options for a U.S. company wanting to set up in the European Community can range from a simple agency/distribution arrangement, through possible co-operation arrangements, to a branch or fully-fledged subsidiary. Other options include licensing and franchising. The effect of EC law on distribution and agency agreements is now considered. Franchising (although a form of retail distribution) is considered separately.

The Block Exemptions

Theoretically, one or more non-exclusive distributors could be appointed for the whole of the Community. In practice, it would be more efficient to appoint separate distributors in each of the major markets, since they have local knowledge of the markets, as well as being familiar with the language and local culture. EC law basically recognizes three types of distribution arrangement:

(1)   exclusive or sole distribution;

(2)   exclusive purchasing; and

(3)   selective distribution.

An exclusive distribution agreement is one in which the distributor is granted an exclusive territory in which it can concentrate its sales. If the agreement is fully exclusive, the supplier will also agree to refrain from competing with the distributor in that territory. In a sole distribution arrangement, the supplier reserves the right to supply either all customers in the distributor's territory or selected categories of customers, so that both the supplier and the distributor can compete for such custom. The agreement is sole in the sense that the supplier agrees not to appoint other distributors in the same territory. Regulation 1983/83 is the block exemption for exclusive and sole distribution agreements (and has to be read in conjunction with the Commission's explanatory notice). It exempts in particular the following restrictions on the distributor:

(1)   not to manufacture or distribute competing goods;

(2)   not to purchase the goods for re-sale from any third party (i.e. to purchase them exclusively from the supplier);

(3)   to refrain, outside the contract territory and in relation to the contract goods, from seeking customers, from establishing any branch, and from maintaining any distribution depot (i.e., a ban on active sales).

The exemption may not apply if a supplier appoints one of its competitors to distribute its goods in another market. Above all, the agreement must not contain restrictions on the distributor's re-sale prices, although the supplier can recommend prices and must not attempt to stop parallel trade (e.g., to stop the distributor's customers from engaging in cross-border trade).

If the supplier wishes to appoint two or three distributors in the same exclusive territory, this is not covered by the block exemption, but such an arrangement would probably be acceptable to the Commission if notified.

Regulation 1984/83 applies to what are called "exclusive purchasing agreements." Title I of the regulation is of general application to all forms of exclusive purchasing agreements. These are similar to exclusive distribution agreements, but the distributor is not given an exclusive territory. He is, however, obliged to obtain all supplies of the products from the supplier. He may be given a "principal sales area" in which sales must be concentrated. The main limitation of this regulation is that the agreement must be for a maximum of five years and must not be automatically renewable. Furthermore, it does not cover supply agreements for industrial processes (e.g., a five-year agreement between a manufacturer and a raw materials supplier) as it only covers agreements for *re-sale*. Exclusive purchasing agreements tend to be rarer than exclusive distribution agreements. There are, however, two industries where such agreements are very common, namely the brewing industry and the petrol industry. For this reason tied house arrangements and solus petrol agreements are specifically exempted under Titles II and III of Regulation 1984/83. Parties have the option of relying either on the general or the specific rules.

Selective distribution agreements are considered below. A specialized regulation

(Regulation 123/85) is also available for distribution agreements between motor manufacturers and their dealers which takes into account the particular conditions of that market. A different kind of regulation altogether applies in the air, sea, and road transport sectors, including a number of block exemptions.

Agency Agreements

A new notice is due to be published by the Commission on exclusive agency agreements by early 1994. These can often fall outside Article 85(1) altogether. It is understood that the Notice will make a distinction between integrated agents and non-integrated agents. If the agent is basically working for one principal (a large proportion of the agent's turnover is for one company) the agent is akin to an employee. The degree of commercial risk accepted by the agent will also be relevant in distinguishing a true agent from a distributor who has sole responsibility for disposing of his stocks. Restrictions on handling competing products and actively supplying products to other agents' territories are then acceptable. If the agent is unintegrated, he is treated more like a distributor (and only restrictions on *active* sales outside the territory would be permitted). Both the integrated and unintegrated agent can be made to sell only at the principal's list prices and on the principal's terms and conditions of sale, but the unintegrated agent must be free to do what he likes with his commission. This means that the agent could offer additional price incentives or other bonuses to potential customers as a way of competing with other agents. This was, in fact, confirmed as correct by the European Court in a case involving travel agents who had offered their own incentives to customers without the consent of the tour operators whose tours they were selling (*Vlaamse Reisbureaus*: case 311/85). If principals attempted to interfere, this would be prohibited by Article 85(1) and could attract fines. The agency route therefore offers a slightly greater degree of control than straight distribution even if the agent is "unintegrated." Agency can however be commercially more risky for a manufacturer or service provider who has to accept primary legal liability for any default by the agent and generally bear the commercial risk.

Selective Distribution

Selective distribution agreements affect mainly consumer goods sold through high class department stores and specialist outlets. It therefore affects perfumes, hi-fi equipment, and other such products requiring some special expertise and handling. Manufacturers who wish to maintain high standards for their products may wish to lay down minimum quality criteria for their retail outlets, e.g., ensure that staff are properly trained, that the outlets are properly laid out and kept to a high standard, etc. EC law makes the somewhat arbitrary distinction between such qualitative restrictions (which are deemed to fall outside Article 85(1)) and any quantitative restrictions (e.g., a restriction on handling of competing products, or a restriction or quota on the number of resellers in a particular district). The law in this area needs to be applied with some care and it will often be necessary to notify the agreement to the Commission, possibly with a view to a comfort letter. As a general rule, selective distribution is only acceptable if one can show that the goods have certain special qualities that require a particular standard of premises or specially trained staff or perhaps facilities for after sales service. The Commission has, for instance, accepted such a system for dinner services but not for plumbing equipment. The Commission will scrutinize any restrictions on cross-supplies between approved dealers, will usually insist on a uniform procedure for dealing with applications for approval, minimum annual purchase levels not exceeding 40 percent of average purchases in a given territory and will satisfy itself that the system for checking whether a dealer is authorized is no stricter than necessary.

A possible alternative to selective distribution (or other forms of distribution) is franchising, which is covered by its own block exemption (Regulation 4087/88). This applies to both distribution and service franchises, where the franchisee is selling a particular franchised product (e.g., Pronuptia wedding dresses or McDonalds hamburgers) and to outlets selling a number of different products under a franchised system (e.g., Computerland).

Parallel Imports

These are imports of products originally sold through an authorized outlet in one part of the Community and imported by a third party dealer or trader to another Member State where the same product is being sold at a higher price, so undercutting the local distributor or licensee there. Very often manufacturers and their dealers or licensors and their licensees, will be tempted to stop such parallel imports in order to ensure 'orderly marketing'. The consequences of such action can be serious. It is worth repeating the fundamental importance of free movement of goods within the European Community. *Any contractual restrictions on trade within the Community are to be approached with great care.*

As has been seen, the block exemption for distribution agreements allows a restriction on *active selling* outside the exclusive territory but provides for automatic loss of exemption if "one or both of the parties makes it difficult for intermediaries or users to obtain the contract goods from other dealers inside the common market or, insofar as no alternative source of supply is available there, from outside the common market. . . ." This could include adding the words "export prohibited" on sales invoices, expressly forbidding customers of the distributor to sell outside the territory, insisting the distributor sells only to retail outlets and not wholesalers who might be able to engage in parallel trade, or even using intellectual property rights (or, in the case of agro-chemicals or pharmaceuticals requiring marketing authorizations, distinct product compositions) to make parallel imports difficult. Any refusal by a distributor to supply a dealer where the dealer is a known parallel importer can cause difficulties: The presumption will be that the refusal was designed to prevent parallel trade, but if there is another good reason for refusing to supply (e.g., that the dealer appears to be insolvent) it is advisable to ensure that accurate written records are kept.

It is possible to combine a selective dealership system with a network of exclusive dealers. The distributor can be restricted to selling only to dealers who satisfy certain qualitative criteria (i.e., sufficient technical training, knowledge of the products, attendance at a number of courses and/or ability to provide adequate after sales, warehousing, advertising or marketing facilities), which fall outside Article 85(1), always provided they remain qualitative.

It will be no surprise that the vast majority of decisions by the Commission have involved restrictions on parallel imports and no surprise either that the Commission will not hesitate to impose severe fines on companies in breach of these rules. The rules make it imperative to consider the EC law aspects early on, so that, whenever possible, problems of parallel trade do not arise in the first place. In the *Konica* case, for instance, the problem arose because the Japanese film manufacturer Konica had decided to market its films differently in the U.K. and in Germany. In the U.K. it competed directly on price with the market leaders, and was marketed as a cut-price alternative. In Germany, on the other hand, it was promoted as a high quality prestige product, sales being restricted to specialist camera shops and prices being correspondingly high. A parallel trade in low-priced U.K. products was quick to develop. Attempts by Konica and its European subsidiary to stop the trade were condemned by the European Community and they were fined.

Active and Passive Sales

It is important to make the distinction between "active" and "passive" sales, which is a distinction which appears in most of the block exemptions. Active selling includes:

- actively seeking customers (by advertising or promoting goods)
- establishing a branch (or a subsidiary)
- maintaining a distribution depot
- engaging in advertising specifically aimed at other territories

Passive sales are sales which are made in response to unsolicited orders received from a customer in another territory.

It is important for non-EC suppliers to be aware of the scope of these rules, so as not to be pressured by a distributor into taking action which would be in breach of the EC rules. Some protection for dealers is clearly possible under the block exemptions, and suppliers should also consider whether they need to lay down qualitative guidelines to ensure that any parallel trade is routed through suitably qualified dealers. As already noted, parallel trade tends only to become a problem where there are wide price divergences between different territories. Suppliers can help themselves by eliminating such price differences as far as possible. Exchange rate fluctuations remain a potential problem, although the existence of the Exchange Rate Mechanism (ERM) of the European Monetary System has helped to keep such fluctuations to a minimum (currently the currencies still within the EMS are obliged to keep within a maximum band of 15 percent either way). Greater currency stability was promised by the timetable for full economic and monetary union and a single European currency laid down by the TEU, but realistically this timetable will not be met and a single European currency in all Member States is not likely until well into the next century. There is nevertheless greater scope for manufacturers to introduce and maintain uniform pricing across all markets, even though a uniform pricing policy may not at the end of the day always be commercially desirable.

Problems will, in any event, still arise in industries, such as the pharmaceutical or motor industries, where prices are heavily regulated in some Member States.

It may also sometimes be possible for a supplier or distributor to rely on national laws governing passing off or unfair trading practices to prevent the entry of parallel imported goods. This whole area, however, raises difficult questions of EC law which are not considered here.

Directive on Commercial Agents

EEC Council Directive 86/653 of December 18, 1986 is worth mentioning as it has a direct effect on the drafting of agency agreements in the Community. It provides, for instance, for minimum compensation levels on termination, guarantees agents certain minimum rights (including information about updated products and potential customers) and generally attempts to lay down minimum standards for agency contracts throughout the Community. In the U.K., the Commercial Agents Regulations 1993 which implement the Directive will only come into force on January 1, 1994 and until that time there are virtually no restrictions on what can be included in an agency agreement under English law.

International Sale of Goods Conventions

The United Nations Convention on Contracts for the International Sale of Goods was adopted on April 11, 1980 and has been in force in several Member States since January 1, 1988. The Convention, as its name implies, lays down rules governing the formation of contracts for the international sale of goods and covers the rights and obligations of seller and buyer arising from the contract.

The U.K. is one of the few remaining Member States of the Community which has not ratified the Convention. The U.K. Government will not promise a date upon which they will make a decision on ratification—a stance which is said to follow from lack of parliamentary time to incorporate the Convention into the U.K. law. The U.S., by contrast, adhered in December 1986 with the reservation that the parties must all be from a contracting state for the Convention to apply.

An important point to bear in mind when selling in any country which has already ratified the Convention is that the Convention automatically applies to a contract unless the contracting parties agree to exclude it. There is a certain amount of suspicion about the Convention in the U.K. and it is likely that any U.K. party would want to exclude the Convention. That will clearly be a matter for commercial negotiation.

X.   LICENSING

Availability of Block Exemption

There are two block exemption regulations which are relevant when licensing in the Community. Regulation 2349/84 basically covers patent licenses, but also covers mixed agreements where know-how (proprietary technical information of a confidential nature) is also transferred. Regulation 556/89 (the know-how regulation) is a more recent, and slightly more liberal regulation which covers know-how licenses (i.e., where there is basically a transfer of *know-how*, although there may also be a subsidiary patent license). The main difference between the two regulations is that the patent license regulation does not allow use of the technology by the licensee to be restricted in parts of the Community where there are no patents and so a licensor wanting to tie the licensee as far as possible to manufacturing or selling in a particular part of the Community will normally be better off under the know-how regulation. It is relatively unusual for companies to go to the trouble and expense of applying for patents in all twelve Member States.

The single Community Patent does not yet exist (a Community Patent Convention establishing Community-wide patent protection has been signed but not ratified). The European Patent Convention is soon to take effect in the majority of Member States, but only gives the applicant a bundle of national patents in those countries which he has designated. Patentees rarely designate all 12 Member States. Pharmaceutical products (and in due course also agro-chemicals) many benefit from a Supplementary Patent Certificate extending the period of patent protection by up to five years beyond the standard 20-year period. The rules relating to patent licenses continue to apply during the extension period.

Parties may often have a choice between relying on one or other regulation. The know-how regulation will obviously only be of use if there is recent, substantial and confidential know-how which can be transferred or licensed.

Both regulations contain lists of white and black clauses. They also provide that grey clauses (i.e., restrictions of competition which are neither white-listed nor black-listed) will be looked at under an expedited procedure known as the opposition procedure. Under this procedure the agreement has to be notified on the normal Form A/B, but the Commission has only six months to decide whether to open a full procedure. If it takes no action within the six month period, the whole agreement automatically benefits from exemption. This can be a useful procedure in cases of doubt, although it should only be used when the parties are interested in receiving a quick decision.

Exclusive Territorial Protection

Under both regulations a license can provide for the grant of exclusive manufacturing and/or sales rights for the full duration of the patents in all or part of the Community or in a territory which is partly in and partly outside the Community. The licensor and licensee can restrict each other from selling in each other's territories. A licensee can be restricted from manufacturing in another licensee's territory. However, a licensee may only be restricted from *selling actively* in other licensees' territories (i.e., must agree to meet unsolicited orders) except for the first five years in the case of new technology. Where the restrictions relate to territories which are covered only by know-how (and no relevant patents) the restrictions must be limited in time. The basic licensor/licensee exclusivity is limited to a maximum of 10 years from the date of the license and restrictions on selling in other licensee's territories is restricted to 10 years from the grant of the first license in the EC of the same technology. The license can continue beyond this period, but in order to continue the territorial restrictions it is necessary for the parties to renegotiate the contract to cover any new technology not included in the original license.

Except for the first five years in the case of new technology, there can be no restriction on passive sales except as authorized by the regulation. In this way parallel trade is likely to emerge if one licensee sells at significantly lower prices than another.

Post-Termination Know-How

One area of controversy concerns the use which the licensee can make of know-how after the license has expired. The European Commission used to take a strict line. It usually considered any such restriction as *prima facie* restrictive of competition and requiring individual notification. The parties in principle had to notify their agreement and persuade the Commission that the ban on post-term use of know-how was necessary and justified. Since Regulation 556/89 has come into force, the Commission has relaxed its attitude. It now accepts that so long as know-how remains confidential and has an intrinsic commercial value which licensees are prepared to pay for, restrictions can be placed on its use. It is therefore possible to have a know-how license for a fixed term and to require the licensee to abandon all further rights to the know-how on termination. However, there has to be a *quid pro quo*. Under Regulation 556/89, if the licensor wants to restrict use of know-how after termination, he must accept that he has no entitlement to utilize any improvement technology which has been granted back to him under the grant back provisions which are commonly included in licensing agreements. On the other hand, the regulation white-lists any provision whereby the licensee must grant back to the licensor (whether in return for royalties or not, but on a *non-exclusive* basis) any improvement technology or new applications technology developed by the licensee in the course of exploiting the license. These provisions attempt to strike a balance between the two parties' interests and to ensure as far as possible that they have an equal bargaining strength when the agreement comes to its term.

It is also accepted by the Commission that the confidentiality of the know-how is of such overriding importance, that confidentiality obligations must be able to survive the duration of the agreement for as long as the technology does not enter the public domain. Once the technology has become public knowledge, however, the licensee can no longer be restricted from using or divulging it unless the publication of the technology was due to the licensee's own default. The license can accordingly also include provisions which restrict the licensee from disclosing its own developments to third parties if those developments *cannot be used independently* of the basic confidential licensed know-how. A licensor will usually want to insert a provision that requires the licensee to obtain consent before making any such disclosure so that the licensor can verify whether the confidentiality obligation is respected. This is white-listed by the regulation.

Black Clauses

In line with the general advice already given, it is advisable to avoid including any black clauses in a license agreement, particularly if there is no intention to notify it. The black clauses in both regulations are similar and include:

- restrictions on the use of know-how in the public domain
- mandatory assignment or exclusive grant back of improvements
- unnecessary tie-ins
- no challenge provisions relating to the technology or (in the case of patent licenses only) the trade marks
- payment of royalties on unlicensed products
- customer restrictions
- quantity and price restrictions
- very importantly, any restriction on the licensee engaging in competing activities (although in the case of the know-how regulation, an agreement can provide for loss of exclusive rights in the event of any competing activities)
- perpetual extensions
- excessive territorial restrictions.

XI. JOINT VENTURES AND CO-OPERATION

The Block Exemption Regulations

Block exemption is available for specialization and co-operation agreements under Regulations 417/85 and 418/85 and, for joint ventures involving cross-licensing of intellectual property, also under Regulations 2439/84 and 556/89.

Regulation 417/85: Specialization Agreements

A specialization agreement is one where each party decides to specialize in *manufacturing* a particular product, but each party sells both its own and the other party's products, so extending the product range of both parties. The parties' market share must not exceed 20 percent. The regulation also has application to joint venture arrangements where one or more of the parties, or a third party, or a joint subsidiary, are given exclusive distribution rights, provided that the relevant market share does not exceed 10 percent. In both cases the parties' turnover must not exceed ECU 1,000 million (U.S. $1,120 million).

Regulation 418/85: Research and Development Agreements

Regulation 418/85 is aimed principally at joint research and development agreements which may, under certain strict conditions, also extend to joint production (subject in general to a 20 percent market share limit) and (subject to a 10 percent market share limit) joint sales. It may cover agreements under which one of the collaborating parties, a jointly owned company or an entirely separate third party is appointed to sell the jointly manufactured product. Parties may also agree to reserve territories to each other (e.g., the U.S. partner may sell exclusively in America and the European party may sell exclusively in Europe) but only active selling outside these territories may then be restricted and the restriction may only last for five years from the start of joint production.

In practice, these rules are difficult to apply: It can be particularly difficult to calculate a market share for new products because of the difficulty of establishing the correct market definition; even when the market share is ascertainable, it will often be exceeded. The five-year time limit on exclusive territorial protection is also likely to be commercially unattractive, especially for innovative products with a slow sales growth. Joint venture and co-operation agreements accordingly often need to be notified to the Commission.

Because of their long-term nature, and the difficulties which could arise if they were found to be unenforceable at a late stage, there is often merit in discussing such agreements with the Commission in advance and, if necessary, notifying them with a view to an informal comfort letter. The Commission is in general well disposed towards joint venture agreements, particularly where this enables foreign technology or investment capital to be introduced into the Community.

Merger Control Regulation

The Merger Control Regulation (Regulation 4064/89 on the control of concentrations between undertakings) which came into force on September 21, 1990 applies to mergers and acquisitions with a Community dimension. These are large-scale mergers and acquisitions where the sales of the parties (both worldwide and within the Community) are above certain thresholds. The relevant thresholds are:

— ECU 5,000 million (U.S. $5,700 million) group turnover of *all* parties worldwide;

— *plus* ECU 250 million (U.S. $285 million) group turnover of *at least two parties* in the Community

— no more than two thirds Community turnover in the same Member State.

Such concentrations must be notified to the Commission within one week of the transaction taking place. The regulation catches some 50–60 transactions per year. The term used in the regulation to describe mergers and acquisitions is "concentration," i.e., a concentration of the activities of two separate entities into one single economic entity involving a transfer or change in control.

Concentrations are prohibited if they are incompatible with the common market: This is deemed to be the case if they strengthen a party's dominant position such that effective competition is likely to be impeded. If the Commission, upon initial enquiry, has *serious doubts* about the compatibility of a proposed transaction with the common market it must launch a detailed investigation (a so-called Phase two investigation). The Commission then has four months to complete its investigation and reach a final decision.

Certain joint venture situations may involve a concentration as understood under Community law, as briefly explained below. The distinction is crucial, particularly in view of the mandatory notification requirement. Moreover the Commission is not entitled to apply Articles 85 and 86 to concentrations within the meaning of the regulation.

There may be procedural advantages in using the notification procedure under Regulation 4064/89, including formal time limits within which the Commission must reach a decision (one month for its initial Phase One decision and a further four months if a full Phase Two investigation is launched). For cooperative joint ventures, on the other hand, there exists only an informal administrative practice limiting the initial review to two months.

Distinction Between Cooperative and Concentrative Joint Ventures

The distinction between cooperative joint ventures and concentrative joint ventures is not easy to grasp, but basically where:

- two or more parties create a joint venture (i.e., any situation of joint control), and not necessarily involving equal shareholdings) which becomes an autonomous economic entity; and

- at least one of the controlling parties drops out of the relevant market on a long term basis or is no longer active on it; and

- the joint venture will not give rise to the coordination of competitive behavior between the parent companies *inter se* or between the parents and the joint venture (unless such effects are minor or are centred outside the Community);

the arrangements will not be considered under the competition rules, but rather as a concentration coming under Regulation 4064/89. If the arrangements involve co-ordination of the activities of the parents, however, it remains a cooperative joint venture subject to Articles 85 and 86. An example is provided by the joint venture, known as European Vinyls Corporation, created by ICI and Enichem in 1986 which was originally treated by the Commission as a joint venture and exempted for a limited period of five years. When the parties applied to renew the exemption, they were told that the joint venture had now acquired an identity of its own, i.e., that the parties had effectively merged their vinyls business and should be treated as a concentration. The distinction between cooperative and concentrative joint ventures is set out in the Commission's Notice regarding the Concentrative and Cooperative Operations under Regulation 4064/84 ([1990] OJ C203/10).

A joint venture owned by two parents may be deemed to be concentrated with both its parents (without the parents themselves being considered as concentrated) or, where one parent is effectively in the position of an investor, the joint venture may be deemed to be concentrated only with one single parent.

In creating a joint venture in the Community, therefore (or even acquiring a minority interest in the capital of a European enterprise amounting to joint control), companies need to be aware that there are EC law issues which will need to be addressed at an early stage. Where there is any doubt about whether the merger regulation applies, it will be necessary to approach the Commission early on to ensure that the correct procedure is followed, as there is an extremely tight timetable for pre-filing of mergers. In the case of cooperative joint ventures, it can often be advantageous to approach the Commission early on an informal basis and possibly obtain a comfort letter.

XII. LITIGATING IN THE COMMUNITY

Euro-defenses

A U.S. plaintiff seeking to enforce a contract in the Community (or even a judgment of the U.S. court following a contract dispute) or seeking to enforce its intellectual property rights in the Community, may frequently be faced with the prospect of a Euro-defense. This is a defence based on one of the EC Treaty provisions or a relevant regulation or directive. The commonest Euro-defenses are that the contract in question is void and unenforceable under Article 85(1), or that the plaintiff is abusing its dominant position, or that the action in question is in breach of the free movement rules in Article 30 of the Treaty.

Unenforceable Terms

As indicated above, one of the commonest Euro-defenses is that the agreement in dispute infringes Article 85(1). The system of block exemptions ensures that for many typical distribution, licensing and agency agreements, the competition rules should present no problem provided the agreement has been properly drafted in the first place. Where the parties have taken the risk of not complying with the relevant block exemption and included restrictive terms which are not covered, it may be possible for the plaintiff to notify the agreement to the European Commission immediately before taking legal action. This is often a useful precaution and gives the plaintiff a much stronger hand in the course of the litigation. However it does mean that the plaintiff will only be entitled to injunctive relief and may not be able to claim damages for a period prior to the date of notification.

Where an Article 85 plea is made, it may be possible for the plaintiff to apply to the relevant court to have that part of the defense struck out as disclosing no reasonable defense. The English courts are ready to strike out such defenses where there is clearly no prospect of the them succeeding. However, under English court procedure, so long as the defense is arguable it will remain as a contentious issue and will add considerably to the costs of the litigation. Where difficult questions of Community law are involved, there is always the possibility that guidance will be needed from the EC Court of Justice under the Article 177 procedure (this enables the national court to ask the Court of Justice for guidance on any difficult question of Community law). It is important to be aware of the possibility that such problems may arise when litigating in the Community.

Statutory Rights

As mentioned in section 5 above, plaintiffs in an intellectual property action will often be faced with a defense based on Article 30 of the Treaty. Although Article 36 provides that measures restricting imports are permitted to the extent that they can be justified by reference to the protection of industrial and commercial property rights, Article 36 contains two important provisos. The measures must be non-discriminatory and they must not be used as a disguised means of restricting competition within the Community. Intellectual property rights such as patents, trade marks, and copyright may therefore become exhausted (and unenforceable). Once goods have been sold through an authorized distributor or manufactured and/or sold through a licensee in one Member State, the basic effect of the EC rules on free movement is that the manufacturer cannot rely on its intellectual property rights in other parts of the Community to stop those products from being imported and the defendant would have an absolute defense to any such action.

There are, however, some difficult areas, e.g. whether rights are exhausted by the mere grant of a right to manfacture (so entitling a licensee who has lawfully manufactured goods to supply them directly in another part of the Community); or what happens in the situation where the rights are not strictly parallel (as where there are different trade marks in different parts of the Community); or whether rights can still be enforced if they are not intellectual property rights (e.g., are based on the law of passing off or unfair competition).

Direct Effect

In many other areas, EC law may become directly relevant because of its direct effect. Not only do EC directives have direct effect (i.e. can be relied by individuals as against Member States once the deadline for implementing them has passed), but also certain provisions in the EC Treaty itself have direct effect. This includes the rules on equal treatment of men and women (which has spawned a great deal of litigation in the area of employment law and pension rights), free movement of goods (as already noted, particularly in the context of intellectual property litigation), free movement of persons and rights of establishment (as exemplified by the fishing cases mentioned above), statutory regulations relating to public monopolies (e.g., relating to German monopoly rights granted to the state executive search agency) and in many other areas. In many cases the principle of supremacy of Community law results in national legislation becoming unenforceable.

Choice of Jurisdiction

Brief mention should be made of the 1968 EEC Convention on Civil Jurisdiction and Judgments (known as the Brussels Convention) which is now applicable throughout most of the Community (and by virtue of the Lugano Convention, will also extend to EFTA states). The Brussels Convention provides that:

- a defendant must in principle always be sued in his place of domicile (in the case of companies this is usually where the company is incorporated or where it has its registered office) and

- judgments given in one Member State must be enforced by courts in all the other Member States.

In certain situations the general rule on jurisdiction may be overidden by specific rules relating, e.g., to insurance or consumer contracts, or tort actions. Article 17 provides a useful exception to the jurisdiction rules. The parties are free to agree a place of jurisdiction, which can either be formally incorporated into the contract or can be orally agreed, or can be inferred as a matter of trade practice. If the parties agree that the courts of one country should have jurisdiction to hear any disputes, then those courts have *exclusive* jurisdiction.

The Convention applies to any agreement involving at least one Community party. In a U.S./EC context it means that if any action is brought within the Community it must be brought in the appropriate place (agreed jurisdiction or, in the absence of any agreement, place of domicile or other jurisdiction specified in the Convention), although it is still open to the parties to agree a non-EC jurisdiction. There may be some scope for forum shopping under the Convention; there can be advantages in bringing proceedings quickly in the forum of one's choice as a court would, if proceedings had already been brought before another court involving the same or a related dispute be obliged to, or have a discretion to decline jurisdiction.

Choice of Law

The governing law of a contract need not necessarily be the same as the jurisdiction chosen. Under the Rome Convention, which came into force in the U.K. in April 1991, there are now Community-wide rules laying down the applicable laws where the parties have not agreed what this should be. It can therefore be important to specify the governing law as this will no longer automatically be inferred from the place of jurisdiction.

Arbitration

The Brussels and Lugano Conventions do not apply to any agreement which is subject to arbitration. Although this is often a convenient way of resolving contractual disputes, it has its limitations and may not always offer the parties the cost savings which they might have hoped for. However, whatever the cost of arbitration, it will not avoid the need to comply with the relevant competition and other rules of the EC Treaty. While arbitration is clearly excluded from the Conventions, the courts have yet to test the issue of precisely which forms of ADR fall within the arbitration exception. This reflects the fact that ADR is less well developed in Europe than in the U.S.

XIII. TRADE POLICY

Common Customs Tariff

As well as creating a common market, the EEC Treaty established a common commercial policy covering the external trade relations of all the Member States. This means that there is a common system of customs tariffs applicable wherever goods are imported into the Community from outside, a common set of rules for valuation and tariff classification, and for determining the origin of goods. As both the Community and its Member States are members of the GATT, common customs policy is subject to GATT rules, but many products are the subject of bilateral/multilateral agreements. Clearly this is an aspect which needs to be looked at in deciding whether to supply U.S. products directly into the Community or to establish a European assembly operation or whether to follow a licensing route. The considerations will depend on the particular product concerned.

In the past, individual countries have been able to retain national quotas, e.g., in the field of motor vehicles and textiles, but these are gradually being phased out and, where appropriate, are being replaced by Community-wide quotas. Under Article 115 of the EEC Treaty, countries could impose restrictions on intra-Community trade where "indirect imports" from outside the Community were involved, but since January 1, 1993 they are no longer entitled to do so.

Anti-Dumping

As part of the common commercial policy, the Community has a well developed anti-dumping legislation based on the relevant provisions of the GATT. There has been a trend in recent years for companies (in particular Japanese companies) affected by anti-dumping duties to set up local assembly plants in the Community in order to avoid having to pay anti-dumping duties. The Community has been very strict with regard to these so-called "screwdriver plants" but this policy has been criticised by the GATT panel. In most cases, however, it should be possible to avoid anti-dumping difficulties by setting up an assembly operation.

XIV. EMERGING AREAS

In this section, various "emerging areas" of EC law are considered which are becoming of increasing importance to companies doing business in the Community. The main areas are as follows:

Environment

Since the 1986 Single European Act, which came into force in 1987, the Community has been extremely active in proposing environmental legislation covering the whole spectrum of environmental protection, from air pollution to water and ground pollution, to national heritage, to eco-labelling systems, to transport of dangerous substances, and so on. The result is that the European Community is slowly acquiring a body of environmental legislation which is becoming as complex and far reaching as that which already exists in the U.S. The European Community legislation is generally in the form of directives requiring Member States to implement national legislation by specified deadlines.

At the same time, Member States continue to take initiatives of their own. The U.K. for instance, recently adopted the Environmental Protection Act 1990 (not all of which is in force) which contains many very important provisions affecting any company doing business in the U.K. In particular, it places a duty of care on all companies to dispose of all environmentally harmful waste to an authorized carrier and imposes personal liability for breach of any of any statutory obligations under the Act upon directors and officers of companies.

Company Law Harmonization and Social Policy

Another important area where developments are likely to arise in future is that of company law harmonization. At the moment, the rules and procedures governing the formation and management of companies tend to differ widely between Member States. Full harmonization is, however, a long way off. Some measures are of direct benefit to small companies (e.g., one of the directives on company accounts specifically excuses small companies from having to comply with all the accounting requirements imposed on large companies). There is also a number of important proposals affecting the social obligations of companies towards their workers, e.g. minimum hours of work, minimum wages and rights of consultation, which have been put forward by the Commission. These have met with considerable opposition from the U.K. in particular and are unlikely to be adopted except in very diluted form. In many cases the U.K. objections are based on a desire to avoid imposing any unnecessary bureaucratic and administrative burdens on small and medium-sized companies. Support for this point of view appears to be growing in other Member States as a result of recessionary pressures.

Harmonization of social legislation is also likely to advance further in the 11 Member States which subscribed to the Agreement on Social Policy attached to the TEU; the U.K. was not a party to this Agreement, although many items of social legislation can nevertheless be introduced under the aegis of the single market program.

Utilities and Public Procurement

The Commission has made strenuous efforts to open up the heavily regulated utility industries (including energy, telecommunications, water and transport) and to open up public procurement generally. This should benefit both companies established in any one Member State of the Community and also, on the international plane, U.S. and other non-EC companies seeking to tender for public supply contracts and works in the Community. A complete set of directives has been introduced, including a directive extending the principles of open, non-discriminatory competition to the water, energy, telecommunications and transport industries which have traditionally been closed to non-nationals. A directive on procurement of services (which might affect e.g., consultancy contracts for government departments) and a directive giving rights to damages for tenderers who have not been treated in accordance with the relevant rules, are also in force.

Eastern Europe and Community Enlargement

It goes without saying that the Community is directly affected by the rapid pace of change in Eastern and Central Europe and the CIS. Specifically, six of the Eastern European states (Hungary, the Czech Republic, Slovakia, Poland, Bulgaria, and Romania) have negotiated association agreements and preferential trade deals, which will give them access to Community markets and which go some way to establishing a single economic zone throughout Eastern and Western Europe. The association agreements offer the prospect of future EC membership, without committing the EC to any firm dates. The twelve states of the former Soviet Union have agreed a negotiating mandate for a partnership and co-operation agreement on similar lines.

The EFTA states (with the exception of Switzerland), which do not currently form part of the Community, and the 12 members of the Community have [now] ratified the Agreement establishing a European Economic Area (EEA), and a protocol containing amendments to the original Agreement following Switzerland's decision to withdraw from the EEA. The EEA Agreement creates an 18-nation free trade area and is designed to strengthen trade and economic relations between the 12 EC Member States and the particating EFTA states (Austria, Finland, Iceland, Liechtenstein, Norway and Sweden). The EEA Agreement will not apply immediately to Liechtenstein to give it time to sever its economic ties with Switzerland. The EEA Agreement effectively extends the single market to the six EFTA members. It covers the free movement of goods, services, capital and persons and other rules, e.g. competition and state aids and cooperation in certain areas, including research and development, environment and education. The six EFTA states automatically agree to give effect to existing Community legislation (the *acquis communautaire*), and several new institutions have been established (including the EEA Council, the EEA Joint Committee and the EEA Court as well as an EFTA Surveillance Authority and an EFTA Court) to ensure all EEA rules are observed.

The EFTA Surveillance Authority and the European Commission have similar responsibilities within their respective jurisdictions and there are rules for establishing which has jurisdiction in case of overlap. A concentration involving undertakings from the EC and EFTA automatically falls under Community jurisdiction, whereas jurisdiction over competition cases depends on the relative turnover of the parties concerned.

The EEA Agreement was signed on May 2, 1992 and was intended to come into force on January 1, 1993. However, the delay caused by Switzerland's failure to ratify has meant postponing the entry into force of the EEA Agreement to [November 1, 1993].

In February 1993 Sweden, Austria, Finland and later, Norway, commenced detailed accession negotiations for full EC membership.

Several Member States, including the U.K., would like to see the Community enlarged to include Eastern European States, but there are others, in particular France, who do not want to see enlargement at the expense of a deepening of the economic and political union within the existing Community framework. However these debates are resolved, the Community undoubtedly provides a useful springboard for any company intending to expand eastwards into the rest of Europe.

Economic and Political Union

The objective of the Treaty on European Union is the promotion of economic and social progress by the establishment of economic and monetary union, and ultimately a single currency. The mechanisms for this are to follow a three-stage process. The first stage looks to closer economic and monetary co-operation within the existing framework and will seek to create greater convergence of economic performance. A new institutional arrangement will commence in the second stage (commencing January 1, 1994) to assist in the process of greater co-ordination of monetary policy and preparation for a single monetary authority. A consultative and advisory body will be created, to be known as the European Monetary Institute, constituted by the Governors of Member State central banks. It is to be replaced by the European Central Bank in the third stage.

The protocol on the transition toward full economic and monetary union, with a common monetary and exchange rate policy, suggests that the movement is irreversible. No Member State is to prevent this third and final stage from being reached, and there is an irrevocable, set date of January 1, 1999, at which point the European System of Central Banks and European Central Bank will commence their operations. The United Kingdom and Denmark are, however, not obliged or committed to proceed onto the third stage without a separate decision to do so. The third stage (which may begin in 1997 if a majority of Member States ratify the relevant convergence criteria) will see the introduction of a single currency. The Treaty lays down a long stop date of January 1, 1999 for the start of the third stage, although Member States who at that date do not meet the conditions for adoption of the single currency are excluded from participation (becoming known, in EC jargon, as "Member States with a derogation."

Here there are wider implications, especially as regards Community trade and investment, given that the notion of economic and monetary union is based on the Single Market (itself largely in place since January 1, 1993). However, these moves have received a set-back, not only because of the stance of the U.K. and Denmark, but also because the exchange rate mechanism which seeks to keep EC currencies broadly aligned has fallen subject to currency speculation, causing, for example, the U.K., Italy and Ireland to suspend their membership of the mechanism, and the currency bands (for most currencies which remained in the system) to be widened at an emergency meeting in August 1993.

In addition to the changes in the economic and monetary sphere, the TEU made a number of other changes to the scope of the Community Treaties and extended the Community's jurisdiction in certain fields, e.g., transport, environment and research and development; it has considerably bolstered the powers of the European Parliament; and it has created certain new rights for European citizens, including voting rights for Community nationals in municipal elections throughout the Community and a right of appeal to a Parliament any Ombudsman where Community institutions are guilty of maladministration. As mentioned above it also effects certain tentative steps toward political union, by creating as two "pillars" of the new European Union common policies in the area of foreign affairs and security, and justice and home affairs. The essential feature of these policies is that they will operate formally on the level of inter-governmental agreement, and therefore legally outside the institutional framework of the Community, although they will be able to make use of many of the services of the Community institutions to help them in their tasks. There is specific provision for a conference in 1996, to review the policies and other forms of co-operation under the Treaty.

XV. CONCLUSION

The aim of this chapter has been to draw attention to the main areas which may need to be considered by any company attempting to do business in or with the Community. Although the paper has concentrated on the competition rules which directly affect the drafting of commercial agreements with European partners, it has also drawn attention to the other important areas of the EC Treaty which have a bearing on a company's European strategy. The advances made since the Single European Act and the launch of the 1992 program in creating a single market and reducing barriers to trade within the Community, have made it easier for a company to establish a base in one Member State as a preliminary to targeting the Community as a whole. There is no reason why U.S. and other non-EC companies cannot also play their part and, in particular, share some of the benefits which the European Community is able to offer.

GOING INTERNATIONAL IN THE
UNITED KINGDOM

Graham N. Arad
Philip D. Beck

I. INTRODUCTION

General

TO PARAPHRASE the well known real estate maxim, there are three important factors to be considered by Americans wishing to do business in the United Kingdom; "language, language and language."

The key to doing business in any country is successful communication. Whether in marketing products and services, negotiating contracts, or resolving problems which may subsequently arise, it is axiomatic that each party must fully understand and appreciate the other's expectations, requirements and point of view. Language is not simply a matter of using the right words. If the prevailing business and social culture is unfamiliar, the words themselves may have no meaning, or the listener may understand something different, or worse, the opposite of what the speaker intended.

The purpose of this chapter, is to indicate to the U.S. lawyer advising on U.K. ventures, when alarm bells should ring. The reader will find that, particularly in commercial matters, the principles of the common law, as separately developed in the U.S. and the U.K., are still remarkably similar. This chapter is intended to highlight some areas where the application of those principles has diverged in the two jurisdictions; namely, where jurists and legislators applying similar principles of law have, over the centuries, found different practical solutions to the same legal and commercial problems.

This is intended to be a "nuts and bolts" guide (rather than an academic treatise) to certain of the practical and commercial legal issues that U.S. businesses and their attorneys are likely to face. English legal and commercial terminology will be used throughout, in order to familiarize practitioners with it, with "translations" given, wherever the authors have found that confusion commonly arises.

Finally, if there is a single lesson which the authors wish to convey, it is that in dealing with U.K. law and lawyers, it should never be assumed that because you understand "the words" you have also grasped their full import and effect.

Legal Environment

U.K. Law

The United Kingdom of Great Britain and Northern Ireland, although not a federal state, comprises three separate jurisdictions; England and Wales, Scotland, and Northern Ireland. All legislation is passed at Westminster, in the bi-cameral Houses of Parliament and there is a single national government, formed by the party having the largest representation in the elected House of Commons. While there is local government at the level of counties, towns and boroughs, there is no separate regional government for the three jurisdictions (although proposals for constitutional change to establish them have been much discussed in recent years).

The administration of justice however, is divided between the three jurisdictions, each having its own court system and legal and judicial qualifications. Most legislation is enacted on a uniform national basis and the majority of modern commercial law, such as taxation and company law is also uniform. However the legal systems are distinct and, particularly in the case of Scotland, quite different in certain respects. For example, Scottish law of property (both real and personal) and trusts is unique and in the important area of real estate transactions, the procedures vary substantially in Scotland from the rest of the country.

These distinctions will have little impact on most of the topics discussed in this chapter but the authors being english solicitors, the English law viewpoint will predominate. Accordingly, practitioners advising on matters involving Scotland or Northern Ireland should be aware of the potential variations and take advice accordingly.

European Union Law

Overlaying the U.K. legal system is the growing body of European Union ("EU") law, for which the final arbiter is the European Court of Justice ("ECJ") in Luxembourg (a more detailed analysis of which appears elsewhere in this work). Recent years have seen an increasing development of the breadth and depth of the effects of EU legislation and ECJ decisions. A major cause of this has been the growth in the number of decisions pursuant to Article 177 references.[1] These are requests from national courts of the member states to the ECJ for rulings on the interpretation, or validity of particular issues of EU law. The national courts then use the ECJ's decision to decide the law governing the case pending before that court. Secondly, the ECJ has also been extending the rights of individuals to rely on the direct effect of EU legislation. That is to say laws enacted in Brussels which the ECJ has held give individuals rights, even though such laws have not been separately incorporated into the law of a member state by its legislature, often through the default of the relevant member state.

As a result, in more and more cases, lawyers advising clients in entirely domestic situations must be mindful of relevant EU law. Whereas this was always evident in such areas as competition law, recent decisions have considerably widened the areas of law to which this applies. For example, in the landmark *Barber* case, the ECJ held that the long standing British practice of using different retirement ages of 65 for men and 60 for women, in the calculation and determination of employee retirement benefits and entitlement, was unlawful discrimination on the ground of sex. The decision has caused enormous turmoil in the pensions industry and amongst employers generally because of the potentially huge costs of compliance with the new regime. Furthermore, the case has spawned a host of related litigation, in various parts of the EU.

Accordingly, the potential pitfalls for even experienced practitioners, in unexpected areas of the law and business cannot be understated.

Business Environment

In the U.K., American businesses will find a modern, market-based economic structure not unlike their own. As a result of the massive privatization program instituted by the Thatcher government in the 1980's (and subsequently followed throughout the world) government's role in business and industry has been substantially reduced to that of regulator or supervisor of specific industries, rather than that of principal.

There has been a significant effort to reduce the regulatory and administrative burden on businesses, particularly those small and medium size enterprises targeted by the 1992 Single Market program. In many areas, such as Value Added Tax ("VAT") and other taxation, corporate accounting and company procedures, recent legislation has cut the financial and administrative costs of compliance for small businesses. There have been some losses in the battle, notably, the voluminous VAT reporting requirements imposed on exporters from January 1, 1993, as a result of the implementation of the Single Market, but the process continues.

There is free movement of capital in and out of the country and no currency exchange controls. Businesses and individuals can hold bank accounts in numerous currencies, restricted only by what banks will offer. There are no restrictions on the repatriation of profits of foreign owned businesses and the applicable tax regime for corporate dividends remitted to foreign shareholders was eased in the Spring 1993 budget. There also exists a Double Taxation Treaty between the U.S. and the U.K., which further mitigates the effect of U.K. taxation on U.S. businesses.[2]

Labor costs are generally acknowledged to be amongst the lowest in Western Europe. Indeed it was generally perceived that an important part of the rationale of the 1994 purchase by BMW of 80 percent of Rover, the last independent U.K. volume, car manufacturer, was to provide the German company access to its cheaper British workforce. The labor market is also less regulated than elsewhere in Europe, although this is changing under continuing pressure from the European Commission and other EU members.

As a result of these factors and the (apparently) familiar language and culture Britain has long been a popular location for U.S. businesses. As of 1991, well over a third of all U.S. investment in the EU was in the U.K.; equal to the total U.S. investment in Germany, France, Ireland and Spain combined. Nearly 3,000 U.S. companies have invested in the U.K, including 96 of the Fortune 100.[3]

II. ESTABLISHMENT IN THE U.K.

Choice of Business Structure

Forms of Business Structure

The forms of business structure most commonly used in the U.K. are the limited liability company, partnership, sole trader (i.e., self-employed individual) and the branch or agency of a foreign company. Although the limited partnership exists under U.K. law, it is rarely used in practice, since the legislation relating to it dates back to the early part of the century and it has never had the tax advantages or the attractiveness as a form of investment, which the limited partnership has enjoyed in the U.S. In general, when advising businessmen as to the appropriate form of entity through which to trade, similar considerations will apply to the U.K., as they do in the U.S. Accordingly, this section will only deal with those considerations less familiar to U.S. practitioners.

The Limited Liability Company

Private and Public Companies

The two principal types of limited company provided for under the U.K. Companies Acts[4], are the Private Company Limited by Shares and the Public Limited Company ("PLC"). Only PLC's are permitted to offer their shares generally for sale to members of the public. As a consequence, the Companies Acts impose greater restrictions and requirements on PLC's. However, many PLC's exist as wholly private companies, whose shares are never traded on any exchange. Many businesses prefer the PLC form, since it gives them greater status in the market place. However, the practitioner should not be fooled. Although a PLC is required to have an issued share capital of £50,000, only a quarter of this, £12,500 need be paid up in cash. Accordingly, although the paid-up share capital of a private limited company may only be £1, it may in fact be of far greater substance than many PLC's.

Public Information

The principal difference between the U.K. limited company and the U.S. corporation is transparency. The U.K. limited company was conceived as one of the most flexible commercial vehicles ever devised. Shareholders and directors (who, with the secretary, are the sole officers of U.K. companies) have almost limitless powers to structure the business as they choose, subject only to completing and filing the required documents, in the required place at the required time. Share capital can be expressed in any currency and in any denomination and may consist of limitless classes, each having different rights. The capital structure can be changed at will, as often as wished, and without any taxation consequences. There is no limit to the type of activity that a company can undertake and in particular, since the Companies Act 1989, which permitted the objects of a company simply to be stated as "a general commercial company." The doctrine of *ultra vires* is practically dead.

However, the corollary to this freedom of action is a level of formality, and disclosure requirements not known in most U.S. jurisdictions. Every U.K. company must make regular filings with the companies registry of its particular jurisdiction (located in Cardiff for England and Wales, Edinburgh for Scotland and Belfast for Northern Ireland). Such filings include details of the appointment and resignation or removal of every director of the company, together with each director's address, date of birth, occupation and a list of all other directorships which they hold or have held during the previous five years. A full shareholders' list must be filed every year, including details of all transactions in the shares. A copy of every special, extraordinary and elective resolution (being resolutions required by the Companies Acts to be passed with a 75 percent majority) must be filed. The Companies Acts require special resolutions to be passed for a wide range of corporate acts, including those effecting changes to capital structure, the Memorandum and Articles of Association (Certificate of Incorporation and By-Laws) and the repurchase or redemption by a company of its own shares.[5] Most importantly, every company must file annual financial statements or accounts, which, in the vast majority of cases, will need to be audited by a registered auditor.

Accordingly, it is axiomatic practice when first dealing with any company, to obtain a search report from the relevant company's registry. This should show who owns and manages the company, give some indication of its finances and also disclose other matters such as mortgages and liens over its assets. This is obviously vital information for potential suppliers and others proposing to enter into business relationships with the company.

In practice, however, such searches are often not so revealing for a number of reasons. Many small companies simply do not comply with their statutory obligations, or comply very late. This, notwithstanding determined efforts by the various registrars of companies to enforce compliance using a computerized "tickler" system, often leading to prosecution and fines. Secondly, in order to ease the burden of compliance for smaller companies, they are permitted to file simplified and abbreviated financial statements, which really only give an overview of the business. Thirdly, there is nothing to stop an owner using nominee shareholders and directors, so that the true owners' names do not appear on the company's file. Their anonymity will thus be protected from the general public and casual observer.

The appointment of nominees may not, however, protect owners from any governmental or regulatory scrutiny, or personal liability for misfeasance, if they are deemed to be "shadow directors," namely persons in accordance with whose instructions the directors are accustomed to act. In such case, they will be deemed to have all of the same duties and obligations as the formally appointed directors. This applies in particular, in insolvency situations. Directors of U.K. companies, including shadow directors, may be held personally liable and subject to disciplinary, as well as criminal proceedings for a wide range of misconduct, including continuing to incur liabilities at a time when it was, or should have been apparent, that the Company would not be able to pay its creditors, even following a liquidation.

Thus in order to have the benefit of limited liability the business must accept that, to a certain extent, persons dealing with it are entitled to have a greater level of information about its internal affairs and financial status, than that to which U.S. businesses are accustomed.

Corporate Taxation

All bodies corporate (U.K. incorporated companies and corporations established in other jurisdictions) are liable to pay corporation tax on their profits. If the body corporate is deemed to be resident in the U.K., then it is taxable on its world-wide income. Any company incorporated in the U.K. is automatically deemed resident in the U.K. for tax purposes. Foreign corporations may be determined to be resident, if the "central place of management and control" is determined to be in the U.K. The Inland Revenue, will look not only at such factors as where board meetings are held and the residences of individual directors, but also at how the company is actually managed and whether that takes place in the U.K.

Under the present system, there are three tax-rate bands, which for the year 1994/95[6] are as follows:

Profits	Tax Rate	Name
Up to £300,000[7]	25%	Small companies rate
£300,001–£1,500,000	35%	Marginal Rate
£1,500,000+	33%	Full rate

The marginal rate band operates as a sliding scale, which increases the rate of tax, from the small companies rate to the full rate, as a company's profits grow.

Presently, corporation tax is payable nine months after the company's year end. However, in practice, it is legally not due and no interest or penalties accrue, until 30 days after Inland Revenue issues an assessment, which may be much later. A new payment and return system will be introduced for accounting periods ending after March 31, 1996, known as "pay and file." Under that system each company will have to pay corporation tax due, on an estimated basis, within six months after its year end and file the tax return within nine months after its year end.

Taxation of Dividends

Dividends and distributions paid by U.K. companies are subject to a particular form of withholding tax, called Advance Corporation Tax ("ACT"). No equivalent to the U.S. "S" Corporation exists in the U.K. and accordingly, the company is liable to tax on all of its profit and shareholders are only liable to tax upon the amount of dividends and distributions received (with certain very limited exceptions, where anti-tax avoidance provisions apply). From April 5, 1994 a company is liable to pay ACT equal to one-quarter of the amount of the dividend paid (i.e., if the shareholder receives a dividend of £100, the company must pay ACT of £25). ACT can be offset against the corporation tax liability of the company on the profits of the period in which the dividend was paid (subject to a maximum of 20 percent of taxable profits). Any excess which cannot be so offset, can be carried forward indefinitely against future tax liability or back for six years against any past tax liability.

In the hands of the individual shareholder, the dividend is treated as received gross, i.e., the amount of the dividend actually received plus the amount of the ACT "withheld" (in the above example, £125) and the shareholder also receives a tax credit equivalent to the amount of the ACT (in the above example, £25). An individual not subject to higher rates of taxation will not be liable to pay any further tax on the dividend. Dividends received by other U.K. resident companies or U.K. branches of foreign companies, are exempt from corporation tax and are, therefore, tax free to such entities. If dividends are paid to a U.S. shareholder then, pursuant to the double taxation treaty, the U.S. resident shareholder will be entitled to the same tax credit (or in some cases a proportion of the same tax credit), as is available to U.K. resident shareholders, subject to a notional withholding tax which varies, but may be as low as five percent, depending on the extent of the shareholding in the U.K. company.

Since ACT is only offsetable against U.K. corporation tax, a particular problem arose for U.K. companies which had extensive foreign earnings from foreign subsidiaries or branches. Foreign earnings were taxed in the relevant foreign countries and by virtue of double taxation relief or treaty, little or no U.K. corporation tax was payable on those earnings. Accordingly, many companies were building up vast sums of unrelieved ACT, commonly referred to as the "ACT Mountain" which they were unable to offset against their corporate taxes, since they had insufficient U.K. earnings. Accordingly, the government has proposed legislation to alleviate the problem in the Finance Bill 1994. The new provisions will permit such companies to "stream" their foreign income and pay dividends out of that income ("Foreign Income Dividend" or "FID"). The company will still be liable to pay ACT on FID's but may reclaim or offset it, on proof that the dividend was paid out of foreign source income. Furthermore, if more than 80 percent of a company's shareholders are non-resident and each owns more than five percent of the share capital, the company can qualify as an International Headquarters Company ("IHC"). IHC's will not have to account for ACT on any Foreign Income Dividends. In the hands of the recipient of an FID, the usual credit for the amount of ACT paid is not available.

Branch

As an alternative to establishing a U.K. subsidiary a U.S. corporation could simply establish a branch in the U.K. However, this will still involve filing requirements, including details of directors and the filing of annual accounts. The particular advantage of a branch over a U.K.-incorporated subsidiary is with regard to taxation and repatriation of profits. A U.K.-incorporated company is deemed resident in the U.K. for tax purposes and is thereby subject to taxation on its worldwide income. A branch is only subject to taxation upon income arising from activities of the branch and the remaining activities of the corporation are not subject to the filing of U.K. tax returns or payment of U.K. taxation. Furthermore, since a branch is part of the same entity as its U.S. parent, repatriation of profits is tax-neutral and is not subject to any U.K. withholding tax. It should be noted that, as in the U.S., transfer pricing is of significant concern to Inland Revenue and all internal trading arrangements need to be very carefully considered.

The disadvantage of the branch, is that since it is part of the same entity as the U.S. parent, recourse may be had to all of the assets of the U.S. corporation in the event of any claims against the branch. A U.S. corporation which is merely a shareholder in the U.K. limited company, will of course, have the benefit of limited liability for the debts and obligations of the U.K. company. That said, this protection is of little help in certain areas, particularly product liability, where numerous successful cases have been brought in the U.S. against manufacturers of products distributed in the U.K. by U.K. limited liability subsidiaries.

Partnerships and Sole Traders

These do not have the benefits of limited liability, but neither are there any formal legal requirements relating to their establishment or business obligations. There are no public filings of information about unincorporated entities, equivalent to those for companies. From a tax point of view, partnership or self-employed status used to be particularly beneficial because of the peculiar "preceding-year basis" of taxation applicable. Under that basis, it was quite legally possible to postpone the payment for taxes on income earned in any year for up to nearly two years. However, under recent legislation, this is gradually being phased out and such businesses are being moved to a basis very similar to that prevailing under the Internal Revenue Code, under which taxes are payable on an estimated basis, by reference to income earned in the current tax year, with severe penalties for late filing and payment.

Foreign Investment

If the U.K. activity is simply going to be the holding of an investment, for example, real estate or shares, then care should be taken to avoid establishing any U.K. presence whether through an office, or by the appointment of an agent with discretionary authority to legally bind the U.S. entity, which could result in the owner being deemed resident for U.K. tax purposes. Non-resident persons are not subject to any tax on capital gains arising on the sale of U.K. investments. It should be noted that the U.K./U.S. Treaty, permits a person or entity to be dual resident. A common example of this is a U.S. national or permanent resident individual who takes up permanent residence in the U.K. Unless, and until U.S. nationality or permanent residence is surrendered, such an individual would be resident for tax purposes and subject to tax on world wide income in both countries. Double Taxation Relief will be available to mitigate any tax liability but it is complex and the taxpayer will still be required to file returns in both countries.

Raising Capital

If it is going to be necessary to raise equity finance for the U.K. business, then the PLC is the only vehicle available. As stated above, PLC's are the only types of entity which can offer their shares to members of the public. Pursuant to the Financial Services Act 1986 ("FSA"), "the public" is very broadly defined and includes almost any group of people (however small) who are not intimately known to the owners and promoters of the company.

In order to offer shares for sale, whether or not they are going to be traded on any stock exchange, a prospectus complying with the provisions of the FSA will be required to be prepared and filed with the Registrar of Companies. A prospectus must be approved by a person authorized to carry on investment business pursuant to the Financial Services Act. Many types of professionals are so authorized either directly by the Securities & Investment Board, the statutory authority created by the FSA or by the various self-regulatory organizations, such as The Securities Association ("TSA"), which governs members of the London Stock Exchange and the Investment Management Regulatory Organization ("IMRO"), which governs investment managers. Solicitors and chartered accountants are also authorized by their relevant professional bodies to approve investment advertisements and offers.

Securities regulation in the U.K. is in a state of turmoil at present. Prior to the FSA, there was very little statutory regulation and the securities industry was largely governed by the codes of conduct of the organizations of the various professions doing business in the City of London. The FSA established an overburdensome regulatory regime, and the system is now creaking under the strain. Following certain spectacular recent failures of regulation, in particular with regard to the alleged looting of pension fund assets by the late Robert Maxwell, which went completely undiscovered by the regulatory authorities, numerous proposals have been floated for restructuring the regulatory regime and a heated debate continues.

However, it is still possible to raise capital relatively cheaply, off market, although clearly, it may be more difficult to find potential investors.

Relations Between Joint Owners

Where the business venture involves more than one principal it is vital at the outset to establish a proper structure for decision-making, ownership rights and profit sharing, and dispute resolution between the owners, whether through a shareholders agreement, partnership agreement or joint venture agreement. Although the Companies Acts provide significant protection for minority shareholders from oppression or unfair prejudice by majority shareholders, partly by way of super majority voting requirements and by extensive rights of recourse to the High Court, in order to avoid expensive and time consuming litigation practitioners are advised to ensure that their clients enter into proper agreements with their partners.

Such protective provisions and the corporate governance and decision-making structure of the limited company, simplify the preparation of such an agreement. On the other hand, a partnership or joint venture agreement will need to deal with every aspect of the operation of the business and the relationship of the owners, due to the relative lack of statutory regulation.

In principle, such agreements will need to cover the same areas as in the U.S., such as provisions relating to the transfer of shares or ownership interests and minority protection provisions with regard to decision making. Particular attention will need to be paid to those areas affected by the particular legal and economic structure of U.K. business entities. Dispute resolution devices such as put and call options, "shot gun" clauses, and other buy-out provisions are commonly used but these will need to be drafted by U.K. practitioners, in order to ensure that they will be effective and enforceable by the U.K. courts. Furthermore, detailed advice will be needed in such areas as non-competition restrictions which, when dealing with large enterprises, may be affected by EU law and, therefore, subject to intervention by the European Commission. Even smaller enterprises need to be concerned with the application of the Restrictive Trade Practices Act, which prohibits certain types of non-competition or exclusivity agreements, or requires them to be filed, failing which they may be void.

Location

The decision as to where in the U.K. to locate the new enterprise will involve numerous economic, commercial, and social factors, most of which are beyond the scope of this work. However those advising businesses establishing in the U.K. should also consider the various incentive schemes offered by both national and local government, as well as the EU. These are intended to promote the development of particular disadvantaged or under-developed areas of the country.

Here follows a brief summary of some of the schemes available to foreign businesses, which is based upon information provided by the British Trade and Investment Office in New York. Each project will require individual assessment and appropriate enquiries should be made at an early stage, since certain grants are conditional on a showing that the project would not proceed without them.

Regional Selective Assistance

This is available, if the project is in an "Assisted Area" and principally consists of project grants. Each grant is based on the capital cost and the job creation or job preservation potential of the project, usually over the first three years. It is necessary to show that the project: (a) is likely to be profitable; (b) will create or safeguard employment in the Assisted Area; (c) will benefit the regional and national economies; and (d) will not be able to proceed without the grant. However, the majority of finance is expected to come from private sources.

The grant is available for various costs associated with the acquisition and improvement of the site for the project and the establishment of the operation. Project

Grant is usually payable in three installments, depending on the extent of project implementation and job creation.

Government Premises

Within Assisted Areas, a number of commercial and industrial properties may be available for purchase or lease from the government. Premises range from small workshops to large factory units, suitable for a range of industries. Terms will be in accordance with local market conditions but almost by definition, real estate in Assisted Areas will not command premium prices and rents.

Enterprise Zones

The U.K. government has designated a number of areas as Enterprise Zones, which offer tax advantages and streamlined real estate development controls, to businesses establishing themselves within the zone. The zones were designed to run for 10 years from the dates of their respective designation and although many zones were established in 1983/84, a number have been designated since 1989.

The principal benefits for businesses available in an Enterprise Zone are:

(a) Exemption from Local Authority Rates;

(b) 100 percent capital allowances for investment in industrial and commercial buildings; i.e., the capital cost may be deducted against income for taxation purposes;

(c) Simplified planning (zoning) procedures, in order to encourage development generally.

If the Enterprise Zone is also in an assisted area then RSA may also be available.

Local Assistance

Pursuant to various national and local powers, local authorities can provide additional assistance to businesses being established in their area, whether by way of grants or loans for the acquisition and improvement of land and buildings; grants to assist the payment of rent on leased premises; grants for the regeneration of inner city areas, provided the project will result in new jobs, industrial space or housing and discretionary, partial, or total relief from local authority rates.

In view of the variety of grants and loans on offer and the discretionary powers of local authorities, it is advisable to consult and negotiate with the relevant local authority at an early stage in any project, in order to maximize the benefits for all concerned.

Northern Ireland

The government has made investment in Northern Ireland a major priority. Accordingly, some of the highest levels of financial incentives and assistance are available for businesses establishing operations in Northern Ireland. The Industrial Development Board for Northern Ireland (IDB) is responsible for administering and coordinating the various schemes and projects.

Some of the benefits available are industrial development grants, providing up to 50 percent of the cost of new buildings, machinery and equipment; employment grants, rent grants; and interest relief grants (in order to subsidize loans from private sector financiers). Secured loans and, in some cases some form of equity participation may also be available.

In addition, there are various management and employee grants, which are intended to enable the company to attract and train top quality management and labor force. Various tax benefits are also available, as outlined above.

In all cases the key elements which will need to be shown to IDB, are that the project has substantial prospects for job creation and structural improvement in Northern Ireland. In many cases, grants are payable only upon achievement of certain targets in these areas.

Finance from EU

Through the European Investment Bank (EIB) the European Regional Fund and the European Social Fund, various types of assistance are available to qualifying projects.

In general, assistance from the EU will be available to finance industrial or infrastructure projects which can be shown to assist regional development. A number of regional development areas have been designated by the EU and businesses must locate within these areas in order to obtain the relevant benefits.

Since most loans are designated in European Currency Units (ECU) which are calculated by reference to a basket of the currencies of the member states, there are exchange risks involved. However, the government has established the Exchange Risk Guarantee Scheme, pursuant to which borrowers for qualifying projects take on only the sterling liability, with the government bearing the exchange risk.

III.   DOING BUSINESS IN THE U.K.

Value Added Tax (VAT)

Chargeable Supplies

VAT is a tax which is much misunderstood in the U.S., as was apparent when the idea of introducing it was floated by the Clinton Administration in 1993, as a way of paying for health care reforms. Firstly, it is technically not a tax but a duty and it is therefore administered by HM Customs and Excise rather than HM Inland Revenue. Furthermore, it is a tax not only on the sale of products but on the provision of services in the widest sense of the word (collectively a "supply"). For example, landlords have the right to charge VAT upon the rent payable by commercial tenants. Finally, there is no real measurement of the value added except in the most notional sense, since it is really a tax on gross revenues. Every member of the EU is obliged to charge VAT, since the EU is principally funded by a proportion of the VAT receipts of each member state. The current rate in the U.K. is 17.5 percent.

Operation of the Tax

VAT is chargeable on the gross invoice price of the product or service supplied, at every state of production and distribution ("output"). That is to say, the supplier of raw materials must charge it to a manufacturer, who must charge it to a wholesale distributor, who charges it to a retail distributor, who charges it to the retailer, who charges it to the consumer. However, every commercial enterprise having taxable supplies in excess of the registration threshold, (£45,000 per annum from December 1, 1993) is required to register for VAT (and to charge VAT on its outputs) and is therefore entitled to deduct from the VAT collected on its income, the VAT which it has paid on its expenses ("inputs"). Only the net amount is required to be paid to Customs and Excise. In theory, for registered businesses, VAT should only have cash flow implications, with the only person who really bears the cost being the retail customer. If a business only has "exempt supplies" e.g., the sale of residential real estate, then it is not entitled to register and neither charges VAT, nor recovers any VAT paid on its expenses.

On the other hand, businesses which are primarily involved in exporting from the U.K. may have a particular cash-flow advantage. Such exports are "zero rated" which means that although they are technically required to collect VAT, the applicable tax rate is zero. Such businesses are still entitled to register for VAT, (as opposed to a business only engaged in exempt supplies, which is not entitled to register; *see* above) and will, accordingly, be able to reclaim the input VAT which they have paid on all of their expenses. This means that every time they file a VAT return rather than paying VAT, they will receive a refund from Customs and Excise.

Accounting for VAT

VAT requires a completely separate accounting system for each business, since it does not go through the usual books of account and does not appear in the profit and loss account (any liability for VAT will, of course, appear on the balance sheet). This can be an enormous administrative burden particularly for small companies, as well as a financial one. Most accounting in the U.K. is done on an accruals basis, which means that the business has to account for VAT based on the date of the invoice not the date of payment. Small businesses in particular may experience major cash-flow problems if they are not receiving timely payments from their customers. Accordingly, businesses having annual sales of less than £250,000 are entitled to cash account for VAT and only pay it to Customs and Excise once they have been paid.

Exports within the EU

Following the implementation of the single market in the EU on January 1, 1993, the situation with regard to dealings with businesses in other member states has become more complex. The system is still in a transitional stage and currently requires an enormously increased amount of paper work by each of the companies involved, since there are no longer border controls at which import and export information can be collected. Furthermore, VAT is payable by the registered enterprise which is receiving the supply upon importation (referred to as an "acquisition" in this context) and at a rate prevailing in its own jurisdiction. Previously, sales to businesses in other member states were simply zero rated (*see* above). There are plans to simplify the procedure but it is believed that this will take some years.

Temporary Imports

When certain classes of goods are imported into the U.K. on a temporary basis and are then re-exported within a short period, relief from duty and VAT may be available. Security is usually required in the form of a cash deposit, guarantee or bond. In addition, if goods are held in bonded warehouses or imported into one of the five free zones, then no VAT is payable unless and until they are moved out of the warehouse or free zone into the U.K. market. Most import controls and duties do not apply in such cases and to a certain extent, such goods may even be processed and bought and sold whilst within the warehouse or free zone.

Prices

Finally, it is most important to note, that contrary to the common presumption with regard to sales tax in the U.S., any price quoted is deemed to *include* VAT, unless expressly stated to the contrary. This generally applies in retail establishments and makes life easier for the consumer. However, in the commercial context, it is usual to discuss prices "ex VAT". In that case, the practitioner and the business person must ensure that the contract specifies that prices referred to are "exclusive of" or "plus" VAT.

Premises—Leasing and Buying

In general, the commercial considerations governing the decision whether to buy or lease premises in the U.K. will be the same as in the U.S. From the tax point of view, as in the U.S., both rental payments and interest on loans by a business to purchase a property are deductible against income, for U.K. tax purposes. This section will, therefore, be limited to a review of some of the differences in the economics and legal procedures involved in leasing and buying real property in the U.K. (Real property law being significantly different in Scotland, this review will deal primarily with the situation in England and Wales).

Leasing

There are fundamental differences in the way in which U.K. commercial leases deal with the prime issues of rent and rent reviews (escalations), service charges (payment for operating expenses), property taxes and renewals.

Rent

A typical English lease will set an initial rent, subject to periodic, upward-only rent reviews to the open market rent prevailing at the date of the review (e.g. a nine-year lease with reviews in the third and sixth years). Accordingly, the rent is only agreed until the date of the first rent review. This contrasts with typical U.S. leases, in which the amount or calculation of all future escalations are agreed at the outset.

At each review date, the landlord proposes a new rent, based on the rent recently agreed for new lettings or reviews under leases of comparable premises in the area. If the parties do not agree the new rent, the lease will normally provide for arbitration by one or more Chartered Surveyors or Licensed Valuers (who carry out all real estate appraisals in England). Rent is payable at the previous rate under the lease, until the amount of the review is agreed or determined, when the accrued deficiency is payable, usually with interest from the effective date of the review.

Service Charges

Rent is generally not inclusive of any expenses incurred in the management and operation of the property. Accordingly, most commercial leases will require the payment of a service charge in addition to rent, representing a proportion (based on area) of *all* of the landlord's expenses in operating the building and not merely the increase in expenses over a base year, as is often the case in the U.S.

The main exception is a "Full Repairing and Insuring Lease" (an "FRI Lease"), under which all of the obligations for repair and maintenance of the building are assumed by the tenant and accordingly, the landlord has no operating expenses. Generally this will only arise where the lease is of an entire building, for a relatively long period, say in excess of 15 years.

Taxes

Property taxes are almost universally paid by the tenant, in addition to rent. The property tax regime in the U.K, was completely revised under the Thatcher government. Under present law, each unit of ownership, whether an entire building, or the area demised under a particular lease will be separately valued by the District Valuer. The local authority (city or borough) then applies to the valuation the Uniform Business Rate (rate of tax), which is set by the U.K. government for each fiscal year (April 1 through March 31) and payments are made to the local authority. It is possible to pay taxes in 10 equal, interest free installments, during the relevant fiscal year.

In addition, a water rate is payable to the local water company, for the provision of fresh water and sewage services.

Renewals

Commercial leases are subject to the security of tenure provisions of Part II of the Landlord and Tenant Act 1954. Most commercial tenants have the right to a renewal of their lease on the same terms, subject only to payment of the then open- market rent.

In summary, the procedures are as follows. Prior to the end of the lease, the landlord is entitled to serve a notice stating that it accepts or opposes the tenant's right to a new lease. The tenant is entitled to serve a notice stating that it wishes or does not wish to exercise its right to a renewal of the lease. In only limited circumstances is the landlord entitled to object to the grant of a new lease, the most common instances being where the landlord requires the premises for its own use or for a substantial reconstruction of the whole building. In the event of a dispute, either party is entitled to commence proceedings for a judicial determination under the statutory provisions.

Since strict compliance with the statutory provisions is required by both landlord and tenant, in order to preserve their respective rights, each party should take detailed advice on their positions at least one year before the expiration of the term. Furthermore, since either party can commence the procedure by service of notice and service of the first notice triggers a statutory timetable, the tactics of who does what and when need to be very carefully considered.

These statutory rights of renewal can be excluded by agreement, subject to approval by the County court. Such exclusions, commonly referred to as "taking the lease outside of the 1954 Act" are generally only agreed in special, short term situations, e.g., a sublease for less than three years.

Delapidations

One feature of English leases can prove very expensive to the unsuspecting tenant and is often the subject of lengthy negotiations and litigation. Under most leases, apart from detailed repairing and maintenance obligations on the part of the tenant, the tenant will also have an obligation to reinstate the premises at the end of the term, to the condition which existed at the commencement of the lease. The landlord is entitled by statute to serve on the tenant a "Schedule of Delapidations" setting forth in great detail all of the construction work and repairs that landlord considers necessary for tenant to comply with its obligations. Compliance could cost the tenant hundreds of thousands of pounds.

Accordingly, Schedules of Delapidations are frequently served prior to the end of the term as a negotiating tactic, in order to give the landlord additional leverage in the negotiations for the renewal of the lease. Careful drafting of the lease is needed to mitigate or limit the effect of the repairing and reinstatement clauses.

Purchase

A majority of real estate transactions in England and Wales involve registered land. Pursuant to the scheme first introduced by the Land Registration Act of 1925, title to registered land has been investigated by the Land Registry for the district in which the land is located and a government guaranteed Land Certificate is issued to the owner for each parcel of registered land. Title insurance, as commonly used in the U.S., is unknown in the U.K. and, indeed, unnecessary in the case of registered land. Since land is only required to be registered when it changes hands, land which has been held by the same owner since before the 1925 Act, remains unregistered. The transfer of unregistered land involves detailed title investigation and therefore the procedure on sale is entirely different. This section will only deal with sales of registered land.

Pre-contract Inquiries and Searches

The normal progression of a real estate transaction involving registered land, would be as follows. Once the vendor and purchaser have agreed terms, they will instruct solicitors to prepare the sale contract. As in the U.S., a contract for dealing in any interest in land is unenforceable unless recorded in writing.

The vendor's solicitor will prepare the contract and obtain from the Land Registry an office copy of the Land Certificate. The purchaser's solicitor will review the contract and the Land Certificate. The Land Certificate will show the present owner of the property, any charges registered against the property (e.g., mortgages and other liens) and restrictive covenants affecting the property. However, the purchaser's solicitor also needs to ask the vendor various questions regarding the use and other detailed legal and practical matters relating to the property, which will not be registered (e.g., leases or subleases, occupants other than the vendor who may have certain rights, boundary disputes, and so on).

In addition, the purchaser's solicitor will carry out a Local Authority Search, in order to disclose the planning (zoning) situation. This would reveal any major forthcoming adverse developments, such as the construction of a highway through the area and any enforcement notices (violations) which may be recorded.

Exchange of Contracts

Once the contract has been agreed and the purchaser is satisfied with the results of all inquiries and searches, the parties may proceed to "exchange contracts." It is only at this point that the parties are legally committed to the transaction and specific performance can be sought to enforce the contract. Both parties sign one part of the contract and deliver it to their solicitor. The purchaser also provides the contract deposit, usually 10 percent of the purchase price. The solicitors will generally deal with exchange by a telephone call, in which they agree that the contract is exchanged (or effective) and undertake to send a copy of the contract signed by their client and, in the case of the purchaser's solicitor, the contract deposit, to the other party's solicitor.

Contracts are rarely conditional, so that all matters which could affect the purchaser's decision to proceed must be resolved prior to exchange. Any physical inspection report (always required where financing is involved) and an unconditional mortgage offer (loan commitment) must be obtained before exchange of contracts.

Completion

Completion (closing) will normally take place one month later. In the case of registered land, a simple two-page transfer document in statutory form is used to convey title to the property. Mortgage documents are also generally simple forms and the solicitor for the purchaser will often act for the bank, except in the case of complex or large commercial loans.

Completion is also often accomplished by a telephone call. The purchaser sends the purchase price to the vendor's solicitor in escrow, in advance of completion (generally on the morning of the completion date). Once confirmation of the wire transfer has been received, the vendor's solicitor will confirm that all necessary documents are in his possession and undertake to send them to the purchaser's solicitor. In most simple transactions, there is no closing meeting as such, or even if there is, the principals frequently need not attend.

Registration of Title

Following completion, the purchaser's solicitor must have the transfer "Stamped" by the Inland Revenue, which evidences payment of Stamp Duty (transfer tax) of one percent of the purchase price (subject to limited exemptions). Only when the document has been duly stamped, can the new owner's title to the property (and any mortgage) be registered at the Land Registry.

Employees

Employment legislation in the U.K. has a different focus than similar legislation in the U.S. A great deal of emphasis is placed upon the protection of employees with regard to the terms and conditions of their employment and the termination of employment. As in the U.S. there is a growing body of law and precedent, much of it coming from the ECJ, intended to counteract discrimination in all forms. The government has strongly resisted further regulation by the EU, particularly with regard to limitations on hours of work and employee representation in management of the business. Indeed, John Major's government considered that it had achieved a major coup, when it negotiated an "opt-out" clause from the recent Maastricht Treaty, with respect to certain social and employment legislation. However, the U.K. is still, to a certain extent, subject to such regulation by virtue of other, pre-existing treaties and legislation. The following is a summary of some of the principal areas of employee relations law, which may be unfamiliar to U.S. practitioners and businesses.

Terms of Employment

Under the Employment Protection (Consolidation) Act 1978 ("EP(C)A"), as amended by the Trade Union Reform and Employee Rights Act 1993 ("TURERA") most employees (excluding among others, employees who work less than eight hours per week) are entitled to written particulars of certain terms of their employment, within two months after the date on which their employment commences. They are also entitled to a statement updating the particulars from time to time.

The EP(C)A and TURERA set forth a detailed list of the matters which need to be notified. A sample statement of particulars appears in Appendix B. Apart from those particulars which state specific facts, e.g., the names of the parties, the date employment commenced, the job description, etc., the law does not mandate what the terms should be, it merely requires that the employee be informed what the terms are. For example, the rate of remuneration or the method of calculating remuneration must be stated but there is no minimum wage. Details of any pension benefits must be set forth, but there is no obligation to provide any. If there are no provisions as to any of the terms of which particulars are required, that fact must be stated.

Certain of the particulars must be given in detail, at the same time, in a "principal statement"; these are indicated by an asterisk in Appendix B. Other information may be given in or by reference to other documents. For example, the employer may issue a separate handbook or memorandum detailing rules relating to disciplinary and grievance procedures, pension and retirement arrangements and agreements with trade unions. The requirements relating to disciplinary and grievance procedures do not apply, if on the date of commencement of employment, the employer has less than twenty employees.

If the employer fails to provide the required particulars voluntarily, the employee is entitled to demand them and if the employer still fails to give them, in the event of any dispute, any ambiguities in the terms will be construed against the employer.

Effect of Statement of Particulars

The written particulars provided under the statute do not constitute a "contract" of employment in the common law sense, nor are they exhaustive. There may be no separate contract of employment, or there may be a very detailed and comprehensive service contract, as is common for senior executives. A business would be well advised to have standard terms and conditions of employment, incorporating the required particulars and including other matters, such as confidentiality, health, and safety codes etc. The statement is evidence of the employment contract but it is not conclusive evidence. The law of contract applies to employment contracts, as it does to other commercial contracts, although a specific body of case law has developed in relation to employment contracts. There is no legal requirement for a contract of employment, nor as to the content of any such contract.

Unfair Dismissal

Every employee has statutory rights not to be "unfairly dismissed". The majority of these rights only arise after two years of continuous employment by the same employer, however every employee has the right, both under U.K. and EU law, not to be unfairly discriminated against when seeking employment, during the course of employment or upon termination of employment. Unfair dismissal focuses on two separate aspects of termination of employment: (a) the reason for the dismissal; and (b) the manner of dismissal.

Reason for Dismissal

Every employee is entitled to a written statement of the reason for his dismissal. The reason must be objectively reasonable and relate to the employee's performance and conduct of duties for his employer. The one exception is dismissal by reason of redundancy. Here, the employer must show that the job for which the employee was hired is no longer needed or available (typically for financial reasons) and that the employer has made every reasonable effort to try to find the employee an alternative position within the business.

Manner of Dismissal

Although there is no statutory procedure for dealing with disciplinary problems, as a matter of practice, the Industrial Tribunal and the courts have required employers to follow a fair and proper procedure, in order to give a non-performing employee, every chance to improve his conduct. If an employer does not follow procedures laid down in any trade union agreement or in the employer's own disciplinary rules, then the employee will be deemed, *prima facie*, to have been unfairly dismissed. In the absence of such rules, the employer will be strongly advised to ensure that the employee was warned about his conduct, probably on more than one occasion and with at least one written warning; and that the particular reason for the dismissal was presented to the employee and that he had the opportunity to have that decision reviewed by an "independent" person in the organization, i.e. one who is not involved in the decision to terminate employment. The employee should be entitled to have someone sit in at such review whether a trade union representative, lawyer or friend, and to present his case.

Legal Recourse

If the employee is dissatisfied with the stated reason for or the manner of his dismissal, then he is entitled to apply to the Industrial Tribunal for review of the decision and redress. The Tribunal is intended to operate under a more informal procedure, and although the parties are entitled to be represented, a "legalistic" form of representation is discouraged. The normal rules of evidence are not strictly applied. As a matter of practice, it must be said that unfair dismissal cases tend to be decided in favor of the employee. The Tribunal has the power to award compensation and to require reinstatement of the employee in appropriate cases. The basic compensation payable, in the event of a decision against the employer, is limited by reference to a maximum weekly level of earnings multiplied by the number of years of continuous employment. The Tribunal is entitled to award additional compensation in appropriate cases, by reason of the conduct of the employer and to compensate for additional losses of benefits such as pension rights but this is presently capped at £11,000.

However, the law in this area is now in turmoil, following the recent landmark decision by the ECJ in the case of *Marshall* v *Southampton and Southwest Hampshire Health Authority* (ECJ 271/91)[1993]. In that case the ECJ held that it was contrary to the EU's Equal Treatment Directive 76/207 for national provisions to prescribe a maximum limit on the compensation recoverable by a victim of discrimination, in respect of loss and damage sustained. At present, it seems that only employees in public sector employment can benefit from this, but the writing is apparently on the wall for this provision. Following the case, the Ministry of Defense has taken the unprecedented step of announcing that about 5,500 women were dismissed from the armed services by reason of pregnancy, in breach of the directive and that it was trying to settle these cases by paying additional compensation.

This area of the law in particular, serves as a salutary lesson to all practitioners, that even apparently wholly domestic U.K. issues, not involving any other more obvious inter-European affairs, may be dramatically impacted by EU law and decisions of the ECJ. Lawyers ignore this at their peril.

Appeal from the Industrial Tribunal lies to a specialized panel of judges of High Court status called the Employment Appeal Tribunal. From there, further appeal lies direct to the Court of Appeal and then to the House of Lords and, in appropriate cases, the ECJ.

Redundancy and Notice

Although redundancy is a good reason for dismissal, this does not mean that employees have no rights in the event of being dismissed for that reason. Apart from any internal redundancy provision that each company may make, every employee who is made redundant after more than two years of continuous employment, is entitled to redundancy pay, calculated at an equivalent level to the basic compensation for unfair dismissal. Redundancy pay is separate and apart from any entitlement to pay, during the period of notice of termination, or in lieu of notice of termination. Every employee has the right to at least one week's notice of termination during the first two years of employment and thereafter, an additional week for every year of employment, up to a maximum of 12 week's notice. Such periods of notice may be increased by contract.

Wrongful Dismissal

Basis of Claim

Wrongful dismissal is a common law claim for breach of contract. The elements required in order to maintain a wrongful dismissal are exactly the same as for breach of any other contract. The fact that an employee may have been held to have been unfairly dismissed, is not conclusive evidence of wrongful dismissal, although it is obviously supportive evidence of such a claim. Since any damages award in a wrongful dismissal action, could be taken into account in assessing compensation for unfair dismissal, in appropriate cases, it is common for employees to pursue their rights through the Industrial Tribunal first, before commencing High Court action.

Damages

The key issue in wrongful dismissal cases (once a breach of the contract has been established) is the calculation of damages. Although this is based upon the usual contract measure of damages, a specific body of law has evolved with regard to damages for breach of employment contracts. Take the example of an employee who has a three year fixed-term service contract who is wrongfully dismissed after one year. *Prima facie*, he or she would be entitled to the equivalent of two years salary and benefits under the contract, representing what they would have received had the employer performed its obligations under the contract. However, there is a strong duty on the employee to mitigate damages by trying to find comparable employment, as soon as reasonably possible. Account may be taken of unemployment benefits received. A further deduction would be made based on the fact that the employee would receive the damages reward as a lump sum, as opposed to a stream of payments over two years and an appropriate discounting factor may be applied. On the other side, the employee is entitled to claim for such additional losses as loss or diminution of pension rights, the value of lost benefits in kind, such as motor vehicles and the loss of the right to exercise any share or stock options.

Discrimination

Under the Sex Discrimination Act 1975 and EU legislation and case law (referred to above), every employee has the right not to be improperly discriminated against in seeking employment and during the course of and on termination of employment. This is an area with which U.S. lawyers are well familiar and although generally, the law in this area is not as developed as it is in the U.S., as can be seen from recent ECJ decisions, U.K. law is rapidly catching up.

Continuity of Employment

Many of the rights granted to employees under U.K. legislation are dependent upon "continuous employment." Accordingly, U.K. law has made additional provision in order to protect employees from having that continuity broken. Particular attention should be paid to the Transfer of Undertakings (Protection of Employment) Regulations 1981. Pursuant to these regulations, where an employer disposes of substantially all of the assets and undertaking of the business (as opposed to selling shares in a company) the employer changes and, in the absence of the regulations, the employee's continuity of the employment would be broken.

The regulations set forth a number of rights and obligations in such cases, as follows:

(a) The new employer is required to offer employment on comparable terms, to all employees of the business.

(b) The employees are not required to accept the offer of new employment and if they do not do so within one month then, subject to certain conditions, they are entitled to be treated as having been made redundant and paid compensation accordingly.

(c) Employees are treated as having continuity of employment from the date when they were first employed by the original employer. The effect of this, is that the new employer inherits a contingent liability in respect of redundancy, unfair dismissal, maternity, and other rights based, on the length of employment by the seller of the business.

The parties are at liberty to apportion the impact of these rights and obligations between themselves, provided they do not affect the rights of the employees. For example, the seller could agree to indemnify the purchaser and to pay the redundancy cost of any employees who do not accept employment with the new owners. Accordingly, in any contract for the sale or purchase of a business it is most important to obtain warranted details of all employees, including their terms and conditions as to salary, notice and the date on which they commenced employment and, in appropriate cases, to make provision for dealing with the effect of the Transfer of Undertaking Regulations.

Payroll Costs

All employers are required to pay their employees subject to withholding tax and National Insurance Contributions ("NIC") (Social Security), under the scheme commonly referred to as "pay as you earn" or "PAYE." As in the U.S., employers are required to deduct income tax and NIC in accordance with tables and codes and to account Inland Revenue for same by the 19th of the month following the month in which the payroll occurs. In addition, employers are required to pay employers' NIC which, for the year 1994/5, is at the rate of 10.2 percent of gross pay. Lower rates apply in respect of lower paid workers, in order encourage employment in that sector of the labor market. Following the enactment of a series of anti-avoidance provisions, NIC will also be payable not only on wages and salary but also upon a wide range of benefits in kind, which were previously used as devices to save the amount of NIC payable.

Notes

[1] Article 177 The Treaty of Rome.

[2] Convention of December 31, 1975 (as amended).

[3] "Britain the Preferred Location," The Invest in Britain Bureau of the U.K. Government's Department of Trade and Industry, January 1991.

[4] The Companies Acts comprise the following: The Companies Act 1985, The Business Names Act 1985, The Company Securities (Insider Dealing) Act 1985, The Companies Consolidation (Consequential

Provisions) Act 1985, the provisions relating to companies in the Insolvency Act 1986 and the Companies Act 1989. These are commonly referred to as the Companies Acts 1985–1989, or simply the Companies Acts.

[5] The Companies Acts permit but do not require, extraordinary and elective resolutions to be passed, although they may be required by the company's Articles of Association, in certain circumstances.

[6] The tax year for companies runs from 1st April to 31st March. Within certain restrictions a company can select and change its own accounting period and pay tax by reference to the accounting period ending within a particular tax year.

[7] The exchange rate as of March 1994 was approximately $1.50 to the £.

APPENDIX A

CHECKLIST FOR COMPANY FORMATIONS

1. Name

2. Registered Office

3. Private Company or PLC

4. Share Capital

    A. Authorized: Classes, Nominal Value and amount.

    B. Issued: Classes, amount, and issue price (Issue Price cannot be less than Nominal Value but may be more. Issue price may be payable in installments).

    C. Shareholders: Names, addresses and number of shares to be subscribed for.

5. Directors: Names, addresses, occupations, nationalities, dates of birth, and details of other directorships.

6. Secretary: Name and address.

7. Auditor:

8. Accounting Reference Date (fiscal year end) and first accounting period.

9. Memorandum and Articles of Association.

10. Shareholders' Agreement.

    Ready made companies may be purchased "off the shelf" and thereby be available for use in a day. Customized formation of companies can take two to three weeks, depending on the extent of the backlog at the Companies Registry.

APPENDIX B

STATEMENT OF TERMS OF EMPLOYMENT

OF

*Name of Employee:

*Address:

*Date of Statement:

*Commencement of Employment
1. Your employment began on:

2. Employment with your previous employer is not included as part of your present period of continuous employment.

*Job Title

3. You are employed as:
   The Company reserves the right to require you to carry out other duties which it is reasonable to ask you to perform. Any long-term alteration in your job title and description will be notified to you personally in writing.

*Place of Work

4. Your principal place of work will be at :

   *The Company reserves the right to require you to work in any of its offices in the Greater London area at any time.

   You may also be required, from time to time, to spend periods of more than month at the Company's offices in New York, U.S.A. and the Company will endeavour to give you at least one month's notice in advance, specifying the dates when such visits will be required. Your salary will continue to be paid in Pounds Sterling in the U.K. during such periods of work overseas but if appropriate, in view of the length of any proposed stay in the U.S.A., the Company will consider any request to pay salary in US dollars. In respect of such periods of work overseas, the Company will be responsible for all travel, accommodation and car hire costs, in accordance with the Company's then current policies. Such periods of work overseas will not affect your job description and position with the Company and you will resume your normal duties upon return to the U.K.

*Hours of Work

5. Your basic hours of work are 9.30 a.m. to 5.30 p.m., Monday to Friday, inclusive, each week with a break of one hour for lunch each day, but there may be times when you will be required to work outside these basic hours and your co-operation in this connection will be expected.

*Remuneration

6. You will be paid at the rate of £ per annum payable monthly in arrears. No remuneration will be paid for overtime working. You will be paid on the last working day of each calendar month.

*Holidays

7. The Company's holiday year runs from January 1st to December 31st in each year and holidays not taken may not be carried forward into the following holiday year. In addition to all Bank Holidays, you will be entitled to 20 working days paid holiday in each holiday year on the basis 1 2/3 days for each completed calendar month of employment in each holiday year, which may be taken only on prior consultation with the Company. In any event, the maximum period of continuous holiday to be taken, without the express agreement of the Company, is 10 working days. No holiday may be taken during any period of notice of termination of employment, except with the specific agreement of the Company.

Absence Through Sickness and Sick Pay

8. If you are absent due to sickness, you will be entitled to receive Statutory Sick Pay, subject to producing appropriate certificates as specified below. If you are absent from work due to sickness or injury, you must inform the Company by telephone as soon as reasonably possible and where you are absent for two or more but less than five working days, continuously, a written self-certificate, in the attached form covering the period of absence must be produced on your return to work. If you are absent for seven or more working days, a Doctor's certificate covering the period from and including the seventh working day of absence must be produced, if requested by the Company.

Pensions

9. The Company does not operate its own Pension scheme for employees. The Statutory Pension scheme operates and no contracting out certificate is in force in relation to your employment.

[OR]

Details of your rights and benefits under the Company's pension scheme are in the attached booklet (as amended from time to time). A contracting out certificate is in force in relation to your employment.

Notice

10. You are entitled to receive one week's notice of termination of employment after you have completed four weeks' continuous employment until you have completed two years' continuous employment and thereafter one week's notice for each year of continuous employment up to a maximum of 12 weeks' notice after 12 years of continuous employment. The Company reserves the right to require you to leave immediately, on payment of salary at the rate stated in Paragraph Six in lieu of notice, for the period of notice to which you are entitled. Nothing in this paragraph precludes the termination of your employment without notice or payment in lieu in appropriate circumstances. Until you have completed four weeks' continuous employment you are required to give the Company one week's notice of termination in writing and thereafter, one month's notice of termination. All notices must be in writing. Notice of termination will not be accepted by the Company if given during any period of absence, unless by prior agreement.

Collective Agreements

11. The Company is not a party to, nor are your terms and conditions of employment affected, by any collective bargaining agreements with any trade union or similar organization.

Grievance Procedure

12. Any grievance relating to your employment, should be referred to the personnel administrator in charge of the office at which you are then employed. If his (her) decision is not acceptable to you, you may request that the matter be referred to a committee of two Directors (neither of which shall be the Personnel Director), for their consideration, and the decision of such committee of Directors, shall be final and binding.

    When stating your grievance you may be accompanied or represented by any fellow employee or close relative of your choice.

13. The Company reserves the right, if appropriate, to suspend you from normal employment during the period of any investigation of any grievance or breach of the terms and conditions of employment, during which time you will not be entitled to access to any of the Company's premises without the Company's prior consent and subject to such conditions as the Company may impose. Notwithstanding such suspension, your contract of employment shall be deemed to continue with all rights, including payment of salary.

Disciplinary Procedures and Rules

14. As part of the terms and conditions of your employment, you are required to comply with any Rules and Regulations that the Company may introduce. Any infringement of these Rules and Regulations or misconduct resulting in disciplinary action or warnings by the Company will be noted in the Company's records. If it is considered that you are guilty of minor misconduct or infringement, you may be given an oral warning; more serious misconduct will result in a written warning. The Company shall have the right to dismiss you if your conduct results in your receiving more than two written warnings. The following infringements or misconduct will be regarded as gross misconduct justifying summary dismissal, but these examples are not exhaustive or exclusive:

(a) Any form of theft or dishonesty.

(b) Any unauthorized disclosure of confidential information or breach of trust.

(c) Any form of violence on the Company's premises.

(d) Gross disobedience, or insubordination and refusal to carry out duties or reasonable instructions.

(e) Wilful interference with or negligence in use of equipment on the Company's premises, or neglect or refusal to comply with safety regulations or regulations for use of equipment, thereby exposing you or fellow employees to injury.

(f) Deliberate absence from the Company's premises during working hours without reasonable excuse.

(g) Repetition of misconduct for which written warnings were previously given.

The Company reserves the right to change these terms and conditions of employment and you will be given written notice of any changes.

_____ _____
Date   Employee's Signature

_____ _____
Date   For [Company]

APPENDIX C

USEFUL NAMES AND ADDRESSES

British Trade and Investment Office
British Consulate
845 Third Avenue
New York, New York 10022
Telephone: (212) 745-0495
Fax: (212) 745-0456

Invest in Britain Bureau
Department of Trade and Industry
Kingsgate House
66–74 Victoria Street
London SW1E 6SW
England
Telephone: (071) 215-8439
Fax: (071) 215-8451

**Office of Western Europe
(Room 3042)**
U.S. Department of Commerce
Washington, D.C. 20230
Telephone: (202) 402-3748
   (U.K. desk direct line)
Fax: (202) 402-2897

British Consulate, New York
845 Third Ave.
New York, NY 10022
Telephone: (212) 745-0200
Visa Section: (212) 745-0202

**Delegation of the Commission of the
   European Communities**
3 Dag Hammarskjold Plaza
305 East 47th Street
New York, New York 10017
Telephone: (212) 371-3804
Fax: (212) 758-2718

**Embassy of the United States of
America**
Grosvenor Square London
W1A 1AE
England
Telephone: (071)499-9000

**British American Chamber of
Commerce**
52 Vanderbildt Avenue
New York, New York 10017
Telephone: (212) 661-4060

GOING INTERNATIONAL IN TAIWAN

Lawrence S. Liu

I. CHANGING FACES OF TAIWAN

THE SUCCESS STORY of Taiwan's economic transformation from a poor, underdeveloped country to today's powerhouse is well known around the world. Scholars cite a strong and interventionist government, economic policies geared at creating a strong private sector, and social policies geared towards development of human capital, as some of the reasons for Taiwan's economic success. Starting from the 1980s, though, Taiwan's economic and social environment gradually changed. Previously interventionist measures which worked well in developing Taiwan's economy became inadequate in the context of an already developed economy seeking global integration.

Taiwan's economic transformation in the 1980's can be summarized into one word: deregulation. The wealthy middle-class, western-trained technocrats and business leaders who control the economy today are more practical and open-minded than their counterparts from the pioneering generation. In addition, the government realized that it needs to change its role from being primarily a leader and conductor of national economic development to being a regulator whose main task is to create and rigorously enforce fair and clear rules designed to maintain an efficient and competitive environment.

Taiwan in the 1990s

Following the deregulation of the 1980s, in the 1990s, the ROC government and the business community of Taiwan will continue to liberalize and integrate the local market into the world economy.

The ROC is currently trying to join the General Agreement on Tariffs and Trade (GATT) and other international economic organizations, as part of the measures towards integration with the global economy. In addition, it carried out three waves of financial reform in the late 1980s. These are: the foreign exchange liberalization since mid-1987, the transformation of the securities market since early 1988, and the banking reform since mid-1989.

Status of Foreign Investment in Taiwan

For the past four decades, the consistent policy of the Republic of China (ROC) government in Taiwan has been to aggressively attract foreign and overseas Chinese investment and technical cooperation. To that end, the government has engaged in several encouragement policies. In the 1950s, with basic necessities still in short supply, the government encouraged import-substitution industry, such as labor-intensive, light industries. In the 1960s, the government shifted its focus to export-oriented economic activities. In the 1970s, the government concentrated on heavy and chemical industries, and in the 1980s, the government once again shifted its focus to capital and technology-intensive industries.

Now in the 1990s, with the economy in transition, there is a need to bring advanced technology to upgrade the domestic industries. Thus, the current focus of the ROC government is on turning the ROC into a base for the research and development of high technology and high value added products and for their marketing, operations, and transportation within the Asia-Pacific region.

Japanese and American investors have been leading investors in Taiwan. In recent years, there are more European investors. In terms of industry emphasis, foreign investment in Taiwan has been concentrated in the following industries: electronics and electric appliance, chemicals, general services, machinery equipment and instrument, basic metals and metal products, trade, banking and insurance, plastics and rubber products, non-metallic minerals, and transportation[1].

II. IMPACT OF 1987 REFORM

The main statute governing foreign investment in Taiwan is the Statute for Investment by Foreign Nationals (SIFN). The SIFN was enacted at a time when foreign exchange was in short supply. As a result, it mainly used repatriation rights as a way to channel foreign investment into desirable industries. That is, only foreign investors whose investment projects contributed to the development of selected industries enjoyed the right under the SIFN to repatriate net earnings and capital gains. Consequently, investment incentive policies in the ROC have been closely connected to foreign exchange control policies.

While the SIFN channeled foreign investment to desirable areas, the Statute for the Administration of Foreign Exchange (SAFE) ensured that the ROC government had complete control over the entry and exit of foreign exchange in Taiwan. SAFE is the basic statute governing foreign exchange control. Before the 1987 reform, it required that foreign exchange earnings resulting from export be sold only to the Central Bank of China (CBC) or "appointed banks" (i.e. banks authorized by the CBC to engage in the foreign exchange business). This restrictive set up lasted only until the mid-1987, when an amendment to the SAFE catalyzed the liberalization of foreign investment regulations in the ROC.

Foreign Exchange Liberalization

By the early 1970s, the excuse used to justify such tight control by the SAFE was no longer appropriate. That is, foreign exchange was no longer scarce due to trade surpluses with the ROC's main trading partners (especially the United States) and the accumulation of foreign exchange assets and reserves in the ROC. In the mid-1980s, excess liquidity and speculative short-term funds, which flowed into the country anticipating the appreciation of the NT dollar, produced an enormous quantity of "hot-monies". The government reacted by adopting administrative measures designed to decrease foreign exchange reserves. But these measures were less than successful.

As a result, in June of 1987 the ROC Legislative Yuan (i.e. its Parliament) amended article 26–1 to the SAFE. Article 26–1 authorizes the Executive Yuan (i.e. the Cabinet of the ROC) to suspend the application of core provisions of the SAFE in whole or in part during long periods of international trade surplus, or when the ROC accumulates substantial foreign exchange, or when there are major changes in the international economy. But following the ROC government's motto of gradual change, the Executive Yuan never intended to fully and suddenly dismantle the foreign exchange control system. In July of 1987, the Central Bank of China (which is under the Executive Yuan) suspended the SAFE's core provisions, set up eight new regulations under article 26–1, but kept the foreign exchange control system.

Of the eight new regulations, the most important are the Regulations for Non-Governmental Inward Remittance ("Inward Regulations") and the Regulations for Non-Governmental Outward Remittance ("Outward Regulations"). These regulations were designed to relax the flow and retention of foreign exchange in the ROC. For instance, the Inward Regulations allow any adult resident to accept remittances of up to U.S. $ 5 million per year for conversion into NT dollars. This quota is the result of several increases from the original amount of U.S. $ 50,000. However, each inward remittance may not exceed U.S. $ 1 million[2]. Moreover, inward remittances for the repatriation of capital and profits of an ROC offshore investment project or for a foreign investor's investment in the ROC, have to be approved by the CBC.

The Outward Regulations permit ROC adult residents and entities to make up to U.S. $ 5 million worth of outward remittances in foreign exchange each year. Outward remittances exceeding U.S. $ 1 million are subject to a ten-day waiting period, though. Moreover, remittances over the U.S. $ 5 million or U.S. $ 1 million limits require special approval from the CBC[3].

Impact on Regulation of Foreign Direct Investments

Foreign investment in the ROC is regulated by the Statute for Investment by Foreign Nationals (SIFN) enacted in 1954. As mentioned above, the SIFN is based on the privilege of an investor with foreign investment approval (FIA) granted by the Investment Commission (IC) of the Ministry of Economic Affairs (MOEA), to repatriate the original capital (whether as equity investment or loan investment), investment yield (whether as dividend or interest repayment on loan investment), and return on investment (i.e. capital gains)[4]. Still, the SIFN does not regulate all types of foreign investment in the ROC. Foreign banks, insurance companies, and other foreign companies can set up branches in the ROC without undergoing the FIA process.

The SAFE reforms have naturally led to changes in the SIFN and relaxation of the foreign investment policy of the ROC. The ROC government began approving foreign investment liberally in the early 1980s, and in 1989, an amendment to the SIFN was promulgated. The 1989 amendment to the SIFN sets forth a negative listing policy which made the foreign investment review process standards more transparent and less intrusive by listing industries and businesses in which foreign investment are prohibited or restricted[5].

Yet, despite this negative listing, the SIFN does provide some advantages over other non-FIA forms of foreign ownership of companies. An FIA company is exempt from cumbersome Company Law requirements on nationality and residence of the certain employees, and rules governing mandatory public offering of stocks and employee stock subscription rights. In addition, the Statute for Upgrading Industries (SUI), a successor to the Statute for Encouragement of Investments (SEI), provides many tax incentives for FIA investors. Still, with the liberalization of foreign exchange controls, the main incentive to seek FIA status disappeared. As the Outward Regulations gave regulatory repatriation privileges to anyone, some foreign investors are skipping the FIA process altogether and setting up non-FIA branches in the ROC.

Impact on Regulations of Direct Outward Investment

The CBC's Outward Regulations have facilitated direct investment abroad by ROC residents and entities, to secure raw materials, technology, and markets. In promoting the outflow of capital, the Outward Regulations have also helped the ROC in offsetting its trade surplus. However, this Outward Regulations-induced should not be overrated.

For many years, ROC companies have had to apply for an Outward Investment Approval (OIA) before investing abroad, according to the Regulations Governing the Review of Outward Investment and Outward Technical Cooperation (OIA Regulations). These regulations apply only to companies. As a result, after July 1987, when foreign direct investment was greatly facilitated for individual investors, these OIA Regulations became an obstacle for Taiwan companies wishing to directly invest abroad. In order to narrow the gap in the treatment of individuals and companies, an amendment adding a three-tier review test in the OIA Regulations was adopted in March of 1989. This amendment states that outward investments of less than U.S. $ 1 million may be implemented before it is reported to the IC. Outward investments projects involving sums between U.S. $ 1 million and U.S. $ 5 million must file an application with the IC. If after a thirty-day waiting period the IC does not disapprove of the project, the latter is deemed to be approved. Finally, outward investments projects involving amounts over U.S. $ 5 million are subject to full scrutiny by the IC[6].

III.   FORMS OF FOREIGN INVESTMENT

There are no specific definition for "Foreign Direct Investment" in the ROC laws and regulations. In practice, however, FDI in the ROC usually takes one of the following three forms: (1) FIA foreign direct investment; (2) Non-FIA foreign direct investment; and (3) Branches of foreign companies.

FIA Foreign Direct Investment

According to the SIFN, a foreign investor can make direct a investment in the ROC after obtaining a Foreign Investment Approval (FIA) by the IC of the MOEA for the following activities: (1) setting up a local subsidiary wholly owned by the foreign investor or jointly owned by the foreign investor and local joint venture investors; (2) buying part of an existing company by subscribing to new shares or buying issued shares; or (3) injecting new capital or capitalizing retained earnings in the activities just described.Most of the FIA foreign direct investments are channeled into the form of subsidiaries, which are often companies limited by shares incorporated under the Company Law, in order to take advantage of the privileges prescribed by the Statute for Upgrading Industries (SUI).

An FIA foreign direct investment can take the form of an inflow of capital; capitalization of machinery, equipment, or raw materials; capitalization of technical know-how or patent rights; or capitalization of investment principal, capital gains, net profits, interest or any other income generated from the transfer of investment, reduction of capital or dissolution and liquidation of an FDI enterprise, as approved by the ROC government.

Non-FIA Foreign Direct Investment

FIA granted by the IC is not a mandatory step in the formation of a local subsidiary by a foreign direct investor. The foreign direct investor may choose to form a local subsidiary by following the regulations prescribed in the Company Law without applying for IC approval. In this case, the investment is not entitled to repatriation of profits rights under the SIFN. The subsidiary's repatriation of profits to its home country is governed by the Outward Regulations. Presently, a U.S. $5 million annual quota of outward remittance is allowed. In order to finance the capital of a local subsidiary, a foreign direct investor must find local funding as it is not entitled to remit any foreign currency into the ROC, according to the Inward Regulations. Moreover, this type of subsidiary is subject to the local residence and nationality requirements under the Company Law.

Branches of Foreign Companies

A third way for foreign entities or individuals to make direct investment in the ROC is by applying for recognition as legal entities with the MOEA and then set up branches in the ROC in order to conduct business.

According to the Company Law, approval for recognition of foreign companies is based on the principle of reciprocity following international practice, with public safety and social order in mind. The Company Law does not contain any disparate treatment between foreign companies trying to set up local branches and local residents trying to set up local companies.This form of foreign investment has been widespread in the banking, securities, insurance, transportation, trading, and general trade-related services. Usually, there is no need to obtain approval under the SIFN. Nonetheless, in certain regulated industries such as banking, insurance, and securities, a prior approval by relevant authorities such as the Ministry of Finance (MOF) or the Securities and Exchange Commission (SEC) is necessary. Foreign companies wishing to set up branches in the ROC must first apply for recognition as legal entities with the Department of Commerce (DOC) under the MOEA. Then, the foreign company is required to remit funds into the ROC to be used as the branch's working capital. Finally, the branch has to set up its own accounting and bookkeeping system, and is liable for all taxes applicable to local profit-seeking enterprises.

The branch establishment process could take up to eight weeks. Moreover, under ROC law, the ROC branch of a foreign company is seen as an integral part of the foreign company, as opposed to being a separate legal entity (except for tax purposes). Consequently, the foreign company is liable for all obligations of the ROC branch and subject to the jurisdiction of the ROC courts. In fact, branch managers of foreign companies usually serve as agents in both litigious and non-litigious matters in the ROC.

Setting up Liaison Offices

A foreign investor who do not wish to maintain a sizeable profit-seeking enterprise in the ROC (such as a branch or subsidiary), may set up a representative or liaison office by appointing a person to act as its representative in the ROC. In practice, there are two forms of such offices, a "386 office" and an office set up by simply appointing a representative and filing an appointment letter with the local tax office for recording and tax registration purposes. A "386 office" is an office set up pursuant to article 386 of the Company Law. It may engage in juristic acts such as signing agreements in the name of the parent company, or conduct other activities such as market surveys and product inspection. A "386 office" allows its representative to apply for a resident visa and alien resident certificate, while a "non-386 office" does not.

The main advantages of setting up liaison offices reside in the simplicity of their application and in the absence of any capital requirement applying to such offices. The drawback is that such offices may not engage in any profit-seeking activities. In fact, some agencies regulating businesses requiring special approval to be set up have, in recent years, requested the MOEA to not even grant permission for such foreign companies to set up "386 offices" in the ROC. As far as taxation goes, liaison offices are not subject to any taxes in the ROC since they are not profit-seeking businesses. The only exceptions are that they are required to withhold income tax on salaries to employees and rental payments to their landlords, and that they are subject to the tax office's verification of the proper establishment of accounting records and the receipt of inward remittances from the parent company.

Agency and Distribution

Foreign investors who do not make any equity or technological investment in the ROC for a variety of business reasons, may set up an agency or distributorship arrangements in the ROC. Despite the fact that foreign investment laws and regulations do not apply to them, these agencies or distributors should still bear in mind relevant provisions of the ROC Civil Code, which may apply when there is no choice-of-law agreement to the contrary.

Portfolio Investment

Aside from foreign direct investment, a foreign investor may choose to make passive investment in ROC. Most often, foreign passive investment in the ROC are channeled into shares of Taiwan Stock Exchange (TSE) listed companies and real estate. But foreign investment in these two properties is subject to many important restrictions.

For instance, the securities markets has not yet been completely liberalized. Only in 1983 did the Legislative Yuan amend the Securities and Exchange Law (SEL) to allow foreign securities and other leading types of financial institutions to set up "securities investment trust enterprises" (SITE) by joint-venturing with ROC residents and companies. Four SITE—there are now 15—companies were then set up to sell mutual funds for foreign investors to indirectly invest in the TSE. The SIFN was also amended so that regulations could be adapted for foreign portfolio investment in Taiwan's securities market[7]. There has been pressure for further liberalization of foreign investment in the ROC's emerging securities market. Another form of portfolio investment is the Qualified Foreign Institutional Investment ("QFII") program administered by the SEC and TSE. It permits qualified foreign institutional investors to invest a total of U.S. $5 billion in TSE, listed companies.

IV. PRACTICAL TIPS FOR FIA

The FIA Requirement and Process

Despite the feasibility of non-FIA forms of foreign direct investment, the "FIA track" is still the one most companies find most advantageous after reviewing their business plans.The agency primarily responsible for reviewing foreign investment applications is the IC of the MOEA[8]. However, in cases where a foreign investor seeks to implement an investment project in special zones such as the Hsin-Chu Science Based Industrial Park or an export processing zone, the IC delegates the review responsibility to agencies in charged of administering foreign investment in such designated zones.The IC is an unique agency in that is was established more than 20 years ago as a "coalition agency" created to streamline procedures relating to foreign investment applications. It is headed *ex officio* by the vice minister of economic affairs as its chairman, and managed by an executive secretary and a deputy executive secretary. The IC' investment commissioners are the following representatives from various other agencies who also serve *ex officio*: vice minister of economic affairs; vice minister of finance; vice minister of foreign affairs; vice minister of communications; vice minister of interior; vice chairman of the Council of Economic Planning and Development (CEPD); vice chairman of the Commission of Overseas Chinese Affairs; deputy governor of the CBC; deputy director general of the National Health Department of the Executive Yuan; deputy director general of the Reconstruction Department of the Provincial Government of

Taiwan; deputy director general of the Reconstruction Bureau of the Municipal Government of Taipei; and deputy director general of the Reconstruction Bureau of the Municipal Government of Kaohsiung.

These commissioners often do not attend commission meetings at the IC. Instead, they send lower level officials to participate in these meetings, unless the meetings involve very important investment projects. During commission meetings, foreign investment applications on the docket are subject to discussion leading to a final decision by the end of each meeting. These meeting are held every other Monday. The views of various governmental agencies are important considerations in the FIA projects reviews. For instance, where an FIA project involves manufacturing activities, the views of the Industrial Development Bureau (IDB) of the MOEA are taken heavily. The IDB is usually present at IC meetings and its position usually favors the foreign investor. Similarly, when an FIA project involves a regulated industry, the views of the relevant regulatory agencies are considered crucial. The IC is supported by staff members who are divided into the following sections: general secretarial, taxation, foreign exchange, import and export, business administration, and supervision. The general secretarial section reviews FIA, TCA, and outward investment applications, and policy issues involving foreign investment, technical cooperation, and outward investment. The taxation sections deals with the tax and duty incentives. The foreign exchange sections takes care of all matters related to inward and outward remittances and conversion of investment funds, earnings, interest, and royalty income. The business administration section is responsible for verifying the status of a foreign investor, reviewing powers of attorney, visa and immigration matters, and corporate, factory, trading, and business registrations. The import and export section is predictably in charged of reviewing the import or export of machinery, equipment, and materials.

Preparing The FIA

A foreign investor seeking FIA status for its investment in the ROC must submit an FIA application to the IC or its designated agencies in certain zones. There are no government prepared FIA application forms. However, drafting the application requires professional legal and business skills. In general foreign direct investors seek experienced legal counsel for initial drafting, are responsible for information about themselves and their companies in the FIA application, and collaborate with counsel on the section regarding the investment project itself. The most important part of an FIA application is where the foreign investor itemizes the various SIFN benefits and investment incentives it seeks to gain. This section is usually drafted by legal counsel. An FIA application for establishing a new investment project must also include necessary exhibits such as certificates of incorporation or good standing in the case of foreign corporate investors, nationality certificates in the case of foreign individual investors, statement of sources of funds, and powers of attorney. The FIA application and attachments must all be written in Chinese. Foreign investors usually request a bilingual binder containing English translations of these filings. It must be stressed that the FIA application is a legal document with representations and undertakings designed to induce the favorable consideration of the IC or its designated counterparts. Foreign investors, and its responsible persons in the case of foreign corporate investors, are liable for false statements in the FIA application. They can be prosecuted for criminal offenses on grounds of inducing inaccurate statement to be recorded by civil servants, for instance[9]. But such prosecution is extremely rare. However, false statements could still lead to rejection of the FIA application or revocation of the FIA, once granted. Similarly, if an FIA investor violated provisions of the SIFN or conditions to its FIA, the IC may suspend its repatriation privileges or revoke the entire investment project and all rights and privileges granted under its FIA[10]. In conclusion, the FIA application is neither a prospectus to offer securities to the public (which is subject to rigorous scrutiny by its regulatory authority), nor simply a business plan. Therefore, foreign investors who deem their FIA applications to be borderline cases should try to make their applications as persuasive as possible. Although the IC has a statutory deadline of two months to review each FIA application and make a final decision[11], it usually only takes four to six weeks to carry out these tasks. In addition, certain FIA applications may receive a fast track review pursuant to a policy adopted by the IC since 1988, if they meet several prerequisites. First, they should not involve activities on the negative list (see below). Second, they should not involve in-kind investment. Third, their investment projects should not be on an industry deemed substantially polluting by the government. Fourth, they may not include requests for tax incentives. Fifth, the total amount of investment involved in each application should not exceed NT$ 30 million. Sometimes, it takes a longer period for the IC to come to a final decision because of supplemental or inadequate fillings by the applicant, heavy work load on the IC and constituent agencies, and sheer difficulties of the issues involved. Prudent foreign investors and legal counsel usually submit very carefully crafted FIA applications, and follow up with these constituent agencies. This follow up is useful in responding to clarification and inquiries, eliminating adverse comments, familiarizing the officials with the investment in question, and controlling the time it takes for the FIA application to be scheduled for the commission-level hearing at the IC.

When a foreign direct investor seeks investment in a regulated industry (which is usually in the restricted area of the negative list), it should either directly seek special approval with the agency having primary jurisdiction over the regulated business, or request the IC to refer the application to the agency[12]. For instance, an FIA application for investment in a securities firm would have to be preceded by an approval with the SEC. Or, an FIA application to set up a "venture capital investment company" should be preceded by an application with the MOF for special approval. In such cases, the IC usually holds the FIA application until the relevant agencies advises the IC in writing to approve the application. Usually, special approvals or special permits are valid for only a short period of time, usually six months. This means that the FIA investor must secure all the certificates and licenses in order to set up the enterprise within this short period of time. The FIA investor may request a one-time extension of this deadline if it has a good cause for extension, such as requiring additional time to complete all preparations and procedures.The IC may set up a time limit for an FIA investor to implement its approved investment in the ROC by making an inward remittance[13]. Failure of the FIA investor to comply with this requirement may result in the cancellation of the FIA by the IC. However, if the FIA investor can demonstrate a reasonable cause for a delay, it may apply for an extension of the implementation deadline anytime before the actual deadline[14]. There is a rule of thumb for the length of time an FIA investor has to make the initial inward remittance[15]. For FIA amounts of NT$ 30 million or less, the deadline for implementation is three years. For FIA amounts between NT$ 30 million and NT$ 100 million, the deadline for implementation is four years, and for FIA amounts over NT$ 100 million, the deadline is five years. Under special circumstances, the deadline could even exceed five years, as long as there is a reasonable basis for such extension[16]. These special circumstances usually involve capital and technology intensive investments and the construction of sizeable plants.

If an FIA investor finds out after receiving the FIA that it cannot proceed further with the investment, it has two alternatives. First, it can transfer the investment from the original project to a new project that is not on the negative list. Second, it can apply to remit the original investment back to its home country[17]. In this second case, it must apply for the liquidation and dissolution of the FIA company before it is able to retrieve the original capital. Just as an FIA investor should be careful in following deadlines, and reviewing whether its investment is on the negative list, it should also be careful in reviewing the FIA letter from the IC to see if it has obtained complete approval of all the activities it seeks to engage in. Failure to obtain complete approval of the business scope of the enterprise could delay its incorporation. Also, carefully defining and confirming the business scope of the enterprise is important because the rights of the enterprise to engage in specific activities must derive from explicit enumeration of these rights in the FIA letter and the enterprise's article of incorporation. As a cardinal principle, the definition of the business scope of an enterprise should be both as specific and as broad as possible. It should be specific enough to include the desirable business activities, and it has to be broad enough to include the entire spectrum of profit-seeking activities of the enterprise.

Negative Listing

The negative listing policy for the ROC's foreign investment application procedure was promulgated by the Executive Yuan on May 4, 1988. This policy includes a list of business categories which are ineligible for investment by foreign nationals and/or overseas Chinese, as well as a list of business categories which are restricted for the same purposes. There is a total of 54 ineligible categories. Applications for investment in these categories are automatically rejected by the IC. There is a total of 55 restricted categories. Applications for investment in the restricted categories are subject to conditions or requirements according to applicable laws, regulations, and policies of the ROC.

The negative listing is intended to facilitate and increase transparency in the FIA application review process. Applications for foreign investment in categories not specified in the negative listing usually receive approval by the IC, although foreign investors are still required to apply for an FIA pursuant to the SIFN. This is so because the negative listing includes certain "catch all" segments which include business activities other than the obviously stated.

The negative listing policy was officially amended into the SIFN on May 26, 1989. As amended, the SIFN prohibits foreign investment in any of the following enterprises[18]:

1. enterprises in violation of public safety;
2. enterprises repugnant to good morals;
3. enterprises involving a high degree of pollution; and
4. enterprises that are legal monopolies or in which foreign investment is legally prohibited.

Also, the SIFN requires that foreign investment in any of the following enterprises be approved in advance by the agencies having primary jurisdiction over these enterprises and pursuant to regulations adopted by these agencies[19]:

1. public utilities;
2. financial and insurance enterprises;
3. news reporting and publishing enterprises; and
4. enterprises in which foreign investment is restricted by laws or regulations.

Foreign ownership of land is also subject to many important restrictions pursuant to the Land Law. This is not surprising, given the scarcity of land area in this tiny island. The main principle governing foreign ownership of land in Taiwan is reciprocity, that is, only foreign nationals from countries where ROC nationals may own real property can own real property in the ROC[20]. Still, many types of land cannot be transferred, encumbered or leased to foreign nationals. These include: farm land; forestry land; fishery land; pastoral land; hunting land; land with ponds to distill salt; mineral land (this restriction may be exempted in the case of a foreign investment receiving FIA); land from which waterways, rivers, or creeks originate; and land within military zone and border territories[21]. After having met reciprocity requirements and passed restrictions on the types of lands that cannot be owned by foreigners, a foreign investor wishing to buy or lease land in the ROC may do so only if the location and space of the land comply with laws and regulations of the local government and the land is for any of the following purposes: residence; shops and factories; churches; hospitals; foreign language schools for expatriates; embassies or meeting places for public-benefit, non-profit organizations; or graveyards[22]. Purchase or lease of land by foreign nationals is subject to approval of the relevant local government. In certain cases, the local government also must report the application to the Executive Yuan. If after the application, the foreign investor decides to modify the use of the land or seeks to transfer it, another approval is required[23].

V.   INCENTIVES AND RELEVANT PROGRAMS

Historically, the ROC government has not given any significant special treatment to foreign investment. Instead, it made a policy decision to provide the same incentives for both foreign and domestic investors. The only significant exception to this was article 16 of the now extinct Statute for the Encouragement of Investment (SEI), which allowed FIA investors to receive a reduced dividend withholding tax rate as opposed to non-FIA investors. This neutral policy has prevailed to this day. Investment projects, whether foreign or domestic, are encouraged on the basis of their merits.

Statute for Investment by Foreign Nationals (SIFN)

The SIFN claims to regulate the administration and protection of all foreign investment in the ROC[24]. However, not all forms of foreign investment fall within the scope of the SIFN. That is, some forms of foreign investment in Taiwan do not need to go through the FIA review process, and consequently, may not receive all the privileges and benefits under the FIA. For instance, neither the establishment of a ROC branch of a foreign company (with the exception of a manufacturing branch) nor the establishment of a representative office need to undergo the FIA process. Geographically speaking, the SIFN is only applicable to foreign investment made in the island of Taiwan. Expansion of the geographical scope of an investment requires further approval by the Legislative Yuan.[25]

Among the incentives for foreign investments approved by the IC under the SIFN are repatriation of annual net profit and capital investment, exemption from government expropriation, exemption from some of the Company Law's nationality requirements, and exemption from the requirement to issue shares to the public or to provide employees with preemptive rights to subscribe to newly offered shares. More specifically, under the SIFN, an FIA investor is entitled to the following benefits:

(a) Repatriation of annual net profits or interest derived from the investment, in foreign currency;

(b) Repatriation of capital investment and capital gains after one year from the start of business operations of the enterprise in the case of transfer of shares, reduction of capital, or dissolution of the enterprise;

(c) Exemption from government requisition and expropriation for 20 years from the start of business operations, and exemption from the statutory requirement of offering newly issued stocks to the public or to employees for subscription, as long as the foreign investors collectively hold 45 percent or more of the total capital of the invested enterprise; and

(d) Exemption from the Company Law's requirements on the ROC residency and nationality of the share holders, chairman of the board, and supervisors, the amount of investment by ROC nationals, and the places of meeting of the board of directors and shareholders of the invested enterprise.

Statute for Upgrading Industries (SUI)

The SEI was enacted in 1960 as a transitional program aimed at incorporating all government investment incentives into one legislation. It has been extended several times by amendment until late 1980s, when the government finally deemed it obsolete. The SEI received many criticisms before it was finally replaced. First, it was argued that the SEI's tax incentives made tax administration more difficult. Second, it was argued that the SEI only promoted growth in certain areas in the economy, especially manufacturing, without trying to balance the economy as a whole. As a result, the government thought of a new legislation which would encourage industries to upgrade into more capital and technology intensive companies able to make higher-end, more value-added products. The Statute for Upgrading Industries, the legislation which replaced SEI, was promulgated in 1991. The most important distinction between the SUI and the SEI is that the SUI claims to involve all domestic companies limited by shares and branches of foreign companies, which engage in certain functions such as research, development, massive export and marketing campaign, and pollution control which are considered to be conducive to upgrading the level of their industry[26]. Most of the incentives under the SUI were tax and duties incentives. The most important tax incentive under the SEI, five-year tax holiday, was not be retained in the SUI. In addition, the SUI imposes a dividend tax on branches of foreign companies, which were previously not required to pay branch profit tax[27].Under the SUI, many incentive programs are available for FDI enterprises, including:

- accelerated depreciation;
- investment tax credit between five percent and 30 percent for investment in automation machinery or technology, purchasing pollution control machinery, equipment or technology within five years, and investing in programs whose expenditures are incurred for research and development, training of employees, or building an international brand name[28];
- incentives for investment in "important technology projects" as classified by the IC, in the form of 20 percent tax credits; and
- income tax deferment on stock dividend distributed in connection with plant expansion or reinvestment project.

Science Park

The Statute for the Establishment and Administration of Science Based Industrial Parks (Park Statute) was promulgated in 1979 as a formal implementation of a proposal by the ROC government to attract high technology investments into the ROC. According to the Park Statute, the government may appoint suitable locations as sites for science parks. So far, only one science park, the Hsin Chu Science Based Industrial Park, has been established[29]. The Park Statute was enacted at a time when the ROC was starting to industriously develop a high technology industrial base. The Science Park is located in the Hsin Chu area, which is about 70 kilometers south of Taipei. It occupies about 2,100 hectares of land space, and hosts close to 100 high-tech companies engaged in areas such as electronics and information, precision instruments and equipment, computer and semiconductor design and manufacturing, biochemical engineering, and material science. As the Science Park was designed with the Silicon Valley of Northern California in mind, it contains standard factories and research faculties, pleasant environment, schools for the foreign born children of returnee Chinese scientists and engineers, two leading universities with a strong science emphasis in their curriculum, and even a research institution.

Similarities with the Silicon Valley go well beyond the physical appearances. Creating an investment environment where government regulation would be streamlined and government assistance maximized was an important theme in the creation of the Science Park. With that in mind, the Park Statute created the Science Industrial Park Administration (SIPA), a new organization under the National Science Council (NSC) of the Executive Yuan. The SIPA consolidates all company dealings with the government into one agency[30]. Thus, the SIPA administers the Park Statute, the SIFN, the SAFE, and other relevant statutes and regulations. It has generally taken a less bureaucratic approach in reviewing and regulating Science Park businesses.

In addition to the reasons outlined above, setting up high-tech investment projects in the Science Park is advantageous for yet another reason: the expiration of the SEI. The Park Statute provides for incentives similar to those of the SEI and which are not in the SUI. Moreover, the Park Statute does not have an expiration clause. Because of its enormous success, the Science Park is now experiencing some problems such as lack of space. Thus, while smaller operations oriented towards research and development can still be accommodated, the Science Park finds it harder now to house high-tech manufacturing plants requiring more space. The SIPA, NSC, and MOEA are all trying to find ways to expand the geographical space of the Science Park or to establish other science parks.

VI.   GAME PLAN

After the high rates of economic growth and liberalization of the 1980s, the ROC is yet going through another transition. This time, the ROC is transitioning from a manufacturing-based economy to one relying on high-tech industry and the services sector. Once more, public and private sectors of the economy are collaborating in a joint effort to bring the country into the 21st century as a fully developed economy. To that extent, following the foreign exchange liberalization, and the banking and securities markets reforms, the next step for the ROC economy to come full cycle is to bring the business decision making cores of the world into the country. This is where the concepts of "Regional Operations Center" and "Greater China" come into play.

Regional Operations Center

Regional Operations Centers are set up as local representatives of multinational enterprises directly under the latter but which controls all of the enterprise's operations in the region it is in charged of, and is fully integrated into the regional economy. A regional operations center is responsible for all subsidiaries, branches, or joint ventures its parent enterprise engages in. Most importantly, should it choose to expand its business operations in the region, a regional operations center has access to local financing. Under this set up, the parent multinational enterprise, which previously exercised direct control over all of its subsidiaries, branches, and joint ventures around the world, and was thus subject to the ups and downs of several economies, now becomes a company holding shares of a few regional profit centers around the world. The economic downturn of one specific region is less likely to affect the economic performance of the parent company because the latter has transferred some of the financial risks of its investments to local investors. In choosing a locale for setting up a regional operations center, some criteria to consider are: productivity of the country, its infrastructure, its market, local financing availability, the initial public offering (IPO) environment, and the regional network. Given these criteria, the ROC is probably one of the best locations for setting up regional operations centers in the Asia-Pacific region. First, the ROC has shown an impressive productivity for the past two decades. From 1976 to 1986, its growth rate averaged nine percent a year. From 1989 to 1990, despite worldwide economic depression, the ROC still maintained an average real growth rate of 6.7 percent. In 1991, the real growth rate escalated to 7.2 percent. In 1992, it was about 6.2 percent. Second, the ROC's economic and political infrastructure is increasingly approaching that of more advanced countries. The ROC already had a well developed manufacturing sector as early as the 1970s. In the late 1970s, it further fostered high-tech industries and the service sector, and in the mid-1980s, three waves of financial reform liberalized foreign exchange control, the banking industry, and the securities market. Throughout these changes, the ROC government has always been extremely favorable to foreign investment. Third, staggering economic growth in the past two decades created both a huge consumer market and the world largest foreign exchange reserve[31]. These two facts makes local financing extremely easy, despite restrictions in the not yet fully liberalized laws and regulations of the ROC.

Finally, with meaningful and peaceful dialogue, many tensions in the Western Pacific region are being gradually diminished and as a result, several markets in this area are being integrated into a regional economy. This integration involves primarily ethnic Chinese from Hong Kong, Taiwan, and certain provinces in the southeast part of Mainland China (particularly Guandong and Fujian), and is based on common culture and tradition as much as rational or purely economic considerations. Along with the geographical location of the ROC (which is situated in the middle of the Asia Pacific region), this integration provides for the regional network criteria mentioned above.

Platforms for "Greater China" Strategies

Another idea derived from the need to fully integrate the ROC into the developed world is to make the ROC into a platform for "Greater China" strategies.

Greater China is traditionally thought of as the business triangle formed by Taiwanese, Hong Kongnese, and Southeast Chinese entrepreneurs mentioned in the previous section. These business relationships have integrated their activities into a regional economy with a population of over 120 million and a gross domestic product of U.S. $320 billion[32]. While Taiwan and Hong Kong provide capital and technical expertise (thus developing the Mainland Chinese market and linking it to the world economy), Mainlanders provide local contact as well as cheap and abundant labor. However, in a much broader sense, Greater China could be understood to be the worldwide network of Chinese business, including primarily overseas Chinese communities in Southeast Asia, and the United States, but also including those communities in South America, and Europe. The business ties among entrepreneurs in these communities provide for a network which is more powerful than any created by a multinational enterprise.

VII.   SELECTED BIBLIOGRAPHY

Hsu, Paul S.P. *Prospects of American Companies Selecting Taiwan as Its Operation and Profit Center for Business Expansion in Asia Pacific Region*. Taipei: Lee and Li, Attorneys-at-Law, 1992.

Kao, John. *The Worldwide Web of Chinese Business"*. Harvard Business Review, March—April, 1993. pp. 24–36.

Liu, Lawrence S. *Financial Developments and Foreign Investment Strategies in Taiwan—A Legal and Policy Perspective"*. The International Lawyer, vol. 25, 1, Spring 1991. Section of International Law and Practice, American Bar Association.

Liu, Lawrence S. *The First Decade of Taiwan's Science Park—A Corporate Practitioner's Perspective. Investment for the Future. Science Park in Hong Kong*. Hong Kong: Society of Hong Kong Scholars, 1992. pp. 36–43.

Notes

[1] "Total Foreign and Overseas Chinese Investment Exceeding U.S. $ 12.3 billion," *Economic Daily News*, August 12, 1990, p.3.

[2] Inward Regulations, Article 4.

[3] Non-Governmental Outward Remittances Regulations, Article 5.

[4] Statute for Investment by Foreign Nationals, Article 7.

[5] Liu, Lawrence S. *Survey of Major Commercial Law Developments in the Republic of China: 1987–1988*," Chinese Yearbook of International Law and Affairs, Vol.7 (1987–88), pgs. 136–152.

[6] Regulations Governing the Review of Outward Investment and Outward Technical Cooperation, Article 3.

[7] Statute for Investment by Foreign Nationals, Article 13.

[8] SIFN, Article 7.

[9] SIFN, Article 20.

[10] SIFN, Article 22.

[11] SIFN, Article 8.

[12] SIFN, Article 8.

[13] SIFN, Article 9.

[14] SIFN, Article 9.

[15] "Key Points on the Treatment of Deadlines for complete Arrival of Funds for Investment by Foreign nationals and Overseas Chinese and Extension Thereof" Article 3.

[16] *Ibid*. Article 4.

[17] SIFN, Article 11

[18] 24. SIFN, Article 5.

[19] SIFN, Article 5.

[20] Land Law, Article 18.

[21] Land Law, Article 17.

[22] Land Law, Article 19.

[23] Land Law, Articles 20–23.

[24] SIFN, Article 1

[25] SIFN, Article 23.

[26] SUI, Article 3.

[27] SUI, Article 4.

[28] SUI, Article 7.

[29] Park Statute, Article 1.

[30] Park Statute, Articles 5 and 6.

[31] By June of 1993, the ROC's foreign exchange reserve amounted to U.S. $ 86.6 billion.

[32] Hsu, Paul S.P. *Prospects of American Companies Selecting Taiwan as Its Operation and Profit Center for Business Expansion in Asia Pacific Region*. Taipei: Lee and Li, Attorneys-at-Law, 1992. p.2.

GOING INTERNATIONAL IN INDONESIA

Darrell R. Johnson[1]

THE PURPOSE of this Chapter is to provide an overview of pertinent laws and regulations affecting foreign investment and business operations in Indonesia. This summary is not intended to be a substitute for specific advice in the case of an actual investment, and the usual admonition applies that the advice of counsel should be sought for specific transactions.

Indonesia offers a number of different alternatives by which foreign businesses may operate in Indonesia. These may be placed in four broad categories: *(i)* equity investments; *(ii)* foreign oil company branch offices; *(iii)* technical assistance and licensing arrangements; and (iv) representative offices.

I. EQUITY INVESTMENTS

General

There are two different regimes by which foreign investors may make equity investments in Indonesian companies: establishment of an Indonesian limited liability company under the Foreign Investment Law and establishment of certain types of Indonesian limited liability financial companies under regulations issued by the Department of Finance.

For all types of manufacturing companies and most types of service companies, the Foreign Investment Law is the method of foreign investment in Indonesia. Joint venture banks, insurance companies and finance companies are service industries that are not regulated by BKPM and are not subject to the Foreign Investment Law, but are subject to the jurisdiction of the Department of Finance. Finally, foreign oil companies are permitted to establish branch offices in Indonesia if they have signed contracts with the state oil company, PN Pertamina. In 1968, foreign banks were allowed to establish branches in Indonesia, but licenses are no longer issued.

Foreign Investment Law Companies

As noted, most foreign investments are made pursuant to Indonesia's Foreign Investment Law, Law No.1, 1967 (January 10, 1967), as amended by Law No. 11, 1970 (August 7, 1970) (collectively, the "FIL"). The FIL has been supplemented by numerous government regulations, the most recent of which was issued in October 1993 and is known as the October Package.

Initial Steps

Verification of the Negative Investment List

The first issue a foreign investor must address is whether the Indonesian Government will permit an investment in a desired line of business. As a general rule, all business sectors are open for foreign investment unless specifically prohibited. For this purpose, the Government publishes a Negative Investment List, known by its Indonesian initials as the "DNI". A copy of the most recent DNI was issued in June of 1993, as Presidential Decree No. 54 of 1993, regarding the List of Business Sectors Closed for Capital Investment (June 10, 1993) and is attached as Appendix A. The DNI specifies the business areas in which foreign investment is prohibited, restricted or conditioned. A business area is open for foreign investment if it is not listed in the DNI, subject only to any specific controls issued by a Government department that may have jurisdiction over the activity concerned.

Selection of an Indonesian Partner

In most cases, foreign investors are required to have a co-investor, commonly referred to as a partner. The selection of a partner is a critical decision, perhaps the most significant the foreign investor will make. The foreign investor is well-advised to conduct a thorough partner search before opening discussions with one or more proposed partners, to avoid raising expectations that may not be met. Once the selection of a proposed partner has been made, the foreign investor must then negotiate a joint venture agreement with the local partner, which sets out the terms and conditions of their business relationship. As a business matter, this document should be agreed, finalized and signed before the investors engage the approval process of the Indonesian Government.

PT Company

A foreign investment approved under the FIL must take the form of an Indonesian limited liability company, known as a "Perseroan Terbatas" or "PT." When this company is established and licensed under the FIL, it is often known as a "PMA" (the Indonesian acronym for foreign capital investment) or "joint venture" company. This term is used loosely: the PT is not a joint venture in the American sense of a temporary business relationship for a specific project, but refers to the corporation to be established.

Required Business Forms for the Investors

A foreign investor must be a limited liability company, whereas the Indonesian investor can be a limited liability company (wholly-owned by Indonesian nationals), an Indonesian individual, or an Indonesian cooperative.

Model I Application

In order to initiate a foreign investment under the FIL it is necessary to file a Model I Investment Application with the Indonesian Capital Investment Coordinating Board (known by its Indonesian initials as "BKPM"). The October Package revised the Model I Application, a copy of which is attached as Appendix B.

With certain exceptions noted below, all approved FIL investments require the foreign investor to have an Indonesian partner, both of which must sign the Model I Application. The Investment Application identifies these participants, describes the proposed project, including the intended name of the company, estimates the company's proposed annual production (or if the company is a service business, its projected annual sales), sets out the land area, if any, required for the company's operations, and specifies the number of proposed foreign and Indonesian employees. In addition, the investors must indicate the amount of the total foreign investment, which includes not only the intended equity capital, but the foreign loans to be obtained for the company. The application must also indicate the shareholding percentages of the foreign and Indonesian participants, the projected time schedule to implement the investment, the proposed date for the commencement of commercial production and the power requirements for the project.

Both the Indonesian and the foreign investors are required to submit certain attachments with the Model I Application. For the Indonesian investors, the attachments are a copy of its articles of association, if a company, a record of its basic rules, if a cooperative, or a copy of the investor's identification card, if an individual, and in any case a copy of the investor's tax registration number. The foreign participant must supply a copy of its articles of incorporation, in English or Indonesian. In addition, the investors must attach a flow chart of the manufacturing process, or the proposed company's business activities if the investment is in the services sector, a draft or executed joint venture agreement (in English or Indonesian), and a power of attorney if the application is not signed by the investor. The power of attorney is invariably required for the foreign investor.

Minimum Investment Levels

General Rule

As a matter of policy, the Indonesian Capital Investment Board requires an investment level of at least U.S. $ 1 million. Article 1 of Government Regulation No. 50 of 1993 on the Requirements for Share Ownership in Foreign Capital Investment

Companies (October 23, 1993) ("GR 50") provides that "approval . . . shall be granted" if the investment amount is not less than U.S. $ 1 million. It should be emphasized that the foreign investment consists of both equity capital and foreign loans. BKPM does not impose strict debt equity ratios and, except as noted below, there is no minimum paid-in-capital requirement. The investors thus have considerable latitude to decide how much of their total investment will be direct equity.

Exceptions

(i) Export, Supply and Service Companies: Article 3 of GR 50 provides an investment level of U.S. $250,000 may be approved if either one of the following applies:

(a) The PMA company is labor-intensive, with at least 50 workers, and:

(i) at least 65 percent of the company's production is for export; or

(ii) the company produces basic materials, complementary materials, or semi-finished products or components for other industries;[1] or

(b) the company is engaged in legally permitted services.

If the FIL company meets one of the conditions in sub-paragraph (a), the Indonesian partner on establishment must own at least five percent of the company's equity. If the FIL company is a service company within the meaning of sub-paragraph (b), the Indonesian investor must own at least 20 percent of the company's equity on establishment. [*See* GR 50, Articles 3(2) and 3(3).]

Examples of permitted investment opportunities in the services sector include engineering and management consulting. Indonesian foreign investment law companies (and foreign companies generally) are not allowed to engage in trading activities, which are restricted to Indonesian nationals and companies (and other business forms) owned wholly by them. Trading activities include the retail sale of goods and, with limited exceptions, the retail sale of services, and distribution activities. In the case of distribution, BKPM allows a foreign investment law company to establish a distribution subsidiary which in turn must be approved by BKPM and follow the application procedure described above. [*See* Government Regulation No. 19 of 1988 (November 21, 1988) Regarding Amendment to Government Regulation No. 36 of 1977 on the Termination of Foreign Trading Activities, as implemented by Minister of Trade Decree No. 376/Kp/XI/1988 Regarding Amendment of Minister of Trade Decree No. 77/Kep/III/1978 on Limited Trading Activities by Investment Production Companies (November 21, 1988).] Again, this distribution subsidiary must itself have an Indonesian joint venture partner. The subsidiary can distribute only the products manufactured by its parent company. It cannot distribute imported products or products manufactured by other companies in Indonesia.

(ii) Large Scale Companies Wholly-Owned by Foreigners: The minimum equity investment is U.S. $ 50 million. (*See* the discussion below.)

(iii) Large Scale Supply Companies Wholly-Owned by Foreigners: The minimum equity investment is U.S. $ 2 million. (*See* the discussion below.)

Investment Incentives

An approved foreign investment law company is provided a range of investment incentives and guarantees by the Indonesian Government. The FIL and BKPM policy permit access to foreign exchange for the free remittance of: *(i)* dividends proportional to foreign ownership; *(ii)* proceeds from the sale of shares to Indonesian nationals; *(iii)* foreign loan payments (principal and interest); *(iv)* compensation in the case of nationalization; and *(v)* repatriation of invested capital in case of liquidation. It must be emphasized there are no foreign exchange controls in Indonesia and these guarantees are thus insurance against their adoption.

Exemptions or reductions are also granted from import duties and value added taxes for certain imports related to the investment. These include: *(i)* a 100 percent exemption on import duties and an indefinite postponement of value added taxes on capital equipment for the approved project (the capital goods being subject to a limit equal to the amount specified in the approved Model I Application); *(ii)* a 50 percent reduction on import duties on support and auxiliary equipment; *(iii)* a complete exemption, for two years' production, from import duties on raw materials, if the import duty is five percent or less, and otherwise a 50 percent reduction; *(iv)* a 100 percent exemption from import duties on consumable materials for one year's operations and on raw materials for one year's production; and *(v)* a total exemption from import duties on personal effects for expatriate personnel, excluding liquor, tobacco, and like items.

Term of Investment Approval

The foreign investment license granted by BKPM is for a period of 30 years from the date of commencement of commercial production. [*See* Government Regulation No. 24 of 1986 on the Validity Period of the Licence for Foreign Investment Companies (May 6, 1986), as amended by Government Regulation No.9 of 1993 Regarding the Period of the Licence for Foreign Capital Investment Companies (February 17, 1993).] This term may be extended at the discretion of the Government. As the FIL is only now approaching its 30-year anniversary, the Government has not yet extended foreign investment licenses, but the Indonesian investment community does not foresee any issue in this connection.

Maximum Foreign Ownership and Divestment Requirements

General Rule

The general rule is that the foreign investor may own only a maximum of 80 percent of the equity, which must be reduced to 49 percent or less within 20 years after the PT's commencement of commercial production. However, the Government has gradually liberalized its limits on foreign ownership as part of its general deregulatory policy, the most recent effort being the October Package.

Specific Exceptions to Limitations on Foreign Equity Participation:

(i)   Export and Supply Companies: As noted above, export or supply companies can own as much as 95 percent of the PT's capital on incorporation. [*See* GR 50, Article 3(2).]

(ii)   Service Companies: A service company must have an Indonesian partner that owns at least 20 percent of the equity on establishment. [*See* GR 50, Article 3 (3).]

(iii) 100 Percent Foreign Ownership: In certain cases, 100 percent foreign ownership is permitted. This is permitted where:

   (a) the foreign investor undertakes a minimum *equity* investment of U.S. $ 50 million; [*See* GR 50, Article 4(1)a. (emphasis supplied).];

   (b) the foreign investor undertakes a minimum *equity* investment of U.S. $ 2 million and the goods produced are raw materials, semi-finished goods or components for supply to other factories in Indonesia; [*See* GR 50, Article 5(1). (emphasis supplied).];

   (c) the investment is located in one of the following 15 designated under-developed provinces of Indonesia: Irian Jaya, Maluku, East Timor, East Nusa Tenggara, West Nusa Tenggara, South Sulawesi, Southeast Sulawesi, Central Sulawesi, North Sulawesi, East Kaliman-tan, Central Kalimantan, South Kalimantan, West Kalimantan, Bengkulu and Jambi; [*See* GR 50, Article 4(1) b.];

   (d) the investment is located in a region being developed by Indonesia in cooperation with a third country or countries. (An example of the latter case is the so-called "Golden Triangle" being developed by Singapore, Malaysia, and Indonesia in the area demarcated by Johor, Batam Island, and Singapore). [*See* GR 50, Article 4(1) c.]; and

   (e) the foreign investment law company is located in a bonded zone or has export production entrepots (EPTE) status. [*See*, GR 50, Article 6(1).] Pursuant to Government Regulation No. 22 of 1986, Regarding Bonded Zones (May 6, 1986), a bonded zone is equivalent to a special customs area. An EPTE is an individual industrial location, such as a factory or building, which produces for export and which has applied for and received the right to receive special customs, tax and import treatment. [*See* Minister of Finance Decree No. 855 KMK.01/1993 Regarding Export Production Enterpots (EPTE) (October 23, 1993), issued as part of the October Package.]

Specific Divestment Requirements:

(i)   Export and Supply Companies with an Approved Foreign Investment of U.S. $250,000: If either type of company commences business with five percent or more local equity, the foreign investor must divest to 80 percent within 10 years. [*See* GR 50, Article 3(2).] Article 3(2) of GR 50 is silent on whether the foreign investor must divest to 49 percent within 20 years, per the general rule.

(ii) Service Companies: This type of company follows the general rule, where foreign divestment to at least 49 percent is required within 20 years. [*See* GR 50, Article 3(3).]

(iii) Large-Scale Companies and Companies Located in Remote Provinces or in Regional Development Zones: For companies with U.S. $ 50 million in equity or located in remote provinces or in regional development zones, the foreign investor is required to divest to not more than 49 percent within 20 years, beginning 10 years after the commencement of commercial production. [*See* GR 50, Article 4(2).]

(iv) Supply Companies with an Approved Foreign Investment of U.S. $ 2 million: For these companies, the foreign investor must divest to 49 percent within 20 years, beginning 10 years after the commencement of commercial production. [*See* GR 50, Articles 5(3) and 5(4).]

(v) Companies Located in Bonded Zones and EPTE Companies: The foreign investor in this type of company must divest to 80 percent within 20 years, beginning 10 years after commencement of commercial production. In other words, the foreign investor in this type of company may retain majority control indefinitely. [*See* GR 50, Article 6.]

In all cases, divestment, may be achieved by a sale of shares to private parties or through Indonesia's capital markets. [*See* GR 50, Article 7.] In addition, Article 4(2) of the Elucidation of GR 50 provides that a foreign investor can satisfy divestment requirements if it sells shares to the International Finance Corporation, the Asian Development Bank or the Islamic Development Bank.[2]

A close review of the foregoing rules indicates some policy positions, and also possible anomalies, that have yet to be clarified by the Indonesian Government. One apparent incongruity is that it appears that supply companies can be formed with as little as U.S. $250,000 in total investment, and the foreign investor is not required to divest majority control at any time, whereas the same company formed with a U.S. $2 million investment requires the foreign investor to divest within 20 years, beginning 10 years after the commencement of business. [*Compare* GR 50, Article 3(3) with GR 50, Articles 5(3) and 5(4).] While Article 3 does not specifically provide that the general divestment rule is not applicable, there is no mention there of any further divestment requirement, whereas other Articles of GR 50 are quite specific. Further, Article 3(3) is specific that service companies must have Indonesian majority control within 20 years and it seems the Indonesian Government would have specifically imposed that requirement—had it intended to do so—on other types of companies regulated by Article 3.

Further, companies wholly-owned at the outset by foreign investors must begin divestment earlier (within 10 years) than companies that begin business with Indonesian partners. [*Compare* GR 50, Article 2 with GR 50, Article 4(3) and Article 5(4).] This may be seen as a policy decision to allow 100 percent ownership for only a limited time. Finally, it will be seen that 100 percent foreign-owned companies located in bonded zones and EPTE companies may maintain majority control indefinitely, having only to divest to 20 percent within 20 years. The obvious policy consideration is to encourage the formation of export-oriented companies. As further encouragement, these companies are permitted to sell 25 percent of their production domestically (except to companies located in bonded zones and to EPTE companies), to allow them access to Indonesia's large domestic market.) [(*See* Article 7(2) of Minister of Trade Decree No. 312/Kp/X/1993 Regarding the Entry of Goods Into and the Release of Goods from Export-Oriented Production Entrepots (EPTE) (October 23, 1993) and Article 7(2) of Minister of Trade Decree No. 313/KP/X/93 Regarding the Entry of Goods Into and the Release of Goods from Bonded Zones (October 23, 1993).]

Investment Application Approval

After an evaluation of the Model I Application, BKPM submits the application to the President of the Republic of Indonesia for approval. Assuming the application is approved, BKPM so notifies the applicants. The Notification of Presidential Approval is known as an "SPPT" and is in effect a temporary business license that permits the investors to go forward with their investment.

Post-Approval Matters

Execution of Articles of Association

After the issuance of the SPPT, the investors are permitted to execute and file the Articles of Association for their company with the Indonesian Department of Justice. This document is executed in notarial deed form by an Indonesian notary. The usual time necessary to complete the Department of Justice's review is between six and 12 months. Only after the Department of Justice has approved the Articles of Association does the PT achieve limited liability. Before that period, the parties operate as a company-in-formation. In legal effect, the investors have a partnership, and for acts taken in the company's name, the shareholders are jointly and severally responsible. Many companies engage in business during this period by acquiring land, constructing manufacturing plants, and so on. They are permitted to do so by virtue of having executed the Articles and submitting them to the Department of Justice, and having obtained the SPPT from BKPM. After the Articles are approved by the Department of Justice, the shareholders' liability ceases, but the company's managers continue to be personally liable for the company's acts until such time as the Articles are filed at the district court of the PT's domicile and are published in the State Gazette. Publication of the Articles of Association in the State Gazette usually takes place more than one year after Department of Justice approval, and the directors' liability continues for this period. Typically, the shareholders and/or the company indemnifies the directors for acts taken in good faith during this period.

All Indonesian companies have a life limited to 75 years, but this term is renewable by the Department of Justice.

Additional Permits

After the SPPT is issued, BKPM also issues additional permits and licenses. This process occurs concurrently while the Department of Justice reviews and approves the

Articles of Association. Those permits and approvals include the following: (a) master list approval, allowing the PT exemptions or reductions from import duties and indefinite postponement of value added tax and sales tax on luxury goods, on the importation of listed capital goods and related materials; (b) a limited import license (APIT), permitting the import of capital goods; (c) a manpower utilization plan (RPTKA) allowing expatriate employment, and (d) a permanent operating license (IUT). The IUT is issued when the PT is certified ready for the commencement of commerical production. [*See* Article 3, State Minister of Investment Funds Mobilization/Chairman of the Capital Investment Coordinating Board Decree No. 15/SK/1993 Regarding the Application Procedures for Domestic Capital Investment and Foreign Capital Investment (October 23, 1993).]

The local office of BKPM issues work permits for expatriate employees, and other regional offices of the Government also issue various permits and licenses.

Other Notable Measures Contained in the October Package

The October Package relaxes custom procedures for goods moving to and from bonded zones and EPTE companies, and permits companies located in bonded zones, and EPTE companies, the right to sell a portion of their production in the domestic market equal to as much as 25 percent of their export production. Again, these sales may not be made to companies located in bonded zones or to EPTE companies. Although existing companies both located inside and outside industrial estates may also apply for EPTE status under the October Package, new companies wishing to gain EPTE status are required to locate their factories in an industrial estate. This is consistent with the Government's encouragement for foreign investment law companies (and domestic investment law companies) to locate their manufacturing facilities in industrial estates.

The October Package also simplifies the procedure that must be followed by foreign investment law companies to complete an environmental impact study. Whereas each company was previously required to produce its own environmental impact study, now, under the October Package, only one such environmental study is required for several companies implementing projects in the same geographical location, as long as certain other requirements are additionally satisfied.

The October Package simplifies import procedures and reduces or eliminates customs duties and surcharge customs duties on over 200 items. The goods affected include automobiles and automobile parts, electronic components, steel, pharmaceuticals, and agricultural products.

Department of Finance Companies

General

The Department of Finance allows the formation and operation of certain types of finance companies. These include joint venture banks, finance companies, securities companies and insurance companies. Because these types of financial institutions are not formed pursuant to the FIL, the repatriation and other guarantees and facilities provided to FIL companies are not furnished to these entities. As these are service companies, the usual facilities for manufacturing companies, such as duty free import privileges, are not important. However, these companies do assume foreign exchange risk, should foreign exchange controls be adopted, and do not obtain other types of investment guarantees.

Specific Financial Insitutions

Joint Venture Banks

Joint venture banks are licensed pursuant to Minister of Finance Decree No. 1068/KMK.00/1988 Regarding the Establishment of Consolidated Banks (October 27, 1988) ("MOF Decree No. 1068"), MOF Decree 1068 provides that a joint venture bank may be formed by a foreign and Indonesian investors, if the foreign bank concerned *(i)* has a representative office in Indonesia and is a major financial institution in its country of domicile and *(ii)* the country in which the foreign bank is established allows Indonesian financial institutions to be established.

The joint venture bank must be established primarily for export credits. Within 12 months after the joint venture bank is established, at least 50 percent of its total loan portfolio must consist of export credits.

The authorized capital of the joint venture bank must be at least Rp. 50 billion (approximately U.S. $24 million). The Indonesian partner, which itself must be a bank, must have a minimum equity of 15 percent. The maximum foreign equity is thus 85 percent. The Indonesian bank must also be certified as financially sound by Bank Indonesia, Indonesia's central bank.

The joint venture can only open office in seven of Indonesia's principal cities: Jakarta, Medan, Bandung, Semarang, Surabaya, Denpasar, and Ujung Pandang.

MOF Decree 1068 does not specify any divestment requirements and provides that divestment is subject to agreement between the investors.

Finance Companies

Indonesian joint venture finance companies are permitted by Presidential Decree No. 61 of 1988 Regarding Financial Institutions (December 20, 1988) ("PD 61") and Minister of Finance Decree No.1251/KMK.013/1988 Regarding Stipulation on the Operation of Financial Institutions (December 20, 1988) ("MOF Decree 1251"), as amended by Minister of Finance Decree No. 1256/KMK.00/1989 Regarding the Amendment of Stipulations on Securities Trading Companies in Minister of Finance Decree No. 1251 of 1988 on the Realization of Financial Institutions (November 18, 1989) ("MOF Decree 1256"), as revoked by Minister of Finance Decree No. 1548/KMK.013/1990 Regarding Capital Markets (December 4, 1990) ("MOF Decree 1548"). Finance companies may engage in five different types of activities: leasing, venture capital, factoring, credit card finance, and consumer finance. Article 9 of MOF Decree 1251 provides that these activities may be carried out by three types of institutions: banks, non-bank financial institutions (i.e., merchant banks), and fincance companies, including joint ventures. If the joint venture finance company wishes to engage in only leasing or venture capital, the minimum paid-up capital must be not less than Rp. 10 billion (approximately U.S. $4.8 million). If the joint venture company is to engage in only factoring, credit card finance or consumer finance, the paid-up capital must be at least Rp. 8 billion (approximately U.S. $3.8 million). Finally, if the joint venture finance company is to engage in more than one kind of financing activity, for example, factoring and leasing, its paid-up must be not less than Rp. 15 billion (approximately U.S. $7.1 million).

Securities Companies

Joint venture securities companies are permitted to be formed by MOF Decree 1256 and MOF Decree 1548. Securities companies are permitted to engage in underwriting, securities trading and brokering and investment management. The minimum paid-up capital is Rp. 10 billion (approximately U.S. $4.8 million) for a joint venture underwriting company, with a minimum net adjusted working capital of Rp 500 million (approximately U.S. $239,000). For securities trading and brokering joint venture companies, and for joint venture investment management companies, the minimum paid-up capital is Rp 1 billion (approximatley U.S. $477,000), and the minimum net adjusted working capital is Rp 200 million (approximately U.S. $96,000). There are no divestment requirements for these companies, but the minimum Indonesian equity percentage on formation is 15 percent.

Joint Venture Insurance Companies

The Department of Finance allows joint venture insurance companies to be established in Indonesia, pursuant to Law No. 2 of 1992 Regarding the Insurance Business (February 11, 1992) (the "Insurance Law"), as implemented by Government Regulation No. 73 of 1992 Regarding Insurance Business Operations (October 30, 1992) ("GR 73") and Minister of Finance Decree No. 223/KMK.017/1992 Regarding licensing of Insurance Companies and Re-insurance Companies (February 26, 1992) ("MOF Decree 223"). Under the Insurance Law, GR 73 and MOF Decree No. 223, joint venture companies can be formed to engage in the insurance business and the insurance support business. The insurance business consists of casualty loss insurance, life insurance, and re-insurance. The insurance support business is limited to insurance brokerage, re-insurance brokerage and insurance loss adjustment, actuarial consultancy and insurance agency. Article 6(3) of GR 73 provides that the total foreign equity of a joint venture insurance company may not exceed 80 percent of its paid-up capital. The minimum paid-up capital required for a joint venture life insurance company is Rp.4.5 billion (approximately U.S. $ 2.1 million), for a joint venture casualty loss insurance company, Rp 15 billion (approximately U.S. $ 7.2 million), for a joint venture re-insurance company, Rp 30 billion (approximately U.S. $ 14.2 million) and for a joint venture insurance brokerage company and a joint venture re-insurance brokerage company, Rp 3 billion (approximately U.S. $ 1.5 million) While neither the Insurance Law nor GR 73 provides any divestment requirement, under MOF Decree 223, the foreign owner must divest to a minority position of not more than 49 percent within 20 years.

Application Procedures

The application procedures for each of the above types of companies are generally similar, yet each differs somewhat from the others. A description of the application procedures for finance companies will provide the reader with a general overview of how these types of companies are formed. MOF Decree 1251 provides that the formation process must begin with an application form specified by the Department of Finance. Attached to the application form must be seven separate documents, as follows:

(i)   The deed of establishment of the company.

(ii)   A receipt of the company's paid-in capital issued by a bank in Indonesia.

(iii)   An example of the financing contract to be used.

(iv)   An indication of the Board members of the company (though not specified, this should include members of both the Board of Directors and Board of Commissioners.)

(v)   The company's tax identification number.

(vi)   The company's balance sheet.

(vii)   A copy of the joint venture agreement between the foreign and Indonesian shareholders.

Because the deed of establishment (i.e., articles of association) of the joint venture finance company must be enclosed with the application, the license application procedure varies substantially from the FIL. In the case of a FIL company, Government approval is first obtained for the investment and then the company is formed; in the case of a joint venture finance company, the company is formed first and then obtains an operating license. The investors must thus first form and fund the company without knowing whether their application will be approved, and the Indonesian Department of Justice must first approve the articles of association before it knows that the technical department concerned, in this case is the Department of Finance, will approve the company. If the Department of Finance does not issue an operating license, the company would have to be liquidated, a time-consuming process.

The operating license for a finance company remains in effect for as long as the company is operative. [*See* MOF Decree 1251, Article 14(2).] As will be noted from the discussion above, this differs from the FIL, which limits the foreign investment license to a renewable 30 years.

Article 13(1) (g) of MOF Decree 1251 addresses the divestment issue. It indicates that the joint venture agreement must reflect the "direction toward Indonesianization" to be taken by the company. Unlike divestment procedures under the FIL, there is neither a time limit nor a requirement that majority control be surrendered to Indonesian shareholders.

II. BRANCHES OF FOREIGN OIL COMPANIES

A foreign oil company which executes a production sharing contract for oil and gas exploration or production in Indonesia with PN Pertamina, the Indonesian national oil company, is permitted to open a branch office in Indonesia by virtue of the contract. The branch office is permitted to employ both expatriate and Indonesian personnel and is subject to Indonesian income tax on its Indonesian operations and to Indonesian withholding tax on after-tax profits remitted abroad. These are the only branch offices of foreign companies that are now permitted to be opened in Indonesia.

III. TECHNICAL SERVICES AGREEMENTS AND
LICENSING AGREEMENTS

Technical service agreements and licensing agreements are often entered into by Indonesian companies and foreign companies. Pursuant to a technical assistance agreement, a foreign company agrees to provide expert manpower to an Indonesian company to assist it with its Indonesian operations. The foreign personnel become employees of the Indonesian company and are paid by the Indonesian company. The foreign company has no business presence in Indonesia and, importantly, also does not have a permanent establishment in Indonesia for Indonesian tax purposes, at least by virtue of the technical assistance relationship. In most of these transactions, certain residual employment ties are maintained between the seconded employee and the foreign company. Such ties may include stock option rights, pension fund benefits and the like. The employment relationship between the Indonesian employer and the seconded employee, and the protection that relationship provides to the foreign corporation from permanent establishment status, appears to be respected notwithstanding such residual ties.

The foregoing does not mean that the foreign corporation is free from tax on the technical assistance fees it receives. If technical assistance is provided in Indonesia to the Indonesian company, fees paid to the foreign company will be subject to Indonesian withholding tax. The tax rate is 20 percent of the gross proceeds remitted, subject to reduction if the foreign recipient is in a country that has a tax treaty with Indonesia. If the foreign corporation performs services for the Indonesian company solely outside Indonesia, fees should not be subject to Indonesian withholding tax. Under Article 26 of the Income Tax Law, Law No. 7 of 1983 (December 30, 1983), fees for services provided outside Indonesia are not subject to withholding. If part of the services are provided both within and outside Indonesia, the tax authorities tend to treat the fees attributable solely to the services provided in-country and subject the entire amount to tax.

Foreign companies also license technology, trade names and trade marks to Indonesian companies. All fees paid on such licenses are subject to Indonesian withholding tax under the same rate mentioned above. The licensing of such technology and related intellectual property does not create a permanent establishment for the foreign company in Indonesia.

In many cases, technical assistance agreements and license agreements are used in conjunction with foreign equity investments. A PMA manufacturing entity may receive a technology license from its foreign shareholder and enter into a technical assistance agreement to receive technical advice on the use of that technology, via seconded employees to the Indonesian company. There is no prohibition on these arrangements under Indonesian law. Such arrangements allow the foreign investor, or often an affiliate, to receive income from the Indonesian entity, the expense of which may be deducted by the Indonesian entity against its Indonesian income tax. The Indonesian tax authorities may view such arrangements as disguised dividends and disallow the deduction in appropriate cases.

IV. REPRESENTATIVE OFFICES

General

A number of Indonesian Government Departments permit the formation of representative offices. Each of these representative offices requires a license from the Department concerned and none (with one exception) may engage in any profit-making activity. The purpose of a representative office is only to represent the foreign company and its business activities. The sole exception is a representative office licensed by the Department of Public Works which is permitted to engage in construction activity for profit, provided it forms what is known as a "joint operation" with an Indonesian contracting company licensed as a contractor by the Department of Public Works.

The Departments which presently issue representative office licenses are:

(i) the Department of Trade (for manufacturing and trading companies), pursuant to Minister of Trade Decree No. 78/KP/1978 Regarding Provisions on the Licensing of Representatives of Foreign Trading Companies (March 9, 1978);

(ii) the Department of Public Works (for construction companies) pursuant to Minister of Public Works Decree No. 50/PRT/1991 Regarding the Licensing of Representative Offices of Foreign Construction Service Companies (February 7, 1991);

(iii) Bank Indonesia (for banks) pursuant to Bank Indonesia Circular Letter No. 5/81/UPPB/PpB Regarding Provisions of Foreign Bank Representative Offices (August 16, 1972), as amended by Bank Indonesia Circular Letter No.11/4/UPPK Regarding the Reporting of Loans, Guarantees and Other Investment Funds Made by the Legal Entity or Individual Abroad to Parties in Indonesia (October 8, 1978);

(iv) the Directorate General of Sea Communications (for shipping companies) pursuant to Minister of Communications No.KM.80/1988 regarding General

Agents and Representative Offices of Foreign Shipping Companies (November 21, 1988);

(v)   the Directorate General of Air Communications (for airlines), pursuant to Director General of Air Communications Decree No. SKEP/02/I/85 Regarding Conditions and Provisions of an Undertaking of General Sales Agent (January 9, 1985); and

(vi) BKPM (For regional representative offices), pursuant to Presidential Decree No.53 of 1987 Regarding Foreign Company Representative Offices (December 24, 1987), as implemented by Chairman of the Indonesian Capital Investment Coordinating Board Decree No. 01/SK/1988 Regarding the Provisions of the Implementation of Presidential Decree No.53 of 1987 Regarding Foreign Company Representative Offices (February 10, 1988).

Among the most common type of representative office is that licensed by the Department of Trade. Although the licensing procedures of each of the various Departments differ, the Department of Trade's procedure is illustrative. In order to qualify for a Department of Trade representative office license the company must manufacture or trade products. The representative office, however, may only engage in market promotion and other activities in support of this business activity in Indonesia. It may not conclude contracts itself.

The first step to form a representative office is to file a letter of intent with the Department of Trade. This letter informs the Department of Trade of the company's intent to establish a representative office in Indonesia, and encloses an application with a number of attachments:

(i)   a letter of appointment, specifying the name of the representative of the foreign company, his foreign address, his Indonesian address, his proposed activities and term of appointment. This letter must be legalized by the Chamber of Commerce in the country of the foreign company and addressed to the Department of Trade;

(ii) a curriculum vitae of the proposed representative must be enclosed with the application, together with his statement addressed to the Department of Trade, confirming he will not engage in trading activities; and

(iii) a reference letter from the local Indonesian Embassy or Consulate in the country of the foreign company concerned.

The licensing process takes approximately two months to complete and the license, when issued, has a renewable term of two years.

There are numerous further details and formalities beyond the scope of this Chapter that must be complied with in order to finalize the application process and to comply with immigration and work permit formalities.

V.   NOTE ON INDONESIAN TAXATION

All companies operating in Indonesia are subject to Indonesian tax on their net profits, pursuant to the Income Tax Law. This Law is modeled on the U.S. tax law, including the latter's self-assessment tax system. Indonesian taxes are graduated to a maximum marginal rate of 35 percent of net income. However, the maximum rate becomes applicable at the level of approximately U.S. $ 25,000. In addition, dividends and after tax profits are subject to Indonesian withholding tax at the rate of 20 percent. The rate of withholding is subject to reduction if the foreign recipient is domiciled or resident in a country that has a tax treaty with Indonesia. Typically, dividends tax rates are reduced to 15 percent. Payments to foreign companies for royalties, technical assistance fees and the like are also subject to Indonesian withholding tax at the rate of 20 percent, if the services are provided within Indonesia. This rate is also subject to tax treaty reduction, typically to 10 percent.

Indonesia also has a value added tax system which imposes a 10 percent value added tax on the purchases of goods and services and on imported goods. An additional sales tax is applicable to luxury goods.

Indonesian taxpayers are also obliged to withhold tax on the payment for services within Indonesia, at rates ranging from nine percent to 15 percent, and to withhold personal income tax from employees' wages.

VI. CONCLUSION

Indonesia has made vigorous efforts to deregulate its economy and to attract foreign investment. The results have been dramatic: Average gross domestic product has increased (in real terms, adjusted for inflation) annually by more than six percent for the last six years. Annual exports have grown to more than U.S. $ 39 billion annually since 1983, an increase of more than 60 percent. Foreign investment has risen from U.S. $ 854 million in 1985 to U.S. $ 12 billion in 1992. To reduce restraints on economic development caused by commercial laws, the Government is also committed to the modernization of its legal system and is currently engaged in the largest economic law reform project in the world: the Economic Law and Improved Procurement Systems (or ELIPS) Project. ELIPS is a multi-year, multi-million dollar project supported by the Indonesian and U.S. Governments. These developments are part of Indonesia's quiet revolution to propel the world's fourth largest nation to the position of a newly-industrialized country by the end of the century.

Notes

[1] The author wishes to acknowledge, with gratitude, the able assistance of the law firm of Soewito, Suhardiman, Eddymurthy & Kardono and particularly Dyah Soewito, Retty Suhardiman, Ira Eddymurthy and Rahmah L.W. Prasetyo.

[2] For ease of reference, in this paper, the companies referred to in sub-paragraph (a) (i) are called "export companies," those in sub-paragraph (a) (ii) "supply companies," and those in sub-paragraph (b) "service companies."

[3] "Elucidations" are commonly enacted with laws, decrees and other promulgations and contain explanations of provisions which the Government considers necessary.

APPENDIX A

PRESIDENT OF THE REPUBLIC OF INDONESIA

PRESIDENTIAL DECREE OF THE REPUBLIC OF INDONESIA
NUMBER : 54 OF 1993
DATED : JUNE 10, 1993

REGARDING
LIST OF BUSINESS SECTORS CLOSED FOR CAPITAL INVESTMENT

THE PRESIDENT OF THE REPUBLIC OF INDONESIA,

Considering: that in the framework of increasing capital investments, it is deemed necessary to review the list of business sectors closed for capital investment.

Bearing in mind:
1. Article 4 paragraph (1) of the 1945 Constitution;

2. Law Number 1 of 1967 Re: Foreign Capital Investment (State Gazette of 1967 Number 1, Supplementary State Gazette Number 2818), as amended by Law Number 11 of 1970 (State Gazette of 1970 Number 46, Supplementary State Gazette Number 2943);

3. Law Number 6 of 1968 Re: Domestic Capital Investment (State Gazette of 1968 Number 33, Supplementary State Gazette Number 2853) as amended by Law Number 12 of 1970 (State Gazette of 1970 Number 47, Supplementary State Gazette Number 2944);

4. Presidential Decree Number 33 of 1981 Re: Investment Coordinating Board (BKPM), as amended by Presidential Decree Number 78 of 1982;

5. Presidential Decree Number 25 of 1991 Re: Status, Tasks, Functions, and Organizational Structure of the Investment Coordinating Board; and

6. Presidential Decree Number 33 of 1992 Re: Capital Investment Procedures;

HAS DECIDED :

By revoking Presidential Decree Number 32 of 1992 re List of Business Sectors Closed for Capital Investment.

To Stipulate: PRESIDENTIAL DECREE OF THE REPUBLIC OF INDONESIA RE LIST OF BUSINESS SECTORS CLOSED FOR CAPITAL INVESTMENTS.

Article 1

(1) The list of business sectors closed for capital investment, constituting an attachment to this Presidential Decree, consists of capital investment business sectors which are closed for all capital investments (ATTACHMENT I), and business sectors, which are reserved for small scale industries/businesses, cooperating with medium - or large - scale businessman/entrepreneurs (ATTACHMENT II).

(2) The list of business sectors as referred to in paragraph (1), shall be valid for the territory of the State of the Republic of Indonesia.

Article 2

The list of business sectors closed for capital investment shall be valid for 3 (three) years and is, deemed necessary, can be reviewed in accordance with the requirement and developments of the situation.

Article 3

(1) The settlement of capital investment licencing in the framework of the Foreign Capital Investment Law, based on the Presidential approval on certain capital investment plans, shall be conducted by the State Minister of Investment Funds Mobilization/Chairman of the Investment Coordinating Board (BKPM), on behalf of the Minister, subordinating/ promoting the relative capital investment business sector in accordance with the provisions of the effective legislative regulations.

(2) The settlement of capital investment licencing in the framework of the Domestic Capital Investment Law, shall be conducted by the State Minister of Investment Funds Mobilization/Chairman of BKPM, on behalf of the Minister, subordinating/promoting the relative capital investment business sectors in accordance with the provisions of the effective legislative regulations.

(3) The settlement of capital investment licencing outside the Foreign Capital Investment Law and the Domestic Capital Investment Law shall be conducted by the Minister, subordinating/promoting the relative capital investment business sector, in accordance with the respective competencies, based on the provisions of the effective legislative regulations.

(4) Especially for Foreign Capital Investment in the general mining sector, in the form of a work contract, the procedure therefore shall be stipulated by the Minister of Mining and Energy.

Article 4

This Presidential Decree shall start to become effective on the date of stipulation.

Stipulated at   :JAKARTA
On   :JUNE 10, 1993

THE PRESIDENT OF THE REPUBLIC
OF INDONESIA,
Signed

S O E H A R T O

ATTACHMENT I TO: PRESIDENTIAL DECREE OF THE REPUBLIC OF
INDONESIA
NUMBER: 54 OF 1993
DATED: JUNE 10, 1993

NO. BUSINESS SECTOR	I	II	III
I. BUSINESS SECTORS, CLOSED FOR CAPITAL INVESTMENTS EXCEPT IF MEETING CERTAIN CONDITIONS			
1. Milk Powder/Condensed Milk, Except Integrated with Live stock Breeding	X	X	X
2. Palm Oil Frying Oil Industry, Except if raw material guarantees are available	X	X	X
3. Block Board Industry, Except if the raw material originates from waste	X	X	X
4. Wood Saw mill, Except in the Provinces of East Timor and Irian Jaya	X	X	X
5. Ordinary Plywood, Except in the Provinces of East Timor and Irian Jaya	X	X	X
6. Finished Goods/Semi-Finished Goods of Rattan, Except in Provinces outside the Island of Java	X	X	X
7. Processing of Finished Goods/Semi-Finished Goods of mangrove Wood, Except integrated with cultivation	X	X	X
8. Printing of Valuable Papers: 1. Stamps 2. Duty/Revenue Stamps	X	X	X

NO.	BUSINESS SECTOR	I	II	III
	3. Bank Indonesia Securities			
	4. Passports			
	5. Stamped Postal Objects,			
	Except for PERUM PERURI (Money			
	Printing Public Corporation)			
9.	Ethyl Alcohol,	X	X	X
	Except technical grade			
10.	Explosives and the like,	X	X	X
	Except for PT. DAHANA (Persero)			
11.	Utility Boiler,	X	X	X
	Except for manufacturing, at least equal to the			
	manufacturing level, already conducted by similar			
	domestic industries at present.			
12.	Motor-Vehicles:	X	X	X
	a. Medium Truck, Light Truck, Pick-up,			
	Bus and Minibus;			
	b. Multipurpose Vehicles/Jeep;			
	c. Sedan Passenger Vehicles/Cars and Station Wagon;			
	d. Two-Wheel Motor-Vehicles,			
	Except manufacturing, at least equal to the manu-			
	facturing			
	level, already conducted by similar domestic indus-			
	tries			
	at present			
13.	Aircraft:	X	X	X
	a. Jet engine or propeller for transport			
	b. Helicopter			
	c. Aircraft engines: Combustion piston engine,			
	turbo jet, turbo propeller, other gas turbo,			
	ram jet, pulse jet and turbo fan			
	d. Aircraft equipment and accessories: aircraft/			
	helicopter propellers and landing gear,			
	Except for / cooperating with PT. IPTN (Nusantara			
	Aircraft Industry)			

II. BUSINESS SECTORS, CLOSED FOR CAPITAL INVESTMENT, EXCEPT FOR NEW PROJECTS, OF WHICH 65% OF THE PRODUCTION IS FOR EXPORT OR EXPANSION

NO.	BUSINESS SECTOR	I	II	III
14.	Machine-Made white Cigarettes	X	X	X
15.	Drug/Medicine Formulation :	X	–	–
	a) Formulation Pharmacy			
	b) Traditional (Herbs).			

III. BUSINESS SECTOR, CLOSED FOR NEW PROJECTS AND EXPANSION CAPITAL INVESTMENT, EXCEPT IF THE ENTIRE PRODUCTION (100%) IS EXPORTED

NO.	BUSINESS SECTOR	I	II	III
16.	Synthetic Sweeteners and saccharine:	X	X	X
	Expansion and new projects shall be in a Bonded Zone			
	or Production Entrepot for Export Destination (EPTE).			

NO.	BUSINESS SECTOR	I	II	III
17.	Hard Liquor and other Alcoholic Drinks : Expansion and new projects shall be in a Bonded Zone or Production Entrepot for Export Destination (EPTE)	X	X	X
18.	Fireworks: Expansion and new projects shall be in a Bonded Zone or Production Entrepot for Export Destination (EPTE)	X	X	X
19.	Disposable Gas lighters: Expansion and new projects shall be in a Bonded Zone or Production Entrepot for Export Destination (EPTE)	X	X	X

IV. SERVICES BUSINESS SECTORS, CLOSED FOR FOREIGN CAPITAL INVESTMENT

NO.	BUSINESS SECTOR	I	II	III
20.	Taxi/Bus Transport	X	—	—
21.	People's shipping (Local)	X	—	—
22.	Scheduled/Charter Flights	X	—	—
23.	Aircraft workshop and components there-of, operating at airports	X	—	—
24.	Retail trade	X	—	—
25.	Trade Supporting Services-Advertising Advertising	X	—	—
26.	Private Television Broadcasting Station and Radio Broadcasting Services	X	—	—
27.	Cinema Building Exploitation Services	X	—	—

V. BUSINESS SECTORS, ABSOLUTELY CLOSED FOR CAPITAL INVESTMENT

NO.	BUSINESS SECTOR	I	II	III
28.	Contractor Services in the field of Forest clearing	X	X	X
29.	Casino/Gambling	X	X	X
30.	Sponge Utilization and Exploitation	X	X	X
31.	"Ganja" (kind of marijuana) and the like	X	X	X
32.	Veneer (Rotary)	X	X	X
33.	Penta Chlorophenol, Dichloro Diphenil Trichloro Ethane (DDT), Dieldrin, Chlordane	X	X	X

Explanation of the columns:

I.: Business Sectors, closed in the framework of Foreign Capital Investment (PMA)

II.: Business Sectors, closed in the framework of Domestic Capital Investment (PMDN)

III.: Business Sectors, closed in the framework of Non-Foreign/Domestic Capital Investment (Non-PMA/PMDN)

PRESIDENT OF THE REPUBLIC OF INDONESIA,
Signed

S O E H A R T O

ATTACHMENT II
(TO BE CONTINED)

GENERAL

PRESIDENT OF THE REPUBLIC OF INDONESIA

PRESIDENTIAL DECREE OF THE REPUBLIC OF INDONESIA
NUMBER : 54 OF 1993
DATED : JUNE 10, 1993

R E

LIST OF BUSINESS SECTORS CLOSED FOR CAPITAL INVESTMENT

(Continued from Warta CAFI Number : 77   Dated: July 1, 1993)

ATTACHMENT II TO :
PRESIDENTIAL DECREE OF THE REPUBLIC OF INDONESIA
NUMBER: 54 OF 1993
DATED: JUNE 10, 1993
NO. BUSINESS SECTOR

NO. BUSINESS SECTOR

1. Non-Pedigree chicken breeding
2. Milk cow-breeding
3. Shrimp seedling breeding
4. Catching of mackerels, flying fish, sea-fish and the like.
5. Shrimp catching
6. Cultivation of escargoes/snails, eels, crocodiles, frogs, "sidat" (large eels).
7. Catching of coral fish, such as "kerapu" (serranus), "lencan" "kurisi" "kakap" (lates Calcarifer) and the like.
8. Catching of cuttle fish/squid, sea-cucumber, yelly-fish and the like as well as catching of sweet-or seawater or namental fish.
9. Estates/Plantations of clove, pepper, "melinjo" cassiavera, candlenut, vanila, cardamom, nutmeg, fan-palm fruits (borassus flabellifer), sugar-palm/arenga and lontar (kind of fan-palm).
10. Herb plantations, except ginger.
11. Fruits and vegetables canning industries (salted and sweetened).
12. Industries of Salting/Drying of fish and the like.
13. Industries of smoked fish and the like.
14. Industries of flour of rice, grains, legumes, and tubers :
    1) Rice flour (all kinds)
    2) Flour of all kinds of grains
    3) Flour of manioc
15. Palm sugar industry
16. Rough Soybean Sauce (Taoco)
17. Fine Soybean Sauce (Kecap)
18. Rough Soybean Cake
19. 6Fine Soybean Cake
20. "Petis" and "terasi" (paste made of shrimp) industries
21. Pastry industries
22. Other foodstuff industries :
    1) Snacks of legumes (roasted peanuts with skin, salted peanuts, "Bogor" peas (kacang Bogor), fried peanuts with garlic).

     2) Salted/preserved eggs

     3) "Peyek" (fried rice chips with peanuts, or soybean, or green beans).

     4) "Kerupuk" (large chips made of shrimp and flour)

     5) "Keripik" (Chips made of sliced young bananas or sliced soybean cake with rice-flour).

23. Yarn spinning industries :
     1) Cocoon production business
     2) Filament production business
     3) Stam fibre decoration
     Except integrated silk textile industries

24. Yarn improvement industries :
     1) Yarn bleaching
     2) Yarn dyeing
     3) Yarn patterned/dye binding
     Using manually operated equipment.

25. Cloth Printing and Improvement industries :
     Printing, using manually operated equipment, unless integrated with the upstream industry.

26. Hand-made Batik Industries

27. Weaving industries :
     1) the ATBM Weaving Industries
     2) the "Gedogan" Weaving Industries

28. Knitting industries, using manually operated means/equipment

29. Skull-cap and fez industries

30. Industries of lime and goods of lime :
     1) Quick lime
     2) "Sirih" quid lime/white-washing lime
     3) Slaked lime/plaster lime
     4) Goods of line

31. Industries of clay ceramics for household use :
     1) Unglazed household utensils
     2) Unglazed household ornaments
     3) Unglazed flower vases of all kinds

32. Industries of Agricultural equipment/tools :
     1) Broad hoes
     2) Spades
     3) Plows
     4) Harrows
     5) Pitchforks
     6) Crowbars
     7) Sickles/grass knives
     8) Curette
     9) Reaping knives
     10) Devices to smoke-out mice
     11) Sprayers
     12) Hand sprayers
     13) Manual rice threshers
     14) Manual maize/corn grain removers from the cob
     15) Manual rice hulling devices

33. Craftsmen tool industries :
     1). Chisels
     2). Hammers (small type)
     3). Planes/wood planes (manual)
     4). Cement trowel

34. Cutting tools industries :
    1). Chopping knife
    2). AX e s
35. Indonesian Traditional Music Instrument industries
36. Handicraft industries, not included in any group :
    1). Handicraft goods, using raw materials from plants
    2). Handicraft goods, using raw materials from animals
    3). Artificial flowers and decoration ornaments
37. Raw Rattan Processing

THE PRESIDENT OF THE REPUBLIC OF INDONESIA
sgd.

S O E H A R T O

APPENDIX B

INVESTMENT APPLICATION
UNDER THE FOREIGN INVESTMENT LAW

An investment application under the Foreign Investment Law No. 1, 1967 and No. 11, 1970 is herewith submitted to the Republic of Indonesia through the Capital Investment Coordinating Board (Badan Koordinasi Penanaman Modal).

I. *DESCRIPTION OF THE PARTICIPANTS*
   A. *Foreign Partticipants(s)*
      1. Name of Company   :
      2. Main line of business   :
      3. Address (incl. phone, telex and fax number) :

   B. *Indonesian Participants(s)*
      1. Name (company, cooperative or individual) :
      2. Tax Registration Code (NPWP) :
      3. Address (incl. phone, telex and fax number) :

II. *DESCRIPTION OF THE PROPOSED PROJECT*
   1. Tentative name of the company :
   2. The proposed line of business :
   3. Location of the project
      a. Region/City :
      b. Province :

4. *Annual Production* (based on . . . . . . shift per day).

Type of Goods/Services	Unit	Designed	Remarks
. . .	. . .	. . .	. . .
. . .	. . .	. . .	. . .
. . .	. . .	. . .	. . .

Note:
For certain services business (c.q. toll roads, hotels) the capacity is rated on other than a time basis.

5. *Annual Sales*

a. Type of Goods/services	Unit	Internal Used Quantity	Domestic Market Quantity	%	Export Quantity	%
. . .	. . .	. . .	. . .	. . .	. . .	. . .
. . .	. . .	. . .	. . .	. . .	. . .	. . .
. . .	. . .	. . .	. . .	. . .	. . .	. . .

   b. Estimated total export value: U.S. $ . . . .

6. *Land Area required*: M2/HA

7. *Employment*   Foreign   Indonesian
   a. Board of Commissioners . . . . . .
   b. Board of Directors . . . . . .
   c. Management staff (excl. directors) . . . . . .
   d. Workers   . . .

7. *Employment*   Foreign   Indonesian
                                                          . . . .
                                        Total   . . . .

Note:

For each management staff (foreigner) provide position title.

8. *Allocation of Investment Funds*
   a. Fixed Capital
      —Land & Land development   :U.S. $. . . . .
      —Building & construction   :U.S. $. . . . .
      —Machinery & equipment   :U.S. $. . . . .
      —Spare parts (5% of machinery & equipment value)   :U.S. $. . . . .
      —Other   :U.S. $. . . . .
                                                             . . . .
                                        Sub Total   :U.S. $. . . . .
   b. Working Capital (for one turnover)   :U.S. $. . . . .
                                                             . . . .
                                        Total   :U.S. $. . . . .

Note:

For an investment project having more than one location/line of business breakdown the Allocation of Investment Funds for each.

9. *Source of Investment Fund*
   a. Equity   :U.S. $. . . . .
   b. Loans   —Local   :U.S. $. . . . .
                     —Offshore   :U.S. $. . . . .
                                                             . . . .
                                        Total   :U.S. $. . . . .

10. *Equity Capital*
    a. Authorized capital
    b. Issued capital   :U.S. $. . . . .
    c. Paid-up capital   :U.S. $. . . . .

The above issued capital will be fully paid-up not later than the commencement of commercial production/operation.

11. *Share Holdings*
    1. Foreign participant(s)
       a.   :U.S. $. . . . . or . . . . % equity
       b.   :U.S. $. . . . . or . . . . % equity
                                                . . . .
                             Sub Total   :U.S. $. . . . . or . . . . % equity
    2. Indonesian partici-
       pant(s)
       a.   :U.S. $. . . . . or . . . . % equity
       b.   :U.S. $. . . . . or . . . . % equity
                                                . . . .
                             Sub Total   :U.S. $. . . . . or . . . . % equity
                                                . . . .
                             Total   :U.S. $. . . . . or . . . . % equity

12. *Project Time Schedule*   :. . . . . months,

(From the date of issuance of the Notification Letter of Presidential Approval (SPPP) until the date of commencement of Commercial Production)

13. *Utilities :*
   a. Electricity   :.......... KVA
   b. Water   :.......... M3/day
   a. Telephone   :............units

III. DECLARATION

1. It is declared that this application has been properly and duly made and that we (all of the participants) are responsible for its accuracy, correctness and completeness, including all data and documents attached hereto.
2. We acknowledge that we are obliged to take preventive measures against any pollution resulting from the operation of our investment project, at our joint venture company's own expense, and in conformity with the applicable rules and regulations.

                                                      ....19......
Foreign Applicant(s)   Indonesian Applicant(s)

                                                  stamp duty Rp 1,000.-

(........................)   (..........................)
Name, Signature, and Stamp   Name, Signature, and Stamp

FULFILLMENT OF THE DATA:

a. Indonesian Participant:
   1) A record of the Articles of Association of the company (Akta Notaris) for Limited Companies (PT), State Enterprises (BUMN/BUMD), CV or Fa.
   2) A record of Basic Rules of the Organization for Cooperatives (Koperasi).
   3) A copy of Identification Card for Individuals
   4) A copy of the Tax Registration Code Number (NPWP)
b. Foreign Participant:
   A record of the Articles of Association of the Company (Akta Notaris) with English or Indonesian translation.
c. 1) A flowchart of the production process with its explanation and kind of raw materials/supporting materials for manufacturing industry.

Editorial Note: The author notes that since the preparation of this chapter, the Indonesian government has promulgated two additional deregulation measures: Government Regulation No. 20 of 1994 (May 19, 1994), which radically changes divestment and other rules pertaining to foreign equity requirements, and the June 27 package, which reduces import tariffs and adopts other measures to ensure increased access to export markets.

GOING INTERNATIONAL IN AUSTRALIA AND NEW ZEALAND

Patrick B. Fazzone

I. INTRODUCTION

THE IMPORTANCE of the U.S. trading relationship with the countries of the Antipodes and particularly with Australia is not widely understood. Far from being a distant and remote outpost, Australia is actually the United State's twelfth most important trading partner. The two-way trade between United States and Australia is nearly U.S. $10 billion annually. The United States enjoys a trade surplus of two-to-one with Australia, its only surplus with a major trading partner in the Pacific Rim. Australia is also one of the principal sites for U.S. investment in the Asia Pacific region. With around U.S. $40 billion invested, the United States is the biggest foreign investor in Australia ahead of Britain and Japan.

New Zealand has also become an increasingly interesting niche export market for U.S companies. The U.S. in turn is New Zealand's fourth largest export market and second largest supplier of goods and services. U.S. investment in New Zealand is also on the rise with several major investments recently by U.S. entities in infrastructure and other areas.

There are many reasons why these trading and investment relationships have developed. Many Americans feel most comfortable dealing in countries where there are some common linguistic and or cultural ties. Not surprisingly, small to mid size companies in particular often make their first export port of call countries like Canada, the United Kingdom, Australia and New Zealand. After these markets are successfully entered, some of the more exotic or difficult markets can then be attempted.

Australia and New Zealand share various cultural and other ties with the United States. Americans generally feel quite comfortable in Australia and New Zealand and vice versa. The system of laws, the regulatory environment, and other key aspects of doing business are, as in the United States, relatively transparent. It is generally not difficult to come to grips with how to do business in Australia and New Zealand and how to get things done.

Importantly, cultural similarities mean similarities in markets as well. Many of the products that are developed in the United States have a natural market in Australia and New Zealand and vice versa. The similarity in life style between Australia, New Zealand and many parts of the United States, for example, means that U.S. leisure goods often

593

have a ready market in Australia and New Zealand without having to be significantly altered. Australia and New Zealand thus can be fairly simple markets to crack, presenting the possibility of a quick win on the export performance charts.

Australians and New Zealanders also have other qualities that are very attractive for U.S. exporters and investors. They are inveterate users of technology. One off-cited statistic is that there are more facsimile machines per capita in Australia than anywhere else in the world. Given its relative isolation (at least from Europe and the Americas) this is not surprising. The affinity for technology in communications has spread to other areas as well. Most of the major U.S. computer companies are present and have been operating for some time in Australia. Due in part to certain Australian government programs, a large number of U.S. high-tech companies have set up subsidiaries in Australia and have even used the country as an export launching pad to other regional markets.

Equally significant is the number of U.S. firms that export directly from North America to Australia and New Zealand. The export of aircraft is the most conspicuous example. However, U.S. high tech exports span the range of computer, telecommunications, and other related products.

The remainder of this chapter covers some practical considerations of doing business in Australia and New Zealand. The first section reviews certain general characteristics of the legal regimes in these countries. The next section provides some further detail on those areas of law likely to be of greatest relevance to exporters and investors. The final section focuses on some further practical aspects of doing business in the Antipodes.

II. GENERAL CHARACTERISTICS OF THE LEGAL REGIMES

The Legal System

Both Australia and New Zealand are common law jurisdictions based originally upon the English system of common law. The notion of stare decisis is an important element in both countries. Overlaying the common law (still important in such areas as contracts and torts) is the statutory law. Just as in the United States, in Australia and New Zealand there has been an increasing tendency to enact statutes to address new issues. Predictably, a substantial portion of the law in such areas as commercial law, tax, intellectual property, trade practices, and labor law is codified.

In Australia, the common law, which was inherited from England at the time of Australia's settlement as an English colony is still a major source of law. It is substantially the same as English common law and until the 1960s Australian Courts regarded themselves bound by the decisions of the English House of Lords. However, recent times have seen the emergence of a distinctive Australian law. This indicates a recognition on the part of the judiciary in Australia to apply principles which may differ from the corresponding principles of English common law by taking into account conditions unique to Australia.

In New Zealand, the English common law which was inherited from England through the statute of Westminster in 1947 and through New Zealand's colonization is also a major source of law. Unlike Australia, New Zealand has tended to continue to follow the development of English common law where there is a nexus with New Zealand law and circumstances are similar. Indeed, New Zealand's highest court remains the Privy Council in London. Like Australia, New Zealand has its own unique legal system. However, as a unitary system, it shares more similarities with the U.K. than Australia. Moreover, New Zealanders are generally less concerned with the "principle" of creating truly independent legal system than Australia. They tend to take a more pragmatic approach, learning from and using laws from other jurisdictions where appropriate.

Existing side by side with the common law in Australia and New Zealand are principles of "equity". The rules of equity were formulated and administered by the English Court of Chancery to supplement the rules and procedure of the common law. It is now administered by Australian and New Zealand courts and where there is any conflict between the rules of law and equity, equity prevails.

Australia, like the United States, is a federal system. The Commonwealth of Australia is a federation of six states in which three levels of government operate. The Australian Constitution gives the central or federal government power in specific areas. These include external affairs, defense, customs and excise, taxation, interstate trade and commerce, currency, insurance, banking, immigration, interstate industrial disputes, bankruptcy, and matrimonial law. The state governments have power in respect of all matters not constitutionally reserved for the Commonwealth. These include education, health, housing, police, harbors, waterways, regulation in mining and other internal natural resources, and tourism.

The third tier of government in Australia is local (or municipal) government. These are a creature of state legislation and are therefore subject to state government control.

Unlike Australia and the United States, New Zealand is a unitary system. It has no single written constitution. Constitutional law in New Zealand springs from United Kingdom statutes, constitutional conventions, common law, the Treaty of Westminster, and the Constitution Act of 1986. The New Zealand central government has all the powers to govern subject to the New Zealand Bill of Rights. New Zealand also has local (or municipal) governments which are empowered and controlled by central government statute and regulation.

Under the Australian Constitution, legislative powers are exercised by the parliament, judicial power by the courts and executive power by the government. New Zealand has followed a similar path, although those powers are not set out in a single, written constitution. Unlike in the United States, there is no separation of powers in either country between the executive (the "government") and the legislative (parliament). Rather, as in England, the system is based on the Westminster system of an integrated executive and legislative branch.

As in the United States, in Australia there has been some tension between an expanding federal law and residual powers and authority within the states. For example, as in the United States, there has been a gradual expansion of the federal power to regulate commerce. Thus far that federal power has expanded more slowly than in the U.S. and a significant amount of control over commerce still falls under state control. In New Zealand, these tensions do not exist, although tensions between the executive and judicial branches of government have arisen from time to time due to judicial interpretation of the law.

As in the United States, both the federal and state governments in Australia have their own judiciary and own system of laws. The relationship between state and federal law and the areas of jurisdiction of state and federal courts are somewhat different in Australia than in the United States. Nevertheless, suffice it to say that there are many more similarities in approach than differences.

The structure of the court systems in Australia and New Zealand is similar to that of the United States. There is the familiar pattern of a trial court (and in some instances the use of magistrates), overlain by one or more levels of appeals courts. Until 1986, it was still possible to appeal some cases from Australia to the Privy Council in London. Appeals to the Privy Council have been abolished completely, and all appeals are heard within Australia before Australian courts. In New Zealand, appeals may still be heard before the Privy Council.

As in the United States, in Australia there has been a steady expansion of government regulation of the various areas of commerce, industry and life generally. In general, however, Australian industry and commercial practices are still less regulated than in the United States.

Interestingly, in some areas Australia and New Zealand have actually built on or learned from the U.S. experience particularly in regulatory law. Both countries have had the opportunity to observe the U.S. experience and to learn from it. This has caused Australian and New Zealand legislators consciously to reject some U.S. approaches. A good example is in the area of product liability law. In Australia, there have been a number of government sponsored inquiries into whether legislation should be enacted imposing greater responsibilities and liabilities on manufacturers, designers and sellers of merchandise. On several occasions, U.S. approaches have been consciously rejected as unacceptably onerous to manufacturers and likely to inhibit the local production of consumer products. New Zealand legislators actually decided to legislate against personal injury actions. In New Zealand there is a system of government compensation to the victim(s) for injuries arising from such accidents. In some cases, criminal penalties may also be imposed against the culpable party.

In other areas, Australian and New Zealand legislators have adopted approaches, techniques and ideas already in U.S. legislation. Perhaps the best example of this in Australia is the Australian Trade Practices legislation discussed more fully in Section III below. The Australian Trade Practices legislation is the equivalent of the U.S. antitrust and consumer protection laws. Much of the trade practices laws were patterned on the U.S. Sherman, Clayton, and Federal Trade Commission acts. Again, with the benefit of hindsight, certain adaptations were also possible. Thus, for example, the sections of the Trade Practices Act dealing with monopolization, attempts to monopolize, and the like are far more detailed than the corresponding U.S. statutes. Much of New Zealand's securities law is drawn from the U.S. experience.

Similarly in the area of environmental law, Australia and New Zealand have gradually increased their regulation of environmentally harmful practices. Various ideas and techniques are quite similar to the approach taken under the key U.S. environmental statutes. U.S. laws should continue to provide an inspiration as Australian and New

Zealand environmental laws become more comprehensive. Various areas of growing concern in the United States such as storm water regulation are as yet unregulated.

The Legal Professions

The Australian and New Zealand legal professions are highly sophisticated. A distinctive feature of these legal systems (as in Canada, the United Kingdom, and other Commonwealth countries) is the solicitor/barrister dichotomy. While there have been some reforms and ongoing calls for change, in practice a clear division of responsibility has been maintained in most areas. In general, solicitors focus on most areas of regulatory and commercial law and as well as on the strategic and documentary aspects of commercial and other types of litigation. Barristers in turn handle actual court appearances, and assist in the development of strategy. Most barristers also have a particular area of substantive expertise. As a consequence, they are often called upon to write "advices" (legal opinions) for solicitors.

All Australian jurisdictions have also maintained the practice of not allowing barristers to market their services, or to deal with clients directly. Rather they must take "instructions" from a solicitor. This is not the case in New Zealand. In addition, all Australian and New Zealand jurisdictions have retained the system of Queen's Counsel (Q.C.), although this is currently under siege in at least one Australian state. Q.C. are distinguished members of the Bar who supposedly have particular expertise and capability. In practice, designation as Q.C. presents a good opportunity to charge premium billing rates. In the Australian state of New South Wales (where Sydney is located) the local Law Society (the equivalent of the local bar association) recently grandfathered all existing Q.C.s but prohibited any new appointments. In the short term, this will merely strengthen the position of those remaining Q.C.s.

Lawyers are admitted to practice both before state courts and federal courts. Each of the six states in Australia and two territories have judicial systems to which solicitors and barristers can be admitted for practice. (Solicitors generally are also permitted to appear in court at least in certain types of matters.) In addition, to state courts, barristers and solicitors can be admitted to the federal courts in Australia.

As in the United States, Australia has spawned a significant number of "mega" law firms comprised of many hundreds of lawyers. New Zealand also has a number of large legal firms. While this development has occurred in other common law jurisdictions, it is still relatively rare in most countries of the world. This evolution in Australian and New Zealand firms occurred principally in the 1980's in part because of a perception that clients demanded multidisciplinary, nationally based capability from their lawyers. As in the United States, these large firms tend to offer a full range of services and to be geared up to handle large complex matters for multinational or large clients. In addition to these firms there are a large number of small to mid-sized firms that specialize in various niche areas and in less sophisticated or complex matters.

Many Australian and New Zealand lawyers have received legal training or have close ties with lawyers in other common law jurisdictions. As a result, the profession tends to be both sophisticated and well-connected internationally. At the same time, at least traditionally the approach of lawyers in Australia and New Zealand has been much closer to the English model than to the American approach. Typically, solicitors act upon "instructions" received from the client and limit their advice and assistance to those instructions received. Barristers in turn receive instructions from the instructed solicitors or in the New Zealand case, also directly from clients. The notion of lawyers acting virtually as business advisers in problem solving for their clients is still relatively new. However, the New Zealand legal profession has generally progressed further in this regard than Australia. The economic downturn in New Zealand in the mid 1980s and in Australia since the early 1990s has put irresistible pressure on the profession to change its approach. As a matter of survival, many firms and lawyers have had to become more aggressive and "pro-active" in their approach to clients and their problems. This development may actually bring the Australian and New Zealand professions more in line with the approach taken by U.S. lawyers, hopefully to the benefit of all involved.

III. KEY AREAS OF LAW

There are certain areas of Australian and New Zealand law of particular relevance to exporters and foreign investors. Following is a brief overview of the relevant principles in these areas.

Foreign Investment Law

In Australia, the Federal Treasurer is responsible for the administration of the government's foreign investment policy. The Treasurer is advised by the Foreign Investment Review Board (FIRB), whose recommendations the Treasurer usually follows.

The FIRB examines certain types of proposals for "foreign interests" wishing to invest in Australia. A "foreign interest" includes:

- a natural person not ordinarily resident in Australia;

- any corporation, business, or trust in which there is a substantial foreign interest. (This means an interest of 15 percent or more in ownership or voting power held by a single foreign person or an interest of 40 percent or more in the aggregate ownership or voting power held by more than one foreign person.)

The following transactions involving foreign interests must be submitted to the FIRB for review prior to implementation:
- acquisitions of interest in urban real estate;
- an off-shore acquisition where both the offerer and the target companies are incorporated overseas but have subsidiaries or assets in Australia valued at $50,000 or more, or where the Australian assets constitute more than half of the total assets of the target company and its subsidiaries;
- acquisitions by foreign interests of shares in Australian companies or assets of Australian businesses where the relevant Australian company or business has total assets exceeding $50,000;
- takeovers of Australian companies and businesses by means other than acquisition of shares, e.g., purchase of assets or agreements in relation to board representation;

- proposals for the establishment of a new business or project irrespective of size in sectors subject to special restrictions, e.g., civil aviation, media and uranium mining projects;
- proposals to establish a new business in other sectors of the economy where the total amount of investment is $50,000 or more; and
- direct investments by foreign governments or their agencies regardless of size.

While other transactions may not require FIRB approval, it is advisable in most circumstances to notify the FIRB of the transaction. Proposals submitted to the FIRB are treated as confidential. Decisions are usually made within thirty days of lodgment of the proposal.

In New Zealand, the Overseas Investment Commission ("OIC") is responsible for the administration of the government's foreign investment policy. The role of the OIC is to examine proposals concerning foreign investment and to advise the government on all matters relating to overseas investment in New Zealand. The OIC must grant consent for an "overseas person" to be eligible to make an investment in New Zealand of over NZ$10 million or obtain a "controlling interest" in a New Zealand company.

An "overseas person" includes:

- a company incorporated outside New Zealand;

- a person not ordinarily resident in New Zealand;

- a company incorporated in New Zealand in which a controlling interest is held by overseas persons and any nominees thereof.

A "controlling interest" means 25 percent or more of a New Zealand company's shares or control of 25 percent or more of the voting power of a New Zealand company.

In certain "specified sectors" such as businesses concerning rural land or fishing within New Zealand's territorial waters, OIC approval must be obtained before any investment may be made. Acquisitions of rural land must also be approved by the Land Valuation Tribunal. The OIC approves almost all proposals it receives and proposals are treated as confidential. Decisions are usually made within one to three weeks.

Business Structures

Investors seeking to establish a business in Australia and New Zealand need to determine the most appropriate form of business entity or vehicle. The most common forms of business structure used in Australia and New Zealand by both residents and non residents are:

- companies;
- joint ventures;
- partnerships; and
- trading trusts.

Companies

Most companies in Australia are formed by incorporation under the Corporations Law. In most cases the form taken is that of a limited liability company having a share capital.

In New Zealand, companies are formed under the provisions of the Companies Act. That law is in the process of being dramatically revised. New legislation is planned to be enacted by the end of 1993. As in the case in Australia, the form usually taken is that of a limited liability company. However, in both countries a number of different company forms exist.

An overseas company may elect to establish a branch rather than form a subsidiary. Under Australian law the company must still reserve the name of the overseas company with the Australian Securities Commission (ASC); lodge copies of its constituents documents (i.e. memorandum and articles of association); provide details of the registered office in Australia and of its company officer; and lodge details of appointment of a local agent to carry out such functions as accepting service of process and certain notices. The procedures are similar in New Zealand.

In both countries, the branch office of a foreign company is not required to have resident directors and secretaries. This is in contrast to subsidiaries. In Australia, for example, the Corporations Law requires a local director and secretary.

Joint Ventures

Foreign investment in Australia and New Zealand often involves the formation of a joint venture between one or more parties. There is no specific legislation which regulates joint venture arrangements.

A joint venture need not be incorporated as an entity separate from that of the parties to the joint venture arrangement. The rights and duties of the participants are usually set out in a detailed joint venture agreement which would be unique to the particular venture. Where a company is used as the vehicle for a joint venture, the participants normally enter into a shareholders' agreement to document arrangements that are specific to the venture.

Partnerships

A partnership under Australian and New Zealand law is an association of persons who carry on business in common with a view to profit. Business partnerships in Australia of more than twenty persons and in New Zealand of over 25 persons are prohibited except for certain professional partnerships. A partnership is formed by agreement between the parties and the rights and obligations of the partners are usually documented in a partnership agreement. In addition, partnership legislation in the various states of Australia and nationally in New Zealand regulates certain rights and obligations of the partners. In most cases, the liability of a partner for the debts of the partnership is unlimited. This means that each partner is fully liable and may be sued personally.

Limited partnerships are permitted under the laws of the Australian states of Tasmania, Queensland and Western Australia and in New Zealand. In this context there are two classes of partners. "Limited partners" are liable only to the extent of a pre-contributed sum. In contrast "General partners" are subject to unlimited liability. It is the general partners who usually undertake any managerial role.

Trading Trusts

A trading trust is an arrangement under which a trustee, usually a limited liability company, conducts a business or holds an investment on behalf of certain beneficiaries. The most common form of trading trusts in Australia and New Zealand are discretionary trusts and unit trusts. In a discretionary trust, the trustee has discretion as to distribution of the income and capital of the trust to the beneficiary named in the trust deed. These are usually established for family tax planning purposes so as to enable the splitting of income among various family members. Discretionary trusts are not often used as investment vehicles by foreign interests.

In unit trusts investors will subscribe for units issued by a trustee. Each unit confers upon the holder a proportionate interest in the assets and undertaking of the trust. A unit trust is often established as a vehicle for publicly managed investment schemes.

Each of the various business structures described above has certain advantages. For example, a corporate structure carries with it the benefit of limited liability. Similarly, a partnership enables a business to be conducted in Australia without the requirement to make public disclosures of reports and accounts as is the case with companies. Foreign investors must consider carefully the most appropriate form of business organization having regard to their particular objectives.

Regulation of Companies

Companies in Australia are governed by a national scheme known as the Corporations Law. Companies in New Zealand are governed by the Companies Act. In New Zealand, the company law is in the process of being revised. New legislation is planned to be enacted by the end of 1993.

Under the Corporations Law, the Australian Securities Commission (ASC) was established for the administration of company and securities law throughout Australia. The ASC regulates the incorporation of companies and the retention of public records.

Foreign investors in Australia will typically acquire a shelf company and change its name by a relatively straight forward procedure involving the registration of the new name with the ASC.

Importantly, the Corporations Law sets out in statutory form the duties and obligations required of a company director. Combined with the general duties imposed by the common law, directors in Australia are required to:

- exercise care, diligence, and skill;
- act in good faith for the benefit of the company as a whole; and
- use the power vested in the directors for a proper purpose and to avoid the possibility of any conflict of interest.

Recent case law has interpreted the duty of care, diligence and skill so as to require directors to take an active role in acquainting themselves with the running of the company. Directors are expected to be capable of understanding the companies affairs so as to reach a reasonably informed opinion as to its financial capacity.

The Corporations Law regulates capital-raising activity of both local and foreign corporations in Australia. A corporation can not generally raise money in Australia unless it first lodges, registers, and circulates a prospectus which complies with certain disclosure requirements. The company bears the onus of ensuring that the prospectus complies with the full and fair disclosure requirements set out in the Corporations Law. In this regard, the prospectus must contain information which investors and their professional advisors would require to make an informed investment decision.

The general principles of New Zealand company law are currently similar to those set out above. However, with the proposed changes to New Zealand's Companies Act, a significant divergence may develop in some areas.

Taxation

In Australia each level of government imposes its own taxes. However, the most significant of these for foreign investors are the federal government taxes. In New Zealand taxes are only imposed by the central government. The principal categories in each country are:

Individual Income Tax

In Australia and New Zealand individual income tax is a tax imposed upon annual taxable income which comprises total assessable income less allowable deductions. All Australian-sourced income is subject to Australian tax regardless of residence of the tax payer. Similarly, New Zealand sourced income is subject to New Zealand tax.

The tax rates for individuals are as follows:

Australia

Taxable Income A$	Marginal Tax Rate %
0— 5,400	0
5,401—20,700	20
20,701—36,000	38
36,001—50,000	46
Over 50,000	47

New Zealand

Taxable Income NZ$	Marginal Tax Rate %
0—30,875	24
Over 30,875	33

Company Income Tax

Resident companies in Australia and New Zealand are liable to pay tax on all income whether from sources within or outside of the countries. Non-resident companies only pay tax on income derived from sources within Australia or New Zealand.

A company is considered to be resident of Australia or New Zealand if:

• it is incorporated in that country; or

• it carries on business in that country and has either central management and control in that country or in the case of Australia its voting power is controlled by a resident shareholder or in the case of New Zealand is controlled by one or more directors in New Zealand.

The Australian and New Zealand corporate tax laws also had a system of "imputation". This means that shareholders receive credit against their tax liability on dividends for taxes paid by the corporation. Dividends representing profits which have been subject to company tax are referred to as "franked dividends."

Withholding Tax

All dividends and interest from Australian or New Zealand sources are subject to withholding tax. The rate of withholding tax on dividends in Australia and New Zealand is normally 30 percent of the gross amount of the dividend paid or credited. The rate of withholding tax on interest paid or credited in Australia is normally 10 percent and in New Zealand is 15 percent. These rates, however, may vary by specific provisions in tax treaties.

Fringe Benefits Tax

Australia and New Zealand both have Fringe Benefits Tax (FBT) introduced to curtail the spread of untaxed fringe benefits in employee remuneration packages. FBT is imposed on employers in Australia at the rate of 48.25 percent, and in New Zealand at the rate of 49.1 percent on the value of deductible non-cash and other benefits provided to an employee in respect to his/her employment, other than salaries or wages. In Australia, although the cost of the benefits remain a deductible business expense, the FBT itself is not deductible. In New Zealand the FBT is a deductible expense for income tax purposes.

Stamp Duty

All the states and territories of Australia impose "stamp duties" at various rates on documents such as mortgages and other securities, insurance policies, leasing transactions, and on contracts affecting the transfer of shares and real estate. In New Zealand, stamp duty is payable only on conveyance of commercial real property and interests in commercial leases.

In Australia, stamp duty varies depending on where the transaction is carried into effect. For example, in both New South Wales and Victoria, the maximum rate for transfers of real property is approximately 5.5 percent.

Trade Regulation

Import Restrictions

Imports into Australia and New Zealand are subject to the customs laws. These laws regulate imports and authorize the Customs authorities to prevent entry of goods found to pose health and safety hazards and other circumstances.

The customs authorities in each country assess customs duties pursuant to national tariff schedules. The rates of duty that apply vary greatly between different classes of goods. As such, it is important to determine the classification of goods. Some goods may be imported free of duty. In Australia, goods which are not manufactured locally may be eligible for a "concession" under which duties are waived. In New Zealand raw materials generally are allowed into New Zealand either duty free or at a low rate of duty.

Australia and New Zealand both have "dumping" laws. These laws authorize the imposition of special duties in the event of "dumping". "Dumping" occurs where an overseas supplier is selling goods of a kind manufactured locally at a price below what is considered to be the normal price at which the supplier would sell the goods in its own country. When this occurs, dumping duties may be imposed on those goods, provided it is also shown that the dumped goods cause or threaten material injury to local manufacturers of the same merchandise. If dumping duties are imposed, they are payable on importation by the importer.

Exporting

For the purpose of fostering economic growth, Australian federal and state governments offer assistance to potential exporters. This assistance can take the form of:

• Export Market Development Grants;

• Export Insurance Funding;

• Assistance for Advanced Manufacturing Technology; and

• Direct concessions to specific industry sectors.

New Zealand offers no direct export incentives but does have a number of enterprise growth schemes to assist New Zealand companies to be more internationally competitive. These schemes are:

• Enterprise Growth Scheme;

• Business Development Investigation Grant; and

• Expert Assistance Grant Scheme.

Intellectual Property Protection

Australian federal legislation and New Zealand national legislation provide for the registration and protection of intellectual property, including patents, trademarks, copyright, and industrial designs.

Patents and Designs

The patent laws in Australia and New Zealand confer upon the owner of a "standard" patent the exclusive right to make, use and sell a patented invention for a period of 16 years from the date of the patent. In order to obtain patent protection the invention must be novel, not obvious and must have utility.

Australia and New Zealand are signatories to the Patent Cooperation Treaty. An applicant for a patent in another convention country may gain date priority for a subsequent Australian or New Zealand application, based on the overseas application, provided the Australian and New Zealand applications are filed within 12 months after the patent was initially filed in the convention country.

Features of products, such as shape, pattern, or ornamentation may be protected from imitation by registration of those features as "designs". In Australia, design registration gives the owner of design protection for a period of up to 17 years in respect of the features provided they are applied to particular products. In the case of New Zealand, protection is granted for up to 15 years. The main prerequisite for design registration is that the design be new or original.

Trademarks

Trademark protection is applicable to distinctive names or marks applied to a particular good or service. In the absence of a reputation in respect of a trademark, no proprietary rights in the particular name or mark are created until it is registered. The basic requirement for registration is that the mark not be substantially identical or deceptively similar to any prior registration in respect to the same goods or services. Further, the mark must be distinctive. The proprietor of a trademark may bring an action for infringement if another person uses a mark which is substantially identical to, or deceptively similar to, the mark.

Copyright

There is no formal registration of copyright required in Australia and New Zealand. However, the Copyright Acts in each country extends protection to owners of certain original literary work and other work such as artistic works, sound recordings, and computer programs. The most common remedies available to the owner of a copyright which has been infringed is an action to seek an injunction and obtain damages or an account of profits.

Australia and New Zealand are signatories to the Berne and Universal Copyright Conventions. As such, copyright works created by a citizen of a member country or first published in the relevant member country are entitled to the same protection as if they had been created and first published in the country. The term of copyright is the life of the author plus 50 years.

Trade Secrets and Confidential Information

There is no legislation protecting trade secrets or confidential information such as customer lists, marketing techniques, software, knowhow, product specifications, and manufacturing processes. There is, however, a general legal principle that a person must maintain the confidentiality of information communicated to him/her in circumstances of confidence.

Trade secrets are typically the subject of an express contractual obligation to maintain secrecy. Indeed, most employment, licensing, and sale contracts will contain a confidentiality clause. Alternatively, the obligation of confidence may be the subject of a separate confidentiality agreement.

Business and Company Name Registration

Legislation in Australia and New Zealand provides for the registration of company or business trading names. An overseas company seeking to establish a branch or subsidiary in Australia and New Zealand should apply to register the company or business name as a matter of priority.

Trade Practices/Competition Law

The Australian Trade Practices Act in Australia and the Commerce and Fair Trading Acts in New Zealand prohibit certain restrictive trade practices. Part IV of the Federal Trade Practices Act in Australia prohibits the following anticompetitive trading practices:

- exclusive dealing;
- misuse of market powers;
- anticompetitive agreements and exclusionary provisions, including primary or secondary boycotts;
- price discrimination which is likely to substantially lessen competition;
- mergers that result in market dominance or an enhancement of market dominance; and
- resale price maintenance.

It is important to note that the Trade Practices Act may apply to off-shore mergers of foreign corporations having subsidiaries in Australia, provided such mergers have anticompetitive effects within Australia.

Penalties under the Trade Practices Act for breaches of Part IV are up to $250,000 for corporations and $50,000 for individuals. The court also has power to impose injunctions and award damages. In the case of mergers the court may order divestiture of shares or assets illegally acquired. Penalties under the Commerce Act are up to NZ$5 million for companies and NZ$500,000 for individuals.

The Trade Practices Act is administered and enforced by the Trade Practices Commission in addition to the courts. The Trade Practices Commission has the power to issue an authorization in relation to a proposed activity which would otherwise breach the legislation, provided the detriment to competition is outweighed by the overall public benefit. The Commerce and Fair Trading Acts in New Zealand are administered and enforced by the Commerce Commission which has similar powers to the Trade Practices Commission in Australia.

Contract Principles / Sale of Goods / Consumer Protection

Basic Elements of Contracts

Australian and New Zealand law recognize the principle of "freedom of contract" which provides the framework within which much of the law still operates. For a contract to be valid and legally enforceful there must be:

Intention to Contract—An agreement is not binding as a contract if the parties had no intention of creating legal relations. For example, an agreement made "subject to contract" or between family members may lack the requisite intent. In the case of ordinary commercial transactions there is a rebuttable presumption of contractual intent.

Certainty of Terms—Courts will strive to give effect to the intention of contracting parties. However, if an agreement is so vague that it is incapable of any sensible meaning, it cannot give rise to a binding contract. A meaningless clause which adds nothing may be severed from the rest of the contract.

Valuable Consideration—Generally, an agreement is not binding unless it is supported by valuable consideration. Consideration may consist either in some right, interest, profit or benefit accruing to the promisor or some detriment, loss, or responsibility given, suffered or undertaken by the promisee.

Consensus—The parties must be contracting about the same thing and must communicate that fact to each other. An offer must be made with the intention to be bound as soon as the offeror accepts. The offeror must accept with the same state of mind and accept exactly what has been offered. A conditional acceptance is merely a counter-offer. Before a contract can become binding the acceptance must be communicated to the offerer. As a business convenience rule, an acceptance sent through the post is regarded as taking effect on the day it is mailed.

Sale of Goods

The United Nations Convention on Contracts for the International Sale of Goods (the Vienna Sales Convention) became part of Australian law on April 1, 1989. Unless the parties provide otherwise, international sales agreements with Australian parties that fall within the convention generally will be governed by the Convention and not by Australian contract law.

All Australian states have enacted sale of goods legislation, many of which re-enact the provisions of Part V of the Trade Practices Act described below. In other words, the state legislation will imply into contracts for the sale of goods the range of conditions and warranties as set out in the Trade Practices Act.

The state laws generally apply to a wider range of traders than is the case with respect to the Trade Practices Act which applies primarily to corporations and sole traders and partnerships whose activities cross state boundaries. The state legislation applies also to sole traders and partnerships whose activities are restricted to operations within a particular state.

Consumer Protection

Part V of the Australian Trade Practices Act prohibits unfair practices including:

* misleading and deceptive conduct in trade or commerce;
* making a false representation with respect to the supply of goods, services, land or employment;
* referral selling and bait advertising;
* unconscionable conduct;
* pyramid selling; and
* coercion or harassment at a place of residence.

Part V also implies certain conditions and warrantees into contracts for the supply of goods or services to a "consumer." These include:

* a warranty as to the title and quiet possession of the goods;
* a condition that the goods will correspond with the description under which they are sold;
* condition that the bulk of the goods will correspond with the sample provided to the consumer;
* a condition that the goods are of merchantable quality;
* a condition that the goods are reasonably fit for the purpose for which they are purchased; and
* an obligation to compensate consumers for the non-availability of spare parts and repair facilities.

The New Zealand legislation covering this area of the law is similar in scope. The legislation provides that a person purchases goods as a "consumer" if the price of the goods does not exceed $40,000, or, where the price exceed $40,000, if the goods are of a kind or are acquired for personal, domestic or household use, or consumption. The implied conditions and warranties do not apply in respect of goods which are acquired for the purpose of re-supply or use in manufacture.

There are many other state laws in Australia dealing with consumer protection issues. These include legislation in respect of the provision, regulation, and enforcement of:

* consumer credit;
* home finance contracts;

- door to door sales; and

- pyramid selling.

Each state's consumer protection laws are administered and enforced by its Department of Consumer Affairs. These departments have the power to investigate violations and impose penalties. In addition, each state also has Smalls Claims Courts or Tribunals to resolve disputes in respect of certain consumer transactions where the value of the transaction is less than a particular amount, e.g., $3000.00.

Employment Law

Terms and Conditions of Employment

The terms and conditions of employment in Australia are governed by:
- federal and state "awards";
- the terms of the relevant contract of employment; and
- legislation affecting employment working conditions such as annual leave and long service leave entitlements.

The terms and conditions of employment in New Zealand are governed by:
- The Employment Contracts Act;
- Collective or individual collective agreements made under the Act; and
- Legislation affecting employment.

In Australia an award is a binding agreement made by an industrial tribunal. The award contains the terms and conditions of employment of employees in specific industries. These include:
- minimum hours of work;
- overtime;
- sick leave;
- expenses; and
- termination of employment.

In New Zealand, besides fairly generous minimum standards for working conditions, negotiated collective agreements set out the terms and conditions of employment.

Historically, the awards regulated virtually all the workforce in Australia. However, recent government changes in the State of Victoria (the capital city of which is Melbourne) have signalled increased use of "enterprise bargaining". Management positions are not usually governed by an award.

Leave Entitlement

All states in Australia have legislation providing for long service leave and annual leave for employees. In general, the following apply to most employees:

- four weeks annual holiday on ordinary pay at the end of each year of employment with the employer;

- long service leave at ordinary pay after a specified period of continuous service with an employer (e.g., 10 years);

- other benefits such as unpaid maternity leave and sick leave;

- most states have legislation that requires an employer to maintain insurance in respect of workers injured in the course of employment.

Unions

Approximately 40 percent of the workforce in Australia is unionized. Dispute between employers and employees are usually referred to the appropriate industrial tribunal. If conciliation fails, the matter is often resolved by way of arbitration before an industrial tribunal.

Superannuation

Australian federal law requires that in specified circumstances three percent of employee earnings be contributed by the employer to a superannuation fund (i.e., a pension fund). Employers may also make additional contributions to a superannuation fund on their employees behalf. Some awards have provision for further superannuation payments.

The requirements of Australian employment law, and Australian labor practices generally are sometimes cited as factors inhibiting foreign investment. Certainly, Australian wages are considerably higher than in neighboring countries in Asia. However, in general Australian labor practices and rules are far less of an impediment to business than in the past. And, the trend is in the direction of fewer restrictions and burdens on business.

Closer Economic Relations

Australia and New Zealand are signatories to a treaty for Closer Economic Relations ("CER"). The CER establishes a free trade area between the countries similar in scope to the U.S.-Canada Free Trade Agreement ("FTA"). Like the FTA, this arrangement provides for the elimination of duties on trade between the signatories. CER also abolishes the application of antidumping laws between the countries and provides for the harmonization of each country's laws in various areas.

Native Property Rights: The "MABO" Decision

In a recent landmark decision in *Mabo v Queensland*, the High Court of Australia held that the common law of Australia recognizes native title to land and decided that native title can continue to exist:

- where Aboriginal and certain island people have maintained their connection with the land through the years of European settlement; and
- where their title has not been extinguished by valid acts of the government.

The implications of the judgment are far-reaching. The Australian courts and the community at large will continue to grapple with what appear to be competing interests, namely the recognition of the significance of land for the indigenous population and the importance for the Australian economy of land-based activities (e.g., exploitation of natural resources).

IV. SOME PRACTICAL CONSIDERATIONS IN DOING BUSINESS IN AUSTRALIA AND NEW ZEALAND

Approach to the Australian and New Zealand Markets

For U.S. companies, it often sometimes is not cost effective to export over the 10,000 miles to Australia and New Zealand. Freight rates can be high. Tariffs also sometimes are an impediment. In addition there may be competition from other countries located closer by. For these companies, it is often more attractive to consider licensing the rights to manufacture and market all or a portion of the product.

Other companies have opted to establish a facility for local manufacture themselves. For these companies, the major issue is whether the Australian / New Zealand markets can support the establishment of a facility. In addition to the local market, however, there is the possibility of expansion regionally as well. While Singapore has received the greatest amount of attention as a regional center in recent years, many U.S. firms have continued to use Australia as a manufacturing base for the Asia Pacific region. In a survey by the American Chamber of Commerce in Australia 300 U.S. firms in all industries indicated that they structured their operation in this way. Other firms are able to export profitably from the United States.

For services companies it is often necessary to establish a facility in Australia in order to service the market effectively. The distance from the United States and the tyranny of time zones makes the provision of services from off-shore difficult. Australia in particular can serve very effectively as a regional center for the rendering of services throughout the Pacific Rim. It enjoys a very relatively good infrastructure, relatively cheap telecommunications, and a good transportation network.

A broad range of U.S. service companies have already established in Australia. Banks, insurance companies, legal firms, accounting firms, software houses, business advisory companies, and engineering and construction firms are all present in the Australian market.

Some Further Practical Considerations

No matter how one does business in Australia and New Zealand, it is important to take time to select a business partner carefully. Deceptive similarities mask many differences. Some are very important. The Australian business culture for example is considerably different from that in the United States. Australians are hard-working. However, they also take their annual vacation time seriously, and tend to take a more relaxed attitude about many issues that are considered quite urgent in the United States. Relative slackness in paying outstanding bills is only one of the many examples of the more laid-back Australian attitude. It is best to understand and appreciate these differences in advance; otherwise doing business in Australia can have its headaches.

There are also some "macro issues" that are concern to many companies and do affect the conduct of business between the countries. In general Australia and New Zealand enjoy very good bilateral relationships with the United States. There are relatively few irritants between the nations. Nevertheless there are some areas of friction. The Australian government and industry have complained loudly about the U.S. program of agricultural subsidies on wheat and other grains. These subsidies have hurt Australian growers.

Of greater relevance to U.S. exporters and their advisors are Australian trade restrictions. Tariffs continue to be high in many areas, although they are coming down rapidly in most manufacturing sectors. Australia also imposes local content requirements on most programs and products that are broadcast. The Australian government also has a well entrenched offsets program. Under the offsets scheme, foreign firms that would like to sell products to the defense sector must meet certain local production or similar requirements.

Other factors also can affect trade and investment between the countries. The exchange rate between the U.S. and Australian dollar is fairly unstable. Rapid shifts in the value of the Australian dollar against the U.S. dollar can occur over short periods of time. The can make business planning a challenge. The overall tax burden in Australia and New Zealand is also slightly greater than in the U.S. This fact should be well understood in advance.

GOING INTERNATIONAL IN THE GULF

Mitri J. Najjar[1]

THE ARABIAN GULF represents a significant area of opportunity for any business seeking to expand internationally. The region has long been a marketplace for American products and its residents are used to doing business with the United States. Most local currencies are pegged in some fashion to the Dollar, so the purchase prices of American products in local currencies are not subject to fluctuation (unlike those of most European and Asian products). Finally, spending on consumer items is high, and American products in the Gulf market have a reputation for being of high quality and are fashionable, which provides a marketing advantage over products from other countries.

Any company seeking to expand its activities to the Gulf will need to decide early on whether it desires to have a presence in the Gulf or not. If it simply wants to sell its products there, then the involvement is relatively limited. On the other hand, if the U.S. company is going to establish a presence overseas, the situation is trickier, both from a legal perspective and from a logistical one. Establishing a presence in the Gulf requires a significant commitment of resources and should not be considered lightly. This chapter considers both the indirect presence and a more formal presence and reviews the legal structures associated with both.

I. THE INDIRECT PRESENCE: COMMERCIAL AGENCY

By far the most common method for U.S. companies to become involved in the Gulf is to sell their products in the region. While one-off sales can be effected from time to time, an effective marketing system usually requires a local presence. The easiest way to establish this local presence is to have a commercial agent in the particular country where the products are to be sold. The commercial agent represents the interests of the principal and assists with local marketing.

Set forth below is a discussion of the rules governing agency and other forms of agency relationships in the various Gulf countries. However, an agency relationship is more than a legal structure. It is, in very basic terms, a business partnership. The local commercial agent represents the foreign company's interests and if there is not full agreement on the fundamental terms of the relationship between the principal and agent, those interests will not be well-served. As such, structuring an agency relationship must be done with care and it is wise to avoid slavish devotion to standard forms, particularly

613

those produced by local chambers of commerce and other organizations, which tend to favor the local agent.

Saudi Arabia

Although it is possible for foreign companies to sell directly to Saudi customers without employing a local commercial agent, it can be beneficial to appoint a Saudi agent or distributor to facilitate the process. Pursuant to the Commercial Agency Regulations, as adopted by the Royal Decree 11 of 1382 (1962), all commercial activities in the Kingdom are restricted to either Saudi nationals or companies that are owned exclusively by Saudi nationals. Distributors who buy from the principal and sell to third parties directly and commission agents who act for the principal in return for a commission are treated alike under the Commercial Agency Regulations.

Commercial agency arrangements generally involve the appointment of a local entity to carry out commercial activities as an agent for a foreign manufacturer or supplier in return for profit, commission, or other benefit. The definition of commercial agency is broadly construed and covers both goods and services. Agency agreements that follow the model agency agreement issued by the Saudi Ministry of Commerce in 1983 are more easily accepted for registration, although this form agreement is generally unacceptable to most Western companies. It should be noted that significant changes can be made to the form agreement and it will still be accepted for registration.

If the agency is terminated without cause, the agent may be entitled to compensation, even where the agency is at will. Failure to renew the contract is tantamount to termination, and may subject the principal to liability. In addition, a foreign principal who has wrongfully terminated an agency arrangement may have difficulty procuring approval for the registration of any subsequent agency agreements in the Kingdom. These problems can be initially eliminated through careful draftsmanship which takes into account terminating the relationship and the consequences thereof.

Kuwait

A foreign company intending to do business in Kuwait, including importing goods directly into Kuwait, must appoint a local Kuwaiti commercial agent, who serves to promote its products and negotiate deals on its behalf. Pursuant to Law No. 36 of 1964 and Chapter Five of the Commercial Law No. 68 of 1980, governing commercial agencies and distributorships generally, only Kuwaiti citizens and corporations established in Kuwait with at least 51 percent Kuwaiti ownership are permitted to act as commercial agents. Similarly, only Kuwaiti citizens and Kuwaiti corporations acting as agents are permitted to import goods under Law No. 43 of 1964. Foreign companies planning to import products directly into Kuwait through an agent must obtain a license from the Ministry of Trade and Commerce.

All commercial agencies must be direct arrangements and must be registered with the Commercial Register within two months of entering into an agreement in order to be effective. The Ministry of Commerce and Industry, however, has the discretion to reject such applications. Significantly, the agency agreement need not be exclusive, and the foreign investor or exporter therefore has the flexibility to appoint more than one agent for both the same product and territory, although in practice, this is seldom done.

The Commercial Law No. 68 of 1980 sets out three types of agency arrangements under the Kuwaiti regulatory system. The first type of arrangement, pursuant to Article 271 of the Commercial Code, is the contracts agency under which the agent agrees in a written agreement to undertake "in a certain area of activity to continuously encourage and negotiate the conclusion of transactions for the benefit of the principal in consideration of a remuneration." The agent thus agrees to assist the principal in obtaining orders for goods in the principal's name in exchange for a payment based on the quantity of goods the principal is able to sell in Kuwait. A contracts agent is entitled to remuneration for all transactions entered into by the principal within the area of activity assigned to the agent even where the agent does not participate in the transaction.

The second type of arrangement is the distribution agency under which the Kuwaiti agent agrees to act as the sole distributor of the principal's product in a limited territory in return for any value it receives on the resale of such goods in the territory.(Article 286 of the Commercial Code).

The final type of arrangement is the commission agency whereby the agent enters into agreements in his own name for the account of the principal. (Articles 287–296 of the Commercial Code). There are two advantages to this type of arrangement. First, the principal has no liability to the agent's customers in that the customers have legal recourse only against the agent. In addition, the agent is required to keep the principal's identity and the identity of the agency agreement confidential from all third parties.

Companies planning to appoint a commercial agent should be aware that principals are restricted by law from terminating the agency without cause and are liable for any damages the agent incurs resulting from the wrongful termination. Thus even in the case of limited term agreements, the principal may be required to renew the agency agreement or face liability for the value of the goodwill the agent has built up as a result of such agreement. In addition, the agent retains a security interest over all goods in its possession, securing the remuneration of and all amounts accruing to the agent on account of the agency. (Article 266).

Bahrain

Foreign companies that intend to export directly to Bahraini customers must appoint a local agent. On July 14, 1992, Bahrain promulgated a new Commercial Agency Law by Legislative Decree No. 10 of 1992, which states that an agent must be either a Bahraini national or a company which has its head office in Bahrain and is at least 51 percent Bahraini owned.

There are two types of agents under Bahraini law. The first are commission agents, who act in their own name for the account of the principal in return for a commission based on the number of goods sold. Third parties contract directly with the agent and have no legal recourse against the principal. The second type of agents are commercial representatives, who act in the name of the principal and may bind the principal to obligations with third parties.

All agents and agency agreements must be registered with the Ministry for Commerce and Agriculture and such registration must be renewed every two years. An agent has an exclusive right to the appointed activity, and in the case of an agent engaging in distributorship and sales activities, the agent has the sole right to the product for which it has been given that right. Under the new law, third parties may import goods and products specified under the agency agreement, however, the agent is entitled to a commission from such goods and products imported into Bahrain.

The agency may not be terminated by either party without cause where the term of the agency is not specified, unless both parties consent to such termination. Where the agency is for a specific term, the agency terminates automatically at the expiration of that term unless all the parties to the agreement agree to a renewal of the agency. However, if the principal refuses to renew the contract, the agent may have the right to compensation relating to its contribution to the increased goodwill of the principal's products arising from the agency. Any disputes arising from unlawful termination are settled by an arbitration board specified in the agency agreement.

United Arab Emirates

Commercial agencies in the United Arab Emirates ("UAE") are regulated by Federal Law No. 18 of 1981, as amended by Federal Law No. 14 of 1988, which permits a foreign company great flexibility in the appointment of commercial agents. For example, the principal may appoint an agent for each of the seven Emirates, or may appoint one to govern the entire federal territory. However, agents have an exclusive right to sell or distribute products within their appointed territory and may appoint sub-agents.

The law of commercial agency is similar to that found in other Gulf states. Agents must be either nationals of the UAE or companies owned 100 percent by UAE nationals, and must be licensed. The agency agreement must be in writing and must be registered at the Ministry of Economy and Commerce. The agency agreement may not be terminated by either party without cause. If the contract is terminated or not renewed without cause, the aggrieved party may be entitled to full compensation for the loss of earnings resulting from the wrongful termination or expiration of the agreement. Under Article 7, an agent is entitled to remuneration for all transactions entered into by the principal within the agent's assigned territory, even if such transactions were not concluded as a result of the efforts of the agent.

Oman

Any foreign company that intends to export goods directly into Oman, or wishes to engage in other commercial acts or open a branch office may only do so through an authorized Omani agent. Commercial agency arrangements in Oman are governed by both the Law of Commercial Agencies of 1977 and the Law of Commerce, Book Three, Part Five of 1990. The 1990 Law broadly defines "commercial agency" to mean any relationship whereby a principal appoints an agent to carry out a specific commercial act for a payment based on the value of the act. Agents must be Omani citizens, or in the case of companies, be at least 51 percent Omani-owned.

All agency agreements must be entered in the Commercial Register before they become effective, and applications must be submitted to the Ministry for Commerce and Industry for authorization of such agency relationship. In addition, all agreements must be in writing and approved by the Chamber of Commerce or the particular foreign chamber of commerce where the agreement was concluded.

Commercial agency agreements are exclusive in both territory and product, and the principal is prohibited from selling its products or supplying its services without paying the agent a commission on such goods. Moreover, the foreign principal must be either the original manufacturer of the goods or the supplier of the goods in the foreign jurisdiction.

The restrictions on the principal's ability to terminate both limited term and at-will agreements without cause is similar to those found in other Gulf countries. The principal is thus liable for all damages suffered by the agency due to either the failure of the principal to extend the contract or to its termination of the agency. The parties may not contract around these restrictions.

The Law of Commerce 1990 sets out three different types of agency arrangements possible for foreign companies doing business in Oman. The rules governing these relationships are very similar to those in Kuwait. The first arrangement is a "contract agency" whereby the agent generally agrees to enter into and promote transactions with parties in Oman on behalf of the principal for some agreed amount of remuneration. Under the second type of agreement, the principal appoints a "commission agent" who contracts with third parties in his own name for the account of the principal. The third option is the appointment of an agent to serve as a "commercial representative" who is authorized to enter into transactions in the name of the principal.

Qatar

Under Qatari law, a foreign exporter who wishes to engage in sales directly with Qatari customers is not required to act through a Qatari agent. However, only Qatari entities will be granted import licenses.

A foreign company may choose, however, to engage the services of a local agent for various business and marketing reasons. A service agent is required for foreign construction companies which intend to engage in economic development projects under a Decree of Exemption. Pursuant to the Foreign Participation Law No. 3 of 1985, only Qatari citizens and 100 percent Qatari-owned companies may be agents. Agency agreements are required to be registered with the Department of Control of Companies, although as a practical matter this requirement is frequently ignored.

Under Law No. 4 regulating commercial agents in Qatar, commercial agents are granted an exclusive license to sell or display the principal's property or to perform certain services, on behalf of the principal, for either profit or commission. The agency agreement is exclusive in both territory and by product. Foreign principals are also limited in their ability to terminate the agency relationship without cause or to not renew limited term agreements, even where the agreement specifically permits such termination. Law No. 4 provides that the terminating party will be liable for all damages "for injury sustained by him as result of the dismissal or withdraw being made at an inappropriate time and without an acceptable reason."

Conclusion

Again, perhaps the most important aspect of structuring the agency relationship is establishing a clear understanding between the principal and agent with respect to expectations and rewards and including sure that such understanding is accurately reflected in a comprehensive, well-drafted agreement. Failure to do so at the outset will result in an unhappy marriage and, inevitably, a failure of the relationship. Most importantly, because business relationships do fail, it is critical that the lawyer preparing the agency agreement pay close attention to termination provisions (especially termination compensation), setting forth a clear mechanism for separating the parties and avoiding costly and time-consuming litigation.

II. DIRECT PRESENCE: JOINT VENTURES, CORPORATE OWNERSHIP AND BRANCH OFFICES

It is very common in the international arena to speak of "joint ventures". Usually this is a misnomer for the creation of a local company owned by both foreign and local investors. Of course, it is possible to create a contractual joint venture that is dedicated to executing a particular project, but more often than not, joint ventures involve a more permanent presence in the local market. There are considerable differences among the Gulf countries, in terms of permitted percentages of foreign participation and also in terms of regulatory hurdles which must be cleared prior to investment.

Creation of a "joint venture company" involves a significant application of resources and considerable follow-through. It is a commitment to the local market place far greater than simply selling ones products there. It has its advantages as well, usually in the form of tax incentives and other governmental encouragement.

For those U.S. companies not ready to make the significant commitment of resources connected with formation of a local company, many Gulf countries offer the opportunity to establish a branch office. Often, these branch offices may engage only in very limited activities, but they do offer a middle ground between formation of a local company and no presence at all.

Saudi Arabia

Foreign investors may want to consider establishing a more direct permanent presence in the Kingdom to take advantage of the incentives offered to investors who participate in the long-term development of the Kingdom. There are basically two forms that such a permanent presence may take: a representative office or a joint venture in the form of a limited liability company with Saudi partners. The foreign investor must obtain a license under the Foreign Capital Investment Code to invest permanently in the Kingdom. The general principle is that approval will only be granted if the project is beneficial to the economic development of the Kingdom. It is unlikely that a license will be granted to companies in which there is no or limited Saudi participation.

The most common form used by foreign companies intending to establish a direct presence in the Kingdom is through participation in a limited liability company as a joint venture with other Saudi partners. As was noted above, it is also possible to enter into a contractual joint venture with Saudi partners. A contractual joint venture has no separate legal identity and each joint venture participant therefore is fully liable for the obligations of the joint venture under any contract to which it is a party. A foreign joint venturer, as signatory of a contract in Saudi Arabia in its own name, therefore, is still required to procure a temporary license to do business in the Kingdom.

Kuwait

The Company Law in Kuwait recognizes joint ventures, but only as a relationship between the participants in the venture and not as having a separate legal identity. Third parties doing business with the joint venture are limited in their recourse to the partner with whom the third party dealt. Thereafter, the joint venture partners have recourse among themselves with regard to the conduct of the business. Because this structure is cumbersome and affords no protection to its participants, it is not much used by foreign companies doing business in Kuwait.

An alternative to joint ventures is for foreign entities to set up a Kuwaiti business structure or to invest in an existing company. There are two possible corporate forms that are open to foreign investors. The first is a limited liability company, which must be 51 percent Kuwaiti-owned and is only available to individuals not corporations. Foreign corporations seeking to own an interest in a Kuwaiti limited liability company circumvent this rule by holding their shares through a "nominee". The advantage to a limited liability company structure is that due to the lack of individual income tax, discussed *infra*, limited liability companies are non-taxable.

Pursuant to Articles 68 and 94 of the Companies Law, foreign companies may also invest directly in majority-owned Kuwaiti closed joint-stock companies, although there are two disadvantages to investing in this type of company. First, the foreign entity would be subject to corporate taxation. Second, the foreign company must apply to the Ministry of Commerce and Industry for permission, which will be granted only where there is a need for capital and foreign expertise, and where the company's purpose is not related to banking or insurance.

Bahrain

Bahrain has some of the most liberal laws governing foreign investment in the Gulf. Bahraini law permits foreign investors to have a direct presence in Bahrain through any of the following corporate structures: limited liability company, joint stock company, general partnership, limited partnership, and joint venture. A Foreign investor may also register as an off-shore company, which has no restrictions on foreign equity ownership but is restricted from doing business with Bahraini residents. These "exempt companies" are normally created to serve as regional headquarters or as regional distribution centers for operations elsewhere in the Gulf, and to take advantage of favorable tax treatment.

Joint ventures are one of the forms most commonly used by foreign companies intending to do business in Bahrain. Joint venture companies must be at least 51 percent Bahraini owned. Foreign investors must have a foreign guarantor for all transactions with third parties entered into by the joint venture or in the name of the foreign investor. The partners in a joint venture must enter into a written Memorandum of Association, which governs only the legal rights between the parties. However, under Bahraini law, a party to a joint venture is restricted from withdrawing from the joint venture unless the agreement so provides.

Under Decree 13 of 1991, amending Article 278 of the Commercial Companies Law, foreign companies may also directly invest in joint stock companies, and in certain cases may own up to 100 percent of the companies. For example, foreign companies may own 100 percent of a closed joint-stock company which only engages in service or industry activities and uses Bahrain as a regional distribution center. Foreign companies may also set up branch offices through a Bahraini sponsor.

United Arab Emirates

A foreign company that intends to establish a legal and continuing presence in the UAE may do so through a number of legal forms, including joint ventures with local companies or individuals, ownership of up to 49 percent of a local limited liability or joint-stock company, or by opening a branch office in the UAE. A foreign company that chooses to use the last two forms will be subject to the licensing, registration, and administration requirements of Decree 58 of 1985, which include the appointment of local auditors and the procurement of a license in all the local municipalities in which the foreign company participates. An agreement may be reached with the federal government to exclude a foreign company from these requirements. The specific regulations governing joint ventures in the UAE are similar to those found in the other Gulf states.

Oman

The easiest way to do business in Oman is through a contractual joint venture arrangement. Generally, the joint venture acts as a partnership between the foreign entity and the Omani guarantors. Third parties deal with the partners individually, not with the joint venture. Therefore, the agreement must be carefully drafted to set out the various duties and rights of each party.

In Oman, all other direct foreign business investment is governed by the Foreign Business and Investment Law, promulgated under Sultani Decree 7/74 (as amended), and the Commercial Companies Law. Under the current laws, foreign companies that wish to invest directly in Oman are required to apply to the Ministry of Commerce and Industry, which permit them to do so only as a participant in Omani-owned corporations with Omani participation of at least 35 percent, and are limited to certain areas of investment, primarily in agriculture, construction, and industry. However, the Ministry of Commerce and Industry has recently set forth new regulations which permit foreign investment companies that engage in tourism, services, and trading, including the import and export of goods—activities which represent a significant sector of Oman's economy.

Although these regulations have not yet been promulgated, foreign companies may soon be permitted to engage in a greatly expanded range of activities. For example, companies with significant foreign ownership may now be permitted to directly import goods into Oman, without the need to engage an Omani agent; under the current law, only Omani companies may tender for supply contracts. In addition, they will also be permitted to engage in the whole range of agency activities.

Qatar

In Qatar, a company or partnership will generally not be qualified to do business if it has any foreign representation, unless it falls within one of the areas not reserved for Qataris. A foreign company that engages in business or representation in Qatar may, however, apply for a Decree of Exemption from the Ministry of Economy and Commerce if it engages in various economic development projects such as industry, agriculture, mining or tourism. Joint ventures remain the best option for companies investing in Qatar, however, as stated above, no foreign equity is permitted except in certain cases.

The Ministry will also license foreign entities to invest in Qatari joint stock companies where there is a demonstrated need for foreign capital or foreign investment.

Conclusion

Because the rules surrounding local investment by foreign companies are reasonably complex, they must be understood well in advance of any investment. Protections can be crafted in order to bolster the foreign company's position, but the rules must be understood and the limitations must be recognized. Again, the role of the lawyer is critical. A well crafted shareholders agreement, joint venture agreement, or other document governing the management of a "joint venture" will prove invaluable to avoiding conflict once the business of the transaction has begun. Again, perhaps the most important section is the termination section. A carefully crafted termination section, taking into account the rights of all the parties and providing for an orderly termination, will alleviate the pangs of litigation. For the business executive, knowing in advance what one's company wishes to derive from the relationship in structuring a relationship that meets those goals will prevent eagerness to do the deal from turning into bitterness over unrealized opportunities.

III. GOVERNMENT CONTRACTING

In a survey of other areas of the globe, this chapter would not necessarily contain a section on government contracting. However, because the government is the central engine of all economic activity within the various Gulf counties, government contracting plays a particularly important role. This is especially true in the construction and defense industries. It is important for both the businessman and the lawyer to have at least a passing knowledge of government contracting rules in the Gulf, as it is a virtual certainty that U.S. businesses will at some point or another become involved in government contracting.

Saudi Arabia

Government contracting in the Kingdom is governed by the Procurement of Government Purchases Law, Decree No. M/14 of 7/4/1391 A.H., the Implementing Regulations to the Procurement of Government Purchases Law issued by the Ministry of Finance and National Economy, and other regulations released from time to time. Unless a foreign company tenders as a participant in a majority Saudi-owned company it will need to have a Saudi service agent to contract with the Saudi government, except in the case of defense contracts and government-to-government contracts with respect to which agents are specifically forbidden. The basic procedural aspects to tendering for a government contract are set forth below.

Bidders must provide a bank guarantee securing one percent of the total contract value accompanying the bid, and if successful, must provide a performance guarantee of five percent of the contract's value. The government will sometimes make an advance payment of up to 10 percent of the value of the contract, where such payment is secured by a bank guarantee in case the bidder fails to perform.

The government has an extensive policy of Saudiazation which favors local bidders through open bidding and other incentives and requirements, and, therefore, it is advisable for foreign bidders to associate closely with local entities in bidding for government contracts. For example, at least 30 percent of all work must be subcontracted to Saudi firms, and whole market areas have been closed to foreign bidders where the level of Saudi expertise is high.

Kuwait

Contacting with a government entity in Kuwait is governed by the Public Tenders Ordinance Law No. 37 of 1964, which establishes who may bid and the procedure for making such bids. Foreign companies should be aware that Kuwait has recently instituted an offset program whereby a percentage of the value of the contract must be reinvested back into Kuwait.

Foreign entities may submit tenders for any government contract, but under Article 5 of the Public Tender Law, must do so through a Kuwaiti service agent pursuant to an officially authenticated agreement. Each bidder must be classified by the Central Tender Board based on the size of contracts which they are deemed able to undertake, and are thus restricted from certain bids. Bidders normally must also pre-qualify for bids with the Central Tender Board by submitting relevant information about their experience and financial resources, before being allowed to even submit a bid for a tender.

All bids must be accompanied by a bank bond valid for the duration of the bid. Successful bidders must in addition sign performance guarantees prior to signing the agreement. An advance payment of 10 percent of the contract value is normally offered by the contracting Ministry. All bids must also conform to the exact conditions of the tender, and must state the exact fixed total costs. Companies wishing to tender for a government contract should note that national companies are granted a significant 10 percent price advantage over foreign bidders for supply tenders.

Bahrain

Any foreign company that intends to tender for a government contract must do so through a Bahraini agent. In addition, foreign contractors need a Bahraini sponsor who has expertise in the field in which the contractor plans to tender. The Ministry of Development and Industry generally invites to tender only those foreign contractors who are specialized in the field, and who have met capital and competency requirements.

United Arab Emirates

Tenders for government contracts are governed by Law No. 4 of 1977. Foreign companies may bid for government contracts either through a local agent, or if they have a continuing presence, through the company or branch. The Tender Board is required to give preference to local products, which is defined as those produced by companies with at least 51 percent local ownership. The laws governing the tender of supply contracts are similar to those found in the other Gulf states.

The UAE has also instituted an offset program for defense contracts, requiring foreign bidders to agree to reinvest 60 percent of the value of the tender back into the local economy. The guidelines require each foreign bidder to submit an investment proposal with the UAE Offsets Group along with its individual bid.

Oman

Pursuant to the Tender Law and the Tender Regulations, issued by the Royal Decree No. 86 of 1984, all government tenders must be through the Tender Board, except for defense contracts. A foreign entity planning to bid for Omani tenders must be both authorized by the Ministry of Commerce and Industry, and registered in the Commercial Register. Although it is not required, it is also advisable to tender through a local agent due to the complexity of the process and the discretion given to the Tender Board to award the bid to persons other than the lowest bidder. An agent would facilitate the process, and increase the bidders chance of being awarded the tender.

As under the government contracting laws of the other Gulf states, a foreign bidder must be classified by the Tender Board according to its prior experience, and financial capital structure, which will determine the kinds of contracts the investor will be permitted to tender for. Finally, each contract is generally non-negotiable after the contract has been tendered.

Qatar

Foreign companies may contract with the government or enter into joint ventures with the government upon registering in the Contractors Register. Generally, a blanket Decree of Exemption will be given in the government contracting context, so the restrictive provisions of the Foreign Participation Law are rarely applicable. The most effective method is to tender through a local agent. Qatar's regulations regarding government tenders are similar to those in other Gulf states.

Conclusion

An entire book could be written on the subject of government contracting in the various Gulf countries. A comprehensive study of those rules is beyond the scope of this chapter. Nevertheless, the foregoing review should provide a summary of the rules and should alert the reader to at least some of the issues involved.

IV. INTELLECTUAL PROPERTY

The Gulf countries have only lately introduced laws governing the protection of intellectual property. Nearly all of the Gulf countries have come under some criticism for weaknesses in their laws or absence of such laws in their entirety. Some rectification of these shortcomings has taken place and continues. Nevertheless, foreign companies who are introducing their intellectual property into the Gulf should be particularly cautious.

Saudi Arabia

Saudi Arabia has in recent years passed a comprehensive series of intellectual property laws covering all areas including trademarks, patents, and copyrights. However, the effectiveness of such laws remains in doubt, and investors should be aware that the Copyright Law, passed in 1989, does not protect foreign works by non-Saudis.

Pursuant to the Royal Decree M/5 of 1404 (1984), trademarks, including service marks, may be registered with the Ministry of Commerce for a renewable 10-year period of protection. A foreign investor may also file a priority claim of a trademark registered outside the Kingdom. Significantly, owners are free to enter into licensing agreements with other parties based on the trademark for the period of registration, and may restrict the licensee's use of the trademark so long as the restrictions are necessary to safeguard the owners rights.

Patents are protected in the Kingdom by the Royal Decree M/38 of 1989, which are defined as any new products or processes or improvements to such products or processes provided they met certain criteria including novelty, and are shown to have an apparent industrial application.[2]

Applications for patents must be submitted to the King Abdulaziz City for Science and Technology, Directorate of Patents and Inventions and must include the name of the local agent. Patents may be licensed to other parties so long as such licenses are authorized and registered.

Kuwait

Under Law No. 2 of 1961, the first applicant is permitted to register trademarks in Kuwait. Any mark a person or entity uses to distinguish the its products or goods in which it deals or offers for sale may be registered in any language. Foreign trademarks that were previously registered outside Kuwait may also be registered in Kuwait. The term for the trademark is 10 years and is renewable at the end of the period for additional 10-year periods.

Non-Kuwaitis residing or doing business in Kuwait, or citizens of a nation giving reciprocal treatment may apply for protection for patents under Law No. 4 of 1962. A patent is generally granted for 15 years, renewable for an additional five years upon application to the Commercial Registration Authority at the Ministry of Commerce and Industry. However, if a foreign registrant does not exploit the patent within three years from the date of the grant of the license, the license may be granted to other third parties. Kuwait has not adopted a copyright law.

Bahrain

Bahrain provides for protection for both trademarks and patents. Pursuant to Legislative Decree 10 of 1991, foreign entities may register with the Commercial Registry at the Directorate of Commerce and Companies' Affairs any mark that takes a distinctive form, if used in distinguishing products, goods, or services. All trademarks are protected for a renewable period of 10 years.

Patents are protected by the Patent, Design, and Trade Mark Law of 1955, as amended by Ministry Decree 22 of 1975 and the Implementing Regulations issued in 1978. Foreign applicants must show a certified copy of an authorized foreign registration in order to register its patent in Bahrain at the Patents and Trademarks Registration Office. Patents may be registered for 15 years, renewable for an additional five-year term if such patent has either "special importance" or if the expenses incurred were not reasonable in relation to the income derived from the patent.

United Arab Emirates

Pursuant to the Trademark Law No. 37 of 1992, and its implementing regulations issued on February 2, 1993 all marks that take a "distinctive form" and are used or intended to be used to distinguish goods or services, to indicate that the product belongs to the owner by reason of their manufacture, or to indicate the rendering of a service are protected as trademarks. A registered trademark is protected for 10 years, renewable for one additional term. The owner may transfer the ownership of a trademark, however the transferee has no rights vis-à-vis third parties until the transfer has been endorsed in the Trademark Register.

Under the Federal Patent Law, various types of industrial intellectual property are protected, including the rights of inventors of new inventions resulting from original ideas or original improvements to previously patented inventions. The new patent law protects the rights of foreign entities only where there is reciprocal treatment offered by the foreign state to UAE nationals. Generally, the Industrial Property Administration of the Ministry of Finance and Industry will grant patents for ideas founded on scientific bases and capable of industrial development for 15 years—renewable for an additional five years. The holder of a patent may prevent third parties from selling, manufacturing, importing, or using the imported idea or product.

The Copyright Law promulgated in 1993, protects the works of foreign persons whose home jurisdiction offers reciprocal treatment and where such persons are publishing their work in the UAE for the first time.

Oman

In 1987, Oman formally adopted the Trademarks and Commercial Data Law, as implemented by the Trademark Regulations promulgated in 1988,[3] however, Oman has not yet adopted any laws to protect copyrights or patents.

Under the Trademark Law, the owner must submit an application to register the trademark with the Director of Agencies and the Trademarks Department of Commerce and Agency. The registration of trademarks is open to both Omani and foreign applicants, including foreign entities with no direct presence in Oman. Only the first registrant is entitled to protection. The registrant is deemed to be the absolute owner of the trademark for a 10-year term, which is renewable for successive terms upon filing notice within three months of the end of the current term. The registrant is protected from any contest to its absolute ownership if its ownership has not been contested for the five years prior to such contest.

Qatar

Pursuant to Law 3 of 1978, as amended by Legislative Decree 17 of 1987 and Ministerial Order 63 of 1987, trademarks may be registered in Qatar by the first applicant to do so. Registrants' trademarks are protected for ten years, which is renewable for additional terms. Qatar has no copyright or patent law.

Conclusion

As can be seen from the foregoing overview, intellectual property laws are not particularly comprehensive in the Gulf. It may be possible to provide for protection on a case-by-case basis, particularly where the foreign company has licensing technology or know-how to a local user.

V. TAXATION

No discussion of doing business anywhere in the world would be complete without at least some discussion of tax issues. While personal income tax is virtually unknown in the Gulf, taxation of corporate entities and other businesses is widely practiced and can often result in a very heavy tax burden. Part of this burden can be alleviated by forming local companies that will attract tax holidays, although this possibility does not exist for every business. Alternative structures can often be found, but careful advice should be taken on tax issues. Local governments have become more sophisticated in tracking and collecting taxes and have developed effective enforcement mechanisms.

Saudi Arabia

Foreign companies doing business in Saudi Arabia should anticipate being subject to taxation on all business income arising or derived from Saudi Arabia, including any share of the capital they own in a Saudi company. Thus, if the business is based in Saudi Arabia or the performance takes place there, all income will be taxable by the Department of Zakat and Income Tax, the administrative body in charge of all taxation. However, foreign companies will not be subject to tax on income earned outside the Kingdom, unless it is related to income or activities conducted in the Kingdom. This is true even where the activities are conducted both inside and outside Saudi Arabia. Foreign exporters may also be subject to taxation if they import the goods directly into the Kingdom. In structuring transactions, one should be aware that there is a significant tax (of up to 50 percent, in some cases) imposed on royalty payments paid by a Saudi company to a foreign entity.

Kuwait

Under the Decree on Income Tax of 1955, foreign companies carrying on a trade or business in Kuwait with income having its source in Kuwait are subject to corporate taxation on that income. These include activities where only part of the economic activity has been carried on in Kuwait. However, a foreign company that restricts its activity to the export of goods directly into Kuwait, as under an agency arrangement, will not be subject any corporate income tax. In addition, American companies that have paid U.S. income tax, will likely be able to claim this amount as a deduction. There are no other significant taxes in Kuwait.

Bahrain

Bahrain has no corporate, individual, or withholding income taxes, except on oil, gas, and petrochemical companies, and does not tax corporate profits. It does however have a customs duty on goods imported into Bahrain.

United Arab Emirates

There is a corporate income tax imposed by each of the Emirates in the UAE, however, the income tax is rarely enforced on companies not engaged in the petroleum business. There are no other significant taxes applicable to foreign companies, except for a customs duty on all products imported into the UAE.

Oman

Under the Royal Decree 47 of 1981, foreign exporters of goods into may be subject to corporate income tax in that such activities constitute the carrying on of a trade or business in Oman. However, foreign exporters who negotiate and finalize the importation agreements outside Oman and who engage in sporadic transactions may be able to avoid this tax. Foreign companies with a direct presence in Oman may be subject to a corporate income tax rate of up to 50 percent of their income. There are no other significant taxes.

Qatar

A foreign company that acts only as an exporter of goods to Qatar is not subject to Quatari corporate or individual income tax. However, a foreign entity that intends to do business in Qatar through a joint venture will likely be subject to a tax, although companies that carry on business in partnership with a local agent who is an individual may be able to avoid taxation.

VI.   CONCLUSION

While there are numerous opportunities for American businesses in the Gulf, care must be taken to structure the transaction properly so as to avoid raising false expectations or failing to protect ones interests adequately. Local laws are deceptively simple; their application may be far more complex. It is important to involve a specialist, particularly one with practical experience in every transaction. Perhaps more than elsewhere in the world, care must be taken in structuring the transaction. Once structured and finalized, local business partners can be generally counted on to abide by its terms, thereby yielding a rewarding experience for all parties.

Notes

[1] The author gratefully acknowledges the generous assistance of Arthur M. Rogers, III, an associate in the Washington, D.C. office of Gibson, Dunn & Crutcher in preparing this chapter.

[2] International Bureau of Fiscal Documentation, *Taxes and Investment in the Middle East*, Saudi Arabia-34 (1992).

[3] Sultani Decree No. 68/87 of October 5, 1987 (effective January 1, 1989); Implementing Regulations No. 103/88; Law Decree No. 635 of April 3, 1991; Royal Decree No. 33/91 of April 6, 1991.

GOING INTERNATIONAL IN AFRICA

Ten Practical Steps for U.S./Africa Trade and Investment Success

Michael E.M. Sudarkasa

INCREASINGLY during the last few years, U.S. corporations have begun to recognize that Africa is one of America's last business frontiers. Although investment in Africa has remained relatively modest, overall trade with Africa during the last five years has grown six percent, led by a 12 percent increase in U.S. exports to the continent. The $5.4 billion earned by U.S. companies in 1992 from exports to Africa was the highest total in a decade. U.S. sales to Africa from 1987-92 grew nearly 75 percent. Behind only France and Germany, America is now Africa's third largest supplier of goods, services and technology.

Notwithstanding the recent exponential growth in U.S. exports to Africa, the continent has still maintained a trade surplus with the U.S. of nearly $36 billion over the last five years. America has become Africa's largest export market. In 1991, the U.S. purchased nearly 20 percent of all products exported from Africa.

As the countries of the African continent continue to move toward democracy and free enterprise, opportunities for U.S. companies to pursue trade and investment opportunities will continue to grow. Unfortunately, securing access to business information related to Africa is still a problem for most American corporations. Professionals who counsel the American business community, i.e., lawyers, bankers, and accountants are also often at a loss for the accurate and timely information needed to evaluate business opportunities in Africa.

For American corporations and business counselors interested in pursuing the growing opportunities to do business in Africa, there are, however, a few practical steps that can be taken to enhance one's ability to: learn about attractive trade and investment opportunities in Africa; get into the information loop about U.S./Africa commerce; and effectively pursue and consummate business deals involving African partners.

Listed below are ten practical steps for U.S./Africa trade and investment success:

Step 1: Become Educated About the African Business Climate

Individuals, corporations, and organizations interested in pursuing business opportunities would do well to learn as much about the overall macroeconomic climate in Africa, the political and economic climate of the region and country that is of interest. Information about the recent performance of companies in the industry of interest is also always beneficial .

Although the common perception is that business information on African countries and

629

industries is difficult to obtain, with a little diligence a great deal of valuable, yet inexpensive information is indeed available. Today, there is an ever increasing number of periodicals featuring business information on Africa. The U.S. government produces a number of inexpensive publications which provide up-to-date commercial information about Africa. This information, gathered by members of the U.S. & Foreign Commercial Service corps and U.S. Department of State economic officers stationed on the continent, includes the investment and political briefs, *Background Notes*, the quarterly periodical *Investment Climates* produced by the Africa Bureau of the U.S. State Department, *Business America, The Commerce Business Daily, Foreign Economic Trends*, and the *Overseas Business Reports* which are publications of the U.S. Department of Commerce and feature selected articles and profiles on African commerce and U.S./ Africa trade and investment.

Along with information produced by the U.S. government, the following periodicals are available in the U.S. and offer pertinent information about economic and political developments in Africa: *Africa Technology Forum* and *African Profiles*. Other useful periodicals published overseas that can be ordered in the U.S. include *African Business, Banking and Finance for Africa, Africa Economic Digest*, and *African Review of Business and Technology*. There are a few reference publications which provide more in-depth analysis of the macro-economic, political, and social climates in Africa and within the respective countries of the continent. These publications include *Africa South of the Sahara, The Economist Intelligence Unit-Country Reports/ Profiles, The African Banking Directory*, T*he Annual Report of the Global Coalition for Africa* and *The [Annual] Book of the Year by Encyclopedia Britannica*. Lastly, *The International Directory of Importers* is also a very helpful publication because it lists, by industry, importers in almost all of the countries of Africa.

Within the last few years there has been a proliferation of "how-to" seminars across the U.S. related to business development in Africa. Frequently these forums are sponsored by local chambers of commerce, universities, district offices of the U.S. Small Business Administration, state economic development agencies, and private consulting firms. Maintaining regular contact with local and state trade promotion offices is the best way to get information about when and where an upcoming conference may be taking place.

There are a number of public institutions that have both useful business information about Africa. These institutions can also be approached for general and specific information. The agencies include the Overseas Private Investment Corporation, the U.S. Department of Commerce, the African Development Foundation, the U.S. Export/ Import Bank, the African Development Bank - North American Regional Office, and the World Bank. Because of the magnitude of information these institutions have on Africa, it is best to approach them for information when pursuing specific projects. This way the project and desk officers of the institutions may feel more compelled to assist you in obtaining the information you desire.

Step 2: Establish Rapport with Africans in the U.S.

Africans living in the U.S. are one of the most underutilized resources available to American companies seeking to explore business opportunities in Africa. Various assessments have placed the African population living in the U.S. at over 1 million people. Many of the Africans living and studying in the U.S. have numerous personal and professional contacts in their countries. Increasingly, Africans are choosing to pursue undergraduate and graduate studies here in America. African business and law students in particular can be very helpful to U.S. companies in doing market research, identifying trade and investment opportunities, making important introductions, and generally introducing U.S. corporations to African markets.

African embassies in the U.S. can also be helpful in providing entry to their countries to American companies. African embassies may not have all of the information that a U.S. company or business advisor may desire, but developing strong relations with members of the African diplomatic corps can be a plus when pursuing business prospects in Africa. Members of the African diplomatic corps can provide useful letters of introduction and they can afford access to African ministers, other important economic offers and business owners when they visit the U.S. They can also offer sage advice about their respective countries' business cultures and about how to consummate transactions in Africa.

African professionals, business owners and staff of multilateral institutions represent other cadres of U.S. residents who, potentially, can be of tremendous help to American companies hoping to explore business possibilities in Africa. Individually and collectively through formal and informal organizations of Africans in America, these persons represent potential business partners, advisors, and sources of information.

Step 3: Identify Market for Your Product/Services

There are tremendous opportunities in Africa for manufacturers and distributors of products made in the U.S. These products include the following: agricultural machinery, telecommunications equipment and technology, transportation equipment (buses, trucks, aircraft), construction material, equipment and technology, educational material, computer hardware and software, new and used clothing, medical equipment and medicine, and energy technology and equipment. The difficulty for U.S. companies desiring to do business in Africa is knowing which countries to target for which products. Identifying the markets in Africa in which U.S. products have a competitive advantage is no small feat. However, there are some institutional resources available which can make the task more manageable. These institutions include African embassies as mentioned above, the U.S. Department of Commerce, the U.S. Department of Agriculture, the U.S. Agency for International Development, the U.S. Trade and Development Agency, the Overseas Private Investment Corporation, United Nations Industrial Development Organization and the World Bank.

The U.S. Department of Commerce tracks export opportunities for U.S. companies through the U.S. & Foreign Commercial Service (U.S. & FCS). The agency also has industry specialists who advise American companies on specific opportunities in various countries. These country and industry desk officers can be contacted via reference from the Department of Commerce's Trade Information Center. This information clearing-house provides useful names and numbers of U.S. federal government agencies that sponsor programs designed to aid U.S. exporters.

The U.S. Department of Agriculture Foreign Agricultural Service, like the U.S. & FCS, helps U.S. agricultural producers to identify export opportunities. FAS annually sponsors a number of trade shows, seminars, marketing opportunities and numerous other activities to help U.S. companies in the agriculture business identify and market their products overseas.

Two institutions, the Overseas Private Investment Corporation (OPIC) and the U.S. Export-Import Bank, have personnel who consistently monitor and appraise trade and investment opportunities in Africa. These organizations can be helpful not only because they finance projects in or involving Africa and African companies, but because they also serve as a clearinghouse for both U.S. and African businessmen and women looking to identify joint venture partners.

The U.S. Agency for International Development (USAID) in conjunction with OPIC has sponsored a number of investment missions to Africa. As the agency has a large number of offices on the continent, USAID has acquired useful information about the political and economic climate in Africa. In preparation for jointly sponsored investment missions to Africa, USAID has also produced a number of comprehensive profiles of business opportunities in selected African countries.

The United Nations Industrial Development Organization has designated the decade of the 1990s as the Industrial Decade for Africa. Toward making that proclamation a reality the institution has mobilized its worldwide network to research and identify investment opportunities throughout Africa. As well, the institution frequently organizes matchmaking forums to highlight industries and markets which hold opportunity in Africa.

The World Bank has compiled exhaustive information about the African private sector and most country desk officers have comprehensive studies of many industries which may be of interest to U.S. firms. Often these studies are available upon request. Additional reports are promoted and sold through the Bank's bookstore located in Washington, D.C.

Step 4: Put Together an International Business Action Team

It is very difficult, although not impossible, to begin international business activities without some counsel from professionals, such as attorneys, lawyers, bankers, accountants and consultants who specialize in advising companies desiring to trade and/ or invest abroad. In Africa, it is almost imperative that you seek advice before pursuing ventures on the continent.

It has been estimated that there are over four hundred U.S. companies which have investments in Africa, and as mentioned above, annually U.S. companies export over $5 million worth of products to Africa. In most, if not all of these transactions there were many professionals in the U.S., and in Africa, who played a role in making the deals happen. These professionals can be of invaluable service in helping your firm avoid costly and time consuming missteps. Finding these professionals is not always easy, but through national professional associations they can be identified.

Other resources that can add to your "International Business Action Team" are the many local, state and federal agencies which have programs to aid U.S. companies in doing business abroad. Some of these institutions include: the Small Business Administration's Small Business Development Centers, Small Business Development Institutes, Export Legal Assistance Network and Service Corps of Retired Executives; the U.S. Department of Commerce's Foreign Commercial Service Officers based in local district offices domestically, and in U.S. embassies in Africa; and the U.S. Agency for International Development's International Executive Service Corps, headquartered in Connecticut. Each of the institutions mentioned above have a network of professionals with international trade and investment experience. As well, the advice they offer is often less expensive than that provided by private firms.

Two additional resources that can help you to identify technical assistance related to doing business in Africa are the Department of Commerce's Trade Information Center and the U.S. Agency for International Development's Center for Trade and Investment Service. Both of these offices have representatives who can provide useful insight on developing international business development strategies and on identifying qualified professionals to assist in your firm's potential project (s) in Africa.

Step 5: Prepare an International Business Development Strategy

There is a saying that those who fail to plan, plan to fail. Nowhere is that more true than when considering expanding one's business to include international trade and/or investment. Developing an action strategy for doing business in Africa should be approached in much the same way as one develops a business plan. Some of the key issues that should be addressed include: a description of the new market/clients, identification of the competition and an analysis about how your company proposes to gain market share, an assessment determining whether it would be more profitable to begin your international foray by trading or investing, identification of possible trade or other barriers which might negatively impact upon your project, and financial analysis projecting the intended growth in sales/revenues from your new trade/investment, with justification for the underlying assumptions which lead to the projections.

It is also useful to identify any and all incentives available which make your proposed venture more attractive and/ or less risky, such as tax concessions, export/ import duty exemptions, and bilateral treaty agreements.

Step 6: Commence Marketing Strategy

There are a number of vehicles through which U.S. products, services and technology can be marketed in Africa. Some involve considerable expense, some are relatively inexpensive. A comprehensive marketing strategy might include some or all of the following activities: placing an advertisement in the U.S. Department of Commerce publication *Commercial News USA* which is distributed through the U.S. & Foreign Commercial Service to all importers around the world, including Africa; participating in one or more of the many trade shows in Africa held annually and bi-annually and listed each year in the December issue of the U.S. Department of Commerce publication *Business America*; participating in one or more of the regional and national domestic trade shows affiliated with the U.S. Department of Commerce's Foreign Buyer Program to which foreign importers are invited; identifying and sending direct mailings to potential importers listed in the Africa Volume of *The International Directory of Importers* compiled by Interdata, a publishing company based in Washington state; and organizing a reverse trade mission (or requesting to meet foreign buyers on a reverse trade mission) organized by another company under the U.S. Trade and Development Agency's Reverse Trade Mission Program through which U.S. companies can seek federal assistance to bring potential customers to the U.S. to look at American technology and products intended for export.

Step 7: Identify Finance for Your Transaction

Perhaps the most important ingredient to a successful international trade or investment transaction is an adequate supply of financial resources. When considering such transactions in Africa or with African partners, questions pertaining to how the project will be paid for often become paramount. Despite appearances to the contrary, there are indeed a number of sources of funds for trade and investment transactions between the U.S. and Africa. Many of these funds are available through bilateral and multilateral sources but there are also private financial institutions that will also consider bankable transactions in Africa.

In the U.S., the primary federal institution which offers trade finance is the U.S. Export Import Bank which puts in place trade finance facilities to either assist governments or foreign private companies in their efforts to purchase American products. Barclays Bank, with branch offices in among other places, Manhattan, New York, also offers trade finance for transactions involving African buyers. Meridien-BIAO Ltd., a Zambian bank which also has a representative office in New York, specializes in financing trade transactions in Africa. Both Barclays and Meridien-BIAO have extensive banking networks in Africa and long standing experience in financing projects in Africa.

In terms of bilateral and multilateral financial support for investments in Africa, the primary federal institution providing assistance to U.S. companies is the Overseas Private Investment Corporation, which offers both investment finance and insurance. The World Bank Group affiliate, the International Finance Corporation also provides investment finance for African projects. Although, the IFC invests primarily in multi-million dollar projects, a special facility, The African Enterprise Fund, provides investment capital for projects requiring as little as US $250,000.00 in debt/ equity finance. Another source of investment resources is provided by the African Development Bank's (ADB) Private Sector Development Unit, a lending facility created in 1990 with the specific aim of allowing the ADB to finance private sector projects.

These are but some of the capital sources available for trade and investment projects involving African partners. A much more comprehensive overview of African banks and world wide bilateral and multilateral sources of finance is provided in The African Banking Directory produced by SIFIDA, a Switzerland-based finance company which provides trade and investment finance for African projects.

Step 8: Develop Risk Limitation Strategy

It is almost impossible to eliminate risk in an international trade or investment transaction. It is, however, possible to mitigate and minimize risk. Because U.S. companies are often less familiar with Africa's companies, business climate and culture, the risk attendant to transactions on the continent can often appear prohibitive. Yet, careful planning and analysis can help the interested American company limit the amount of risk in transactions involving buyers or investment partners in Africa.

Determining whether one's partner has sound credit references is one initial way to minimize the risk involved in international transactions. There are a number of public and private agencies that provide business reference checks and credit checks in Africa. The U.S. Department of Commerce Foreign Commercial Service offers the World Trade Data Report service. Dunn and Bradstreet, the Foreign Credit Interchange Bureau and Piguet International are three private companies that also provide reference and credit verification services. In the event that these institutions do not provide satisfactory references requesting bank references from a potential partner is another good way to obtain financial references on a potential partner.

Two institutions, the Multilateral Investment Guarantee Agency and the Overseas Private Investment Corporation offer investment insurance to help mitigate risk in the investment transaction itself. The Export-Import Bank through the Foreign Credit Insurance Association offers credit insurance for trade transactions. Lastly, requesting payment in advance or an irrevocable confirmed letter of credit can provide additional security in a trade transaction.

Step 9: Visit the Country of Choice: Target Market

In transactions involving business opportunities in Africa, it is extremely beneficial to actually visit the country or countries in which one intends to do business. There really is no substitute for first hand knowledge of the market and those who direct its flow. Personal relationships and the trust that grows out of them are crucial to long term success in doing business in Africa.

There are an increasing number of vehicles that one can pursue to visit Africa. The Overseas Private Investment Corporation periodically organizes investment missions to African countries. These missions provide valuable access to senior U.S. officials in Africa and to African governmental economic officers. The National Association of State Development Agencies in conjunction with the U.S. Agency for International Development offers a Business Development Seed Fund program through which non-profit organizations and trade promotion agencies can request funds to offset the expense of trade and investment missions to developing countries.

If a firm desires to travel to Africa individually, the Africa Travel Association based in New York can provide a list of travel agents around the country who specialize in U.S./ Africa travel. Often ticket consolidators such as Magical Holidays in New York offer very reasonable packages for travel to Africa. Air Afrique, whose U.S. offices are also based in New York, offers flights to Africa three times a week.

Step 10: Identify Local Partner

For both investment and trade transactions finding a reliable local partner is an important part of long term success when doing business in Africa. Establishing business relationships, however, often can be very time consuming and involve significant expense in the form of travel costs, telephone and fax costs and postage fees spent strengthening ties with partners on the African continent.

Fortunately, there are a few ways to identify prescreened potential partners in Africa which ultimately may save one time and money. The U.S. Department of Commerce U.S. & FCS service offers information on potential agents and distributors through their Agent/ Distributor Service. African embassies in the U.S. and U.S. embassies in Africa often receive inquiries from African business men and women seeking American joint venture and trading partners. Commercial and economic counselors in these institutions can play needed match maker roles. As was mentioned above, the Directory of International Importers is also a good reference for identifyimg local partners. For investment projects, the United Nations Industrial Development Organization is a good reference for potential partners as is the International Finance Corporation's Africa Project Development Facility which undertakes feasibility studies for African investment project promoters and molds them into bankable studies. At any given time, APDF has a portfolio of projects waiting to be financed and often in need of foreign partners. Lastly, the United Nations Development Program's Private Section Division which assists African promoters in developing feasibility studies for investment and privatization projects is another source of information about potential business partners for U.S.-Africa ventures.

The steps mentioned above are by no means the only way that one interested in doing business in Africa can proceed, but they do present a systematic method that will lead to the development of a measurable action plan which will vastly increase the likelihood of lasting success in efforts by American companies to do business in Africa.

10 PRACTICAL STEPS
FOR U.S./ AFRICA TRADE AND INVESTMENT SUCCESS
RESOURCE PROFILE

STEP	SOURCE	RESOURCE	TELEPHONE #
One-Education	U.S. Department of State	Background Notes	(202) 647-6575
		Investment	(202) 647-6575
		Climates—Africa	
	U.S. Department of Commerce	Commerce Business Daily	(202) 482-0632
		Business America	(202) 482-5487
		Foreign Economic Trends	(202) 482-5487
		Overseas Business Report	(202) 482-5487
	African Technology Forum	African Technology Forum	(617) 225-0339
	African Profiles International	African Profiles International	(212) 765-5004
	IC Publications	African Business	[44] (71) 404-433
	World Publications Services	Bank. and Fin. for Africa	(201) 365-1278
	Media International	African Economic Digest	(202) 338-4440
	Alain Charles House	African Rev. of Bus. & Tech.	[44] (71) 834-7676
	Europa Publications, Ltd.	Africa South of the Sahara	18 Bedford Square, London
	WC1B3JN, England		
	Business International	Economist Intelligence Unit	(203) 655-1007
	SIFIDA	The African Banking Directory	[41] (22) 348-60-00
	The Global Coalition for Africa	Annual Report	(202) 842-0408
	Encyclopedia Britannica	Annual Book of the Year	(703) 222-7100
	Interdata	Int'l Directory of Importers	(707) 433-3900
	OPIC	General Information	(800) 424-6742
	U.S. Dept. of Commerce	General Information	(800) 872-8723
	African Dev. Foundation	General Information	(202) 673-3916
	U.S. Export/ Import Bank	General Information	(800) 424-5201
	African Dev. Bank	General Information	(202) 429-5160
	World Bank	General Information	(202) 473-4619
Two- Networking Three-Find Market	U.S. Department of State	Diplomatic List	(202) 647-6575
		U.S. & FCS	(202) 482-6220
	U.S. Department of Commerce		
	U.S. Department of Agriculture	FAS	(202) 720-3448
	U.S. Agency for Int'l. Dev.	CTIS	(800) 872-4348
	United Nations	UNIDO	(202) 659-5165
	World Bank	General Information	(202) 473-4619
Four-Business Action Team and Five-Strategy	U.S. Small Business Admin.	Small Business Dev. Ctrs.	(800) 827-5722
		Small Bus. Dev Institutes	(800) 827-5722
		SCORE	(800) 827-5722
		ELAN	(800) 827-5722
	U.S. Department of Commerce	US & FCS and TIC	(202) 872-8723
	U.S. Agency for Int'l. Dev.	IESC	(203) 359-6000
		CTIS	(800) 872-4348

10 PRACTICAL STEPS *(Continued)*
FOR U.S./ AFRICA TRADE AND INVESTMENT SUCCESS
RESOURCE PROFILE

STEP	SOURCE	RESOURCE	TELEPHONE #
Six-Marketing	U.S. Department of Commerce	Commercial News USA	(202) 482-4918
		Business America	(202) 482-5487
		Foreign Buyer Program	(202) 872-8723
	Interdata	Int'l Directory of Importers	(707) 433-3900
	U.S. Trade and Dev. Agency	Reverse Trade Mission Program	(703) 875-4357
Seven-Finance	Barclays	Trade Finance	(212) 412-4000
	Meridien	Trade Finance	(212) 980-9110
	World Bank	IFC	(202) 477-1234
	African Development Bank	PSDU	[225] 20-41-68
	SIFIDA	African Banking Directory	[41] (22) 348-60-00
Eight-Insurance	U.S. Department of Commerce	World Traders Data Rep.	(800) 872-8723
	Dun and Bradstreet	Credit Information	(908) 771-7500
	For. Cred. Interchange Bur.	Credit Information	(212) 947-4368
	Piguet International	Credit Information	(203) 584-8088
	World Bank	MIGA	(202) 473-6168
	OPIC	Investment Insurance	(202) 336-8593
	U.S. Export-Import Bank	FCIA	(212) 306-5000
Nine-Missions	OPIC	Investment Missions	(800) 424-6742
	NASDA	Trade Missions	(202) 898-1302
	Africa Travel Assoc.	Travel Agents	(212) 447-1926
Ten-Partners	U.S. Department of Commerce	Agent/ Distributer Service	(800) 872-8723
	UNIDO	Investment Projects	(202) 659-5165
	World Bank	Africa Proj. Dev. Facility	(202) 473-0508
	United Nations	UNDP - PSD	(212) 906-6310

GOING INTERNATIONAL IN CHINA

Thomas L. Shillinglaw

I. EQUITY JOINT VENTURES

Introduction

CHINA ESTABLISHED its basic law on equity joint ventures early in its economic decentralization—the Law of the PRC on Sino-foreign Equity Enterprises, dated July 1, 1979. This basic Law was then implemented by regulations on September 20, 1983. These two basic provisions have been subsequently supplemented by laws and regulations on such related matters as taxation, foreign exchange, accounting, labor, minimum equity requirements, and company dissolution. Since there is no separate company law in China, the rights and obligations of the parties to the enterprise are regulated by the above joint venture legislation and related specialized subject matter regulations, as well as by the provisions of the joint venture agreement itself. Since there are fewer basic western type corporation law provisions in the above referenced Chinese laws and regulations than would be found in a typical U.S. state's corporation law, it is prudent to add more of these basic provisions into the joint venture agreement documents than a western investor otherwise would consider doing. There are two of these documents—the joint venture agreement itself, which contains most of the business issues the parties to the joint venture want to address; and the articles of association, which typically contain procedural and management issues (such as board meeting procedures and officers' responsibilities). In theory it would be possible to collapse both of these agreements into a single document, but the Chinese government's approval authority, the Ministry of Foreign Trade and Economic Cooperation ("MOFTEC") insists that they be kept separate.

The basic 1979 joint venture statute provides that a joint venture is a limited liability entity, with registered capital. The registered capital constitutes the capital contributed to the new company by the parties, both in cash and in kind. Of course, the foreign party's contribution is typically in the form of equipment and cash, and possibly technology. The foreign party can own from 25 percent to 99 percent of such a company. A threshold issue for the foreign party is whether it should contribute its technology to the joint venture as part of the capital or should license the technology to the joint venture. U.S. tax considerations will probably favor a license agreement, since U.S. foreign tax credits favor royalty income to dividend income. In any event, the parties are required to make their respective contributions within a prescribed time period.

In addition, by licensing technology to the joint venture the foreign party can negotiate a royalty stream based on joint venture product sales. The rationale for this is that the foreign party will be updating the technology on an ongoing basis during the term of the joint venture and it should naturally be compensated for doing this. The Chinese will ask to have this royalty stream end after 10 years, at which time the license would be treated as being paid up. However, the foreign party can justifiably maintain that its updating the licensed technology on an ongoing basis in effect is entering into a series of annual license agreements with the joint venture for newly developed technology, and hence any arbitrary 10-year limitation should not apply.

Upon the signing of the joint venture contract, articles of association and any related agreements, all of them are submitted to MOFTEC for approval. It is important for the foreign party to realize that MOFTEC's approval is usually conditioned on the parties to the joint venture making changes (required by MOFTEC) in documents which have already been negotiated and signed by the parties. This MOFTEC set of amendments is sent back to the Chinese party, and the foreign party has very little if any ability to negotiate changes to this set of MOFTEC changes. Thus, it is important for the foreign party to realize that the signed joint venture contract and articles are going to be further changed, and not to the benefit of the foreign party. In addition, if Bank of China financing is involved, it is quite conceivable that the Bank will also ask for changes in any of the payment provisions of the already signed documents.

After the MOFTEC (and Bank of China, if relevant) approvals have been received and the documents amended accordingly, the parties must apply to the State Administration for Industry and Commerce for a business license. The date of issuance of this license is the date of formal establishment of the joint venture company.

U.S. Tax Laws

At an early stage in the negotiations, the foreign party should satisfy itself whether under U.S. tax law the joint venture will be treated as a corporation or as a partnership. There are four criteria for treatment as a corporation: limited liability, centralized management (i.e., an elected board of directors), free transferability of interest, and continuity of life. A Chinese joint venture would in all probability satisfy the first two criteria, but the second two are more problematic. In particular, regarding continuity of life, a Chinese equity joint venture has a pre-established term: it is not established with an indefinite term, as is the case of a U.S. corporation. The statutory maximum term is 30 years, but in any event the term agreed upon by the parties should not be less than 10 years because the joint venture may therefore not be eligible for certain tax preference treatment. The joint venture contract should contain a straight-forward procedure for the parties to extend the term of the joint venture. Typically, an off-shore joint venture must sufficiently satisfy enough of these criteria to be treated as a corporation rather than as a partnership.

Operational Control of Joint Venture

The contributions of the foreign party to a PRC joint venture must equal at least 25 percent of the entity's total capital, but there is no maximum percentage contribution.

Typically, as is the case with an equity joint venture in any other country, majority equity control gives the party with that control a majority of the seats on the joint venture's governing board of directors. The foreign party having or not having control is a question of the facts of any particular negotiation. However, a western company should try to get majority control of the joint venture—even at only 51 percent. For one thing, with the possible political instability in the country within a few years majority control could be very helpful in permitting the western investor to have more to say in the management of the joint venture under conditions which could be very different from those existing when the joint venture was consummated. In addition, even without any future political upheaval, on an ongoing basis it is beneficial to have control of the board due to the difficulties of operating a joint venture in China—even in the more developed coastal regions or Shanghai environments (for example, frequently inadequate infrastructure, potential differing views between the parties regarding future commercial directions of the joint venture and potential differences regarding uses of the joint venture's foreign exchange).

Control of ongoing management of the joint venture is clearly a matter for negotiation. However, it would certainly be prudent to have the joint venture general manager appointed by the foreign party. In addition, the foreign party should appoint the financial manager and the technology/operations manager. To be effective, especially at the outset, these three managers should be resident at the joint venture in China. Of course, this presents some very important housing and other logistical issues (especially if the joint venture is located in other than a developed special economic zone along the coast).

Board of Directors

The above discussion concerning control of the joint venture speaks in terms of control of the board. The board is the highest governing body of the joint venture; there are no shareholders' meetings. Therefore, the board should be viewed as an operating board and the western company's board members should be selected accordingly. The company's articles of association should provide for: *(i)* not less than quarterly board members (to permit sufficiently detailed oversight); *(ii)* meetings either inside or outside of China; *(iii)* the appointment of substitute directors (including another director) in case a director cannot attend a meeting (a frequent problem for the western company); and *(iv)* board votes being on the basis of the western company or Chinese company (i.e., if there is only one board member at the meeting from either investor that member automatically has all the votes for the investor, including for his or her absent colleagues).

Regarding sales of equity interests, China permits the parties to a joint venture (in the case of any sale of existing interests in the joint venture or the sale of additional equity) to have what a western investor would consider to be the typical rights of first refusal in favor of the existing parties to the joint venture.

Memorandum of Understanding

At the outset of negotiations, the foreign party should determine from the prospective Chinese party if it needs to have a preliminary memorandum of understanding in order to begin the processes in China to obtain any preliminary required local, provincial and national governmental approvals for the proposed joint venture, as well as to permit the Chinese party to apply for the land, utilities and any financing which may be needed for the joint venture. All of these initial approvals should be spelled out in the memorandum, as well as a provision regarding any financing or other approvals from the Bank of China. Of course, the memorandum should explicitly state that it does not create any legally binding obligation, and that such an obligation can only result from a formal joint venture contract which has become effective according to its terms.

Following any such memorandum of understanding, the key first step in the process is to negotiate a feasibility study for the joint venture. This will be done in conjunction with the negotiation of the joint venture contract, articles of association and license contract. Of course, this is an important exercise for the foreign party because (as is the case with an equity investment anywhere) it forces both parties to formulate at the outset a realistic financial plan for the venture. In China, the feasibility study serves an additional role in that it is the vehicle for the Chinese party to obtain formal allocations of resources to the joint venture (as opposed to the preliminary commitments from the memorandum of understanding). Two key legal issues concerning the feasibility study are; *(i)* to state in the joint venture contract that the financial projections contained in the study are just that, and that they do not constitute legally binding commitments of the joint venture; and *(ii)* since the foreign party, in particular, will be disclosing its confidential design and production information while developing the feasibility study it is important to have a confidentiality agreement concluded with the prospective Chinese party to the joint venture (and have the trust that this party will respect the confidentiality undertakings in the agreement).

Foreign Exchange Availability

Foreign exchange availability is an ongoing concern for joint ventures with foreign equity participation, especially since many such joint ventures are set up (certainly in the eyes of the foreign investor) as a means to establish a presence in the Chinese market. Joint ventures in China manufacturing industrial products have often found it difficult (at least initially) to export, due to a combination of high production costs and the lack of international marketing expertise. Of course, joint ventures have ongoing convertible currency expenses: royalties and dividends to the foreign partner, raw materials which can only be sourced abroad, salaries of the foreign party's expatriates at the joint venture, etc.

Due to this need for convertible currency (especially with the current unsettled situation with the Chinese RMB following the January 1, 1994 unification of the Chinese currency by the elimination of the so called Foreign Exchange Certificates), it is critical for the joint venture's feasibility study to have a realistic plan for maintaining an ongoing favorable balance of convertible currency. One potential source which has received much attention is the system of foreign exchange adjustment centers (commonly called "swap centers"). These are foreign exchange markets where in theory Chinese RMB can be exchanged for foreign currency, and vice versa. However, in practice these centers (even prior to the currency unification) have not in general provided the ongoing access to foreign currency as had been expected. Exchange rates at these swap centers have become increasingly volatile and there has been a substantial decline in the availability of convertible currency at the centers. In addition, the swap centers are localized so that at times it can be difficult for a joint venture in one city to trade at a swap center in another city. However, this concern is mitigated if the joint venture's Chinese party has had a history of accessing swap centers on its own (in particular to purchase foreign exchange to finance its imports). The exchange rates between centers in different cities will vary—sometimes fairly markedly. In fact, the ongoing strong demand for foreign exchange reinforces the tendency of the local State Administration of Exchange Control officials to discourage these transactions in which convertible currency leaves their jurisdiction. Thus, it is a risk for a joint venture's feasibility study to rely solely (or even primarily) on these swap centers as a source of foreign exchange. Adding to the liquidity problem of swap centers is that in 1993 government imposed rate ceilings significantly reduced the pool of dollars at the centers. Also, there is a question of how these centers will operate on an ongoing basis following the above mentioned January 1, 1994 unification of the Chinese currency. One aspect of this unification was to set the official exchange rate at the swap rate, which amounted to a 50 percent devaluation of the yuan (RMB) against the dollar. This devaluation will also affect valuation of joint venture assets. Under the old dual rate system, most foreign investments in China automatically lost approximately a third of their value since the investment made at the lower official RMB rate per dollar (for example) could only be recovered at the higher swap rate per dollar.

In fact, it is unclear at present the degree of ongoing access by joint ventures to swap markets. The government, for example, could mandate that all foreign currency transactions must be done through banks, thereby closing the swap markets. In addition, it is not clear under what rules banks will sell foreign currency to foreign invested enterprises. For example, at present companies seeking to sell dollars through banks must present import authorizations to the banks.

In order to discourage proposed foreign investments from being too much of a drain on the country's own foreign exchange reserves, the Chinese governmental approval authorities often encourage an export commitment to be a part of the proposed joint venture's feasibility study. These commitments may either be binding or written as non-binding targets. The former, of course, carry a substantial risk of the joint venture not being able to meet its commitment. In addition, if there is such a commitment, MOFTEC may require that the commitment be fulfilled before the joint venture may receive authorization for a foreign exchange purchase.

A more realistic approach to this key issue of balancing the joint venture's foreign exchange is to have a number of well thought out sources, including a portion from swap market trading (if in fact this source even remains available) and a portion from a non-binding export commitment. A controllable source is for the foreign party to use the joint venture as a source for components or parts to sell to the foreign party's affiliates abroad. Three other foreign exchange sources would be for the joint venture: *(i)* to purchase Chinese goods or materials for RMB and resell these abroad for convertible currency; *(ii)* to sell the joint venture's output to Chinese customers for convertible currency (once the joint venture receives the approval to do so from the State

Administration of Exchange Control—which approval is routinely granted); or *(iii)* to sell its output in China as part of a World Bank or Asian Development Bank sponsored project.

Article 75 of the 1983 Equity Joint Venture Law Implementing Regulations, as well as 1987 import substitution measures adopted by the Chinese government, had encouraged potential investors to expect that the government would allocate foreign exchange to joint ventures which produced and sold products to replace imported goods. It had not been clear in the regulations what the mechanism would be to calculate the amount which would be eligible for import substitution, but in any event the regulations were in fact not widely implemented in practice. It would, therefore, not be prudent for a proposed joint venture's feasibility study to assume any convertible currency based on import substitution.

As referred to above, the entire issue of foreign exchange availability for equity joint ventures has been made somewhat uncertain due to the January 1, 1994 unification of the RMB and foreign exchange certificates. As of yet, implementing regulations for this currency unification have not been published.

A related foreign exchange issue is the nature of the Chinese party's capital contribution. This contribution is typically in RMB, since it is usually used to purchase locally sourced needs for the joint venture (such as the right to use land and the cost of building construction/renovation). In fact, the foreign party should encourage that this local contribution be in RMB, since a joint venture party's dividend payments are in the currency of its capital contribution. Thus, if the Chinese party were to contribute dollars, this would be another requirement for convertible currency which the joint venture would have to satisfy on an ongoing basis. With the Chinese party contributing RMB, it is important that this contribution be phased in over time on an as needed basis since the exchange rate of these RMB contributions into U.S. dollars would be calculated at the time of the actual contribution and not at the joint venture's effective date. With the real possibility that the RMB will depreciate against the U.S. dollar, this type of staged valuation of RMB capital contributions would be more equitable for the foreign party.

Real Estate

An equity joint venture (or any other type of business entity) does not obtain title to real estate, but rather obtains a right to use the realty. If a joint venture is to obtain such right to use for residential purposes it is for 70 years, for industrial/manufacturing purposes 50 years and for commercial purposes 40 years. The joint venture would typically be obtaining its certificate for its right to use from the local municipal government, and (as noted above) the payment for this right is often a part of the Chinese party's capital contribution (since it is paid in RMB).

Employees and Unions

The foreign party should actively participate in the selection process of joint venture employees. The joint venture should include a confidentiality provision in its employment agreements, and rely on this following the employee's termination to protect the company's trade secrets, rather than relying on a formal non-compete provision (which would be very difficult to enforce in China). Although the joint venture establishes salary levels, the Joint Venture Law provides for a percentage range for these salaries above the range of equivalent domestic Chinese companies located in the same geographic area. There may also be local municipal and province level regulations for employee benefits. However, a joint venture is not responsible for providing housing for the joint venture's employees.

The joint venture will have a union. Two percent of each employee's salary goes into the union fund. An employee's participation in the union, however, is voluntary. Although union representatives do not formally participate in the joint venture's management or on the board of directors, these representatives are expected to give suggestions to management and to the board concerning safety and worker welfare issues. Specifically, if a board meeting is to discuss labor issues or key operational issues for the company, then the chairman of the joint venture's union is expected to attend the meeting as a guest (and therefore be non-voting).

In part, due to local passport and local housing permit requirements, recruitment for the joint venture's domestic Chinese employees tends to be from the general geographic location of the venture.

Joint Venture Funds

A joint venture has to have a reserve fund for future contingencies. This fund is built up on an ongoing basis from payments equalling not less than 10 percent of the venture's after tax profits, until the fund equals not less than 50 percent of the venture's registered capital. In addition, there is a discretionary expansion fund which does not have required contribution amounts (if in fact the joint venture decides to establish such a fund). Finally, there is a required welfare and bonus fund—although the amount to be paid into this fund is not set by law, but rather by the company's board of directors based on the company's policies in this regard. One frequent use of this welfare and bonus fund is to pay a housing subsidy for employees.

Equipment as Equity Capital

When the foreign party is contributing equipment as part of its equity capital, there is no customs duty or any tax (either VAT or Consolidated Industrial and Commercial Tax) on the importation of this equipment if the importation is done within the first two years after the joint venture's effective date.

II. WHOLLY FOREIGN-OWNED ENTERPRISES AND COOPERATIVE JOINT VENTURES

In lieu of forming an equity joint venture with a Chinese party, a foreign company that wants to have a corporate presence in China can establish its own wholly-owned company. Such a wholly-owned company is not a frequently used method of doing business in China, but it can be used by a foreign company which because of the nature of its business does not perceive a need for a Chinese partner; or because it (either as a matter of corporate policy or strong preference) prefers to maintain the latitude of operations which a wholly-owned subsidiary provides. In addition, the foreign investor could conclude that it is concerned about protecting its proprietary technology and that it wants to have as little outside interference as possible with the operation of the company.

The original law governing Wholly Foreign Owned Enterprises was adopted by the National People's Congress on April 11, 1986. This Law specifies that a condition for governmental approval of such an enterprise is that it must either use "advanced technology and equipment" or "export all, or the majority of its products." The Law also specifies that "an enterprise with sole foreign investment shall itself resolve its balance of foreign exchange income and expenditures" which implies that such an enterprise cannot turn to other means of foreign exchange balancing.

In 1990, the Chinese government issued implementing rules for the Law on Wholly Foreign Owned Enterprises, which provided a mechanism for the government to be increasingly selective about approving such enterprises. The regulations stipulate these approval criteria, methods of capital contribution, land use, taxation, and grounds for termination. A key concern about a wholly foreign owned enterprise is that in order to obtain approval (which could be time consuming) access to the domestic Chinese market may in fact be precluded since these regulations do (with some province level discretion) provides for 100 percent export from such companies. Of course, how such a 100 percent requirement could be administered would be a real issue.

III.   OTHER FORMS OF INVESTMENT

Cooperative Joint Venture

In 1988 a law governing so called cooperative joint ventures was adopted, and in 1991 tax laws relating to these ventures were introduced. These joint ventures permit the same 99 percent-25 percent foreign ownership and the same types of possible management control and types of operation, but they lack the detailed set of regulations which equity joint ventures enjoy. For a cooperative joint venture, there is no need to refer to the original authority for approval.

Holding Company

Traditionally, a foreign company's investments in China were held separately in individual equity joint ventures. However, it is possible to form a holding company which in turn can hold more than one of the foreign company's Chinese investments. There are significant benefits to doing this. For example, profits from one of the operating joint ventures can be invested through the holding company into another operating joint venture. There can be operating company foreign exchange balancing through the holding company and purchasing of needed operating company product inputs and personnel training can be centralized. However, such a holding company has to have a defined business license, and it cannot act as a general trading company. It must have at least U.S. $10 million in registered capital, at least 25 percent of which is in foreign exchange. Holding companies are basically governed by the equity joint venture law, and obtaining MOFTEC approval may be difficult—not to mention the approval of the Chinese parties to the operating joint ventures.

IV. TAXES

Company Income Taxes

China initiated its system of tax incentives in 1980 when it established a series of so called Special Economic Zones ("SEZ"). In 1984 14 Coastal Cities were added as tax preference areas, and these in turn were followed by other geographic areas inland. All of these areas were created to attract foreign investment, in large part by offering tax incentives. On January 1, 1994 China adopted an overhaul of its entire tax system, a primary goal of which was to unify the tax burden for foreign invested enterprises ("FIE") and for Chinese owned companies. Prior to these reforms, Chinese state-owned and municipal-owned enterprises paid higher income taxes than did FIE's. The base rate for FIE's had been 33 percent, but as noted above this rate had been significantly reduced for companies in SEZ's, the 14 Coastal Cities, and certain other areas. The January, 1994 reforms do not at present adversely impact the preferential tax treatments granted to FIE's under the prior tax regime.

The first step in the tax reform is to reduce the top bracket for Chinese enterprises to 33 percent. There is now a question of whether the federal tax authorities will grant to Chinese enterprises in selected locations the same types of tax incentives currently enjoyed by FIE's in similar locations, or if the authorities will eliminate in whole or in part these incentives already granted to FIE's. However, in this effort to create an even financial playing field between FIE's and state owned companies, it is to be noted that the latter still have preferential access to key raw materials and to government loans.

An important tax incentive which is not based on the geographic location of the joint venture is for the joint venture to be designated as having advanced technology status. To obtain this, the joint venture as promptly as possible after it is formed has to apply in writing to MOFTEC, followed up with a verbal presentation to MOFTEC explaining the venture's technology in greater detail. If a joint venture (i) obtains this advanced technology status, and (ii) is located in an SEZ, Coastal City, or any inland location which has established the same tax preferences as an SEZ, then the company income tax effect would be as follows:

(i)   the basic 33 percent rate (30 percent national and three percent local surcharge) is for a manufacturing joint venture of at least 10 years' duration;

(ii)   the first two profit making years are exempt from income tax;

(iii)   for the next three years the joint venture pays the federal tax at one-half the normal rate; and

(iv)   for the following three years the joint venture (with advanced technology status) continues to pay the federal tax at one-half the normal rate.

Sales Tax

As of January 1, 1994, there was also a complete change in the country's sales taxes. Prior to January 1, 1994 state companies paid a product tax while FIE's paid a Consolidated Industrial and Commercial Tax ("CICT"). Both of these taxes were paid by the seller, were commodity specific, and were levied both at the time of a product's import and at each domestic sale and resale. A new value added tax will replace both of the above taxes, and it will be applicable to domestic and to foreign companies. Although it is not clear at this time how much this new VAT will be, it will probably be higher than the CICT which it is replacing for FIE's. On the other hand, an FIE will be able to deduct any VAT already paid on an item, so the net effect may not mean an increase over the superseded CICT.

Personal Income Tax

The Personal Income Tax Law of the PRC, enacted October 31, 1993, took effect on January 1, 1994. This new Law unifies domestic and expatriate employee individual income taxes into a nine tier system with rates from five to 45 percent. The deductible income for expatriates has yet to be decided by the State Council.

IV. OTHER LEGAL ISSUES

Accounting and Auditing

For foreign invested companies, the accounting methods are specified in the Accounting Regulations for Joint ventures using Chinese and Foreign Investment, issued by the Ministry of Finance. These Regulations were updated in 1992 in order to bring them closer to international standards. International accounting firms are allowed to establish joint venture companies in order to perform statutory audits in PRC.

Arbitration

PRC adopted rules for arbitration in 1989. Arbitration may be held in PRC by the Arbitration Commission of the China Council for Promotion of International Trade. Foreigners are allowed to act as arbitrators. Of course, parties by contract may select third country arbitration.

Banking

The Bank of China, the PRC's central bank, has five specialized banks under its control. The China International Trust and Investment Corp ("CITIC") was formed in the early 1980's and has developed into a major international financial services organization. In addition, foreign banks and joint venture financial companies are allowed to operate in the SEZ's and in certain Coastal Cities.

Contract Law

Contracts covering business relationships between Chinese and foreign entities are subject to the PRC's Foreign Economic Contract Law of 1985.

Customs

China National Foreign Trade Corporation and China Ocean Shipping Agency, both of which are state owned entities, arrange for Chinese customs clearance for imports and exports. The PRC Customs General Administration publishes tariff schedules with import and export duty rates. PRC purchasing contracts typically stipulate that one of the shipping documents for imported goods is a certificate of quality (including a confirmation that the goods conform to applicable specifications), which certificate is confirmed by the Commodities Inspection Bureau when the goods reach the PRC.

Foreign Exchange Controls

The State Administration of Exchange Control ("SAEC") and the Bank of China are responsible for the management and control of foreign exchange. All foreign exchange transactions must ultimately be cleared through the Bank of China. All enterprises with foreign investment in PRC are required to open both RMB and foreign exchange accounts with the Bank of China or with other approved banks.

Insurance

China's principal insurance company is the People's Insurance Company of China ("PICC"). PICC conducts reinsurance relations with insurance companies throughout the world. All foreign invested enterprises are required by statute to be insured by PICC.

Patents and Trademarks

PRC's Trademark Law dates from 1983, its Patent Law from 1984 (it is now being revised) and its Copyright Law from 1991. At present, China has not become a member of either the Berne Convention or the Universal Copyright Convention (the two main multilateral copyright conventions).

Payments to and from PRC

If any payments from a PRC entity is to be done by a letter of credit, it should be noted that the PRC is not a member of the International Chamber of Commerce ("ICC") and therefore is not under any obligation to conform to the ICC's Uniform Customs and Practices for Documentary Credits. PRC letters of credit are normally only advised, not confirmed, and all transactions must be cleared through the Bank of China.

GOING INTERNATIONAL IN SINGAPORE

Margaret L.H. Png

I. INTRODUCTION

SINGAPORE is an island nation of three million people[1] located at the crossroads of international trade routes between the Pacific and Indian Oceans. In the north, the island is separated from Peninsular West Malaysia[2] by the Straits of Johor and in the south, it is separated by the Straits of Malacca from the Indonesian island of Sumatra.[3] Although Singapore has no natural resources, its strategic location in the heart of the resource-rich region of Southeast Asia has enabled the island to become a major economic force. It is therefore not surprising that Singapore, the smallest nation (land size and population) among the membership of the Association for Southeast Asian Nations (ASEAN), exerts considerable influence over economic issues within ASEAN.[4]

Singapore is characterized by a multi-ethnic society made up primarily of Chinese (76.4 percent), Malays (14.9 percent), Indians (6.4 percent), and others (2.3 percent).[5] This multi-ethnicity is reflected by the nation's four official languages: Malay, Chinese-Mandarin, Tamil, and English.[6] The first three languages are representative of the three major races in the country, and English was included for practical reasons. Malay is the national language[7] and English is the language of administration.[8]

During the first two decades of its independence, Singapore developed as a low-cost center for off-shore manufacturing and assembly. With development, prices of land, labor and material inputs in the country escalated so that Singapore is now priced out of being a low-cost center. In response to the change in the island's comparative advantage, the government's strategy for continuing expansion into the next century shifted to high value-added manufacturing and provision of international financial services. To this end, government policies now emphasize upgrading skills of the workforce, automation (with a view to shifting labor-intensive production off-shore), and development of indigenous research and development capability. The government is positioning the country to be a high-tech managerial and service hub for the rapidly growing Southeast Asian economies.

The ensuing sections will provide a brief history of the Singapore legal system and discuss issues of interest and concern to foreign investors. An understanding of the island's legal heritage is helpful, because many of the laws applicable to investment are in fact vestiges of the island's colonial past.

II.   HISTORY OF THE SINGAPORE LEGAL SYSTEM

The Singapore legal system is predicated on the English common law system. This is the result of the island's colonial history. The story began in 1819, when the English East India Company established a trading post in Singapore.[9] Then the island was virtually uninhabited, except for some 150 Malay fishermen and a few Chinese inhabitants.[10] During the initial years, there was no known body of law that was uniformly administered on the island. Instead, the officers of the East India Company administered justice according to the dictates of conscience and applied local Malay and Chinese laws, if they existed, to local inhabitants.

This legal chaos ended on November 27, 1826 when the English Crown granted the Second Charter of Justice. Under the Second Charter, a system of courts, fashioned after the English system, was created in Singapore with the applicable law being English law. However, not all English law was applied in the island. Common law was applied regardless of the date of its creation but only statute law promulgated on or before November 27, 1826 could be applied. *See Ponoghue v. Stevenson*, (1932) AC 562. Further, English law was not given *carte blanche* application in the island. Three qualifications were imposed on its application: (1) only laws of general application and policy were applied. *Yeap Cheah Neo v. Ong Cheng Neo*, (1875) LR 6 PC 381; (2) where applicable English law had to be adapted to suit the religions, manners, and customs of the local population in order not to work injustice and oppression. *See Cheang Thye Phin v. Tan Ah Loy* (1920) AC 369, *Khoo Hooi Leong v. Khoo Hean Kwee* (1926) (1926) AC 529, *Khoo Hooi Leong v. Khoo Chong Yeok*, (1930) AC 346; and (3) English law could not be applied if local law on the subject existed. The qualifications ensured that only English law that was suitable or adaptable to local conditions were applied in Singapore.

Today, English common law, regardless of its vintage, continues to be applied in Singapore. The only exception is where local statute law on the subject exists. Then local statute law takes precedence. With regard to English statute law, statutes that were enacted on or before November 27, 1826 are applicable in Singapore. The only exception is where local statutes expressly incorporate English statute law by reference.

There is no separate body of law governing investment in Singapore. Neither is there a separate body of law governing *foreign* investment. Instead, investment is governed generally by contracts law (English common law), company law (the local Companies Act[11] is based on English statute), intellectual property law (mixture of English common law, local statute based on English statute, and English statute law), and income tax law (local statute).

III.   INVESTMENT IN SINGAPORE

Singapore has one of the world's most open investment regimes. Its investment policy is designed to overcome land, resource and labor limitations, and to propel the island into the league of developed countries by selectively encouraging firms that can build up the country's technological base and bring about improvments in the skills of its labor force.

Generally, there are no restrictions on foreign investment in Singapore, except in sensitive sectors, such as arms manufacturing, airlines, and real estate.[12] Foreign investment is prohibited or limited in these sectors. Also, foreign investment in the financial, legal, insurance, shipping, and stockbroking sectors[13] require special approval or specific licenses from the government.[14] Aside from the sectors listed, Singapore maintains an open door policy to foreign investment.

Vehicles for Investment

Foreign investors may elect to operate their businesses in Singapore through one of four vehicles. First, an investor may establish a sole proprietorship. This form of business is established under and regulated by the Business Registration Act.[15] Second, where more than one investor wish to conduct business together, they may set up a partnership. The maximum number of partners permitted under the Business Registration Act is twenty.[16] Third, investors may also establish a company, limited by shares or guarantee, to conduct their business. A company can also be set up in an unlimited liability format. This form of business is governed the Companies Act.[17] Finally, a branch of a foreign parent company may also be established under the Companies Act.[18] Although the choice of the investment vehicle rests with the investor, the decision is usually governed by the particular circumstances of the investor, the nature of the business, and tax considerations.

There is another alternative for investors who do not wish to conduct business in Singapore but want to establish a presence in the country: a representative office. A representative office's activities are restricted to promotion and liaison functions on behalf of its parent company. The office is prohibited against concluding contracts, providing consultancy for a fee, undertaking trans-shipment of goods or opening or negotiating letters of credit, directly or indirectly, on behalf of its parent company. Representative offices are regulated by licenses issued by the Trade Development Board of Singapore.

Investment Incentives

The Economic Development Board operates as the "business architect" of Singapore and is entrusted with the role of promoting foreign investment in the country. The Board identifies sectors with high potential for contributing to the economy and draws up a variety of tax and fiscal incentives to encourage investment in these sectors. The centerpiece of the incentive scheme consists of grants of tax concessions and tax holidays for investment in selected areas. Currently, incentives are directed largely at encouraging existing investors to become more competitive through: (1) automation and improvement of their operations; (2) acquisition of new technology and processes; and (3) development of new products and capabilities. New investment in the manufacturing sector is still encouraged, particularly in the design and production of higher value-added products and which employ medium- or higher-range technology. Biotechnology and information technology related activities are also welcomed by the government, as are investments in the services and trading sectors.[19]

The following are some of the incentives available to investors:

- *Pioneer Status.* New manufacturing and service investment that introduce qualifying high technology are exempt under "Pioneer Status" from payment of the thirty percent (30%) tax on profits arising from pioneer activity for a period of five (5) to ten (10) years.[20] This tax incentive may be further extended on a case-by-case basis.

- *Post-Pioneer Incentive.* As an incentive to firms with pioneer status, if such firms make additional investments on or after April 1, 1986, they are eligible to apply for a concessionary tax rate of ten percent (10%) for a period of up to ten (10) years upon the expiration of their pioneer status.[21] Profits after this period are assessed at the normal rate of thirty percent (30%).

- *Expansion Incentive.* To encourage existing companies to expand their operations, tax exemptions are offered to companies that invest a minimum of S\$10 million[22] (approximately U.S. \$6 million) in new production equipment and machinery.[23] Qualifying companies are exempt from the normal thirty percent (30%) tax on that portion of profits earned in excess of their pre-expansion level.

- *Investment Allowance Incentive.* This incentive is designed to stimulate investment in new production equipment that will increase productivity by automation.[24] This incentive is an alternative to the pioneer incentive, and qualifying companies enjoy tax exemption on a portion of their income, based on a specified percentage (not exceeding 50 percent) of fixed, capital expenditure incurred for projects or activities.[25]

- *Operational Headquarters Incentive.* To encourage investors to locate their operational headquarters in Singapore, income arising from the provision in Singapore of approved services to overseas subsidiaries is taxed at a concessionary rate of ten percent (10%).[26] Other income from overseas subsidiaries and associated companies may be eligible for effective tax relief also. These tax reliefs are available up to a period of ten (10) years, with provision for extension.[27]

- *Research and Development Incentive.* Liberal tax incentives are provided to encourage research and development (R&D) organizations to locate in Singapore and to encourage existing investors to conduct R&D on the island. The incentives include double tax deduction for R&D expenses on approved projects, tax depreciation allowance on R&D buildings as "industrial buildings," and tax deduction for R&D expenses which are not usually tax deductible.[28]

- *Other Incentives.* Other incentives offered include: the Approved Foreign Loans Scheme, which exempts withholding of interest on minimum loans of S\$200,000 from a foreign lender for purchase of production equipment; the Approved Royalties incentive, which exempts royalties in whole or part from withholding tax; the Venture Capital incentive, which permits deduction of investment losses, resulting from the sale of shares, from taxable income.[29]

Tax Considerations

The major taxes and levies[30] that investors should be aware of are income tax, property tax,[31] stamp tax,[32] skills development levy,[33] estate duty,[34] and customs duty.[35] There is no capital gains, gift or wealth tax in Singapore. However, unlike the United States, income tax in Singapore is imposed on a territorial basis. Generally, income is taxable if it accrues in or is derived from Singapore, or it is received in Singapore from sources outside Singapore.

Foreign companies are taxed at the same rate as local companies: that is, 30 percent on profits.[36] But, unlike the United States, there is no "double taxation" in Singapore. Dividends paid by companies are not considered taxable income in the hands of shareholders.[37] Instead, corporate tax paid by companies are imputed to their shareholders, so that no tax is payable by shareholders on dividends received.

Individuals who are residents are subject to a income tax on a sliding scale, ranging from three and a half percent to 33 percent. Non-residents pay a flat income tax rate of 15 percent on assessible income or the graduated rates applicable to residents, whichever is greater. However, non-residents are exempt from tax on interest for funds deposited in Singapore banks and Asian dollar bonds.[38]

Protection of Intellectual Property Rights

Historically, Singapore has been dependent on British legislation for the protection of intellectual property rights on the island. Until 1987, it did not have its own copyright laws. Prior to that date, copyright protection was available only under British laws, which were incorporated by reference into the Singapore legal system. Even today, protection of patent rights in Singapore is only possible through registration of patents in the United Kingdom.

Copyright

In 1987, the Singapore Parliament enacted the Copyright Act.[39] The Act provides comprehensive protection for all literary and artistic works, including computer software, motion pictures, sound recordings, books, and other modern and traditional works. Protection is divided into two levels: the first level covers musical, literary, dramatic, and artistic property and the second level covers sound recording, films, broadcasting, and published editions of works. Enforcement of copyright laws lies primarily with the industry.

At the international level, Singapore recently became a member of the World Intellectual Property Organization (WIPO). However, it has yet to join the membership ranks of the Universal Copyright Convention and the Berne Convention.

Patents

As mentioned above, Singapore does not have its own patents legislation. Instead, protection is accorded through registration under the United Kingdom Patents Act.

Although this system generally provides adequate protection, Singapore's Compulsory Licensing Act (1968)[40] exempts the government from the 20-year rights monopoly by the patent owner. The Act permits the Singapore government to engage in parallel imports from sources other than the patent owner, thereby avoiding the need to pay royalties.[41]

Trademarks

Singapore's Registry of Trade Marks and Patents maintains a list of trademarks registered under the United Kingdom Trademarks Act of 1938 as patents. Patents that have been registered in the United Kingdom are registrable at the Singapore trademarks office[42] and anyone who has applied for registration in the United Kingdom or other country, which has reciprocal trademark relations with Singapore, may also apply for the mark in Singapore. An amendment to the law was passed recently, extending trademark protection to a wide range of service industries.[43]

Trade Secrets

There is no provision under statute law for the protection of commercial trade secrets. The only legislations in existence, the Official Secrets Act and the Internal Security Act, protect government trade secrets. Therefore, commercial trade secrets are left to the protection of common law.

Semiconductor Works

Protection in this area is provided under the Copyright Act[44] and the Registered Design Act to the extent of its registration. The Patent Act is applicable for the protection of the layout design as an invention.

Land Rights

Most commercial properties are leaseholds (as opposed to fee simples) in Singapore. Commercial properties, especially industrial estates, are generally leased from the government for periods of 30 years and only 99 year leaseholds are available for purchase.

Residential property on the island is limited as the country has a land area of 240 sq. miles.[45] Preference is therefore given to local residents for residential property. This is achieved by requiring foreigners to obtain special approval for the purchase of residential property.[46] The only exception is the purchase of private apartments located in buildings with more than six levels.[47] Title in residential property generally takes one of two forms: estates in fee simple (that is, absolute ownership for an indefinite period of time) or leasehold titles, which generally are granted for periods of 99 years or 999 years.

Labor Regulations

Unlike most developing countries, there is generally no restriction on the employment of expatriates in foreign investment companies. There is no requirement that specific positions or numbers be filled by domestic workers, but the government discourages dependence on unskilled foreign labor.[48] To this end, an employer must pay a levy of S$300 per month to the government for every foreign worker that it employs. Further, foreign workers may not exceed 45 percent of a company's workforce in the manufacturing sector, 75 percent in the construction industry, and 66 percent in the marine industry.[49]

At the executive level, The Companies Act requires that every company have at least two directors,[50] one of whom must be resident in Singapore, and expatriate-employees must obtain the approval of the immigration authorities before they are permitted to work in Singapore. Such employees are subject to the same regulations as other immigrants.[51]

Both employers and employees are required to contribute to the Central Provident Fund, which is a state-managed social security plan. Generally, employees contribute 22 percent of their total wages to the fund, and employers contribute an amount equal to 18 percent of employees' wages. The contributions earn interest in the account and may be withdrawn in a lump sum on retirement at age 55 percent years. However, employees may use monies in the fund to purchase residential properties, to purchase blue-chip shares, and to pay for of medical expenses and education.[52]

The minimum conditions of employment in Singapore are regulated by the Employment Act.[53] The Act specifies the number of hours of work,[54] the public holidays,[55] required overtime and bonus payments, and the amount of annual leave,[56] sick leave and maternity leave.

Exchange Controls

There is free movement of profits and capital in Singapore. In 1978, the government lifted all restrictions on exchange transactions and international capital movements. As a result, no approvals or formalities are required for any payment, remittance, or capital transfers in any currency into or out of the country.

Double Taxation Agreements

Singapore has entered into double taxation treaties with 25 percent countries. These countries are Australia, Bangladesh, Belgium, Canada, The People's Republic of China, Denmark, Finland, France, Germany, India, Israel, Italy, Japan, Korea, Malaysia, Netherlands, New Zealand, Norway, Philippines, Sri Lanka, Sweden, Switzerland, The Republic of China (Taiwan), Thailand, and The United Kingdom.[57] Pursuant to the treaties, double tax relief on foreign-sourced income is provided in the form of tax credits granted for income received in Singapore by a resident individual from a tax treaty country.

Apart from tax treaties, double taxation relief is also provided under domestic law.

A Commonwealth tax relief is given on a reciprocal basis for income arising from certain British Commonwealth countries, such as Brunei and Hong Kong.[58] Further, a unilateral tax credit is granted to Singapore residents for tax paid in Indonesia, The United States, and certain Middle Eastern countries with regard to income derived from prescribed professional, consultancy, and other services.[59] A deduction is also granted by way of concessions so that only net income derived from nontreaty countries is taxed in Singapore. This has the effect of allowing foreign tax paid as a deduction.[60]

IV. CONCLUSION

Singapore is generally an open economy. The government's policies are pro-business and very supportive of free enterprise. This is evident from the wide range of investment incentives available coupled with relatively few rules governing businesses in the country. Except for sensitive sectors, there is no restriction on business ownership, international trade, repatriation of capital and profits, and expatriate employment.

Although Singapore's economy has gradually slowed from the feverish pace of the late 1980's, with real GDP growing at 6.7 percent in 1991,[61] the country still holds promise for investors. The government has demonstrated an ability and a willingness to adapt to changing conditions in the country and the world. For example, when the island's comparative advantage as a low cost manufacturing center diminished, the government quickly shifted its emphasis to high value-added manufacturing and international financial services. Similarly, the government recognized the limitations of a small domestic market and is currently encouraging local companies to invest overseas and become "international." This ability to recognize the country's own limitations has enabled Singapore to mature from a third world country to a developing nation. This ability will also help propel the country into the ranks of a developed nation in the future.

Notes

[1] *World Tables 1992*, The World Bank, at 528.

[2] Malaysia is a federation of 13 states divided into two distinct geographical regions: Peninsular West Malaysia, which consists of 11 states, and East Malaysia, which consists of 2 states located on the island of Borneo.

[3] Sumatra is one of the 13,000 islands that make up the archipelago of Indonesia.

[4] *Investment Climate Statement—Singapore 1992*, American Embassy in Singapore, at 1.

[5] *The World Factbook 1991*, Central Intelligence Agency, at 279.

[6] *Singapore, Facts and Pictures*, Ministry of Communications and Information, 1990 at 4.

[7] *The World Factbook 1991*, Central Intelligence Agency, at 279.

[8] *Id.*

[9] See generally, Myint Soe, *The General Principles of Singapore Law.*

[10] *Id.*

[11] Compliance Act (Cap 185).

[12] *Investment Climate Statement—Singapore 1992*, American Embassy in Singapore, at 2.

[13] *Asia Pacific Regional Investment Guide*, The Second Asia Pacific Investment Conference organized by Euromoney, Singapore 1991, at 18.

[14] *Id.*

[15] Business Registration Act, 1973.

[16] *Id.*

[17] Companies Act (Cap 185).

[18] *Id.*

[19] *Doing Business in Singapore*, Price Waterhouse 1993, at 26.

[20] *Investment Climate Statement—Singapore 1992*, American Embassy in Singapore, at 3; *see Doing Business in Singapore*, Price Waterhouse 1993, at 27.

[21] *Investment Climate Statement—Singapore 1992*, American Embassy in Singapore, at 3; *Doing Business in Singapore*, Price Waterhouse 1993, at 28.

[22] "S$" denotes the Singapore dollar.

[23] *Investment Climate Statement—Singapore 1992*, American Embassy in Singapore, at 3; *Doing Business in Singapore*, Price Waterhouse 1993, at 29.

[24] *Id.*

[25] The list of qualifying activities include: manufacturing activities; engineering or technical services, research and development; construction operations; reducing the consumption of potable water; computer-based information and other computer-related services; development or production of any industrial design; services and activities that relate the provision of entertainment; leisure and recreation; publishing services; medical services; services that relate to the provision of automated warehousing facilities; services and activities that relate to agrotechnology; services that relate to the organization or management of exhibitions and conferences; financial services; business consultancy, management and professional services; services and activities that relate to international trade; venture capital fund activity; operation or management of any mass rapid transit system; services for the promotion of the tourism industry (other than a hotel) in Singapore; and textile and garment makers. *Doing Business in Singapore*, Price Waterhouse 1993, at 30.

[26] *Investment Climate Statement—Singapore 1992*, American Embassy in Singapore, at 3.

[27] *Id.*

[28] *Doing Business in Singapore*, Price Waterhouse 1993, at 30.

[29] *Id.*, at 32.

[30] Other minor taxes include license fees and motor vehicle (road) tax.

[31] Property tax rate is standardized at 16 percent of the annual value of the property, but owner-occupied property attracts a concessionary rate of four percent tax. *Doing Business in Singapore*, Price Waterhouse 1993, at 162–163.

[32] Stamp tax is imposed on certain written documents at rates that vary according to the nature of the document and the values referred to in the documents. *Id.* at 164.

[33] A skills development levy of one percent is imposed on employees earning a monthly salary of S$750 and below. *Id.* at 107.

[34] Estate tax is levied on all movable and immovable property located in Singapore that passes on death. The estate tax is five percent for estates valued at S$10 million or less and 10 percent for estates valued at more than S$10 million. Exemptions are granted for certain types of assets.

[35] The primary tax and levy provisions are embodied in the Income Tax Act and the Economic Expansion Act.

[36] *Doing Business in Singapore*, Price Waterhouse 1993, at 117.

[37] *Id.*

[38] *Id.* at 151.

[39] Copyright Act (Act 63).

[40] Patents (Compulsory Licencing) Act (Cap 221).

[41] *Investment Climate Statement—Singapore 1992*, American Embassy in Singapore, at 5.

[42] Application for a Singapore patent has to be made to the Singapore Registry of Trade Marks and Patents within three years from the date of sealing in the United Kingdom. The Singapore patent is valid for the life of the United Kingdom patent.

[43] U.S. Department of State Briefing Paper, Singapore at a Glance, EAP/EP SEEP 40 3/14/91 at 4.

[44] Copyright Act (Cap 63).

[45] *Singapore*, 1992 Ambassadors' Tour, at 24.

[46] Residential Property Act, no. 18 of 1976.

[47] *Id.*

[48] Singapore has a small workforce of 1.3 million, and this limits the supply of labor at all skill levels. *Singapore*, 1992 Ambassadors' Tour, at 34.

[49] *Doing Business in Singapore*, Price Waterhouse 1993, at 94.

[50] Companies Act (Cap 185).

[51] Qualification and background checks will be conducted on expatriate employees.

[52] *Doing Business in Singapore*, Price Waterhouse 1993, at 90.

[53] Employment Act (Cap 91).

[54] Ordinary hours of work are limited to 44 hours per week.

[55] Eleven paid public holidays are mandated under the Act.

[56] At least seven days of annual leave must be provided for employees in their first year of employment with a company. An extra day is mandated for every subsequent year of employment up to a maximum of 14 days.

[57] Doing Business in Singapore, Price Waterhouse 1993, at 181.

[58] Neither country has a tax treaty with Singapore. *Id.* at 100.

[59] *Id.* at 101.

[60] *Id.*

[61] *Investment Climate Statement—Singapore 1992*, American Embassy in Singapore, at 1.

The Editor:

Alan S. Gutterman has had over a decade of experience in counseling entrepreneurs, managers, investors and small and large business enterprises in the areas of general corporate and securities matters, venture capital, mergers and acquisitions, international law and transactions, strategic business alliances, technology transfers, and intellectual property law. For most of his professional career, Mr. Gutterman has been affiliated with internationally recognized law firms and has served in a number of capacities within the American Bar Association Sections of Business Law, International Law and Practice, and Science and Technology. He has published numerous articles on a diverse range of topics, including international law, technology transfer and business financing. Mr. Gutterman has also been an adjunct profesor and lecturer on corporate finance, venture capital and corporations law at Hastings College of the Law, Golden Gate University and Santa Clara University. He received his A.B., M.B.A. and J.D. from the University of California at Berkeley, has completed all of the coursework and examinations for a D.B.A. in international business from Golden Gate University and is currently pursuing a Ph.D. in Law and Economics at the University of Cambridge.

The Contributors:

Graham N. Arad is a partner in the firm of Frydman Beck King & Arad in New York, NY.

Philip D. Beck is a partner in the firm of Frydman Beck King & Arad in New York, NY.

Leslie Bertagnolli is a partner with Baker & McKenzie in Chicago, IL.

William A. Burck, III is Deputy General Counsel International and Director of International Government Affairs for Data General Corporation.

Frederick Brown is a partner in the law firm of Orrick, Herrington & Sutcliffe in San Francisco, CA.

David L. Dubrow heads the tax practice group and is a shareholder and director of Sheehan Phinney Bass & Green, Professional Association, in Manchester, NH.

Patrick B. Fazzone is an International Trade Partner with Collier, Shannon, Rill & Scott in Washington, DC and is Resident Partner of the firm's Asia Pacific office in Sydney, Australia.

Kathy Woeber Gardner is an associate with Mayer, Brown & Platt in Chicago, IL.

Howard B. Gee is an associate with Thompson, Hine and Flory in Cincinnati, OH.

Albert S. Golbert is a founding partner of Golbert Kimball & Weiner in Los Angeles, CA.

Mark C. Hendricks is a principle of the Christian Hendricks law office in Glendale, CA.

Lee H. Hsu, former summer associate with Steptoe & Johnson, Washington, DC, is presently a third year student at Yale Law School, class of 1995.

Darrell R. Johnson is a Partner of the Business Advisory Group with offices throughout South East Asia.

William Kunze is an associate with Steptoe & Johnson in Washington, DC.

K. Russell LaMotte, former summer associate with Steptoe & Johnson, is a law clerk for Judge Judith Rogers, U.S. Court of Appeals for District of Columbia Circuit, Washington, DC.

Robert Lee is Director of Research at Wilde Sapte in London.

Eleanor Roberts Lewis is Chief Counsel for International Commerce at the U.S. Department of Commerce.

Peter Lichtenbaum is an associate with Steptoe & Johnson in Washington, DC.

Lawrence S. Liu is a counsel and senior attorney with Lee and Li Attorneys-at-Law in Taipei, Taiwan.

Andrew J. Markus is a shareholder of Popham, Haik, Schnobrich & Kaufman, Ltd., in Miami, FL.

Drake D. McKenney is an associate with Thieffry & Associés in New York, NY.

Amy Meldrum is an associate in the law firm of Orrick, Herrington & Sutcliffe in San Francisco, CA.

Vincent Mercier is a partner in with Thieffry & Associés in New York, NY

Mitri J. Najar is a partner with Gibson, Dunn & Crutcher in London.

William K. Norman is Managing Partner of Ord & Norman and is Chair of its Business Transactions Department in Los Angeles, CA.

Michael R. Oestreicher is Partner-in-Charge of the Cincinnati office of Thompson, Hine and Flory.

William Park is Professor of Law at Boston University, Counsel to Ropes & Gray, and Vice President of the Court of International Arbitration.

Daniel J. Plaine is the manager of Steptoe & Johnson's Antitrust and International Trade Group in Washington, DC.

Magaret L.H. Png is an associate with Akin, Gump, Strauss, Hauer & Feld in Washington, DC.

Robert Shanks is a partner in the Washington, DC office of Latham & Watkins and was formerly Vice President and General Counsel of the Overseas Private Investment Corporation.

Thomas Shillinglaw is an Assistant General Counsel of Corning Inc., in Corning, NY.

James R. Silkenat is a former chair of the American Bar Association Section of International Law and Practice, and is a partner in the New York office of Winthrop, Stimson, Putnam & Roberts.

Michael E.M. Sudarkasa is the president of 21st Century Africa, Inc. in Washington, DC.

Patrick Thieffry is a partner in the Paris and New York offices of Thieffry & Associés.

Edward Wiatzer was a partner of Stikeman, Elliott in Toronto and New York until November 1993, when he was appointed Chairman of the Ontario Securities Commission.

Robert Walker is a partner with Wilde Sapte in London in Shipping and Trade Related Law.

Philip Wareham is a partner with Holman, Fenwick & Willan in London where he leads the European and Competition Law practice.

Tom Zych is a partner with Thompson, Hine and Flory in Cleveland, OH.